NEW HISTORY
OF
THE MARATHAS

NEW HISTORY
OF
THE MARATHAS

VOLUME II

THE EXPANSION OF
THE MARATHA POWER

[1707-1772]

BY

GOVIND SAKHARAM SARDESAI

GYAN

ISBN : 978-81-212-1570-1(Set)

ISBN : 978-81-212-1572-5 Vol.2 (HB)

First Published, 1946

Published, 2018

Published by

Gyan Publishing House
5, Ansari Road
Daryaganj, New Delhi-110002
Phone: 011-47034999, 9811692060
www.gyanbooks.com
E-mail: books@gyanbooks.com

Printed at: G. Print Process, Delhi.

To the Memory of

Sayaji Rao Gaekwad

Sena-Khaskhel Samsher Bahadur,

Grand Commander of the Star of India.

Maharaja of Baroda

[1875-1939]

to whom I have given all my life's years of Service, and who had led my young steps into the pleasant path of History.

G. S. Sardesai

PREFACE

I feel great relief in being able to send out this second volume of my New History of the Marathas not very long after the first, and I have little to add by way of a prefatory word to what I have said before. I hope I shall be equally fortunate in completing the third volume as well in quick succession and along with it my last great task. The matter of these two volumes has increased beyond my expectation, as I considered a full statement necessary in justice both to the achievements and the failures of the Marathas. The reader will notice that many new characters and episodes have been here dealt with, which had not hitherto received proper treatment. The vast amount of Marathi sources and the records in the recently published Persian Calendar and the Poona Residency Correspondence, have made this amplification necessary.

A full chronology for each chapter and thus for the whole of Maratha history is a novel feature which I have for the first time introduced here and which, I am confident, will be appreciated by students of history and general readers alike, although it has materially increased the size of my book.

I must repeat my keen sense of gratefulness both to Sir Jadunath Sarkar and to Dr. V. G. Dighe for the unstinted help and care which they have readily extended to me in the execution of what I have always felt as an ambitious undertaking for a solitary worker like me.

KAMSHET,
DIST. POONA.
February, 1948.

G. S. SARDESAI

CONTENTS

ABBREVIATIONS

A detailed bibliography is not considered necessary here, as the fullest references are given in my Marathi Riyasat volumes. The reader should note the following abbreviations :—

AIT. PATR.	=	Aitihasik Patravyavahar;
AIT. SAN. SA.	=	Aitihasik Sankirna Sahitya vols.;
BHAU S. BAKH.	=	Bhausaheb Bakhar;
BHAU S. KAIF.	=	Bhausaheb Kaifiyat.;
GWA. PAPERS	=	Papers of Mahadji Sindia, Gwalior Darbar;
HINGNE PAPERS	=	Vols. 1 & 2.
HIS. REC. COM.	=	Historical Record Commission Proceedings.
INDORE VOLS.	=	Sources of the Holkar State history, vols. 1 & 2;
ITI. SANG. P. D.	=	Peshwa Daftar Papers published by Parasnis in his Itihas Sangraha; Aitihasik Tipne etc.
PATRE YADI	=	Kavyetihas Sangraha letters, new edition by G. S. Sardesai;
PER. CAL.	=	Persian Calendar vols. published by Govt.;
PESHWA DIARIES OR Roz Vols by Vad	=	—Shahu Roz; Nana S. Roz; Mad. Roz; Sa. Mad. Roz; Baji. Roz. etc.
P. D. S.	=	Peshwa Daftar Selections—vols. published by the Bombay Govt.
PHALKE VOLS.	=	Vols. of Sindhia Papers published by Sardar Phalke of Gwalior;
PUR. DAF.	=	Purandare Daftar vols.;
RAJ. VOLS.	=	Volumes of Sadhanen published by Rajwade;
SATARA PAPERS	=	Two vols. published by Satara Hist. Society;
SHIV. CH. SA.	=	Shiva Charitra Sahitya vols. published by the Poona Mandal.

CORRECTION

P. 216, line 20, read exhibition for expedition.

P. 248, line 22, read influenced for inflamed.

P. 385, lines 2 and 10, exchange words succour and suspect.

P. 394, line 3 bottom, read January 14 for February 5, as on p. 403, (refer to Hingne Daftar II. 42).

P. 396, line 1, read Rajputs for Rajput.

P. 418, line 2 bottom, read who after Shuja.

P. 507, line 13 bottom, read Kholapur for Kolhapur.

NEW HISTORY OF THE MARATHAS

VOLUME II

CHRONOLOGY

CHAPTER I

1682, May 18	Shahu born.
1689, November 3	Shahu is captured at Raigad.
1696, June 9	Tarabai's son Shivaji born.
1698, May 23	Rajasbai's son Sambhaji born.
1698, May 23	Kanhoji Angre made Sarkhel.
1707, February 20	Aurangzeb dies at Ahmadnagar.
1707, March 5	Azam Shah proclaimed Emperor.
1707, March 13	Shahu meets Azam Shah at Burhanpur.
1707, May 4	Azam Shah reaches Sironj.
1707, May 8	Shahu leaves Mughal Camp for south.
1707, May 25	Shahu in Khandesh joined by Maratha Chiefs.
1707, June 8	Battle of Jajav : Azam Shah killed, Bahadur Shah proclaimed.
1707, August 3	Jotyaji Kesarkar receives Imperial sanads in Shahu's name.
1707, August-Sept.	Shahu at Ahmadnagar : Parad reduced ; Fatehsinh taken under protection.
1707, October 12	Shahu wins victory at Khed.
1707, October 27	Shankaraji Narayan Sachiv dies ; Shahu wins forts.
1708, January 1	Shahu captures Satara.
1708, January 12	Shahu crowned king.
1708, May 17	Bahadur Shah crosses Narmada for the Deccan.
1708, June 27	Dhanaji Jadhav dies.
1708, November 20	Balaji Vishvanath made Senakarte.
1709, January 3	Kam Baksh falls fighting.
1709, May	Bahadur Shah returns north.
1709, May 16	Lodhi Khan killed near Poona.
1709, August 23	Raybhanji Bhosle dies.
1710	Parsoji Bhosle dies.
1710, December	Rao Rambha Nimbalkar Mughal Faujdar of Ahmadnagar.

M. H. II—2

1711	Chandrasen Jadhav, Damaji Thorat and Vithoji Chavan rebel against Shahu.
1711, August 17	Chandrasen joins Mughals after his quarrel with Balaji Vishvanath.
1711, October 1	Santaji Jadhav is made Senapati.
1711, November 20	Shahu arrests Pratinidhi.
1711, December 2	Krishnarao Khatavkar put down.
1712	Mansinh More Shahu's Senapati.
1712, February 17	Bahadur Shah dies.
1713, February	Nizam-ul-Mulk appointed Subahdar of the Deccan.
1713, November 17	Balaji Vishvanath appointed Peshwa.
1714, February 28	Balaji Vishvanath and Kanhoji Angre meet and arrange treaty of peace.
1715, January 30	Siddi of Janjira makes peace with Shahu.
1715, March 25	Kanhoji Angre visits Shahu at Satara.
1715, December 26	Charles Boone President of Bombay.
1718—1724	English War against Angria.
1718, November 2	Boone attacks Khanderi.
1721, December	Bajirao defeats the English near Kolaba.

Shri Shahu Chhatrapati

CHAPTER I

SHAHU'S POSITION STABILIZED

[1707—1715]

1. **Shahu's home-coming.**—The death of Aurangzeb on 20th February, 1707, marks a distinct break between the old order that was passing and the new that was coming. The Emperor had spent full twenty-five years of his long reign and the vast resources of his extensive dominions in a vain attempt to subdue the Marathas. This long drawn war of independence won an imperishable place for them in the annals of India. We have to begin our study of it with the life of Shahu as a prisoner in the Mughal camp.

On hearing of Aurangzeb's death his second surviving son Azam Shah hastily returned to Ahmadnagar and performed the funeral rites. Next, on 5th March, he proclaimed himself Emperor and at once started with all his father's camp for the north, to put down his elder brother Shah Alam who was coming from Lahore to contest the throne. Shahu had no choice but to accompany Azam Shah. His mother and party numbered about two hundred. He had long formed a friendship with the generalissimo Zulfiqar Khan who looked upon the Mughal Deccan as his future charge. After reaching Burhanpur Zulfiqar Khan presented Shahu to Azam Shah, pleaded his cause and begged that he might be released and sent back as a contrivance for keeping the Marathas divided by a domestic feud. Several Rajput princes of the camp were friendly to Shahu and urged the same course upon Azam Shah's attention. Azam Shah honoured Shahu with gifts and dresses, but put off the actual release for one reason or another. His attention was focussed on the contest he was going to have with his brother, and he little cared for the feelings of a harmless mendicant that Shahu appeared to him to be. Leaving Burhanpur on 13th March, Azam Shah crossed the Narmada at the end of April and reached Sironj on 4th May.

With the increase of distance from his home, Shahu began to grow impatient and restless about his release and was advised, in the midst of his gloom by his never failing guardian angel the Begum Zinat-un-nisa and other friends, not to wait for formal sanads of appointment from Azam Shah, but to quit the camp at once and proceed to his home country. He readily acted upon this advice and left the Mughal camp on 8th May at Doraha about 20 miles north-west of Bhopal. The Muslim writers assert that he ran away, the Maratha writers that he obtained permission to go back, leaving behind, as hostages, a small party including his mother, wife and Madan Sinh, an illegitimate brother, in case he should upon his return home assume a hostile attitude. Jotyaji Kesarkar was left behind to obtain the formal sanads which were under preparation, when completed. That Shahu was not pursued shows that Azam Shah either tacitly consented or was helpless under the circumstances. The terms of his release as they had come under discussion from time to time were (1) that he was to rule the small *swarajya* of his grandfather as a vassal of the Mughal Empire; (2) that he was to serve his liege lord whenever called upon to do so with his contingent of troops; and (3) that he was also permitted to collect Chauth and Sardeshmukhi from the six Mughal provinces of the south. It may be noted in passing that the first two of these are the same terms which Aurangzeb himself had granted to Shivaji in 1667, and all three of which later on, Shahu obtained from Muhammad Shah in 1719 in formal sanads, notwithstanding all the wars and wranglings during the intervening period.

A month after Shahu's departure from Azam Shah's camp in Malwa, the contest between the two sons of Aurangzeb was decided on the battlefield of Jajav near Agra on 8th June 1707, where Azam Shah was killed and Shah Alam became Emperor under the title of Bahadur Shah. After his accession Bahadur Shah came to the Deccan during 1708, killed his youngest brother Kam Baksh in a fight near Haidarabad on 3rd January 1709, went back to Delhi and died three years later on 17th February 1712. With these events in view we must here follow Shahu's career to his homeland after leaving Doraha with only a couple of hundred followers and servants.

Mahadaji Krishna Joshi, a banker, and Gadadhar Pralhad Nasikkar a priest, were the only men of note who accompanied Shahu on his return journey. By their advice he addressed formal letters to several Mahratha chiefs informing them of his expected arrival and demanding their help and obedience. After crossing the Narmada he purposely took the shorter route through Bijagad and Sultanpur into Western Khandesh so as to avoid the eastern highway via Burhanpur, the principal seat of the Mughal Government in the Deccan. He arrived at Bijagad about thirty miles south of the Narmada and was there joined by its ruler Mohansinh Rawal, who had long rebelled against Aurangzeb and co-operated with the Marathas. Mohansinh was the first to espouse the cause of Shahu and help him with troops and funds. From Bijagad Shahu proceeded to Sultanpur on the river Tapti, where he was joined by several Maratha chiefs, such as Amritrao Kadam Bande, Sujansingh Rawal of Lambkani, the Bokils, the Purandares and other representative Brahmin families, who although serving the Mughal government nominally had favoured the cause of this declared heir of Shivaji. The Purandares possibly brought with them their friend Balaji Vishvanath, who had for long been a moving diplomatic figure at Poona and round about.

Thus Shahu came to be cordially welcomed in Maharashtra, as the legitimate scion of the Bhosle family, for whose liberation a long and tough war had so long been waged. But Shahu's greatest help came from Parsoji Bhosle, the ancestor of the later Bhosle rulers of Nagpur, who was then in possession of the territory of Berar. Parsoji's example was quickly followed by Nemaji Sindia, Haibatrao Nimbalkar, Rustumrav Jadhav (Shahu's father-in-law), Chimnaji Damodar and others who were then working in Khandesh and Baglan. Having spent the two months of June and July in Khandesh in collecting troops and strengthening his position, Shahu proceeded to Ahmadnagar early in August with high hopes of a smooth passage to the capital of Satara, where he wished to rule as the Maratha sovereign.

2. **Battle of Khed.**—But Shahu was soon disillusioned. He received intimation from his aunt Tarabai that she looked on him as an impostor, that he had no right to the Maratha throne, that the kingdom which his father Sambhaji had once enjoyed had been lost by him, and that the present domain was a fresh acquisition made by her husband Rajaram and had now descended to her son, the young Shivaji, who had been duly crowned a few years ago. Thus the plan long contrived by Aurangzeb himself of effecting a schism among the Maratha nationals and bringing about a civil war between the followers of Shahu and Tarabai, came into operation and in consequence Shahu had to face a difficult situation. He halted at Ahmadnagar for three long months preparing for a contest with his aunt and organising his forces.

One point that he was careful about was to secure the good will of the local Muslim Government officials by deferring to their claim to overlordship. He visited the dead Emperor's tomb at Khuldabad walking there on foot, rendered pious obeisance to his memory and exhibited in an unequivocal manner his deep gratitude and devotion to the royal house of Delhi. During this absence from Ahmadnagar he had an accidental little skirmish with the villagers of Parad, about 25 miles north of Daulatabad. The Patil of the village was killed and his widow brought her little son to Shahu and sought his protection. Shahu looking upon the encounter as his first victory, gave the boy the name Fatesinh and brought him up as his own son. This boy of the Lokhande family came to play an important part at Shahu's court, was brought up as an heir apparent and would possibly have inherited Shahu's throne, if he had not declined the position himself. His family still rules at Akalkot.

This little incident illustrates the soft and kindly vein in Shahu's character. It influenced not only his personal actions throughout his long reign, but the fortunes of the whole Maratha nation. He had given his sacred word to the dying Emperor that he would run to the rescue of the Emperor's descendants whenever they needed help. In fact, Shahu never for a moment forgot that he owed what he was, entirely to the kindness of the Emperor, who could as well have put an end to his life and inflicted miseries upon his mother and other relations. He did not leave Ahmadnagar until circumstances compelled him and would even have preferred in order to avoid an open recourse to arms, to rule from that town itself, if it were possible. But Satara had behind it the claims of a legitimate Maratha capital while Ahmadnagar which had figured for centuries as a Muslim possession and more recently as the seat of Aurangzeb's government, was now ill-suited to the requirements of a Maratha king. When at Ahmadnagar Shahu learned in October 1707 that Tarabai's forces were marching against him, he moved from that place southward towards Poona and halted at Khed where he found himself confronted by a powerful army drawn up on the opposite side of the Bhima ready to attack him.

Shahu's following was after all a heterogeneous mass with no capable general to lead them into action. On the opposite bank were ranged against him seasoned troops commanded by the veteran Dhanaji Jadhav the hero of a hundred fights, and Parashuram Pant Pratinidhi a devoted partizan of Tarabai. Afraid of certain annihilation by risking a precipitate attack, Shahu had recourse to diplomacy in which the hereditary Chitnis Khando Ballal, Balaji Vishvanath Bhat, a Brahman Sar-Subahdar, and Naro Ram, all close helpmates of Dhanaji, played a conspicuous part. These and several others had already been well convinced of Shahu's identity and impressed by his charming personality. He managed through these agents to call Dhanaji to a secret personal interview and succeeded in winning him over to his cause. Dhanaji agreed to wage a sham battle and desert to Shahu at a convenient moment. An action took place the next day on the plain of Khed on the north bank of the Bhima, in which Shahu appeared at the head of his troops in a manly deportment confident of success. The Pratinidhi fought valiantly but having been deserted by the Senapati after the action had been joined, was routed and fled for safety across the river. Shahu thus won the day and encamping on the battlefield, received Dhanaji and conferred upon him the honours of the Senapati and upon Khando Ballal the office of the Chitnis. The whole episode disclosed the weakness of Tarabai's position. The Maratha nation was solidly rallying behind Shahu and acclaimed him with full heart as against a lady, who, however competent, could not occupy the throne and whose son the young Shivaji was known to be altogether incompetent and incapable of conducting the affairs of the State.

3. **Coronation at Satara.**—After this first success Shahu lost no time in marching on Satara, halting a short while at Shirwal, near which another faithful adherent of Tarabai, the redoubtable Sachiv Shankaraji Narayan, had his official residence in fort Rohida near Bhor. Shahu called upon him to surrender or take the consequences of refusal. The Sachiv confounded by this peremptory summons, put an end to his life by swallowing poison on 27th October, 1707. As he failed to appear, Shahu personally marched against him and, to his dismay, while ascending the heights met the Sachiv's dead body being brought down for cremation on the banks of the stream below. Feeling very sad at heart, he directly went up to the Sachiv's palace, comforted with soothing words the dead Sachiv's shrewd wife Yesubai, conferred the hereditary office of Sachiv upon her young son then about a year old, and with singular tact and judgment gained the affection of a large section of the Maratha populace in those homelands of the Mawals.

From Shirwal to Satara is only 35 miles, which Shahu did not take long to cover. Having secured the forts of Chandan and Vandan on the way, he appeared before Satara some time in November. The capital had already been deserted by Tarabai and her son, who had taken shelter in the fort of Panhala about 60 miles further south, leaving the defence of Satara to the Pratinidhi, whom Shahu called upon to submit. The Pratinidhi refused and defied Shahu to an open fight. The commandant of the garrison was a Muslim officer of the name of Shekh Mira, who on receiving an assurance of safety and emoluments from Shahu, put the Pratinidhi under confinement and opened the gates to the rightful heir of the Maratha raj. Shahu entered the capital on a Saturday in December, within seven months of his leaving the Mughal camp.

Thus the nation got back their king after a long and heroic struggle. The coronation ceremony was duly performed on 12th January, 1708 with all the customary pomp and ritual.

Shahu made fresh ministerial appointments on the occasion and thus ending the preliminary stage of captivity and hardship, began a new era of success and moderation, with which his name came to be associated during succeeding generations. Even at this day his name is a household word in Maharashtra signifying the king's piety and simplicity of life and good will towards all.

Almost the first act of his new regime was an attempt to appease his aunt Tarabai in order to put an end to the domestic strife, and with that object he offered her very liberal terms, consistent with his own position as Chhatrapati. But the proud lady far from accepting the proffered hand of friendship, prepared to carry on the struggle, using all the powers of craft and diplomacy that she singularly possessed. Shahu marched on Panhala in March. Upon his approach Tarabai left that fort and fled to Rangna about 60 miles further south. Her only adviser was now the veteran Ramchandrapant, who continued to support her cause in spite of her fast dwindling resources. When Shahu arrived before Rangna in summer, Tarabai ran away to Malvan on the west coast. But the approaching monsoon compelled Shahu to give up the pursuit and retrace his steps to Panhala where he spent the rainy season.

4. **Rise of Balaji Vishvanath.**—While thus engaged in his operations against his aunt, Shahu had not neglected his main object of securing the northern portions of his patrimony. He had deputed his Pratinidhi Gadadhar Pralhad and his Senapati Dhanaji Jadhav to Baglan and Khandesh with his trusted confidant Balaji Vishvanath. They vanquished the local Mughal officers like Karim Beg of Junnar and plundered that city of its accumulated riches. They were now recalled by Shahu for the monsoon. On the way to Panhala, Dhanaji was suddenly taken ill and died in June 1708 at Wadgaon on the Warna, thereby dealing a severe blow to Shahu's cause. Although Shahu at once conferred the Senapati's office upon Dhanaji's son Chandrasen, he was already suspicious about the latter's loyalty on account of his well-known leanings towards Tarabai's party. As a safeguard against possible treachery by the new Senapati, Shahu appointed Balaji Vishva-

nath to the post of Senakarte (organizer of forces), a new office that encroached to some extent upon the province of the commander-in-chief. Chandrasen had never taken kindly to Balaji's views and policy of supporting Shahu, and had possibly condemned his father for having deserted Tarabai's cause on the field of Khed. Balaji on his part did his best at this crisis to carry out Shahu's wishes by raising funds, enlisting men and bringing to obedience such elements in the kingdom as were hostile, so that he soon outstripped all the other ministers and helpmates of Shahu in efficiency and speed of execution. In a few years, Shahu conferred upon him the office of the Peshwa or Prime Minister, a consummation which soon changed the whole character of the Maratha administration and government, and in course of time caused the position of the Chhatrapati himself to be eclipsed. Subsequent history speaks of the Peshwa as the de facto ruler of the Marathas. In order to understand the significance of this change it is necessary to go back a little and review the antecedents which raised Balaji so high in Shahu's estimation.

The early career of Balaji Vishvanath is little recorded in history. We know that his ancestors were Deshmukhs of Shrivardhan on the west coast under the jurisdiction of the Siddi of Janjira, a naval officer first of the Nizamshahi Kings of Ahmadnagar and, after its extinction, of the Emperor of Delhi. While Balaji's elder brother Janoji looked after the Deshmukhi work of Shrivardhan, he himself was employed as a clerk in the salt works at Chiplun also owned by the Siddi. Tradition says that having been persecuted by the Siddi, Balaji left his home and went out in search of employment to the upper regions of the Western Ghats, where Shivaji was then just opening fresh fields of activity for those who were strong in arm. We cannot say definitely whether Balaji had the chance to work in any of the offices established by Shivaji: the earliest recorded notice we get of him refers to the year 1689, the year when Sambhaji was put to death by Aurangzeb, wherein Balaji is mentioned as a revenue clerk or writer under Ramchandrapant Amatya. Many letters have been discovered for the twelve years 1695-1707 in which Balaji is addressed by Ramchandrapant and other ministers of Rajaram as the Sar-Subah of the districts of Poona and Daulatabad, just the districts in which the Emperor was conducting his war against the Marathas. He is also mentioned as a revenue collector working under the Senapati Dhanaji Jadhav.

We know that the Mughal Emperor conducting a relentless war against the Marathas, had cantoned his armies at Poona and Khed during the two successive monsoons of 1703 and 1704, and that Balaji Vishvanath as a Maratha officer executing orders of the Chhatrapati and his ministers, had also his headquarters at Poona at the same time. A question arises how could Balaji escape being captured and put to death by the hostile Emperor. Perhaps the answer is that Balaji did not belong to the fighting force, was probably helpful as a revenue officer of the district and as such was expected to supply the various necessaries of life, draft animals, carts, labourers and other requirements as much to the vast Mughal camp as to his own employers. Scanty scattered evidence proves that Balaji had made friends with the various officials of Aurangzeb and was possibly introduced even to his daughter Zinat-un-Nisa Begam's notice.[1] Balaji looked after the captive Shahu's concerns and supplied means to convey and bring him news of happenings outside. One may presume that he was privy to the affair of Shahu's proposed conversion and may have been consulted in the selection of brides for his marriage. In 1703 when the Emperor captured the fort of Sinhgad, it was stoutly defended by the Marathas against Tarbiyat Khan's formidable artillery, and a letter printed in the Purandare Daftar mentions how Balaji Vishvanath tried to save this famous stronghold from falling into the Emperor's hands. From such circumstantial evidence it would not be unfair to conclude that during the five years of arduous campaign conducted by the Emperor personally between 1699-1704 against the hill forts round about Poona and Satara, Shahu and Balaji Vishvanath became well attached to each other. Possibly the young Sawai Jaya Sinh who had distinguished himself in the capture of Vishalgad in April 1702 was also equally acquainted with them both. Prominent figures working together in a narrow field of action, cannot long remain utter strangers. Balaji rendered invaluable service to Shahu on the eve of the

1. An unpublished Maratha Bakhar at Osmania University.

battle of Khed and he in return rewarded him with the Peshwaship after a full trial of years, in which Balaji had exhibited an uncommon grasp of the political situation as it developed between the Marathas and the Mughals and a rare capacity for handling it to the best advantage of the Mahratha nation. History has justified Shahu's choice and done credit to his discernment.

5. **Shahu and Bahadur Shah.**—Shahu's fortunes during these early years of his kingship were severely controlled by the Emperor Bahadur Shah, a clever and conciliatory ruler, who had gained long and varied experience of war and government under his exacting father, so that to all appearances he gave promise of a long and prosperous reign avoiding the extremes which had ruined his father and fully controlling the disruptive forces that had set in. His early death was a blow to the Empire. But during his five years rule Shahu had to reckon with this Emperor's policy in controlling the Marathas.

Bahadur Shah's first concern after his coronation was the recovery of the southern Mughal dominions which his brother Kam Baksh had seized. He immediately started from Agra and arrived on the Godavari in June 1708 when Shahu was conducting operations against his aunt Tarabai. Bahadur Shah called upon Shahu to join him with his forces. Shahu sent excuses for his absence. Kam Baksh prepared for the contest and in a sanguinary fight met his death near Haidarabad on 3 January 1709. After arranging the administrative affairs of the conquered territory, Bahadur Shah started back from the Deccan, and reached Ahmadnagar in May, where Shahu's Pratinidhi Gadadhar Pralhad and Raybhanji Bhosle offered him obeisance and begged for sanads or written undertakings, confirming the grants of Chauth and Sardeshmukhi for their master Shahu in order to have his position legalized. Tarabai too was not inactive in this respect. Through her agents she made a similar request for the grants, contending that Shahu was not the rightful heir to the Maratha throne.

In this predicament Bahadur Shah's Wazir Munyim Khan, rejecting Zulfiqar Khan's advice to confirm Shahu's nomination, went through the details of the representations and ordered that Shahu and Tarabai should settle the dispute by fighting it out and then the sanads would be issued to the party that would win. This decision fully answers those critics who argue that Tarabai was fighting for the principle of complete independence as established by Shivaji and denounce Shahu for accepting subordination to the Emperor. Tarabai followed the tactics of Shahu. Raybhanji Bhosle, one of Shahji's illegitimate sons, was during these negotiations Shahu's main support and adviser pleading his cause at the Emperor's Court. He had served Aurangzeb for several years and obtained a rare insight into the various political currents of the Mughal-Maratha relations. Raybhanji died on 23rd August, 1709 soon after Bahadur Shah had left the Deccan, so that Shahu had none in the Mughal camp to support his cause.

6. **Chandrasen's defection, rise of Kolhapur.**—Shahu's activities in the region of Poona had not ceased during the new Emperor's presence in the south. A capable Mughal officer named Lodi Khan from his seat at Chakan used to harass the Maratha agents, but he was killed in an action at the pass of Purandar on 16th May 1709, by Shahu's troops under Gadadhar Pralhad. Lodi Khan's collaborator the powerful Karim Beg of Junnar was captured alive and kept in confinement. These two notable successes which at once established Shahu's authority in the region between Satara and Junnar, were however, of short duration, and Shahu's position quickly received a set back chiefly through the machinations of Chandrasen Jadhav, who out of spite towards Balaji's rising power, began open hostilities against him. A trivial incident aggravated the tension between them. During the summer of 1711, as both Chandrasen and Balaji were conducting an expedition near Karhad, a deer being pursued and wounded by one of Balaji's troopers, casually entered the kitchen tent of Chandrasen's Brahman clerk (one Vyasrao), who sheltered it and refused to give it up. The dispute soon reached the principals and incited them to open hostilities. Balaji was worsted by Chandrasen and had to flee for life when closely pursued. Balaji escaped capture and sought Shahu's protection through intermediaries. Chandrasen sent a strong threat to the king that unless Balaji was delivered into his hands for punish-

ment, he would quit his service and join the standard of Tarabai. Shahu had no alternative. He determined to support Balaji against the insolent Senapati whose loyalty was never firm and who was beyond hope of appeasement.

A very serious situation at once developed for Shahu. Chandrasen moved heaven and earth against him in all directions. Tarabai greeted him with expressions of the warmest respect and fed his vanity with all the arts of flattery. Shahu sent Parasurampant and Khanderao Dabhade to mediate and settle the dispute. The former was released and promised the coveted office of Pratinidhi if the mission proved successful. But these two noteworthy figures were easily won over by Chandrasen and they deserted Shahu's cause. Several local chiefs such as Damaji Thorat, Krishnarav Khatavkar, Udaji Chavan and others of lesser repute, seized this opportunity of rising against Shahu in order thereby to gain their own selfish ends. Not one of these had a moment's thought for the national interests as such. Thus the latter half of 1711 filled the cup of Shahu's misery to the brim. His only hope was centered in Balaji, who, though by no means a soldier, possessed unrivalled fortitude, power of planning and resourcefulness.

But Tarabai's main weakness lay in the want of solidarity or cohesion between the various elements that formed her following. She had absolutely no funds and an army cannot march on empty stomachs. Chandrasen was a mere braggart without any capacity for leadership. Ramachandrapant, her former minister and adviser, had been too much offended to feel enthusiasm or interest in her concerns. He was secretly negotiating for a place in the newly formed ministry of Shahu. Balaji rose to the occasion. Through friends and bankers he borrowed large sums, engaged and organized what later on came to be styled the Huzrat, or the King's own troops, and with a rapid stroke put down Khatavkar and sufficiently checked Thorat and Chavan. He also won a phenomenal diplomatic success against Kanhoji Angre, another formidable adherent of Tarabai, as will be described later. Thus within two years 1712 and 1713 Shahu's difficulties were settled to a large extent.

But the severest blow to Tarabai came from the jealousies in her own family. Rajaram's second wife Rajasbai and her son Sambhaji II were not content to remain nonentities. During the monsoon of 1714 Rajasbai contrived to put Tarabai and her son Shivaji in confinement and place her own son Sambhaji in the Chhatrapati's seat. In this connection Tarabai wrote long afterwards, " In the course of time we were compelled to undergo a sad experience. Rajasbai and her son Sambhaji managed through some of their agents to put us in confinement and inflict hardships upon us. Sambhaji was seated upon the throne." Evidently there was a strong opposition to Tarabai's domination, and she had to pass the remaining 47 years of her life practically behind prison walls, a spectacle of great regret and commiseration for such a gifted and heroic lady. As Chandrasen does not figure in this revolution, he was perhaps not trusted by either party.

This change in the Kolhapur government must have been supported, if not initiated by Ramchandra Nilkanth himself, the only man of capacity and experience in that party. The famous *Ajnapatra,* completed on 19th November 1715, expounding Shivaji's policy, is addressed by Ramchandrapant to Sambhaji II, then 17 years old as to a beloved pupil, conveying lessons in the art of governance and pouring forth all the accumulated wisdom of Shivaji's policy in which the Amatya was the principal instrument of execution. The language and diction are in harmony with the exalted subject, so that this treatise is considered of singular value in disclosing the high ideals of the founder. Ramchandra Nilkanth either died or retired after the issue of this Ajnapatra.[2]

The dual monarchy in the Chhatrapati's line has been the source of perennial evil affecting the unity of the Maratha nation. Sambhaji established his seat at Kolhapur, having found the fort of Panhala suitable for the close guarding of Tarabai and her son. Although Sambhaji did not entertain a more conciliatory attitude towards Shahu, the rigour of his rivalry certainly declined in the course of time. He now and then disturbed Shahu's peace by playing into the hands of

2. An inscription has been recently discovered pointing out the spot where his funeral took place in fort Panhala.

Nizam-ul-mulk: but the Peshwa Bajirao proved a match for them both, and relieved Shahu of his anxieties. Shahu defeated his cousin in open fight after enduring from him repeated acts of treachery, but gave him generous terms by the treaty of Warna in 1731, which forms the foundation charter of the present house of Kolhapur, as the sequel will show.

Shahu desired to inflict severe punishment upon Parasuram Pant for his treachery, but was induced by the mediation of his devoted Chitnis Khando Ballal to relent and to restore him to his old office of Pratinidhi. After his death on 26 May 1716, his second son Shripatrao was appointed to the Pratinidhi's post, the eldest son Krishnaji having already accepted the same office under the Kolhapur branch.

7. **Balaji wins the Peshwaship.**—How Balaji contrived to secure his appointment to the Peshwa's office is an interesting story. He won over to Shahu's cause another opponent greater in resources and valour than Chandrasen, viz. Kanhoji Angre, the warden of the west coast and head of the Maratha navy, whose career has become well-known in Anglo-Indian history. Kanhoji had vastly extended his power during the regime of Tarabai and readily joined Shahu on his arrival from the imperial camp and tendered his obedience and help to him. But after the defection of Chandrasen Jadhav, he went over to Tarabai's party and started war upon Shahu. He captured several forts above the Ghats belonging to Shahu, who sent his Peshwa Bahiropant Pingle to put him down. But Bahiropant was no match for Kanhoji, who seized and confined him at Kolaba and almost threatened Shahu's capital of Satara. Tarabai's triumph during the monsoon months of 1713 knew no bounds. At this very moment the highly capable Nizam-ul-Mulk was made the Emperor's Subahdar in the Deccan, thereby menacing Shahu's position still more.

Shahu was at a loss how to curb Angre's aggression. He asked the Sena-Karte Balaji to proceed against him and promised him the Peshwaship if he succeeded. Balaji thereupon urged that he was quite willing to execute the king's commands, provided he went out as the accredited Peshwa possessing powers to decide delicate issues of war and peace. "Here is an enemy," he added, "who has dared to capture and confine your Peshwa, and insinuates thereby that he would deal similarly with the Chhatrapati himself. Is it not then necessary to impress upon Kanhoji that another Peshwa has already taken the place of the one that is gone and that the king's government goes on without interruption? This is the only way to put him down." This argument was irrefutable. Balaji gained his object, Shahu immediately conferred upon him the office of the Peshwa with due ceremonies of investiture on the field of Manjri, 8 miles south of Poona, where they were then camping. Thus the 17th of November 1713 was a proud and momentous day not only for Balaji and his family but for the Maratha nation as well, as it marked the beginning of the transfer of power from the Chhatrapati's to the Peshwa's hands. In due course the other ministerial posts were also filled up out of the new Peshwa's partizans whose loyalty and devotion had been found unshakable. Ambajipant Purandare was appointed the Peshwa's Mutalik or Vice-Peshwa, and Ramajipant Bhanu his Phadnis or purser, an office which later descended to another well-known member of the family named Nana Phadnis. Thus the Bhats, the Purandares, the Bhanus and several other families of future note, came to be locked together in a revolutionary change for weal or woe, jointly bearing the responsibilities of the Maratha State in future.

Kanhoji Angre and Balaji had long been known to each other as friendly neighbours inhabiting the same coastal region of the west. Through common friends and secret agents Balaji appealed to Kanhoji's conscience, how both their personal and national interests would be highly promoted by their acting jointly under Shahu's suzerainty and how they would be ruined by adhesion to the Kolhapur party then like a broken reed. He urged that the Maratha raj was a sacred legacy left behind by the Great Shivaji, which it was their duty at the present crisis to preserve through common co-operation and harmonious working of the two forces, the army and the navy: that Shahu was a generous and large-hearted ruler incapable of harming even an adversary; that Kanhoji himself was surrounded by enemies, like the Siddis, the British and the Portuguese, against whom he could not hold his position long single-handed, unless he had at his back the full support of the central Government. Reasons both of policy and interest, therefore, required that Kanhoji should not alienate Shahu's sympathies, and at the same time Balaji promised to stand guarantee as the Peshwa to see that all promises made to Angre would be solemnly carried out.

This forceful appeal had its effect at once. Shrewd words proved effective where arms had failed. Kanhoji agreed to receive Balaji with the respect due to a Peshwa and personally arrange terms for their future relations. Balaji marched from Poona some 30 miles west to the vicinity of Lohgad where Kanhoji had taken his station. The latter came down from the fort and they had a cordial meeting at Valvan, a suburb of Lonavla, early in January 1714. They held a long conference discussing terms of a lasting peace between the Chhatrapati and the Sarkhel, which later proved a basis for a similar settlement with the other feudatories, thus gradually building up a fresh constitution for the future Maratha expansion, as the old constitution had fallen into utter confusion during the period of war and unrest that followed Shivaji's death. The terms having been solemnly agreed to with Shahu's knowledge and approval, the two chiefs proceeded together to Kolaba where the treaty was ratified on 8th February and the ex-Peshwa Bahiropant was released from confinement. Kanhoji came to pay his respects to Shahu at Satara, where the Holi festival of 1715 was performed with particular rejoicing.[3] In the main the treaty demarcated the Angrian and the Chhatrapati's possessions and provided for mutual co-operation and common defence.

This happy conclusion of what at first had appeared a calamity had its natural effect upon the policy of the Siddi of Janjira and the English at Bombay, two constant enemies of Kanhoji, who had all along shown determined opposition to any Maratha ambition. The Siddi readily concluded a peace with Angria on 30th January, 1715, an engagement which was not disturbed for seventeen years.

But the English of Bombay would not so easily give up the game and needed a lesson, particularly their pugnacious

3. The full text of the treaty can be studied in Mawji and Parasnis' printed collections.

President Charles Boone, who assumed office on 20th December 1715. Shahu's power and prestige were fast improving all round and were resented by the impulsive and aggressive temperament of Boone, who organized a strong naval expedition to extirpate the pirate, as Angria was then styled by the English. As special histories have fully detailed what followed, there is no need to treat the episode here at length. Clement Downing's published diary is eloquent and describes how miserably the English venture failed and how it was repeated year after year. Ultimately the English formed a coalition with the Portuguese of Goa and launched a conjoint attack against Angria during 1721, when Balaji Vishvanath was dead, and his son Bajirao who had just entered his new office, earned his first laurels by suddenly swooping upon the English by land and routing them near Kolaba. The English thought it wise to retrace their steps by concluding a treaty of peace with the Peshwa, which was not disturbed for several years.

CHRONOLOGY

CHAPTER II

1671, August 11	Nizam-ul-Mulk born.
1708	Mughal Subahdars of the Deccan.
1708-13	Daud Khan Pani.
1713 Feb.—1715 April	Nizam-ul-Mulk.
1715 May—1718 Nov.	Saiyad Husain Ali.
1718 Dec.— 1720 Aug.	Alam Ali.
1720 Aug.—1722 Jan.	Nizam-ul-Mulk.
1709-10	Rajput alliance against the Emperor.
1711	Wazir Munyim Khan dies.
1712 February 17	Bahadur Shah dies.
1713 January 12	Zulfiqar Khan put to death.
1713 January 19	Farrukhsiyar becomes Emperor.
1713 Nov.—1714 July	Saiyad Husain Ali invades Marwar.
1713	Jayasinh Sawai appointed Subahdar of Malwa.
1715 May 10	Jayasinh defeats the Marathas in Malwa.
1715 August 26	Daud Khan Pani killed in battle.
1717 January 11	Khanderao Dabhade appointed Senapati by Shahu in the place of Mansinh More.
1718	Shankaraji Malhar negotiates Maratha help for Saiyad Husain Ali.
1718 August 1	Shahu enforces terms of agreement.
1718 November	Balaji Vishvanath leads Maratha expedition to Delhi.
1719 February 13	Emperor meets the Saiyad Brothers.
1719 February 28	Emperor deposed: some Marathas massacred near Delhi.
1719 March 3	Grant of Chauth ratified.
1719 March 15	Grant of Sardeshmukhi ratified.
1719 March 20	Balaji Vishvanath leaves Delhi on return.
1719 July 4	Balaji Vishvanath reaches Satara.
1720 April 2	Balaji Vishvanath dies.

CHAPTER II

NEW ERA DAWNS

[1715—1720]

1 Imperial politics favour Shahu.
2 The friendly Rajput Princes.
3 Saiyad Husain Ali in the Deccan.
4. Husain Ali secures Maratha help.
5 Conditions of Maratha vassalage.
6 Balaji's Expedition to Delhi.
7 Clash of arms.
8 Release and death of Yesubai.
9 Chauthai and Sardeshmukhi explained.
10 Origin and evils of Jagirdari.
11 Hereditary Offices.
12 Death of Balaji, character estimated.

1. Imperial politics favour Shahu.—Shahu's position as King of the Marathas came to be stabilized during the six years that elapsed between his release and the appointment of Balaji Vishvanath to the Peshwaship. But Maratha politics received special vigour not so much through domestic occurrences, as from the many momentous and rapid changes that came over the Court of Delhi after Bahadur Shah's death on 17th February 1712. His successor Jahandar Shah suffered a sad fate within less than a year, and Farrukhsiyar came to occupy the throne on 17th January 1713, mainly with the support of the well-known Saiyad brothers, Abdulla and Husain Ali, who put to death the old experienced general Zulfiqar Khan, who had an eye on the Deccan and who, if he had lived, would possibly have established his rule at Haidarabad. The six years of Farrukhsiyar's reign were taken up by intrigues and counter-intrigues between him and these two powerful ministers, each doing his utmost to contrive the other's ruin. The Saiyad brothers possessed not only power but talents of a rare order combined with administrative capacity. If they had been given a free hand, they could possibly have raised the tone of the decaying Mughal administration, and brought it to the level of that of Bahadur Shah. But the Mughal house came to be hopelessly divided and afforded the Marathas their coveted chance to expand themselves in all directions outside their national frontiers.

Daud Khan Pani had governed the Mughal Deccan since 1708 as the deputy of Zulfiqar Khan. When Farrukhsiyar ascended the throne and Zulfiqar Khan came to be assassinated, Chinqilich Khan Ghazi-ud-din Firuz-jang, then 42 years old (born August 1671), was appointed to the government of the Deccan with the title of Nizam-ul-Mulk Khan-i-Khanan. Daud Khan was then transferred to Gujarat and he left Aurangabad in July 1713 ; and in the following October Nizam-ul-Mulk took charge of his office : at this very moment Balaji Vishvanath was invested with the Peshwaship, so that these two great men and their descendants between them made up the history of the Deccan for nearly a century, developing relations sometimes of amity, at others of enmity towards each other, with the result that whilst no trace of the Peshwas exists in Maharashtra at this day, the dominions of His Exalted Highness the Nizam are flourishing under the aegis of Britain. How this happened is fully explained by Maratha history.

Chinqilich Khan, however, held office in the Deccan only for two years, 1713-1715, owing to a sharp antagonism between the Emperor and the two Saiyad brothers. Farrukhsiyar appointed Husain Ali to the charge of the Deccan in 1715, and removed Nizam much against his will to the insignificant Foujdari of Moradabad. During these two years of his office Nizam-ul-mulk could not do much to consolidate his power. He encouraged his local assistants and befriended Rambhaji Nimbalkar, Chandrasen Jadhav and others who had risen against Shahu, and tried to strengthen the Mughal hold on Poona and its environs as a means of checking the activities of Shahu and his Peshwa. He lived during this period a life of almost regal splendour at Aurangabad, and lavishly spent on the ceremonies of circumcision of his two sons, Ghaziuddin and Nasirjang, the latter about five years old at the time. Shahu on his part continued to be harassed on all sides, particularly by Chandrasen Jadhav ; and the Peshwa Balaji was occupied in saving his master's position against heavy odds. His critical situation is clearly evidenced by the following letter addressed by Shahu to his Peshwa some time in 1715 :—

" We have had no news for some time about your movements and plans. As regards our situation here, we have already communicated to you in detail the rebellious activities of our cousin of Kolhapur incited thereto by Nizam-ul-mulk. Thus the short-sightedness of the one and the treachery of the other, have now combined to our detriment : but we are by no means daunted by this development : our only fear is how you can counteract these intrigues from the distance that you are now at ; but we are perfectly easy and calm having full confidence in the incomparable prowess of a servant of your type. We have called together all the scattered troops posted in different stations and would feel greatly relieved if you can run up here immediately, leaving aside your ordinary engagements."

The departure of Nizam-ul-mulk for the north for a time removed the anxieties of Shahu, whose situation took a different turn with the arrival of Saiyad Husain Ali. The Emperor called upon Daud Khan Pani of Gujarat to march against the Saiyad and do away with him. He also instigated Shahu for the same purpose. As a result of this incitement Daud Khan and the Saiyad met in a deadly combat near Burhanpur on 26th August, 1715, wherein Daud Khan was killed and the Saiyad came out victorious, so that Shahu's prospects came to be affected by the policy that Saiyad Husain Ali Khan would now adopt in co-operation with his brother Saiyad Abdulla at Delhi. The two brothers' instinct of self-preservation was the factor which moulded Shahu's policy during the next two years.

2. **The friendly Rajput Princes.**—Another powerful factor at the Imperial Court, which affected Shahu's interests was the attitude of the prominent Rajput princes towards the struggle between the Emperor and his powerful ministers. Akbar's policy of conciliating the Rajputs had been reversed by Aurangzeb, whose death afforded them a welcome opportunity of throwing away their allegiance to the Emperor. The princes that counted most in such a revolt deserve to be carefully noticed. Amar Sinh, the Rana of Udaipur ruled from 1700 to 1716 and his son Sangram Sinh from 1716 to 1734, both strong and clever, refusing obedience to the Muslim sovereign. Jodhpur was ruled by Ajit Sinh Rathod, who although a nominal ally of the Emperor was at heart no better

friend than his brother princes of Udaipur. Ajit Singh ruled his state from 1678 to 1724 and was succeeded by his son Abhay Sinh the most terrible of all Rajput kings, who ruled from 1724 to 1750. The Jaipur state was ruled, however, by a genial and accomplished ruler named Sawai Jaya Sinh, fourth in descent from the great Mirza Raja, the devoted general of Aurangzeb. Sawai Jaya Sinh in early youth served the Emperor in the Deccan and rendered conspicuous service to Aurangzeb at the capture of fort Vishalgad between the months of November 1701 and April 1702, although then quite young. He attained immense influence and prestige in the imperial counsels after Aurangzeb's death mainly through several precious qualities of head and heart, which he acquired by assiduous labour, viz., a fondness for letters and learning, a study of science, particularly astronomy, a congenial compromising spirit guided by high ideals in life and a sound judgment about men as well as a reforming spirit far in advance of his age. In this connection the particular attachment that existed between Shahu and Jaya Sinh deserves to be noted, as it led to far-reaching political relations between the two Hindu races—Rajputs and Marathas. Jaya Sinh patronized poets and writers from all parts of India, while Shahu patronized saints and warriors. Several Maharashtrian names have recently been discovered among those whom Jaya Sinh revered and promoted. His family priest and his guru were Deccani Brahmans, of whose capacity he evidently formed a high opinion during his residence in Aurangzeb's camp.

What great significance such a typical contact between the Maratha Shahu and the Rajput Jaya Sinh, must have carried in the long run during those revolutionary times, had better be imagined. What could have been the ideal that stirred their hearts and the hearts of the society they moved in? The Hindus have always cared more for religion than politics. The destruction of the Kashivishveshwar temple of Benares by Aurangzeb in 1669, was an unforgettable shock to the average Hindu mind. We know how it affected Shivaji and his mother, and how it nerved the Marathas during their memorble struggle against the Emperor through a quarter of a century. In other respects they had no quarrel with the Emperor. They only needed an assurance that their religious liberty would not be interfered with. They were not covetous of political domination beyond their home. The expansion of power which they later acquired was an indirect result of their zeal for preserving their religion. Shivaji had made this clear in his famous letter to Aurangzeb on the subject of Jazia. That Emperor's bigoted policy of destroying Hindu temples, of conversion under pressure, of the imposition of Jazia and of administrative depression of the Hindus, had exasperated and alienated the whole Hindu community, who severely resented this attack on their religion. This is all they wanted to prevent. The dream of Hindupad Padshahi was not territorial ambition but mainly limited to the religious field.[1]

At any rate Shahu and Jaya Sinh freely exchanged views on this policy of the Mughals and later each tried in his own way to bring about a kind of compromise, that is, non-interference or toleration as inculcated and practised by the great Akbar. When Bahadur Shah started his religious war against the Sikhs, the above mentioned prominent Rajput princes held a prolonged conference on the border of the Pushkar lake and after full deliberation proclaimed a solemn concerted policy,—that they would not thenceforth give their daughters in marriage to Muslims and that if any prince acted contrary to this resolution, the others should join and put down the deserter by force if necessary. The declaration went further. The Ranas of Udaipur were acknowledged to be of purer blood, having all along refused to give their daughters in marriage to Muslims ; so the Pushkar conference laid down that if any Rajput prince had an issue from a daughter of the Udaipur family, that issue should be given preference over those born from other wives in choosing a successor to the vacant throne. This stipulation made the remedy worse than the disease, as, in the long run, it led to a crop of wars of succession throughout Rajputana. The famous story of Krishna-Kumari is an illustration of such results. But in our present discussion of Maratha activities, it is enough to note how the religious element prevailed over politics.

1. This is well explained by Sir Jadunath in his History of Aurangzeb, Vol. 3, Chapter on Islamic State-Church. Jazia means substitute-tax, price of indulgence, i.e. a tax or fine levied in return for liberty in religious matters.

The Saiyad brothers were by no means less enthusiastic than Aurangzeb in putting down the religious claims of the Hindus, and used their power in sternly enforcing the traditional Muslim policy. To counteract the results of the Pushkar conference, these ministers carried sword and fire into Rajputana and compelled Ajit Sinh of Marwar to give his daughter Indra-Kumari as a wife to the Emperor. The marriage was later on solemnized at Delhi with great pomp. The other Rajput princes submitted to the inevitable and bowed down before the powerful Saiyads, who doubtless possessed valour and talent of a high order, which Farrukhsiyar had not the wisdom to direct towards beneficial ends. He kept on plotting incessantly for their ruin and when he found himself foiled at every step, he separated them by appointing Husain Ali to the government of the Deccan, as we have already mentioned.

3. **Saiyad Husain Ali in the Deccan.**—To make room for Saiyad Husain Ali, Nizam-ul-mulk was recalled from the Deccan, thereby giving him unnecessary umbrage. The Saiyads and Nizam-ul-mulk far from being on cordial terms with each other, passed through Malwa without observing the customary formality of an exchange of visits as brother officers. Immediately on arrival, Husain Ali as has been already noticed, encountered Daud Khan in an action near Burhanpur and killed him. The Emperor had called upon the Marathas also, to oppose the Saiyad, but they were discreet enough not to take any active part on either side. Shahu, Balaji and Khanderao Dabhade, his Senapati mostly occupied themselves at this time in wresting the region of Poona from the hands of the Mughal officials who were then in charge.

The main object of both the Emperor and the Saiyads was to put down the rising Maratha power in the Deccan and to oust them entirely from Malwa, where they had been acquiring a foot-hold. Malwa being the main highway between the north and the south, its possession had always been considered essential for the security of the Empire. Aurangzeb himself was watchful about Malwa and as early as February 1704 had inflicted a crushing defeat through his trusted general Ghaziuddin upon several Maratha chiefs such as Nemaji Sinde, Parsoji Bhosle, Keshopant Pingle and others near Dipalpur and Ujjain. Later on the Marathas, by no means entirely checked, had continued their depredations so persistently that in 1713 Farrukhsiyar appointed Jaya Sinh Sawai to the government of Malwa, which the Rajput was ambitious to annex to his own patrimony of Jaipur. Khanderao Dabhade and Kanhoji Bhosle entered Malwa in the early months of 1715, burnt and plundered Ujjain and the regions round about ; Jaya Sinh was ready to meet them and inflicted upon them a crushing defeat on 10th May and recovered all the goods and property that had been plundered. But Jaya Sinh's success proved temporary and when he was recalled soon after, the Marathas renewed their aggression with impunity.

The Emperor had about him capable generals and efficient resources : the Sayid brothers, Nizam-ul-mulk, Amin Khan, Saadat Khan, Jaya Sinh, Ajit Sinh were all men of valour and capacity, but their efforts were never combined and thus proved ineffective, mainly on account of the Emperor's intriguing policy and his want of trust in them. Every one of his officers and courtiers remained in imminent danger to life and was prevented from putting forth his best effort in the imperial service. Historians often criticise the Saiyad brothers for allowing the Marathas a free passage right up to Delhi. But this was not really the case. They tried their best to put down the Marathas ; and Husain Ali during his first two years in the Deccan made strenuous efforts to prevent Maratha inroads in Baglan and Khandesh. But when ultimately they found they stood in the greatest danger to their life and position from their master, they were compelled to reverse their policy and seek Maratha friendship.

Shahu's position likewise remained insecure for long. He was not as fortunate in securing a competent Senapati as he was in his choice of the Peshwa. Dhanaji's son Chandrasen was put into that office, but he practised open treachery : his brother Santaji whom Shahu gave the office in 1711, was an idiot with no capacity to plan campaigns. He was replaced by Mansinh More in 1712, a faithful servant, but quite a mediocrity in his profession ; and he too unfortunately broke down in health. Shahu then had recourse to Khanderao

Dabhade whom he appointed to the office of the Senapati on 11th January 1717. For a time he worked well, but age and infirmities soon disabled him for the growing intricacies of the political situation, particularly for meeting the demands of a new era created by the revolutionary changes at the Court of Delhi. Khanderao Dabhade's failure to enter wholeheartedly into the plans and schemes of the Peshwa, soon made him lose his ground and gave a welcome chance to the rising star of the future young Bajirao.

For two years Saiyad Husain Ali struggled hard in the Deccan to put down the Maratha encroachments as best he could, and to meet the intrigues which the Emperor was assiduously devising in order to ruin him. His brother Saiyad Abdullah's position at Delhi was steadily deteriorating and became so precarious, that being afraid of his own life, he recalled Husain Ali from the south with all expedition and with a strong military equipment to save their position at Court. Husain Ali thereupon took full counsel with his friends and followers, and came to the conclusion that his only chance of success lay in securing the goodwill and co-operation of the Marathas, particularly of Shahu and his supporters. He could not afford to antagonise them, if he were to remain absent from the Deccan: for the two ministers could easily be crushed between the Marathas in the south and the Emperor's clique in the north. The author of Shahu's chronicle[2] writes :—

"When the Emperor Farrukhsiyar recalled Nizam-ul-mulk and appointed Saiyad Husain Ali to the chief Subahship of the Deccan, the latter selected for his chief adviser one Shankaraji Malhar, a renowned old Maratha diplomat who had migrated long ago from his attendance as Sachiv upon Rajaram at Jinji and resided at Benares. The Emperor learnt of this clever and serviceable person, brought him to Delhi under personal persuasion, and sent him to the Deccan with Saiyad Husain Ali as his confidential adviser upon matters concerning the Marathas. The Emperor made a suitable provision for Shankaraji's services as an ambassador."

2. Pages 26, 36.

4. **Husain Ali secures Maratha Help.**—This Shankaraji Malhar, a Maharashtra Brahman surnamed Nargundkar possessed a rare genius for political affairs. He had in 1689 accompanied Chhatrapati Rajaram to Jinji and on some irritation had retired to Benares. But a spirit of restless ambition took possession of his mind, and he readily accepted the Emperor's mission to the Deccan to accompany Saiyad Husain Ali, whose good graces he soon managed to secure and he made himself invaluable in his new office, as Husain Ali himself was an utter stranger to the Marathas. Shankaraji's presence soon became known to Shahu and his Peshwa Balaji, through personal agents and commanders. When Saiyad Husain Ali received a peremptory call from his brother at Delhi, his first concern was not only to close his war with Shahu, but also to gain his friendship and military help in order to prosecute his future plans with success. He deputed Shankaraji to proceed to Satara and secure a friendly arrangement with Shahu. Shankaraji arrived at Satara early in 1718. Shahu and his counsellors grasped this mission almost as a heaven-sent opportunity for establishing a direct contact with Delhi, and for putting an end to the vexatious wars which were sapping their strength and resources practically ever since the release of Shahu.[3]

Shahu and Balaji had already come to their wits' end in putting their house in order. Ten years had gone by and they were in no way better off. Internal and external troubles, dissension and treason among their followers, the unstable character of the imperial administration, disorder all round, were eating into the vitals of the small afflicted Maratha nation with hardly any prospect for it to live and revive after the fashion of their revered founder.

The Marathas possessed brain and nerve, which had been well exercised and disciplined during their long war with Aurangzeb. Leaders of their martial bands were roving the land, crying for work and adventure, and wasting their energy in cutting each other's throats, swearing one moment to uphold the cause of Shahu, and deserting the next moment to

3. This mission of Shankaraji is clearly explained both by Khafi Khan and the author of Siyar-ul-Mutakherin.

Kolhapur or to the Mughals; and all the time seeking nothing but their selfish ends, preying upon the hapless toiling population, the real producers of food and wealth. How was this anarchy to be ended? This was the problem which Balaji and Shahu with all their wisdom had proved impotent to solve. Shankaraji when he arrived at Satara, suggested the solution. He urged that if these roving bands of Maratha soldiery could be supplied with some suitable employment out of their accustomed routine, their attention would be diverted to new prospects outside and the chaotic conditions in Maharashtra would be at once changed.

Shankarajipant like a prophet assured the doubters and hesitators that the Mughal power was at that time only a make-believe; that there was no less anarchy and turbulence in the north; that races and principalities in those quarters were ready to greet any power that would come and relieve them; that these lessons of adventure and self-reliance were bequeathed to them by the great Shivaji and that they must follow in his foot-steps. "Here," said Shankaraji, "are the two powerful Saiyads holding out their hand for friendship: grasp it by all means without hesitation: offer your own terms: they would be ungrudgingly granted: they are hard pressed by danger at this moment. Your king is pious and generous at heart. He will not sanction a policy that would do harm to the Emperor. This is an advantage in itself. The Saiyads themselves do not personally contemplate any harm to the Emperor: they are only anxious to set matters right in the administration which must run smoothly. They only seek to gain sufficient control over the government machinery. Shahu had given his solemn word to the dying Aurangzeb that he would never rise against the Empire, and that he would help it with all his power in its sore need."[4] That was just the course that Shankaraji advocated. So a treaty of peace and good will, an agreement with definite terms, ensuring the interests of both parties, was advocated. Shahu and his Court were called upon only to stand by the Saiyad ministers as supporters.

4. P. D. 30. 222.

5. **Conditions of Maratha Vassalage.**—Such was the nature of the peace parleys that were held for some days at Satara. The actual details have not been recorded. But Shahu had another personal reason for falling in with the plan. His mother Yesubai, wife Savitribai (for his second wife Ambikabai was already dead) and his brother Madansinh with a number of followers were still held at Delhi as hostages whom he was naturally most anxious to get back. Balaji and Shankaraji managed to put in a clear stipulation to that effect in the treaty that was arranged for the approval of Saiyad Husain Ali. The terms agreed to by both the parties were :—

1. That all territories known as Shivaji's *swarajya* (original dominions); together with the forts therein, should be delivered to Shahu in full possession ;

2. That such territories as had been recently conquered by the Marathas in Khandesh, Berar, Gondawana, Haidarabad and Karnatak as described in the annexure to the treaty, should also be ceded to them as part of the Maratha Kingdom.

3. That the Marathas should be allowed to collect Chauth and Sardeshmukhi from all the six Mughal Subahs in the south ; in return for the Chauth the Marathas were to serve the Emperor with a contingent of 15 thousand troops for his protection ; and in return for the Sardeshmukhi the Marathas were to be responsible for maintaining order by preventing robbery and rebellions ;

4. That Shahu should do no harm to Sambhaji of Kolhapur ;

5. That the Marathas should make a cash payment annually of ten lacs of Rupees to the Emperor by way of tribute ; and lastly

6. That the Emperor should release and send back from Delhi Shahu's mother Yesubai, his wife and his brother Madansinh with all the followers that were detained there.

Saiyad Husain Ali agreed to these terms and promised to get them formally ratified by the Emperor in due course. On 1st August 1718, Shahu issued orders to his local officials to enforce the terms of the above agreement and make collections of Chauthai and Sardeshmukhi. An order issued by Balaji to the Deshmukhs and Deshpandes of Poona dated 30th July 1718 exists which calls upon them to stop the payment of these dues to the Mughal official Rambhaji Nimbalkar. Balaji, immediately upon the agreement being confirmed, toured through the districts and took possession of them in the name of Shahu and raised a special corps of troops for the service of the Emperor which along with what he already possessed. later came to be termed the Huzarat, i.e. the King's troops.

Such was the welcome stroke of policy and good fortune which through Balaji's state-craft at once raised Shahu's prestige and established his position as the lawful ruler of the Marathas, in contrast with his cousin Sambhaji. It was this legal status which Shahu had all along been trying to acquire since his release and which Balaji's supreme efforts succeeded at last in confirming. An orderly government for Shahu's *swarajya* came to be immediately organized in place of what was till then a casual operation based upon force. Divided loyalties were thenceforth removed and a legal status for all Maratha governmental measures established. Thus this treaty enabled the Marathas to become masters of their home and to obtain fresh facilities for expansion outside from their base in the Deccan. The exact interpretation of the terms agreed upon remained vague in several points for a long time, and often varied with each fresh official dealing with the subject on either side.

Shahu unlike Shivaji never claimed to be an absolutely independent king, but agreed to remain like a vassal paying annual tribute and rendering nominal obedience to the Emperor whom, however, he undertook to protect with his own troops. But when a sovereign seeks protection from a vassal it means in actual practice, that the comparative strength of the two contracting parties is reversed. The Marathas hereafter obtained freedom to go about in search of fresh fields and pastures new.

For years past Shahu was seeking such a development. For this very purpose he had deputed his Parasnis Yadavrao Prabhu to Delhi to arrange matters as long ago as 1715. He now addressed the following letter on 24 February 1718 to this Parasnis :—

"From what Shankaraji Malhar and you have written, the three important concessions, viz., of Swarajya, Chauthai and Sardeshmukhi have been satisfactorily secured. The only matter that yet remains to be executed is the release and return of our revered mother Yesubai, Madansingh and their staff. When this is effected, then only will all the strenuous exertions and mediations which Shankarajipant and yourself have been so selflessly rendering, have been profitably employed. Please do not neglect this point; urge it incessantly upon the Saiyad's attention and have it quickly carried out. I have written fully on the subject to Shankarajipant from whom you can gather what my special anxiety is."

6. Balaji's Expedition to Delhi.—Although a satisfactory agreement was formally executed with the Saiyad, it remained to be ratified at Delhi, where the Emperor was already involved in his struggle with his ministers. There was no knowing that he would readily assent to the terms. The Emperor was by no means a friend of the Marathas. He had his own counsellors and advisers and the Maratha hopes depended upon the turn affairs might take at Delhi. They would gain their ends only if the Saiyad brothers came out victorious in the contest that was impending between them and the Emperor. When Husain Ali and Balaji met and discussed the situation, they must have talked fully and plainly what preparations were needed, how they were to act and how the expenses were to be met in the venture they were jointly undertaking. The irresistible urge came from Shahu on account of his anxiety for his mother, and Balaji could not refuse to undertake the risk.

Khanderao Dabhade, Shahu's Senapati arrived at Aurangabad in June 1718 with his contingent of 15,000 troops, in fulfilment of the contract. Husain Ali had already kept the Emperor informed of his new move of conciliating the Marathas and requested his assent to it. The Emperor, in reply, however, wrote to state his disapproval of the whole transaction and appointed his own nominees to several important offices in the Deccan. Husain Ali on his own part put down these officials and arranged his affairs with a high hand. The Emperor realized the danger he was running into by antagonising his powerful ministers and hastily called back to his presence Nizam-ul-mulk from Moradabad, Sarbuland Khan from Patna and Ajit Sinh from Gujarat. When these grandees arrived at Delhi with their large followings, Saiyad Abdulla also strengthened his fighting resources and sent urgent calls to his brother to repair to the capital from the south without a moment's delay.

Husain Ali quickly grasped the situation. He had not a moment to lose. He arranged his plans in consultation with Balaji who was asked to accompany the expedition. Shahu and his Court supported the project heartily and left nothing undone that discretion and foresight could suggest. Khando Ballal Chitnis and Yadavrao Munshi Parasnis accompanied the party as Shahu's personal agents to watch the conduct of affairs. Khanderao Dabhade Senapati, with Udaji, Keroji and Tukoji Pawar, Ranoji and Santaji Bhosle, were the principal Maratha leaders of the fighting arm. Shekh Mira, Baji Kadam, Naro Shankar, Chimnaji Damodar, Mahadeo Bhat Hingne, Ambaji Trimbak Purandare, Balaji Mahadev Bhanu, these and other rising spirits of the future, were ordered by Shahu to accompany the expedition, which, headed by the Peshwa with his promising youthful son Bajirao by his side, formed, as would be seen, the best brain and arm of the Maratha king.

Husain Ali posted his own spirited nephew Alam Ali Khan at Aurangabad with his brother Saif-ud-din Ali to support him. He also left with them Shankaraji Malhar by whose advice they were to be guided during his absence. At Balaji's special pleading, however, Shankarajipant was taken to Delhi for a short time and was allowed to return very soon. Husain Ali's sole hope rested upon the cordial support he secured from the Marathas and he boldly left Aurangabad in high hopes and confidence in November 1718, and Burhanpur in the middle of December, reaching Delhi on 16th February next year. Each Maratha trooper received from the imperial treasury one rupee per day for his expenses.

7. **Clash of Arms.**—As news of Husain Ali's approach reached the Emperor, he became extremely apprehensive for his life and forwarded repeated messages and special agents to turn him back. Thereupon Husain Ali asked the Maratha commanders to return or halt where they were, but they refused to do so unless Shahu's mother and party were delivered into

their hands. Husain Ali reported the matter to the Emperor adding that it was now impossible for him to offend his Maratha allies and that they would create fearful trouble for all, if their wishes were opposed. Thus they all pushed on and the two Saiyad brothers met together at Delhi and at once concerted sound plans for mastering the situation as it developed. Details of the revolution that followed are plentiful and can be studied in the pages of Irvine's *Later Mughals*, in *Siyar-ul-Mutakherin* and other contemporary accounts. Here only the relevant portions touching the Maratha doings need be adverted to.

During February and March the capital of Delhi wore a dreadful appearance, due to large Maratha forces and others belonging to the several Rajput rulers and Muslim grandees, having assembled there. The populace of Delhi and the environs took serious alarm at the obvious portents of what was to come next. The Emperor to ease the situation tried to send away Jaysinh and Ajit Sinh to their dominions, but they only left the city and remained encamped in the vicinity. During the last week of February the Emperor and the two brother ministers had many stormy meetings at which the latter gained the upper hand. The news that the Emperor was trying to get rid of Husain Ali Khan, infuriated the brothers so highly that they determined to depose him and place on the throne another Shahzada of their choice, who would be more amenable to their measures and policy.

On 27th February the brothers besieged the palace and the fort and posted their own guards at the gates for preventing ingress or egress. The strategic points in the city were also similarly guarded. The Maratha troopers were posted not far from the main entrance to the palace. Saiyad Abdulla and Ajit Sinh remained closeted all night with the Emperor, exchanging hot words and angry epithets which grew in tone and temper as the night advanced. The imperial city exhibited a ghastly appearance in the early morning of 28th February, the ministerial cavalry men riding through the principal streets and killing all who opposed them. Muhammad Amin Khan a partizan of the Emperor tried with his few determined followers to force open the palace gate and had a severe skirmish with the Maratha guards posted at the entrance. In this encounter some 1500 to 2000 Maratha horsemen were cut to pieces, prominent among whom were Santaji Bhosle of Nagpur and Balajipant Bhanu the grand-father of the famous Nana Phadnis. The ministers arrested the Emperor and confined him; and successively put on the throne two Shahzadas after short intervals. Muhammad Shah was ultimately installed who ruled until his death in April 1748. The deposed Farrukhsiyar was put to death two months later.

In this revolution Ajit Sinh the Raja of Marwar sided with the Saiyad ministers and with his strong support facilitated their measures, so that they became supreme masters for a time able to make whatever arrangements they thought best. They appointed Nizam-ul-mulk to the government of Malwa whom Balaji Vishvanath particularly befriended, as he was likely one day to be the governor of the Deccan. While at Delhi Balaji and Nizam-ul-mulk exchanged *Bhaichara* or brotherly dinners in token of mutual friendship. They at this time cultivated such esteem and regard for each other that the Nizam himself recommended Balaji and Ambaji Trimbak to the notice of the Emperor. Similarly Jaysinh and Ajit Sinh both willingly supported the Maratha claims as embodied in the treaty contracted by the Saiyad and thus legalized what in actual practice was being enacted by the Marathas ever since the days of Shivaji. As soon as the palace revolution was over, the Saiyads prepared formal grants for the three items of Swarajya, Chauthai and Sardeshmukhi and delivered them to Balaji duly ratified under the imperial seal. Shahu's mother and the rest of the party who had been in confinement at Delhi for nearly twelve years, were released and delivered over. The Sanad for the grant of Chauthai is dated 3rd March 1719 and that of Sardeshmukhi 15th March. Writes Sir Richard Temple,—

"Balaji Vishvanath carried victoriously all his diplomatic points and brought back to western India a political instrument which is one of the most noteworthy state documents in Indian history and constituted the Magna-Charta of the Maratha Dominion." These sanads were long in the Chhatrapati's possession at Satara and were examined by the historian

Grand Duff. They are now available in print, but not in the original Persian.[5]

Shahu had instructed Balaji and others to try and obtain similar sanads for the Subahs of Malwa and Gujarat, but the circumstances at the Court of Delhi were not yet favourable for such a consummation. What they already obtained was by no means a small gain. Balaji was given a hearty send off back from Delhi which he and the party left on 20th March and reached Satara early in July, after the Peshwa himself had paid a hurried visit to Benares and performed the customary rites of a pious Hindu. The Maratha stay at Delhi did not extend for over a month. Ajit Sinh of Marwar was rewarded by the Saiyads for his services with the grant of the Subah of Gujarat, which he had long coveted and which he at once went to take possession of.

Shahu journeyed a long way from Satara to offer a grand welcome to the Peshwa and his party on their arrival. He felt highly gratified at the success of the expedition which had all the while caused him no small anxiety. The joy he felt at meeting with his mother after twelve years of separation can only be imagined. He profusely complimented the Peshwa on this remarkable achievement. It is said that Balaji received from the Saiyads about 50 thousand rupees cash daily for the expenses, out of which he actually paid 30 lacs into Shahu's treasury in addition to a large number of presents of dresses and curios of various kinds, which each member of the expedition must have separately obtained. All received their wages regularly in cash and the usual complaint of the salary of troops remaining in arrears was not heard.

A grand Darbar was held at Satara where Balaji presented his colleagues and co-workers to Shahu bringing to his notice their particular services. A new era of hope and aspiration had begun for Maharashtra. The pretensions of Shahu's cousin of Kolhapur were now curbed. As Santaji Bhosle had lost his life at Delhi, his brother Ranoji was given the title of Sawai Santaji with fresh inams and rewards for the sacri-

5. "*Treaties and Agreements*" edited by Mawji and Parasnis, Nirnay Sagar Press, 1914.

fices he had made. The two brothers were the sons of Shahu's first benefactor Parsoji Bhosle.[6]

The social results of this first Maratha venture into the north were no less important. It gave a new turn and a fresh vision to Maratha ambitions. Delhi had hitherto been supposed to be far off. They had only heard of it, they had never seen the imperial Court, or its grandeur and etiquette. They now felt the striking contrast of the splendour of Delhi to the poor and half-naked life of an average Maharashtrian in the south. The Marathas for the first time experienced the remarkable difference in the whole life, dress, food, manners and ways, which hereafter widened their outlook and excited their greed for conquest and expansion. This is typified in the life of the first Peshwa's son Bajirao, whose nerve came to be entirely different from his father's. Shahu quickly noticed the change in this promising youth and did not hesitate to invest him with the robes of Peshwaship when Balaji suddenly died a few months after his return home.

8. *Release and death of Yesubai.*—The story of Yesubai the pious and revered mother of Shahu, deserves to be concluded here. Daughter of Pilaji Shirke of Shringarpur, she was married probably at the age of 8 to Sambhaji about the year 1669 and passed her early life under the direct eyes of the great Shivaji. She bore two children, the elder a girl named Bhavanibai, the younger, a son named Shahu. They and their followers about 200 in all were captured at the fall of Raigad and kept in strict confinement in the Mughal camp and carried from place to place wherever it moved during the 18 years of war, a period in which she had to suffer such misery and want as would excite one's pity for her misfortunes and admiration for the patience and fortitude which she exhibited

6. The following letter written by Shahu on 2 August 1719 to Balaji Mahadev Bhanu's son is typical of the way in which he rewarded the services rendered to the State.

'Your father Balajipant who had accompanied the Peshwa on duty as an accountant (Phadnis), lost his life in the confusion that occurred at Delhi. In recognition of his loyal services you are hereby granted the village of Banksai in inam which you should share along with your uncle Ramaji Mahadev the brother of the deceased."

under severe trial. After Aurangzeb's death at Ahmadnagar the party were forced to follow his son Azam Shah in his journey to the north and were taken to Delhi as hostages. After the long and wearisome detention at the capital Yesubai was released in March 1719 and soon after reached Satara to find her son securely seated on the Maratha throne. After her return to Satara she seems to have lived for at least 12 years more. Yesubai ended her chequered life very happily, leaving behind a pious memory of a pure and selfless soul. Sambhaji wrote the following letter of condolence to Shahu on learning of the death of Yesubai. It discloses the unusual reverence in which the lady was held by all.

"The sad news of the illness and consequent death of your revered mother Yesubai has occasioned to us no less sorrow than to you. It is a matter beyond human control and we have all to put up with it. You as an elder doubtless possess the fortitude to bear the calamity calmly. What more comfort can I offer on this sad bereavement?" Shahu and Yesubai live in Maratha memory almost as much as Shivaji and his mother Jijabai do. Shahu ever felt that he owed all his good fortune to the blessing of his mother.

9. **Chauthai and Sardeshmukhi explained.**—It is now time to review the actual results of the policy and efforts of the first Peshwa for the revival of the Maratha State from the condition in which it existed at the time of Aurangzeb's death.

The three main points secured by Balaji Vishvanath under the Emperor's seal and on which the future policy of the State came to be based, were three distinct claims which Shivaji had out of his own strength and under no outside sanction long ago enforced upon the Mughal Empire. That Shahu and Balaji obtained fresh grants from the Emperor for these old claims clearly means that while Shivaji considered himself an independent sovereign, the ruler of the Maratha State became henceforth a vassal and an obedient servant of the Emperor. This patent and striking distinction, while certainly plain and unquestionable, made little difference in actual practice, since we know that the Maratha soldiers and people in general under the regime of Shahu and his Peshwa, were by no means less independent than they had been during the days of Sambhaji and Rajaram. If these latter two conducted wars directly against the Emperor, Shahu and his Peshwas waged similar wars against the provincial governors of the Mughals. Shahu's position was doubtless more delicate and precarious. Having been compelled to pass the prime of his life in the Emperor's confinement, he owed his life mainly to his kindness and became the head of the Maratha State. With the help of Balaji he turned to the best advantage of his nation the peculiar difficulties of the Mughal Court and struck the best bargain possible under the circumstances. If he were to oppose openly the Mughal power and its numerous local agents and keep the old sore of war open, he would have failed in his attempt. He had no money, no men, no resources. He, therefore, took the path of conciliation and goodwill, thereby practically obtaining results more brilliant and lasting than he would have secured by any other method. He knew his own limitations and deliberately departed from the policy of complete independence followed by Shivaji.

In the mind of an average student the close association of the three charters, *Swarajya, Chauthai* and *Sardeshmukhi* has perhaps created a confusion about their origin and import. They are three entirely different items : their juxtaposition is a mere chance brought about by the three documents having been drawn up and executed at one and the same time at Delhi in March 1719 and thereby having thenceforth continued to be mentioned together in official records first at Satara and subsequently in Grant Duff's *History*, so that their co-existence has become almost proverbial in text-books and studies.

Swarajya[7] is a term applied to those territories of central Maharashtra, which were originally formed into an independent kingdom by Shivaji out of the possessions of the Adilshah of Bijapur and the Mughal Empire of Delhi. It practically extended from the river Tapti in the north to the Krishna in the south with a few glaring exceptions round about Aurangabad and Burhanpur. On the west Shivaji's swarajya was bounded by the sea and on the east the boundary was not quite

7. In Persian documents the term is translated as *mamalik-qadim*, meaning "old dominion", i.e. lands originally held by Shivaji. It did not mean Hindu raj.

definite, as it often shifted according to circumstances. The Marathas continued to claim this region as their legitimate patrimony acquired by Shivaji and it was to preserve this precious acquisition that they waged that long and relentless war against Aurangzeb for a full quarter of a century. The sanad for *Swarajya* obtained by Balaji enumerates the particular districts included in the term. A few isolated outposts subjugated by Shivaji such as Kopbal, Gadag, Bellari and even Vellore, Jinji and Tanjore were also supposed to be included in the swarajya established by Shivaji. These distant posts formed a link to hold the southern regions in sway. Shivaji did not himself live to realize his dream of full Hindavi-swarajya.

The next puzzling term is Sardeshmukhi. This has nothing to do either with Swarajya or with Chauthai. Its origin goes back to the far off ancient days when Maharashtra came to be first colonized and agriculture was taxed for revenue, to collect which, village or district officials called Deshmukhs or heads of the land were appointed. They were entrusted with the duty of collecting the land-tax, receiving a commission of ten per cent for their services. If a village was assessed say at one thousand rupees, the Deshmukh was to collect the amount due from each land-holder, pay Rs. 900 into the Government treasury and appropriate for his own labour the remaining one hundred. This was found in those old days to be the easiest, cheapest and most convenient method of collecting the revenue rather than appointing fully paid government servants, whose honesty could not be taken for granted and whose knowledge of the holders and tillers of the soil might not be close. It was the interest of the Deshmukhs to bring under cultivation fallow lands by inducing suitable persons, to inhabit and cultivate them, as their own commission increased with the increase of the cultivation. These Deshmukhs were supposed to exercise a general supervision over village administration and afford facilities to the ryots to prosper by their labour.

Thus the interests of all parties came to be safeguarded by the employment of the Deshmukhs all over Maharashtra since remote pre--Maratha and pre-Muslim rule. Many fresh conquerors came, occupied the country in succession, but the

'Deshmukhs did not change with the change of rulers as their existence was indispensable to all. A head Deshmukh controlling a group of several villages or one district, was styled Sardeshmukh, and he was responsible for the peaceful and orderly government throughout the district. These Deshmukhs and Sardeshmukhs considered their profession a *vatan* or a hereditary preserve, which could not be affected by political revolutions or changes of government. Shivaji, however, made a slight change in this conception. In the capacity of a Chhatrapati he styled himself the supreme Sardeshmukh of the whole *swarajya* and took powers for himself to distribute the Deshmukhi vatans to his own followers and favourites in order to ensure his revenue and to prevent treachery towards the *swarajya* which he was establishing. He laid down that the Chhatrapati was the Sardeshmukh of the whole country; and this practice was adopted by Shahu, who upon his being crowned as Chhatrapati assumed the function of the Sardeshmukh and had it legalized by the sanction of the Emperor in 1719. The Sardeshmukhi cess was confined only to territories of the Maratha swarajya and the six Mughal Subahs of the Deccan.

Chauthai again is another separate levy quite different from the two mentioned above. A practice existed during pre-Shivaji days in some of the territories conquered by the Portuguese on the west coast, where the Portuguese settlers agreed to pay to the adjoining chieftains, to avoid incessant inroads and to ensure their protection, one-fourth of the revenue of their possessions. When the Portuguese conquered the districts of north Konkan between Bassein and Daman, the local chiefs and landlords often attacked them and they offered to pay them a fourth part of their assessed income to buy their protection or immunity from further attack.[8] Such a practice or contract existed in some other parts of the country and later Shivaji adopted it for his own gain when conquering foreign territories. He first established his swarajya over the few lands which he had inherited and which were distinctly Maratha in character. Thereafter he began to extend his

8. See Dr. Sen's *Military system of the Marathas*, Chapter II. Refer to *Storia do Mogor* (under Chutia).

dominions by raiding outside territories, which although Maratha in character formed part of the Muslim kingdoms of Bijapur, Golkonda and the Mughal Empire. As soon as he subjugated a certain portion of these regions, he offered their chieftains or leaders the choice of entirely coming over to his rule or the payment of a fourth of their annual income, for which he would thereafter bind himself not to molest them further and also to protect them from any other conqueror. Thus there arose a category of semi-conquered territories which paid the Chauth and thereby acknowledged their allegiance to him, but for whose internal welfare and administration he was not directly responsible. It was essential for a conqueror of the type of Shivaji to find methods of consolidating his conquests. He had to incur expense for keeping an army of occupation and devised the method of Chauth as an alternative to *swarajya*, the principle involved in the process being that the subjugated peoples bore the cost of their protection. Students will notice how this same principle was later on adopted by the British Governor General Lord Wellesley when he formulated his famous Subsidiary System, which was nothing but a well-defined and minutely conditioned development of the system of Chauth prevalent in the country and practised by the Maratha Governors from Shivaji on to Nana Phadnis.[9]

In the hands of Balaji Vishvanath and the succeeding Peshwas this system of Chauthai proved a convenient means for the rapid expansion of the Maratha power, as it had done during the reigns of Sambhaji and Rajaram for waging a successful war against Aurangzeb, whose territories they raided on the plea of collecting Chauth. Khandesh, Malwa, Karnatak and other parts of the Mughal Empire were subjected by the Marathas to the levy of Chauth. Aurangzeb never acknowledged these Maratha claims, nor did the various Mughal governors of later times, like Nizam-ul-mulk, care to execute the formal grants of 1719 which, they urged, had been exacted under pressure of a military threat. This gave rise to a never-ending struggle throughout the eighteenth century between

9. Note the case of the State of Sondha, *Shiva—C. Sahitya* III No. 497; also Ranade's *Rise of the Maratha Power*, Chap. IX.

the Maratha leaders roaming about for the collection of Chauth and the Mughal governors resisting these claims. The history of the 18th century of Indian politics is a record of this struggle.

Let us now dispassionately consider how these instruments worked in practice. On the face of them they amount to a clever dissimulation between the two opposing parties, the Marathas and the Mughals, the latter trying to preserve their prestige as suzerain, concealing the important fact of their seeking Maratha protection against internal and external enemies; while the former accepted and avowed specious vassalage or the position of tributary chiefs, outwardly obedient to the Emperor but in reality possessing the actual power of managing the imperial affairs as suited their own interests best. The Marathas agreed to serve the Emperor with fifteen thousand troops and pay an annual cash tribute of ten lacs. In return they were allowed to collect 25% Chauth and 10% Sardeshmukhi from the six Subahs of the Deccan which were supposed on paper to yield a nominal yearly revenue of 18 crores, of which 35% was to go to the Marathas. It is obvious that in practice the figures actually realized fell far below the paper calculations. Governments like individuals accepting foreign protection virtually admit their weakness and consequent loss of liberty.

10. **Origin and evils of Jagirdari.**—This collection of Chauthai was the direct cause of Maratha expansion through the system of jagirdars of which the merits and evils must now be set forth. It was fortunate that Balaji's young son Bajirao proved himself capable of enforcing the terms contained in the three grants. He got together a band of enthusiastic associates, Pawar, Holkar, Sindia and others, and within a few years managed to expand the Maratha power beyond the six Subahs of the south. For this purpose separate spheres were assigned as the exclusive preserve set apart for each army chief's independent activity. This practice had become altogether essential during the seventeen years of war which the Marathas waged against Aurangzeb over the vast region of several thousand square miles between the Narmada in the north and Jinji in the south. The necessities of this

long war compelled each Maratha leader to act on his own initiative and devise whatever means he thought best to meet the situation in which he found himself. Santaji, Dhanaji, Parshuram Trimbak, Shankaraji Narayan and a host of other leaders all acted under the nominal direction of Ramchandrapant Amatya at Panhala in Maharashtra and the Chhatrapati Rajaram at Jinji in the Karnatak, when practically there was no central government nor easy communication to enforce definite orders and plans on these subordinates.

Unconsciously a situation came to be developed in the course of time in which the Maratha leaders and captains of fighting bands, came to establish their sway over distant parts of the country and gradually settled down in them as their own exclusive spheres of influence. The Ghorpades subjugated most of the Karnatak lands south of the Krishna and received the titles of Mamalkat-madar, Hindurao and Amir-ul-umrao. Kanhoji Bhosle, Senasaheb-subah, controlled Berar and Nagpur. Baglan was seized by the Sarlashkar Nimbalkars. Senapati Dabhade established himself in west Khandesh and parts of Gujarat, while the Peshwa tried to capture several intervening tracts as if to control and supervise the activities of all in his capacity of the Prime Minister of the State.

This state of things had come into being before Balaji obtained the formal grants at Delhi in 1719, so that most of the lands south of the Narmada had been already parcelled out among the various Maratha chiefs. Thereafter fresh leaders and captains flocked to Shahu's Court and begged him to supply them with fields of work and employment elsewhere. The Peshwa's return from Delhi with success gave a new impetus to Maratha aspirations. Almost a craze for exploitation, expansion and conquest seized every youthful soldier's mind.: the soft-hearted obliging king allowed them liberty to spread out. He stationed Fatesinh Bhosle his god-son, at Akalkot on the southern frontiers of the Maratha kingdom by way of check upon the Nawab of Haidarabad. Fatesinh's descendants are today ruling the small state of Akalkot. Shahu's bosom friend and favourite the Pratinidhi was allotted a few districts round about the capital and his line today holds sway at Aundh. Kanhoji Angre the Sarkhel of Kolaba became the naval guardian of the west coast, and his line has become extinct. Each of these leaders was supposed to keep a certain number of trained fighters for the service of the State whenever called upon, to defray his expenses out of the Chauth he collected, and pay the balance into the Government treasury rendering regular accounts of his transactions to the Chhatrapati.

This was roughly the arrangement that was found most convenient by Balaji and the king. They could not at once institute a perfect new system of their own. They had to build upon the system that existed with the material they had at hand. Balaji was not oblivious of the evils of this arrangement, which later developed into the Maratha system of Jagirs and Saranjams. For the rapid expansion of the Maratha power no other arrangement could have served so well. The jagirdars had no easy task to perform. They had to hold their own in a distant land surrounded by enemies and to collect Chauthai dues mostly by armed force, which they had to keep ready at hand and for which they had to incur huge debts in order to pay the wages of their troops. They had all sorts of trouble in realizing the expected amounts. Their troops could never be paid in time and were always clamorous for their pay.

Shivaji the founder of the Maratha raj had never countenanced such a system of jagirs. He made regular cash payment to his troops and never alienated the state lands for military services. On the contrary he rigorously confiscated land gifts and inams for government service that had come down from previous regimes. This salutary principle of Shivaji was abandoned by Shahu and his Peshwas on account of various considerations. The jagirs had come into being during the recent war. They could not be at once done away with. Shahu himself owed his position to the help which these jagirdars rendered him in the first instance. He could not deprive them of their possessions at his will. They would have revolted and created confusion in the midst of the civil war which was not of his seeking. He had no regular army of his own for putting down feudal disaffection and revolt. The case of Chandrasen Jadhav is a glaring instance of this.

But there is no doubt the system carried with it the seeds of decay, although for a time it conduced to the rapid spread of the Maratha power. The jagirdar chiefs offered all kinds of excuses and troubles when called upon to render service. They did not often entertain the stipulated quota of troops and accoutrements; sent a thousand excuses for non-attendance and always exhibited the usual separatist tendency and selfishness so ruinous to the interests of the State. Their accounts were never perfect, could not be settled from a distance and this fact caused tremendous vexation to all concerned.

But in able hands the system worked admirably. Particularly the second Peshwa Bajirao, possessing most of the qualities of leadership, personal valour, circumspection, and winsome ways, collected a band of young enthusiasts and in the short space of a few years succeeded in putting down his veteran experienced antagonist Nizam-ul-mulk Asaf Jah, occupied Malwa, Gujarat and Bundelkhand and carried the Maratha arms right up to the gates of Delhi under the plausible excuse of collecting Chauth. His able commanders soon acquired small hereditary holdings or dependent kingdoms with suitable well fortified capitals of their own. Dhar, Dewas, Indore, Ujjain, Gwalior, Saugor, Nagpur, Baroda and other towns in non-Maratha regions became essentially Maratha colonies which have existed to the present day. To hold the Maratha raj together no other method could have worked so admirably, particularly when distant parts were to be held by strength of arms with no military roads for easy communication with the seat of the central government at Satara, from which reinforcements could be sent in case of emergency. The main prop of this system of jagirdars was the competency of the Chhatrapati and the Peshwa to exact obedience. Shahu and his first three Peshwas, and after the third Peshwa's death his son Madhavrao succeeded in keeping the jagirdars under proper check and in looking after the numerous concerns of a growing empire with strictness and justice. But when disorders started in the Maratha government after the murder of the Peshwa Narayanrao, the edifice toppled down for want of a competent master. We as students of history should properly weigh the pros and cons of the system before pronouncing a final judgment on it.

11. *Hereditary Offices.*—There was also another pernicious principle, that of hereditary posts, which had then taken deep root not only in Maharashtra but throughout the country, and of which students of history must take careful note. High and low alike, private or public, looked upon all offices and services as hereditary claims. When an officer, say the Senapati, died, his son or other relation claimed the office as of right, whether he was competent or not. This practice of hereditary appointments to public offices was sternly put down by the wise Shivaji, who looked to merit alone in making his selection. But the practice could not be completely rooted out from society and was revived during the years of the Mughal war with redoubled force. All offices, grants of land or cash emoluments of whatever nature, came to be looked upon as personal property, or *vatan* as it is termed, to be claimed in hereditary succession in private as well as in public transactions. A few landed *vatans* like those assigned to certain village officials, the Patil or the Kulkarni, had probably existed since ancient times. But however essential the system might have been for village administration, it certainly proved harmful to the public service where capacity and efficiency must be the essential qualifications. A Senapati's son, unlike the son of a carpenter or goldsmith, was not necessarily competent to conduct his father's duties after him. Commanders and administrators cannot be produced at will. They have to be trained in external experience.

To reward a person's good service is a commendable policy ; but for a person to claim the same reward for services rendered by his predecessors, is an intolerable evil which encourages idleness and sloth, kills initiative and ruins the whole society. Innumerable papers have been published in Marathi wherein constant applications are seen pouring in, the tone and substance of which may be thus summarized. Writes the Peshwa to an applicant,—

"You (such and such a person) came and represented to us at such and such a place that your father and grandfather &c. loyally served the State and that you too wish wholeheartedly to continue to do the same, that you have a large family and have no means for their support and that therefore some lands and villages may be kindly granted to you in inam. Taking into consideration this humble prayer, it has pleased us to bestow on you the following lands or villages &c. &c."

Thus what at first was granted for loyal and meritorious service and for valour and sacrifice, came to be demanded for maintenance and support of large families, a form of beggary which ruined both the State and the recipients of the alms. So long as there was a competent Peshwa or master exercising healthy control from above and exacting obedience, the system of rewards worked well and yielded satisfactory results. A comprehensive and reasoned review of later Maratha activities alone would correctly explain the results and implications of the three memorable imperial grants obtained by the first Peshwa in the early months of 1719 and would supply the corrective in estimating the worth of the deeds or misdeeds of Maratha nationals working their way to northern India during the first half of the 18th century.

12. **Death of Balaji, character estimated**—Unfortunately Balaji Vishvanath did not live long enough to put into practice whatever aims and intentions he had formed or expressed during his discussions with the Saiyad ministers and with other officials in authority at Delhi. While Balaji was away on his expedition to the north, Sambhaji of Kolhapur seized the opportunity of the Peshwa's absence to create mischief against Shahu, so that if Balaji had not achieved the success he did, some serious trouble would have ensued in Maharashtra. Shahu lost no time in leading his troops against Sambhaji, whom he worsted on the Warna near Wadgaon in the early months of 1719. Immediately upon his return Balaji took possession of Poona and the surrounding districts and of those of Kalyan and Bhivandi in north Konkan. Shahu and Balaji together carried their arms against Sambhaji during the closing months of 1719 and besieged his capital Kolhapur, without however putting a permanent stop to Sambhaji's nefarious activities. In March 1720, Balaji returned to Saswad where the Peshwas had temporary residence before the

palace in Poona came to be constructed. Balaji's first home was at Supa whence he shifted to the shelter of his friends the Purandare family at Saswad. Here he suddenly expired on 2nd April 1720. His age is nowhere mentioned, but may be presumed to have neared sixty or probably exceeded it.

Balaji left behind him his wife Radhabai, a shrewd and revered lady, coming from the Barve family, who survived her husband for thirty-three years and materially helped the cause of the Maratha raj, which he had toiled to rear up. During the regimes of her son and grandson Radhabai's voice and influence were powerful, particularly in social and religious matters, in the construction of the Peshwa's palace and their numerous shrines in Poona and outside. She bore four children, two sons and two daughters, all married before Balaji's death, the eldest Visaji alias Bajirao succeeded Balaji in the Peshwaship. The second was a brother Antaji alias Chimnaji Appa who became equally famous with his brother in managing the affairs of the Maratha State. Next came a daughter named Anubai married to Vyankatrao Ghorpade of Ichalkaranji, where her descendants are still ruling a small principality under the Kolhapur jurisdiction. This Anubai was a great favourite of the two brothers who ever tried to please her with gifts of rare cloths and fancy articles. The youngest was a daughter named Bhiubai married to Abaji Naik Joshi of Baramati. Bajirao was married to Kashibai daughter of Mahadaji Krishna Joshi of Chas, a rich banker who had helped Shahu in his difficulties and whom the Chhatrapati appointed his treasurer. Chimnaji Appa was probably two or three years younger than Bajirao and was married to Rakhmabai sister of Trimbakrao Pethe, known later as Trimbakrao Mama who commanded the Peshwa's force in many subsequent campaigns. The two brothers Bajirao and Chimnaji were extremely attached to each other and much of their success in political life is due to the wise circumspection and enthusiastic co-operation they rendered to each other through weal and woe. The whole family of these Peshwas had handsome features and a very fair complexion.

The phenomenal success which the Peshwas attained in their careers is in no small measure due to the development of character and enterprize so rigidly enforced particularly by the ladies in the domestic life of the Peshwa's palace and its surroundings, a feature which rapidly pervaded the upper strata of Maharashtrian society for nearly a century, in severe contrast to the decadent life of the contemporary Muslim households.

Balaji Vishvanath was entirely a self-taught man. It was under Ramchandrapant Amatya that he received his best training in the politics of the day and in the organisation of national resources by actually handling different problems and temperaments. He not only studied the Maratha character and capacity, but he was as intimately acquainted with the life and ways of the Mughal Court and its agents. Thus it was Balaji alone who could chalk out the future course of Maratha policy. He observed the last days of Aurangzeb and foresaw that the best chance for the Maratha nation lay in upholding Shahu in preference to Tarabai. He seconded Dhanaji Jadhav and secured the co-operation of other prominent individuals and families, such as the Purandares, the Bokils, &c. Khanderao Dabhade, Parsoji and Kanhoji Bhosle, and Shankaraji Malhar were his intimate colleagues. He also secured the financial support of most of the bankers of the day through friendship or family connection, so that he could cope with the treachery of Chandrasen Jadhav and Damaji Thorat. It is futile to attempt to discover in him any special genius like that of Shivaji, but barring such exceptional and gifted personalities, one might put down Balaji Vishvanath as a statesman of a high order, comparing favourably with the other eminent personalities of his day. Sir Richard Temple remarks :—

"He was more like a typical Brahman than any of his successors. He had a calm, comprehensive and commanding intellect, an imaginative and aspiring disposition, an aptitude for ruling rude nature by moral force, a genius for diplomatic combination, a mastery of finance. His political destiny propelled him into affairs wherein his misery must have been acute. More than once he was threatened with death for which he doubtless prepared himself with all the stoicism of his race when a ransom opportunely arrived. He wrung by power of menace and argument from the Mughals a recognition of Maratha sovereignty. He carried victoriously all his diplomatic points and sank into premature death with the consciousness that a Hindu Empire had been created over the ruins of Muhammadan power and that of this Empire the hereditary chiefship had been secured for his family."[10]

The following contemporary estimate of the high reverence in which this Peshwa was held is available. "The most ardent desire of Balajipant Nana was to secure the weal and prosperity of the common masses and to this aim he studiously devoted all his powers of head and heart. He restored peace and plenty to the Maratha territory which had been utterly ruined by the long devastating war. He put down with a high hand all turbulent elements and repopulated the country by means of special concessions. Thus the ryots came to look upon Nana as their great benefactor. His fame spread in uncommon measure to all quarters."[11]

Some critics have charged this Peshwa with sowing the seeds of ruin of the Maratha State by departing from the wise constitution laid down by the founder. It is contended that the three instruments which Balaji brought from Delhi were nothing short of shackles of slavery inasmuch as they acknowledged the Emperor's supreme power. It has already been explained how circumstances justified the policy of Balaji for securing Maratha expansion by aiding the Saiyad brothers. An exact parallel can be discovered in Clive's acceptance of the Diwani of Bengal leaving mere phantom power in the hands of the Emperor. The British secured the substance and continued to utilise the Emperor's name long after he had become quite a non-entity. Even their currency continued to be issued in the Emperor's name right upto 1835. By offering Maratha help to the Emperor Balaji secured real power, a plan which deserves to be acclaimed as consummate. He succeeded in cutting a new path out of a vicious circle of civil war and stagnation. For the ultimate fall of the Maratha State Balaji can in no way be held responsible.

10. *Oriental Experience*, pp. 389-90.
11. *Hingne Daftar* I. 15.

CHRONOLOGY

CHAPTER III

1700 August 18	Bajirao born.
1720 April 17	Baji Rao appointed Peshwa.
1720 June 19	Battle of Ratanpur, Dilawar Ali Killed.
1720 July 31	Battle of Balapur, Alam Ali killed, Shankaraji Malhar died.
1720 October 8	Saiyad Husain Ali murdered.
1720 November 14	Saiyad Abdulla confined (put to death on 11th October 1722).
1720 December 15	The Mughals defeated by the Marathas on the Godavari.
1721 January 4	Bajirao and Nizam meet at Chikhalthan.
1721 February	Wazir Amin Khan dies.
1721 October 21	Nizam leaves Deccan for Delhi.
1722 January	Nizam becomes Wazir.
1722 October 2	Nizam starts for Malwa.
1722 December 5	Bajirao meets Aiwaz Khan in Khandesh.
1723 February 13	Bajirao and Nizam meet at Bolasha.
1723 May 15	Nizam-ul-mulk returns to Delhi.
1723 December 23.	Nizam-ul-mulk resigns Wazirship and marches to the south.
1724	Mubariz Khan opens war upon Shahu.
1724 May 18	Bajirao and Nizam meet at Nalchha.
1724 June 11	Nizam takes possession of Aurangabad.
1724 July 27	Qamr-ud-din Khan becomes Wazir.
1724 September 30	Nizam wins victory at Fateh Kherda; Mubariz Khan killed, Nizam assumes independence. Entertains Baji Rao at Aurangabad.
1725 June 20	Emperor confirms Deccan to the Nizam.
1726 September 21	Khando Ballal Chitnis died.
1734 August 25	Ambaji Purandare died.

Malharrao Holkar and Peshwa Bajirao I

CHAPTER III

NIZAM AND BAJIRAO, FIRST CONTACT

[1720—1724]

1 Investiture and position at Court
2 Fall of the Saiyad Brothers.
3 Maratha claims opposed by Nizam-ul-mulk.
4 Bajirao faced with a new danger.
5 Nizam asserts independence.

1. **Investiture and position at Court.**—Balaji's sudden death was indeed a national loss, but Shahu had special reasons to mourn it since he owed his position and fortune entirely to this devoted servant. Happily for the Maratha nation, however, Bajirao then 19 years of age had been associated with his father in all his later movements, including the expedition to Delhi, and had closely watched its implications. The general opinion considered him to be a raw, inexperienced and impetuous youth, because none had yet any occasion to judge the genius that he possessed. But Shahu was a shrewd judge of men and possessed the power of detached observation. He often acted on his own intuitive but unerring judgment and now did not take long to make up his mind on the question of appointing a successor to the departed Peshwa. He always appreciated the adventurous spirit of a youthful and aspiring soul and resolved to invest Bajirao with the responsible office of the Prime Minister.

Many a veteran of Shahu's Court possessing experience and merit was not prepared to support or acquiesce in such a choice. Shripatrao Pratinidhi, Anandrao Sumant, Naro Ram Mantri, Khanderao Dabhade, Kanhoji Bhosle and others of a similar bent of mind, opposed the appointment with all the vehemence they possessed. What irritated them most was the idea that they would have to be controlled and commanded by a young lad of Bajirao's type. Shahu properly gauged this feeling of the public and was at a loss to silence the clamour of his courtiers and advisers. He also realized the usual prejudice against the Chitpavan Brahmans coming from the

Konkan, and attaining prominence. In such a dilemma Shahu took all his immediate courtiers into his confidence and made a personal appeal to one and all to support the choice which his mature thought and best judgment dictated. One particular merit he urged upon all was the resourceful character of Balaji and his family, saying that they would carry to success every venture that they undertook, and that they would never accept discomfiture, whatever the odds against them. History proved that Shahu was right.

The robes of Peshwaship were conferred upon Bajirao in Shahu's camp at Masur, 30 miles east of Satara on 17th April 1720, exactly a fortnight after his father's death. For this purpose he held a special Darbar and asked the assemblage to give a cordial support to the course he was following, and assured them at the same time that if Bajirao proved unworthy in his future plans and actions, he would himself remove him and make a fresh appointment. But to place Bajirao in the post, was the only way, Shahu explained, in which he could repay the heavy debt of gratitude he was under to the deceased Peshwa Balajipant Nana.

Bajirao fully entered into the spirit of the times, and was intimately acquainted with the policy and measures of his father. He possessed, as the great historian Grant Duff puts it, the head to plan and the hand to execute. He had fully acquired the traditional training in athletics and horsemanship, was well versed in reading, writing and accounts, and conversant with the ancient Sanskrit learning then current among the Brahman class. The members of Balaji's family were all smart and intelligent and generally possessed handsome features in addition to courteous manners, which produced a favourable impression wherever they went. This was particularly the case with Bajirao, whose visits to Nizam-ul-mulk are known to have evoked a peculiar enthusiasm among the crowds of the places through which he passed. It is recorded that when this Brahman warrior of thirty whose name had become famous throughout India for valour and diplomacy and who had so quickly overcome such experienced officers of the Mughal court as Giridhar Bahadur, Daya Bahadur and Muhammad Khan Bangash, rode through the cities of Aurangabad, Burhanpur, Ujjain and Jaipur, crowds of men and women instantly flocked to their windows to have a view of this remarkable figure. Such striking qualities as Bajirao possessed are rarely to be met with.

The life stories of Shivaji and Sambhaji, of Ramchandrapant Amatya and Santaji Ghorpade were, we may be sure, well-known to Bajirao and must have inspired him to deeds of valour and sacrifice, for reaping the fullest advantage of the great war of independence, in the midst of which his father the first Peshwa had lived his life of hazard and unrest. Bajirao's training and mentality can be correctly gathered from the large number of published and extant letters and papers, which a recent calculation reveals to be more than 3,500 inclusive of the official correspondence of all the Maratha writers and workers of that period. Of these at least five hundred are from the pen of Bajirao and his brother alone.[1] It is certain that a considerably larger number has perished through the action of time and neglect. But what remains is sufficient to enable a student to arrive at a correct estimate of his life and work.

Bajirao possessed a robust and hardy constitution. His younger brother Chimnaji was, however, most unlike him in this respect. He constantly suffered from cold, cough and asthma. His mother and near relations always entertained great fears about his health and frequently cautioned him on that score. The two brothers did their utmost to win the favour and good opinion of their master Shahu, and with this object kept some one in their own confidence about the royal person, not only to keep him fully informed of all that was happening outside, but to counteract any adverse influence or counsel which their numerous opponents at Court were apt to exercise on the open, pliant and unsuspecting mind of Shahu. For to Bajirao and his brother their master's full

1. Of these 3,500, about 3,100 are dated and the remaining 400 have no dates. Moreover, only 550 of these pertain to the first eight years of Bajirao's regime; and over 2,800 to the last 12 years. About 900 belong to the wars and affairs of the west coast. By far the major portion of these letters has been only recently discovered in the Peshwa's Daftar and published by the Bombay Government. No accurate and connected account of Bajirao could have been written before these letters came to light.

support and implicit confidence were essential for their success abroad. It was a practice in those days to appoint a Mutalik or deputy-minister for every cabinet post. When the chief was out on duty, it was the Mutalik who acted for him at Court for the execution of orders and measures coming for the King's consideration. Ambajipant Purandare was made his Mutalik when Bajirao was invested with the Peshwaship and continued to support him loyally right up to his death in 1734, and so did his relatives after him.

The Konkanastha Peshwa family and that of the Deshastha Purandares, though differing in their origin, were closely attached to each other, a fact to which much of the Peshwa's success is certainly due. When both Bajirao and Ambaji had to be away on duty abroad, Chimnaji Appa remained with Shahu as the keeper of his conscience. In a few years when the young son of Bajirao, Balaji alias Nanasaheb, was grown up, he used to remain at Satara and thus relieve Chimnaji for work outside. The Peshwas had another strong supporter at Court in the revered saint Brahmendra Swami, whose role in the war against the Siddi of Janjira will be explained in a subsequent chapter, and who wielded great influence by reason of his being the guru to Shahu and to several members of his Court. The veteran Khando Ballal Chitnis was Shahu's obedient secretary, regularly submitted papers and petitions for orders and co-ordinated the work of the various officers engaged in distant expeditions and matters of state. When Khando Ballal died in 1726, his son Govindrao took the father's place and performed his duty with zeal and probity for a long time. Govindrao, a shrewd and loyal supporter of the Peshwas, carried out with candour and persuasiveness the King's orders in a sweet conciliatory spirit, always trying to secure the highest good of the State.

Immediately on receiving the robes of office Bajirao formed his own band of devoted followers of equal age and companionship. There was doubtless a large party of elders around Shahu's person whose susceptibilities Bajirao cautiously avoided offending. But there was also a large number of youngsters whom he managed to attract by his brilliant and vigorous policy, and who followed his lead with devotion and intelligence. The Purandares, the Bhanus, the Bokils, the Hingnes, the Pethes, and other families that were to attain prominence in later days now joined heartily in Bajirao's undertakings and largely contributed to his success. One of Shahu's experienced favourites was Pilaji Jadhav, who at the instance of his master offered his sincere co-operation to Bajirao. Pilaji's genial temper and shrewd foresight proved immensely helpful to Bajirao's early activities, and even later on Pilaji continued his best endeavours to support Bajirao in several arduous campaigns and delicate missions. Fateh Sinh Bhosle was another great favourite of Shahu and was brought up by him almost as his heir-apparent. He possessed an upright and honest character, was conscious of his own limitations, and the two being nearly of the same age he fell in readily with Bajirao's views and never raised a dissentient voice.

2. **Fall of the Saiyad Brothers.**—The new Emperor Muhammad Shah whom the Saiyad brothers had raised to the throne (in 1719), soon started against them the same old intrigues to ruin their power. How these imperial concerns affected Bajirao's plans at the beginning of his career is a question that deserves careful consideration. Chin Qilich Khan Nizam-ul-mulk, the only powerful opponent of the Saiyads at Court, was then appointed by them to the government of Malwa. He left Delhi on 15th March 1719 and after reaching Ujjain collected a large number of troops ostensibly to drive away the Marathas from Malwa, but in reality to put down the Saiyads at an opportune moment. His cousin Muhammad Amin Khan, an equally powerful noble, who was the Governor of Agra, also prepared for a contest against the Saiyads. Feeling extremely alarmed at such developments the Saiyads decided to take the offensive and despatched with adequate provision, Dilawar Ali Khan, one of their own trusted and spirited partizans, to put down Nizam-ul-mulk, and at the same time instructed their cousin Alam Ali Khan, then the Subahdar of the Deccan, to march from Aurangabad with all his armed forces towards Malwa, so that, it was arranged, Nizam-ul-mulk might be crushed between the millstones of the two powerful armies, one under Dilawar Ali marching from the north and the other under Alam Ali marching from the south. These movements suddenly plung-

ed the central and southern provinces of India into a severe panic. The Emperor and his mother, intending the ruin of the Saiyads, wrote personal letters to Nizam-ul-mulk urging him with promises of honours and rewards to release them from the tyranny of those powerful Saiyad ministers : the two youths Dilawar Ali and Alam Ali were quite equal to the task entrusted to them, but lacked coolness and circumspection against the tactful and consummate veteran Nizam-ul-mulk, calculating and collected to a degree, who arranged his moves with the utmost caution. He was recalled by the Saiyads to Delhi, but he declined to obey the summons and proceeded instead to the south, crossing the Narmada in May 1720, i.e., just when Bajirao had received the robes of the Peshwaship. Nizam-ul-mulk managed to take possession of Asirgad, a fort that guarded the gate of the south and entrusted it to the care of his son Ghaziuddin. Thereafter he took his post at Burhanpur on the north bank of the Tapti river. Here Aiwaz Khan from Berar came and joined him.

Alam Ali learned of these aggressive moves of Nizam-ul-mulk and at once despatched Anwar Khan and Rao Rambha to recapture Asirgad and Burhanpur. As these two chiefs came within range of his moving forces, Nizam-ul-mulk captured and kept them both in confinement. Alam Ali himself left Aurangabad early in June with a view to joining Dilawar Ali, who had crossed the Narmada near Handia and was coming upon the Nizam with great impetuosity. The Nizam decided to prevent their junction by all means and bring about their destruction by meeting them separately. Both the antagonists solicited the Peshwa's help : but Shahu ordered Bajirao to remain neutral and watch the game from a distance so as to turn it to his own advantage.

Nizam-ul-mulk took post near Ratanpur, about 30 miles north of Burhanpur and not far from the present railway station of Khandwa. Dilawar Ali on the other hand instead of waiting for the arrival of Alam Ali from the south, and finding the Nizam ready for a fight, at once attacked him rashly on 19th June and suffered a crushing defeat after three hours of severe fighting. Dilawar Ali himself with most of his followers was killed and Nizam-ul-mulk gained a decisive victory. The battle is known in history as that of Khandwa.

Alam Ali who was then nearing Burhanpur, felt extremely confused at the news of Dilawar Ali's fall, while Nizam-ul-mulk now flushed with victory and playing his game with deep calculation, without allowing himself rest, marched against Alam Ali and did not give him time either to retreat or to rearrange his battle front and plan of action. Nizam-ul-mulk arrived at Burhanpur on 27th June and wrote to Alam Ali that he cherished no hope of obtaining the Subahdari of the Deccan and only wanted to visit Mecca to end his days there peacefully, after discharging his troops and settling his monetary affairs.

Alam Ali was strongly advised by his own intimate friends and by his Maratha allies not to risk a battle in the midst of the severe rains that had started, but to retire to a convenient position towards Aurangabad or even back to Ahmadnagar, continuing to harass the enemy during the interval after the Maratha fashion. Alam Ali, however, did not accept this advice and developed his own strategy. The Nizam played a cool game. The two armies marched towards Balapur along the flooded river Purna, the Nizam by the northern bank and Alam Ali by the southern. The former soon managed to cross over by means of a bridge of boats and came face to face with Alam Ali in the environs of Balapur. The latter had for his allies a Maratha contingent led by Khanderao Dabhade, Santaji Sinde, Kanhoji Bhosle and others numbering about 18,000 in all. The Saiyads' agent Shankaraji Malhar did his best to bring Maratha support to Alam Ali much against Shahu's explicit orders. On 10th August 1720 Alam Ali in a high spirit of personal valour and self-confidence, led an attack upon the Nizam's position. Fighting with desperate courage he received a mortal wound from a bullet while goading his elephant, which had got out of control. At this critical moment one of the Nizam's captains rushed upon the mad elephant, cut off Alam Ali's head and carried it to his master in great triumph. The general being thus killed, all his followers fell fighting for him on the field of battle, giving a decided victory to the Nizam. Shankaraji Malhar who was also in the thick of the fight became wounded and was captured alive. He died a few days later. The Marathas lost altogether about 700 men in their ardent endeavour to save the day for Alam Ali.

The victories of Khandwa and Balapur within a few weeks of each other at once created an important change in the politics and history of India, as they marked the beginning of the Saiyad Brothers' fall from power and the rise of their opponent Nizam-ul-mulk. Most of Alam Ali's followers such as Mubariz Khan, Turk-Taz Khan and others, as also his Maratha allies submitted to the victorious Nizam and offered him their homage and congratulations. The Nizam possessed a wonderfully discreet and thoughtful temperament. He treated Alam Ali's family and relations with kindness and courtesy, gave them pensions for support, and assured them that he was their best friend and that having won his object, he had no longer any personal rancour towards them. It was this policy of the Nizam to win the good opinion even of his enemies, which in the long run helped him to gain success in his attempt to carve out an independent kingdom.

The news of the defeat and death of Alam Ali following close upon that of Dilawar Ali, threw the Saiyads into utter consternation. The root cause of their ruin was the clever and insidious intrigue of the two cousins Amin Khan and Nizam-ul-mulk, both acting in perfect concert to encompass the Saiyads' fall. They were secretly instigated by the Emperor who pretended to march against the rebellious Nizam and asked Saiyad Husain Ali to accompany him, leaving Abdulla at Delhi. Thus the two brothers came to be separated. The Emperor left Agra on 11th September for Jaipur, all the while secretly plotting to murder Husain Ali at an opportune moment. As the party were camping at a spot about 60 miles east of Jaipur, Saiyad Husain Ali was suddenly assassinated on 8th October 1720 by agents instigated by three high officers of the Emperor. Overjoyed at this event the Emperor held a grand Darbar and distributed presents to those who had contrived to bring it about. He at once appointed Muhammad Amin Khan to the Wazirship and retraced his steps towards Delhi. During the march the Emperor was joined by Muhammad Khan Bangash, another powerful opponent of the Saiyads. Abdulla thus left alone fell an easy prey to his enemies. He did his best to oppose the Emperor for a time but after his devoted Hindu cashier Ratan Chand

Nizam-ul-mulk Asaf-Jah I

had been put to death, Abdulla also came to be captured and imprisoned on 14th November. He was put to death after about two years' confinement, on 11th October 1722.

3. **Maratha claims opposed by Nizam-ul-mulk.**— After the fall of the Saiyad brothers the Peshwa and his colleagues at Shahu's Court realized that they stood on slippery ground as regards the execution of the imperial grants that had been obtained by Balaji Vishvanath and which, they well knew, Nizam-ul-mulk and the other members of the Emperor's Court would strongly oppose. Moreover, Nizam-ul-mulk was not the man easily to forget that the Marathas had helped Alam Ali at Balapur. He, however, at this time showed not the least irritation towards the Marathas. On 15th October 1720 Bajirao's cousin and agent Malharrao Barve thus reported from Delhi, "Saiyad Husain Ali Khan has been murdered by Amin Khan. The field is now open. You must not allow your enemies to capture it." In this letter the ambassador suggests that steps must be taken to counteract the evil effects of the fall of their supporters the Saiyads. At this very moment Mubariz Khan wrote pressingly to the Nizam from Haidarabad, that "Maratha pressure for collecting Chauth was daily increasing in that part of the Karnatak, and that it must be promptly put down by their joint efforts." Nizam-ul-mulk took the hint and employed Chandrasen Jadhav to instigate Sambhaji of Kolhapur to prefer claims for Chauth similar to those which Shahu and his Peshwa were already trying to enforce. Thereupon Nizam-ul-mulk informed Bajirao that as he had received demands from Sambhaji similar to his, he did not know who the rightful claimant was; and as the domestic dispute between Shahu and Sambhaji had not been settled, he would withhold the payment, until the issue between them was decided.

This fresh development, a device of Nizam-ul-mulk, became a positive impediment to the realization of Maratha claims. Shahu had already directed his Sarlashkar Sultanji Nimbalkar to collect Chauthai from the regions between the Godavari and Aurangabad. Nizam-ul-mulk accepted the challenge and despatched Chandrasen, Rao Rambha and Muhkam Sinh against the Sarlashkar. A severe battle took place on

15th December 1720 in which Sultanji obtained a decisive victory over the Mughals.

About this time Shahu and Bajirao held a consultation together about the attitude they should hereafter adopt towards Nizam-ul-mulk's refusal to respect the Emperor's grants. Bajirao advocated an immediate armed conflict as the only effective remedy for a final decision. He said, "It is the duty of the Peshwa to undertake such ventures. If I cannot assert myself, I have no right to the high dignity of that office. I only crave Your Highness' commands. Do order me to go against the enemy, and see what I can do under your blessings. I will put down this Nizam-ul-mulk and assert our claims throughout north India, where my revered father had established political connections with the Rajput princes." Upon this representation Shahu gave Bajirao the necessary permission and asked him first to meet the Nizam personally and try if the dispute could be amicably settled.[2]

Anandrao Sumant, Shahu's foreign secretary, went to the Nizam and arranged the place and time for the Peshwa's visit. Accompanied by Pilaji Jadhav, Khanderao Dabhade, Kanhoji Bhosle and Fatehsinh Bhosle with their full quotas of troops, Bajirao proceeded to Chikhalthan, a few miles east of Chalisgaum, where a meeting took place between him and Nizam-ul-mulk on 4th January 1721. For four days all the pomp of a grand ceremonial visit dazzled the spectators. Greetings and presents were lavishly exchanged : long discussions on vital questions took place : but so far as actual results were concerned, all this proved of no avail. Bajirao concluded that the Nizam would not yield the Maratha claims unless compelled to do so by force of arms. Shahu and Bajirao's mother having apprehended danger from a personal meeting of the two chiefs, showered hearty congratulations upon the Peshwa for the visit having passed off quietly without any untoward incident.

Soon after this visit Bajirao went his own way and the Nizam and his trusted lieutenant Mubariz Khan turned their attention to the Karnatak, where the Marathas had been asserting their power for some time past. Mubariz Khan who

---

2. *Chitnis Life of Shahu*, p. 45.

bore a bitter enmity towards the Marathas, was a formidable antagonist for them, having worked successfully and efficiently for several years in the government of Gujarat and Malwa and having been specially commissioned by the previous Emperors to punish the Marathas for their encroachment.[3] Thus in 1721 these two powerful chiefs, Nizam-ul-mulk and Mubariz Khan became Bajirao's bitter opponents.

4. **Bajirao faced with a new danger.**—Muhammad Amin Khan whom the Emperor had appointed his Wazir upon the fall of the Saiyads, died in February 1721, within a few months of his receiving the office. A vacancy was thus created for filling which the Emperor considered none among the elderly noblemen at Court, so well fitted by character and capacity as Nizam-ul mulk, who was not at all keen on playing a part in the Central Government. The Wazirship was not a bed of roses as recent experience had amply proved. Such powerful men as Zulfiqar Khan and the Saiyads had to pay for it with their lives. The frequent changes of government since the death of Aurangzeb had clearly disclosed to public view the decadent condition of the Mughal power. The Emperor with a view to improving his position begged Nizam-ul-mulk to come and accept the Wazir's post and do all he could to uphold the prestige of the Chaghtai dynasty. For some time the Nizam hesitated. His friend and counsellor Mubariz Khan also pressed him not to leave the Deccan. But the Emperor continued to repeat his call, so that it became impossible for Nizam-ul-mulk to resist his master's wishes. At last he entrusted the government of the Deccan to Mubariz Khan as his deputy and left Aurangabad on 21st October 1721 for Delhi.

Once more the Nizam's transfer to Delhi meant a break in the arrangements the Marathas had effected as to their claims. They were destined to suffer further disturbances on account of the Nizam's insecure tenure of the Wazirship. He reached Delhi in January 1722 and was formally invested with

3. This Khan is mentioned under various names in Marathi papers. His original name was Amanat Khan. Farrukhsiyar conferred on him the title of Mubariz Khan and appointed him the Nazim of Haidarabad, an office which he held for many years.

the Wazir's robes on 13 February following. During the next ten months that he held this office, he found that he could not pull well together with his master who cared for nothing beyond personal pleasures. They soon so severely disagreed that Nizam-ul-mulk found his position intolerable and had to part company finally. His clever moves during this disagreement and the plans he was intent on pursuing during the next two years, affected the Maratha interests vitally. Nizam-ul-mulk's ambition was to break away from the Empire and secure for himself an independent position in the Deccan with, if possible, Malwa and Gujarat added to it. For Malwa was the doorway to the south. He began with this object to consolidate his position but in this daring plan he encountered opposition not only from the Marathas, but from the two Rajput rulers of Jaipur and Marwar, who coveted for themselves Malwa and Gujarat respectively. The Marathas also had planted their power in these two provinces and were not going to give up their hold easily in the Deccan either. His agents at Delhi kept Bajirao fully informed of the Nizam's discussions with the Emperor and the schemes and projects he was there forming.

Towards the end of 1722 Nizam-ul-mulk collected a large force and arrived in Malwa, having given out that he intended to drive the Marathas out of that province. This was a direct challenge to Bajirao who readily accepted it and proceeded into Malwa with adequate preparations. But no open clash between him and Nizam-ul-mulk then took place. Both were eager to avoid direct hostilities and arranged through intermediaries for a second personal meeting in order to reach some basis of adjustment and peaceful settlement. They had a week's conference from 13th February 1723, at Bolasha, about 25 miles south of Dohad on the borders of Malwa and Gujarat. It is not recorded what actual conclusions were formed during the meeting : it is not wrong to infer, however, that once more they tried to conceal their real aims from each other under a profuse display of good will and complimentary ceremonial. How could two opposite extremes of aggression meet ? At this and other meetings of a similar character ample warning was conveyed to Bajirao of a possible attempt on his life. But he always put on a bold appearance. On the present occasion, it is recorded, that he had consulted a Muslim Fakir named Jyotiling Bawa and obtained an assurance from him that no harm would result from the meeting.[4]

During the period between February and May 1723 Nizam-ul-mulk effected a kind of loose hold upon Malwa and Gujarat and returned to Delhi to explain to the Emperor what he had accomplished in restraining the aggressive Marathas. But the disagreement between them assumed the same violent form as that which had grown a few years ago between Farrukhsiyar and the Saiyads. The Emperor getting alarmed at the growing power of Nizam-ul-mulk now in possession of three large provinces, Malwa, Gujarat and the Deccan, transferred him to the government of Oudh in order to ward off the danger. This irritated Nizam-ul-mulk so bitterly that on 27th December 1723 he resigned his Wazirship in disgust and under pretence of proceeding to his new charge of Oudh, marched straight to the south, informing the Emperor that he felt it his imperative duty to drive away the Marathas from Malwa and Gujarat. By long and rapid marches he quickly reached Ujjain, little dreaming that he would have to encounter there the Peshwa in full force. In the meantime the Emperor decided to punish the rebel, nominated Mubariz Khan to the government of the Deccan, and called upon him and Raja Shahu to do their best to put down the Nizam with all the forces at their command. This proved a welcome opportunity to Bajirao. Having been accurately informed by his agents at Delhi of the Nizam's activities, Bajirao left Satara in January 1724 and passing some time in north Khandesh, organizing his forces, crossed the Narmada on 8th May, and arrived in close proximity to the Nizam's camp at Sihore.

Mubariz Khan had in the meanwhile fallen into grave doubts as to what attitude he should adopt in the contest that was developing between the Emperor and the Nizam. Should he join the latter and punish the Marathas or should he execute the Emperor's commands by putting down the Nizam ? The three parties had their own personal objectives and watched the situation with caution. Shahu alone sincerely tried for peace, for averting open hostilities and reconciling the various conflicting interests. During February Shahu sent

4. P. D. S. 10. 25.

round urgent calls to his Sardars to come with all their troops as hostilities were imminent against the Mughal Chief of Bhaganagar, that is, Mubariz Khan, to whom he despatched his ambassador Anandrao Sumant offering a basis for peace and declaring that if those terms were rejected, hostilities would be immediately opened. Shahu and his Court determined to reap the best advantage out of the ensuing contest provoked by the Nizam.

A very important paper printed as No. 1 of the P. D. Volume 10, gives some clue to the Maratha aims and their attitude towards this three-sided contest. A broad and imperative call by Shahu repeatedly occurs in this document enjoining the well-wishers of the Emperor "to put down this rebel Nizam-ul-mulk by joining their forces with those of Raja Shahu." The Nizam however, considering Mubariz Khan as his enemy No. 1, tried to conciliate the Marathas, as he found it beyond his power to fight the two enemies simultaneously, particularly when he himself was declared a rebel by the Emperor. So on his way to the south, the Nizam had his third meeting with Bajirao at Nalchha, near Dhar, on 18th May 1724, wherein they once more professed friendship towards each other, concealing their real designs for the time being, without committing themselves to any definite terms.

Maratha help was similarly sought by Mubariz Khan also in his struggle against Nizam-ul-mulk. Shahu seems to have put before him some definite terms, probably through his Sumant Anandrao. These terms occur in the paper referred to above. It is necessary to state them in full, as they clearly explain the aims of the Marathas in creating an exclusive field for their activities :—

1. The grants of Swarajya, Chauthai and Sardeshmukhi already sanctioned under the imperial seal should be ratified and given effect to.

2. In addition, the right to collect Chauthai and Sardeshmukhi from the provinces of Malwa and Gujarat should be conceded.

3. The kingdom of Tanjore which had been annexed to the Mughal Empire should be restored.

4. The forts of Shivner, Chakan, Mahuli, Karnala, Pali, Miraj together with the lands attached to them should be handed over to the Marathas.

5. The Deshmukhi of Sinnar should be granted personally to Shahu.

6. The appointment of the Mughal Subahdar of the Deccan should be made upon the recommendation of Shahu.

7. The three Mughal officials of the Deccan, Diler Khan, Abdul Nabi Khan and Alaf Khan should be asked to join the Marathas in putting down Nizam-ul-mulk.

8. No protection should be extended to Shahu's cousin of Panhala.

9. Maratha deserters should not be entertained in Mughal service.

10. Maratha deserters already in Mughal employ should be handed back.

11. Those Mughal and Maratha chiefs who hold land-grants should be continued in their possessions if they zealously exerted themselves in putting down Nizam-ul-mulk.

12. Fatehsinh Bhosle should be appointed to the viceroyalty of Haidarabad.

13. The forts and territories captured by the Siddi of Janjira should be restored to the Marathas.

14. Maratha troops on duty with Mubariz Khan should be paid their wages at the same rate as was paid by the Saiyads to Balaji Vishvanath.

15. The present of Rs. 50,000 promised by the Emperor to Shahu should be delivered.

It is obvious that these terms, while similar in form to those which had been offered to the Saiyads are on a much higher pitch. The Maratha aims amount in substance to this that they wished to be the masters of the Deccan and protectors of the Emperor beyond it. The reference to Sambhaji, to the Raja of Tanjore and the Nawab of Janjira foreshadows the contests waged against them a few years later, and upon which Shahu had set his heart as personal objectives.

5. **Nizam asserts independence.**—Immediately after his visit to the Nizam in Malwa, Bijirao returned to Poona to prepare for the part he was to play in the approaching con-

test. The Emperor openly declared Nizam to be a grand rebel, removed his son Ghaziuddin from the Wazirship and appointed Qamruddin Khan to that office. He also appointed Giridhar Bahadur to the government of Malwa, lest Nizam-ul-mulk should appropriate it.

During June and July 1724 Shahu's Court had a busy time at Satara, discussing the probable consequences of the impending struggle and the attitude they should adopt in regard to it. On 29th July Shahu writes to Kanhoji Bhosle. "A war is impending between Nizam-ul-mulk and Mubariz Khan ; you must not join either party."[5] Shahu felt it wise to remain perfectly neutral, not being sure which party would win. Bajirao, however, prepared to reap the best advantage from the affair and immediately seized the province of Burhanpur, which was the main theatre of war between the two Mughal grandees. He wrote to Chimnaji Appa, "The Mughals have evacuated Burhanpur. As you have to pass that way, you must not neglect to seize the territory even by force if necessary."[6]

Mubariz Khan at Haidarabad learned that Nizam-ul-mulk was fast making towards him for a decisive encounter. The Khan did not at first realize that his safety lay in quickly proceeding to meet and oppose the Nizam and firmly securing in his hand the key-post of Aurangabad, then the centre of Mughal power in the Deccan. His deputy Aiwaz Khan was in charge of it and was not suspected to be a traitor. Aiwaz Khan, however, had leanings towards Nizam-ul-mulk to whom he at once surrendered the place before Mubariz Khan had any inkling about it. At the end of May the Nizam was near Dhar in Malwa and in three weeks he reached Aurangabad. Mubariz Khan was completely outwitted by the rapidity of his opponent's march. By losing this capital town, the Khan lost all valuable stores and supplies and thereby considerably weakened his own position. Nizam-ul-mulk used another artifice to keep Mubariz Khan off his guard. He wrote[7] to him frequent letters to this effect : "Why should we fight between ourselves ? I have come only to chastise the Marathas who are our common enemies. I have besought the

5. *Shahu Rozuisi* 22. 6. P. D. 10. 30. 7. Irvine II.

Emperor to appoint me to some other post. As soon as I receive his commands, I will quit the Deccan and proceed to my charge. We should not uselessly shed Muslim blood."

In the meantime Mubariz Khan received formal commands from the Emperor confirming him in the viceroyalty of the Deccan and calling upon him to attack and annihilate Nizam-ul-mulk. He also promised a quick despatch of reinforcements from the capital for the purpose. Young and impetuous as Mubariz Khan was, he neglected all caution and started boldly to oppose the Nizam, confident that he could crush him between his own army and the other that was to come from the north. He slighted the Maratha contingents when they demanded the cash payment of their wages. Instead of going directly to Aurangabad Mubariz Khan marched northward from Haidarabad, thereby giving Nizam-ul-mulk the chance to select his own terrain for the ensuing action. When he learned that Mubariz Khan had gone towards the north, the Nizam left Aurangabad on 3rd September, proceeding eastwards. At a distance of about 50 miles he found Mubariz Khan encamped at a place called Sakharkhedla in the district of Mehkar on the banks of the Purna. On 9th September Bajirao thus writes to one of his lieutenants, "You inform me that Mubariz Khan has taken shelter in the village of Sakharkhedla. This proves he is not in a position to take the offensive. Perhaps he would run away unobserved during the night. You must, therefore, closely watch his movements and keep me fully informed. I have advised Nizam-ul-mulk to halt at this place for a day."[8]

The two armies manœuvred for a few days in search of a suitable moment of attack. On 30th September a bloody battle took place between them, the actual details of which can be studied in the eloquent narrative of an eye witness quoted by Irvine. Mubariz Khan fought with the greatest fury and determination, but he lacked calculation and foresight in a critical situation where patience avails more than personal valour. Most of the Nawabs and chiefs of the Karnatak, of Arcot, Kadappa, Karnul, were present in support of Mubariz Khan to whom they were personally attached. They all fought

8. P. D. 30. 34.

hard and dauntlessly. Mubariz Khan fell fighting along with two of his sons, and practically the whole of his army was annihilated. Nizam-ul-mulk won the day and thereby changed the course of the subsequent history of India. A large number of elephants, animals and baggage was captured by him. The severed head of Mubariz Khan he sent on to the Emperor with an explanatory letter of apology, saying "With your Majesty's blessing I have succeeded in killing this rebel." He changed the name of the battlefield from Sakharkhedla to Fathkherda.

It is difficult to determine what actual part the Marathas played in this famous battle. Bajirao and some others remained close by, watching the result and ready to make a bargain with the winning side. Bajirao's personal sympathies were for Nizam-ul-mulk, as probably he had had bitter experience of Mubariz Khan's antagonism towards the Marathas. Mention is made in an account paper "of Rs. 10 having been paid to Ranoji Sindia and others for dressing their wounds received in the fight against Mubariz Khan." Other payments of a similar nature are also recorded, mentioning the rising stars of future history. Raghuji Jadhav of Sindkhed, one of the family from which Shivaji's mother Jijabai came, was killed fighting for Mubariz Khan. His son Mansing Rao Jadhav, born from Ambikabai (Rajaram Chhatrapati's daughter) was afterwards brought up by Shahu and became a partizan of Tarabai in her contest with the Peshwa after Shahu's death.

Nizam-ul-mulk's practical skill and far-sighted wisdom were well exemplified in his handling of the situation after the actual fighting was over. He did all he could to assuage the grief of the family and friends of Mubariz Khan by keeping them contented in all possible manner and thus extinguishing the rancour of a fallen enemy. The dead bodies were given proper funeral : the wounded were carefully looked after. The Nizam remained four days on the spot and then he returned to Aurangabad where he received Bajirao in a ceremonial visit of courtesy and good will and conferred upon him the title of a commander of seven thousand with personal honours and cash rewards including robes and jewellery of a rare quality. This was possibly a reward for the neutral attitude which Bajirao had adopted before the battle.[9] Nizam-ul-mulk was certainly anxious to disarm all opposition and bitterness in Bajirao's mind and to conciliate the Maratha sentiment, at the commencement of his career of independence in the Deccan. He also similarly rewarded Maratha Sardars like Rao Rambha Nimbalkar and Chandrasen Jadhav who were in the Mughal imperial employ.

Having made the necessary arrangements for the security of Aurangabad and the northern regions, Nizam-ul-mulk started for Haidarabad to subjugate the southern territory. On his way Udaji Chavan, one of the arch-enemies of the Maratha Government, came and offered his submission at Pandharpur, agreeing to serve him. In due course the Nizam stabilized his position at Haidarabad, after taking possession of that place by appeasing those who had tried to oppose him. He then wrote a long explanatory letter to the Emperor with profuse expressions of loyalty and obedience and begging pardon for his offences. The Emperor made a virtue of necessity, accepted the Nizam's professions and confirmed him as Subahdar of the Deccan. At the same time the provinces of Gujarat and Malwa were taken away from his charge, Sar-buland Khan and Raja Giridhar Bahadur being respectively nominated for them. The imperial *firman* of these changes arrived in due course and was received by Nizam-ul-mulk with proper ceremony on 20th June 1725.

Thus, the battle of Sakharkhedla proved a turning point for the fortunes of the Asaf Jahi[10] dynasty. It at once marks the assumption of independence for all practical purposes by the Nizam, a political change by which the future of the Marathas came to be closely linked up with the fortunes of the rulers of Haidarabad. He certainly for a time concealed his new position and shrewdly avoided outward signs and open declarations, that might have indicated his severance from the Central Government of Delhi ; but he ceased hereafter to refer to Delhi for orders on administrative matters or to send the

9. What passed at this visit is narrated in Purandare Daftar I. 77.

10. The title of Asaf Jah was given to Nizam-ul-mulk by the Emperor later on in 1737, when he was called to Delhi to put down the Marathas. Some writers mention that it was given in 1725. See Ashob, Irvine II—p. 301.

surplus revenue into the imperial treasury. He declared wars and concluded treaties on his own account. He made appointments and conferred honours, titles and dignities after the fashion of the Emperor.[11] But he did not establish a throne for himself, nor did he strike coins in his own name. In his Friday prayers he kept up the name of the Emperor. In all formal correspondence, he took care to use forms of language avowing the Emperor as his master. It cannot at the same time be denied that the actual dismemberment of the Mughal Empire started with this example of open revolt set by the Nizam. When a suggestion was made to him that he should set up an independent throne, he retorted, " May thrones and umbrellas bring good to him who has them. My business is to preserve my honour, and if this be mine, what need have I for your Imperial throne? " Doubtless this example came soon to be copied by others.

The Asaf-Jahi dynasty at Haidarabad became thus a permanent factor to be reckoned with in the future policy of the Marathas with diminishing interference from Delhi. The fortunes of the Marathas hereafter came to be controlled by one dominant personality for whom Bajirao alone proved more than a match. He thought it the best policy under the circumstances to bar out Nizam-ul-mulk's activities from the north by securing a permanent footing in Malwa and Gujarat. In his Aurangabad visit Bajirao had offered his full co-operation to Nizam in jointly carrying out measures of government and in settling mutual claims and disputes. For this the Peshwa proposed a joint expedition into the Karnatak, where urgent matters now invited his attention.[12]

11. See above, the title of Seven thousand Commander conferred upon Bajirao.

12. See Purandare Daftar 1. 77.

CHRONOLOGY

CHAPTER IV

1725 Nov.—1726 May	Bajirao's 1st expedition into Karnatak.
1726 Nov.—27 April	Bajirao's 2nd expedition into Karnatak.
1726	Shahu assures Chief of Sunda of protection.
1726	Nizam-ul-mulk marches into Karnatak.
1726 February	Sambhaji rises against Shahu.
1726 Nov. 19	Sarlashkar Sultanji Nimbalkar joins Nizam, is dismissed by Shahu.
1726 November	Chandrasen, Rao Rambha, Udaji Chavan raid Shahu's territory.
1727 April	Maratha armies suffer from cholera at Shrirangapattan.
1727 April	Karnatak chiefs submit to Bajirao.
1727 April	Bajirao effects settlement with Nawab Sadatulla Khan of Arcot.
1727 August 27	Bajirao starts against Nizam-ul-mulk.
1727 Oct-Dec.	Nizam joined by Sambhaji attacks Shahu's territory.
1728 January	Bajirao raids north Khandesh, threatens Burhanpur; proceeds to Ali Mohan.
1728 February	Nizam declares Sambhaji Chhatrapati at Poona; ravages Poona territory; Shahu and Chimnaji Appa take shelter at Purandar.
1728 February 14	Bajirao on the Tapti in Khandesh.
1728 February 28	Bajirao humbles Nizam at Palkhed.
1728 March 6	Nizam accepts terms from Bajirao at Mungi-Sheogaon.
1728 June	Chhatrasal besieged by Muhammad Khan Bangash at Jaitpur.
1728 October 25	Chimnaji Appa leaves Poona for Malwa.
1728 November 25	Chimnaji reaches the Narmada.
1728 November 29	Battle of Amjhera, Giridhar and Daya Bahadur killed.

1728 December 13	Chimnaji besieges Ujjain.
1729 February	Bajirao enters Bundelkhand *via* Deogad and Garha.
1729 March 12	Bajirao meets Chhatrasal.
1729 April 18	Bajirao routs Bangash and receives a portion of Bundela dominions.
1729 May 23	Bajirao returns to the Deccan.
1729 December	Marathas capture Mandavgad
1730 March 31	Mandavgad returned to the Emperor.
1731 December 14	Chhatrasal dies.

CHAPTER IV

RAPID SUCCESSES SOUTH AND NORTH

[1725—1729]

1 Consolidation in Karnatak.
2 Nizam-ul-mulk sets up Sambhaji as Chhatrapati.
3 Nizam overcome at Palkhed.
4 The quick action of Amjhera.
5 Chhatrasal rescued.

1. Consolidation in the Karnatak.—How Maratha interests developed in the Eastern Karnatak or the region south of the river Krishna ever since the days of Shivaji and Rajaram, has already been told. Apart from the wish of maintaining a strong Maratha hold on places and stations that had been his ancestral possessions so long, Shahu personally entertained a deep sentimental attachment towards his cousins of Tanjore, where at this time Raja Sharfoji ruled on a precarious tenure in the midst of unsettled and hostile surroundings. Out of revenge for the murder of Santaji Gorpade in June 1697 his brothers and nephews waged stern and continuous fights against the imperial forces under Zulfiqar Khan and other imperial generals, who tried to expel the Marathas from those distant regions. The Ghorpades practically conquered and held them almost to the time we are now talking of. Santaji's brother Bahirji Hindurao, his son Sidhoji and grandson Murarrao became for a time household words in the annals of the Karnatak.[1]

Shahu and his Peshwa as arbiters of India's destiny and confident of their righteous aims, now felt called upon to control the political situation, as they entertained high and noble hopes of creating order and establishing a congenial peaceful government by regulating the

1. A vast amount of literature recording the activities of the Ghorpades has been recently unearthed and irregularly printed; it is awaiting a careful and patient study for extracting a connected story from it. Murarrao made Gutti his permanent seat, and his history of half a century has yet to be constructed. See Shir. Ch. Sa. III. Sondha.

conflicting claims of the various chiefs and exacting obedience from them by force of arms, if necessary. During his visit to Nizam-ul-mulk after the battle of Sakarkhedla Bajirao freely discussed with him his aims and views, and suggested a joint tour of the Karnatak, in which the Nizam agreed to offer his co-operation. The matter was discussed at Satara during the autumn of 1725 and Shahu issued commands to Bajirao, so that two successive Maratha expeditions took place during the years 1725 and 1726, the first extending from November, 1725 to May 1726 and the second from November 1726 to April 1727. The first campaign is named after Chitaldurg and the second after Shrirangapattan. Both were led by Bajirao personally, although Shahu gave the nominal command to his favourite Fatehsinh Bhosle. Nizam-ul-mulk sent Narso Kusaji the Maratha agent at his court to Bajirao in February 1725 inquiring what the Peshwa's object was in going to the Karnatak.[2]

From this scheme of proposed joint expedition in settling the Karnatak affairs, Nizam-ul-mulk deliberately kept himself aloof and tried to counteract whatever harm might possibly occur to his interests from the Peshwa's move, only sending his own deputy Aiwaz Khan with a considerable force to act independently of the Peshwa. From this very moment Nizam-ul-mulk began to apprehend a clash with the Marathas and commenced deep underhand intrigues against both Shahu and Bajirao, which culminated at Palkhed. In the present expedition Fatehsinh Bhosle was accompanied by Trimbakrao Dabhade, Sultanji Nimbalkar and the Pratinidhi in addition to the Peshwa, totalling between them about 50,000 troops. Murarrao Ghorpade joined them later from Gutti. Fatehsinh Bhosle at the special behest of Shahu proceeded to Tanjore and explained to Sharfoji the object of the Karnatak undertaking.

The Marathas proceeded via Bijapur, Gulburga and Kopbal on to Chitaldurg. They collected arrears of tribute, obtained promises of regular payment in future, put down those who opposed them and re-established Maratha rule in places which had thrown it off. The chief of Sunda (Sondhe)

---

2. P. D. 30, 36.

was taken under Maratha protection at Shahu's special instance.[3] The campaigning season having ended, the Maratha armies returned to their headquarters for the rains. During the winter of 1726 they again moved into the Karnatak to complete the remaining work of collecting the Chauth and meeting the possible opposition from the Nizam. In this connection Shahu addressed the following letter to the Deshmukh of Lakshmeshwar on July 20, 1726 :-

"We have received your request for help against the tyranny that the Nawab Nizam-ul-mulk has been practising upon you and your territories and have pleasure to inform you that we have arranged to send you the required succour about the next Dassarah season, when troop-movements become practicable. The Senapati, the Peshwa and the Sar-Lashkar will proceed to the south, and you must try to defend your position till they arrive, with whatever resources you possess and prevent the Nawab's entry into your state."[4]

This partially explains why a second expedition became necessary. Nizam-ul-mulk commenced open encroachments upon the Maratha spheres of influence when Bajirao was absent; and Shahu undertook to restrain him and protect his feudatories. Bajirao went this time by the western route via Belgaum, Sunda and Lakshmeshwar, on to Bednur. From thence he proceeded to Shrirangapattan, where he arrived on 4th March and after spending a month at that place returned rapidly to Satara on receiving an urgent call from his master for meeting the trouble that Nizam-ul-mulk had then started in various parts of Maharashtra. Through heat, lack of water and a sudden outbreak of cholera, the Maratha armies suffered terrible losses during 1727. While at Shrirangapattan Bajirao arranged a treaty of friendship and alliance with the Nawab Sadatulla Khan of Arcot settling the rights of the Tanjore Raja. The arrangement was scrupulously honoured by the Nawab for the next 15 years and evinces the true Maratha spirit of conciliation and amity towards neighbouring states. This

3. Vide Shiva-Charitra-Sahitya, 3. 497.

4. S. R. 27.

example and the cases of Sunda and Lakshmeshwar already mentioned, testify to the general trend of the Maratha system of collecting Chauth and offering protection in return.

Shahu and Bajirao were now bent upon consolidating Maratha rule all round. Murarrao Ghorpade was struggling alone to maintain his precarious position at Gutti and was now induced by Bajirao to accept the Peshwa's leadership. Henceforth he became a friend and loyal member of the Maratha power. Similarly the Poligar Chiefs of Surapur, Kanakdurg, Chitaldurg, Gadag, Lakshmeshwar came to meet Bajirao, and paid him their homage and tribute. The Raja of Shrirangapattan also offered his submission by paying a tribute of 21 lacs in cash. The extension of Maratha power in the extreme south thus started, necessarily required a longer time to consolidate and was unavoidably interrupted by Bajirao's presence being required urgently in Maharashtra. Years passed before Shahu could take the work up again; but he had not forgotten it and when in 1739 he sent Raghuji and Fatesinh Bhosle again into the Karnatak, the object was to complete the work of consolidation which had been begun by Bajirao in these two expeditions of 1725 and 1726.

2. **Nizam-ul-mulk sets up Sambhaji as Chhatrapati.**—From February 1725 to February 1728 or roughly from Sakharkhedla to Palkhed is a period of three years, which in miniature discloses the nature of the relationship which the two neighbouring powers, the Maratha and the Nizami, were to develop towards each other for some three generations, culminating in both being subjected to the paramountcy of Britain. The Marathas all along tried to enforce the rights granted to them by the Emperor in 1719. The Nizam opposed them on the ground that they had been won through their unholy alliance with the Saiyads, who had defied the Emperor and ultimately put him to death. Nizam-ul-mulk did not, however, precipitate matters and required over one year to consolidate his own position in the Deccan before openly challenging the Marathas. The two expeditions of Bajirao into the Karnatak were construed by the Nizam as an encroachment upon his own government, for he considered that as all the regions south of the Krishna had once belonged to the old kingdoms

of Bijapur and Golkonda, they had come into the Emperor's possession by right of conquest, and now naturally formed his own jurisdiction. At the same time the Marathas maintained that these territories were subjugated by them at an enormous cost of blood and effort, during the long war which they had successfully conducted against the Emperor Aurangzeb. This is indeed the origin of the whole dispute which in the last resort came to be decided by an appeal to arms. Bajirao had well anticipated this clash of policy and had suggested an immediate offensive against Nizam-ul-mulk. But Shahu long hesitated to give any offence to the Nawab and feared that Bajirao might not be able to cope with the task of putting him down. Matters took an ominous turn for Shahu when Bajirao was absent in the Karnatak during the early months of 1727 and Shahu's patience was sorely tried.

Let us here review the resources of the two parties. Aiwaz Khan, Turk-Taz Khan and Ghias Khan were the three principal agents whom Nizam-ul-mulk employed to harass the Maratha collectors of Chauth and their local agents, by subtle pinpricks, which soon became intolerable. The three abovementioned officers of the Nizam were guided in their work by some Maratha deserters, such as Chandrasen Jadhav, Rao Rambha Nimbalkar and Udaji Chavan, whose only principle had always been an uncompromising opposition to Shahu and his Peshwas. Moreover, Nizam-ul-mulk was not slow in seducing some of Shahu's intimate supporters, notably his Senasaheb-Subha Kanhoji Bhosle and his Sar-Lashkar Sultanji Nimbalkar, who had grown jealous of Bajirao's increasing ascendency in the Maratha Government.

Sambhaji of Kolhapur and his mother Rajasbai were no less hostile than Tarabai, and continued their intrigues against Shahu by playing easily into the hands of Nizam-ul-mulk, through the agency of men like Chandrasen and Udaji Chavan. A letter written by Sambhaji to the Senapati's agent Rayaji Malhar on 23rd July 1721 clearly reveals this intrigue. It runs thus :—

"Chandrasen Jadhav must have already communicated to you the deep interest he takes in our affairs and the efforts he is making to promote our cause. We have no doubt that you too with your great attachment for us would do your utmost towards the same end."[5]

Such a move against Shahu had clearly been afoot since 1721 ; but it could not gain material strength until Nizam-ul-mulk lent it weight by espousing Sambhaji's cause openly in 1725. Bhagwantrao Amatya, son of the famous Ramchandrapant, also joined the conspiracy then being formed against Shahu. One of Shahu's faithful commanders Nilkanthrao Jadhav was captured in a fight and kept in confinement by Nizam-ul-mulk. An order of Shahu dated 23rd August 1725 exists describing his anxiety to get Nilkanthrao released. On 25th November Bajirao thus writes to Shahu, "I am perfectly aware of Your Highness's intentions not to create suspicion in Nizam-ul-mulk's mind by my assemblage of troops near Pandharpur. These are meant for our Karnatak undertaking, and I am taking no action direct or indirect that would give offence to Nizam-ul-mulk. I cannot, however, omit to convey to you my strong suspicion that the signs are ominous and that I apprehend trouble.[6]

In February 1726 Sambhaji writes to Chandrasen, "We are exceedingly happy to receive your letters and to learn that you have succeeded in inducing Nizam-ul-mulk to espouse our cause and promote it in every possible way. Acting upon your valuable suggestion, we led an expedition towards the south right up to the river Tungabhadra, having been joined by the influencial following of Hindurao and Sagunabai Ghorpade and of Piraji and Ranoji also. As Shripat Rao Pratinidhi has marched against us, please come quickly for our succour. Nizam-ul-mulk has marched towards Adoni and asked us to send him our contingent. Accordingly we have despatched our minister Nilkanth Trimbak with orders to join the Nizam quickly ; and now we are waiting at Torgal to meet you. We cannot ourselves go and join the Nizam, as the Peshwa and the Pratinidhi are both coming to oppose us. You have indeed done us a great service by inducing Nizam-ul-mulk to break off his relations with Shahu and take up our cause. We are confident that Murarrao Ghorpade, Udaji Chavan, Appaji Suro and others would soon join us. Aiwaz Khan has also

5. Raj. 3. 559. 6. S. R. 14, 157.

earnestly commenced operations in a different direction. Thus the moment is now ripe for action, and we are only waiting for you to join in as quickly as possible."[7] Here is clear evidence of the intrigue which Nizam-ul-mulk fomented against Shahu. Sambhaji fell into the trap and allowed himself to become a tool in Nizam-ul-mulk's hand. Was Sambhaji doing all this to preserve Maratha independence?

Sambhaji, however, did not possess a single capable follower, nor the high character necessary in a master to maintain his position. Jealous of Shahu's increasing popularity and prosperity, he resorted to mean intrigue and sedition, which ultimately ruined him. Shahu left no stone unturned to wean Sambhaji from his evil course, and when he despatched Bajirao into the Karnatak, he sought Sambhaji's co-operation by offering him the following terms on 30th Dec. 1725,—

" Let us both exert ourselves in co-operation to recapture Mughal territories and add them to our swarajya in the way our ancestors did. You may work in the south, we will work in the north. We shall give you a fair share of what we acquire in the north and you should also similarly give us a share of what you would acquire in the south."[8]

But Sambhaji did not see the wisdom of falling in line with Shahu and allowed himself to be duped by self-seeking agents of Nizam-ul-mulk, on the advice of his minister Nilkanth Trimbak Prabhu Mahadkar, and another vainglorious officer of Shahu, his Rajadna Chimnaji Damodar Moghe, who with a record of 20 years faithful service behind him had been directed by Shahu to persuade Nizam-ul-mulk in a personal discussion to desist from the harmful course he was following. A letter of 30th July 1726 mentions that Shahu deputed Chimnaji to meet the Nizam.[9]

This Chimnaji Damodar had the vain dream of rivalling Bajirao both in war and diplomacy, and out of spite towards him fell into Nizam-ul-mulk's snare. The latter induced him to accept Sambhaji's Peshwaship. Chimnaji light-heartedly deserted Shahu's cause and agreed to serve Sambhaji for which he had to pay dearly in the end. Shahu at first never

7. Dalvi's History of the Jadhav Family, p. 81.
8. Patre Yadi 14.
9. S. R. 28.

suspected that a strong opposition was being formed against him but was rudely awakened to his danger towards the end of 1726 during Bajirao's absence in the Karnatak.

About the Dassara of 1726 (24th September) Sambhaji left Kolhapur and joined Nizam-ul-mulk, leaving his mother Rajasbai behind to conduct the usual administration. He was away from his capital for about three years.[10] Hostile activities against Shahu immediately commenced in different quarters. Turk-Taz Khan committed terrible atrocities near Sangamner during the fair season of 1726-27. Nizam-ul-mulk long kept up professions of amity and good will, which he communicated to Shahu through the Pratinidhi and the Sumant. He alleged that he had nothing to urge against Shahu personally, but that his Peshwa was the principal source of mischief. Along with Turk-Taz Khan, other officers of Nizam-ul-mulk, such as the Nimbalkars, Rao Rambha and his son Janoji, and Udaji Chavan, began to create trouble in the neighbourhood of Satara itself. They attacked Rahimatpur a few miles east of Satara, where in an action in August 1726 one of Shahu's Sardars Rayaji Jadhav was killed. Happily Shahu managed to win over Chandrasen's brother Shambhusinh and the Kolhapur Senapati Piraji Ghorpade with his lieutenant Dharrao Nimbalkar. The veteran Vyasrao, an old servant of Dhanaji Jadhav, who was strongly attached to Shahu, brought about similar defections in the ranks of Kolhapur to the advantage of Shahu. Early in 1727 Sambhaji toured through the district of Poona as the de facto ruler receiving homage from and granting sanads to the local officials. When this report reached Shahu's ears, he felt shocked and realized the far-reaching game that Nizam-ul-mulk had begun to play. So he wrote to some of his northern chiefs inviting them to come to his relief without a moment's delay, as all his troops were away in the Karnatak.[11]

3. **Nizam overcome at Palkhed.**—At this juncture Shahu's counsel was divided. The only man of courage and foresight who could save the situation was away, and those

10. Raj. Vol. 8 Nos. 94 and 96. 11. S. R. 25, 26.

who were near advised him to effect a compromise with Nizam-ul-mulk by mild and submissive measures. In a weak moment Shahu accepted their advice and asked his Sumant and his Pratinidhi to negotiate a peaceful understanding with the Nizam. The latter proposed that he would make cash payment of the Chauthai dues and that the Maratha agents stationed for the purpose at different places should be withdrawn. He also communicated to Shahu his own friendly and salutary advice to rid himself of the pernicious influence of the Konkanastha Peshwa.

Shahu was almost on the point of accepting the proposal of cash payment, when Bajirao returned and remonstrated with him strongly on the subject, explaining that such a course would destroy all hold of the Marathas upon the outlying districts already subjugated. While this discussion was going on at Shahu's court, he was informed that even the proposed cash payment of Chauthai could not be made, since Sambhaji now claimed it as head of the Maratha State. This meant an immediate danger to Shahu's position as the Maratha sovereign and he indignantly ordered Bajirao to open a war against Nizam-ul-mulk. Bajirao left Satara on this task on 27th August 1727.

The following letter addressed by Nizam-ul-mulk to Sawai Jaysinh clearly explains his evil designs.

"It has been repeatedly reported to the Emperor that these Marathas raid Gujarat and Malwa at my suggestion and instigation. I have performed all the necessary exertion in this matter. I have again and again written to Shahu Rajah giving him the good counsel that the Marathas should not plunder Gujarat and Malwa. Although thus pressed and threatened, nothing has resulted from it and the Marathas have not given up their raids. Therefore with a view to carrying out the Emperor's order I have called to my side Raja Sambhaji, who is Shahu's rival. I have conciliated him and engaged him in punishing and exterminating Shahu. Sultanji Nimbalkar, the Sar-i-Lashkar of the enemy's army came and saw me and has been appointed to command Sambhaji's army. By the grace of God I am hopeful that the other partizans of Shahu would equally desert him. As at this time autograph letters from the Emperor have repeatedly reached me, asking me to chastise Shahu, I have taken on my shoulders this grand enterprise, in order to satisfy the Emperor and give him proof of my loyalty and devotion. Otherwise it would be highly inexpedient for me to break my relations with the Marathas. And now that they have permanently planted their claws in all the imperial territory and their strength and power have increased beyond limit, I have challenged them to fight solely out of reliance upon the grace of God and the Emperor's favour."[12]

On October 13th Shahu declared war upon Nizam-ul-mulk.[13] The Nizam readily took up the challenge. He kept his movements entirely secret. Giving out that he was going to Aurangabad he marched towards Junnar and Poona. At the beginning of 1727 he was encamped at Bid and spent the three months from June to August at Dharur. On 21st September 1727 Purandare informed Bajirao that Nizam-ul-mulk was marching upon Satara, via Mhaswad, guided by Sultanji Nimbalkar. At this crisis Bajirao was the only strong support of Shahu. His Senapati Khanderao Dabhade was both old and involved in domestic dissensions. Besides, Dabhade entertained a secret grudge against the Peshwa, possibly because the latter entirely usurped the Senapati's official functions. Operations were opened on both sides.

Turk-Taz Khan and Aiwaz Khan were the two able lieutenants of Nizam-ul-mulk, while Bajirao relied on Malharrao Holkar and Ranoji Sindia. The latter declared to the Peshwa that he "was ready for any eventuality, even to sacrifice his life if it became necessary. God is the protector of all." The Pawar brothers were also equally loyal and served Bajirao with perfect devotion. Aiwaz Khan marched towards Poona from Aurangabad but was encountered by Tukoji Pawar near Sinnar, whose Deshmukh Kuvar Bahadur was an old landholder in Mughal service. Kuvar Bahadur was defeated and made to join the Peshwa's banner. Fatehsinh and Raghuji Bhosle encountered Chandrasen Jadhav and defeated him after a sanguinary action.

---

12. Trans. & text printed in *Islamic Culture* by Sir J. N. Sarkar.
13. S. R. 30.

But Nizam-ul-mulk made the Poona district his main objective, and ravaged it through his trusted Maratha commanders. They attacked Lohgad and came upon Chinchwad and Poona. Shahu's garrisons at most of his posts deserted them and ran away for safety in different directions. Accompanied by Sambhaji, Nizam-ul-mulk himself entered the Poona district from Junnar and after capturing most of the fortified places on the way came and took up his residence at Poona. Here in February 1727 Sambhaji was married to a Rajput lady of the Sisodia clan of Ramnagar and was there openly declared the Chhatrapati of the Marathas. Appointing Fazal Beg to hold Poona, Nizam-ul-mulk proceeded to Loni Pargaum, Patas, Supa and Baramati, creating fearful havoc at all these places by means of his efficient artillery.

Bajirao on the other hand had no artillery and depended solely on his usual guerilla tactics of long marches and sudden swoops upon the enemy at different spots. Leaving Poona in September, he crossed the Godavari near Puntamba and plundered Jalna and Sindkhed, defeating Aiwaz Khan who opposed him on November 5. Thereupon Bajirao proceeded through Berar, ravaged Mahur, Mangrol and Wasim, and then suddenly directing his course to the north-west entered Khandesh, crossed the Tapti at Kokarmunda, and with lightning speed proceeded through eastern Gujarat in January 1728 to Alimohan or Chhota-Udaipur. Sarbuland Khan, the governor of Gujarat befriended him in opposition to the Nizam. Here learning that the Nizam had turned towards Poona, Bajirao gave out that he would devastate Burhanpur, the principal Mughal mart in the north, and reached Betawad in Khandesh on 14th February.

Bajirao rightly calculated that his sudden descent upon Burhanpur and Aurangabad would draw away Nizam-ul-mulk from Poona for the protection of his northern possessions. Chimnaji Appa was stationed to watch the Nizam's movements and to manœuvre him away towards Bajirao's position. Chimnaji Appa and Shahu had in the meantime taken up their residence in the Purandar fort both for safety and for watching the movements of the enemy. Nizam-ul-mulk found his occupation of Poona extremely costly. His allies Sambhaji and Chandrasen having no efficient troops or sufficient funds, proved only a clog on his own movements and a fearful drain on his resources. When he heard that his northern territories were being devastated, he left Poona about the middle of February and directed his march towards the Godavari with the object of destroying Bajirao and his light-footed army in an open plain where his artillery could be effectively employed. Both parties now played their own tactics with the utmost care and watchfulness. But the Marathas proved more alert and agile. Their spies obtained useful information about the enemy's plans and quickly communicating it to their various chiefs, managed to keep the Nizam off his guard and get him into an inextricable position like a hunted beast of prey. In order to carry out swift movements Nizam-ul-mulk left his cumbrous artillery behind and crossed the Godavari to find Bajirao near Aurangabad. During the course of his march, on February 25, the Nizam found himself suddenly entrapped in a maze near Palkhed about 20 miles west of Aurangabad and some ten miles east of Baizapur, a difficult hilly place in which he could get no water or provisions. Here he was quickly surrounded on all sides by the Maratha bands; his communication with the outside world was entirely cut off and he soon found it impossible to extricate himself and escape to a place of safety. Bajirao thus writes of this situation : "Today I have come within sight of the Nawab. A distance of four miles separates us. Please point out to me the best route for bringing him to bay. Instruct all men to be extremely cautious and join me without a moment's loss." Malharrao Holkar was stationed to watch and arrest the Nawab's movements.

Aiwaz Khan and Chandrasen understood what had happened and appealed to Bajirao for relief, as the situation daily grew more desperate for Nizam-ul-mulk. Bajirao demanded hostages before any relief could be offered. Thereupon the two parties moved to Mungi-Shevgaum where water and provisions were offered to the Nawab in plenty. On 6th March 1728 a settlement was signed, the terms of which were :—

(1) All administrative or diplomatic measures for the government of the six Mughal Subahs should be executed through the agency of the Marathas, who would fully guard the imperial interests.

(2) Anandrao Sumant should not be employed as an intermediary for transacting political business, as he no longer enjoyed the Peshwa's confidence.

(3) The Nawab should withdraw his protection from Raja Sambhaji and allow him to proceed to Panhala.

(4) Poona, Baramati, Khed, Talegaum and other places captured by the Nawab should be restored to Shahu.

(5) The previous grants of Swarajya and Sardeshmukhi should be confirmed.

(6) Balavant Sinh (?) and others should have their jagirs restored.

(7) No more jagir should be bestowed on Sambhaji than had been already provided for him by Shahu Raja between the Krishna and the Panchaganga.

(8) Sultanji Nimbalkar who had deserted to the Nawab should not be allowed to create mischief.

(9) Tributes illegally collected by Sambhaji should be paid back to Shahu Raja.

(10) The vatan and Patilki of Shahgad should be continued to Pilaji Jadhav as before.

(11) The prisoners captured by Turk-Taz Khan out of the Maratha swarajya should be sent back.

(12) The five villages of Peta Nimbone should be granted to the Pawar brothers, Krishnaji, Udaji and Keroji.

(13) Raja Sambhaji should not be allowed to collect Chauth from districts north of the Krishna."[14]

When these terms were negotiated Bajirao and Nizam-ul-mulk met and ratified them by a formal exchange of dresses and presents, completely restoring a cordial spirit of mutual relationship. This was the fifth meeting of these two chiefs, the fourth having taken place at Aurangabad after the battle of Fatehkherda.

This narrative of the Palkhed campaign wherein Bajirao successfully overcame Nizam-ul-mulk discloses the important results which accrued to the Marathas for all the strenuous labours, preparations and anxieties of a year's hostilities. The main point they gained was a formal acknowledgment by Nizam-ul-mulk of the Maratha claims long ago ratified by the

14. See P. D. 15. 86 p. 89. Four unimportant articles are omitted.

Saiyads. This was now unequivocally conceded by Asaf Jah. He would no longer openly support Sambhaji and repudiate Shahu's claim to be regarded as the head of the Maratha raj. The Nizam's power was certainly not finally broken, nor was that the avowed object of Maratha policy. Nizam-ul-mulk fully realized Bajirao's capacity as an opponent and what he would have to expect from him in the future. This was a signal outcome of this short but successful episode of Palkhed, in which Bajirao overcame the greatest strategist of the day, thirty years his senior.

Another indirect result of this victory was the restraint that came to be imposed upon Maratha deserters like Chandrasen Jadhav, Udaji Chavan, Kanhoji Bhosle, even the Dabhade Senapati and the Sar-Lashkar Nimbalkar, who were merely self-seekers, plying between the two powers and making a personal bargain out of divided loyalties. Bajirao and his brother now obtained full control to restrain these disturbers and their treacherous intrigues, as they made capital out of the difficulties of Shahu and his Peshwa. Guerilla tactics triumphed over artillery. It should, however, be clearly noted by those who carelessly accuse the Peshwa of inability or neglect to uproot the Nizam finally from the Deccan, that Shahu was mainly responsible for preserving the Haidarabad State. He thus writes to Bajirao, " You must on no account inflict any loss upon Nizam-ul-mulk or injure his susceptibilities. We enjoin this on you as a sacred obligation to the memory of your revered father." At the same time Shahu allowed his Peshwa to exercise full control over the Maratha government and the State.[16]

It is also clear incidentally that those stand self-condemned, who accuse Shahu and his Peshwas of having sold Maratha independence to the Mughals by accepting their vassalage. What better results could have been achieved by Tarabai and her party, if Shahu had not gained the leadership of the Maratha State?

4. **The quick action of Amjhera.**—Palkhed forms a landmark in the career of Bajirao. The eight years from April

15. P. D. 10. 75, S. R. 188, P. D. 17. 13.

1720 when he was invested with the Peshwaship, to March 1728 when he scored his first notable victory against a veteran soldier and diplomat of the character and capacity of Nizam-ul-mulk, may be termed a period of probation in which he felt his ground, collected his own party, and proved his capacity for the leadership in the Maratha State. Above all he secured the confidence of his master Shahu and belief in his own powers. At the same time he seems to have made his choice of expansion of his power in the north in preference to the south, in which latter direction the Pratinidhi, the Sumant, Fatesinh Bhosle and even Shahu himself would not have allowed him a free hand. Tired of constant personal jealousies and court intrigues, he selected Malwa and Bundelkhand as the field where he could leave a permanent mark.

During the rainy season of 1728 the two brothers and their immediate associates deliberated long and anxiously, and made up their minds to strike first, strike hard and strike effectively. Possibly they did not disclose their plans to Shahu for fear of provoking his disapproval; perhaps they had no full and detailed plans of what was going to be achieved. They had only one pressing object before them. Shahu had long since contracted debts which he was most anxious to pay off. If the Peshwa was not to find funds to release his own master from the constant pressure of creditors, who else could do it? Whom else was Shahu to look up to? So by some means or other money must be procured at once. Malhar Rao Holkar and Ranoji Sindia who had previous acquaintance with Malwa, had estimated its resources and revealed to their master the prospect of some signal achievement and quick gain. Gujarat was rich enough, no doubt, but it was a preserve of the Senapati whom the Peshwa dare not touch.

Giridhar Bahadur was at this time the Mughal Subahdar governing Malwa. He was an able and tried officer with a prestige for upholding Mughal predominance and traditions. He had by his side an equally energetic and resourceful coadjutor in his own cousin Daya Bahadur. They had vowed to oust the Marathas from Malwa and had received for that task all the support they asked for from the Emperor. Bajirao had despatched his trusted diplomat Dado Bhimsen to interview Sawai Jaysinh and find out how the venture into

Malwa was likely to turn out. Jaysinh had long been on friendly terms with Shahu and being covetous of securing Malwa for himself, he was not immediately concerned in supporting Giridhar and his cousin. Dado Bhimsen wrote from Jaipur on 17th August 1728 communicating Jaysinh's advice that the time was opportune for the Peshwa's entry into Malwa and that he should not lose a moment in undertaking it.

Bajirao and his brother formed their plans for an invasion of Malwa and each separately made a formal start on an auspicious day from Poona, Chimnaji by the western route through Baglan and Khandesh, and Bajirao by the eastern through Ahmadnagar, Berar, Chanda and Devgad towards Bundelkhand, keeping in close touch so as to render help to each other in case of emergency. Baji Bhivrao Retrekar, Ganapatrao Mehendale, Naro Shankar, Antaji Mankeshvar, Govindpant Bundale accompanied Chimnaji in addition to the three trusted lieutenants Malhar, Ranoji and Udaji. These three proceeded long before in advance to prepare the preliminaries of a sudden swoop upon Malwa. The actual march of Chimnaji did not commence till the Divali (October 23), and Bajirao's indeed much later, he having been called away by Shahu to accompany him to Tuljapur on his devotional visit to his tutelary deity. The veteran Pilaji Jadhav and Davalji Somavanshi, the new Sar-Lashkar accompanied Bajirao.

Chimnaji reached the banks of the Narmada on 25th November, and four days after, on 29th he won the grand victory of Amjhera (near Dhar) after a stiff fight in which both Giridhar Bahadur and Daya Bahadur lost their lives. The news of this fateful event flashed like lightning across India and shocked the Mughal Court as much as it gladdened Maratha hearts. Bajirao received the news in Berar and at once despatched further instructions to his brother quickly to follow up the action of Amjhera. How such a reverse could so suddenly overtake the powerful Mughal forces led by two gallant and experienced generals and fortified by an efficient artillery, is a mystery which cannot be correctly solved in the absence of full details. The first announcement of the Mughal defeat runs thus :—

"Daya Bahadur marched to meet the Marathas and awaited their advance at Amjhera blocking the narrow pass of the Vindhia range. But the Marathas avoided that pass, ascended by the pass of Mandavgad and attacked the Mughals unexpectedly from behind. Daya Bahadur found himself in a fix but had no alternative, except to meet the onslaught. He faced it bravely and was killed along with many noteworthy followers. Elephants, horses, drums and all the standards were captured by the Marathas, and the whole Mughal camp plundered." Chimnaji Appa writes on 30th November, "Giridhar Bahadur came treacherously upon us and a stiff battle raged for six hours (2 prahars). He was routed and killed along with his whole army.[16]

The Jaipur letters run thus :—

" Keshavrao's Arzdast to Maharaja Sawai Jaysinh dated 29th November 1728. You must have already learnt the account of Malwa and I also intimate the same to you. Kantha Maratha (Kanthaji Kadam) with ten thousand horse wandered in Malwa and went to Gujarat. On hearing the news of his wandering, Raja Giridhar Bahadur who had encamped at Mandsaur, sent his personal staff to Ujjain and started in pursuit of the villain. When the Raja Bahadur was camping at Amjhera, Chimna Pandit brother of Bajirao and Uda Pawar with a force of 22 thousand horse suddenly crossed the Narmada and travelling 30 cos in one day, left part of their troops at the fort of Dhar to prevent Muhammad Omar Khan, who was stationed to guard the fort, coming to join the Raja Bahadur, and with the rest the Marathas fell upon the Raja Bahadur's army. In an engagement that followed, first Rao Gulab Ram, and then Jamadar Salabat Khan were killed. Raja Anand Ram received two musket wounds and was captured by the Ghanim with his brother Shambhu Ram. The Raja Bahadur discharged arrows with his own hand until the

16. The recently discovered letters from the Jaipur records contain a similar account and leave no doubt that the two nobles met their sad end in one and the same action of 29th November, although possibly the fact took a little time to be accurately ascertained and reported. It is necessary to note that for years past the exact time and details of the death of these two chiefs had exerçised the ingenuity of many research students and it is a relief that the mystery surrounding the event has been finally solved by Dr. Raghuvir Sinh.

four quivers became empty, when he suddenly received a shot in his breast and lost his life in his master's service."

There are further letters giving an account of the subsequent siege of Ujjain, which was valiantly held by the imperialists against desperate attacks by the Marathas.

Not content with this first success Bajirao wrote back to his brother, "I am happy to learn the news of your victory at Amjhera, which is due to the blessing of our master and our revered father. May God continue to grant you similar victories ever more. You must take forethought about the future: press upon the capital Ujjain with all speed so as to obtain funds with which to pay the Chhatrapati's debts. I note what you say about the strenuous services rendered by Udaji Pawar and others. We rely upon them all for following up this first achievement with equal persistence. Convey to them all my congratulations and an assurance of our good intentions. You must in particular be very circumspect. Allow no slackness in discipline, nor feel unduly elated by your success. Your first concern should be money and more money. We intend marching towards Bundelkhand via Chanda and Devgad."

Similar congratulations were showered upon Chimnaji from all quarters. It became also known that it was Holkar and Pawar who had obtained information beforehand about the dispositions of the Mughal forces, and the suitable routes for fording the river and crossing the passes beyond. This striking success at once created a name and a pre-eminent position for the Peshwa. The local Rajput element welcomed Maratha penetration and rendered valuable help in the adventure which the Marathas had undertaken. The ancient fort of Mandavgad which commands the passes and passages into Malwa, was at once captured by Udaji Pawar but was restored to the Emperor's authority by Shahu at the special request of Sawai Jaysinh.

5. **Chhatrasal rescued.**—We must now turn to the movements of Bajirao himself. The moment was full of both danger and hope for the Marathas. A new era was dawning in Indian politics. The Rajputs of north India had become thoroughly disaffected towards the Mughal Empire. The

Bundelas in particular had long contracted friendly relations with the Marathas, having been imitating the latter in their fight for liberty and in the many difficult adventures and trials for national uplift. One valiant son of Champat Rai, named Chhatrasal, had established his capital at Panna and waged intermittent war against the Mughals ever since the days of Aurangzeb and Shivaji. Born on 26th May 1650 and facing misfortunes and adverse circumstances, Chhatrasal early came to the Deccan seeking employment in the train of Mirza Raja Jaysinh when that powerful general was sent by the Emperor to conquer Shivaji. He was since then more or less in touch with that hero's activities and like him aspired to win independence for his own land, which was then included in the Subah of Allahabad for administrative purposes. A Pathan general of valour and ability named Muhammad Khan Bangash, who afterwards made a name in Indian history as the founder of the house of the Nawabs of Farrukhabad, was then the Mughal Subahdar of the province and severely restrained Chhatrasal from the national activities he was conducting. A strong antipathy thus arose between the two often leading to open fights and bloodshed for several years.

Just about the time that Nizam-ul-mulk and Bajirao were engaged in hostile operations during the early months of 1728 in the south, Muhammad Khan Bangash attacked the Bundela king with a large force commanded by himself and his three valiant sons and defeated him on several occasions. After a sanguinary action in June 1728 Chhatrasal betook himself to the fort of Jaitpur, which the Bangash at once invested. The siege was long and arduous. In December 1728 at the moment when Chimnaji Appa invested Ujjain after his signal success at Amjhera, Chhatrasal was so hard-pressed at Jaitpur that he desperately attempted to fight his way out and came to be captured severely wounded along with the fort. He sent urgent messages and piteous calls both to Chimnaji Appa at Ujjain and to Bajirao, to come with all speed and save his life and fortunes. Muhammad Khan Bangash was a consummate politician and seasoned soldier devoted to the imperial cause. He knew what the Marathas were doing in Malwa but possibly did not expect Bajirao to march by the unfrequented eastern route towards Bundelkhand with another large army. Chimnaji was fully occupied with his operations for consolidating the Maratha positions and acquiring booty out of the riches of Ujjain. Bajirao was at Devgad when he received the news of the posture of affairs. He thus wrote to his brother in January : " Do not waste time and energy upon Ujjain. There are other places and surrounding districts equally alluring. Let me at once know if you require me to join you. If I do not hear from you, I shall go directly into Bundelkhand." In the meantime Chhatrasal managed to send urgent and confidential emissaries to Bajirao calling upon him to come to his relief without a moment's delay.[17] Bajirao received this S. O. S. at Garha in February, 1729 and at once wrote to Chimnaji, " I am proceeding to succour Chhatrasal. You may arrange your movements independently of me as suits you best."

Bajirao had with him about 25,000 horsemen commanded by trusted lieutenants like Pilaji Jadhav, Naro Shankar, Tukoji Pawar and Davalji Somavanshi. On 12th March he reached Mahoba where Chhatrasal's son met him. The next day Chhatrasal himself arrived having contrived to escape from his confinement and brought him presents and marks of honour.[18] Bajirao boldly pushed forward against the Bangash and having set in motion his plans for the contest he was undertaking, inflicted severe reverses upon his adversary, considerably adding to the glory of Maratha valour already won by Chimnaji Appa at Amjhera. The Bangash also met the danger boldly, sent urgent calls for help to the Emperor and requisitioned his son Qaim Khan to come with fresh troops. Bajirao learnt that Qaim Khan was coming in hot haste and so he proceeded against him before the father and the son could effect a junction. Qaim Khan was routed near Jaitpur and ran away from the field with only 100 followers to save his life. Writes Pilaji

---

17. This imploring call has been immortalized by the poet in a Hindi verse recalling a mythological story now well-known to every school boy. It means " Know you, Bajirao, that I am in that same sad plight in which the famous elephant was when caught by the crocodile. My valiant race is on the point of extinction. Come and save my honour.

जो गति ग्राह गजेन्द्रकी सो गति जानहुं आज ।
बाजी जात बुंदेलनकी राखो बाजी लाज ॥

18. P. D. 22. 36.

Jadhav from the place of action: "Having conciliated the chief of Devgad, the Peshwa proceeded to Garha where he learnt of the Bangash coming to attack Chhatrasal with a strong force of 20 thousand well equipped troops. We then effected a junction with Chhatrasal's men and have now surrounded the Bangash. In the meantime Qaim Khan Bangash with a fresh succour of 30 thousand marched against us. We prevented him from effecting a junction with his father and handled him so roughly, that after a sanguinary action he was completely routed. A large amount of booty has been secured, among which are 3,000 horses and 13 elephants. Enclosed is a list of our killed and wounded. Please do communicate the news to their relations. We hope soon to finish this affair and return home. Muhammad Khan still remains besieged and will be vanquished if he ventures out. If to save himself from starvation he asks for terms, these will be granted in order to conclude operations quickly as the season is fast expiring."[19]

Muhammad Khan was humbled and "allowed to return safe to his headquarters upon his giving a written undertaking that he would never again return to Bundelkhand or embarrass Chhatrasal in any way." Thus was Bundelkhand lost to the Empire in the same way that Malwa had been four months before. The defeat and disgrace of Muhammad Khan Bangash the bravest and most spirited of the Mughal nobles of his time were complete. The Emperor deprived him of his government of Allahabad and appointed Sar-buland Khan to that office.

The old Chhatrasal could now afford to have a peaceful and glorious end. He lavished all honours and riches upon Bajirao, who became so endeared to him that he held an open Darbar in Bajirao's honour, brought his two young sons Hirdesa and Jagat Raj before him and entrusted them to his care for the future. At the same time he assigned out of his dominions a large jagir in perpetuity to Bajirao, and extracted from him a sacred promise that he would look upon his two sons as his younger brothers and protect them from harm in the midst of the ferocious enemies round them. Bajirao readily assented. It was very possibly at this time that Chhatrasal

19. Raj. 3. 14.

made a unique present of the young Mastani[20] to Bajirao following the traditional usage of honouring a guest in high position, who had rescued him from instant ruin.

Bajirao left Jaitpur on 23rd May 1729 for Poona. The aged Chhatrasal died two years later on 14th December 1731, happy in the thought that his descendants would be free from the distress that he had to put up with during his long and chequered life. The example of Bajirao like that of Shivaji inspired the Bundelas and other Rajputs in north India and even the Sikhs of the distant Punjab caught the spirit of revolt against the religious persecution of half a century. The Mughal Empire was in dissolution.

Upon Bajirao's return to his native land lavish praises and hearty congratulations were showered upon him. But what must have been the feelings of Shahu? Was he elated at these grand successes? No. His sense of justice and good will could not welcome such excesses as he thought the two brothers had committed in a distant land. He was afraid, they would bring disaster and retribution. On 12th April 1729 he wrote, "It is now the season for the troops to return. We have to convey to Bajirao certain imperative admonitions and command him to repair to our presence at once along with Udaji Pawar and Holkar. Please do not delay."

The disposition made by Chhatrasal proved more troublesome than beneficial for the ends it was intended to serve. Chhatrasal's agents Haridas Purohit and Asharam came to Poona to adjust the points in connection with the jagir that was promised to Bajirao. In the meantime Chhatrasal expired and his two sons agreed to hand over to Bajirao territory worth Rs. one and a quarter lacs each. Next year when Chimnaji Appa went to Bundelkhand he took charge of the assigned districts and appointed Govindpant Kher known thereafter as Bundele to manage the acquisition. They are enumerated as Kalpi, Hata, Saugor, Jhansi, Sironj, Kunch, Garhakota and Hirdenagar.[21]

20. Mastani's story will be narrated later.

21. Later on some of the districts were transferred by Bajirao to Mastani's son Shamsher Bahadur who made Banda his chief town of residence, thus giving his descendants the title of the Nawabs of Banda. It is said that the Jagir of Banda later on yielded an annual revenue of 33 lacs of rupees.

CHRONOLOGY

CHAPTER V

1717 January 11	Khanderao Dabhade made Senapati.
1726-28	Rajasbai administers the Kolhapur State.
1728 March	Sambhaji deserts Nizam, returns to Panhala.
1729	Malwa, Bundelkhand, Gujarat pass under Maratha influence. Jaysinh advocates appeasement of Bajirao.
1729 September 27	Senapati Khanderao Dabhade died.
1730 January 8	Trimbak Rao Dabhade appointed Senapati; Chimnaji Appa levies Chauth in Gujarat.
1730	Sarbuland Khan recalled from Gujarat; Abhay Sinh appointed Subahdar.
1730 August 8	Sambhaji offers submission to Shahu.
1730 Sep.—Oct.	Deep Sinh's mission to Satara and to Nizam at Aurangabad.
1730 November	Shahu sends a deputation to fetch Sambhaji from Panhala to Satara.
1730 closing months	Senapati Dabhade and other Maratha Chiefs join Nizam and form a strong combination against Shahu and Bajirao.
1730 October 10	Under orders of Shahu Bajirao left Poona to fetch Dabhade to Satara.
1730 December	Muhammad Khan Bangash appointed Subahdar of Malwa and Abhay Sinh of Gujarat.
1731 February	The two royal cousins meet near Karhad and proceed to Satara.
1731 February	Bajirao and Chimnaji Appa join forces in Gujarat. They meet Abhay Sinh at Ahmadabad and proceed to Baroda.
1731 March 17	Nizam and Bangash meet at the Narmada and concert measures against the Marathas.
1731 April 1	Battle of Dabhai : Trimbak Rao killed : his mother seeks justice from Shahu.

1731 April 13	Treaty of Warna concluded between Shahu and Sambhaji.
1731 May	Umabai Dabhade reconciled to Bajirao.
1732 April 14	Abhay Sinh murders Pilaji Gaikwad at Dakor.
1732—40	Five visits of Sambhaji to Satara.
1751 April 26	Sambhaji's mother Rajasbai dies.
1760 December 20	Sambhaji dies.
1761 December 9	Tarabai, Rajaram's Rani, dies.

CHAPTER V

FURTHER TRIUMPHS

[1730—1731]

1 The mission of Deep Sinh.
2 Sambhaji brought to submission.
3 Ceremonial meeting of the royal cousins, agreement.
4 Exit Senapati Dabhade.

1. The mission of Deep Sinh.—We must now go back to Shahu's Court and review how he and his immediate advisers were faring during the year 1729 when Malwa, Bundelkhand, and Gujarat were being subjugated by the Peshwa and his brother. The affairs of Gujarat will be narrated elsewhere. Nizam-ul-mulk, though temporarily checked at Palkhed, did not give up his efforts of putting obstacles in the way of Maratha progress in the south. The defeat and death of Giridhar Bahadur and the set back that the Bangash had sustained, created quite a consternation in the heart of the Emperor and his responsible advisers, among whom there was a sharp division of opinion about their future policy. One party headed by Khan Dauran and Jaysinh was for appeasing the Marathas and trusting to their honour for the preservation of the Empire. The other party headed by Saadat Khan, Muhammad Khan Bangash and Abhay Sinh &c., were for a united offensive to be at once launched against the Marathas to drive them out by force of arms. The Wazir Qamruddin Khan and the Emperor himself could not make up their minds either for the one or the other course.

The Court of Delhi had lost all their former vigour and felt themselves too weak for an offensive war, particularly when they remembered that heroic efforts against the Marathas by Aurangzeb, Bahadur Shah and the Saiyads for half a century had proved of no avail. At the same time they could not in all conscience think of an abject surrender. At this juncture Jaysinh came forth to undertake the responsibility of dealing with the Marathas, and as an earnest of his efforts succeeded in getting back Mandavgad by a personal appeal to

Shahu. Before any decision was taken, it was necessary to find out what the Maratha aims actually were, how far they were disposed to come to terms with the imperial Court and most of all how Shahu Raja was personally inclined towards the Emperor. Reliable information on these points was vital for any step to be taken and had to be obtained personally through trustworthy agents. It was, therefore, resolved by the Emperor and his Court to send a deputation to meet Shahu and the Peshwa at Satara, discuss personally with them the points of a lasting settlement and also gather at the same time the views and inclinations of Nizam-ul-mulk whose voice and experience as an accredited governor of the south, was of supreme importance for any decision. The deputation was empowered to arrange definite terms of a solemn agreement to be ratified at a later date.

Jaysinh himself took the lead in this negotiation and after consulting Rana Sangram Sinh of Udaipur, chose the personnel of the mission. He himself nominated Deep Sinh and Mansaram Purohit and Sangram Sinh added his own nominee Bagchi (Vyaghraji). These ambassadors with a suitable retinue arrived at Satara in the autumn of 1730 and were courteously received. The Peshwa, Fatesinh and Raghuji Bhosle, the Pratinidhi, the Sumant, the Purandares and others were all openly and privately consulted by these delegates in the month of September; and after finishing their business at Satara, the mission proceeded to Aurangabad to interview Nizam-ul-mulk, who also treated them with equal hospitality. They left Aurangabad early in November and on return made their report to Jaysinh and the Emperor's Court. Bagchi the representative of Udaipur died on the way back near Ajanta. The ambassadors formed a flattering opinion of the Maratha Court and its policy. One of them Mansaram Purohit was indeed so taken up with Shahu's ways and the life at Satara, that he soon after came and lived with Shahu for the rest of his life. He was highly respected in the Deccan.

The impression formed by the mission was that the Marathas had no aggressive or grasping ambition of a wicked character, that they only insisted upon collecting the Chauth and were ready in return to serve the Emperor and run to his protection whenever required. They demanded 11 and 15 lacs for the annual Chauth of Gujarat and Malwa respectively. If such an arrangement were formally approved by the Emperor, no trouble would be created by the Marathas in future. The views of Nizam-ul-mulk were, however, found entirely different. He had no good opinion of Bajirao and declared openly that he could not trust his word, although at the same time he could not suggest how he could be put down by means of force in the face of repeated failures in the past. Nizam-ul-mulk tried to influence the ambassadors and induce them to make a strongly unfavourable report about Maratha ambitions. He said, agreeing to pay them 15 lacs a year for Malwa would ruin its governor Bangash, as he was not in a position to save that amount out of the usual collections. As regards Gujarat, the situation according to Nizam-ul-mulk was more depressing, as the Gaikwads, the Bandays, Abhay Sinh and others laid claim to that province, and the Peshwa could not keep all these under control. Deep Sinh suggested that the Peshwa and Jaysinh together would repel the Bandays and the Gaikwads. Nizam-ul-mulk replied, they professed to do so, but who could trust Bajirao? Deep Sinh replied, "I consider Bajirao's word of honour fully trustworthy, as he and Jaysinh were traditional friends and admirers of each other."

Nizam-ul-mulk could not refute Deep Sinh's conclusions and in indignation asked, "Whom do you find worthy of trust and respect at Satara? Who do you think commands the Raja's confidence?" Deep Sinh replied, "Of course Bajirao. It was to find this out that I was particularly deputed from Delhi. No one else at Shahu's court can equal Bajirao in valour, probity, diplomatic talents or organizing capacity. He is the only man who pre-eminently rules the Maratha Court." "How did you find the Raja himself?" asked the Nizam.

Deep Sinh—The Raja too is a capable ruler.

Nizam—I do not think so. He is too light-hearted and fond of gossips.

Deep Sinh—If he were not wise and capable, how could his raj flourish so well? He is indeed a considerate and wise ruler and knows his craft well.

The Maratha agent at the Court of Nizam-ul-mulk thus comments on this subject :—

" Nizam-ul-mulk felt severe irritation at the lavish praise which Deep Sinh bestowed upon Bajirao and replied,--I have absolutely no good opinion of Bajirao's faith or humanity."

Deep Sinh—You may have your own grounds for forming this opinion about him. I for myself feel sure that Bajirao is a capable man, well-experienced and honest, who would respect his plighted word. Of all the Raja's counsellors he alone bears a pre-eminent character. His army trusts him as a superior person.

Nizam—But he is inordinately arrogant and deserves to be severely handled.

Deep Sinh—I do not consider it wise on your part to think of antagonising such an able person as Bajirao, particularly when the Emperor himself looks upon you as a rebel and deserter. Bajirao can at any moment collect a lac of troops to oppose you.

Nizam—Is not Nar Bawa (Naro Ram) an equally capble person at Shahu's Court ? I sent Ghiyas Khan to Satara and he reported that he could easily put down Bajirao by taking Nar Bawa into his confidence. You will soon see how we shall accomplish this end of bringing Bajirao down to his knees. We have already been promised about 50 thousand men to be collected by Sidhoji Nimbalkar, Kanthaji Banday, Udaji Pawar, and Kanhoji Bhosle and the Gaikwads, who are all ready to join us and with whose co-operation we shall either capture Bajirao alive or put him to such a rout and plunder, that he would never raise his head again.

Deep Sinh—I have communicated to you what appeared to me right and just. You are at liberty to take whatever measures you consider necessary.

This account of Deep Sinh's mission supplies a recorded explanation of the lifelong contest that raged between Nizam-ul-mulk and Bajirao with results which are well-known. Jaysinh possibly wished to secure Maratha friendship in order to acquire the provinces of Malwa and Agra. So far as any direct results are concerned, Deep Sinh's mission proved a failure. It only presents a graphic picture of the political situation of the times and explains the turn of future events.

Nizam-ul-mulk was the ablest old representative of the Mughal power and Bajirao, thirty years his junior, was the young rising star of the Marathas. Bajirao's agent residing with the Nizam thus reported to him (November 1730), "Anandrao Sumant has addressed to Nizam-ul-mulk a sadly vituperative abuse of you. This certainly spells danger. Nizam-ul-mulk takes these reports as true. He entertains venom in his breast; is full of wiles and stratagem. Kanthaji, Udaji and Kanhoji are frequent visitors here and are being seduced by Anandrao Sumant, who has assured the Nizam that King Shahu would not be sorry at all if Bajirao is put down, and that not a dog would bark at such a result." The agent then warns Bajirao against remissness or neglect. "One must take warning even from a casual dream," says he, and adds, "two of the Nizam's prominent helpers Hamid Khan and Aiwaz Khan are dead and gone; a few others have lost faith in him. These openly declare that he is fast losing his senses and approaching his end, which he is destined to meet with at your hands. You are fortunate in possessing the blessings of a pious king like Shahu. Those who oppose him will surely court ruin. Such a foolish move on the part of the Nizam only indicates there are higher successes in store for you. Pride will have its fall. God works on the side of truth. Yesterday Deep Sinh was given his final send-off, when a coldness between them became perfectly visible. Chandrasen Jadhav was sulking and is being assuaged. Dabhade and Banday have written to the Nizam asking for assurance of shelter, if they succeed in humbling the Peshwa and in putting an end to Shahu's raj. They contemplate making Sambhaji the Chhatrapati, Dabhade his Senapati and Kanthaji Banday his Sar-Lashkar. Letters to this effect were received through Ghiyas Khan, upon which the Nawab declared, "I have Sambhaji's interests next to my heart; if we can, we should raise him to the throne and remove Shahu, thus aggravating their family dissensions; that will conduce to our interest. Such a chance has been presented to us without our asking. Which of the two, Shahu or Sambhaji, loses is immaterial, one opponent will be the less for us. Therefore we won't reject the proposal."

Another agent of Bajirao writes to him from the Nizam's headquarters, "You must be closely on your guard. The Pratinidhi is setting up an intrigue against you here. It is a wilful mischief, which you must as wilfully counteract. The

Nizam is afraid of forfeiting Shahu's friendship; outwardly he speaks sweet words, as the terror of Bajirao has taken possession of his heart."

As reports like this poured upon Bajirao's attention from various quarters, it would have been madness for him to remain off his guard. The safety of Shahu and of the Maratha raj was in his keeping, and he lost no time in bringing to Shahu's mind a lively sense of the dangerous situation that Nizam-ul-mulk was creating in collusion with Dabhade and other traitors. Thus arose the necessity of restraining both Sambhaji and Dabhade, a task which occupied Bajirao during the two years 1730 and 1731, and which now deserves our attention.

2. Sambhaji brought to submission.—Shahu's domestic struggle which commenced with his advent into the Deccan in 1707, had since passed through various phases and had not yet ended. How the unprovoked attack by Nizam-ul-mulk which ended in his discomfiture at Palkhed, arose through Sambhaji has been already narrated. Bhagwantrao Amatya and Udaji Chavan thereafter half-heartedly upheld his cause; Chandrasen Jadhav did not venture any longer to take an active part against Shahu and Bajirao. Shahu did his best all along to conciliate his royal cousin. When he openly revolted and sought the shelter of Nizam-ul-mulk in 1727 Shahu addressed the following letter to him, which deserves to be quoted in full as it sets forth the ideals which Shahu as the Maratha king was pursuing and the method he employed in dealing with his antagonists :—

"This kingdom is a gift from God How can you hope to win success by seeking the protection of a Muslim? If you wanted to have a separate kingdom of your own, you could have communicated your desire to us. We possess men of pre-eminent capacity some of whom would have accompanied you and procured for you a kingdom of your own; or you should have acquired one by your own prowess. We are at present acquiring fresh territories to add to our kingdom out of those seized by the Mughals. You could have followed a similar course and made your own mark. But to ask a share out of what we have gained is not right. Your revered father the late Rajaram Maharaj went as far as Jinji and eventually obtained a kingdom through great personal effort. He then returned to his home in Maharashtra, plundered rich and renowned cities and made a name for himself. You must be well aware what a keen interest he took in our welfare, and what efforts he made to get us released from the imperial confinement. Knowing all this, your seeking the protection of a Muslim governor was not at all proper. You should at once quit the Mughals and come back to us. We will ourselves grant you whatever you need most willingly. But to claim a share in a kingdom has no religious sanction. You must give up this evil course. Chandrasen Jadhav's conduct in proving faithless to us and accepting service under a Mughal government, is most reprehensible; coming as he does from the Jadhav family of Ramdev Rao of Devgiri, he openly acted against the Maharashtra Dharma, i.e., the sacred policy enjoined by our religion. It was the height of folly on your part to have acted upon the advice of such a renegade and served the Muslim ends."

But this remonstrance had no effect upon Sambhaji. Soon his Senapati Ranoji Ghorpade and his Amatya Bhagwantrao and other officials openly deserted him out of disgust and came over to Shahu for service. Udaji Chavan of Athni already a broken reed remained Sambhaji's only supporter for a time. When Bajirao and Chimnaji Appa were engaged in Malwa and Bundelkhand during 1729, Udaji at the instigation of Sambhaji plundered Shahu's territories and created trouble for him. Then Shahu himself undertook a campaign against Udaji Chavan early in 1730. One day as Shahu was out hunting, some agents employed by Udaji came up with the intention of murdering him. The plot was discovered and the culprits punished. Thereupon Shahu flung aside his usual equanimity and ordered a march straight upon Sambhaji's territory with a large force commanded by Trimbakrao Dabhade. Shahu himself remained encamped on the Warna. In March 1730, the Pratinidhi attacked Sambhaji's camp on the other side of the Warna. Both Sambhaji and Udaji were separately routed and escaped to Panhala. When Sambhaji's camp was plundered, his ladies including his aunt Tarabai, his Rani Jijabai and the whole staff of the household, were captured and brought before Shahu as prisoners. The occasion revealed Shahu's nobility of heart, to the astonishment of the royal ladies. He paid due respect to them all and after conversing with them affably, allowed them to go back to Sambhaji at Panhala. Tarabai was already under Sambhaji's confinement and elected to live with Shahu at Satara, having for her manager Yado Gopal Khatavkar who was appointed to look after her comfort. She was to have the same restraints upon her liberty that she had to put up with at Panhala. Thereupon Shahu and Tarabai returned from the camp to Satara for the monsoon, giving up the plan of pursuing Sambhaji in favour of conciliation. Sambhaji now found that his position had become hopeless. Writes Bhagwantrao Amatya, "The affairs of Sambhaji sank lower day by day. Justice, character, wisdom and similar virtues became conspicuous by their absence in his administration. There exists not a single person here who can be called a gentleman."

Sambhaji was strongly advised by his well-wishers and perhaps by his Rani Jijabai in particular, to throw himself on the mercy of Shahu and obtain the best bargain he could from him, rather than continue hostilities which promised no success against the resources of Shahu, who had already despatched forces for the capture of Vishalgad and other places belonging to Sambhaji. Udaji Chavan also deserted Sambhaji and accepted service under Shahu.

Tarabai's presence at Satara opened a channel for communication and exchange of views. Sambhaji was urged to make a personal visit to Shahu. They had never met before. Shahu wrote to him a cordial personal letter assuring him of a warm reception if he would come in a penitent spirit. In October 1730 Sambhaji wrote the following reply to Shahu:—

"Your very warm greetings and your sincere and hearty wishes for a cordial and lasting understanding between us, conveyed by the revered Matushrisaheb (Tarabai) have reached me and gladdened my heart immensely. Coming from an elderly person of your eminence, the message is most welcome and in the fitness of things. I reciprocate your sentiments with equal warmth. What can redound to our credit more than that our differences should be finally settled and that perfect amity should for ever exist between us? Her Highness had long since advised me to send Babaji Prabhu to discuss and arrange an agreed course. But ill-health prevented him from undertaking the journey earlier. He is now better and takes this letter from me as a token of my sincere wish for a happy termination of the troubles between us."

Bhagwantrao Amatya also wrote at the same time to Shahu that "as the Court of Kolhapur has become a refuge of mean and ill-mannered beings, I would feel grateful if your Highness would allow me to serve at your feet."

Babaji Nilakanth Prabhu Parasnis of Kolhapur mentioned in Sambhaji's letter was a clever and commanding personality, who heartily worked for bringing about a lasting reconciliation between the royal cousins of the Chhatrapati's house. Shahu practically agreed to everything that Sambhaji asked for and sent back the ambassador with dresses and presents along with a reply couched in such flattering terms, that they melted even the hard heart of Sambhaji, whose answer will ever remain a model of both language and sentiment. He wrote back this short message : "Your divine grace and extraordinary affection have touched me to the quick. You are a father to me. It behoves you in that capacity to take care of me. This conduct will redound to your lasting credit."

3. Ceremonial meeting and agreement.—Sambhaji thus gave up his former high pretensions and agreed to accept what Shahu out of his generosity would willingly offer. But the latter did not stint himself in any way and rose to the occasion without showing the least rancour for all the past sins of his cousin. During November 1730, Shahu sent to Panhala a large party of his high officials and men of influence to escort Sambhaji to Satara. Fatesinh Bhosle, the Pratinidhi, Nar Bawa Mantri, Balaji Bajirao, Bhavani Shankar Munshi, Ambajipant Purandare, Krishnaji Dabhade, Nimbalkar, and others with a large body of troops proceeded to Panhala and were received with equal respect in a Darbar where they all offered to Sambhaji *nazars* and presents of elephants, horses, jewellery and dresses. In return they were each given similar dresses at a parting ceremonial. They left Panhala on December 16 escorting Sambhaji and his party, travelling back

by easy marches. After crossing the Warna at Wadgaon they reached the vicinity of Karhad in due course.

Shahu on his part had already proceeded to Karhad, about 30 miles south-east of Satara, where a grand camp was pitched on the banks of the Krishna. The meeting place of the two royal cousins was arranged at a village a few miles off, at Jakhinwadi, where a large open tent or *shamyana* splendidly decorated, was pitched near the river. The large assemblage consisting of the Sardars, troops and followers of the two parties is said to have numbered over two lacs. An auspicious moment on the afternoon of 27 February, 1731, Saturday, Falgun Shudh 2 of the Shak year 1652, was fixed for the actual meeting. Amidst the music of bands and instruments, Shahu and Sambhaji rode on their richly caparisoned elephants towards each other through long files of well appointed troops, receiving their homage. As soon as they sighted each other, they dismounted from their elephants and coming closer embraced each other warmly, punctiliously observing the traditional forms prescribed in the shastras. They then proceeded to the Darbar where the members of the two parties made their bows. After the Darbar the two sovereigns again mounted an elephant and together drove to the camp of Shahu. A grand dinner was arranged in the evening after which rich presents were distributed. The two princes spent a few days in the camp freely conversing and enjoying the amusements of hunting, music, games and other pastimes, each doing his utmost to please the other. Some novel programme was arranged every day. The merriment of the occasion was heightened by its synchronising with the celebration of the Holi festival which commenced on 12th March and for which the host and the guest moved to Shahu-nagar for additional rejoicings. The whole of Maharashtra glowed in rapture at the unaccustomed sights of spendour that characterised the celebration which long lived in the memory of that generation.

Thus the civil war that had started with the release of Shahu came to a close. A treaty of peace consisting of nine articles was concluded and formally ratified on 13th April 1731. It is known as the treaty of the Warna, for that river was made the boundary line between the two kingdoms. The territory to the south of this river and stretching right up to the bank of the Tungabhadra was assigned to Sambhaji's independent sovereignty in all essentials, but subordinate to Shahu as far as his foreign relations and safety were concerned. It was also stipulated that the southern districts beyond the Tungabhadra right up to Rameshwar should be supposed common for joint endeavour. Sambhaji never once moved out or endeavoured to extend his dominion. What Shahu allotted to him in 1730 has practically been the extent of the Kolhapur State right up to the present day, without much change in spite of the vicissitudes of more than two hundred years. Possibly Belgaum and a few other places have been lost by Kolhapur.

Sambhaji's character and capacity were limited and he sank into insignificance in comparison with the high position of Shahu and his rapidly rising Peshwas. If he had delayed longer to submit to Shahu in a spirit of humble acquiesence, he would probably have been extinguished altogether. During the 23 years of the civil war, one clearly notices three stages of an approach to settlement, the earliest in 1708 just after Shahu's coronation, the next in 1725 and the last during this visit in 1731. At each stage Shahu's terms grew less liberal on account of the continued opposition which Sambhaji openly offered to him. Thus the civil war started by Tarabai and continued by Sambhaji availed them nothing, nor did it materially affect Shahu's prospects. He rose all the more in public estimation on account of his high personal character and the latitude for service he offered to the able persons he collected about himself.

This result of Shahu's relations with Sambhaji has proved historically noteworthy for the Maratha raj. A separate kingdom came to be permanently created in the heart of Maharashtra, which proved a perennial source of discord. The Kolhapur rulers claimed equality of status with those of Satara, so that the creation of the Kolhapur raj resulted in perpetuating the division of the Maratha nation. In 1740 upon the death of Bajirao, Sambhaji came to visit Shahu at Satara, when the new Peshwa executed a secret understanding with him for uniting the two branches of the Chhatrapati's house. Shahu had no male issue and it was proposed that Sambhaji should succeed him at his death. If such a consummation had come about, a perpetual source of factious trouble would have been permanently removed.

Sambhaji's affairs did not improve by the treaty of the Warna. Nor could his relations with Shahu remain entirely cordial. He paid frequent visits to Satara mostly at Shahu's invitation and was every time treated with all respect and cordiality. But he remained sullen and discontented owing to various trifling causes. He found himself openly defied by some of his own subordinates who, he considered, were instigated against him by persons in Shahu's employ. Sambhaji was born on 23rd May 1698 and died on 20 December 1760. It is curious that Shahu or Tarabai never once visited Panhala and Kolhapur again after the treaty was concluded. Sambhaji's mother Rajasbai died on 26th April 1751 ; and the aged Tarabai, Chhatrapati Rajaram's wife also died ten years later on December 9, 1761.

4. Exit Senapati Dabhade.—It has already been mentioned how the principle of hereditary appointments proved ruinous to the Maratha State. Khanderao Dabhade, who had been appointed Senapati by Shahu on 11th January 1717, had no doubt been a capable leader at one time, but soon became a spent force, unable to execute the new policy and fresh enterprizes which the dashing Peshwas inaugurated. Bajirao necessarily usurped the Senapati's function by raising his own independent armies and leading expeditions in which the services of the Senapati came to be gradually discarded. Thus the Dabhades slowly came to be pushed into the back-ground and spent their time and energy in sulking and recrimination, which Shahu could not prevent. Khanderao declined in health and became personally unfit for carrying on the duties of his office. His own household became a hot bed of intrigue and vice. His wife Umabai and son Trimbakrao, both spirited and able in their own way but jealous of the Peshwa's predominance, only worsened the situation, by their overbearing ways and antagonism to the Peshwa. When Khanderao died on 27th September 1729, matters began to assume a grave aspect for the Senapati's house. Trimbakrao received from Shahu the robes of his father's office on 8th January 1730 at Satara.

The province of Gujarat and parts of Khandesh had been assigned by Shahu as the Senapati's sphere of activity. Chimnaji Appa had already entered Gujarat and secured it from Sarbuland Khan, so that the Peshwa on that account claimed a half share of it. Shahu could not adjust their claims: mutual antagonism followed, leading ultimately to a clash of arms. During the early months of 1730 Chimnaji Appa entered Gujarat with a large force and wrested from Sarbuland Khan the Maratha claims of Chauth and Sardeshmukhi for that province. The terms were modelled on those of Malwa and Maharashtra. For his incompetency to hold Gujarat against the Marathas, Sarbuland Khan was recalled by the Emperor and Abhay Sinh of Marwar appointed in his place. This only introduced a further complication into the situation. Trimbakrao lodged before Shahu a strong complaint against the Peshwa for having interfered with his sphere of activity, and when he found that Shahu was too soft to control Bajirao effectively, he began open preparations for an armed conflict. The dispute was agitating Satara during the autumn of 1730 at the very time when Deep Sinh the imperial envoy was there discussing the affairs of Malwa with Shahu.

Dabhade had under him several powerful local chiefs of Baglan, Khandesh, and east Gujarat whom Bajirao seduced from their allegiance by offering them better prospects. Bhausinh Thoke of Mudane, Dalpatrao Thoke of Abhone, Kuvar Bahadur Deshmukh of Sinnar, Lakshadhir Dalpatrao of Peth, along with Bajaji Atole, Avji Kavde and others were induced to accept service under Bajirao. This enraged Trimbakrao and his mother Umabai, both bitterly resenting Bajirao's conduct and they started negotiations with Nizam-ul-mulk for help in order to counteract the Peshwa's insidious aggression. It has already been mentioned how Nizam-ul-mulk smarting under his humiliation at Palkhed, was himself trying to seduce some of Bajirao's and Shahu's adherents, such as Kanhoji Bhosle, Sar-Lashkar Nimbalkar and so on; and when Dabhade approached him with a proposal to put down Bajirao, we may imagine how cordially the Nizam must have welcomed it. If the abovementioned local chiefs espoused Bajirao's leadership, they would materially affect the security of Nizam-ul-mulk as his territory was intermixed with theirs.

So he started crushing them one by one by means of his powerful artillery. Thus towards the end of 1730 the atmosphere of north Deccan became surcharged with serious unrest and impending signs of war.

Bajirao and Chimnaji Appa foresaw the danger, gauged its force, and prepared to meet it boldly. Shahu on his part, however, began his usual method of persuasive reasoning and conciliation. He sent his personal agents to Dabhade to induce him to accept a reasonable compromise and called upon Bajirao to appease Dabhade by conceding all that he claimed. Upon this Chimnaji sternly replied, "If Dabhade creates trouble for us, we are quite equal to stopping him from doing mischief; but if he goes over and joins the Nizam, your Highness must not hesitate to deprive him of his office of the Senapati." Thereupon Shahu despatched his own trusted agents Ambaji Trimbak, Naro Ram, and Naro Gangadhar Muzumdar to meet Trimbakrao and Umabai and bring them to reason for a peaceful accommodation. Dabhade, however, instead of coming to the point, wasted time in vague discussions and general accusations, setting forth his grievances against the Peshwa and showing no disposition to come to terms. He was all the while secretly intriguing with Nizam-ul-mulk and concerting plans of a rebellious character. His hollow professions of loyalty put the Peshwa on his guard, who in his heart decided to take time by the forelock. The Senapati declared to Shahu's agents, "We shall not give up an inch of the lands we own and will render only such service as we can." When Shahu learnt that Dabhade was in league with Nizam-ul-mulk, he sent him the following strong remonstrance.[1]

"You have been a loyal Hindu servant of the State and as such we have all along dealt with you most kindly. You have nevertheless deserted to the enemy, taking offence at something we are not aware of. You must know what fate traitors meet with. We urge you, therefore, to forget all wrongs, to remember how your ancestors behaved, and serve the State instead of the enemy, so that the nation may be proud of your conduct. You must exert yourself to execute our commands

1. P. D. 17. 12.

and win increasing favours from us. Such a conduct alone will be noble. You have to subdue the nation's enemies and not join them. You must work to extend the Maratha raj. This warning is addressed to you in full confidence that you will remain a loyal servant of the State and not molest the poor innocent ryots." This letter besides being an admonition explains incidentally the objects of the Maratha raj and the policy of Shahu in pursuing them. This remonstrance, however, had no effect and the affair of Dabhade soon assumed a threatening aspect.

The Nizam formed a grand plot to remove Bajirao altogether from Shahu's counsels, and in this plot Dabhade and several other prominent sardars readily joined, so that the supreme power in settling political questions not only of the Deccan but of Malwa and Gujarat also, would have been snatched away from Shahu's hands and gone to Nizam-ul-mulk. Udaji Pawar and his brother Anandrao, Pilaji Gaikwad and the Banday brothers, Chimnaji Damodar, these and others joined in the plot with Nizam-ul-mulk and Dabhade, thus creating a serious threat to Shahu's position by crushing the Peshwa. Bajirao could not quietly submit to such dictation and prepared to meet his enemies with foresight and caution.

Shahu then ordered Bajirao to proceed to Gujarat and bring Dabhade to his presence at Satara, as he would not obey the written commands or the messages sent with accredited agents. At this time Shahu was engaged in settling his dispute with his cousin Sambhaji ; and realizing the value of persuasion, believed that if Dabhade could by some means be brought to Satara like his cousin Sambhaji, he would personally settle their quarrel with equal success in an atmosphere of peace and goodwill. To bring Dabhade to Satara was the mission which Shahu entrusted solemnly to Bajirao, when all other means failed. Bajirao found himself in a most delicate situation.

The two brothers left Poona on the auspicious day of the Dassara, 10th October 1730, intending to dissuade Dabhade from the evil course he was following and compelling him to repair to Satara for a personal adjustment. But when they proceeded on their business, they became aware of the deep-laid plans which had been arranged by Dabhade in full consultation with Nizam-ul-mulk, and which spelt immediate danger to Shahu personally and to the vital interests of the Maratha State.

At this very time the Emperor appointed Muhammad Khan Bangash to the government of Malwa and Abhay Sinh to that of Gujarat in order to stop the Maratha aggression in these provinces. Bangash arrived at Ujjain and offered his wholehearted co-operation to Nizam-ul-mulk in putting down the Marathas. In order to concert effective measures towards this end and make a grand united effort to achieve sure success, the two chiefs decided to meet before moving their forces to support Dabhade, who was not expected to precipitate a fight with the Peshwa until a fully concerted plan was arranged between them all. Bajirao and Chimnaji Appa kept themselves well informed of the movements of their opponents and acted quickly to neutralize their plans with matchless dexterity and intelligent anticipation.

Towards the end of 1730 Nizam-ul-mulk left Aurangabad to open the campaign and join Dabhade in good time. He went as far as Burhanpur, where he learnt that Bangash was at Ujjain. After a preliminary consultation they decided to meet personally and mature their plans for winning a sure success. Two responsible governors of high status could meet only on the border : so they both proceeded to the Akbarpur Ferry on the Narmada, where they had long conferences from 17 to 28 March 1731 ; and having settled the details of their project they parted, Bangash returning to Ujjain and the Nizam hurrying into Gujarat where Bajirao was already on the track of Dabhade. Malharrao Holkar with his trusted lieutenants and a corps of spies remained in the vicinity of the Narmada watching the plans and movements of the Bangash and the Nizam, and promptly communicating vital information to Bajirao. Holkar incessantly harassed Bangash during the time of the above mentioned conference.

The Emperor, on the other hand, looked upon this secret conference of the Nizam and Bangash with grave suspicion. The former was a notorious rebel and intriguer, and the Emperor had called upon Bangash to bring him to book. So while the two nobles were forming secret plans to reduce the overgrown power of the Marathas, Muhammad Khan Bangash was urged to work the ruin of his colleague. It was this factor of the complicated situation which weakened Dabhade and proportionately strengthened the astute Peshwa. Shahu at Satara hardly understood this involved situation in the northern regions. His only method of composing a quarrel was to bring the disputants together in his presence. But Dabhade, relying upon the help promised to him by the Nizam, refused to accompany Bajirao to Satara. Shahu therefore feared a clash, and on 15th December, 1730, cancelled the half share of Gujarat which he had granted to the Peshwa, hoping that this would satisfy Dabhade. The Peshwa did not at once give effect to this order and waited on the course of events.

Bajirao and Chimnaji with their loyal followers Avji Kavde, Ambaji Trimbak, Ayaba Muzumdar and others marched towards Khandesh, where Chimnaji remained behind to watch the movements of Nizam-ul-mulk ; and Bajirao proceeded towards Baroda via Nasik, Peth, Surat and Broach in December. Chimnaji too joined Bajirao soon after in Gujarat, having made sure that Nizam-ul-mulk had proceeded to the Narmada and would possibly bring large forces including those of the Bangash to help Dabhade.

During February the two brothers met and weighed the possibilities of a future action. Bajirao sent overtures to Abhay Sinh at Ahmadabad for his friendship and advice. Abhay Sinh returned a cordial message inviting Bajirao to a personal meeting. Bajirao readily consented and immediately proceeded to Ahmadabad where in a full conference at Shahibag, he won the support of Abhay Sinh. The latter concluded a pact with Bajirao, agreeing to pay him 13 lacs annually in lieu of Chauth ; six lacs were paid immediately and the balance was to be paid when the Peshwa would expel Pilaji Gaikwad and Banday from Gujarat. For this purpose Bajirao left Ahmadabad with a contingent and a park of artillery supplied by Abhay Sinh and marched upon Baroda to oust Pilaji from that place. Although the actual value of Abhay Sinh's contingent was not much, the moral support of the Subahdar of Gujarat proved certainly effective.[2]

2. H. R. C. Proceedings 1939, Abhay Sinh's letters.

Coming near Baroda Bajirao encamped at Savli a few miles to the north, where he learned that Dabhade and Gaikwad had made preparations for an open fight on the plain of Dabhoi and Bhilapur with a force numbering some 40 thousand, while Bajirao's numbers hardly reached 25 thousand in all. From Savli Bajirao sent repeated messages to Dabhade to proceed to Satara and have the dispute composed amicably in the presence of the Chhatrapati, reminding him that it was not proper that the two prominent servants of the king should engage in a personal contest. Finding Dabhade stiff and unyielding the Peshwa precipitated matters by suddenly falling upon the Senapati's camp on 1st April 1731. Dabhade fought with determination and fury. The actual issue for a time hung in the balance, when a chance musket shot[3] pierced Trimbakrao's head killing him instantly, and turning the day in favour of Bajirao, who thus reported the event to his guru Brahmendra Swami :—

"Dabhade with his allies came forward for an encounter on 4th Shavval. Trimbakrao himself, Javji Dabhade, Maloji Pawar, and Pilaji Gaikwad's son Sambhaji, were killed outright. Udaji Pawar and Chimnaji Damodar were captured. Pilaji Gaikwad and Kuvar Bahadur escaped wounded. A large booty was secured. Our side too lost a few brave ones in the battle."

Bajirao wisely showed no rancour after the victory. He captured the elephants carrying the Senapati's dead body and the standards, but handed them back to his brother Yashvantrao, who had just arrived with fresh succours, and who after performing the funeral rites during the night came on the next morning for renewing hostilities. But Bajirao did not tarry a moment after that bloody day and returned with all haste to Satara with the plunder he had secured. On the way, he had a brush with a party of the Nizam's troops near Surat. Bajirao was anxious to report to Shahu the details of his encounter, before others could poison his master's mind against him.

The news shocked Shahu beyond measure. The Sena-

3. The shot that killed Dabhade was later reported to have been fired by Trimbakrao's maternal uncle Bhausinh Thoke of Abhone possibly seduced by Bajirao.

pati's mother Umabai (coming from the Thoke family of Abhone), was heartbroken at the death of her valiant son, attributed it to the Peshwa's treachery and peremptorily required Shahu to inflict adequate and instantaneous retribution. Shahu himself immediately hastened to Talegaum to meet the lady and brought her to Satara for confronting her with Bajirao. The task of adjusting blame or punishment was not at all easy. The peculiar position and predicament of the parties had stirred the whole Maratha nation as never before.

It is said that Shahu called Umabai and the Peshwa to his presence and in a Darbar asked Bajirao to prostrate himself before the lady, and giving her a sword asked her to sever his head if that would satisfy her feeling of revenge. The lady was mollified when the Peshwa humbly begged her pardon and offered all possible compensation for the loss. Shahu conferred the Senapati's office upon the deceased's younger brother Yashvantrao, but he proved utterly incompetent, so that the Dabhades soon sank into nonentity notwithstanding every effort on the part of Shahu until the day of his death, to resuscitate the declining fortunes of that house. Pilaji Gaikwad and his son Damaji both capable lieutenants trained under the Senapati, took up the latter's work in Gujarat and managed it through varying fortunes so ably, that their dynasty still rules over Gujarat. No permanent reconciliation came about between the Peshwa and the Dabhades; and the latter after Shahu's death made unsuccessful efforts to oust the Peshwa from his position.

Before the Nizam could render help to Dabhade, Bajirao had already disposed of him as is shown by a Persian letter written by Asaf Jah to Abdul Nabi Khan. It seems this account refers to an encounter which Bajirao had with the Nizam's troops near Surat on his return journey from Dabhoi.

Asaf Jah to Abdul Nabi Khan,—April 1731.

"The accursed Bajirao finding the province of Gujarat unoccupied by defenders laid siege to Baroda a city that is in the hands of dispersed i.e., mutually antagonistic people.

"I reflected that if, God avert it, this rebel got Baroda, it would be a great disgrace and loss, and our work would be ruined, while his disturbance would become perpetual in that Subah and utter ruin would seize the prevalence of the religion of Muhammad. Therefore, in the spirit and pride of Islam and fidelity to [the Emperor's] salt, I decided upon this religious duty, that after crossing the Narmada I should engage at the full gallop in rooting this black wretch out and thus perform the tasks of holy war and cutting off the roots of disturbance. Immediately on hearing rumours of the approach of the Islamic army by way of Ali Mohan, the wretch, casting off all at once his plans of dominion, withdrew from the siege [of Baroda] and with a view to interposing a long distance between the Islamic army and the rebel horde, in terror of the Muhammadan army, in utter bewilderment at midnight quickly crossed the Narmada and entered the limits of the Deccan. Through his short sight, seeing that the Muslim army was very distant from his, he began to disturb the pargana of Ankleshwar and plundered and burnt the country, land and water alike.

"Therefore, this follower of Mustafa's precepts [i.e., Asaf Jah] from the ford of Akbarpur near the fort of Mandu, sent off his baggage and camp with the big guns to Burhanpur and by favour of the strength and power of God, with great rapidity and in a short time I arrived at Nandurbar, a second time disburdened myself by leaving there other surplus baggage and artillery which were hindering my rapid marching, and reached the environs of Surat in a few days. Leaving my light guns at Kathor, our army arrived near the enemy's horde after undergoing great exertions.

"We surprised the Marathas when they were sleeping in great negligence and ignorance of our whereabouts and they fled away in the utmost disorder, while the Muslim army slew and pursued them with deafening shouts. The dead were countless. Our troops made spoil of their property. During their confused flight they were also plundered by the Kolis and the Bhils in the jungles and deserts, especially at night, when the rebels moved losing their way, much booty fell into their hands and the wretches suffered total losses.

"The Subah of Gujarat has been freed from the disturbance created by Bajirao and the Subah of Malwa too has remained safe from that wretch's mischief-making ; and the holy port (of Surat) has been saved from falling into the clutches of the villain."[4]

The deplorable end of the Dabhades at Dabhoi was indeed the result of the separatist tendency of the Marathas, which the Peshwa as the head of the administration felt it his duty to check. It must also be said to Bajirao's credit that he wisely restored the Pawars, the Bandays, the Gaikwads and others to their former offices, although for a time they had joined the hostile faction.

Abhay Sinh's vacillation cost him his position in Gujarat. His alliance with Bajirao was short-lived, and when he found to his cost that Dabhade's rout at Dabhoi instead of benefiting him, strengthened the Gaikwad who became his opponent, Abhay Sinh managed to encompass Pilaji's murder by treacherous means at Dakor on 14th April 1732. This act was fully avenged by Pilaji's able son Damaji who after capturing Dabhoi and Baroda marched upon Ahmadabad, when realizing his danger Abhay Sinh agreed to pay the annual Chauth to the Marathas and hastened home to protect his patrimony of Marwar then threatened by other enemies. He left behind him in Gujarat his brothers Anand Sinh and Rai Sinh, but they could not check the increasing power of the Gaikwads. Thus Abhay Sinh's ambition of holding Gujarat came to nothing.

4. Extracted from the text published by Sir Jadunath in *Islamic Culture*.

CHRONOLOGY

CHAPTER VI

1649—1746	Brahmendra Swami's life-time.
1727, February 8	Siddi Sat desecrates the shrine of Parashuram at Chiplun.
1729, July 4	Kanhoji Angria dies.
1729, July 29	His son Sekhoji becomes Sarkhel.
1730, December	Jaysinh removed from Malwa, Muhammad Khan Bangash appointed Subahdar.
1731, March	Bangash arrives at Ujjain, confers with Nizam-ul-mulk.
1732, February 12	Bajirao and Sekhoji meet at Kolaba.
1732, July 29	The Peshwa effects division of Malwa between Sindia, Holkar and Pawar.
1732, December	Jaysinh reappointed to Malwa.
1732, December 27	Nizam and Bajirao meet in a conference at Rohe-Rameshvar.
1733, early months	Chimnaji Appa in Northern India
1733, February	Holkar overcomes Jaysinh near Mandsor.
1733, February	Siddi Rasul dies.
1733, March-April	Chimnaji Appa and Holkar capture part of Bundelkhand.
1733, April	Bajirao opens operations against Janjira.
1733, June 8	Pratinidhi captures Raigad.
1733, July 8	A severe action takes place at Govalkot.
1733, August 28	Sekhoji Angria dies.
1733, December 6	Bajirao closes Janjira operations.
1734, early months	Pilaji Jadhav with Sindia and Holkar plant Maratha rule in Malwa and Bundelkhand.
1734, April 12	They take possession of Bundi.
1734, Monsoon	Jaysinh heads a Rajput league against Marathas.
1734, November	Pilaji Jadhav enters Bundelkhand with Balaji Bajirao.
1735, Early months	Khan Dauran and Qamr-ud-din Khan open offensive against Marathas.

1735, February 13	Sindia and Holkar defeat Mughals near Rampura.
1735, February 14	Radhabai leaves Poona on pilgrimage.
1735, February 28	Holkar plunders Sambhar.
1735, March 2	Qamr-ud-din Khan is routed by Pilaji Jadhav in Bundelkhand.
1735, March 4	Khan Dauran accepts peace on Maratha terms of Chauth.
1735, May 6	Radhabai at Udaipur.
1735, June 21	Radhabai reaches Jaipur.
1735, October 17	Radhabai arrives at Benares.
1735, Nov.	Bhagwantsinh Adaru fell fighting.
1736, February	Bajirao at Udaipur.
1736, March 4	Bajirao meets Jaysinh at Kishangad.
1736, May	Emperor declines to receive Bajirao's visit; he returns to Poona, leaving Sindia and Holkar in Malwa.
" June 1	Radhabai returns to Poona.
1736, November	Bajirao leaves Poona for a dash on Delhi.
1737, February 18	Marathas capture Bhadawar and Ater.
1737, March 12	Saadat Khan routs Holkar and Baji Bhivrao in the Doab.
1737, March 13	Mughals encamp near Mathura.
1737, March 28	Bajirao's surprise attack upon Delhi.
1737, April 5	Bajirao returns to Jaipur.
1737, April 7	Nizam leaves Burhanpur for north.
1737, May 28	Nizam and Bajirao near Sironj.
1737, July 2	Nizam meets Emperor at Delhi.
1737, October	Nizam starts from Delhi to recapture Malwa.
1737, November	Chimnaji prevents Nasir Jang proceeding north to support his father.
1737, December 13	Bajirao and Nizam face each other near Bhopal.
1737, December 16	Bajirao besieges Nizam at Bhopal.
1737, December 26	Raghuji Bhosle routs Shujaat Khan in Berar.
1738, January 7	Nizam accepts Bajirao's terms and concludes peace at Sarai-Doraha.
1738, February 13	Kota raided.

CHAPTER VI

THE MUGHAL POWER HUMBLED

[1732—1738]

1 War on Janjira, Brahmendra Swami avenged.
2 Bajirao's visit to Nizam.
3 Jaysinh's attempt to check the Marathas.
4 Radhabai's northern pilgrimage.
5 Emperor refuses to meet Bajirao.
6 Bajirao's dash upon Delhi.
7 Nizam humbled at Bhopal.

1. **The war on Janjira, Brahmendra Swami avenged.**—As with the Nizam so with the Siddis of Janjira the Marathas had to carry on perpetual warfare ever since the days of Shivaji. These Siddis were Muslims of Abyssinian descent and had planted their small colony on the west coast of India in the days of Malik Ambar. From their impregnable island fort since known as Janjira, situated about 50 miles south of Bombay, they ruled a small independent principality which has existed to the present day through strange vicissitudes. Aurangzeb took them under his protection against the aggression of Shivaji and entrusted to them the task of convoying Muslim pilgrims from Surat to Mecca and back. They captured the islet of Underi at the entrance of the Bombay harbour and thence raided Maratha territories along the coast, particularly that portion of it which belonged to the Angria of Kolaba, the admiral of the Marathas. The Siddis often allied themselves with the Portuguese power of Goa and with the British at Bombay. All these foreign elements usually combined against the Marathas and obstructed their legitimate ambitions. It therefore became almost a creed with the Marathas to make the Siddi perfectly innocuous.

But the immediate cause of the hostilities was the meddlesome activity of an influential Hindu ascetic named Brahmendra Swami, who was looked upon as the *guru* or spiritual guide by Raja Shahu and most of the Maratha gentry including the Peshwas. A celebrated orthodox preacher, wielding a fluent pen and an equally powerful tongue, he took up his residence in a lonely jungle near Chiplun, where Balaji Vishvanath in his early days at the time, was employed. Balaji was struck with the saint's miraculous powers and paid devotion to him. The Swami built a large temple for Parashuram, which still stands on a high hill adjoining Chiplun, and collected funds for that purpose from most of the Maratha chiefs. He himself accompanied them for collecting alms in their military expeditions. The Angrias and even the Siddis held the Swami in high reverence and contributed money, lands and other gifts for the shrine he thus raised. He held a grand annual celebration at the place on the Shivaratri day, which in 1727 fell on February 8. At this time the Siddi governor of Govalkot and Anjanvel, two fortified posts not far from the shrine, was one Siddi Sat, a competent, if rather rough, officer, who probably for some personal reasons, had developed an aversion towards the Swami, and made a sudden attack on the Parashuram temple, on that day of celebration in 1727 during the saint's absence, desecrated the idols, and plundered the property, subjecting innocent priests and Brahmans to unspeakable atrocities. This wanton and certainly premeditated violence by a Muslim on a centre of Brahman orthodoxy, roused the whole of Maharashtra as if from a dream, and a cry for vengeance arose on all sides. The chief ruler of Janjira at once apologized for the foolish action of his subordinate, and restored whatever property was left intact. In a few days the Swami arrived on the spot, vented his wrath against the Siddi and left the place for good, having been granted another spot by Shahu up the Ghats at Dhavadsi near Satara, where he then erected new edifices and where an annual celebration for his deity is still held.

The Swami appealed pathetically to Shahu and the leading Maratha commanders, calling upon them to wage a relentless holy war against the Siddi of Janjira. Time passed as no one was free to undertake the venture. When Bajirao returned victorious from his campaign of Dabhoi, both Shahu and the Swami became insistent on his punishing the Siddi for the unwarrantable crime he had committed. Perhaps Bajirao was not keen on that point, as it promised no immediate gain and involved naval operations in which he himself was not very proficient. During 1732 the plans for war were seriously discussed at Satara and the campaign was determined upon in the next season. The main objects of the war were to release the Maratha capital Raigad, from the Siddi's control to whom it had been delivered for protection by the Emperor Aurangzeb after its capture in 1689. Similarly the forts of Anjanvel and Govalkot held by the Siddi in the vicinity of the shrine at Chiplun, were also to be captured. Janjira itself was to be attacked and taken, if possible, and the power of the Siddi to hamper the Maratha government in future was to be completely broken. Bajirao moved into Konkan, met the admiral Sekhoji Angre in February 1732 and formed plans in consultation with him for a simultaneous war on the Siddi by sea and land.

But the wheels of Shahu's Court moved very slowly and not a soul arrived at the appointed places till the beginning of May 1733. Bajirao opened vigorous operations against Janjira in May and quickly captured several places and strongholds on the land side and destroyed the Siddis' navy in the creek of Rajpuri. The Pratinidhi also arrived soon after and through bribery or some diplomatic contrivance captured Raigad at the very first stroke on June 8, 1733, a sudden and sensational achievement, which brought temporary glory to the Pratinidhi.

But either flushed with the pride of this achievement or standing on ceremony, the Pratinidhi did not care to go and meet Bajirao at Rajpuri and arrange with him a concerted plan of operations. Their differences were well known and Siddi Sat of Govalkot was not slow to take advantage of them. Bakaji Naik a valiant subordinate of the Angrias, proceeded from Suvarnadurg and worked for the capture of Anjanvel and Govalkot, then ably defended by Siddi Sat. The Pratinidhi arrived at Chiplun and was approached by Siddi Sat for the surrender of the two places by negotiation. As the Pratinidhi had succeeded at Raigad, he thought he would do the same with Govalkot and asked Bakaji Naik to raise the siege. But Siddi Sat played a successful game and kept the Pratinidhi long under delusion spinning out the negotiations. In the meantime the monsoon started with fury making all warlike operations impossible. Bakaji Naik was recalled by

Sekhoji Angria at the instance of Bajirao and the Pratinidhi soon realized that he had been outwitted.

It was unfortunate that the campaign was opened in an unsuitable season, when no naval and hardly any land operations could be undertaken on account of the violent rains and more violent seas. Bajirao and Sekhoji Angria met at Rajpuri and held prolonged deliberations on the situation. Sekhoji explained that they must wait for the dry season before any effective action could be launched against the Siddi. Bajirao was thus forced to sit down idly before Janjira in which the Siddis had taken shelter and against which no effect could be made by the navy or by the land forces during the rains. In August Bajirao wrote to Shahu, " The Siddi is not an ordinary enemy : you know how often in the past, heroic attempts to humble him have failed. A tremendous effort is necessary if he is to be finally overcome. Without a complete naval blockade combined with carefully arranged operations by land, it is not possible to overcome him. This means enormous expenditure of money, which is not available. We need at least fifteen thousand expert footmen for an effort of this kind, working through a period of at least two years. Janjira is receiving support from Anjanvel and Underi ; these places must first be secured before an attack on this principal stronghold could succeed. We have already exhausted all our money and resources, so that unless you send us ample funds at once, we cannot make any movement. We are putting forth our utmost effort, but that is not enough. The Siddis are getting help from Surat and Bombay also. The Pratinidhi has not come to Rajpuri. I await further orders."

These were highly practical suggestions, but Shahu could not work up to them. The four months of the inoperative season proved a welcome respite for the Siddi. He made urgent appeals to the Portuguese, to the British at Bombay, and to his colleagues at Surat and even to Nizam-ul-mulk and the Emperor of Delhi. Bajirao realized this too late and a re-arrangement could not be quickly effected. He felt disgusted with the undercurrent of intrigue, which sapped the force of his own command and initiative. Shahu got so confused with the conflicting reports and complaints that reached him through his several favourites, that he was quite nonplussed and could do nothing beyond a strongly worded remonstrance to Bajirao to which the latter replied with equal warmth. These documents are well worth study as they fully illustrate the strength and weakness of the Maratha character.[1]

Another unexpected mishap, the sudden death of Sekhoji Angria, proved also a serious impediment to the conduct of the war. Sekhoji died of a short illness at Kolaba on 28th August 1733, almost in the prime of youth. He was a man of uncommon sobriety and foresight and exercised a wholesome check upon his three capable and valiant brothers, Sambhaji, Manaji and Tulaji, and exacted from them all the best work they were capable of. His death proved the ruin of the house of the Angrias and with it that of the Maratha navy. It at once let loose the forces of disruption and compelled Bajirao to abandon the campaign. Bakaji Naik had already been recalled : and in September the Pratinidhi also returned to Satara. So in December Bajirao himself withdrew after patching up a temporary understanding with the Siddi. He personally explained to Shahu the difficulties of the situation and never again himself led a campaign on the west coast. For the present the effort ended in failure with the year 1733.

To redress the wrong done to the shrine of Parashuram at Chiplun, it was necessary to capture from Siddi Sat the two important posts of Govalkot and Anjanvel, and since a dispute had started among the Angria brothers over the succession issue after Sekhoji's death, Shahu declared that he would confer the office of Sarkhel on whichever brother should capture those places. Of the three Sambhaji, Manaji and Tulaji, the Peshwa found Manaji more pliant, while Sambhaji although more daring, refused to obey the Peshwa on account of his interference with the succession issue. Precious time thus came to be wasted in settling the dispute of succession with the result, that a kind of slow desultory fighting continued against the Siddi during 1734 and 1735 near Bankot and Govalkot. The former changed hands several times, and in

1. P. D. S., Vol. 3. 43 contains Shahu's remonstrance, which though addressed to Sekhoji Angria is meant for Bajirao. The latter's reply, a forceful but dignified protest, is conveyed in Vol. 33. 79.

this struggle for the possession of Bankot many Maratha commanders distinguished themselves.

Shahu became all the more impatient for subjugating the Siddis and called upon Chimnaji Appa and Pilaji Jadhav to save Manaji from a serious attack on Kolaba by Siddi Sat which was reported early in 1736. Chimnaji Appa undertook the work seriously and learning that Siddi Sat had left his base at Anjanvel and moved with all his forces threatening Kolaba, the renowned stronghold built by Shivaji, diverted his course towards the enemy's quarters and suddenly attacked Siddi Sat as he was encamped near Rewas. The latter had no alternative but to face Chimnaji Appa in an open fight. A bloody action ensued at the villages of Charegaum and Kamarlen, in which Siddi Sat was killed while defending himself valiantly. More than 1300 of his brave followers were slain, including Siddi Yakut the defender of Underi, and a much larger number wounded. This signal victory over the implacable Siddi who had destroyed the famous Hindu shrine of Parashuram, roused all Maharashtra to heights of ecstasy and earned an imperishable fame for Chimnaji Appa. He was congratulated on the victory by the Swami in the following terms :—

"By killing Siddi Sat, a demon of the type of Ravana, you have uprooted the very life of the Siddis and earned an undying fame." Shahu showered upon Chimnaji honours, costly ornaments and dresses, including a sword set with diamonds. The event naturally unnerved the Siddis of Janjira and induced them to seek a humiliating peace with the Peshwa. Anjanvel and Govalkot alone remained as their mainland posts, and came to be captured much later by Tulaji Angria in January 1745, so that Brahmendra Swami could have a happy death in 1746 after seeing his wrongs fully avenged. His temple of Parashuram still commemorates his life's endeavour in its pristine grandeur. These Konkan regions were looked upon by the Peshwas as their homeland and were always dearest to their heart even during their distant wanderings.[2]

The activities of Brahmendra Swami were inter-mixed

2. See P. D. 33. 142.

with the Maratha politics of Shahu's days for nearly half a century. His was a powerful figure not to be easily ignored by any one who aspired to share the fortunes of the Maratha State. Although possessing neither deep scholarship nor unerring foresight, he yet was gifted with sound common sense and a passion for notoriety. Most of the sardars and commanders of Shahu's court paid homage to him as their *guru*, and the guru never lost an opportunity of exacting from his zealous disciples, gifts of rare articles of all kind, when they returned from the distant parts where they roamed. But he gave away these articles to his devotees, ladies and commoners and the most exacting scrutiny of his dealings does not reveal any wrong or immoral use or a sinister motive on his part in bestowing them thus. He collected funds as alms, often lent them at interest which he rigorously exacted even from his dearest devotees like Bajirao. The proceeds of his accumulations he utilised in building temples, tanks, roads, wells, and similar conveniences for travellers and the people in general.[3] He is said to have enjoyed the life of a full century.

2. Bajirao's visit to Nizam.—The Maratha penetration into Malwa and Bundelkhand created a sharp division of opinion in the Emperor's counsels. One party headed by Jaysinh and the Mir Bakhshi Khan Dauran advocated appeasement and conciliation : the other party, headed by Saadat Khan, Muhammad Khan Bangash and others, advocated an immediate concerted drive against the Marathas. The Wazir Qamr-ud-din Khan, the Nizam and even the Emperor himself could not at once decide upon the one course or the other, and bided their time in the hope of better days. The Deepsinh mission arrived at Satara in August 1730 and communi-

3. The Swami had a voluminous correspondence of a historical character, portions of which have been published by Parasnis, Rajwade and others. A full life of him has also been published in Marathi. In a sense what Ramdas was for Shivaji, Brahmendra was for Shahu, although the latter saint can stand no comparison with the former in point of selfless patriotic work of national uplift. A mediocrity like Brahmendra Swami figures in history because he long swayed the politics of the first three Peshwas under the direction of Shahu.

cated their views, upon their return. Acting on the advice of his delegates Jaysinh arranged a compromise with Shahu, (1) that an annual payment of ten lacs be made to the Marathas for the Chauth of Malwa; (2) in return for this amount one of Shahu's sardars was to reside for service at the Emperor's court. Dado Bhimsen, Shahu's envoy with Jaysinh submitted this compromise to the Emperor, but it was not accepted. Jaysinh, thereupon made the following representation to the Emperor.

"You have been trying this game of driving away the Marathas from Malwa for the last twenty years. If you take into account what it has cost you and what success you have attained, I am sure my plan would appeal to you as the only way out of the difficulty."

The Emperor, however, decided otherwise, transferred Jaysinh from the government of Malwa and appointed Bangash to that office towards the end of 1730. The arrival of Bangash at Ujjain and his conference with Nizam-ul-mulk in March 1731 have been already referred to. For a time Bangash seemed to succeed, as Bajirao was engaged in a war with the Dabhades. Holkar and Antaji Mankeshwar were then acting in Malwa; the latter was defeated near Ujjain by Bangash. Later in the year when Ranoji Sindia joined Holkar, Bangash realized that he was not equal to the task of holding the Marathas back and sent urgent appeals to the Emperor for more reinforcements and funds. This demand severely upset the Emperor, who was expecting to receive a substantial addition of income from Malwa. At the same time serious complaints poured in from several landholders and officials of Malwa, directed against the mis-government of Bangash, to whom both Khan Dauran and Qamr-ud-din Khan were opposed from the beginning. The Emperor, therefore, to save the situation recalled Bangash and once more appointed Jaysinh to that province at the end of 1732. The latter held that post for the next four years.

The year 1732 happened to be one of comparative quiet for the Peshwa. During the rainy season, while discussing preparations for the Janjira campaign, he invited Sindia and Holkar to Satara and effected a kind of working division of the districts of Malwa between them and the three

Pawar chiefs, in a solemn document dated 29th July 1732.

The defeat of the Dabhade-Nizam combine at Dabhoi, paved the way for an understanding between the Peshwa and Nizam-ul-mulk. The latter proposed a personal meeting in order to put a stop to the frequent clashes between them which made neighbourly relations impossible. Bajirao was not personally sanguine about any good coming out of a personal visit, as neither of them could rely upon the other's word. Nizam-ul-mulk repeated his desire to Shahu through the Sumant. Shahu called upon Bajirao to go and visit the Nizam at once. Under such circumstances a report went round that Nizam-ul-mulk had some foul intention in asking for a visit from Bajirao ; that he had offered Shahu the amount of two crores for sending Bajirao on a personal visit. Letters poured into Bajirao's hands from friends and colleagues calling upon him to decline the invitation point blank. But Shahu became insistent and would brook no delay. At last Bajirao accompanied by a few select friends and guards and faithfully served by a number of able spies, boldly advanced into the Nizam's dominions and the two chiefs met on Wednesday 27th December 1732 at a place called Rohe-Rameshwar on the upper Manjira, in the neighbourhood of Ausa, about 8 miles north of Latur. Only a few details of the visit are available. The visit proved quite cordial. The Nizam presented Bajirao 7 dresses, 2 beautiful pairs of costly pearls, two horses and an elephant. The successful termination of the visit sent a thrill of joy throughout Maharashtra and was announced by a salvo of guns from the various forts and the distribution of sugar by Shahu and others.

Bajirao himself wrote the following account of this visit to his brother. " I proceeded by rapid marches towards Latur, where I learnt that the Nawab was at Koti near Vagir about twenty miles away. On 25 December I despatched Anandrao Sumant to meet the Nawab and arrange the details of my visit. An immediate reply was received from the Sumant, and as I advanced, the Nawab cancelling his journey to Haidarabad came specially to meet me and halted at a convenient open plain. Next day, 27th December, I proceeded with my full force to the Nawab's camp. Upon my arrival the Nawab removed the usual armed guard from his gate and posted

Sumant, Rao Rambha and Turk-Taz Khan to wait at the gate to receive and admit me. I left my troops outside and went in with two hundred followers. The Nawab sent a party of a few special officers to conduct me in and himself with Aiwaz Khan and Hamid Khan stood in front of his tent. As I advanced, I first accosted the receiving officers and they introduced me to the Nawab. He then received me with great respect and cordiality. After spending a few minutes together in the open Darbar exchanging enquiries of welcome, the Nawab took me by the hand and led me to another tent for a confidential talk where only Rao Rambha, Turk-Taz Khan and four of my companions were present. Here we talked long and freely upon many topics in a vein of the utmost cordiality and happiness. The Nawab highly applauded me and our Chhatrapati. After an hour's conversation he offered me *pan* and the same was distributed to all our party outside. Thus the visit was concluded and I returned to my quarters an hour before evening. Thereupon we received from the Nawab grand and sufficient rations for our dinner, baskets of sweetmeats and fruits, these extending in a long line from his camp to ours. I had made before now three visits to the Nawab, but those were only formal with no opening of hearts. This time, however, we discussed many questions openly, cementing our mutual good will and friendship. Whatever suspicions and fears had existed formerly, have now been completely removed. The Nawab repeatedly expressed a desire that our cordiality and pleasant relations would go on ever increasing. He specially called Sultanji Nimbalkar and Chandrasen Jadhav for my visit and asked me to extend my kindly attention to them."[4]

The outcome of this momentous visit is thus related by

4. Both these chiefs of weight and standing in the Maratha State had deserted to the Nizam, Chandrasen in 1711 after quarrelling with Balaji Vishvanath, and Sultanji Nimbalkar in 1726. They were now in the Nizam's service and feared retribution at the hands of Bajirao. This is the sixth recorded visit of Bajirao to Nizam-ul-mulk. These can be thus enumerated:— 4th January 1721, Chikhalthan ;, 13th February 1723, Bolasha ; 18th May 1724, Nalchha ; October 1724, Aurangabad ; 6th March 1728, Palkhed ; and 27th Dec. 1732 Rohe-Rameshwar. Cambridge History of India, Vol. IV, page 382 ; Irvine's Later Mughals Vol. 2, page 252 ; P. D. S., Vol. 15 page 94 ; Ait Sankirna Sahitya VI. p. 11.

Elphinstone. "The Nizam entered into a secret compact with Bajirao by which the Maratha government promised to leave the Deccan unmolested and to levy nothing beyond Chauth and Sardeshmukhi from them; while the Nizam agreed to remain neutral during the projected Maratha invasions of Hindustan provided they did not injure the province of Khandesh in their northward march through it."

3. **Jaysinh's attempt to check the Marathas.**—While the Peshwa and the Nizam were at Rohe-Rameshwar, Jaysinh arrived at Ujjain and took charge of the government of Malwa. At this time Chimnaji Appa advanced from the Deccan to meet the Rajput Prince and complete with him the compact which had been long discussed. But as Jaysinh's orders were to drive the Marathas out of Malwa, a settlement became impossible. Chimnaji, therefore, despatched Vithoji Bule, Holkar's principal lieutenant, and Anandrao Pawar to overcome Jaysinh. For a time a tenacious fight ensued in which Jaysinh found himself suddenly surrounded and hard-pressed on all sides by the troops of the two Maratha chiefs. No reinforcements arrived from the Emperor and Jaysinh extricated himself from a difficult situation by paying a fine of 6 lacs in cash in addition to the tributes that had already been collected. The business was handled entirely by Holkar as Chimnaji had proceeded to Bundelkhand in order to take charge of the districts which had been ceded to Bajirao by Chhatrasal three years ago. Two Bundela agents, Asharam and Haridas Purohit had come to Poona to settle the affair of partition; they were sent to Chimnaji Appa by Bajirao with his agent Mudhaji Hari. Chimnaji employed Govindpant and Mudhaji Hari to confirm the Maratha hold upon Bundelkhand and exact tributes from the several States. At the end of the season Chimnaji returned to the Deccan with Sindia and Holkar about June 1733, at a time when Bajirao was occupied in the Janjira campaign.

Much had, however, to be done in the north, and as both Bajirao and his brother were detained in the south, they deputed Pilaji Jadhav with Sindia and Holkar to proceed to Malwa at the end of 1733. These Chiefs had a large following with which they marched right upto Bhadawar beyond

Gwalior collecting tribute, and returned home for the monsoon in May 1734. Jaysinh as the Governor of Malwa tried his best to avoid an open clash with the Maratha commanders. He was involved at the time in a dispute about the succession to the rulership of the state of Bundi, which he coveted. One of the claimants Pratapsinh Hada repaired to Satara and implored Shahu for help against Jaysinh. Shahu asked Sindia and Holkar to capture Bundi and entrust it to Pratapsinh. The two Sardars accordingly took possession of Bundi on 12th April 1734. But upon the return of the Maratha armies to the south, Jaysinh managed to take it back. At Jaysinh's entreaty the Emperor sent him additional troops with funds and supplies under an able commander Muzaffar Khan, the Mir Atish and brother of Khan Dauran. In addition Jaysinh formed a strong league of the Rajput princes during the monsoon of 1734 and with such formidable preparations earnestly started to drive the Marathas out of Malwa.

When this fresh danger was reported to the Peshwa, Pilaji Jadhav was again despatched with young Nanasaheb (Balaji Bajirao) then 14 years of age, with special instructions to Sindia and Holkar to practise their usual tactics and confirm their hold on Malwa. Thus the year 1735 opened in Malwa with grand preparations on both sides, for a final decision in which the Emperor and his able officers readily joined. They marched from Delhi in two divisions, one under Khan Dauran by the western route into Rajputana, and the second under the Wazir Qamr-ud-din Khan by the eastern route into Bundelkhand. During January and February several Rajput princes headed by Khan Dauran fought many stiff battles with Sindia and Holkar near Rampura, after the Marathas had descended into Malwa through the Mukundara pass. Sindia kept them engaged while Holkar moved rapidly into the north, devastated the territories of Marwar and Jaipur, and on February 28 carried away an enormous amount of plunder from the rich commercial town of Sambhar. Jaysinh and the imperialists found themselves so hard pressed by the guerilla methods of the Marathas, that they paid Rs. 22 lacs in cash and purchased peace by a solemn agreement mutually effected at Kota on 24 March 1735. Twenty thousand Marathas proved superior to the Mughal army of 2 lacs, a unique triumph of Maratha strategy.

The campaign in Bundelkhand under the Wazir did not prove more successful. He was encountered by Pilaji Jadhav, Ranoji Bhosle and Vyankatrao Narayan Ghorpade. On 2nd March 1735, Pilaji thus reported the result. "The Wazir came upon us with 25 thousand troops; we had three severe battles with them. We captured 300 horses and camels and fell back upon Kolaras. Qamr-ud-din Khan agrees to pay 5 lacs; but we have not accepted this offer and await further results. We wish soon to return home for the monsoon."

At this time occurred the affair of Bhagwant Sinh Adaru, a small jagirdar of Ghazipur near the northern bank of the Jumna in the Fatehpur district. It illustrates to what a low level the Mughal power had sunk. One of Qamr-ud-din Khan's near relatives was killed by Bhagwant Sinh, and for four years the Wazir exerted himself to punish him but without success. At last Saadat Khan was ordered to march against Ghazipur when a severe encounter took place in which Bhagwant Sinh fell fighting in November 1735; but his son Rup Sinh sought Maratha protection in Bundelkhand and the affair dragged on for a long time.

4. *Radhabai's northern pilgrimage.*—The year 1735 was pregnant with far-reaching consequences to the Mughal-Maratha contest. The Peshwa's mother Radhabai made a peaceful and most successful pilgrimage through northern India during this same year, when the valiant Jaysinh was conducting a serious campaign against the Marathas. Radhabai left Poona on 14th February 1735 and returned there on 1st June of the following year. The lady had a large following and her son-in-law Abaji Naik of Baramati and his brother Babuji were in charge of the arrangements of the journey. When the lady's intention of going on pilgrimage became known, such was the awe that Bajirao's name had created that invitations from the Rajput princes and Mughal officials in north India poured into Poona requesting the revered lady's visit to their States and shrines. The Emperor himself ordered an escort of one thousand troops of his own body-guard to accompany the lady during the period of

her stay beyond the river Narmada. Even Muhammad Khan Bangash whom Bajirao had routed only a few years before, offered a cordial welcome to the lady when she would pass through his jurisdiction.

Radhabai reached Burhanpur on 8th March, crossed the Narmada on 18th April, was received at Udaipur on 6 May. Nath Dwara was visited on 18th May, the party arriving at Jaipur on June 21. Here at the special request of Jaysinh she made a halt of three long months. During September and October she travelled hurriedly to Mathura, Brindawan, Kurukshetra and Prayag, reaching Benares on October 17, where she spent over two months, enjoying the blissful spiritual atmosphere of the sacred place. She proceeded to Gaya in the last week of December, and started thence on her return journey in January 1736, travelling straight west through Bundelkhand and after making a short stay at Saugor returned safely to Poona. The Peshwa's agent at Jaipur thus describes her journey : "The revered mother arrived at Jainagar at the beginning of Ashad under the care of Babuji Naik. She is being pressed to stay here till the Dassara, an event of special celebration. All things go well for her on account of her pious personality. The journey further will, I am sure, prove equally successful. Bajirao's stars are most propitious and no harm can come to her. The Maharaja Jaysinh has deputed Ray Narayandas to accompany her throughout the journey. Narayandas's relation Ray Haraprasad is the Diwan of Muhammad Khan Bangash, who entertains such high esteem for the Peshwa, that Haraprasad came to meet us at the Jamuna, and having escorted the party during the crossing took us for a visit to the Khan, his chief. We all received a cordial welcome from him. The Khan expressed his hearty pleasure that he was honoured by a cordial letter from Bajirao and that he trusted his mother to his care. "She is to me," he says, "just like my own mother." He has sent orders round to his district officials to accord the party full reception through his territory. Haraprasad had brought her a present of Rs. 1,000 in cash with saries of cloud-colour (suitable for a widow). Sawai Jaysinh too expressed his high and sincere regard for the Peshwa. The Rana of Udaipur did the same and has sent his agent Samant Sinh to Poona on a special mission. Your very name has struck a reverential awe in the minds of these potentates."[5]

This pilgrimage of the Peshwa's mother without any untoward incident during a year of unrest and Mughal-Maratha war, discloses the great awe in which the Peshwa's name was held in north India. For this happy result Jaysinh alone was responsible as "he acted exactly like a son to the lady, escorting her with a strong guard and personally entertaining her in his own capital, supplying all her needs and comforts in the minutest detail.[6]

5. **Emperor refuses to meet Bajirao.**—Sawai Jaysinh was a shrewd observer of events and could form an unerring estimate of the comparative strength of the Maratha and the Mughal forces, having been himself long involved in war and diplomacy. He was perhaps the only person capable of bringing about an adjustment of a lasting character after the vexatious hostilities that had continued for so many years. He was essentially a man of peace, tired of incessant war which hampered the peaceful occupations of the people. He directed his energies towards bringing about a lasting and peaceful solution. He had sincerely conducted offensive operations against the Marathas during the years 1733-35, putting forth his own utmost effort along with that of several Mughal chiefs, such as the Wazir and the Mir Bakhshi. Jaysinh fully realized the futility of trying to stop the Maratha aggression by force of arms, and once more used his influence with the Emperor to bring about a reconciliation. He advocated direct negotiations with the Peshwa himself to avoid the mischief and misunderstanding which middlemen on both sides were prone to create. If Bajirao and the Emperor could, he urged, meet face to face in a friendly conference, many vexatious and immoderate demands would be avoided. Jaysinh discussed these views freely in the Emperor's counsels and with his permission invited Bajirao to come over for personal talks

5. P. D. 30 134—Such Maratha contact with north India created revolutionary changes in the social and commercial life of Maharashtra and forms a subject which deserves a special and careful study from the ample sources now available in print.

6. Hingne Daftar Pt. I. 19.

first with the Rajput princes and then with the Emperor. Bajirao himself was not very sanguine about the outcome of such spectacular visits and conferences, but agreed to the proposal out of his great regard for Jaysinh and also for a chance of winning over the Rajput princes through friendly discourses.

Bajirao obtained Shahu's consent for such a venture, left Poona during the auspicious Divali time of 1735 and reached Udaipur in February of the following year. Lest his troops should do wanton damage to the crops and the peaceful pursuits of the inhabitants, he diverted the route of his main army in a different direction and entered Rajputana with only a small personal escort. Says one writer, "The Peshwa's name exercises such a terror over the minds of the people in the north, that he could easily remove the Emperor from his position and install the Chhatrapati on the throne of Delhi." Mahadev Bhat Hingne, the Peshwa's agent at Delhi, came to Udaipur with the draft treaty proposed by the Emperor with gifts and presents for Bajirao. Jaysinh's Divan Ayamall, alias Rajmal popularly called Malji, also accompanied Mahadev Bhat.[7]

Bajirao was everywhere welcomed with plentiful demonstrations of joy and respect. He had a great reception at Udaipur, the Champabag palace having been appointed for his accommodation. He was the next day honoured by the Maha Rana in a grand open Darbar, where two gold-embroidered seats were arranged for the guest and the host. When Bajirao approached the seat which the Rana pointed to him, he politely declined to accept the position of equality with the Rana, the scion of the ancient godly sovereign of India, and occupied a seat just below. They had a long and free conversation together. Dresses and presents were offered and entertainments took place for five days from 3 to 7 February. Bajirao inspected the various sights and monuments of the State and then left for Nath-Dwara. The Rana agreed to pay a lac and a half annually as Chauth.

During his tour through Rajputana presents and tributes

7. P. D. 30. 134; 14. 50, 35-37.

poured upon Bajirao from all quarters. Khan Dauran the Mir Bakhshi sent five to ten thousand Rupees every day. At Nath-Dwara Bajirao and his wife Kashibai offered their joint devotion to the celebrated deity, and proceeding further he and Sawai Jaysinh had their first personal meeting on 4th March at Bambhola near Kishangad.[8] They arrived both riding on their elephants and as soon as they sighted each other, they dismounted, embraced and sat down on the same musnad in an open Darbar. Their visit lasted for several days up to 8th March when they discussed the peace terms and arrangements for the visit to the Emperor regarding which a communication was expected from Delhi. Jaysinh offered to pay 5 lacs Chauth annually for Jaipur and promised to obtain from the Emperor written grants for the provinces of Malwa and Gujarat. The Peshwa's agents Mahadev Bhat Hingne, Yadavrao Munshi, and Jaysinh's envoy Kriparam proceeded to Delhi for arranging Bajirao's visit to the Emperor and as time was hanging on his hand before the reply could come, Bajirao moved into the neighbouring territories on his own account. Ranoji Sindia and Ramchandra Baba powerfully exerted their influence upon the Peshwa in gaining his object.

In the meantime the Emperor not caring to receive Bajirao in a personal visit at Delhi, sent his own agents Yadgar Khan and Kriparam to Jaysinh with certain proposals tending to effect as advantageous a bargain as possible. Bajirao at once rejected the offer and sent his own agents Dhondo Govind and Baburao Malhar to Delhi with counter proposals on his part, the high tone of which displeased the Emperor so much, that he declined to reply and prepared for an offensive against the Marathas. The season also advanced and as there seemed no prospect for Bajirao of a visit to the Emperor, he at once returned to the Deccan fully determined soon to compel the Emperor to grant his demands.[9]

8. Some papers mention Manoharpur as the place of their meeting.

9. Hingne Daftar Pt. I recently published contains graphic pertinent details of the Peshwa's negotiations with the Imperial Court, see letter No. 3. (Dec. 1735), No. 4 (31 May 1736), No. 5, (20 June 1736), No. 6 (11th July 1736) and No. 7. Ranoji Sinde and Ramchandra Baba are mentioned as having only one soul in two bodies.

6. **Bajirao's dash upon Delhi.**—Yadgar Khan reported to the Emperor his impressions, which were by no means agreeable to him. So the atmosphere at Delhi and Satara during the monsoon of 1736 was full of preparations for a stiff campaign. Bajirao asked Ranoji Sindia and Malharrao Holkar to encamp in Malwa and prepare for the coming hostilities. This was indeed the first time that Maratha troops encamped in the north away from home during the rainy season. Hereafter these chiefs formed their permanent camps in Malwa.

Bajirao himself was not long away. He took full counsel with Shahu and his colleagues and after completing his arrangements entered Malwa early in January 1737. Ranoji met him at Bhilsa on January 13 and they deliberated over the details of the impending campaign of a whirlwind type. Duties were definitely assigned to the various commanders for laying under contribution the vast territories between the Narmada and the Jamuna. Baji Bhivrao and Holkar advanced through Bundelkhand, and Bajirao himself with Sindia followed by slow marches to render succour wherever needed. Bhadawar and Ater were captured and an enormous amount of booty was obtained. Nana Phadnis's father Janardan Baba kept a stern supervision under Bajirao's directions upon the accumulation of funds and economy in expenditure.

In the meantime Saadat Khan who had been ordered by the Emperor to oppose the Marathas, proceeded against them and attacked the corps of Holkar and Baji Bhivrao who had crossed over the Jamuna for ravaging the fertile imperial territories of the Doab. They plundered Itimadpur and other places opposite Agra, when they were suddenly attacked by an overwhelming force of Saadat Khan. The Marathas fled for life but were overtaken and a few were slaughtered; and the remainder recrossed and joined the main army. It was indeed an insignificant skirmish with a few advanced stragglers. But Saadat Khan took them to be the main Maratha army, and at once sent to the Emperor a boastful account that he had met and destroyed the Maratha army completely. The Emperor lost no time in sending congratulations to Saadat Khan and other officers and heaped honours and rewards upon them. All the Mughal commanders including the Wazir and the Mir Bakhshi and also Muhammad Khan Bangash, formed an extensive camp near Mathura and started joyous festivities in honour of their victory, entirely oblivious of the coming storm.

Bajirao was at this time in Bundelkhand watching the course of events and meditating upon the best course of undeceiving the Emperor and exposing the boast of his vain satellites. He gathered accurate information of the Mughal concentration, of the routes leading to Delhi and the defences of the capital. In this respect his agents Dhondo Govind and Hingne imparted to him valuable hints and suggestions. What followed has been well summarized in the long account written by Bajirao himself to his brother from Jaipur on 5th April 1737.[10]

"Saadat Khan sent a false report to the Emperor that he had routed the main Maratha army, slaughtered two thousand and drowned another two thousand in the Jamuna. He also reported that Malharji Holkar and Vithoji Bule were killed and that he had thus repelled the so-called furious onslaught of Bajirao. The Emperor was so highly gratified with this news that he sent him hearty congratulations with dresses, and a pearl necklace, elephants and other gifts. My agent Dhondo Govind sent me frequent messages with correct news of these transactions at the Emperor's Court. You know how hollow are the professions of these Mughal grandees. I, therefore, decided to teach the Emperor a wholesome lesson by letting him know that Holkar and Bule were still alive. Two ways were open to me, to attack Saadat Khan and destroy him ; or fall upon Delhi itself and burn its outlying parts. But Saadat Khan would not venture out from Agra. So I took the latter course. Avoiding the main Mughal concentration, I advanced through the Mewati territory while Khan Dauran and Bangash marched towards Agra and joined Saadat Khan on 23rd March. Our agent Dhondo Govind was expelled from their camp as a supposed mischief-maker. He came and joined me.

"In two long marches I reached Delhi on 28, and encamped outside the city. I gave up the idea of setting fire to

10. *Brahmendra Charita*—No. 7.

the adjoining suburbs, considering it a sacrilege to commit such a wanton outrage upon the ancient city. March 29 happened to be the day of Rama's birth, for which celebrations were going on in the city when we created a sensation by falling upon the crowds and carrying away some light plunder. This was enough to strike terror. The news reached the Emperor who on 30th March sent his agent to me, with a request that I should send back Dhondo Govind. I sent word saying that an escort may be sent for Dhondo Govind's safe journey through the infuriated crowds of the city. In the meanwhile to allay the scare created by our presence, we withdrew to a position away from the city and formed our camp at the Jhil Lake. As we started back a force of about 8,000 was despatched by the Emperor to drive us away. Our Sardars, Holkar, Sindia and the Pawar brothers, at once faced them gallantly and inflicted upon them a crushing defeat. A dozen Mughal officers were killed and Mir Hassan Koka was wounded. Several others fled away to save their lives. Our own loss was insignificant. After repairing to the Jhil Lake, we discovered in the afternoon that the Wazir Qamr-ud-din Khan was coming to face us. We at once attacked him, but it soon became dark and we were compelled to retire. On Thursday 31st March we received news that all the combined Mughal army was coming upon us. In order to draw them away and attack them piecemeal we marched towards Rewari and Kotputli, and now we hear the Emperor has called them all back. Jaysinh has written to me requesting me not to molest his territory. We are now proceeding towards Gwalior for collecting arrears : if the Mughals pursue, we are quite equal to the task of facing and destroying them. We have practically desolated the environs of Delhi. If Nizam-ul-mulk tries to cross the Narmada and come to the help of the Emperor, you must prevent him and hold him in check. Such is the outcome of this great offensive." Bajirao considered this chastisement sufficient and retraced his steps towards the Deccan before the rainy season.

Bajirao received unbounded congratulatiomen from his friends and co-workers for this phenomenal dash. "The princes of Rajputana now gave up their vacillation and tried to make friendly approaches to him in order to gain his favour," writes Vyankaji Ram from Jaipur. "The raja", continues the agent "has sent Jawahar Sinh with Rs. 5,000 cash in lieu of a feast for you and has expressed through him his utmost gratification at the brotherly affection which you have exhibited towards him. I read to him every word of your letter, after which he replied "We are the Peshwa's loyal servants: all our raj is his: it behoves him to take care of us in every possible way. His revered mother has given us her blessings and he must continue to do the same."

While Bajirao was in the north, the Emperor sent Muhammad Khan Bangash hurriedly to Jaipur to inspect the raja's military preparations and report what chance there was for a combined and bold stand against the Peshwa. Shahu on the other hand felt extremely nervous at the conflicting reports that reached him from the north and wrote to Bajirao urgent letters calling him back, lest his rashness should launch him into ruin, inflicting permanent harm upon the Maratha cause. He wrote, "a servant of unparalleled capacity like you is a great asset for us. You must not seek a personal interview with the Emperor. The Nizam and other grandees, we are informed, are not at all friendly towards you. They are all bent upon your ruin. So please take the utmost care and caution and send us prompt news of your immediate plans."[11]

7. Nizam humbled at Bhopal.—The two and a half years from the beginning of 1736 may be rightly styled as a period of Mughal-Maratha war, in which Bajirao handled the operations in the north and his brother did the same in the south, helped by Avji Kavde, Raghuji Bhosle, Vyankatrao Ghorpade and others, whose names frequently appear in the documents of the day. The climax was reached in 1738 when Bajirao and Nizam-ul-mulk came face to face for a final trial of strength. The Emperor, terrorized by Bajirao's raid of the summer of 1737, sent repeated and urgent calls to Nizam-ul-mulk to repair to Delhi and stop the Maratha nuisance. Since the secret understanding arrived at during their meeting of December 1732 at Rohe-Rameshwar, Bajirao and Nizam-

11. *Shahu's autograph letter*, author's vol. on Bajirao, p. 308.

ul-mulk had both faithfully kept their word and not crossed each other's path in any flagrant manner. Even now when summoned by the Emperor, the Nizam intimated to Bajirao that his object in going to Delhi was to remove the taint that had long attached to his own name as being the first rebel to assert independence of the central authority. So leaving his dominions in the spring of 1737, he reached Sironj on 10th May and found Bajirao camping in the vicinity for several days on his return journey to the south after devastating the environs of Delhi. It was indecorous for them to remain utterly indifferent being in such close proximity; an intermediary was discovered in the pliant Pilaji Jadhav, who visited Nizam-ul-mulk on behalf of Bajirao on 28th May and offered him the formal customary greetings, though one may be sure, Pilaji was deputed to get some inkling of Nizam-ul-mulk's future plans. The latter was shrewd enough to conceal his real intentions by a grant of lavish presents. But silence was more eloquent and Bajirao was not slow to take the hint and prepare immediately for the impending contest.

In Malwa Nizam-ul-mulk was first occupied in exacting obedience from the local chiefs who had deserted to the Marathas since the battle of Amjhera. It is also possible that Bajirao purposely avoided an open encounter in that hot season, his troops being already worn out by the arduous campaign of several months and impatient to reach their houses before the commencement of the rains and to deposit safely the booty they had collected. From Sironj Nizam-ul-mulk proceeded to Delhi to mature his plans. Heavy clouds began to gather on the political horizon. Once more was Nizam-ul-mulk received in the imperial capital with great but feigned jubilation. The Emperor accorded him a hearty welcome and so did the whole Court. Nizam-ul-mulk made his humble homage to the Emperor and received in return unprecedented courtesy and lavish honours. The latter bestowed on him his own robe and *sirpao* with the title of Asaf-Jah, the highest among the Mughal nobility, and sent him choice dishes from his own kitchen every day, during the period of his stay. Writes Vyankaji Ram from Delhi on 10th August,—

"Nizam-ul-mulk has demanded from the Emperor the government of the five Subahs in addition to a crore of cash to finance his preparations, for removing the Maratha pest from north India. The Emperor has freely granted him all he asked for. His son Ghazi-ud-din has been given the Subahs of Agra and Malwa. His son Nasir Jang has been commanded to prevent Maratha succours coming into Malwa from the Deccan. The three Subahs of Allahabad, Ajmere and Gujarat are to be bestowed on the nominees of the Nizam." Bajirao rightly interpreted the import of these events as reported by his trusted agent and prepared to oppose the Mughals.

Well equipped with his requirements in every detail Nizam-ul-mulk left Delhi in October with thirty thousand select troops, a powerful park of artillery and full authority to act in expelling the Marathas from Bundelkhand and Malwa. He took the easier route to the south crossing the Jumna into the Doab near Agra and recrossing it into Bundelkhand near Kalpi. The Peshwa had already a war on his hands at the time against the Portuguese in north Konkan : but the two brothers rose equal to the occasion and faced a second war of a more gigantic proportion in Malwa. Never was such an anxious time experienced before by Maratha warriors and their helpmates. Never since Aurangzeb's days was such a supreme co-operative effort put forth against the Marathas by the Mughal imperialists. The prospect was appalling even for the stoic equanimity of Shahu, who held frequent and serious deliberations with his Peshwa at Satara and who had specially invited to his presence Ranoji, Malharrao and other responsible leaders from the north for a full consultation. Bajirao enthusiastically took up the challenge and cheered up his sovereign's drooping spirits. The die was cast. On the auspicious day of 15 October Bajirao took his departure for the north along with his master's blessings and the best wishes of his nation, now united as never before.

In the meantime Nasir Jang, a worthy son of a worthy father, had not been idle. He raised fresh levies for use in Malwa and spent lavishly in preparations to crush the Marathas between two pincers, himself moving from the south and his father from the north. Bajirao, foreseeing the game, stationed his brother Chimnaji Appa at Varangaum on the Tapti with instructions to prevent Nasir Jang from proceeding beyond Burhanpur. Chimnaji performed this duty excellently.

Some other tried Maratha chiefs such as Raghuji Bhosle, Damaji Gaikwad and Avji Kavde faithfully supported Bajirao's plans and unflinchingly carried out the duties assigned to them.

Bajirao himself crossed the Narmada early in December with a huge force and keeping his communications under strict control through agents and spies well posted in different directions to report the enemy's moves, watched for an opportunity to push the Mughals by his guerilla tactics into an untenable position. It was the momentous struggle of his life. Before his arrival in Malwa Nizam-ul-mulk had reduced Bundelkhand and arranged his camp with strict attention to compactness and supervision. From the beginning of December the Maratha bands started hovering about the Mughal camp and harassing them from a distance, keeping well out of the range of their artillery. The advanced Maratha troops gradually drove the Mughals towards the south into Bajirao's net, as soon as he had arrived on the tableland of Malwa. The Maratha tactics soon proved effective and the Nizam realized early enough that he could not pursue the Marathas and retaliate swiftly with his huge camp, whose necessaries of life came to be rapidly cut off. He, therefore, decided to find shelter in a well fortified place wherein he could keep his army secure and deal piecemeal with the various Maratha bands.

He was coming towards Bajirao, and as he neared Bhopal he took shelter in that fortified town without first assuring himself of plentiful provisions and remained fully entrenched. This was just the trap Bajirao was trying his utmost to drive his adversary into. Bajirao besieged the Mughals in that small walled place and stopped provisions reaching them from outside. The siege commenced on 14th December and in less than a week's time the Mughals came to an extremity for want of food. Artillery alone served them well and kept the Marathas out of the range of their fire. Nizam-ul-mulk soon found his position intolerable and tried to move out with his whole camp under the shelter of his guns. But he could hardly travel more than four or five miles a day. Thus nearly a fortnight elapsed under extreme pressure, and when he learned that his longed for relief under his son had not even reached

Burhanpur, he was overwhelmed with despair and in agony of heart sent for Anandrao Sumant, his friend in the Maratha camp, and through him begged Bajirao for terms of peace. Bajirao refused to negotiate through the Sumant whom he did not trust and offered to send instead his own agents Pilaji Jadhav, Baji Bhivrao and Baburao Malhar. In the meantime Jaysinh's minister Ayamall arrived on behalf of the Nizam with Saiyad Lashkar Khan and other agents to see Bajirao and arrange terms of peace. They urged that if Bajirao would release the Nizam from the present difficult position, without inflicting any disgrace on him, the Nizam would grant any compensation that would be demanded. After long and vexatious conferences, Nizam-ul-mulk affixed his signature to the following terms on 7th January 1738 at Doraha Sarai about 61 miles north of Sironj :

1. Nizam-ul-mulk solemnly undertook to grant the Marathas a formal cession of Malwa under the imperial seal ;
2. To deliver over to them all the territory between the Narmada and the Jamuna ; and
3. To pay 50 lacs in cash from the imperial treasury by way of expenses to the Marathas.

All the chiefs and jagirdars within the coded region who had formerly accepted Maratha suzerainty but who had during the recent campaign deserted to the Nizam, were sent back by him and received in open Darbar by the Peshwa where they took an oath of loyalty to him.

Thus once more did Bajirao show his phenomenal magnanimity by staying his hand and desisting from proceeding to extremities towards an enemy, who had more than once broken his plighted word and who was out to crush the Marathas finally. This was one more instance of the Chhatrapati's policy towards the Emperor and his provincial governors. They were not to be extirpated but to be supported in their positions. Indeed, the Marathas had at this time a splendid opportunity of inflicting a crushing blow upon Nizam-ul-mulk, but they allowed him to escape lightly, thus conforming to their traditional policy of "live and let live." Writes Bajirao to his brother, "Fortified as the Nawab was with a strong artillery and with the Bundella and Rajput princes as his staunch allies, I accepted your advice and agreed to much lower terms than could have been exacted. You can realize what a severe mortification it must have been to Asaf Jah to sign a document with his own hand parting with Malwa and the rights therein of Chauth and Sardeshmukhi, of which he never allowed even a mere mention till then. It was the height of shame for him to be compelled to yield these. Even this much success is the result of the blessings we have secured both from our revered Chhatrapati and our late parent. The highest noble of the Mughal Empire has been brought to his knees. He has taken sacred oaths on the Koran to abide by the terms agreed upon."

Read between the lines, this letter clearly reveals the policy of Shahu, which was communicated to Bajirao through the mediation of his brother. Bhopal was thus the last and the highest triumph of Bajirao, glorious on account of the very moderation displayed by him in the moment of victory. After the treaty was signed, every facility was allowed to the Mughals to depart without molestation, but Bajirao spent a few months in the north waiting for a formal ratification of the terms by the Emperor.[12] When the negotiations were completed, Bajirao left the vicinity of Bhopal and proceeded to Kota whence he exacted ten lacs of tribute and returned to Poona in July to the immense gratification of Shahu and the nation. The credit of the successful campaign is equally due to Chimnaji Appa who had so intelligently supported his brother when absent in the north.

12. Before ratifying the treaty the Peshwa and the Nizam must have exchanged formal ceremonial visits at this time. If so, this would be the seventh but unrecorded visit between them. See note 4 page 144.

CHRONOLOGY

CHAPTER VII

1730, January 11	First mention of Mastani at Poona.
„ July 5	Sadashivrao Bhau born.
1732, April	Count of Sandomille Portuguese Governor of Goa.
1734,	Sandomille starts fortifications of Thana.
1734, Aug. 18	Raghunathrao born.
1734	Shamsher Bahadur born to Mastani.
1735, Feb. 4—April 3	Bajirao at Kolaba, divides Angrian estate into two portions between Sambhaji and Manaji.
1737 Summer	War opened against the Portuguese.
1737, March 27	Chimnaji Appa captures Thana, Dharavi and other places.
1738	Nadir Shah occupies Kabul.
1738,Nov. 27	Pedro de Mello killed at Thana.
1738, December 29	Battle of Tarapore.
1739, January 9	Mahim and other places captured.
1739, January 12	Vyankatrao Ghorpade attacks Goa, the Portuguese heart.
1739, January 12	Nadir Shah captures Lahore.
1739, January 18	Emperor leaves Delhi to face Nadir Shah.
1739, February 13	Nadir Shah defeats the Emperor near Karnal, keeps him under arrest.
1739, March 7	Nadir Shah arrives at Delhi.
1739, March 9	Saadat Khan takes poison, dies.
1739, April	Nadir Shah plunders Delhi and the environs.
1739, April 25	Nadir Shah calls upon Indian potentates to support the Emperor.
1739, April 27	Goa accepts Maratha terms of peace and saves itself.
1739, May 1	Nadir Shah leaves Delhi for home.
1739, May 1	Marathas attack Bassein violently.

1739, May 5	Bassein surrenders, peace concluded.
1739, May 31	Shahu asks Bajirao to defend the Emperor.
1739, May 12 to July 14	Capt. Gordon's mission to Satara.
1739, June	English envoy Inchbird meets Chimnaji Appa at Thana, concludes a friendly agreement.
1739, December	Mastani kept under confinement at Poona. Nasir Jang invades Maratha territory on the Godavari.
1740, Jan.—Feb.	Bajirao and Chimnaji rout Nasir Jang, and besiege him at Aurangabad.
1740, January 14	Inchbird meets Bajirao near Paithan and concludes a friendly understanding.
1740, February 4	Raghunath Rao's thread ceremony.
1740, February 7	Sadashivrao married to Umabai.
1740, February 17	Nasir Jang accepts Maratha terms, treaty of Mungi-Shevgaon.
1740, March 12	Chimnaji Appa meets Nasir Jang.
1740, April 28	Bajirao dies at Raver Khedi.
1740, Sep. 7	Treaty with the English ratified by Balaji.
1740, Sep. 7	Marathas capture Chaul.
1742, January 12	Sambhaji Angria dies.

CHAPTER VII

BAJIRAO'S LAST PHASE

[1739—1740]

1. Nadir Shah's invasion, Hindu Sovereignty ?
2. War upon the Portuguese, Capture of Bassein.
3. Repercussions in Bombay.
4. Minor episodes, the Angrias.
5. The romance of Mastani.
6. Nasir Jang routed.
7. Sudden death.
8. Bajirao's character.

1. Nadir Shah's invasion, Hindu Sovereignty ?— The invasion of Nadir Shah and its devastating effect upon the Mughal Empire are too well-known to require any elaborate treatment here. How the affair reacted upon the general trend of Maratha history is our concern. Nizam-ul-mulk returned to Delhi after his discomfiture at Bhopal. What he reported to the Emperor about his doings we have no means of knowing, but that he took no pains to fulfil his promise to Bajirao and obtain from the Emperor a full ratification of the terms of the agreement of Doraha Sarai, is perfectly clear. In December 1738 the Maratha envoy Baburao Malhar reported from Delhi, " I had an interview with the Emperor who has exchanged solemn oaths of friendship with Nizam-ul-mulk. Disconcerting news conveying Nadir Shah's threats on account of some frontier disputes, has disturbed the peaceful atmosphere of the Court of Delhi. Rumour has it that Saadat Khan and Nizam-ul-mulk have conducted treacherous underhand parleys with Nadir Shah, instead of supporting the Emperor in the measures that he was concerting to meet the danger." It is clear at any rate if these two most prominent nobles of the Mughal Court had wholeheartedly exerted themselves in resisting Nadir Shah's onslaught, by fully co-operating with the Emperor, the danger would certainly have been averted. The ministers in power made light of the threat from Persia and tried to seek selfish ends rather than undergo the least sacrifice for the imperial cause. These nobles all severally detested the Marathas and possibly conceived the idea of putting them down with the welcome aid of Nadir Shah when he would arrive. There was a widespread belief that the implacable invader undertook the invasion with the sole object of saving the Mughal power from the aggressive Marathas.

Nadir Shah's intentions had been well-known at Delhi for a year in advance. He occupied Kabul in 1738, and at once sent his agents to the Emperor at Delhi, calling upon him to suppress the disturbances of the border tribes who had been ravaging his territory. No notice was taken of these complaints and Nadir Shah started from Kabul in November and after capturing Peshawar and Attock approached Lahore early in January 1739. What was Nizam-ul-mulk doing all this time, if he had sincerely repented, as he alleged, of his rebellious conduct towards the Emperor since 1723? Zakaria Khan the able governor of Lahore tried his utmost to keep away the invader, but was overpowered and Lahore was lost on January 12. There was no stir at Delhi yet. On 18th January Muhammad Shah left Delhi with all his forces and nobles to oppose him. He formed a huge camp at Karnal and with the excellent equipment and fighting material that he possessed, could have easily put down the invader, if he had the determination, grit and above all the unity of command and counsel. Disunity and intrigue, particularly among the principal nobles, were the bane of the Mughal Court and it collapsed like a house of cards. Nadir Shah reached Sarhind on 5th February. On 13th February the imperialists advanced from their base at Karnal and attacked the Persians, but were easily repulsed with great slaughter. Khan Dauran the Mir Bakhshi received mortal wounds and died two days after. Saadat Khan was wounded and captured. Nizam-ul-mulk remained vacillating to the last, and took no part in the actual operations, although everybody looked up to him for guidance as the most sober and experienced grandee of the Empire.

Nadir Shah contrived to obtain useful information by secret personal talks with the captive Saadat Khan about the wealth of Delhi, with a view to satisfying his inordinate greed, which was the principal object of his undertaking, like his great predecessor, Mahmud of Ghazni. Saadat Khan pointed to Nizam-ul-mulk as the custodian of imperial affairs. Thereupon Nadir Shah summoned Nizam-ul-mulk to his camp and asked him how it was that " with such consummate counsellors as you about the Emperor's person, the Marathas could not be driven out?" He replied, "I have no voice in the matter. The Emperor is guided by young inexperienced men; that is why I had to carve out an independent field for myself in the Deccan." It was then agreed to between Nadir Shah and the Nizam that the former should receive Rs. 50 lakhs and retire without creating trouble. The next day Nadir Shah invited the Emperor to his camp for dinner. Upon his return the Emperor learned that Khan Dauran had expired and appointed Nizam-ul-mulk to the post of Mir Bakhshi a position to which Saadat Khan was aspiring. The latter felt mortally disappointed and commenced his intrigues. He represented to Nadir Shah why he should not retire with only a paltry sum of 50 lacs, whereas, if he proceeded to Delhi, he could easily obtain twenty crores. Saadat Khan added, "there is none with the Emperor who can oppose him except the Nizam, but he is a mere cheat and a philosopher." Nadir Shah was not slow to realize the force of this suggestion; he besieged the Mughal camp in order to starve it out, summoned the Nizam for a visit and kept him under arrest, demanding twenty crores as the price of his release. Thereafter Nadir Shah kept the Emperor himself under confinement and plundered his whole camp.

Baburao Malhar, the Maratha envoy at the Court, fled for safety to Jaipur. He writes, "Nizam-ul-mulk seeking his own selfish ends, contrived to pay a visit to Nadir Shah and gain his favour." Thereupon Nadir Shah made captives of the Emperor, Qamruddin Khan and Nizam ul mulk, and proceeding to Delhi he took possession of the capital where he arrived on 7th March. He immediately called upon Saadat Khan to procure for him the 20 crores he had promised, on pain of death. As Saadat Khan could not face the situation, he put an end to his life by swallowing poison.[1] On 10th March Nadir Shah occupied the Mughal throne and proclaimed himself Emperor. Immediately after he began to perpetrate those atrocities upon the hapless populace of Delhi which have continued fresh in Indian memory. From 9th March to 1st

1. Irvine II—356. An estimate of Nadir Shah's plunder is mentioned as three and three-quarters crores in *Hingne Daftar* I. 16.

May men of all grades of society suffered indescribable cruelty, hardship and public humiliation. Instead of 20 crores, it is said, Nadir Shah amassed very nearly a hundred crores worth in cash and goods, including the Peacock Throne of Delhi constructed by Shah Jahan and the famous diamond Kohi-noor, all of which he carried back to Persia.

Competent Maratha agents and observers of events posted throughout northern India sent detailed accounts to Maharashtra, to Bajirao, Shahu and other leaders of the Maratha State, with suggestions each in his own way, as to the course they should adopt in the future. The Hingnes and Baburao Malhar sent their own advice. Jaysinh had stationed his own agent Kriparam at Delhi. Pilaji Jadhav was posted by Bajirao in Malwa to prevent further advance of Nadir Shah. Anandrao Sumant remained with Nizam-ul-mulk at Delhi watching the course of events. All contemporary reports from Delhi and Rajputana agree that there was unprecedented anarchy throughout northern India with no ruler who could impose his will upon the distracted land then entirely filled with stupefaction, with every soul crying out, "What next?" Some called upon Bajirao to come forth boldly and drive away the invader. Others advised a more cautious policy, waiting for eventualities and stepping in at an opportune moment. While more fanatical extremists were not wanting who advised immediate fulfilment of the long delayed dream of placing a Hindu monarch on the vacant throne of Delhi. But all eyes turned to Bajirao, the only man of nerve for the moment, who could face the situation valiantly and command the confidence of all.

At heart Jaysinh and Bajirao were friends and acted in concert, being now happily relieved of the several mischievous elements about the Emperor's person. The Emperor in his distress peremptorily summoned Jaysinh to come to his aid : but Jaysinh did not move from his home. On the contrary he sent congratulations to Nadir Shah by means of courteous letters. Dhondo Govind, a shrewd observer of events, wrote to Bajirao from Delhi advising him to station himself in Malwa, fully prepared for a conflict, adding "Nadir Shah is no God that he could destroy the earth. He possesses sense enough and knows his business. He will not wish to break with you, but will effect a friendly understanding when he knows you are strong enough to oppose him. Please let us have directions as to how we should act. You must first assert your power and then follow it with a soft and sweet attitude. I don't expect actual hostilities to break out between him and you. Important results are often obtained by a mere show of strength and sternness. Jaysinh and yourself aided by the Bundela chiefs will be quite a strong Hindu front which Providence in its wisdom will surely crown with success. Jaysinh is anxiously waiting for your arrival to take the lead. Nizam-ul-mulk is playing a mischievous game. Some of his spies who were found roving about prying into Jaysinh's secret counsels, were captured by him. They confessed they were deputed by Nizam-ul-mulk. They were discharged with their noses and ears cut. When such a powerful noble as Nizam-ul-mulk behaves so treacherously towards his master, how can you expect Nadir Shah to return quietly without punishing the Hindus? All voices agree that the two nobles Nizam-ul-mulk and Saadat Khan alone induced Nadir Shah to undertake the invasion of India. The latter has met the fate he deserved. The former still lives, but lives a life worse than death. He is forced to ride a mule, while proceeding to pay his respects to Nadir Shah. Victory at this moment crowns the Peshwa alone. Many here desire that the Rana of Udaipur should be seated on the throne of Delhi and made Emperor of the Hindus. The northern Rajas are anxiously expecting the Peshwa's arrival : a momentous change appears to be in sight. The world is going to rack and ruin. Let us face the situation boldly."[2]

In the midst of this confusing predicament Shahu alone kept his vision clear and exercised the final voice on the strength of his power. At his instance the Maratha Court and the nation in general did not feel themselves competent to undertake the risk of sustaining a Hindu Emperor at Delhi. Shahu and his Peshwa were not prepared to provoke another contest at a time when they were already involved in a deadly struggle

2. This long letter supplies valuable contemporary evidence not only on the momentous event of Nadir Shah's invasion, but on the relative estimate of the two principal characters acting on the stage of history—Bajirao and Nizam-ul-mulk. Ait. Charcha 4.

with the Portuguese on the west coast. The fall of Bassein and the departure of Nadir Shah from India were synchronous; and then Bajirao following the advice of Pilaji Jadhav prepared immediately to go to the north, a course which Shahu himself dictated, remembering the solemn promise he had made to the dying Emperor Aurangzeb, that he would hasten to the rescue of the Empire whenever it was threatened by an invader from outside. The opportune moment had arrived for Shahu to make his plighted word good. When Bajirao reached Burhanpur he received advices from Delhi that Nadir Shah had departed for his native land, having restored Muhammad Shah to the throne of Delhi and issued emphatic commands to the Indian potentates to render obedience to him.

Shahu reposed implicit faith in Bajirao. He had previously issued orders that "all should obey Bajirao faithfully and should do nothing to disturb his temper."[3] When questioned about creating a Hindu monarchy at Delhi he issued the following clear warning on 31st May 1739, that is just about the time that Bajirao was proceeding to the north. Purandare communicates to him Shahu's sentiments :—

"God has helped Muhammad Shah to regain the imperial position which he had lost, and now that Nadir Shah has gone, the question arises what attitude the Marathas should adopt towards the Mughal Emperor. In this respect His Highness the Maharaja Chhatrapati wishes to impress upon you the following line of policy, viz., that it should be our duty to resuscitate the falling Mughal Empire; that the Chhatrapati, as you are already aware, does not aspire to secure the imperial position for himself; that he considers it a higher merit to renovate an old dilapidated edifice than to build a new one. If we attempt the other course (of aggression), it would involve us in enmity with all our neighbours, with the consequence that we should be exposed to unnecessary dangers and court a crop of trouble all round. Hence the wisest course for us under the circumstances would be to wholeheartedly support the present regime; secure only the administrative management for ourselves as the Amir-ul-Umra of the State : in that capacity we should collect the revenues of the country, out of

3. P. D. 17 13

which we should recover our expenses for the troops and pay the balance into the imperial treasury. This is the general policy I have been asked by His Highness to impress on you for your guidance." This clear definition of the Maratha aims by Shahu deserves the careful attention of students of Mughal-Marātha relations. Is this not exactly the policy that Clive later adopted in securing the Diwani of Bengal ?

Bajirao fully complied with these commands in his journey to the north, but his task became light when he learnt that Nadir Shah had left India. Bajirao sent written assurances to the Emperor with expressions of loyalty and respect and a present of 101 mohurs. The Emperor returned an equally cordial answer, confirming all former agreements and renewed promises of executing them faithfully. Before leaving India Nadir Shah addressed a circular letter to the rulers of India including the Chhatrapati of Satara and the Peshwa, calling upon them to obey and serve the Emperor of Delhi.[4]

2. **War upon the Portuguese, capture of Bassein.**— The conquest of the island of Salsette[5] and the strong fortress of Bassein from the possession of the Portuguese is one of the most glorious episodes of Maratha history. It receives added importance from the fact that the Marathas proved victorious over a strong foreign naval power adept in the art of sea-fight, and invincible on account of their artillery. The Portuguese held their sway over a few points in a strip of the west coast extending from Goa to Daman, a distance of nearly 400 miles; a few fortified places which they held at intervals served as bulwarks of defence impregnable to any invader using antiquated arms like the spear and the sword.

The Peshwa's ambition to extend Maratha supremacy and protect the Hindu religion is responsible for the friction that existed between them and the Portuguese on the west coast. The religious fanaticism of the Catholics and their persecution of the Hindus embittered their mutual relations and frequent complaints reached the Peshwa from the Hindu in-

4. Kincaid, *History of the Maratha People*, Vol. 2, p. 236 : P. D. 22. 399 and P. D. 15 p. 83 ; Satara Hist. Society, Vol. 2. No. 268.

5. Salsette is the name given to the island extending from the creek of Bandra to that of Bassein, a corruption of Sasasti, 66 villages.

habitants of north Konkan crying for redress. The religious zeal of the Portuguese manifested itself in atrocious persecution of the non-Christian residents in their territory. They demanded tribute from ships plying on the west coast and interfered with the native chiefs in their legitimate spheres. Thus the Portuguese government became a scourge and a terror to the natives of the coastal regions. They forced whole villages to embrace Christianity at the point of the sword. On the death of the head of a family the minor children were taken possession of by the priests and compelled to kiss the cross. The Hindus were forbidden to practise their religious rites and ceremonies. Temples were pulled down and churches raised on their sites. Men of position and standing were falsely accused by the priests and forcibly converted. These methods although lately much softened, had become so intolerable that the Peshwa had to take up arms in defence of his religion.

In 1719 Bajirao's father had reconquered the district of Kalyan and gradually extended his conquest to Jawhar and Ramnagar. During 1730 Pilaji Jadhav carried war into the Portuguese territory. He took Kamba, a Portuguese outpost near Bhivandi. A new Portuguese Governor Count de Sandomille, a man of a strong and stern character arrived from Europe and took charge of the Portuguese possessions in India in April 1732. He continued to hold the office for nine years, and assumed such a high handed irritating attitude towards the Marathas that they were compelled to open immediate hostilities. The two important posts which the Portuguese held in their government of the north were Bassein and Thana, the former already strongly fortified but the latter was vulnerable. Apprehending trouble from the Marathas of Kalyan, the new Viceroy hurriedly started to build a strong fort at Thana, a threat directly aimed at the Maratha possessions of Kalyan and the north Konkan districts, which they could not ignore. Before the fortifications of Thana were completed, the Marathas opened hostilities against that place in the summer of 1737. Chimnaji Appa sent bands of selected men and captured Thana on 26 March. The Marathas quickly completed the fortifications and organized the defence of the place so that it might serve as a strong base for operations against Bassein. Several other places in the island of Salsette surrendered to them in April ; Dharavi was secured in May and Santa Cruz in June. There was, however, no naval action so far.

The citadel of Bassein the main symbol of Portuguese power in this part of the country, resisted all the landward attacks that were launched by the Marathas. A mile and a half in circumference and triangular in shape, the fort had strong stone walls rising to a height of 30 to 40 feet from the ground and about 5 ft. in thickness. Four-sided bastions rose from each corner on which strong artillery was mounted. To the south of the fort ran the Bassein creek, the west was washed by the open sea. The eastern side was bounded by a belt of marshy land overflown by tidal waves, while the north supplied the only land passage for attack. Shankaraji Phadke immediately after the capture of Thana tried to surprise the place but failed with the consequence that the Marathas lost heart, at least during the season of 1737, a critical year for the Maratha fortunes, in which the Mughals had put forth their last supreme effort against the Marathas under the sole command of their veteran leader Nizam-ul-mulk. Chimnaji Appa had thus to attend to two arduous campaigns, Bassein and Bhopal simultaneously. So all action against Bassein came perforce to a standstill during the early months of 1738. The interval, however, was a welcome relief to Chimnaji Appa to some extent, as it afforded him leisure to mature his plans and deliver his final attack with no chance of failure. The return of fair weather at the end of 1738 was availed of and the best and most valiant Maratha leaders and soldiers were directed with singular effect against the fortress of Bassein. Holkar, Sindia, Pawar and other renowned captains of the north were summoned for this heroic effort.

But the Portuguese had not been idle. They fully utilised the interval of Maratha distraction during 1738. Fresh-succours arrived for them from Europe. and they started a great offensive against the Marathas in 1738. Mahadaji Pant Phadke, a daring Maratha captain lost his life in the attempt against Mahim, another Portuguese post and thereby caused a sort of general depression among the Maratha soldiery. So when Chimnaji resumed operations towards the end of 1738, he had to face a serious situation. At the risk of ruining his failing health, Chimnaji proceeded to the theatre of war and started a determined campaign, a life and death struggle regardless of losses. The Portuguese made a last heroic effort to recapture Thana, in which a chance shot from the Maratha garrison killed the valiant Portuguese commander Pedro de Mello, while inspecting the defences from his boat rowing through the creek. This was a portent of coming events to the Portuguese and served to cool their ardour. It at the same time roused the Maratha spirits to an unprecedented height: nor was the lure of pecuniary reward neglected by Chimnaji at this critical moment, as he held plentiful funds collected during several years of profitable expeditions by Bajirao in north India. In the month of December Chimnaji descended into Konkan with his very best commanders and select troops and occupied the marshy regions traversed by the various creeks, examined the terrain and formed concerted plans for simultaneous storming, assigning duties with definite instructions and inculcating care and caution. All conceivable preliminaries and precautions added to a spirit of buoyant hope and pre-vision, alone yielded the desired result. The Portuguese contested every inch of the ground and defended their positions with the courage of desperation, so that even if overcome, they would make victory as costly to the Marathas as possible. Chimnaji was ever on the move like lightning throughout the difficult months from November to June.

The Maratha successes began with the capture of Mahim on 9 January 1739, followed a fortnight after by that of Tarapur and Asheri on 24th. The capture on 6 March of Dharavi a small island at the mouth of the Bassein creek, sealed the fate of that main fortress, as it gave the Marathas a position of vantage for an effective attack.

The stiffness with which Mahim and Tarapur were defended, was only second to that of Bassein. Baji Bhivrao the most trusted lieutenant of the Peshwa, lost his life while storming Tarapur, causing severe pangs to the Peshwa's family: for he was considered one of it. Several others like Ramchandra Hari Patwardhan[6] received more or less serious wounds. Bajirao wrote a comforting letter to Baji Bhivrao's

6. Father of Parshuram Bhau of future history.

mother, in which he significantly mentioned that her son was still living.

By the middle of March most of the Portuguese posts in the region of Bassein had fallen into Maratha hands, so that a last concentrated effort against that stronghold became possible. In order to prevent reinforcements reaching Bassein for its relief, Chimnaji had in the previous year despatched his sister's husband Vyankatrao Ghorpade against Goa, who played his part so splendidly that he could have captured the whole of the Portuguese possessions in that region. But this certainly was not the Maratha aim, and when Bassein fell, Vyankatrao was called back.

Chimnaji himself arrived before Bassein on 7 February and immediately began preparations for storming the place. A passage had to be forced by demolishing the strong stone walls mounted with terrific guns of the best Portuguese make. This passage was possible only on the landward line from the north. Mines were excavated under the foundations of the walls and the workers met with volleys of fire and shot from the garrison. Bombs and combustibles were rained upon the approaching miners, who notwithstanding pushed on with grim determination. The Maratha cannon and mortars silenced the enemy's guns. The siege was relentlessly pressed and at last the Marathas succeeded in springing thirteen mines on the cortines and the bastions.[7] On the fateful morning of 2nd May the Maratha drums beat a loud peal, the mines were ignited and an explosion blew up the northern tower, making wide breaches through which heroic Maratha bands quickly rushed in, but were thrown into confusion by some of the mines catching fire late. But they pressed on recklessly against the opposing defenders : a terrible carnage in a hand to hand fight ensued. Another big mine was sprung the next day which made a fresh breach for Maratha parties who quickly made a lodgment in the bastions. This proved the end.

The final engagement lasted for two days. Eight hundred of the Portuguese officers and men had been killed : their ammunition was exhausted and the survivors lost all hope of further defence. On 4th May they hoisted the white flag and

7. *Forrest's Selections, Mar. Series*, Vol. I, p. 39.

a Portuguese officer met Chimnaji Appa for arranging terms of surrender. The capitulations were signed on 5th and a week was allowed for the evacuation.

Towards a fallen foe generosity was an invariable policy of the Maratha chiefs, and it was well exhibited in the present instance. Chimnaji in this affair raised his reputation for valour and magnanimity by granting most honourable terms to the Portuguese. The remaining garrison was allowed to depart unmolested with all their families and belongings and with full military honours. War vessels in the harbour were allowed to remove the artillery without molestation and full religious liberty for practising one's religion was proclaimed throughout the district of north Konkan, which was indeed the main purpose of the war. An exchange of prisoners was also satisfactorily effected and all Portuguese churches were granted full liberty of worship and prayer according to Christian rites.

3. **Repercussions in Bombay.**—The campaign of Bassein lasting over two years proved a resounding success for the Marathas in general and the crowning glory of the Peshwa and his brother in particular. The Marathas took possession of the place on 12th May and on the auspicious day of 23rd the ochre-coloured Maratha flag was ceremoniously unfurled from the ramparts of Bassein, with a proclamation of having annexed the mighty fortress and the province to the Maratha dominions. The gains and losses of both the combatants can be judged with tolerable accuracy. The Portuguese power, which had flourished and overawed the Indian coastal regions in the sphere of commerce and religion for two centuries, was practically destroyed and came to be circumscribed to two or three small spots, Goa, Daman and Div. Soon after the loss of Bassein, Chaul and Korlai, two small Portuguese possessions near Alibag came into Maratha possession through the mediation of the English.

After finishing the necessary adjustments required by the late war, Chimnaji Appa and Vyankatrao Ghorpade returned from Bassein and Goa respectively, to Satara by the end of June 1739, and were both heartily complimented upon their success and profusely rewarded by the Chhatrapati for the victorious conclusion of an anxious and arduous war.

An immediate effect of the conquest of Bassein was the alarm that the English settlement of Bombay received from the Maratha power being planted in its neighbourhood with a fine naval arsenal. The English in their anxiety to remove all chance of offensive Maratha plans against Bombay, sent Captain Inchbird to conciliate Chimnaji Appa, while he was occupied at Bassein in settling its administrative affairs. Inchbird and Chimnaji met in June 1739 and arranged a general treaty of peace and friendship in their mutual interest. But not satisfied with this particular settlement, the English Authorities of Bombay wishing to gauge the inherent strength of the Maratha power, particularly the exact relations of the Chhatrapati and the Peshwa, sent another mission to the authorities at Satara under Capt. Gordon with particular instructions to find out what chance there was of possible antagonism between the King and his Peshwa. Gordon left Bombay on 12th May, visited Shahu on 8th June, remained there till the 30th of that month and returned to Bombay on 14th July. He carried with him presents for Shahu and his courtiers, whom he severally interviewed and gathered minute information of the strength and weakness of the central Maratha Government, for which he was specially deputed. He reported his impressions that Bajirao alone was all powerful and that there was no likelihood of his being dislodged from power.

The Bombay authorities then realized that it was necessary in their own interest to conciliate Bajirao and with this view they deputed Capt. Inchbird to see Bajirao and arrange affairs with him. Inchbird left Bombay towards the end of 1739 and having learnt at Poona that Bajirao was touring outside, he proceeded towards him and saw him near Paithan on the Godavari on January 14, 1740. A treaty of peace and friendship was discussed and arranged. It dealt mainly with the offshoots of the late Maratha war against the Portuguese. The actual ratification of this treaty of 8 articles was executed by the next Peshwa Nanasaheb on 7th September 1740, as Bajirao had died on 28th April. Chaul or Revdanda came into Maratha possession as a result of this treaty and was subsequently dismantled by them. These transactions between the English and the Marathas now only possess a historical interest in point of the relative strength of the two powers.

4. **Minor episodes, the Angrias.**—The author's aim has been to deal only with the main points of Bajirao's singular career and not to study in detail every incident of his life of diversified activity, an adequate treatment of which would require a very much larger volume. A large number of capable leaders whether acting with or against Bajirao contributed in no small measure to the history of the period, and they deserve some notice. One was the founder of the principality of Nagpur, Raghuji Bhosle, whose uncle Kanhoji and Kanhoji's father Parsoji had been the first to espouse Shahu's cause when he returned from the Mughal camp after Aurangzeb's death. When soon afterwards Shahu appointed Balaji Vishvanath to be his Peshwa and practically surrendered all his powers to him, it came to be the Peshwa's duty to bring about uniformity of plan and action and co-ordination of effort among the various scattered leaders and chiefs acting in different localities on behalf of Shahu. These Bhosles, like the Dabhades and the Angrias began to resent the controlling authority exercised on them by the Peshwa, as they were all direct creations of the Chhatrapati and in no way indebted to the Peshwa for their positions. The Peshwas too by way of counterpoise raised to prominence in the state business their own trustworthy helpmates such as the Sindias and the Holkars. With all their valour and capacity the Marathas as a race have always betrayed a separatist tendency which can brook no central control. Concerted action, the very soul of a powerful government, is a rare phenomenon in Maratha history. This inherent weakness clearly explains why the Marathas failed to build a permanent empire over this vast continent. Much of Bajirao's energy came to be wasted in keeping under control these recalcitrant elements at home. The civil war between Balaji Vishvanath and Chandrasen Jadhav, followed by a similar war between Bajirao and Trimbakrao Dabhade and later the third Peshwa's vindictive operations against Tulaji Angria, are all typical illustrations of the delicate domestic politics the Peshwas had to manage, while at the same time they were seriously occupied with expanding the Maratha power into distant provinces outside. Raghuji Bhosle, however, knew his limitations and managed to restrain his jealousy without allowing it to provoke a rupture with Bajirao. The two kept

up an attitude of mutual respect and dignity and often also co-operated in their undertakings.

The Angrias were the wardens of the west coast which they guarded with the help of the Maratha fleet. Kanhoji and his son Sekhoji were both influential members of the Maratha government and employed the navy so dexterously that they were feared and respected by the foreign powers planted on the western coast. After Sekhoji's death his two brothers Sambhaji and Manaji found it impossible to agree to a peaceful succession. Bajirao being called upon by Shahu to settle the dispute went to Kolaba, examined the situation patiently and as the conflicting claims of the two brothers could not be reconciled, he divided the Angrian estate into two sections, the larger extending from Suvarnadurg to Vijayadurg was allotted to Sambhaji with the title of Sarkhel : the northern portion was given to Manaji with his headquarters at Kolaba and the title of Wazarat-Maab. This division certainly weakened the strength of the Maratha navy and perpetuated the family jealousy instead of ending it. The two brothers started an open war, of which the English and the Portuguese were not slow to take advantage. The affair of the Angrias proved a perpetual sore in the Maratha polity, which the death of Sambhaji on 12th January 1742 did not heal. Sambhaji's brother Tulaji proved more intractable to the next Peshwa, who put him down with the help of the English navy, a course, which in the end proved ruinous to Maratha national interests.

Thus, it should be realized that from the beginning all was not well with the internal management of the Maratha power, and although outwardly it expanded rapidly, it contained insidious germs of decay to which it soon fell a prey. The root cause can certainly be traced to Shahu's softness of heart which grew with his age. He hardly ever moved out of his groove round about Satara. Only once did he make bold to wipe the stigma by personally undertaking a child's play which is known as the Miraj campaign for the conquest of that outpost, a remnant of the old Mughal power almost bordering on the Maratha capital. After two years slow campaigning the place was captured on 3rd October 1739. But this small achievement did not in any way restore Shahu's prestige in the State, beyond giving him an opportunity of visiting some holy places like Pandharpur. The Peshwas managed to entrust Miraj to their own partizan, the Patwardhans whose family still continues to hold it through many vicissitudes of fortune.

Students of history will note how the year 1739 was crowded with events of outstanding importance to the fortunes of the Maratha raj. Nadir Shah convulsed India, the expulsion of the Portuguese from north Konkan and the weakness of the Angrian house improved the chances of the English for a slow rise in which the missions of Inchbird and Gordon served as the first cautious feeling of the ground. But nobody dreamt that the heroic Peshwa to whose phenomenal career the rapid expansion of Maratha power was mainly due, would be prematurely cut off. The mystery of his unexpected death is heightened by a domestic affair of a romantic character to which we must now advert.

5. **The romance of Mastani.**—It is now well-known that in the midst of his glowing successes on every side, all was not well in Bajirao's family. His infatuation for a Muslim dancing girl named Mastani since 1730, impaired his reputation in orthodox society, including his nearest kith and kin. The origin of Mastani is shrouded in obscurity. Tradition makes her the offspring of a Hindu father and a Muhammadan mother, but highly accomplished and trained in the cultivated arts of blandishment. The first mention of her name in authentic papers occurs in the accounts of the marriage ceremony of Bajirao's eldest son Nanasaheb which took place on 11th January 1730. In the same year Bajirao built his Shaniwar palace in Poona and later added to it a portion named after his ladylove. In 1734 she bore him a son who was named Shamsher Bahadur. *Tarikh-i-Muhammadshahi* mentions that "she was a Kanchani (a dancing girl) skilled in riding and handling the sword and spear. She always accompanied Bajirao in his campaigns and rode stirrup to stirrup with him." She was adept in music and gave public performances during the annual Ganapati celebration at the Peshwa's palace. Bajirao was passionately attached to her and felt in her company all the inspiration of his eventful life. She dressed, talked and lived in Hindu fashion and looked after Bajirao's comforts

with the devotion of a wife. No wonder that Bajirao's infatuation for her grew with years and led him into meat-eating and wine-drinking so repugnant in a Brahman household. Bajirao had sons by his Hindu wife and naturally the favour shown to the social outcaste seriously disturbed the peace of the Peshwa's family. Popular voice attributed Bajirao's love of wine and meat to his association with Mastani. But a man of Bajirao's type leading the life of a soldier could not retain the rigid rules of his Brahman caste, as he had to mix freely with all kinds of people. The narrow exclusive life of a Maharashtra Brahman must naturally undergo sudden changes by marching to distant lands and coming into contact with Rajput courts where wine drinking, flesh eating and smoking were freely indulged. This supplies a clue to Bajirao's lapses. Maratha society in general doubtless underwent immense transformation during the process of their expansion.

The published papers supply us with only a few glimpses of what actually happened in Bajirao's family. Possibly the contemplated thread ceremony of Raghunathrao and the marriage of Sadashivrao were the immediate occasion of the trouble. Bajirao then became a topic of public criticism and the priests were not prepared to officiate at the ceremonies if such a tainted person as he were present. While Bajirao was absent from Poona on a campaign towards the end of 1739, Mastani was suddenly seized and kept in confinement by Nanasaheb and Chimnaji Appa. This broke Bajirao's heart so completely that the world became all misery for him. He could not outrage society and public opinion by returning to Poona to rescue his beloved one by force. Mahadoba Purandare, Morshet Karanje and other well-wishers of the family visited Bajirao at Patas and counselled him as to the best course to follow. The orthodox party meant possibly to do away with Mastani altogether as the sole cause of trouble in their opinion, and wrote to the King's secretary Chitnis, to obtain his sanction for the violent course. The King was wiser. On 24th January 1740 writes Govindrao, "I have privately ascertained His Highness's pleasure on the subject of Mastani. He strongly objects to the proposal of forcible separation or personal restraint. He will not tolerate any offence being given to Bajirao, who should be kept entirely pleased. The evil does not abide in that lady. It can be stopped only when he himself feels so inclined. On no account can His Highness advise any violence to the feelings of Bajirao." Bajirao was away fighting his last war with Nasir Jang : Mastani was kept under restraint in an out of the way place and the ceremonies of Raghunathrao's thread and Sadashivrao's marriage were performed at Poona on 4 and 7 February 1740, when Shahu specially came down from Satara to grace the occasion with his presence.

6. Nasir Jang routed.—Perhaps, the affair of Nasir Jang supplied Bajirao with a plausible excuse for absence from Poona during this important ceremony in his family. Nasir Jang was doubtless the ablest of Nizam-ul-mulk's six sons. To help his father at the time of the Bhopal campaign, he had built up a large disciplined force which he had not yet disbanded. During the early months of 1739 there existed the threat of Nadir Shah marching to the south and it seems after that invader's departure, Nizam-ul-mulk, smarting under the discomfiture he had met with at Bhopal, once more tried his game of an underhand intrigue at Satara through his willing instrument, Anandrao Sumant, who according to the stipulations of Palkhed, was no longer to be entertained at the Nizam's Court. This Sumant had been with him at Delhi during the period of Nadir Shah's invasion and now returned to Satara to instil a prejudice against Bajirao in the Chhatrapati's mind. The province of Berar, which the Nizam considered as his own exclusive possession, was recently seized by Raghuji Bhosle. In retaliation Nasir Jang advanced from Aurangabad towards the end of 1739 and crossing the Godavari invaded the Peshwa's domain. Bajirao had already deputed Tubaji Anant to capture some of the Nizam's forts in the upper reaches of the Godavari, and now when Bajirao heard that Nasir Jang was advancing, he immediately moved against him and was soon after joined by his brother. Nasir Jang finding his game unprofitable retraced his steps, fighting rearguard actions. He was relentlessly pursued and surrounded near Aurangabad and soon finding himself at his wits' end, agreed to the terms Bajirao chose to impose upon him. The treaty was formally concluded at Mungi Sheogaon on 27th February

and was ceremoniously ratified at a personal meeting between the two chiefs on 3rd March at Pimpalgaon. Nasir Jang ceded to Bajirao two of his districts, Handia and Khargon in Nemad south of the Narmada, and Bajirao immediately proceeded to the north to occupy them. Chimnaji Appa also paid a visit to Nasir Jang at Aurangabad on 12th March.

7. **Sudden death.**—Nobody then knew that Bajirao was fast nearing his end. But a letter dated 7th March 1740 from Chimnaji Appa to Nanasaheb strikes the following alarming note, which gives a faint suspicion that Bajirao was quite ill at heart. "I have had no news from the revered Rao since we parted. I did my utmost to console his distracted mind, but God, it seems, willed otherwise. I do not know what fate is in store for us. We should send *her* to him upon my return to Poona." It is obvious that Bajirao was greatly upset not only on account of being deprived of Mastani's company, but of his inability to get her released from confinement or save her from worse harm. Things remained in this unsettled condition, when on Monday 28th April Bajirao expired suddenly at Raver on the south bank of the Narmada, where a small, stone terrace still preserves his memory. He was taken ill on the previous Friday with a strong fever, the first and the last ailment, which he ever suffered during life. Hopes were given up on Saturday when he fell unconscious. His wife Kashibai arrived at his death-bed with their little son Janardan. There is no mention of Mastani. Possibly Bajirao drowned his afflictions in excessive drinking. Any way his end was tragic and sudden.

As soon as the news of Bajirao's death reached Mastani she died in the palace of Poona, whether by suicide or of shock it is difficult to say. Her dead body was removed to Pabal, a village about 20 miles east of Poona, which Bajirao had granted her in inam and where an unpretentious tomb reminds passers by of the story of her love and her tragic end. By common consent she was known as the most charming woman of her time.

Bajirao's permanent memorial exists at Poona in the shape of the Shaniwar palace which was first constructed by him, and of which only the surrounding wall and the front gate now survive. The construction was started on 10th January 1730 and the ceremony of actual residence took place on 2nd February 1731. It cost Rs. 16,110. Bajirao's father had recovered the old outpost of Poona from Muslim hold and intended to make it his family's permanent residence in preference to Saswad, where he had lived with his friends the Purandares in his early career. Unfortunately a bald, open barren square plinth is all that remains today of the great Peshwa's edifice, to remind the present day visitor of its pristine glory.

8. Bajirao's character.—It is not necessary to write separately about Bajirao's character and achievements. His deeds speak for him. He stands next only to Shivaji in military genius. Shahu's discernment in selecting him for the Peshwaship at the early age of nineteen was more than justified. That a boy in his teens assuming the highest position under the Maratha Chhatrapati, should be able within twenty years to extend the Maratha dominion in all directions, north, south, east and west and to overcome great antagonists both at home and abroad, is an achievement which stands to the permanent credit of the Maratha race. Twenty years spent in breathless activity and tireless journeys across the Indian continent from Srirangpattan to Delhi and from Ahmadabad to Haidarabad, wore out the iron constitution of this great man of action. The twenty years of his active career witnessed a complete revolution in the character of the Maratha State and an entire redistribution of political power throughout India. At his death in 1740 the political centre of gravity shifted from the Court of Delhi to that of Shahu. The system introduced by Bajirao's father and executed by him and his son, equally transformed the constitution laid down by Shivaji and dotted the map of India with numerous centres of Maratha power. Thus Bajirao became the creator of greater Maharashtra. Shahu was no longer the petty raja of a small self-contained one-race, one-language kingdom, as his father and grandfather had been ; he was now monarch over a far flung and diversified dominion. Shahu was a good judge of the character of men and followed the wise rule of choosing the best instruments and allowing them full latitude and initiative without interfering with their plans and actions. This is well illustrated in the

case of Bajirao's appointment to the Peshwaship. He was a matchless cavalry leader and introduced his own technique in the art of warfare which long served the Maratha nation. While Bajirao possessed a hardy robust constitution himself, which never knew what ailment was, his brother Chimnaji was entirely unlike him, being always ailing, sickly and asthmatic. When Chimnaji returned from his victorious campaign of Bassein, Shahu was impatient to hear every detail first hand from his own mouth and called him to Satara : but Chimnaji was so severely bed-ridden, that the pathetic letter he wrote in excuse is a sample of both sentiment and language.[8]

Dr. Dighe in his special study of "Bajirao and Maratha Expansion" gives a penetrating and accurate analysis of that Peshwa's relations with his master. He writes, "the methods of the Sovereign and the Minister were different but their objective was the same. Shahu looked not to supplant the Mughal Emperor ; he would rather be the Emperor's friend and mentor, would lend his sword arm to his support and thus acquire control over the imperial policy. The reverence felt by him for the throne of the Chagtais expressed not the servility of a subordinate to his superior but the sympathy which a man of culture--a noble soul—feels for an ancient relic, for a fallen cause. In the hands of Bajirao this attitude was rightly transformed into an attempt at political hegemony in the north : the sword arm of the Maratha State was wielded so ably by his Peshwa as to fulfil the wildest dream of the monarch. The Peshwa never forgot that his authority emanated from the crown and had its roots in the confidence placed in him by the Sovereign. Some of the lesser chiefs resented the power thus acquired and failed to realize that what gave the Peshwa his preponderance in the royal council was the military strength acquired by him through years of successful warfare. It was equally open to them to raise armies and lead them to foreign conquests, but, like their master, they loved the repose of the Court and in consequence slowly faded into insignificance. Even the Raja on occasions felt the overgrown power of his Minister and expressed his displeasure in sharp reprimands."

8. P. D. 17. 98.

Bajirao had to wage an implacable war against Nizam-ul-mulk, the first rebel to succeed against the Mughal Empire. The Emperor never trusted Nizam. The mischievous part he played during Nadir Shah's invasion is clear. Saadat Khan called him a cheat. He well realized his weakness before Bajirao and avoided an open conflict with him. Chhatrapati Shahu, however, respected Nizam-ul-mulk as the last representative of Aurangzeb's rule and never entertained the thought of removing him from his position. On the contrary he severely checked Bajirao whenever the latter was found to commit the least aggression against Nizam-ul-mulk, and as a set off against Bajirao employed the Sumant and the Pratinidhi to keep the Nizam at ease of mind. This situation of the Peshwas should be clearly borne in mind by those who ask why the Nizam was allowed to remain a permanent factor of disturbance in the Deccan.

Sir Richard Temple, a wise student of history and politics, has rightly assessed the greatness of Bajirao in a passage breathing exceeding enthusiasm. He remarks : "Bajirao was hardly to be surpassed as a rider and was ever forward in action eager to expose himself under fire if the affair was arduous. He was inured to fatigue and prided himself on enduring the same hardships as his soldiers and sharing their scanty fare. He was moved by an ardour for success in national undertakings by a patriotic confidence in the Hindu cause as against its old enemies the Muhammadans and its new rivals the Europeans then rising above the political horizon. He lived to see the Marathas spread terror over the Indian continent from the Arabian sea to the Bay of Bengal. He died as he lived in camp under canvas among his men and he is remembered among the Marathas as the fighting Peshwa, as the incarnation of Hindu energy."[9]

A contemporary, Marathi letter thus speaks of Bajirao's achievement : "Along with his father's blessing Bajirao inherited from him the great task of regeneration that he had undertaken and he spent his life's effort in accomplishing it, viz., to bring peace and prosperity to the country, north of the Narmada as had been done to the territories south of that river.

9. *Oriental Experience*—page 390.

Bajirao tried to restoré the Hindu religion to its former grandeur. It was his ambition to rebuild the great shrine of Kashivishveshwar at Benares. In these efforts he outshone his father in a far higher degree. He possessed uncommon valour and his fame spread widely as a re-creator of his nation."[10]

---

10 *Hingne Dafter* I. 15.

CHRONOLOGY

CHAPTER VIII

1710	Ghaziuddin, eldest son of Nizam-ul-mulk born.
1721, December 12	Balaji Bajirao born.
1731, January 11	Balaji married to Gopikabai.
1740, June 25	Balaji invested with robes of Peshwaship.
1740, June 25	Babuji Naik claims Peshwaship.
1740, August	Mahadev Bhat Hingne visits the Peshwa at Poona.
" "	Nizam-ul-mulk leaves Delhi, for Aurangabad to put down his son Nasir Jang in rebellion.
1740, June 2 to Mar. 30, 1741	Sambhaji of Kolhapur's visit to Satara: makes a secret pact with the Peshwa.
1741, January 5	Holkar captures Dhar.
1741, January 7	Peshwa meets Nizam at Edlabad.
1741, May 12—19	Peshwa's visit to Jaysinh at Dholpur.
1741, July 4	Emperor ratifies grant of Malwa to the Peshwa.
1741, July 23	Battle of Khuldabad, Nizam victorious over his son.
1741, September 7	Emperor confirms the cession of Malwa.
1743, April 21	Sindia, Holkar and Pawar guarantee observance of the terms of the grant of Malwa.

The Peshwa's northern Expeditions:

1. December 1740 to July 1741, Dholpur;
2. December 18, 1741 to July 1743, Bengal;
3. November 20, 1744 to August 1745, Bhilsa;
4. December 10, 1747 to July 9, 1748, Newai.

Peshwa Balajirao

CHAPTER VIII

PESHWA BALAJI RAO, SUCCESSFUL START

[1740—1741]

1. Accession to Peshwaship, Death of Chimnaji.— When Bajirao died at Raverkhedi his eldest son Balaji, popularly called Nanasaheb, and his brother Chimnaji Appa along with Mahadoba Purandare were at Kolaba, negotiating an adjustment of the dispute of the Angria brothers. Unperturbed by the sad event, they continued the task in hand, at the same time performing the obsequies for the thirteen days. Thereafter they returned to Poona on 26th May where the condolence Darbar was held on the 28th. Balaji's widowed mother Kashibai returned from Bajirao's camp on 3rd June. In the meantime he received a summons from Shahu at once to repair to Satara to receive the robes of Peshwaship. He left on 13th and on the auspicious morning of June 25 (Ashad Shudh 12) was invested with the robes of the office.[1] He was then 18 years and six months old, about a year younger than his father when the latter was appointed to that post.

Mahadoba Purandare was appointed Balaji's Mutalik or deputy to look after the duties of the Peshwa's office in the absence of his principal abroad. To cover the emoluments of the Peshwa Shahu conferred on him the revenues of thirty villages in different places, and issued to him the following specific instructions :—

" Bajirao served the State loyally on the lines laid down by his father and expanded the Maratha dominions by means of many a heroic deed. When Nadir Shah devastated Delhi, Bajirao was despatched to restore the Emperor to his seat, but was cut off by fate in the midst of his life. You are his son

1. Sh. R. 112, 113, 134 ; N. R. 1. 133.

and must carry to completion his half-finished work by extending the Maratha prestige to the frontier of Attock."

Perhaps this young Peshwa's path of work was smoother than his father's. Bajirao was commonly dreaded by his friends and foes, but Balaji was loved. Nevertheless he too had to contend against several hostile elements, such as Babuji Naik, Raghuji Bhosle and Tarabai. But he managed to get over them by his innate tact and sweet temper.

Duff is wrong in asserting that Shahu hesitated in appointing a successor to Bajirao and conferred the robes on Nana Saheb in August. Babuji Naik Joshi, a banker and a favourite of Shahu came forth as a competitor of Balaji for the Peshwaship. A small faction, particularly Raghuji Bhosle of Nagpur, supported Babuji's claims. But both were in the Karnatak conducting important operations before Trichinopoly where they learned of Bajirao's death and they hastily repaired to Satara for a few days in June. Shahu, however, turned a deaf ear to Babuji's request and conferred the robes on Balaji without delay. The two thereafter returned to Trichinopoly to continue their work.

Born on 12th December 1721 Balaji Rao was in his 19th year at his investiture, but had given ample proof of his capacity. He had keenly watched and occasionally participated in the rising political career of his father Bajirao, but the moulding influence on him was the personality of his uncle Chimnaji rather than his father. He inherited none of his father's dash or leadership for conducting military operations. As a rule he never accompanied his father in his campaigns, and associated mostly with his uncle in the various transactions of administration and diplomacy. He possessed a suave temper and a naturally commanding appearance which brought him easy success in whatever he undertook. On 11th January 1730, he was married to Gopikabai then about 7 years of age, daughter of Bhikaji Naik Raste, an eminent banker of Wai, in whom the Maharaja Shahu took great interest. During 1735 Balaji was present with Pilaji Jadhav in north India and from an early age understood and promoted the policy of Maratha expansion projected by his predecessors. In 1737, he accompanied Shahu in his southern expedition, which ended with the capture of Miraj in 1739. Early in 1740 in his father's absence he supervised the thread ceremony of his brother Raghunathrao and the marriage of his cousin Sadashivrao, which Raja Shahu attended as a special favour.

Immediately on his accession to power a number of pressing problems required the young Peshwa's attention. They may be thus enumerated. Bajirao aspired to the Subahdarship of Malwa, which had almost come into his grasp by his victory over the Nizam at Bhopal. Nadir Shah's invasion, and the Peshwa's sudden death prevented the consummation. Nana Saheb tried and obtained the grant from the Emperor. During the disturbance of Nadir Shah's invasion, the Maratha prestige at the court of Delhi had received a set back, and it had to be immediately re-established. The affairs of the Deccan suffered from the interference of Nizam-ul-mulk, who had now to be made perfectly innocuous. The Siddi and the Angrias, the Portuguese and the English, still obstructed the smooth working of the Maratha Government on the west coast. Some kind of a settled understanding with them had to be quickly arrived at.

It will be noticed that the Peshwa steadily kept these objects before his mind during the twenty-one years of his office, which fall into two clear divisions, the first of nine years ending with the death of Shahu, and the second of twelve years when he acted as the practical head of the Maratha Government, having removed the whole administration from Satara to Poona.

As soon as Balajirao received the robes of Peshwaship, he planned an expedition to the north for the purpose of examining the situation there, which had been disturbed by Nadir Shah's invasion and of securing the grant of the Subahdarship of Malwa which had been promised by Nizam-ul-mulk. Balaji and Chimnaji both started together from Poona early in December, but the latter was compelled quickly to return on account of ill-health. Chimnaji Appa died at Poona on 17th December. This premature death was severely mourned by the whole nation. Writes Kashiraj Shivdev (author of the future Panipat Bakhar) to the Peshwa, "I am unable to conceive the magnitude of the loss occasioned by Appa's death." Nana Saheb reported Chimnaji's death to Brahmendra Swami as a stunning blow, coming as it did within 8 months of

Bajirao's death.[2] It was indeed a national loss, for much of the phenomenal success which Bajirao attained was due to Chimnaji's hearty co-operation and silent, ungrudging selfless effort. It is hard to find a brother of such capacity and high moral character as Chimnaji was to Bajirao. He possessed very poor health and he willingly sacrificed it for the service of his nation.

One important secret transaction effected by the new Peshwa at this time deserves mention. He had realized the necessity of uniting the two branches of the Maratha State, Satara and Kolhapur, into one. Shahu had no longer any prospect of a son being born to him and the question of succession had begun to press itself upon the attention of the Peshwa. The only surviving male member of the great Shivaji's family was Sambhaji of Kolhapur, who happened to pay a visit to Shahu at Satara and stayed there from 2nd June 1740 to 30th March 1741. There was not much love lost between the two cousins; and Shahu would never consent to Sambhaji succeeding him. But the new Peshwa formed a secret compact with Sambhaji for his succeeding Shahu at Satara on the latter's death. Although for various reasons beyond the Peshwa's control the arrangement proved futile, it none the less discloses a very desirous stroke of policy on the part of the young Peshwa and his advisers, who thus tried although eventually in vain to close the rift which for long marred the unity of the Maratha nation.[3] At his death Shahu left a definite order that Sambhaji should not succeed him and that Ramraja should be made the Chhatrapati.

2. **The new master at work.**—The new Peshwa was no soldier either by inclination or profession, and managed to execute military operations through loyal and trusted subordinates of his own. He never stood in danger of military adventurers usurping his power and setting up their independence. Balaji's cousin Sadashivrao Bhau was trained from the beginning to lead military expeditions and the two pulled

2. P. D. 40. 25, *Patre Yadi* 36, 38.

3. The student is referred to *Patre Yadi*, 246, 249, *Nana Roz*, 193; *Shahu Roz*. 178.

together in full co-operation for the service of their State, which under their joint supervision became a school of training for many youngsters working enthusiastically in all its varied activities.

Control over the finances was perhaps the special feature of Balajirao's administrative capacity. In the policy of increasing the resources of the State and utilising them to the highest advantage, this Peshwa attained remarkable success. He noticed the weakness of his father's position on account of his embarrassing debts and always kept himself above dire want, exercising careful supervision over all financial transactions. A minute study of his itinerary discloses that he was constantly on the move, receiving explanations, granting interviews, reprimanding offenders and rewarding merit wherever it was discovered. During his travels and expeditions, during sieges and battles he is constantly seen working quietly and unperturbed, inspecting accounts, adjusting treaties and guarding the interests of the State in every respect. Every day brought new problems to be solved, which the Peshwa faced boldly. He proved equal to the strain and achieved the largest expansion of the Maratha State under his regime. Unlike Sadashivrao, Balaji loved compromise and conciliation. He knew when to recede and yield if necessary even at some sacrifice of prestige and interest. He was unequalled in diplomatic skill and a writer of great capacity. His eye constantly moved to distant places in all quarters of India. Of all the Peshwas Balaji has to his credit the largest number of extant letters, mostly in his own hand : as a rule every letter going out in his name has at least a few lines of his own added at the end. The earliest letter extant is dated 20th March 1731 when he was just nine years old.

But this Peshwa's success is in no small degree due to the efficient training of his own family and the co-operation of his own kith and kin. In this respect the training of the Peshwa's family was indeed exemplary, particularly under the supervision of Radhabai, Bajirao's mother, who for nearly half a century efficiently managed the private relations not only of her own family but influenced those of several sardars, Brahman and Maratha alike. Balaji's own brothers Raghunath and Janardan and his cousin Sadashiv imbibed this training fully and learned to co-operate heartily and ably in the work of the State. Unfortunately Raghunath did not develop the unselfish spirit of work and service displayed by the other members. Janardan was highly promising, but was carried away by death at the early age of 14. Sadashivrao proved the best example of the family group we are talking of. It was necessary to have some member of the family always in attendance on the Chhatrapati at Satara, as the keeper of his conscience, in order as much to post him with correct information of all happenings outside, as to prevent opponents from poisoning his ears. Sadashivrao, Raghunathrao and others in turn used to reside with the King at Satara whenever the Peshwa happened to be away.

Satara contained the residence of the ministers and high officers and sardars with their personal advisers and self-seekers. These constantly carried on secret intrigues affecting the policy and actions of the Peshwa, which had to be watched for and counteracted. Satara with Shahu's increasing age and infirmities became a hot-bed of factions and intrigues, requiring the Peshwa's close attention. The saving feature of this situation was the close intimacy and hearty co-operation that existed between the two families, the Peshwas and the Purandares. To counteract these intrigues the Peshwa created new workers in his own confidence. Sakharam Bapu Bokil, Gangadhar Yashvant, the Barves, the Chaskars and other future lights of the Maratha State received their early training under the direct eye of Nana Saheb and became attached to him through weal and woe.

Young men ardently came forward to undertake the fatigues of long marches and distant expeditions. Nana Purandare, a mere lad felt deeply grieved when the Peshwa refused to let him accompany his expedition of 1741. His elder cousin Mahadoba was at great pains to persuade the boy to remain at home. This was the enthusiastic spirit that stirred every young soul to serve the State and seek his fortune in what is termed Mulukgiri or expansion of power.

As soon as the Peshwa received the robes of investiture he called his envoy Mahadev Bhat Hingne from Delhi and they met at Poona in August along with Malharrao Holkar and Ramchandra Baba. Pilajirao Jadhav and Avji Kavde also returned from their duties in Bundelkhand. It was agreed that the Peshwa should proceed to the north at once, personally ascertain the views and secure the co-operation of Jaysinh, then the most powerful Rajput chief of the north. The Peshwa left Poona on 23rd November 1740, accompanied by his wife Gopikabai and after paying a visit to Jaysinh at Dholpur for a week from 12 to 19 May 1741, returned to Poona on 7th July. The first expedition of the Peshwa is named after Dholpur. The second expedition generally known as the Bengal expedition was more important and lasted from 18th December 1741 to 30th July 1743, the Peshwa having his monsoon camp of 1742 at Orchha in Bundelkhand. His third expedition termed the *Bhilsa* lasted from 20th November 1744 to August 1745; and his fourth and last one called the *Newai*, from December 10, 1747 to 9th July 1748. These are the only expeditions which the Peshwa personally led to northern India. He never again went to that side and this perhaps accounts for the neglect of Maratha affairs in that quarter which culminated in the disaster of Panipat. We shall now deal with these four expeditions in detail.

Nizam-ul-mulk had not given effect to the agreement he had contracted with Bajirao after his defeat near Bhopal. How to deal with him now was the main concern of the Peshwa. The Nizam's hostile attitude had already necessitated his presence urgently in that quarter. At that time Nizam-ul-mulk was involved in the rebellion of his own son Nasir Jang which indirectly favoured the Maratha cause. The Nizam otherwise would have assumed a very formidable attitude. It is necessary to go into this affair in greater detail in order that the comparative positions of the Marathas and Nizam-ul-mulk may be well grasped.

3. *Nasir Jang's rebellion.*—Briggs mentions that Nizam-ul-mulk had one married wife and four concubines. The former bore him two sons Ghaziuddin (born about 1710) and Nasir Jang and two daughters. He had four more sons, Salabat Jang, Basalat Jang, Nizam Ali and Meer Mughal, from his mistresses. All these have played important parts in later history. The first two were men of ability and valour. The eldest Ghaziuddin was brought up at the Court of Delhi,

while Nasir Jang lived mostly in the Deccan with his father. When during 1737 the Emperor called Nizam-ul-mulk to Delhi for opposing Bajirao, the Nizam stationed Nasir Jang to watch the Marathas in the south and prevent Maratha succours reaching Bajirao in the north. Chimnaji Appa foiled Nasir Jang's efforts and prevented him from crossing the Tapti and helping his father during the action at Bhopal. Thereafter Nasir Jang and Bajirao had an open war during the early months of 1740, which has been already described.

The Emperor and his Court had been utterly disgusted with Nizam-ul-mulk owing to his vacillating conduct and intrigue with Nadir Shah. The report of his having fallen out of favour with the Emperor reached Nasir Jang in the Deccan, and the youth endeavoured to snatch away all power from his father's hand and declared himself independent. This rebellious attitude of his son so disconcerted Nizam-ul-mulk at Delhi that he suddenly left the city in August 1740 with a large force and reached Burhanpur in November, all the while trying persuasive methods to wean his son from his evil designs. He also prepared, if necessary, to oppose Nasir Jang in open war. Nasir Jang was firm, managed to obtain the support of several influential officials of Aurangabad and with a large army took his station at Ajunta to oppose his father. He addressed to his father defiant and insulting letters. He said, "You should remain at Delhi and look after the imperial concerns, leaving me the sole power to manage the affairs of the Deccan. I have no desire to go to war with you; but if you don't deliver to me the sole management in the Deccan, I will become a faqir and resort to the shrine of the saint Shah Burhan-uddin of Khuldabad." The Nizam then came quickly against his son. This was indeed a delicate time for the Peshwa. Both parties appealed to him for help and whatever be the result of the civil war between the father and the son, here was an opportunity for the Peshwa to make the best bargain out of that affair as victory was sure for the side which the Peshwa would espouse. He had already decided to proceed to the north and try to take possession of Malwa by force of arms if the Emperor would not himself appoint the Peshwa to the Subahdarship. While the Peshwa was proceeding to the north, he learned in Khandesh that Nizam-ul-mulk was coming to the south with an army to put down his son. Both were anxious to arrange a personal meeting, Nizam to keep the Peshwa from joining his son; the Peshwa to secure the grant of Malwa. Baburao Barve called on the Nizam on behalf of the Peshwa whose armed help was humbly besought. After full deliberation the Peshwa decided to support the Nizam. Pilaji Jadhav brought about a meeting between them at Edlabad on the Purna in Khandesh on 7th January 1741. At this meeting the Nizam induced the Peshwa not to join or help his rebellious son.[4] A week was spent in cordial entertainments on both sides. The appearances looked entirely cordial, but the two parties were suspicious of each other. The Peshwa demanded possession of Malwa as agreed to in the convention of Bhopal, but the Nizam urged that he was powerless to influence the Emperor to abide by that decision. The Peshwa writes to Brahmendra Swami on 14th January: "A dispute arose between the Nizam and his son Nasir Jang. I supported the former; the latter lost the fight and has become a faqir. The Nizam personally acknowledged deep obligations to me, and added that the Emperor has entrusted the Subah of Malwa to him (the Nizam); and if I (Nana) were prepared to remain in obedience to him, he would appoint me there as his deputy." Thus the hopes of securing Malwa from the Nizam were foiled. The Peshwa, however, thought it best to utilize the occasion for seizing Malwa, took no part in the civil war in the Nizam's house, beyond ensuring that Maratha interests did not suffer on that account, and rapidly proceeded to the north.

In the meantime Nizam-ul-mulk reached Aurangabad and began measures to put down his son. Nasir Jang commenced hostilities against his father and marched upon Aurangabad itself. A severe action took place between the father and the son on 23rd July 1741 on the plain between Khuldabad and Daulatabad in which Nizam-ul-mulk's cannon proved so effective against Nasir Jang's troops that most of his supporters were either killed or captured and he was himself severely wounded. He was taken captive in this helpless condition by Saiyad Lashkar Khan and delivered over to his father. Nasir Jang's main supporter was Shah Nawaz Khan, who

4. Full details of the visit in *Hingne Daftar* I. 20; Br. Ch. 60.

fled and saved his life by hiding himself secretly for five years, a period which he spent in writing the famous biographies of the grandees of the Mughal Empire entitled *Masir-ul-Umrah*. He was ultimately pardoned and restored to his former post.

After winning this victory over his son, the old Nizam prayed on the battle-field, offering sincere thanks to Providence for the three gifts he had received that day : viz., (1) success in the battle, (2) the life of his own son being spared, and (3) the joy he felt for the great valour displayed by him. Nasir Jang was kept a close prisoner for some six months, after which at the urgent solicitations of his wives and relations, the Nizam pardoned and restored him to favour. A touching scene is described when the father and the son met, embraced each other with tears and were finally reconciled.

4. **Malwa secured.**—The aims and policy of Balaji Vishvanath in expanding Maratha influence beyond the Narmada, later executed by his sons Bajirao and Chimnaji Appa have received fresh light in the Hingne papers recently published. There are some very significant papers in this collection which disclose the measures adopted by Bajirao, both stern and persuasive, to bring about a healthy tone between the distracted warring elements and conflicting counsels of Muhammad Shah. Bajirao's friendship with Sawai Jaysinh stands out in glowing colours and was the creation of the shrewd Maratha ambassador Mahadev Bhat Hingne who was first stationed at Jaipur and later transferred to Delhi. The several Maratha expeditions of Bajirao to the north after the fall of Giridhar Bahadur and the peaceful and friendly manner in which Bajirao all along proposed to set right the imperial affairs to the best advantage of the parties concerned, can now be studied in their proper perspective by means of these valuable documents. Some of these papers faithfully recount the inside story of Maratha penetration into the north, which till now could be illustrated only on the basis supplied by *Siyar-ul-mutakherin* and "*The Later Mughals*" of Irvine. The Maratha version was nowhere in evidence.

Chimnaji Appa soon after Bajirao's death on 28th April 1740 eloquently recounts what grand services Bajirao made to the Indian world and how the same policy would be faithfully pursued by his son who was succeeding to the Peshwaship. Chimnaji writes to Mahadev Bhat on 2nd June 1740, "Sawai Jaisinh, Nizam-ul-mulk and Khan Dauran were all of one mind in enlisting the sympathies of Bajirao and entrusting to him the management of the imperial affairs. Bajirao was asked to bring to obedience all those who had flouted the authority of the Emperor; to nourish the interests of the poor ryots, to effect peace and prosperity in the distracted lands, to replenish the imperial treasury and thus to deserve favours from the Emperor and earn for himself transcending fame for having set his power right. For this the late Peshwa exerted himself assiduously for eight long years in co-operation with Sawai Jaysinh. The undertaking was all but completed, in spite of severe trials and obstacles caused by disloyal elements. The Nawab Asaf Jah has supported the scheme and recently sent to me in confirmation his trusted agent Saiyad Lashkar Khan. Every detail having been thus arranged, the late Peshwa marched towards Malwa having first deputed you (Hingne) to meet Sawai Jaysinh to arrange the whole affair in advance. But as soon as the Peshwa reached the Narmada in the district of Khargon he was suddenly taken ill and expired. God's will be done! His young son Nana has now assumed the same responsibility. He and I are ready to carry to completion the unfinished programme of the onerous undertaking, the basis of which was first laid down by my revered father (Balaji Vishvanath, the first Peshwa) whose most ardent concern was to improve the lot of the ryots. Our great Chhatrapati (Shahu) blessed him with all his heart, and treated him with the highest reverence. He thus earned a great name and left the precious heritage of his blessing to his son (Bajirao), who faithfully carried out the benevolent programme chalked out for him, viz., the regeneration of religion, of gods and Brahmans, of the sacred places of Hindu pilgrimage like Benares. He so worked for the good of the people that he improved their lot and earned their good wishes. Having completed the task in the south, he turned his attention to the north. His great ambition was to restore the Kashi Vishveshwar shrine of Benares to its pristine glory and greatness. The late Peshwa has left in tact the whole machine behind, a well disciplined army and a number of capable chiefs, who are all now anxious to work on the same lines. We hope without delay to overcome all difficulties and carry to completion the aims and ideals of our revered predecessors.

"We are now on our way to Satara to meet our revered monarch and hope within a couple of months to get together an army of a hundred thousand men. And since Nizam-ul-mulk seems to oppose our scheme, you must assure Sawaiji and through him the Emperor, that we shall carry out their wishes unreservedly and put down the pretensions of Nizam-ul-mulk as desired by the Emperor; and that we shall faithfully execute every item of the scheme arranged by the late Peshwa. We have every desire to meet the Rana of Udaipur and Abhay Sinh of Marwar in order to enlist their sympathies and co-operation in executing the plans agreeably to the wishes of the Emperor. If chiefs life Nizam-ul-mulk feel that now the field is open for them as the brave Peshwa is dead, we are prepared to disabuse their minds and to show that the death of the Peshwa makes absolutely no difference to the position of affairs. We are more than a match for Nizam-ul-mulk or others that come in our way. We count on the brotherly support of Sawaiji and will with his co-operation soon execute our cherished schemes. We have received Sawaiji's invitation that a strong body of Maratha troops be permanently stationed in Malwa. We are alive to this project and in anticipation have already ordered Vithoji Bule and Pilaji Jadhav to proceed to Malwa immediately; in addition either Malharrao Holkar and Ranoji Sindia or both will soon follow."

Indeed, Ranoji conveys the following threat through Mahadev Bhat on 13 July 1740. "You intimate that Azamulla Khan is coming rapidly upon Malwa. Please note that we are ready to welcome him as servants of the Peshwa. Under God's favour he will receive the reward he deserves at our hands. You should feel entirely at ease as to the result."[5] Again on 26th February 1741 the Peshwa writes to Hingne, "I have already informed you of my visit to Nizam-ul-mulk. You must have communicated to Raj Rajendra Sawai Jaisinh how I am earnestly striving to carry out the imperial undertakings of my father. Sawaiji has agreed to obtain im-

5. *Hingne Daftar*, Nos. 15, 17, 18 and 19.

perial sanads for the Subah of Malwa together with all the fortified places therein, and the acknowledgement of our sovereignty over the local chiefs on this side of the Chambal. He has also agreed to obtain a cash payment of twenty lacs from the imperial treasury, the remittance of the pilgrim tax at Prayag and the cession of Benares. You must impress upon Sawaiji that in our hearty co-operation lies his interest as well as ours."[6]

His visit to the Nizam ended early in January and the Peshwa then proceeded to the north. He crossed the Narmada on 7th March and made for Bundelkhand where he appointed Naro Shankar as the permanent Maratha agent. The Sindia and Holkar were already operating in Malwa. On 5th January Malharrao Holkar captured Dhar from its Mughal keeper; Dhar was the gateway into Malwa and its possession proved a prelude to the complete absorption of that province in the expanding Maratha Empire. On 16th February the Peshwa wrote to Hingne :—" In compliance with your suggestion, I have given strict instructions to our troops not to molest Jaysinh's territories. Assure him of my deep regard for him and enlist his sincere co-operation in obtaining the grant of Malwa from the Emperor. He is our great elderly friend and we depend upon him to look after our interests."

The capture of Dhar by the Marathas led the Emperor seriously to decide upon his future course. He called Jaysinh to his presence and consulted him along with his ministers. The Maratha agent reported to the Peshwa on 17th May, " The Emperor has decided to offer armed opposition to Maratha aggression. He has appointed Jaysinh to lead the expedition. Jaysinh has reached Agra." The Peshwa prepared to meet the situation. He at once despatched Avaji Kavde and Govind Hari with some light troops to devastate the Doab up to Allahabad, and himself proceeded to Dholpur, as Jaysinh had now decided upon conciliating the Peshwa by a personal visit.

Ever since the arrival of the Peshwa in Malwa, negotiations had been going on with the imperial Court, through Jaysinh. Mahadev Bhat Hingne managed the affair with the

6. P. D. 21. 2 ; Raj. 6. 152.

utmost prudence. He impressed upon the Emperor that if the two Subahs of Gujarat and Malwa were at once conferred upon the Peshwa by a formal *firman,* the Peshwa would serve the Emperor loyally : but that a recourse to arms would plunge the imperial affairs into chaos. The Emperor agreed to the suggestion and asked that a written petition be submitted by the Peshwa to that effect. Out of this proposal came the visit of Jaysinh to the Peshwa, which lasted for a week from 12th to 19th May 1741, in a camp between Agra and Dholpur in the presence of Mahadev Bhat Hingne. The Peshwa called on Jaysinh first in his camp, and the next day Jaysinh returned the visit in the Peshwa's camp. The occasion proved a great triumph for the Peshwa.[7] Long conferences were held the outcome of which was an agreement on these three points viz., (1) That the Peshwa and Jaysinh should act in complete friendship and help each other in all circumstances ; (2) that the Marathas should behave with strict loyalty towards the Emperor and that (3) the grant of Malwa to the Peshwa be secured within six months." Having accomplished his object the Peshwa immediately returned to the south and reached Poona on 7th July.

Jaysinh acted promptly and kept his word scrupulously. He had long realized the futility of opposing the Marathas by arms, and from Dholpur he at once repaired to Delhi and explained the situation to the Emperor, who took counsel with his advisers and issued a *farman* appointing Shahzada Ahmad as the Subahdar of Malwa and the Peshwa as his deputy acting on the spot. On 4th July the deed was ratified under the Emperor's seal. A few details which were vague were cleared up and a subsequent explanation was issued on 7th September 1741, entrusting the whole management of the Subah of Malwa to the Peshwa including the civil and criminal jurisdiction. The grant was confined to Malwa only and did not apply to Gujarat. But as this latter province was already in Maratha possession the absence of a formal grant was immaterial. What was commenced on the battle field of Amjhera at the end of November 1728, came thus to fructify after 12 years of war and wrangling. Malwa and Bundelkhand became practi-

7. Raj. 6. 151 ; *Purandare Daftar* 1. 149.

cally Maratha possessions hereafter. The terms of the grant of Malwa stipulated that the Marathas should not encroach upon any other imperial territory : that the Peshwa should station at Delhi one of his commandants to serve the Emperor with 500 horse and if the necessity occurred, four thousand more troops should be provided at the expense of the Emperor ; the Marathas should respect all the previous Muslim grants to individuals and religious institutions, and that they should not enhance the taxes upon the ryots.

On 21st April 1743 Ranoji Sindia, Malharrao Holkar, Yashwantrao Pawar and Pilaji Jadhav endorsed this imperial grant pledging themselves as sureties to guarantee that the terms would be strictly adhered to by the Peshwa.

The new Peshwa's regime came thus to be inaugurated by a great triumph, as he ultimately carried out by a diplomatic stroke what war had long tried to secure, but without success.

CHRONOLOGY

CHAPTER IX

1726	Aliwardi Khan enters Nawab of Bengal's service.
1726	Mir Habib appointed Governor of Orissa by Murshid Quli Khan.
1726, June 30	Murshid Quli Khan dies, his son-in-law Shuja Khan succeeds.
1739, March 30	Shuja Khan dies, son Sarfaraj Khan succeeds.
1741, Monsoon	Bapuji Naik expelled from Poona.
1741, October	Raghuji Bhosle despatches Bhaskar Ram to Bengal.
1742, February	Peshwa at Chanda on way to the north.
1742, March	Peshwa captures Garha and Mandla.
1742, April 15	Bhaskar Ram forms his camp near Burdwan, harasses Aliwardi Khan and gradually reduces Bengal.
1742, April	Babuji Naik prevented by Holkar and Pawar from entering Malwa.
1742, May 6	Marathas raid and plunder Murshidabad.
1742, June 29	Peshwa cantons at Orchha.
1742, July	Peshwa restores Dhar to Yashvant Rao Pawar.
1742, September 27	During Durgapuja celebration Bhaskar Ram's camp raided by Aliwardi Khan.
1742, September 30	Raghuji leaves Nagpur for Bengal.
1742, November 8	Peshwa leaves Orchha for Bengal.
1743, Jan.—Feb.	Peshwa performs pilgrimage to Prayag, Benares and Gaya.
1743, March	Raghuji meets Peshwa at Gaya.
1743, March 31	Peshwa and Aliwardi Khan hold a conference near Plassey and conclude a pact.
1743, April 10	Raghuji being routed by the Peshwa near Pachet, returns to Nagpur.
1743, May 20	Peshwa reaches the Bhagirathi on his return journey.

1743, August 31	Shahu reconciles Peshwa and Raghuji at Satara on solemn oaths.
1744, January	Bhaskar Ram leaves Nagpur for Bengal.
1744, March 30	Bhaskar with 21 other generals is massacred by Aliwardi Khan at Mankara near Katwa.
1745, February	Raghuji marches on Bengal.
1745, May 6	Raghuji captures Cuttack, possesses Orissa and sends Durlabh Ram prisoner to Nagpur.
1745, December 21	*Raghuji routed near Murshidabad and re*-turns to Nagpur.
1747, January	Janoji Bhosle marches upon Bengal, and returns after being defeated.
1747, Summer	Raghuji visits Nizam at Aurangabad and Shahu at Satara.
1748	Sabaji Bhosle marches on Bengal.
1751, March	Aliwardi Khan makes peace with Raghuji by yielding Chauth of Bengal. Shivabhat Sathe appointed first Governor of Orissa and Bengal.
1752, August 24	Mir Habib dies.
1755, February 14	Raghuji Bhosle dies.
1756, April 10	Aliwardi Khan dies.

CHAPTER IX

MARATHA PENETRATION INTO BENGAL

[1742—1752]

1 Orissa the Origin of trouble.
2 Bhaskar Ram at Katwa.
3 Raghuji and the Peshwa clash together.
4 The Reconciliation.
5 Massacre of Maratha Generals.
6 Chauth imposed upon Bengal.

1. Orissa, the origin of trouble.—While engrossed in attending to foreign affairs, the Peshwa had always on his hands several matters of a domestic character. One such that he had to attend to upon his return to Poona in the monsoon of 1741, was the rupture of his relations with Babuji Naik his unsuccessful rival for the Peshwaship and since then his sworn enemy who had now to be forcibly expelled from Poona. He was a banker who had advanced loans to the Peshwa ; and his brother Abaji was married to a sister of Bajirao. Although thus a close old relation of the Peshwa's family, his presence at Poona became troublesome. He demanded from the Peshwa the immediate return of his loan. Mahadaji Purandare collected funds from the other bankers and paid off Babuji, who then quitted Poona finally. Babuji had the support of Shahu, while Raghuji Bhosle and Damaji Gaikwad were his friends. Shahu granted him lands at Baramati, where he built his residence and embellished his chiefship. Even here, however, Babuji's descendants could not continue in peace. They were finally expelled by the Peshwa Bajirao II, as will appear in subsequent history.

North-Indian affairs now demanded the Peshwa's serious attention, as they came to be complicated by the jealousy which Raghuji Bhosle now began to develop towards the Peshwa. The presence of both at Satara in June 1741 created some sensational developments with which Shahu could not cope and which he with his usual weakness allowed to drift towards serious consequences. The Peshwa explained to the Chhatrapati the necessity of strengthening the Maratha position not only in Malwa and Bundelkhand but in the territories lying beyond towards the east. He took counsel with his advisers and prepared for a long and arduous expedition, which proved a vexatious affair lasting from December 1741 to June 1743.

It was Bajirao who had formed dreams of Maratha expansion in all quarters, in which several capable Maratha leaders came forth to secure a share. As early as 1738 Raghuji Bhosle secured a sanad from Shahu, entrusting to him the eastern field of Bengal as his exclusive sphere for the levy of Chauth. The actual words in the document are, "The Subahs of Lucknow, Maksudabad, Bundelkhand, Allahabad, Patna, Dacca and Bihar are made over as Raghuji's field of activity." This was indeed a rough demarcation, with no notion of a definite boundary or geographical accuracy on the map. A scramble thus arose between Raghuji and the Peshwa, each trying to secure the eastern sphere. The latter had already occupied Bundelkhand and appointed Naro Shankar to its management, thus giving sufficient umbrage to Raghuji as an encroachment on his sphere. When the Peshwa returned to Satara for the rains of 1741, Raghuji precipitately left for Nagpur, and was determined, now that Bajirao was no more, to assert his power by exercising a check upon the Peshwa if the latter tried to encroach upon his sphere in the east.

There soon arose an inevitable clash between the Peshwa and Raghuji Bhosle, as the latter's conquest of Trichinopoly now gave him prominence in the Maratha Court. His brilliant successes in the Karnatak and capture of Chanda Saheb naturally gave him a high place in the Raja's favour. He was upon his return received with special honours, gifts and dresses in an open Durbar and soon returned to Nagpur to attend to the affair of Bengal, to which we must now turn.

After Aurangzeb's death the hold of the Central Mughal government at Delhi upon the provincial administrations became very loose and the local governors began to assert their independence. What Nizam-ul-mulk did in the Deccan was imitated in the Karnatak and in Bengal. This last province consisted of three separate units of the present day, Orissa, Bihar and Bengal proper, all then under the jurisdiction of the

Nawab who resided at Murshidabad. This was the richest of the Mughal provinces and had once supplied funds for the costly wars of Aurangzeb. After that Emperor's death Murshid Quli Khan became the governor of the province and ruled it wisely until his death on 30th June 1727. He was then succeeded in the government by his son-in-law Shuja Khan who also carried out his duties efficiently, making regular payment of annual dues to the Emperor. Shuja Khan died on 13th March 1739 and his son Sarfaraz Khan who succeeded him, being incompetent, was defeated and killed by Aliwardi Khan.

This Aliwardi Khan was a Turk who had come to India and accepted service in Bengal in 1726. Clever in the art of war and diplomacy alike, and calculating in his manœuvres, he soon rose to be the principal military officer of Bengal and secured for himself the government of Bihar. He earned the good opinion of the Court of Delhi by his work and the Emperor conferred on him the title of Mahabat Jang, by which name he is known in Marathi papers. When disorder broke out in the government of Sarfaraz Khan, Aliwardi Khan was not slow in taking advantage of it. Possessing full control of the army in Bihar, he marched from Patna upon Murshidabad, when Sarfaraz Khan came out to oppose him. A battle was fought at Gheria on 10th April 1740 in which Sarfaraz Khan was killed and Aliwardi Khan seized the Nawabship. Taking possession of the accumulated hoards of wealth at the capital, he paid two crores of rupees to the Emperor and obtained from him a confirmation of his appointment. The Emperor and his new subahdar thus for a time became essential to each other.

Aliwardi Khan's usurpation was not at all welcome to the partizans of the old Nawab. The English traders in Bengal were flourishing and had then become a power in the land controlling money transactions. Aliwardi Khan secured their good will by granting them concessions and securing their sympathy for strengthening his assumption of the Nawabship. We find in the contemporary English documents Aliwardi Khan's regime highly applauded on account of his sobriety and good administration. But there was a strong faction at the Nawab's Court headed by Mir Habib and some other officials who could not forget the new Nawab's treachery to the son of his benefactor.

Mir Habib, a clever Persian of Shiraz, had long ago migrated to India and from humble beginnings, risen to the deputy Nawabship of Orissa in which post he served his master another Murshid Quli Khan, Governor of Orissa with devotion and distinction. He remained loyal to his master to the last and after the latter's defeat by Aliwardi, had unsuccessfully attempted to engage the Marathas in his master's cause. Raghuji Bhosle was then in the Karnatak and his deputy, Bhaskar Ram, in his master's absence was disinclined to undertake major operations in Bengal. Mir Habib being compelled by circumstances re-entered Aliwardi's service though he continued to nurse severe hatred for the usurper.

Raghuji Bhosle of Nagpur looked on this eastern province of Bengal as his special sphere and had showed deep resentment when Peshwa Bajirao made demands on the revenues of Bengal in his negotiations with Nizam-ul-mulk at Bhopal in 1738. Raghuji's Karnatak expedition had added to his reputation and on his return to Nagpur, in 1741, he was informed of the political changes in Bengal and of the offers received from Mir Habib and the disgruntled section of the new Nawab's officers. Raghuji dreaded the new Peshwa's ambitious views towards the province and decided to forestall him by at once sending his army eastward. He was naturally anxious to have an independent field for his activities and readily grasped the offer made to him by Mir Habib. At Satara, therefore, he hurriedly took his leave of Shahu. At this very time the Peshwa himself conceived the plan of taking a hand in the affair of Bengal, being jealous of Raghuji's rising power.

Immediately after his arrival at Nagpur, Raghuji formed plans in consultation with his trusted lieutenant Bhaskar Ram, who had directly arrived there from Trichinopoly with Chanda Saheb in his custody. A strong expedition was fitted out for proceeding into Orissa and Bengal. It started on the Dassara day of 1741, with about ten thousand troopers. Bhaskar Ram headed the party and himself left Nagpur in November. He marched through Ramgad and plundered the district of Pachet (60 miles east of Ranchi).

2. **Bhaskar Ram at Katwa.**—Aliwardi Khan was surprised to learn of these Maratha movements and the activities of Mir Habib, when the Nawab was leisurely returning from Cuttack. Realizing that he was unable to hold his own against the strong Maratha hordes, he by a rapid march with a slender force reached Burdwan on 15th April 1742, where he formed his camp on the bank of the Rani's lake outside the town. To his dismay, however, he found himself early next morning completely surrounded by the Marathas and was faced with utter starvation. During the following days Bhaskar Ram employed half his men in plundering and devastating the adjoining districts. To escape the miseries of his unbearable situation, Aliwardi Khan sent his agents to Bhaskar Ram begging for terms. The latter demanded 10 lacs which the Khan declined to pay; and on the advice of some of his trusted lieutenants, he secretly set out by night with a select escort for Katwa about 35 miles north-east of Burdwan. The trick was soon detected and the Khan was pursued hotly, his baggage and tents were burnt making him utterly helpless on the way. He again sent piteous appeals to the Maratha commander to release him. Bhaskar Ram now demanded one crore as the price of the Khan's release. Again the terms were refused, but by fighting desperate rear-guard actions the Khan managed to reach Katwa. In the meantime Mir Habib came by a different route and joined Bhaskarpant.

It was now the month of May and the signs of the approaching monsoon appeared so unmistakable, that Bhaskar Ram wished to retire to Nagpur immediately. This proposal was strongly opposed by Mir Habib, who offered an alluring plan of a sudden attack upon Murshidabad and seizing its immense wealth, a prospect which Bhaskar Ram after some persuasion accepted. Mir Habib himself undertook the venture. On 6th May with a contingent of his own and a select body of Maratha horse, he came upon the suburbs of the city, rapidly plundered its treasures, particularly its wealthy bankers, the Jagat Sheth and others, and released his own brother and family who had been imprisoned there by Aliwardi Khan. The Mir returned to Katwa and joined the Pant with the accumulated plunder amounting to between two and three crores of rupees.

Aliwardi Khan being informed in time of the Mir's movements followed upon his track but reached Murshidabad only a day too late, i.e. on 7th May. The Bhagirathi being in flood, Bhaskarpant could not cross over in pursuit of him. During the next three months the Marathas assisted by Mir Habib established their sway right up to the neighbourhood of Calcutta and Hugli and recaptured Orissa. It was in fear of the Maratha raid upon their factory at Calcutta at this time, that the English traders hastily constructed a long ditch round their establishments, which is still known as the Maratha Ditch and which has now been filled up. Bhaskar Ram's violent methods were deeply resented by the populace of Bengal as the sequel will show.[1]

Bhaskar Ram's greed was whetted by the immense wealth he had gained; and he fell a prey to the wily plan of revenge which Aliwardi Khan now contrived. Maratha troops were small in number and came to be scattered at long distances holding the extensive territory which had been subjugated. He had been incessantly asking Raghuji for more men. In order to please the local sentiment the Maratha general decided to hold a grand celebration of his victory during the Durga-puja festivities commencing on 18th September 1742, the 26th being the principal day. While Bhaskarpant and his band were engrossed in the rejoicings of the occasion, Aliwardi Khan planned a surprise attack upon the Maratha camp. During the night of the 26th as the Marathas after a long vigil were fast asleep, the Nawab early in the morning of the 27th having secretly crossed over the river during the night, suddenly fell upon the unwary Marathas and started an indiscriminate massacre. Bewildered by this unexpected havoc the Marathas to save their life fled in various directions from the camp of Katwa. Mir Habib too had to flee for his life, and did his best to help the Marathas to escape safely through bypaths and private agencies. Bhaskar Ram instantly sent news of this disaster to Raghuji and requested immediate succour. On 23rd September Raghuji writes to his Muzumdar, "Enclosed you will find urgent letters received from Bhaskarpant. I

1. See Maharashtra Puran by poet Ganga Ram. English translation in, "*Bengal Past and Present.*"

have immediately to proceed to his succour, and am starting on the Dasara day. Bhaskarpant has undertaken the laborious project of Maksudabad, for the completion of which he is in sore need of further forces, which must reach him quickly. Therefore you must drive all stragglers to join in immediately."

This letter despatched four days before the actual raid upon Bhaskarpant by Aliwardi Khan, proves that the Pant was neither vain nor incautious, as is generally believed. He knew what risk he was running and had already fully reported to his master the perilous situation he had been driven into. That Raghuji for various reasons could not send him succours in time is obvious. However, the Pant bravely faced the situation and saved himself and his forces from complete ruin and to that extent foiled the enemy's object. He escaped towards Pachet cleverly waging a running fight with his pursuers. From Pachet he fled to Midnapur. The outposts of Burdwan, Hugli and Hijli were abandoned and the scattered Maratha forces were collected together. The Pant plundered Radhanagar and sent a detachment to attack Cuttack. Shaikh Masum the Governor of Cuttack was killed and the post was captured by the Marathas, but Aliwardi Khan coming quickly upon his track recaptured Cuttack, provided for the defence of Orissa and returned to Murshidabad on 9th February 1743. It is now necessary here to narrate why Raghuji could not at once go to the relief of Bhaskarpant.

While the Peshwa was strengthening his position in the north, he came to a severe clash with Raghuji Bhosle, mainly on account of his having claimed the revenues of Bengal and just then captured Garha and Mandla, which Raghuji considered as his sphere. On this point Raghuji lodged through his agent at Satara the following strong protest before Shahu on 4th May 1742. "After my return to Nagpur I found that the Peshwa had encroached upon the sphere assigned to me. He had captured my posts Garha and Mandla, plundered and devastated my territory, and ruined my parganas of Shivni and Chhapar. The ruling king of Mandla burnt himself alive to avoid the disgrace. Upon this the Peshwa marched into Bundelkhand. I have heretofore studiously avoided crossing his path. But now my patience has been tried beyond measure. Please inform the Chhatrapati that I am determined to take full revenge. I have already kept under restraint Trimbak Vishvanath Pethe the Peshwa's commandant, for having violated my domains." This Trimbakrao suffered imprisonment for a short time and was released after Shahu had sent his own emissaries to Raghuji for that purpose. The estrangement between the Peshwa and Raghuji was complete. Let us now go back to the Peshwa's movements.

3. **Raghuji and the Peshwa clash together.**—The Peshwa left Poona at the end of 1741 with the object of checkmating Raghuji in Bengal, and slowly proceeded northward, having secured the Emperor's backing in his projected journey to Bengal. On February 20, 1742 a writer from the Peshwa's camp says, "He was accompanying the Peshwa into Bengal." This is written from Vairagad in the district of Chanda (eastern Berar), so it is clear that the Peshwa was watching Raghuji's moves. Thereafter he marched along the southern bank of the Narmada, and after taking possession of Garha and Mandla stepped into Bundelkhand. In the mean time he asked Sindia and Holkar to collect tribute from the Rajput princes, Abhay Sinh and others. In April these two sardars were in Rajputana, executing the Peshwa's commands. In June the Peshwa wanted to return to the south, but finding the Narmada in flood, decided to canton in Bundelkhand. He had good reason for making such a halt. Babuji Naik smarting under his expulsion from Poona and with a view to avenging himself on that score, rushed into Gujarat and in conjunction with Damaji Gaikwad tried to harass the Peshwa's flank from Malwa in the summer of 1742. But Holkar and Pawar got scent of this attempted mischief and prevented Babuji's entry into Malwa through Gujarat. Babuji had to return discomfited.

It thus became necessary for the Peshwa to make his possession of Malwa and Bundelkhand firmly secure against any hostile attacks, before he moved on to Bengal. Dhar, commanding the western and southern entrance of Malwa, had been entrusted to the care of the Pawars after its first capture in 1729 but it had been restored to the Emperor next year at the desire of Shahu. For ten years this strategic post remained in the Emperor's possession, but when Malwa was formally handed over to the Peshwa by the Emperor, Holkar under orders from the Peshwa took possession of that place on 5th January 1741 and appointed Yashvant Rao Pawar as its guardian. The Pawar brothers had long been estranged from the Peshwa, as they had joined his opponent Dabhade at the battle of Dabhoi. Yashvant Rao now came back to the Peshwa's allegiance on condition that Dhar was given to him for his permanent residence. The Peshwa complied with this request and gave him possession of Dhar, which has since continued to be the seat of this family. Yashvant Rao was a spirited man who had at this time adjusted the longstanding dispute between Sawai Jaysinh and Abhay Sinh of Marwar, thus helping the smooth working of the Peshwa's rule in Malwa and Rajputana.

So the Peshwa planted him firmly in Malwa along with Holkar and Sindia, where these three Maratha Chiefs still hold their sway. Raghuji had his agents, at Delhi, Poona, Satara and elsewhere. On the strength of the information received from them, he plainly asked the Peshwa on 30 September 1742 what his project was, and informed him that he himself was proceeding through Devgad to Bengal to succour Bhaskar Ram. In the mean time Aliwardi Khan too was actively strengthening his own position, expecting an onslaught both from Raghuji and the Peshwa. He applied to the Emperor for military help to ward off the danger and warned him that if no help came, the Emperor must consider Bengal as entirely lost to him. The Peshwa on his part communicated his readiness to help the Emperor if the Chauth of Malwa, Bundelkhand and Allahabad was granted to him. The Emperor agreed to the Peshwa's proposal and asked him to proceed to Bihar and Bengal in order to help Aliwardi Khan to resist the Bhosle's aggression. The Emperor also ordered Aliwardi Khan to pay the Peshwa's expenses. This was highly advantageous to the Khan, as it led to a discord between the two leading Maratha chiefs,—the Peshwa and the Bhosle of Nagpur. Aliwardi Khan at once sent some money to the Peshwa and invited him for a conference. The Peshwa received the Emperor's commands in November and began a cautious and adroit game, on the one hand to put down the recalcitrant Bhosle and on the other to deal effectively with the northern possessions of the Emperor. He tried to reap the greatest advantage out of Bhaskar Ram's trouble. The Peshwa had undertaken to protect the Emperor's territories by driving away all those who had become aggressive. A news-letter of 1st February 1743 from the south bank of the Ganges at Prayag, states "The Shrimant has advanced from Bundelkhand to this place with the object of proceeding to the territory of Patna. He had a holy bath along with his whole following of 75 thousand at Triveni near the Allahabad fort. The boats were provided by the Muslim Subahdar of the place. What a wonderful achievement never before attempted by anybody else, for such a concourse to have a successful pilgrimage thus attaining the highest bliss of life. God is great." From Allahabad the Peshwa proceeded to Benares, to which place he paid a hurried private visit simply for taking a bath in the holy waters, wisely refraining from reconstructing the famous temple.

In the mean time some well-wishers of the Maratha cause attempted to bring about a reconciliation between the Peshwa and Raghuji Bhosle. Obviously it was a grievous prospect for two Maratha principals to make an expedition of domestic feud before the world. From Benares the Peshwa proceeded about eighty miles beyond Gaya where Raghuji himself came and paid a hurried visit to him. For four days they stayed together and deliberated on their differences, but no tangible result came out of this visit.[2]

From Gaya the Peshwa marched to Murshidabad and had a meeting with Aliwardi Khan near Plassey for a week from 31st March. The preliminaries of the meeting were arranged in advance by Pilaji Jadhav on behalf of the Peshwa and Mustafa Khan on behalf of the Nawab. These two met their principals in advance and settled the details including sacred oaths against treachery or foul play. Aliwardi Khan had his camp at Lavda about 7 miles south of the present Berhampur Cantonment. The meeting took place in a gorgeous tent pitched on the west bank of the Bhagirathi near Plassey between the camps of the two chiefs. Malharrao Holkar, Pilaji Jadhav and some others were present at the

2. See *Purandare Daftar*. 1. 152. Unpublished papers of the Vaidya collection, of which one letter is quoted on page 72 of the author's Riyasat Volume on "Peshwa Balaji Bajirao and Shahu."

meeting with the Peshwa. The Nawab presented four elephants, some horses and she-buffaloes to the Peshwa. An agreement was arrived at, purporting (1) that the Nawab should pay 22 lacs of rupees to the Peshwa for his expenses, (2) that he should pay the annual Chauth of Bengal to the Chhatrapati and (3) that both should jointly expel Raghuji from the Province. This last item they at once set about to perform.

The details of their next move are rather conflicting and cannot be accurately determined. Raghuji realizing the danger from this combination, dismantled his camp at Katwa—and formed a plan for retreating while fighting rear-guard actions, confident of the superior activity of his cavalry. The Peshwa finding his helpmate the Nawab's troops utterly useless for a pursuit of Raghuji's active cavalry, parted company with him and alone undertook to bring Raghuji to action.

The Peshwa encountered Raghuji on 10th April in the narrow pass of Bendu near Pachet. The main part of Raghuji's army had already escaped through the pass : only his baggage and pack bullocks and other non-combatants were attacked and plundered while passing through that small pass, quite a trifling loss in reality, although apparently it was deliberately magnified into a serious and severe action. From Pachet Raghuji bent his way to Nagpur and the Peshwa to Gaya on his return to Poona. On 20th May the latter from his camp on the Bhagirathi wrote thus to Ramchandra Baba : "By the grace of God I had a successful expedition into Bengal : R. was routed and my authority established. The Nawab was convinced of my power and I have received ample return in money both from him and the Emperor. R. had invaded Bengal and having established his cantonment in the province, had asserted his strength. The Emperor desires that I should oppose and expel him."[3] Raghuji himself writes on 5th June :—

"I had been to the district of Gaya for succouring Bhaskar Pant, who had during the previous year defeated Ala-Birdi Khan and cantoned in Bengal. The Peshwa came into the same region. He sent me trustworthy agents inviting me to go and meet him. I journeyed to Gaya and had conferences

3. Parasnis collection unpublished. R=Raghuji.

with him. I then travelled back, marched against Ala Birdi Khan and halted at Katwa Gunj on the Bhagirathi, outside Maksudabad. The Khan sent me emissaries for an accommodation promising a peaceful settlement of the dispute. In the meantime the Peshwa arrived on the scene, declaring he had come at the behest of the Emperor to succour Ala Birdi Khan and that he would co-operate with him in driving out R. The two marched against me with the consequences which I have already reported. I then came to Ramgad and the Peshwa after dismissing Ala Birdi's troops started for Gaya via Pachet. There is Nizam-ul-mulk's agent one Shesharao residing with Ala Birdi Khan. He wrote to me Ala Birdi's desire to effect a compromise requesting me to send back Bhaskar Ram for that purpose. Accordingly I sent Bhaskar Ram back to the Nawab and myself started on the return journey with some troops and the non-combatants. As I crossed the Bendu pass, the Peshwa attacked my non-combatants who were behind. Some two hundred of them were killed. I at once came back and drove away the attacking party of the Peshwa. Thereafter I arrived at Nagpur by easy marches."

This affair of a clash between the Peshwa and Raghuji is well summarised by Chitnis in his life of Shahu. The same subject is described by Hingne in a letter to his son Bapuji dated 27th April in which he says, 'the Peshwa declared that he was proceeding for a visit to Raghuji and plundered several places on his way, exacting tribute. A number of people with their wives put an end to their life to avoid oppression. This action was highly resented by the general populace. Then came the news that the Peshwa and the Nawab had a long visit and conferences. They swore mutual friendship by taking sacred oaths. The Peshwa then started to chastise Raghuji. This news gladdened the Emperor's heart, who appreciates the Peshwa's loyalty."[4]

These are all the authentic details that we can get of this memorable affair.

4. *The reconciliation*.—In this long drawn account the reader recognises on the one hand the Peshwa's desire to assert

4. Raj. vol. 3. 217.

central control over all the sardars and execute the policy of the Maratha State in the name of the Chhatrapati, and Raghuji's desire on the other hand like many others before him and after, to carve out an independent sphere of action for himself without interference from the Peshwa. This fissiparous tendency of the Maratha sardars proved the greatest weakness of their position. Raghuji realized that he could not hold his own against the Peshwa and that it was his best interest to adjust matters with him. The difference of the two had already alarmed Shahu, lest they should lead to consequences like the clash of Dabhade with the Peshwa at Dabhoi. He sent urgent calls to both immediately to repair to his presence. Expansion of the Maratha dominion in all quarters of India was the avowed aim of his policy. The defining of spheres was not a serious obstacle : and both parties well understood how the Emperor, and Aliwardi Khan took advantage of these internal dissensions. There were wiser counsels in both the camps, and it did not take long for a reconciliation being effected in the presence of Shahu. It was soon reported that the Peshwa waived his claim on Bengal and was willing to abstain from molesting Raghuji in his legitimate sphere. An agreement was signed by both on 31st August 1743 at Satara by which all the territory from Berar to the east right up to Cuttack, Bengal and Lucknow, was assigned to Raghuji, with which the Peshwa bound himself not to interfere : and the territory west of this line including Ajmere, Agra, Prayag and Malwa were to be the exclusive spheres of the Peshwa."[5]

Another paper thus defines the Peshwa's sphere. "All the territories previously acquired by the Peshwa, Mokasa and Jagirs, the Government of the Konkan and Malwa, the tributes from Agra, Prayag and Ajmere, three taluks from the Patna district, the Inam villages granted to the Peshwa of the revenue of 20 thousand, within Raghuji's jurisdiction of the Karnatak, these are to be the exclusive assignments of the Peshwa to which Raghuji or any one else should not object. Lucknow, Bihar, lower-Bengal, i.e. all the lands from Berar

5. Chitnis Bakhar page 79, Aitl. Patravyavahar 35-39 ; N. R. 1-10 ; Raj. vol. 2 pp. 98-99.

to Cuttack are assigned to Raghuji from which he should realize his tributes and other claims."

Thus the Peshwa and Raghuji both bound themselves to respect each other's boundaries and not to encroach on the spheres assigned to them. The Peshkash or presents from these territories were also regulated. The Peshwa and Raghuji were completely reconciled in the presence of the Chhatrapati and exchanged dinners. Shahu called upon them both to lay their hands on his feet and swear that they would never more entertain suspicions about each other. They entertained the Maharaja at dinner, and after all assurances for a firm friendship had been secured, they were given leave to depart. A separate agreement was also effected about the disputed districts of Garha and Mandla. So this long standing rivalry of Raghuji with the Peshwa was closed for the present, and it must be said to the credit of both that their relations never came to be appreciably strained during their lifetime.

5. Massacre of Maratha generals.—Thus during the rainy season of 1743 the Peshwa and the Senasahib Subah Raghuji Bhosle both became strengthened in their friendship, and about the next Dassara time each undertook his own premeditated tasks. Raghuji at once proceeded from Satara to Nagpur and despatched Bhaskar Ram to complete his unfinished work in Bengal. Bhaskar left Nagpur on his journey early in 1744, fully equipped with men and material. The news of this fresh invasion roused Aliwardi Khan to a sense of his danger and drove him to adopt a dastardly plan of treachery against the Marathas. Since his accession to the subahdarship the Khan had been so overwhelmed by worries, difficulties and disasters of an unprecedented character that he found himself altogether helpless to meet the present danger. Bhaskar Ram and Mir Habib did their utmost to harass him in all possible ways. A demand for Chauth arrived from Bhaskar, with a threat of dire consequences in case of refusal. Out of his fertile brain the Khan formed a dark plan of vengeance for overcoming Bhaskar Ram. He decided to entice him to a private meeting and have him murdered with all his party. For this he took into his confidence his Afghan commandant Mustafa Khan and his private counsellor Janki

Ram, both bitter haters of the Marathas. They were induced by the Nawab on specious promises to join in the conspiracy and developed all minute details for its execution. They arranged the plan with consummate dexterity. Bhaskar Ram had his camp at Katwa and the Nawab had his at Amaniganj about 20 miles north of that place. Mustafa Khan sent his agents to Bhaskar Ram and opened negotiations offering submission and declaring that the Nawab had no desire to fight. He proposed that they should both meet in an open conference and come to some amicable arrangement acceptable to both as regards the amount of Chauth. Bhaskar Ram was allured to this course as he hoped to gain his object without recourse to arms.

Bhaskar Ram's agents and those of the Nawab discussed and fixed the details of the meeting. The Qoran and the Ganges water were both profusely used in their oaths. Mir Habib at every moment warned Bhaskarpant against deceit, but in vain. A grand decorated tent was erected on the plain of Mankara between Amaniganj and Katwa, enclosed all round by high double walls of tent-cloth between which armed men were kept concealed, ready to rush out at a given signal and cut down all the Marathas they could lay their hands on. Friday 30th March 1744 (Chaitra Vadya, 13th of Shak 1666, Safar 26) was fixed for the meeting. The Nawab arrived before the Marathas and taking his seat on his dais waited to receive Bhaskar Ram. The enclosure had several doors at which armed sentries were posted as guards. At the appointed hour Bhaskarpant arrived with his retinue, was received at the entrance by Mustafa Khan and Janki Ram, who held his two hands and conducted him to the Nawab inside, uttering expressions of welcome during the interval. As soon as the Pant reached the front of the Nawab's seat, the latter rose and asked loudly "Which is the brave Bhaskar Ram?" In answer to this Bhaskar Ram was pointed out and introduced; when the Nawab in a loud voice called out 'Cut these marauders down." At this signal the concealed Muslims rushed out of their places and began an indiscriminate slaughter; among the perpetrators being Mir Jafar Khan and Mir Kasim Khan of future notoriety in history. The Maratha chiefs though equally armed were taken by surprise, and before they could draw their swords in self-defence were cut down to a man. Mir Kasim cut down Bhaskarpant himself. The whole place became a heap of mangled dead bodies, which the Nawab watched with satisfaction from his seat. The Muslims cut down the ropes of the enclosure and prevented Maratha troops waiting outside from coming to help their leaders. Of the 22 chiefs killed, 20 were Hindus and 2 were Muslims. Of the Hindus three were Brahmans and seventeen Marathas.

The news of this dreadful occurrence reached Raghuji Gaikwad, who was guarding the Maratha camp behind. He exercised great presence of mind in saving the camp and enabling the inmates to escape with as much property as they could carry. Gaikwad eluded the pursuers and reached Nagpur with the broken remnants of Bhaskar Ram's army and communicated to Raghuji Bhosle, graphic details of the dastardly attack on the leaders. The Nawab returned to Murshidabad from Amanigunj and celebrated his triumph with great rejoicing, feeling happy at having got rid of his mortal enemies so easily. What a wave of indignation raged through Maharashtra when the news of the occurrence arrived, had better be imagined. Raghuji was for a time stunned with the blow, but soon recovered and concerted quick measures of revenge, after holding anxious deliberations with his sons and Bhaskar's brother Konher Ram and his large family.[6]

For various reasons, however, no immediate steps could be taken to avenge the dreadful murder of the Maratha Chiefs. Men, money and material most essential for a grave undertaking could not be easily obtained and although Raghuji did not waste a moment in idle speculation, he could not organize a proper expedition for at least a year. Mir Habib was all the while there to urge and advise him. In the mean time

6. Bhaskar Ram's wife Kashibai alias Taibai then a few months advanced in pregnancy had been left behind at the camp of Katwa ; her life was saved by a Muslim lady of the Pathan clan. A palanquin was immediately provided in which she was secretly conducted to Benares. Here she later gave birth to a son who was named Kashirao Bhaskar. Bhaskar's brother Konher Ram was utterly overwhelmed with grief which Raghuji and his sons did their best to assuage. Taibai was given the Subahdarship of Berar with suitable provision. Baburao son of Konher Ram served the Nagpur state with distinction.

Mustafa Khan and Aliwardi Khan came to be severely estranged from each other, and the former solicitated Raghuji to come quickly and crush the wicked Nawab.

Even Mir Jafar rose against the Nawab, with the result that there were again unrest and confusion throughout Bengal. Raghuji left Nagpur in February 1745 and thus reported about his move : "Leaving Nagpur I arrived straight against Cuttack and after a couple of months siege and incessant bombardment captured the place on 6th May. Now I am proceeding towards Maksudabad. I have captured Durlabh Ram, son of the Nawab's treacherous minister Janki Ram." This Durlabh Ram was sent a prisoner to Nagpur whence he effected his release in January 1747 after paying Rupees three lacs for ransom.

6. Chauth imposed upon Bengal.—Raghuji demanded from Aliwardi Khan a fine of three crores for the murder (mund-katai, heads cut) of his 22 brave captains. As Raghuji was proceeding against Maksudabad, Mustafa Khan and Aliwardi Khan came to open blows and the former was killed in a battle at Jagadishpur near Arrah in June 1745. Raghuji cantoned in Birbhum for the monsoon. After the rains a running fight ensued between him and the Nawab. Raghuji had to sustain a defeat near Murshidabad on 21st December, and hastened back to Nagpur, leaving a party of 3,000 troops for the assistance of Mir Habib,[7] who remained in possession of Orissa. The Peshwa also sent his agents demanding Chauth from Aliwardi Khan in accordance with the Emperor's grant. Thus the Nawab now came to be pressed between two enemies, the Bhosle and the Peshwa. The realisation of the fine for the murders, however, was put off for a long time, as Raghuji was overwhelmed in financial difficulties. By the end of 1746 he made his preparations and despatched his son Janoji against the Nawab. Janoji reached Cuttack in January 1747 and was joined by Mir Habib ; and the combined forces inflicted a defeat upon the Nawab near Burdwan. But soon after Janoji having been again defeated by the Nawab, retraced his steps to Nagpur.

7. P. D. 20. 26.

The Nawab, however, did not fare better for all his measures to obtain relief from the Bhosle menace. Mir Jafar and other officers formed a plot to assassinate him, but it failed. Raghuji got so involved in troubles of various descriptions that for long he could not attend to Bengal. Nizam-ul mulk and Shahu were both nearing their graves and engrossed Raghuji's attention. Shahu invited him to Satara in 1747 asking for his son Mudhoji in adoption and Raghuji had to respond to the call. In the meantime Janoji who was campaigning in Bengal had to return to Nagpur on account of his mother's death. Raghuji, therefore, despatched his third son Sabaji to Bengal. He joined Mir Habib and the two did their best to harass the Nawab in all possible ways. The situation became so intolerable to the Nawab that his shrewd wife pressed him to come to an accommodation with the Marathas. He accepted her counsel and deputed Mir Jafar to meet Mir Habib and Janoji personally and settle the terms of peace. The protracted negotiations were brought to a close in March 1751 by a solemn treaty containing the following terms :--

(1) That Mir Habib be confirmed in the government of Orissa, as the Naib or deputy of the subahdar of Murshidabad;

(2) That the Nawab should annually pay twelve lacs of rupees to the Bhosle of Nagpur for the Chauth of Bengal and Bihar;

(3) When these amounts are regularly paid, the Bhosles should no longer harass the two provinces by their expeditions;

(4) That the district of Cuttack, i.e. territory up to the river Subarna-rekha be considered Bhosle's possession.

For the arrears of Chauth the Nawab paid 32 lacs to the Bhosle at once. Immediately the treaty was signed, Janoji returned to Nagpur, withdrawing all his troops, and appointing Shivabhat Sathe as his agent to manage the affairs of Orissa. Sathe thereafter executed his task satisfactorily and maintained an efficient government in the province for a long time. No amount was, however, recovered by way of fine for the murder of Bhaskar Ram and his colleagues, but the main purpose of that general's expedition, viz. the imposition of the Chauth upon Bengal and Bihar, was accomplished and the possession of Cuttack was ensured. Mir Habib did not live long to enjoy the peace for which he had all these years exerted. He was killed in a fracas with some Maratha guards on 24th August 1752. Some allege that he was killed by Janoji Bhosle. Raghuji's tenacity and perseverance are well exemplified in this ten years struggle for the conquest of Bengal. He gradually lost his health, contracted illness and died on 14th February 1755, followed soon after by Aliwardi Khan on April 10, 1756.

CHRONOLOGY

CHAPTER X

1727	Son Madhosinh born to Jaysinh.
1742, January 12	Sambhaji Angria dies.
1742, November	Jotiba Sindia and party assassinated by Birsinh Dev of Orchha.
" "	Naro Shankar razed Orchha to the ground and formed his seat at Jhansi.
1743	Tulaji Angria made Sarkhel.
1743, September 23	Sawai Jaysinh dies.
1744, February	Mahadev Bhat Hingne dies at Delhi.
1744, December to June, 1745	Peshwa's expedition to Bhilsa.
1745, January 15	Tulaji captures Govalkot and Anjanvel.
1745, March 11	Ranoji Sindia captures Bhilsa.
1745, July 3	Ranoji Sindia dies.
1745	War of Jaipur succession started.
1747, February 9	Rajmal minister of Jaipur dies.
1747, March 1—2	Battle of Rajmahal, Ishwarisinh victorious over Madhosinh.
1747, May 3	Tulaji Angria visits Shahu at Satara.
1747	Nadir Shah assassinated ; Ahmad Shah Abdali succeeds.
1748, January 15	Rajkot of Chaul captured by the Peshwa.
1748, Jan.—March	Battle of Mudagad ; Tulaji Angria defeated.
1748, March 3	Battle of Manupur, Ahmad Shah Abdali defeated.
1748, April 1	Mudagad recaptured from Tulaji.
1748, May 21	Peshwa and Madhosinh meet for a week at Newai.
1748, May 28	Manikgad taken by the Peshwa.
1748, August 10	Holkar exacts terms from Ishwarisinh.

1750, Monsoon	Sindia and Holkar in Rajputana.
1750, August	Ishwarisinh assassinates his minister Kesho-das.
1750, December 14	Ishwarisinh commits suicide.
1751, January 10	Fearful massacre of the Marathas at Jaipur, Rajput-Maratha friendship ends.

Sawai Jaysinh

CHAPTER X

ON TO FURTHER SUCCESSES

[1744—1747]

1 Consolidation of Bundelkhand, Jhansi.
2 Two notable deaths.
3 The Rajput war.
4 Social contact.
5 The Angria brothers, Manaji and Tulaji.
6 Pilaji Jadhav.

1. **Consolidation of Bundelkhand, Jhansi.**—To confirm the Maratha hold on Malwa and Bundelkhand Balajirao permanently placed the three valiant Maratha chiefs Holkar, Sindia and Pawar to guard the region between the Narmada and the Jamna. From Bundelkhand it was easy to exercise a check upon the Rajputs in the west, to descend in a moment into the Doab and Oudh to the north and advance to Benares, Patna and even Bengal to the east. If a large Maratha army were permanently posted in Bundelkhand it could be quickly moved to any place outside where required. The Peshwa thus realized the necessity of creating a strong base in the north and deliberately spent more than a year in accomplishing this purpose. Unremitting efforts were made to obtain possession of the central post of Orchha, strategically convenient for exercising control around. Orchha is now a railway station about six miles east of Jhansi on the railway line running to Banda. The famous ancient fort of Chanderi is thirty miles south-west of it, and Gwalior about 50 miles north, while sixty miles to the east are Jetpur and Kalinjar, all more or less fortified places which the Marathas now tried to possess. There were two high roads for entering Bundelkhand from the south, one by crossing the Narmada and proceeding by way of Ujjain along the present Sironj-Bhilsa railway route. The other was to proceed along the Narmada to the east and enter Bundelkhand direct after crossing the river at Garha. It will be recalled that when the first Maratha success in the north was effected in 1728-29 by Bajirao and his brother Chimnaji, the latter took the first route and Bajirao the second.

Although Bajirao had obtained a footing in Bundelkhand, since the Chhatrasal incident in 1729, the Marathas hardly made any headway in that region for several years. Chhatrasal's numerous descendants who held the main chiefships in Bundelkhand were not disposed to accept the Maratha domination without demur. Govind Ballal Kher was the officer appointed by Bajirao to manage the affairs of Bundelkhand. He took up his station at Sagar and tried to collect the annual Chauth. Orchha was then governed by a small Bundela king named Birsinh Dev, who also possessed another small post about 6 miles to the west named Balavantnagar, which had a large hill adjoining it. Birsinh Dev built a fort in this hill which came to be called Jhansi.

In the rainy season of 1742, when the Peshwa had established his camp in the vicinity of Orchha, he despatched a small detachment under Jotiba Sindia, son of Ranoji, and a revenue accountant named Malhar Krishna demanding Chauth from Birsinh Dev, who had not paid it for some time. Jotiba and Malhar proceeded and took up their quarters in Jhansi where one dark night in November 1742, Birsinh Dev suddenly attacked the Maratha camp, killed several men and carried away the heads of Jotiba Sindia and Malhar Krishna, after plundering all their belongings. This was an outrage which the Peshwa could not allow to go unpunished. He quickly despatched Naro Shankar to avenge the wrong. The latter took severe measures, attacked Orchha and carried away Birsinh Dev a prisoner in chains and kept him closely confined on the hill-fort of Jhansi. Orchha was burnt and razed to the ground. The Peshwa's power was asserted to the full and all resistance was violently put down. Negotiations were thereafter opened by the raja, who was released and restored to Orchha, after having given up Jhansi to the Marathas, and a suitable fine for the murders of Jotiba Sindia and others. Thus Jhansi henceforward became the principal Maratha post in this province and Naro Shankar was appointed its first governor. He proved a strong and capable ruler and held the office till 1756. He soon conquered the post of Churkhi (Charkheri) in the neighbourhood where some of Birsinh Dev's relatives lived. The descendants of Birsinh Dev removed their seat to Teheri, as Orchha was in ruins, and there the family still rules.

Naro Shankar established a town at the foot of the fort of Jhansi and invited there many Brahman and other families from the Deccan, so that Jhansi became an essentially Maratha colony in Bundelkhand and acquired a permanent name in Maratha history.[1]

The year 1743 proved memorable in the new Peshwa's career. He had met Sawai Jaysinh the year before and obtained through him the imperial grant of Malwa. He then descended into Bihar and Bengal as already narrated and adjusted his differences with Raghuji Bhosle and Aliwardi Khan, thus ensuring an extension of Maratha power in the east. From the beginning he had set his heart upon the subjugation of Bundelkhand, and would have stayed longer in the north, had he not been abruptly called away to Satara by Shahu who was then suffering from a severe illness. The Peshwa at Satara was relieved to find that Shahu had recovered. The months of July and August were spent at the capital in effecting a lasting reconciliation between him and Raghuji Bhosle. Pilaji Jadhav writes to Ramchandra Baba on 2nd August, "The Peshwa has been restored to the favour of the queen Sagunabai, who had taken offence at his conduct towards Raghuji." For the first time the Maratha sardars made their monsoon camp in the north, breaking the usual Maratha practice of returning home for the rains. The Peshwa was requested by Mahadoba Purandare to order Holkar and Sindia to stay in the north in view of the necessity of the situation. The Peshwa accepted Mahadoba's proposal and the sardars from 1743 onward took their permanent residence in Malwa and Bundelkhand with all their military following.[2]

2. Two notable deaths.—The Peshwa was anxious to complete his work in the north, but for over a year could not disengage himself from the affairs of the Chhatrapati and of

1. After Naro Shankar the following Maratha officers held sway at this place :

Mahadaji Govind Kakirde, 1756-1760 ; Baburao Konher Kolhatkar, 1761-1765 ; Vishvasrao Lakshman (Naro Shankar's nephew), 1766-1769. Raghunath Hari Newalkar, 1769 on, in whose family the chiefship became hereditary and whose last descendant was the Rani Lakshmibai the heroine of the mutiny.

2. P. D. 21 9.

the Nizam. The Bundelas were up in arms, against whom both Sindia and Holkar did their best to hold the ground. Bhilsa which had some time back come into Maratha possession was wrested by the Nawab Yar Mohammad Khan of Bhopal. Ranoji Sindia after a strenuous effort recaptured it on 11th March 1745. Bhilsa forms the centre of Malwa and continues Sindia's main outpost to the present day.

Towards the end of 1744, the Peshwa again started on a journey to the north and took up his residence at Bhilsa. He had not only to deal with external enemies but also to remove the differences and internal jealousies which were growing in intensity between the three principal sardars, Sindia, Holkar and Pawar and a number of minor subordinates all more or less bent upon personal gains, with the result that severe mutual conflicts became common to the detriment of the public interests.

The Peshwa first settled the affairs of Malwa and then turned his attention to Bundelkhand, where a number of chiefs such as those of Datia, Chanderi, Jetpur, Kalinjar, Panna and other places, offered a stern opposition to the present Maratha penetrations. It required long years of labour and expense before these opponents could be overcome. Their internal jealousies proved their greatest weakness of which the Marathas did not fail to take advantage.[3] The Peshwa could not stay long in the north, but returned to Poona for the monsoon, leaving the affairs to the care of Ranoji Sindia and Malharrao Holkar. Damodar Mahadev Hingne thus reports the Emperor's view of the Peshwa's doings in a letter dated 23rd June 1745 : "The Emperor asked me to take to the Peshwa his presents, elephants, horses, ornaments, &c., which I delivered to him in Bundelkhand and which he received with due ceremony. The Peshwa felt highly gratified at this signal honour coming to him from the Emperor. Having settled the affairs of Bundelkhand, he left for the south and I am accompanying him."[4]

At this time Ramchandra Bawa Suktankar and Gangadhar Yashvant Chandrachud acted as the Peshwa's agents

3. As an instance, note the case of Arjun Sinh Dhandhere in K. S. Patren Yadi Nos. 50, 57 and 58.

4. Raj. vol. 6. 174.

with Sindia and Holkar respectively, and watched over the execution of the Peshwa's orders for guarding the best interests of the Maratha State. Both were able men and had worked faithfully since Bajirao's days. Ramchandra Bawa was particularly adept in the collection of tributes and taxes, and inspired awe and respect for the Maratha government among northern peoples by his methods of economy and diplomacy. Gangadhar Yashvant was of a different type, possessing the qualities of an intrepid soldier and serving Holkar with loyalty and devotion. These two men for long executed the Peshwa's policy in the north.

Ranoji Sindia and Ramchandra Bawa pulled together well and kept on cordial terms with each other. Ranoji died suddenly on 3rd July 1745 at Shujalpur, about 30 miles north west of Bhopal. He had long served the Maratha State with valour and integrity, having started his career under the first Peshwa Balaji Vishvanath, and is rightly regarded not only as the founder of the present house of the Sindias but also of having been a principal helpmate of Bajirao in establishing Maratha power in Malwa and Bundelkhand. Ranoji left behind him four sons, equally valiant and capable, Jayappa, Dattaji, Tukoji and Mahadji who all distinguished themselves in later history. Minabai alias Nimbabai was the mother of the first three and Chimabai was the mother of Mahadji. Ranoji had a fifth son Jotiba who was killed before his father at Orchha. After Ranoji's death Jayappa became the head of the family and his relations with Ramchandra Bawa soon came to be severely strained as the sequel will show.

It is necessary here to advert to another important death, that of Mahadev Bhat Hingne, the first Maratha ambassador at the Court of Delhi, a distinguished diplomat, who accidentally lost his life on 1st February 1744. He left his priestly profession at Nasik and accompanied Balaji Vishvanath in his first expedition to Delhi in 1718 and came to be permanently posted there to look after the Maratha interests. For twenty-five years he conducted his onerous duties with courage and satisfaction, built up a tradition and a diplomatic reputation at the Mughal Court which long survived his death. His house continued to serve the Maratha State through generations adding to their ambassadorial duties the successful branch of banking. Mahadev's end was curious. He had gone on a visit to Mansur Ali Khan, the grand Bakhshi of Delhi. During conversation on a vital subject of politics he lost his temper and called names which the Bakhshi bitterly resented. He was at once cut to pieces by the Bakhshi's guards, while his son Bapuji was wounded in the scuffle. Mahadev Bhat's sons Bapuji, Damodar (Dada), Purushottam (Nana), and Devrao (Tatya), all earned reputation for ability and probity in later history.

The settlement of Bundelkhand was not at all an easy affair. The fort of Jetpur resisted for a long time and round it raged a severe struggle. The place was besieged by Sindia and Holkar and captured by them on 5th May 1746. They reported, " the Bundelas had stored an immense amount of ammunition at Jetpur. We lost a thousand men killed and some four thousand wounded." The chief of Datia took long to be reduced. Antri was captured on 24th January 1747. The plan adopted by the Maratha sardars was to prevent a strong Bundela combination. Each was singly combated and reduced. In this arduous campaign Ramchandra Baba's genius proved most useful. But after the death of Ranoji Ramchandra Bawa became estranged from Jayappa, and for a time it seemed that on this account the Maratha interests would suffer a severe drawback. As soon as the Peshwa came to know of this unhappy development, he invited both Jayappa and Ramchandra Baba to Poona and brought about a reconciliation between them.

3. **The Rajput war.**—Two outstanding personalities, Raja Shahu and Sawai Jaysinh, growing up together in a spirit of mutual respect and friendship, created the cordial relations that long subsisted between the Marathas and the Rajputs and which facilitated the rapid extension of Maratha power in the north during the regimes of the first two Peshwas. Soon after Bajirao's death, affairs began to take a different turn between the Rajputs and the Marathas. The reader should note the Rajput rulers contemporary with Shahu mentioned in an earlier chapter. For a time the Marathas and the Rajputs had acted in concert and risen against the religious persecution practised by Aurangzeb. It has already been

Madhosinh

narrated how in 1710 the Rajput potentates held a two years conference at the Pushkar Lake and executed an important agreement for preserving the hereditary purity of Hindu blood, viz., that no Rajputs should offer their girls in marriage to the Muslims and that if any prince had more than one male issue, precedence should be given to the son born of an Udaipur mother in determining the succession. This contract, however noble in principle, proved disastrous in practice. This is well illustrated in the case of the Jaipur Raj.

The renowned ruler Sawai Jaysinh of Jaipur, for long a great figure in Rajputana, the builder of his new capital, a great social reformer and patron of learning, died on 23rd September 1743, at the age of 55, leaving behind him two sons, Ishwarisinh, the elder and Madhosinh the younger : the latter born of an Udaipur Princess claimed the kingdom in consonance with the agreement of Pushkar. He was born in 1727 and Sangramsinh the Rana of Udaipur conferred on him his Pargana of Rampura and entrusted its management to Sawai Jaysinh, in order to make good his future claim to the Jaipur throne. Madhosinh spent most of his childhood and youth at Udaipur in the company of his mother. As soon, however, as Sawai Jaysinh died, Ishwarisinh seized the throne and obtained the Emperor's recognition for his succession. But Jagatsinh the Rana of Udaipur supported Madhosinh's claim even at the risk of an armed conflict. Thus a war started which continued intermittently for some seven years.

As soon as Ishwarisinh occupied the throne after his father's death in 1743, Jagatsinh of Udaipur collected his troops and with Madhosinh marched upon Jaipur. Ishwarisinh came out to meet the forces of Udaipur. For nearly two months the two armies remained facing each other on the plain of Jahajpur, conducting peaceful parleys, as a result of which Ishwarisinh agreed to hand over a few more parganas to Madhosinh ; but the latter demanded quite a half and half division of the kingdom. Ishwarisinh enlisted the sympathies of Sindia and Holkar and in 1745 defeated Madhosinh who then sent his agents to Poona to obtain the Peshwa's support. In the meantime Ranoji Sindia died and there arose serious differences of policy between his son Jayappa and Malharrao Holkar.

Madhosinh's agents succeeded in obtaining the armed help of Malharrao, while Jayappa supported Ishwarisinh's cause. Both Sindia and Holkar were heavily bribed by the rival Rajput parties and fell a prey to personal greed. At such a juncture the capable minister of Jaipur, Ayamal Khatri, popularly known as Rajmal or Malji died on 9th February 1747, an event which caused serious confusion in the affairs of Jaipur. Ishwarisinh's troops marched against Madhosinh and his ally the Rana of Udaipur; a bloody battle took place for two long days, 1st and 2nd March 1747, at Rajmahal on the river Banas near Deoli in which Ishwarisinh scored a decisive victory, and the Marathas secured much plunder. Rana Jagatsinh humbly sued for peace. Ishwarisinh in his distress had already sent his vakils to Poona, pressing the Peshwa to support his cause and agreeing to offer large amounts in return. On 7th March 1747, the Peshwa writes to Ramchandra Baba from Poona, "The Rana of Udaipur's vakils have come here. They urge that both Madhosinh and Ishwarisinh are equal sons of Sawai Jaysinh and must be justly treated. Ishwarisinh should fulfil his promise of handing over parganas worth 24 lacs to Madhosinh. You must support this claim and obtain from the Rana [for me] 15 lacs or more which his vakils agree to pay.[5]

Upon this Ramchandra Baba replied, "Madhosinh's offer is unreal. There is no chance of getting any funds from him. People here very well know that we have so long supported Ishwarisinh. It would now be scandalous to shift our ground." There was here a clear clash between Sindia and Holkar, and the Peshwa became confused. Ishwarisinh's exasperation knew no bounds. He sent an emphatic protest to the Peshwa. Holkar would not yield. He steadfastly supported Madhosinh, whose minister Kaniram proceeded to Poona towards the end of 1747. The situation became so tragic that the Peshwa decided at once to go to the north and himself decide the dispute on the spot. This is known as the Peshwa's expedition to *Newai*, for here Madhosinh paid to him a visit.

The year 1747 was full of grave happenings in the north. Nadir Shah was assassinated in Persia and his position and

5. *Aitihasik Patravyavahar*, 68.

power were usurped by Ahmad Shah Adbali, with whom future Maratha history came to be linked. Ahmad Shah claimed the Indian conquests of Nadir Shah and threatened the Emperor with an immediate expedition, unless his claims were speedily granted. In his sore need the Emperor sent an urgent appeal for help to Shahu who ordered the Peshwa at once to proceed to Delhi and extricate the Emperor from his difficulties. He started on 10th December, but before he reached Delhi,[6] the Emperor's forces had met Abdali and defeated him at Manupur, on 3rd March 1748. The Peshwa, however, arrived and was cordially received by the Emperor. Raja Shahu was highly gratified with this account.[7]

At this time the dispute between Mādhosinh and Ishwarisinh had reached its height. Ishwarisinh had gone to join the Mughal forces at the call of the Emperor, but was disgraced for having run away from the battlefield as soon as the action joined. The Peshwa had large forces at his command and went from Delhi to Jaipur in order to coerce the two claimants into a reasonable agreement. Of a brave but haughty temperament, Ishwarisinh remained sullenly aloof, while Madhosinh paid a visit to the Peshwa and was cordially received at Newai, 39 miles south of Jaipur. Conferences took place for a week from 21st May 1748. A workable compromise was effected between Madhosinh and Ishwarisinh. The latter at the pressure of the Peshwa agreed to hand over four of his districts to his brother, and Malharrao Holkar stood guarantee for the observance of the terms by the two brothers. Rupees 3 lacs was paid as nazar to the Peshwa; and he returned to Poona on 9th July. In the meantime as Ishwarisinh would not fulfil his contract, Malharrao Holkar marched against him with his force and exacted fulfilment of the terms on 10th August 1748.[8]

The Emperor Muhammad Shah was hastening to his grave, carrying away with him whatever semblance of imperial power and prestige there remained at Delhi. The Pathans were rising in power to give the death-blow to the Mughals.

---

6. P. D. 27. 29, 30.
7. P. D. 2. 9.
8. Raj. vol. 6—190, 191, 581.

The Wazir Safdar Jang was powerless to relieve the situation. In the south, king Shahu was similarly in his last moments, causing grave anxiety to all those who had so long sustained Maratha power.

Jayappa was in open disagreement with Malharrao and they between them lost the Rajput friendship for which they had to pay dearly at Panipat. The Peshwa was keenly conscious of this situation and wrote from Newai a strong admonition to Ramchandra Bawa condemning the open rupture that had developed between Sindia and Holkar and of which the enemies of the Marathas did not fail to take advantage."[9] The Peshwa recalled them both to Poona for effecting a compromise, but no amount of paper advice or sentimental appeals could heal the sore differences. The want of cordial co-operation between the sardars is indeed the root cause of the Maratha disaster at Panipat.

It would be convenient at this place to close the episode of Ishwarisinh, although it overlaps the period after Shahu's death to a small extent. The year 1749 passed peacefully in the north. Sindia and Holkar were in the south and the Wazir Safdar Jang was trying to establish his position with the new Emperor Ahmad Shah. The Maratha vakils pressed Ishwarisinh for payment of the promised amounts, and as these were not forthcoming, the Peshwa despatched Sindia and Holkar during the rainy season of 1750 to the north with orders to exact the tribute from Ishwarisinh, who was then deserted by his erstwhile allies and was driven to desperation. In a fit of rage he poisoned his minister Keshodas in August 1750 and persecuted his artillery officer Shivnath, and thus became odious to all. There was no one in the state who could control the situation. In the midst of these troubles Malharrao Holkar approached Jaipur with his hordes in November and put severe pressure against Ishwarisinh for payment. " The latter would offer only a lac or two. Malharrao's wrath knew no bounds. He talked of wreaking vengeance for the death of Keshodas. Ishwarisinh's officials would not venture to meet Malharrao for fear of reprisals. Ishwarisinh

9. This is a long unpublished letter lent by the late Parasnis and is printed at pages 70-73 of the Riyasat Madhya Vibhag 2.

was at his wits' end. Hearing that Malharrao was rapidly marching on, Ishwarisinh ordered a cobra and some deadly poison to be brought in. He swallowed it at midnight and got himself bitten by the cobra. In the early hours of the morning he expired. Three of his wives and a concubine similarly swallowed poison and died (December 14). These four, and 20 other maids burnt themselves on the funeral pyre. There was consternation in the city. Madhosinh arrived and pacified Holkar. Jayappa Sindia also arrived in due course when Madhosinh played a dastardly game against the friendly Marathas. Pretending outward friendship he invited Jayappa and Malharrao for dinner and served them poisoned food. Jayappa detected the mischief in time and the sardars managed to escape death. It was a providential relief. Another plot to destroy the Marathas was hatched the next day. Five thousand Marathas along with Jayappa were invited to view the city. Following a pre-arranged plan after their entrance, the gates of the city were suddenly closed and a general massacre of the Marathas ensued, for about 12 hours from midday to midnight on 10th January 1751. About three thousand Marathas were killed and a thousand wounded, including 25 prominent commanders of Jayappa, a hundred Brahmans, and a number of women and children. Several tried to escape by jumping over the rampart, receiving severe injuries in the attempt. One thousand good horses, ornaments of gold and pearls and other valuables were plundered by the Rajputs. Two days after, the Marathas organized themselves in a camp a few miles away from the town. Madhosinh started negotiations, which proved of no avail.[10]

After these dreadful occurrences, which only served to create bitter resentment between the Rajputs and the Marathas, an accident alone prevented Jayappa and Malharrao wreaking severe vengeance on the Jaipur city. Safdar Jung at this moment was threatened by the Pathans of the Gangetic Doab, as will be narrated later, and sent urgent appeals and piteous solicitations for Maratha help, to which Jayappa and Malharrao, now acting in perfect amity, responded and marched directly from Jaipur into the Doab; and thus the affairs of Jaipur

10. P. D. 2-31 and P. D. 27. 64, 65.

came to be relegated to the background. The Jaipur episode closed, leaving serious rancour behind. The friendship which had lasted between the southern invaders and the Rajput chiefs had given place to enmity and bitterness.

The Peshwa on his way back from Newal halted at Dhar and formally handed that place back to Yashvantrao Pawar, along with Mandavgad and its adjunct Songad. Yashvantrao thereafter remained perfectly loyal to the Peshwa and sacrificed his life at Panipat. Thus a sort of consolidation of Maratha power in the north was effected during the life-time of their revered monarch Shahu.

4. Social contact.—The cultural exchange between Maharashtra and the other parts of this Indian continent must have been immense and is an interesting and useful field for special research. Such an exchange had commenced in the days of Shivaji and continued uninterrupted for half a century particularly during Aurangzeb's invasion of the south and the first Peshwa's expedition to Delhi in 1718. Thereafter it received an immense impetus during the stirring twenty years regime of the Peshwa Bajirao, who developed particularly cultural relations with the Court of Sawai Jaysinh. The latter performed a horse-sacrifice for which he invited learned Pandits from all parts of India. Jaysinh's personal Guru was a Maharashtrian pandit of Paithan named Ratnakar Bhatt Mahashabde. Ratnakar's brother Prabhakar Bhatt and the latter's son Brajanath were Jaysinh's family priests, who all exerted themselves to bring about the famous visit of Bajirao to Jaipur in March 1736. Jaysinh's minister Dinanath visited Satara. The mission of Deepsinh sent by that prince to Satara which has been already dealt with, was a great cementing factor, as also the memorable pilgrimage of the Peshwa's mother. A Kanarese Pandit named Harikavi was for long the chief judge (Prad-vivaka) of Sawai Jaysinh. This kind of common life and thought exchange continued to grow side by side with the Mughal-Maratha struggle which Bajirao so strenuously conducted. It is a subject which deserves a careful and independent treatment, how several cities of India, Satara, Poona, Bhaganagar, Burhanpur, Jaipur, Benares, Delhi, Tan-

jore and others were linked together by an exchange of social life and trade.

This social and cultural contact attained fresh strength during Nanasaheb's regime owing to many Maratha families now taking up their permanent residence in Malwa and Bundelkhand. Large numbers of men had to migrate from their homes for military, diplomatic and religious purposes and move from one place to another as duty and convenience dictated. These frequent and rapid movements could not but have materially affected their social life. The poverty of the Maratha lands was much relieved. People's life became expanded and enriched. Changes silently took place in their language, dress, food and manners by contact with the world outside. Large edifices and palaces on the northern model came to be constructed in Maharashtra for residential and religious purposes with well laid-out gardens attached to them. New flowers and fruits were imported and planted. Deccani Brahmans rapidly assimilated military training and avidly took to a new life of war and diplomacy, giving up the exclusive religious pursuits of their ancestors' days. The third Peshwa himself felt extremely charmed with the novel ways and varied pleasures of life in the north as compared with its simplicity and ruggedness in the south. A letter written in a high flown sanskrit style by this Peshwa to his friend Nana Purandare from Bundelkhand on 22 December 1742, accurately reflects this social change and expansion of ideas that were rapidly coming over Maharashtra. It is here reproduced in substance :

"You see here visibly the old Aryan Culture, Hindu kings well-versed in Sanskrit, not addicted to but averse to the pleasures of drink and sex, fond of music and dancing. They alone experience real enjoyment, being devoted to their religion and respectful towards Brahmans. Life here is rich and full. One finds here large gardens growing varieties of flowers and lotuses. The rivers of these regions are full of healthy sweet water, which enrich the lands and their people, in comparison with which our Deccani rivers would appear to be poor slender streams. The people here are rich and fair in conplexion : they earn more than they have to spend. I wish you were with me here to enjoy and experience this highly pleasant life. I hope you will take an early opportunity to visit these regions and enjoy the pleasures of life to which we have been strangers in our land. As regards politics, my father and grand-father of revered memory had made a river of gold run from the north to the south now for 24 years. Even now that river continues to flow and serve the leaders of our armies and the guardians of our posts: but it goes on increasing our thirst all the more. A similar stream of gold was brought into the Maratha country from the extreme south by Raghuji and Fatehsinh Bhosle, but it mostly vanished in its distant journey. Fortunately this year that stream of gold has been well kept up by our armies; but when it courses through the arid regions of Poona, I fear it will disappear before reaching home. When the two streams, the one from the north and the other from the south, will have their uninterrupted confluence at Poona, as if the mighty sea-stream should come to meet a poor well, then only shall we be freed from our harassing debts and attain salvation both in this world and the next. The river Bhagirathi took its birth for meeting the ocean, but goes on fertilising the valley through which it flows ameliorating the peoples' lot in its course. Similarly, most rivers flow to the ocean, but like the Kaveri benefit the regions through which they pass. This river of wealth also must essentially serve the peoples' cause most. Men like you should exercise their minds in this direction and do their utmost to relieve the miseries of our Maratha country."[11]

Some other features of this social revolution become obvious when one reads the published materials referring to the activities of this Peshwa. The military profession is hardly conducive to the development of a moral tone in life. It is bound to bring with its successes many evils and draw-backs, such as then particularly prevailed in the north. Writes the Peshwa on 11th June 1744 to Damodarpant Hingne: "I asked you at your departure for the north to acquire and send me two handsome Hindu girls aged about ten years. Please do not forget this mission and send the girls as quickly as possible." By asking Hindu girls only, the Peshwa probably meant to avoid the trouble that the Muslim Mastani's pre-

11. Raj. vol. 6. 160.

sence in Poona had previously caused to his household. There are many similar requests from the south to the north for girls being purchased, trained in music and dancing and sent to Poona and other places. There was also a constant demand for various articles of utility and luxury to be imported into the Deccan, e.g. *attars* or scents from Peshawar, saddles from Lahore for horses &c. Any rare article unknown in the south was specially requisitioned by various persons.

Pilgrimage to holy places in the north became quite frequent in these days of the expansion of Maratha power. Pilgrims required protection on the way and took advantage of the constant movement of troops that journeyed to and back from their homeland for military purposes. That is how the practice arose of ladies accompanying military expeditions, often encumbering the operations as in the case of Panipat. The Peshwa's mother Kashitai performed her famous pilgrimage for four years in the north. Mathura, Prayag, Ayodhya, Benares and other places of Hindu worship were usually owned for prestige by Muslim powers who derived revenue from the taxes on the devotees. Kashitai accompanied Babuji Naik to the Karnatak and performed visits to the southern shrines returning to Poona in May 1742. She immediately afterwards went to Benares when the Peshwa was camping in Bundelkhand. At Benares she spent some four years, often causing trouble to the Maratha agents at different places. Her brother Krishnarao Joshi Chaskar who looked after her affairs, was a man of eccentric and irascible temper, who posing as the favourite of the Peshwa created trouble and noise which for a time became unbearable to the Muslim governors of the holy places. Safdar Jang who controlled the places as ruler of Oudh received intelligence that Kashitai had left her home in disgust after having quarrelled with her son, the Peshwa. She was unwilling to return home even after finishing her devotions and it was with difficulty that she could be persuaded at last to go back to Poona some time in May 1747.[12]

The Brahmans before Bajirao's days had the surname *Pant* (Pandit) added to their names, but it changed into Rao

12. P. D. 2. 1, 2; 18. 134-140, 152, 158; 20. 28; 27. 27; 40. 37-42, 44, 47, 49, 50; Raj. vol. 6. 163, 169-1.

quickly and denoted that priesthood had given place to a soldier's life, which most young men from Maharashtra now rapidly adopted. What kind of education these rising lights received in their formative period, is a question which the curious might like to have correctly answered. There were then no schools like the ones we have under British regime. There used to be at certain places Pathshalas or private classes, where lessons were imparted in Vedic and Sanskrit studies. But here only a few young members of the upper classes of society attended. Education was not then regarded as a public duty. It was entirely left to private initiative, each family making its own arrangements according to its needs. Writing and reading the Balbodh and Modi characters, arithmetic and accounts and a working knowledge of the Sanskrit language were the subjects which were usually taught to the generality of the boys and in a few cases to girls also. The great Shivaji had not received much literary education himself, but tutored his son Sambhaji into a master of Sanskrit.

Most of the high placed families had each an officiating priest, a *Puranik*, and also the staff of the accounts office. These formed the teachers of the youngsters of the family; the priest taught recitations from the Vedas; the *Puranik* explained the epics (the *Mahabharat* and the *Ramayan*) and the *Puranas* to the ladies and boys of the household and taught Sanskrit grammar in addition. Widows of the household spent much of their time in studying Sanskrit philosophy. Sagunabai Peshwa a pious widow had a large private MS library of rare Sanskrit works of all varieties. The head clerk probably taught reading and writing in the vernacular and account-keeping. The Peshwas had in their palace a large accounts office called the Phad,[13] where a large number of apprentices was entertained and which proved the principal training school for future officers of the accounts, diplomacy and clerical departments in which the members distinguished themselves in later life according to their aptitude. This *Phad* or

13. From this comes the word Phadnis, one who handles the *phad*. Nana Phadnis took his early training in this office. His surname was Bhanu. *Phad* is a local corruption of the Persian word, *fard*, meaning a list or a slip of paper in general.

secretariat was thus an institution of unique value which built up and manned the various branches of the Maratha administration along with the home training directly under the supervision of the elderly members of the family to which they belonged. Life at home and abroad supplied the supreme practical basis of all training in those days. The Marathas had no institutions to their credit after the model of the Universities of Oxford and Cambridge.

A few papers are available such as the recorded advice offered to young Sawai Madhavrao by his grand-mother Gopikabai or the code of morals enunciated by Madhaorao Vedanti and Daryabai of Nagpur.[14] These papers disclose the traditional type of education which an average Maratha was expected to possess. One particular letter addressed to his younger brother Raghunathrao by the Peshwa from Udaipur in May 1748 deserves to be reproduced in this connection, as much to elucidate the sort of educational preparation of those days as to explain the evil tendencies to which Raghoba was subject from the beginning of his life.

"I hope you will well remember the various instructions I gave you at our last parting. Do not forget to keep up the daily revision of the Vidurniti, selections from Chanakya and other portions that you have learned. You must also learn more every day from the Shastris, and read the Mahabharat whenever you have leisure from the Virat Parva onward, and not waste time in constant reading. You must also keep up the practice of memorizing accounts in weights and measures. Do not fail to render implicit obedience to dear Bhau, and to secure his good will in every point. You must promptly execute whatever he tells you. You should take your food along with him and have no separate stable for your horses either. Now and then you must spend some time in the company of Bai, Tai and Anubai. Your health is not robust, and so you must not neglect to take medicine. Whenever you wish to ride out, you must go in Bhau's company. If you are asked to visit Satara, you must obtain Bhau's permission and take with you Chimangiri or Ganghadhar Bhatt with his consent. When you reach Satara you must not call on the queens of

---

14. *Patre Yadi* 183, 393; *Ait. Patravyavahar* 432; Raj. vol. 1 p. 96.

your own accord, unless they send for you or unless Govindrao Chitnis advises you to do so. You must dress properly as becomes your position and age. In point of worship, meditation and prayer, you must do the needful quietly and in solitude : and while so engaged you must keep absolute concentration and not talk of other matters. Whatever little you do, do it regularly and unostentatiously. Always keep active a desire to learn and a readiness to obey and to earn the good opinions of all elders. Be ever alert, and store your mind with knowledge, inquiring from elders whenever they are disposed to teach. You should always exhibit a spirit of humble pupilship. Your younger brother Janardan works more and learns more, and in this way he will soon outstrip you. How can you then command respect in life ?"

Another letter addressed by Sadashivrao Bhau to Bajaba Purandare on 17th April 1760 tells us a little more about the system of education then prevailing ;—"You must write to me frequently and communicate your news. We have now arrived at the Narmada and are marching on. You must learn to read, write and ride and go to Poona whenever required. You must not while away your time in play. The grandma will fondle you too much and spoil you by keeping you from studies. Therefore you must attend to reading, writing and riding in particular."[15]

5. **The Angria brothers, Manaji and Tulaji.**—The Angria brothers' dispute at Kolaba proved a perennial source of trouble to the Peshwa and to Shahu's court in general. Sambhaji Angria Sarkhel died on 12th January 1742 when a dispute once more arose about the succession to his office. He had been posted to Vijaydurg with the title of Sarkhel and his brother Manaji at Kolaba as Wazarat Maab, thus the Angrian estate came to be divided into two. As soon as Sambhaji died, Manaji went to Satara and requested Shahu to make him the Sarkhel, as the eldest surviving member of Kanhoji's family. Shahu was ever anxious to get back from the Siddi's possession the two important posts of Anjanvel and

15. P. D. 21. 2 ; 18. 134-140, 152, 158 ; 20. 28 ; 27. 27, 40. 37-42, 44-50. Raj. 6. 163, 169.

Govalkot, which even the Peshwa Bajirao had failed to capture during the war of 1733 and which still remained as outposts of the Janjira State. Shahu had to choose between Manaji and his brother Tulaji, and declared that he would confer the Sarkhelship upon him who would capture those two places. Tulaji at once undertook the enterprise, Yamaji Shivdev, the Pratinidhi's mutalik stood guarantee for him, and Shahu conferred the Sarkhel's dignity upon Tulaji some time in 1743 and helped him with funds and troops, so that Tulaji with great heroism captured Anjanvel and Govalkot on 25th January 1745 and immediately communicated the happy news to the Chhatrapati.[16]

Tulaji thereupon went to Satara and paid a visit to the Maharaja on 3rd May 1747 when great respect was shown to him. To all appearances, the visit passed off very cordially, but Tulaji's grievances against the Peshwa were not removed to his satisfaction, as evidently the king was in his last stage of dotage and powerless or incapable of handling state affairs. Tulaji was a man of haughty temperament and would not bend before the Peshwa in the least. The dispute about fort Manikgad near Panvel assumed an aggravated form. It belonged to Manaji Angria and was forcibly taken out of his hands by Ramaji Mahadev at the instance of the Peshwa on 28th May 1748. Manaji at once proceeded to Satara and worked his way through the influence of Rani Sagunabai. The storm assumed such violent proportions that the Peshwa had to yield and after three months wrangling, gave back the fort to Manaji. In the meantime Tulaji started depredations openly in the Peshwa's territory. At the end of 1747 he captured Mudagad, on the top of the Sahyadri range at the entrance to the Kajirda pass, a little to the south of Vishalgad. As in this region the Pratinidhi, the Amatya of Bavda, the Savant of Wadi and the Peshwa had each their respective jurisdictions and as they all suffered more or less on account of Tulaji's aggression, they combined their resources and waged a severe war against Tulaji from January to March 1748.

16. Unpublished letter Vaidya Coll. Shahu was highly gratified at this success and named the places Gopalgad (Anjanval) and Govindgad (Govalkot) but these new names did not come into popular use. The places still go by their old names.

Naro Rayaji Thakur Gode, the Peshwa's keeper of Mudagad led the attack valiantly and recaptured the fort on 1st April.

It is a pity that the two brothers Tulaji and Manaji could not act in unison: otherwise they would have proved invincible being both brave and capable commanders on land and water. They became bitter enemies to each other so that Manaji took shelter with the Portuguese at Chaul, or fort Rajkot as it was then known. Lest Manaji should prove troublesome, the Peshwa at once ordered Ramaji Mahadev to proceed against Rajkot. He performed his task well and captured Rajkot on 15th January 1748. By order of the Peshwa Rajkot and the Masjid in it were all pulled down and Chaul came into the possession of the Peshwa from the Portuguese. Manaji had no longer any support outside and fell back upon the good will of the Peshwa.

6. **Pilaji Jadhav.**—History has not done justice to the meritorious services rendered to the Maratha state by Pilaji Jadhav both in war and diplomacy during the regimes of the first three Peshwas, much of whose initial success in the expansion of Maratha power is due to the loyal support and devoted co-operation of this chief of Wagholi. The sober policy of Shahu was doubtless inflamed by Pilaji's views. They present a severe contrast with those of Dabhade, Chandrasen Jadhav and others, no less prominent in Shahu's Darbar. Pilaji with his conciliatory temperament and deep understanding of human nature, cleverly and successfully handled many a delicate situation arising out of antagonisms which developed between Bajirao and the Mughal chiefs. For over thirty years he acted almost as the accredited Maratha plenipotentiary negotiating peace now with Nizam-ul-mulk and again with Aliwardi Khan and other grandees of the Mughal Court. The rapid rise of some younger men like Holkar and Sindia eclipsed the part which this veteran worker played during the difficult times of Shahu's early career. Towards the end of his life Pilaji was an invalid and died some time after 1752.

CHRONOLOGY

CHAPTER XI

1732	Raja of Trichinopoly dies.
1736	Chanda Saheb takes possession of Trichinopoly.
1737	Shahu undertakes an expedition into the Karnatak.
1739	Shahu deputes Fatesinh and Raghuji Bhosle to collect tribute from the Karnatak and defend the Raja of Tanjore against Chanda S.
1740, April	Fatesinh and Raghuji come upon Arcot.
1740, May 20	Dost Ali falls fighting against the Marathas : his son Safdar Ali takes shelter at Vellore.
1740, May 25	Ladies and valuables of the Nawab seek protection at Pondicherry.
1740, June	Raghuji comes upon Pondicherry.
1740, November 16	Secret pact between Raghuji and Safdar Ali.
1740, December	Raghuji besieges Trichinopoly.
1741, January 16	Pratap Sinh of Tanjore purchases Raghuji's help.
1741, February	Chanda Saheb's brother Baba Saheb falls fighting against the Marathas.
1741, March 14	Trichinopoly surrenders to Raghuji : Chanda Saheb and his son Abid Ali sent prisoners to Nagpur : Murarrao Ghorpade appointed to the charge of Trichinopoly.
1742, August	Safdar Ali murdered.
1743, early months	Nizam-ul-mulk descends into the Karnatak.
1743, August 20	Nizam takes possession of Trichinopoly from Murarrao.
1744, September	Chanda Saheb transferred to Satara.
1744, December	Babuji Naik starts for the Karnatak.
1745, February 15	Muzaffar Jang and Anwaruddin rout Babuji Naik near Basawapattan.

17

1746	Babuji Naik again sustains failure in the Karnatak.
1746, December 5	Sadashivrao leaves for the Karnatak.
1747, May	Sadashivrao returns from the Karnatak with success.
1748, May 21	Nizam-ul-mulk dies.
1748, June	Chanda Saheb effects his escape from Satara and returns to the Karnatak.

CHAPTER XI

CONTEST FOR TRICHINOPOLY

[1740—1748]

1. **The rise of Chanda Saheb.**—The part of India known in history as the Karnatak or Kannad, is the country inhabited by the people who speak the Kanarese language. It is bounded on the north by the river Krishna and extends southwards through the Indian peninsula from sea to sea. It is traversed by the Sahyadri range in the west as in Maharashtra, and in the east by the Eastern Ghats which is a lower line of hills, the lands above this line are known as Bala-Ghat or uplands and those below as the Pine-Ghat or lowlands.

This region of the Karnatak was assigned by Aurangzeb to the Subahs of Bijapur and Haidarabad and when after the Emperor's death, Nizam-ul-mulk became independent in the Deccan, he claimed all this region of the Karnatak as his Mughal heritage. It was divided among themselves by several local Nawabs, who had been originally the governors appointed by Aurangzeb. Five of these Nawabs were comparatively more powerful, viz., those of Arcot, Shira, Kadappa, Karnool and Savnur. Along with these Shivaji's father Shahji held a jagir from the Bijapur rulers, consisting of the five parganas of Bangalore, Hoskot, Kolar, Balapur and Shira, which descended to his sons and continued as the principality of Tanjore, for the rulers of which the Chhatrapatis of Satara ever entertained an affectionate kinship and extended their helping hand whenever they needed it. There were, besides, some ancient chiefships more or less independent such as those of Mysore, Bednur, Chitaldurg, Raidurg and Harpanhalli. The Peshwa Bajirao arrived on the scene to exact the Maratha claim of Chauth during the years 1726 and 1727. Shahu had always been anxious to establish Maratha rule in this region.

In 1737 he himself started on an expedition into the Karnatak, but as he possessed neither the capacity to lead armies nor the personal valour necessary for success, he could only proceed as far as Miraj within two years. In 1739 he deputed Raghuji and Fatesinh Bhosle to exact tribute from the southern principalities, on the stipulation that half the proceeds should be utilised for their expenses and the other half should be remitted to the treasury at Satara. The express instructions are these :—

"As you are the trusted servants of the State, His Highness has no doubt that you will achieve success in this enterprise. The Maharaja's cousin of Tanjore is being harassed by Chanda Saheb of Trichinopoly. Fatesinh Bhosle is ordered to meet the Tanjore Raja and chastise Chanda Saheb."[1]

Nawab Dost Ali was the Mughal governor of the Karnatak with Arcot as his capital. His son-in-law Hussain Dost Khan, popularly known as Chanda Saheb, rose to prominence in the Nawab's administration after the year 1732. He effected reforms in the revenue system and with the help of the French at Pondicherry improved his army, so that his power soon increased on all sides. There ruled at Trichinopoly a petty Hindu chief, whom Chanda Saheb managed to suppress and from whom he acquired that rich and strong post, where he took up his own residence in 1736.[2]

The story of Chanda Saheb's aggression on Trichinopoly is typical of his character and is thus recorded in "*Madras in Olden Times*":—

"In 1732 the Raja of Trichinopoly died without issue. His second and third wives burnt themselves with his body, but the first senior Rani Minakshi succeeded to the government, in conformity with the desire of the deceased Raja. Disputes subsequently ensued between the Rani and a prince of the Royal blood. Dost Ali the Nawab of Arcot was prevailed upon to take advantage of the confusion to subject the kingdom of Trichinopoly to his own authority. Accordingly he sent an army under his son Safdar Ali and his son-in-law

---

1. Ait. Patrav. 26; Raj. 6. 149; Nagpur Bakhar.

2. Wakaskar's *History of Tanjore*, p. 295; Love's *Vestiges of old Madras* II, p. 278.

Chanda Saheb to seize any opportunity which might offer of getting possession of the capital.

"The result was tragical. Chanda Saheb who already owed his advancement to his matrimonial connections alone, was fortunate enough to excite the tender regard of the Rani. Accordingly he was enabled to prevail on the love-stricken lady to admit him with a body of troops into the city of Trichinopoly, having first taken an oath on the Qoran that he would act in nothing to her detriment. But the loves of middle-aged queens are not always fortunate and Chanda Saheb proved cruel to the Rani. He broke the heart of the Rani by remaining where he was. He seized the city of Trichinopoly and there imprisoned the lady, who thereupon died of grief and the kingdom of Trichinopoly yielded to the authority of the faithless Chanda."

2. **Raghuji Bhosle captures Trichinopoly.**—From Trichinopoly Chanda Saheb cast his covetous attention on Tanjore and Madura. In his extremity Pratapsinh the Raja of Tanjore threw himself upon Shahu's protection. Chanda Saheb's ambition and audacity proved so inordinate that he became an enemy also of the Nawab Dost Ali and his whole household. So when the sad tale of Chanda Saheb's aggression reached Shahu, he despatched Raghuji and Fatesinh Bhosle with large forces and with instructions to oust Chanda Saheb from Trichinopoly and make Pratapsinh's position secure. In April 1740 these Maratha forces came sweeping upon Arcot, when its Nawab Dost Ali encountered them at the pass of Damalcherry. The Marathas offered to settle their demands by negotiation, but as the Nawab would not accept a compromise, ten thousand Maratha troops fell upon the Nawab and besieged him. A stiff and prolonged fight ensued in which Dost Ali, his son Hasan Ali and several prominent commanders lost their lives; the Nawab's army was scattered and his Diwan Mir Asad was taken prisoner. This happened on 20th May 1740.

This Maratha success at once electrified the southern atmosphere. Bajirao had already subjugated northern India and now it was believed that Raghuji had conquered the southern portion of the continent as well. The late Nawab's son Safdar

Ali, who was hastening to succour his father, learnt of the latter's fate and took shelter in the fort of Vellore. Chanda Saheb quietly waited at Trichinopoly watching the turn of events. But fearing that the late Nawab's ladies and all his precious property would fall into Maratha hands, both Safdar Ali and Chanda Saheb despatched them immediately to the protection of the French at Pondicherry (25 May). Dumas, the French Governor of the place hesitated for a moment whether he should accept this risk and face possible Maratha vengeance. But the French bonds of friendship with the Nawab were strong and Dumas took charge of the zanana and the wealth of the Nawab. From Damalcherry the Marathas rapidly came to Arcot and captured the place without difficulty. They were, however, extremely disappointed that the hoarded wealth of the place had been already removed. Raghuji at once wrote a threatening letter to Dumas, who made a dignified and firm reply, urging that he knew no other master but his King in France whose commands he should obey. At the same time he presented Raghuji a few bottles of the best Champagne of France, which, as the story goes, so pleased Raghuji's wife that she asked for more of that foreign nectar, and Raghuji's wrath was pacified. The incident reached Shahu's ears and shook his faith in Raghuji's integrity.[3]

Chanda Saheb fired with the desire of securing the Nawabship for himself after Dost Ali's death, entrenched himself at Trichinopoly and prepared to proceed against Arcot. In this predicament, Safdar Ali sought Raghuji's support against Chanda Saheb's aggression. A secret agreement took place between them on 16th November 1740 purporting that Safdar Ali should pay by instalments one crore of Rupees to Raghuji, if the latter succeeded in capturing Trichinopoly and the person of Chanda Saheb and in making Safdar Ali's position as Nawab safe. It was also agreed that the Raja of Tanjore should be protected from all outside molestation.

---

3. An interesting account is available of this episode of Raghuji's attack on Pondicherry. See Sardesai's *British Riyasat*, Vol. I, p. 409 and also Khare's *Aitihasik Lekhsangraha* Vol. 8, page 4439. Purandare Diary in Raj. 6 gives details of this Maratha expedition.

Chanda Saheb felt extremely alarmed when he received the news of this secret agreement. He lost no time in supplicating Dumas to help him in his sore need. This is indeed the first example of European Powers directly intervening in Indian politics. Raghuji too made common cause with the Hindu Poligars and was joined by Pratapsinh of Tanjore with whatever forces he could get together. Two agents of Pratapsinh, Timaji Rangnath and Gangappa visited Raghuji and formed a compact with him to this effect :—"Capture Trichinopoly, remove Chanda Saheb, and Pratapsinh would readily give fifteen lacs cash, three lacs of which would be a personal nazar to Raja Shahu, two lacs to his Ranis, two lacs to Fatesinh and Raghuji, and eight lacs for the expenses of the troops (16 January 1741)."

Raghuji invested Trichinopoly in December 1740, having been joined by most of the Hindu Poligars and potentates. Chanda Saheb too did his utmost to defend the place ; but he could not long hold out as his supplies were exhausted. He called his brother Bada Saheb urgently from Madura : the Marathas got scent of his coming to raise the siege and destroyed his whole army after putting Bada Saheb to death. Chanda Saheb thus became altogether helpless and delivered the place to Raghuji on 14th March (Ramnavami). It was a grand success for the Marathas. Murarrao Ghorpade was immediately placed in charge of this new acquisition and ordered to defend it at all cost. Chanda Saheb was taken into custody.

3. Chanda Saheb's confinement.—Murarrao Ghorpade was a valiant and resourceful soldier, well acquainted with the internal affairs of that region. He sent a request to Shahu to grant him the office of his Senapati, but Shahu declined the request as he did not wish to deprive Dabhade of that post, although the latter was quite incompetent for it. These hereditary offices had now lost their original purpose. Raghuji was in sore need of money at Trichinopoly, and for that purpose demanded a heavy ransom from Chanda Saheb and his son Abid Ali, who were prisoners in his hands. They were unable to pay the amount, and Raghuji, well knowing how dangerous it was to leave this wily politician free to pursue his never-ending intrigues, at once despatched the prisoners to

Nagpur under close guard of his capable captain Bhaskar Ram. Chanda Saheb's family escaped this fate as they had been already removed to French protection at Pondicherry.

A recent discovery of original correspondence on the subject of Chanda Saheb's imprisonment in the Deccan enables us to determine its details with accuracy.[4] Bhaskar Ram took the father and the son to Berar direct and not to Satara, in order, it seems, that no one else might lay a claim to a share in the ransom, for which the captive was being constantly pressed. Chanda Saheb had no funds and so had to put up with his captivity for nearly seven years. Beyond the security of his person there was absolutely no restriction on his contact with the world outside. In fact he was given all facilities for this purpose to enable him to procure his fine. He freely negotiated on this account with the French at Pondicherry, with the Court of Shahu and also with that of Nizam-ul-mulk. For a time Chanda Saheb thus became a pawn of value in the hands of several bankers. He seems to have passed his first three years in Berar, the actual place not found mentioned. In September 1744, Raghuji agreed to accept 7½ lacs, 4½ on Chanda Saheb's account and 3 on account of Abid Ali. The bankers of Satara advanced the amount to Raghuji and took charge of the prisoners. Thus they were removed to the Satara fort towards the end of 1744. He wrote constantly to Pondicherry to pay him the amount as a loan on the security of the jewellery that he had left in French custody. But it seems he received no money from the French Governor Dupleix. He then made friends with the Peshwa and tried to obtain release through him. The death of Nizam-ul-mulk on 21st May 1748 created a stir in the Deccan and early next month Chanda Saheb effected his escape from Satara and proceeded to the south collecting troops on the way. Probably, the Satara bankers never received back the loan they had advanced, as they continued to press the demand upon Chanda Saheb for a good long time after his escape.[5]

Shahu personally took no interest in Chanda Saheb, be-

4. Vaidya Family papers, Modern Review, December 1943.

5. Proceedings H. R. C. 1942—Paper on Chandasaheb by C. S. Srinivasachari.

yond insisting that Trichinopoly should be permanently transferred to Maratha rule. The performance of Raghuji and Fatesinh gave them a high place in public estimation among the Marathas. "It brought in large funds. The two leaders were received by Shahu at Satara with high encomiums. Shahu was highly gratified that his cousin Pratapsinh of Tanjore was freed from the danger of his enemies, and conferred the mokasa of Berar and Gondwana upon Raghuji right upto the frontiers of Cuttack."

4. Trichinopoly lost.—When Trichinopoly was lost in 1741 Nizam-ul-mulk highly resented this Maratha encroachment upon what he considered as his own preserve. Ever since the disaster of Bhopal this nobleman was fast losing his power and prestige. While Raghuji was engaged in reducing Chanda Saheb to humiliation, Nizam-ul-mulk was having a war with his son Nasir Jang. When Nasir Jang was put down, in July 1741, there arose a kind of bitter jealousy between the Peshwa and Raghuji Bhosle, which to some extent relieved the Nizam's anxieties. He even felt secret satisfaction that one of his competitors in the Karnatak, Chanda Saheb, had been happily removed. But what the Nizam resented most was that Murarrao Ghorpade and Pratap Sinh came to be firmly planted at Trichinopoly and Tanjore respectively, so that when the Peshwa and Raghuji came to oppose each other in Bengal during the early months of 1743, the Nizam utilised the opportunity of their absence in undoing the Maratha work in the Karnatak. The Nawabs of that region did not acknowledge Nizam-ul-mulk's authority. Dost Ali had never paid tribute to the Nizam. The latter now demanded it from his son Safdar Ali, but he was murdered in October 1742 by his cousin Murtaza Ali, who seized the Nawabship. In the midst of these disorders Nizam-ul-mulk started from Golkonda in January 1743 with a large force and descended into the Karnatak aiming at the recapture of Trichinopoly.

Murarrao Ghorpade the guardian of that place learnt of this danger and applied to Shahu for help. But all Maratha forces were then engaged in Bundelkhand and Bengal under the Peshwa himself and no succour could be spared for Murarrao. Nizam-ul-mulk reached Arcot in March with an enormous army computed at 80 thousand horse and two hundred thousand foot, whom the poor Nawab could not oppose. The Nizam took possession of Arcot and appointed his own nominee Anwar-uddin Khan[6] to the governorship. At the same time he called upon Murarrao to deliver up Trichinopoly. The latter could not resist the demand and spent four months in negotiations, at the end of which the Nizam granted him the post of Gutti and took from him the possession of Trichinopoly on 29th August 1743.[7]

Nizam-ul-mulk retraced his steps from Trichinopoly and halted for some time at Arcot, where the English and the French traders sent him presents as the over-lord of the southern regions. His large forces quickly reduced the country around, causing thereby enormous loss to the European traders. In the following year Nizam-ul-mulk posted his grandson Muzaffar Jang at Adoni with instructions to look after the government of the eastern Karnatak, and himself returned to Golkonda in February 1744.

5. **Babuji Naik and the Peshwa.**—King Shahu was distressed to hear of the loss of Trichinopoly. He had then by him only two men of some weight, Fatesinh Bhosle and Babuji Naik, both of whom were incompetent to undertake an enterprize, particularly as the Peshwa was not inclined to co-operate with them. Babuji Naik thrust himself forward, and in a weak moment Shahu allowed him to proceed against Nizam-ul-mulk. But the Naik suffered a severe set back after some two years campaigning, in which only the bitter antipathy between the Naik and the Peshwa became more marked; this produced a vast literature, which the inquiring student may notice.[8]

---

6. This Anwar-uddin was an experienced and capable nobleman who had migrated to Delhi and made friends with Nizam-ul-mulk during the period that the latter was Wazir (1722). He accompanied Nizam-ul-mulk to the Deccan and was appointed by him to the management of the Subah of Haidarabad, a work which he carried out efficiently since 1725.

7. *Parasnis Itihas Sangraha*, Ait. Sthalas, Trichinopoly.

8. The tangled web of Karnatak politics is well illustrated in the following documents:

P. D. 40. 32-35, 45, 48, 52, 53; P. D. 28. 17, 17A, 20-34, 36-44;

Babuji Naik started from Satara towards the end of 1744 with the intention of taking Trichinopoly back from Nizam-ul-mulk's possession. Muzaffar Jang and Anwar-uddin with a large following of most of the Nawabs and Jagirdars opposed the Naik's slender forces near Basawapattan, about 15 February 1745 and inflicted a severe defeat upon him. The Naik returned to Satara in discomfiture, renewed his effort, and suffered a similar miserable failure again during the year 1746. He incurred huge debts which he was unable to pay and had to endure great ignominy and misery, which he attributed to the apathy of Shahu and his Peshwa towards his interests. He threatened to starve himself to death and had even recourse to poison. It was detected in time and his life was saved.

In the end the Peshwa's silent diplomacy triumphed. He won over the Nizam's minister Saiyad Lashkar Khan and through him nullified all the efforts of the Naik to improve his position either at the Nizam's Court or anywhere in the Karnatak. Shahu became helpless in the matter, and ultimately consigned the whole affair to the discretion of the Peshwa, who thereupon equipped an expedition and despatched his cousin Sadashivrao Bhau into the Karnatak on 5th December 1746, with Mahadoba Purandare and Sakharam Bhau as his advisers.

Sadashivrao possessed superior resources and performed his task with efficiency. He quickly established Maratha government in the western Karnatak and returned in May from Basawapattan after gaining the first valuable experience in leading an independent expedition. Trichinopoly, however, never again came back to Maratha possession.

P. D. 25. 10-72.; P. D. 26. 12-29; Patre Yadi 45, 48, 52, 53, 54 (dated 18-9-1744) Ait. Patrav. 53, 56, 58, 59, 65; Purandare Daftar, 1. 155, 162, 166.

CHRONOLOGY[1]

CHAPTER XII

1721	Shahu builds a palace at Shahunagar below the fort of Satara. This palace burnt down in 1874.
1727	Rani Sagunabai bore Shahu a son who died when three years old.
1734, November 26	Gangadhar Swami of Chaphal dies.
1740, December 24	Shahu's mistress Virubai dies.
1743, January 6	Jivaji Khando Chitnis dies.
1746, November 25	Shripatrao Pratinidhi dies.
1746, December 17	Jagjivan made Pratinidhi.
1746	Sambhaji of Kolhapur at Satara for six months.
1747, Feb.—April	Balajirao out of office.
1747, May	Raghuji Bhosle at Satara.
1748, April 25	Emperor Muhammad Shah dies.
1748, May 21	Nizam-ul-mulk dies.
1748, August 25	Rani Sagunabai dies.
1749, August	Shahu's condition grave.
1749, Oct. 10	Shahu nominates Ramraja to succeed him.
1749, Dec. 15	Shahu dies, Sakwarbai becomes Sati.

1. The student should note that there often occurs a confusion of 11days in the dates assigned to events by the various writers, some using the new style and some the old one about the middle of this century.

CHAPTER XII

END OF A GLORIOUS REIGN
[1748—1749]

1. The last days of Shahu.—Since 1743 Shahu's health had been visibly declining. In that year his life was despaired of for some days and the Peshwa was summoned to Satara precipitately from his important occupations in the north. Happily the king recovered for a time, although his infirmities went on increasing. What preyed on his mind most was his failure to obtain a male issue to succeed him.

The year 1748 witnessed a big void in Indian politics. Emperor Muhammad Shah died on 25th April followed immediately after by Nizam-ul-mulk on 21st May. Ahmad Shah Abdali a rising Pathan sovereign appeared on the scene. Sindia and Holkar developed a mutual antagonism which cost them the friendship of the Rajputs. In the midst of these occurrences in the north king Shahu died on 15th December 1749. Shahu's successor on the Maratha throne proved an utter imbecile. As the Peshwa wielded the supreme power of the Maratha State, he could not escape the responsibility for any eventual deterioration in Maratha power and prestige.

Many factors combined to sadden the last years of Shahu. His two queens, Sakwarbai the elder and Sagunabai the younger, interfered in the administration and carried on incessant intrigues thereby often worrying their husband to death. He loved the younger wife better as she was soft-hearted and not so violent openly. Shahu's household was for long satisfactorily controlled by his illegitimate wife Virubai, a capable woman, who most carefully and lovingly looked after the personal comfort of the king and who exercised a healthy control over the two queens. This Virubai's death on 24th December 1740, caused a rapid decline in the management of the royal household. Gradually Shahu became so enfeebled and helpless that he would not allow the Peshwa to move away from his side for fear of some unforeseen danger overtaking him all of a sudden. His own ill-health, his two queens' intrigues, Tarabai's independent move to secure power, the selfish animosities of some of the powerful chiefs such as Raghuji Bhosle, Murarrao Ghorpade, the Angria brothers &c., these and other subjects the Peshwa was called upon to handle, and it must be said to his credit that he did all that was possible to safeguard the public interests under the circumstances, with the counsel and co-operation of some of his own supporters, such as Sindia, Holkar, the Purandares and Chitnis. Let us review how the final position developed.[2]

On 21st October 1746 the Peshwa wrote to Ramchandra-baba, "I have been unavoidably detained at Court. The debts contracted by the Maharaja, the enormous sums required by the queens, and their constant quarrels, have so engrossed the Maharaja's attention, that he has no time to consider the matters of State which I put before him. I have a great desire to journey to the north, but that does not seem possible. I am now given leave to proceed to Poona, as I have the Konkan affairs of urgency on hand."[3]

On 25 November 1746 Pratinidhi Shripatrao, Shahu's friend and companion in life died. He was politically a non-entity, but in private life he was a constant associate for over thirty years to Shahu, who thenceforward seriously felt that he must soon follow his friend. The Maharaja appointed his younger brother Jagjivan alias Dadoba to the vacant post, (17 December 1746). Shahu felt great respect and love for the holy seat of Chaphal founded by the revered Ramdas. Gangadhar Swami was a pious occupant of the institution for a long time. When he died on 26th November 1734 disputes arose about the succession, which Shahu settled by a personal visit; and he appointed the deceased's son Lakshman Bawa

2. Read also *Purandare Daftar*, Vol. I. 159 and sequels. The Maharaja thought Nanasaheb alone his support and agent for extricating him out of his difficulties.

3. P. D. 18. 85, 86.

to the headship of that holy place. Jivaji Khanderao Chitnis, Shahu's hereditary secretary died on 6th January 1743. Another devoted servant of Shahu, Naro Ram fortunately outlived him by a year. Shahu had a favourite elephant named Madari. He was a huge beautiful animal, and always most docile even when in ruts. One night he got loose, fell into a well in the city and died, an incident which threw Shahu into the deepest despair about his own future. His Court was of the nature of a private family, and these incidents deprived him of all relish in life. On 2nd August 1746 Mahadoba Purandare thus describes Shahu's condition : "For the last few days His Highness has been getting a little temperature in the afternoon. Blisters have been applied to his stomach. Every day he receives one complaint or another from the palaces (the two queens). When such a complaint comes, he loses all nerve and cries out, 'Why does not God take pity on me and end my days?' In such a state he does not take medicine and neglects his health. He often gives vent to his feelings by crying out, 'These two ladies will starve me to death.' Recently the bankers have become impatient, lest they should lose their advances in the event of the king's demise. Hence they are using all contrivances to have their loans repaid. These are bad omens for the State. God knows what these will lead to ?"[4]

There always existed a faction at the royal Court opposed to any measures that the Peshwa might propose to relieve the situation ; and the moment Shahu was in extreme exasperation, the Peshwa's opponents poured into the king's ears all sorts of bitter complaints against the Peshwa and attributed mischievous motives to him. Shahu got disgusted with such repeated complaints, and much against his will yielded only once to the pressure of the opposition and made a trial of how matters would fare by depriving the Peshwa of his office in the early months of 1747. The Peshwa willingly acquiesced. He resigned office and for a time kept aloof from the affairs of State, watching the course of events from outside. Tradition mentions that the Peshwa was residing in a tent near Satara waiting to receive a call from the king. Shahu sent him a message by Govindrao Chitnis that he was deprived

4. P. D. 8. 60, 63.

of his office and that he need not come to wait upon His Highness. Instead of rebelling, the Peshwa quietly accepted the order and returned all the insignia pertaining to his office. The report did not take long to reach the public. Officers and bankers were altogether upset to see the administration breaking down; for, to the world outside it was the voice of the Peshwa that was dominant. There were visible signs of chaos: all trust and confidence disappeared in a moment. The Peshwa wisely sent a timely warning to the king.

Within a couple of months all people and the public felt convinced that the Peshwa was the only loyal and honest servant of the State, and without him the administration could not go on. On 13th April 1747 he was given formal leave to go on his mission with the robes and powers of his office. How cautious the Peshwa was, is well illustrated by a note written by him evidently for the king's information to Govindrao Chitnis plainly indicating the issues at stake :-

"I was sorry to hear you could not get an audience of His Highness and explain to him the position of affairs. I have very nearly settled the demands of the two queens. I am not sure they will not put forth new claims, which I cannot help. As regards His Highness' personal debts I will certainly do my best to relieve His Highness' anxieties if I am allowed to go out. My being tied down to his presence would not help the situation at all. To say that I should first pay off the debts and then move from hence, is an impossible proposition beyond my power to execute. I want at least a couple of months time to move about and arrange matters.

"As for Babuji Naik's complaint, I am ready to give whatever undertaking is needed that I shall never encroach upon the province definitely set apart for him. At present Sadashivrao Bhau is in the south; the Nizam also is obstructing our operations in that quarter. Let me go from here, despatch Pilaji Jadhav with succours for Bhau and then I will immediately return to execute whatever His Highness wishes.

"The news of my having been dismissed from office has spread widely : it will encourage the Nizam and other enemies. Speedy measures are required to counteract the evil consequences.

"If with all these plain issues before His Highness, he will not grant me leave to go, I will understand that Providence is wrath against the Maratha State and completely resign myself to whatever fate may bring.

"Please explain this to His Highness and let me have a reply."

This note clearly explains the trouble raging between the King and the Peshwa.[5]

At this time Shahu hurriedly sent for Raghuji Bhosle from Nagpur with a view to entrusting the management of the State to him in preference to the Peshwa. Raghuji arrived in May 1747 with his son Mudhoji, whom Shahu wished to adopt as his successor. Mudhoji's mother was the sister of Shahu's Rani Sagunabai. This visit of Raghuji appears to have been all too short; he did not consider it worth his while to undertake the responsibility of managing the concerns of the Maratha State, as his own independent field of Nagpur supplied him with a more lucrative arena for his talents than Satara, where he had nothing to gain and possibly everything to lose. Raghuji had a secret understanding with the Peshwa, which kept him from meddling with the affairs of Satara. Nor did Raghuji aspire to secure the succession of the Maratha State for his son Mudhoji.[6] Shahu knew he was dying and like a pious Hindu he ardently desired that he should pay off his debts before his death; otherwise he would be doomed to eternal perdition. So Shahu restored the Peshwa to his office, himself going to his tent and effecting a complete reconciliation with him. This was done in April 1747.[7]

2. Search for a successor.—When the Peshwa fell out of favour with Shahu his numerous opponents suddenly rose on all sides, causing an unprecedented confusion in the affairs of the State. The Angria brothers started fresh troubles in Konkan. Sambhaji of Kolhapur and his Rani Jijabai invited

5. *Aitihasik Patravyavahar* 65 and 59. The details of the king's debts can be read in *Purandare Daftar* 1. 214-218

6. The Vaidya papers mention Mudhoji's presence at Satara. For the Peshwa-Raghuji relations vide *Nagpur Bakhar*, new edition pp. 63-64.

7. P. D. 31. 137 and A. P. 61.

Murarrao Ghorpade and planned an attack upon Shahu's territory out of revenge for Sadashivrao Bhau's intervention in the Karnatak. Nizam-ul-mulk and his sons were not slow to take advantage of this deteriorating situation. Abdali's invasion of Delhi at this very time was for the Peshwa an additional distraction. Evidently a crisis developed in the fortunes of the Maratha State.

The Peshwa could easily reconcile Sambhaji of Kolhapur. This prince came to Satara in 1746 and stayed there for six months. During this visit, the Peshwa assured him that he would support his (Sambhaji's) succession after Shahu's death. Rani Sakwarbai also supported this secret move. It was not then known that Tarabai would play a different game by putting forward as an heir, Ramraja whose existence even was not then suspected. Sakwarbai, it should be remembered, declared from her funeral pyre at the time of her Sati, " that Ramraja was a pretender and that Sambhaji alone was the rightful claimant to the Satara throne." Thus Nanasaheb quietly pacified nearly all his antagonists and started on his Newai expedition at the end of 1747. He even effected in a personal interview, a very friendly understanding with Nasir Jang immediately after the death of Nizam-ul-mulk in May 1748. He conciliated Muzaffar Jang also in a private visit.

Gradually the dying Shahu became quick-tempered and peevish. Writes his personal attendant Nagorao Meghashyam, " The king's health is growing very delicate every day. He does not tolerate a large number of men about him. The Rani Saheb alone is in constant attendance. Even Sukhanand (the jester) is excluded. He has started the work of building a permanent structure at Mahuli as Virubai's memorial. He talks of visiting Pratapgad and Jejuri."

Purandare writes probably from Jejuri to the Peshwa in 1748,—" The younger Rani Sagunabai has been ailing with fever and headache for some days. She is not able to talk and has grown very weak. Physicians say that the malady cannot be quickly cured. If she does not improve, the Maharaja will have to come here. She has hardly any stamina left in her."[8]

---

8. P. D. 18, 88, 153.

A news-letter of 23 June says, "His Highness had been for some time at Medhe. He wanders from village to village and finds no rest. He likes to live in a grass-hut. The rain adds to his troubles. Most of the attendants have erected similar huts for themselves. Out of regard for the King, Deorao alone is in constant attendance. Ramoji Shirke, his father-in-law (father of Sakwarbai) expired on 21st June 1748. It seems the King will live in the hut all the rainy season. His fondness for hunting continues. The Rani lives in the palace at Satara and visits him here twice every day."

Thus Shahu ardently longed for retirement to a forest (Vanaprasth ashram as it is called) in accordance with the Hindu scheme of life. He got finally disgusted with palace life and its intrigues and selfish bickerings. During these last two years he was constantly attended by his confidential secretary Govindrao Chitnis and his intimate advisers, Devrao Meghshyam and Yashvantrao Potnis. The Peshwa was called up from Poona whenever necessary. At last the ailing Rani Sagunabai was removed to Jejuri as well for a change as for seeking divine favour at that famous shrine. But here she grew worse and died on 25th August 1748. The Maharaja himself escorted her dead body to Mahuli where the funeral took place the next day.

The last bond of Shahu's earthly affections was thus finally snapped and it plunged him into a deep gloom, although he retained his keenness of perception and judgment to the last moment.[9]

During August 1749 his condition became grave; and as there seemed a chance of disturbances occurring over the question of succession, Shahu sent for the Peshwa from Poona, with a sufficient armed force to preserve peace. During September and October, various plans about a successor were suggested and considered by the King and others, the outcome of which may thus be briefly summarized.[10]

---

9. P. D. 8. 60, 63.

10. There is ample literature on this subject. The *Chitnis Bakhar* is full and authentic and is usefully supplemented by the other bakhar published in Bharata-Varsha by Parasnis which goes under the name of Govindrao Chitnis. The Shedgaon Bakhar and the bakhars of the Prati-

Shahu had a son from Sagunabai in 1727, but the child had died at the age of three. Thereafter he had several daughters but no son. He tried to adopt an heir from the Rajput families of the north and brought to Satara one Nathaji, brother of Rana Jagat Sinh of Udaipur. But Nathaji was called upon to succeed to the Jagir of Bagor and Shahu's plan failed. Jaipur papers say that he similarly tried through Sawai Jaysinh to adopt another Rajput heir. Shahu gave due weight to the claim of Sambhaji of Kolhapur to succeed to the Satara raj and unite the two houses. But Shahu had never found any special capacity or discerning power in Sambhaji; the latter too had already advanced in age and had no son himself, so that he again would possibly have to adopt a successor a few years later. Therefore Shahu declined to support the proposal of Sambhaji being entrusted with the headship of the Maratha government. He had heard of the many descendants of Vithoji and Sharifji Bhosle living at different places, out of whom he thought of selecting a suitable boy and for that purpose sent round trusted men for enquiry. He conducted this search through his intimate advisers, Govindrao Chitnis, Yashvantrao Potnis, Devrao Meghashyam and others who were in close attendance on him.

There was then living at the fort of Satara, the aged queen Tarabai, nominally a prisoner, but otherwise a respectable old relation. When she learned that Shahu was looking out for a boy to take in adoption, she sent the King a message that she had a grandson, who was born of her son Shivaji and who had been brought up secretly at Pangaon for fear of Sambhaji of Kolhapur making an attempt on his life. It was obvious that if such a son was indeed available, he would certainly be the rightful heir, being closer to Shahu in relationship than boys of distant families. Shahu sent his Chitnis Govindrao to Tarabai and got in writing the statement given by her. Then he invited Bhagwantrao Amatya to Satara who was privy to the secret bringing up of Shivaji's posthumous son Ramraja[11]

---

nidhi and the Amatya, Itihasa-Sangraha, P. D. Selections, Bavda Daftar, the volumes of the Peshwas' Diaries, the chronologies &c. contain relevant matter on the last days of Shahu.

11. His real name was Rajaram, but as Tarabai according to Hindu

Bhagwantrao was asked to vouch for the truth of the story by a solemn oath taken in the holy waters of the Krishna at Mahuli. When this was done, Shahu's natural doubts were removed. But his Rani Sakwarbai openly declared that the whole affair was a hoax, concocted by the wicked Tarabai in order to satisfy her vanity and ambition of securing power in her own hands. Sakwarbai also plainly told Shahu that she would adopt another boy and frustrate the plan of Tarabai. She took the Pratinidhi and his Mutalik Yamaji Shivdev into her confidence and plotted against the advisers of Shahu such as Govindrao, Yashvantrao and even the Peshwa. With this object Sakwarbai began to enlist troops and increase her following, preparing for an armed conflict if that would be found necessary. Shahu perceived the danger of his position and sent quick orders to the Peshwa at Poona to collect a strong force of trusted men and repair to Satara without delay in order to meet the danger. The Peshwa left Poona on 21st August with his brother Janardan and his trusted Sardars Holkar and Sindia. He then stayed at Satara for full eight months, performing the obsequies of Shahu after his death in December, then bringing in Ramraja, placing him on the throne and thus preventing what might have developed into a war of succession. It is obvious this was a time of unprecedented anxiety, on the part of the Peshwa.

Sakwarbai remained in immediate attendance on Shahu in his last days. Nobody could keep her away. She brought Shahu from his thatched cottage outside into the palace of Rangmahal, on the slope of the Satara fort and exercised full control by closely watching him and his plans. She prevented Chitnis, the Peshwa and any of their partizans from having access to Shahu's presence. She even attempted the life of the Chitnis and the Peshwa. In the meantime Shahu matured his own plan of bringing in Ramraja and ascertained the views of all responsible leaders interested in the future management of the Maratha raj. Whenever Sakwarbai talked to Shahu of her own plan of an independent adoption, he quietly reasoned with her and tried to convince her that her plans far from

custom would not herself utter the name of her husband, she transposed the letters and made it Ramraja.

meeting with success, would simply create trouble for her and implored her to desist. But Sakwarbai was a woman of a strong unyielding bent of mind and would not listen to the sober advice of her husband. In the meantime Shahu sent Govindrao Chitnis round to all prominent leaders such as the Sarlashkar, Fatesinh Bhosle, the Pratinidhi, and the rest and asked their advice if there was any better plan for them to suggest and if any one of the outsiders was ready to accept the responsibility of government in opposition to the Peshwa. Every one replied that the Peshwa alone possessed the resources and the capacity to meet the situation and look after the interests of the Maratha State. Govindrao Chitnis faithfully reported to Shahu the various individual opinions that the impartial national leaders entertained on this vital subject. Shahu explained to his Rani the details of the situation as suggested by the public opinion and the general interest, but she was obdurate to the last moment, although she realized very well that any bold step on her part undertaken in opposition to the Peshwa and the wishes of Shahu, could not succeed and that she alone could not conduct the affairs of the State. She therefore called Sambhaji from Kolhapur immediately and arranged to take charge of the government. When Shahu learnt that Sambhaji was coming to seize Satara, he immediately despatched Bapuji Khando Chitnis with an armed force to prevent Sambhaji from coming on. Sambhaji wisely returned, and happily a civil war was averted.

3. **Final decision.**—Although weakened in body, Shahu fortunately retained his mental powers to the last. He realized that if he brought in Ramraja and completed the adoption in his presence, Sakwarbai would most certainly create trouble; and grave mischief or even bloodshed would be the result. He, therefore, wrote in his own hand two small orders commanding the Peshwa, definitely to take certain steps in regard to his succession. These two small papers have since been published in their original form and leave no doubt that they are in Shahu's hand and represent his genuine disposal of the knotty problem in agitation for over three years. Both the papers seem from internal evidence to have been issued about the 1st October 1749 or possibly on the 10th October, that is the

Dassara day of the year. They bear no date.

Rescript No. 1:

"Balaji Pradhan Pandit is hereby commanded—You should collect troops; several others were similarly asked but they do not accept (the responsibility). I could not write this before. Nor do I now hope to recover. The concerns of the State must be protected. Therefore you should take steps to continue the succession. Do not bring in Kolhapur. I have explained matters to the Chitnis. You should conduct the affairs of the State under the orders of the one who would succeed to the throne. I have every confidence in the Chitnis. You should work in co-operation with him. Whoever becomes the Chhatrapati, he will not interfere with your management. May you act wisely."

Rescript No. 2:

"Balaji Pandit Pradhan is commanded. We feel confident you will carry out the responsibility of the raj. I was sure of this myself, and the Chitnis confirmed me in my view. You have my blessings, and my palm is laid on your head. Whoever comes as Chhatrapati will continue you in the office of minister. If he does not, my curse be on him. You should continue your service in obedience to him. Do preserve the State. What more can I write? You are wise enough."[12]

Shahu survived this decision by a little over two months from 10th October to 15th December. It is clear from this that he deserves credit for having made the best possible arrangement for the future of the Maratha State in the circumstances then obtaining. The Peshwa's attitude too appears perfectly clear. His sole concern was to faithfully carry out the wishes of his dying master. It is unjust to charge him with having purposely brought forward an incompetent successor and thereby usurping the Chhatrapati's power. Ramraja was not more incompetent than any other average Maratha of his day, or even a real son of Shahu would have been. The Peshwa or anyone else knew little of the man then.

4. **The death of Shahu.**—The death of Shahu is thus recorded in the Chitnis and other bakhars. "Shahu expired at

12. *I. S. Ait. Sphut Lekh*, 4. 5.

his palace of Rangamahal at Shahunagar on 15th December 1749."[13], when all were very sad. He was a father and protector to young and old, to man and woman, to officers and servants, great and small. Such a king never lived. Under his government even criminals were not harshly treated. He had no enemy. Unprecedented lamentations were heard. Shahu's aunt Tarabai came down from the fort to have a last look at him. Govindrao Chitnis went and conversed with her. She advised Govindrao "to arrange that Sakwarbai should become Sati. If she lives, she will create trouble for the raj. Nor should Sambhaji be asked to come from Kolhapur. I have a young grand-son brought up at Pangaon. He should be fetched and placed on the throne."

The Chitnis reported this proposal to the Peshwa who consulted the Pratinidhi, Fatesinh Bhosle and others. They unanimously supported Tarabai's suggestion about Sakwarbai's becoming Sati. Her brother Kanhoji Shirke was sent for. He went and communicated the proposal to his sister. She revolved it in her mind and concluded that if she refused and lived after her husband, she would have to suffer untold miseries at the hands of the Peshwa, who was strong enough to control the situation. The brother returned and communicated her assent. Then preparations were made." Along with Sakwarbai two of Shahu's concubines, Lakshmi and Sakhu also burnt themselves on the same pyre. A statue of Shahu was afterwards erected on the burning ground, where it still stands."

There is no evidence to show that Sakwarbai was forced by the Peshwa to burn herself. The latter immediately on Shahu's death put Sakwarbai's partizans under arrest, viz., the Pratinidhi and his Mutalik Yamaji Shivdev. When she saw that she could not manage to snatch power out of the Peshwa's hands she preferred to die. The Peshwa had no need to compel her to that course. He could easily have restrained her, if she had lived and made mischief. The custom of Sati had a strong hold on the higher society of those days, as we notice several prominent Maratha sardars such as Kanhoji Angria, Raghuji Bhosle and others being followed at their death by

13. Friday morning 8 o'clock, Margashirsha Krishna 3 of Shak 1671 Shukla Samvastar, 67 years and 7 months old.

a number of their wives and maids burning themselves on their husband's funeral pyres as a mark of respect for the dead. An elderly lady like Sakwarbai, the only Rani then living of the pious king was bound to follow the time-honoured custom, the merits of which have to be judged by the moral standard prevailing at that period.

5. Shahu's progeny.—Shahu's mother Yesubai bore two children from Sambhaji, the elder a daughter named Bhavanibai married to Shankaraji Mahadik of Tarla. She became Sati. Sambhaji had an illegitimate wife, who with her son Madansinh was also captured at Raigad by Zulfiqar Khan and taken to the Emperor's camp. Shahu took in all four legitimate wives, Ambikabai Sinde, Savitribai Jadhav, Sakwarbai Shirke and Sagunabai Mohite; while Virubai, his highly honoured, although illegitimate wife presided over his harem. His marriage with the first two took place some time about 1703 in the Emperor's camp. Ambikabai died shortly after and the other wife was taken to Delhi whence she returned to the Deccan in 1719. Shahu on his return home married two wives in the Deccan below fort Purandar, Sakwarbai the elder and Sagunabai the younger. He had besides two concubines Lakshmibai and the younger Sakhu. From Sagunabai Shahu had a son in 1727 who died at the age of three. Sakwarbai had a daughter Gajrabai who was married to Malharrao Bande of Wadgaon. Sagunabai had also a daughter named Rajasbai, who was married into the family of the Nimbalkars. Two illegitimate sons Yesaji and Kusaji were born to Shahu from Lakshmibai. They were given the jagir of Shirol and came to be known as Shirolkar. Yesaji had a son named Balgopalji. After Shahu's death Ramraja discovered four young girls, Santubai, Gajrabai, Lakshmibai and Gunavantabai in the palace who claimed to be Shahu's daughters. Ramjara turned them out in June 1750.[14]

6. Contemporary opinion.—Writes Malhar Ramrao Chitnis, "Shahu by his kind and obliging disposition, attracted the love of all his subjects; every one supposed that he alone

14. P. D. 6. 69, 97, 99.

had the full measure of his master's favour. He freely rewarded whatever service was rendered to the State, by means of inams, stipends or gifts, carefully concealing the shortcomings of his officers and servants, and making the highest use of their good and strong points. He fully realized how his father Sambhaji had injured the interests of the State by his cruel ways, by harshly punishing the various qualified servants whom the great Shivaji had with immense pains reared. Shahu in his policy avoided all such harsh measures and invariably employed soft and conciliatory means to gain the hearts of his people. He evinced great regard for the Hindu gods and holy Brahmans, passed his time in the company of gifted and qualified servants, avoiding levity and low associations. He carefully continued the inams and gifts previously enjoyed for temples and holy purposes. He picked up men of merit and turned them to the highest service of the Maratha State. The poorest had free access to him and received quick and impartial justice. He never disregarded even the lowest applicant. On his tours he stopped his palanquin or horse whenever he saw any one making an appeal to him. He disliked harsh and cruel punishments : even in cases of murder his kindly heart revolted against inflicting the capital punishment, such as dropping a criminal from a high precipice."

Muzaffar Jang, Nizam-ul-mulk's grandson is recorded to have said when he heard of Shahu's death, "Shahu at the Maratha Court, and Nizam-ul-mulk at the Mughal Court, are the only two great men, the like of whom is hardly to be met with. He carefully looked after the interests of his State : There has been no equal to him. He rightly deserves the title of "enemy-less" (*Ajata-shatru*).

"By selecting right men for right duties Shahu increased the valour of his soldiers and giving them ample field for expansion, extended the Maratha dominions in all quarters of India, thus fulfilling the ardent wishes of his grandfather Shivaji."

"One peculiar trait of Shahu's character was that he felt the highest pleasure in making others happy, not only his dependents and subjects, but even aliens in race, religion and rule. Himself living a plain frugal ascetic's life, he felt highly rejoiced in seeing people enjoying their various trades and avocations. Indeed he could be called a saint in this respect. Even when faced with murderers that came to attack him, he let them go unpunished and thus created a genuine feeling of reverence for his personality in the minds of the public."[15]

7. Estimate of character.—Personally Shahu was neither a clever politician nor a capable commander, but his innate common sense and sympathetic heart enabled him to detect these qualities in others and utilise them for his service. He rightly judged men's capacities and gave them a free hand without grudge or hindrance. He particularly advanced the interests of the ryots, brought barren tracts under cultivation, encouraged the plantation of trees, relieved the sufferings of the poor, removed irksome taxes. He wrote to his brother-in-law Shankaraji Mahadik, "Your management of the territory is peculiarly harsh, the like of which is nowhere to be seen between the Narmada and Rameshwar. Do the ryots belong to you, that they should be freely robbed?"[16]

Shahu ever considered himself one of the people. He freely mixed with them, partook of their joys and sympathised with their sorrows. During festivals, celebrations, dinners, marriage ceremonies &c., he took an active part with outsiders and observed how they fared. The rich and the poor alike invited him to their marriage or other celebrations and he heartily joined them, spent for them and helped them whenever help was needed.

Shahu is rightly styled *Punyashloke* (of pious memory) by more than one contemporary writer. He appointed fit officers and trusted them. Nor was he remiss in punishing any of them if he did wrong. He always appeared in public in the same plain white garments as in private life, with a bare head, the long grey hairs of which hung down gracefully on the shoulders. He moved about sometimes riding horses, at other times in a palanquin with only a slender retinue, but his secretary and clerks always accompanied him. His daily routine was a permanent fixture. As a rule he went out hunt-

15. *Patre Yadi* 36, 38; Raj. vol. 6. 16, 85, 86; *Rumal*, pp. 120-136.
16. *Itihas Sangraha P. D.* pp. 275-286; Ait. Tipne. 2. 5; 2 Chitnis p. 88.

ing every morning, that was his only exercise and diversion. After breakfast he sat down to office work, carefully disposing of every matter that came before him, and patiently hearing every petition that was submitted. This continued till it was lighting time in the evening when a full Court was held, after formal obeisance had first been made to the deity of light. It is computed that he passed orders on at least 500 matters or cases every day. A little music and dancing closed the occupations of the day. He never had a serious ailment in his long life, till three years before his death, exposed himself freely to sun, wind and rain, and kept his head bare even during the hunt.

One, however, notices some peculiar traits also in Shahu's character. Having been brought up in the midst of Muslim surroundings of the imperial camp, in the most impressionable period of life, he was inclined towards Muslim manners and customs in preference to the Hindu ones of which he was ignorant at first and which he picked up only in later life. He had a large harem full of maids and female servants with eunuchs to guard them.[17] With all this his personal life was scrupulously clean, quite after the austere example of Aurangzeb. He certainly smoked the hukka. He was similarly fond of hunting wild game and shooting birds. He used to have a daily ride outside into the jungles for this purpose, thereby getting both fresh air and exercise. During the monsoon season he amused himself by fishing. There was nothing private or secret in his life; he was accessible to anyone at all times. He had on his staff singers, instrument-players, bards and actors. He kept well-trained hounds and was particularly keen on their breed.[18] He was equally fond of well-bred horses and birds and knew their qualities and features. Rarities of various kinds such as candles, scents, knives, swords, tobacco, gunpowder are also found to have been ordered by him through Kanhoji Angria from the European traders.[19] For tusks of elephants he paid high prices. He was equally fond

17. The eunuch Basavant Khoja was then a familiar figure at his Court.

18. P. D. 18. 70, 71, 19. Full details in P. D. 8 and 18.

19. P. D. 8. 51, 62, 54, 55; 18. 17, 21. *Itihas San*. P. D. pp. 275-288.

of good gardens and ordered the planting of rare fruit and flower trees brought from different places. Entries like the following are numerous. "You have been ordered to sow twenty-thousand seeds of Shivapur mangoes every year. Let me have a detailed return where, when and how these trees have been planted and what the actual outcome is. The district of Poona has no mango groves. This should be quickly attended to."

The winning power of Shahu's kind heart was in evidence throughout his life. Few notable figures in history approach Shahu's personality in the rule of the heart. The motto he adopted for his seal is itself eloquent in this respect : "A small man like me is after all a part of the all-pervading Divine Power."[20] It is the generous selfless policy of Shahu which enabled the Maratha power to expand so quickly.

8. **Shahu's benevolence.**—Few realize the severe agony of Shahu's captive lot in the Mughal camp for seventeen years during the entire formative period of a man's life. The result was that when at last he came to the throne he never chose to shine on the field of battle like his father and grand-father ; added to this his surrender of all power into the hands of the

---

20. वर्धिष्णुस्त्रिक्रमो विष्णोः सा मूर्तिरिव वामनी ।
शंभुसूनोरियं मुद्रा शिवराजस्य राजते ॥
Raj. 20. 60, 194.

An anecdote of Indroji Kadam is well worth reproducing. He was a small leader of a band of troops in the service of the Peshwa, and having been invited to pay his respects personally to Shahu, he marched with a large and splendidly dressed following beating his drums right up to the King's palace, contrary to the usual practice of walking on foot from a long distance and stopping all music. Shahu's master of ceremony suggested that this arrogant captain should be forcibly restrained. This would possibly have resulted in some kind of a deplorable incident. Shahu said, "Never mind, let him come as he chooses. I will see to it myself." Then Shahu came and took his seat in the Darbar, with his favourite dog by his side, upon whose head he placed his own turban. Indroji walked in with his proud salutations right up to the Maharaja's presence. Shahu quietly said, "come Kadam Raje, you are indeed a brave man," and pointed him to a seat nearby. Indroji at once noticed the strange way in which these words were uttered and the manner in which the dog sat near the throne with the turban on. He felt mortified, rose and profusely apologized for his rudeness thus learning a lesson which he never afterwards forgot. (*Rumal* 1. p. 126).

Peshwas, made people light-heartedly credit Shahu with all kinds of blemishes, that he was no judge of men, that he was too soft to wield power and rule men, that he was ignorant of Indian politics, void of the sternness required in managing the intricate concerns of a large growing state. But can such a judgment be borne out by the evidence we now possess in plenty? The story of Shahu's active life is fully narrated in the preceding pages. The very fact of his recognizing the great qualities of Bajirao and giving a free scope for their play, gives a lie to that narrow view. He ensured the expansion of Maratha power by conciliating the Emperor. He effected a lasting friendly understanding with Sawai Jaysinh and other Rajput princes in the interests of a general Hindu regeneration. There came to be an immense exchange of cultures between the north and the south for nearly a century, the authorship of which goes doubtless to Shahu.

Shahu succeeded in achieving brilliant results through a mild persuasive policy dictated by rigid justice and good will towards all. From the moment he came to occupy the Maratha throne, he made this policy the principle of his life, which enabled him to say truly on his death-bed that he had done wrong to no one. When at the death of Aurangzeb Shahu came to occupy the Maratha throne, there was hardly any raj and regular government in existence in the Deccan. Maratha leaders roamed all over the land with their predatory bands and ravaged what they called the Mughal Empire. They had received military training and wide experience in warfare and mostly spent their energies in cutting each other's throats. How were these to be pacified? Unless they were given suitable occupation away from their home, they were sure to kill themselves in the civil war which Tarabai had already started. This was the problem which faced Shahu and his farsighted minister Balaji Vishvanath. Shahu called these leaders together and, let us imagine, thus harangued them:

"Look here, you have no money in hand, nor have we: Your own strong bodies are your only asset. But if you read the situation aright, you can create lucrative fields for yourselves and help build up a Maratha dominion into the bargain. All the Mughal territory is yours if you will go and capture it. Borrow funds, form your fighting material, roam wherever you like, establish posts, settle and colonize them, build your own palaces and your capitals : hold them tenaciously against all odds ; start your own banks, and trading businesses, foster agriculture, capture distant markets. But do all this in a spirit of self-help and good-will to all. Do no wanton injury to anybody and make yourselves welcome wherever you go. Thus will our nation rise." This is the method Shahu personified in his own example and preached to his nation.

Shahu's precept was heartily accepted and acted upon. Dabhade worked in Gujarat, Raghuji Bhosle established Nagpur, the Pawars settled at Dhar and Dewas, the Holkars and the Sindias at Indore and Ujjain, and later Bundelkhand was similarly colonized. All the Maratha colonies, communities, and culture that we notice today at various centres outside Maharashtra, were thus the creation of Shahu and his Peshwas. It was by no means an accidental, haphazard development, but a studied plan of philanthropic non-violent principles applied to the politics of the day. Shahu simply continued the work that was begun by Shivaji and that was for a time interrupted by unforeseen circumstances. The Hindus and their religion had no room, no supporter in India. Providence supplied one in Shivaji. As soon as time came, Shahu rose to the occasion, took up the cue, and dropping those elements out of Shivaji's policy, for which he found himself incapable, transformed the traditional Maratha activities in a new channel where the Hindu interests were safeguarded not in a policy of hate but of good will which he extended in equal measure to Muslims also. More than once did Bajirao offer to extinguish Asaf Jah's rule in Maharashtra, but Shahu restrained him. On 9th February 1740 Bajirao communicating his victory over Nasir Jang wrote to his son, "I am at this moment in a position to eradicate the Mughal completely if only His Highness will immediately order all his chiefs to run to my support. If he does not respond to my call, I shall close this affair by negotiating only an advantageous peace."[21]

The vein of this kindly spirit of Shahu is fully disclosed in such sentences as these which he wrote to a host of his supporters,—"You are an old servant of the Chhatrapati, you

21. Sh. Ch. S. 7 p. 7.

have rendered loyal and selfless service and undergone severe labour, ever since the days of Raigad (i.e. since Raigad became the Maratha capital). It is therefore my bounden duty to look after you and your family's welfare, &c., &c." Words like these doubtless fill one's heart with reverence and admiration for the king.

As already mentioned Shahu certainly felt as great a respect for the Muslim practices as for his own. He started the practice of reciting the Khutba at Satara for which he brought with him the preacher known as Khatib from the Emperor's camp. The sanad conferring an inam on this Khatib mentions,—

"You are one of my select sardars, of high respectability, professing the Muslim faith. I am therefore allowing you the possession of the Satara fort for the accommodation of the throne with the title of Sardeshmukh. The Begam Zinat-un-nisa looked upon you as a son." This Khatib brought with him the gold palm of the Emperor given him by the Begam which Shahu worshipped faithfully during his life. The Khatibs still live at Satara. Shahu made no difference between Muslim saints and Hindu ones. Brahmendra-swami, Kacheshvar Bawa, Thakurdas Bawa, the Ramdasis, the Gosavis and others were all equally respected by him. He conferred inams and gifts upon all without distinction. He extended his patronage to the Christians also. After the fall of Bassein he took utmost care of Christian priests and places of worship. Equal respect for all religions was fully ingrained in his blood. Aurangzeb's daughter Zinat-un-nisa treated him like a son and he always respected her as his own mother.

It cannot however be said that Shahu was a perfectly spotless ruler. He had weaknesses and faults. Many of his campaigns miscarried through vacillation and mismanagement where sternness and prompt action were called for as in the case of the Janjira expedition. Another drawback of his policy was that his administration did not become progressive; his conservatism pervaded the whole Maratha administration.

9. **Shahunagar.**—Satara the capital of Shahu was the name of the fort and not that of the town, which now stands at the foot of the hill. Shahu in 1721 first took up his

residence below the fort and caused his courtiers to build their own separate quarters adjoining his own. A town thus soon grew up which he named after himself as Shahunagar. When he was crowned in 1708 he took his seat on the throne in the fort, which he removed to his palace of Rangamahal in this new rapidly rising town about the year 1721. This original palace of Shahu was burnt down in 1874, and on its site only the old well now exists, known as "the well of the throne". The other old structures that one sees today were erected by Maharaja Pratapsinh, a hundred years after Shahu. The various wards of the old town are named, like those of Poona, after the days of the week, in addition to Yado Gopal Peth, Vyankatpura (named after Vyankatrao Ghorpade, who had married Bajirao's sister Anubai), Chimanpura (named after Chimnaji Damodar Moghe) Durgapura, Rajaspura, Raghunathpura, &c. Shahu supplied the new city with good drinking water brought in pipes from the Mahadara and Yavteshvar hills. The temple of Krishneshwar still reminds visitors of Krishnarao Joshi of Chas, a brother of Bajirao's wife Kashibai. There was a mint established by Shahu in the city. It was entrusted to a well-known firm of bankers, headed by Tanshet Bhurke.

Space forbids a more detailed account of Shahu's activities which have received ample notice in Marathi books.

CHRONOLOGY

CHAPTER XIII

1750, January 4	Ramraja crowned and married.
1750, March	Tarabai departs for Sinhgad.
1750, April 1	Raghuji Bhosle arrives at Satara.
1750, April 18	Peshwa leaves Satara for Poona.
1750, April 26	Sadashivrao married to Parvatibai.
1750, June	Tarabai at Poona from Sinhgad.
1750, June 14	Chimnaji N. Sachiv under arrest.
1750, July 6	Sinhgad taken from him.
1750, July 24	Sachiv liberated.
1750, August	Ramraja with Raghuji Bhosle at Poona ; a grand assemblage held, and resolutions taken.
1750, September 8	Raghuji leaves for Nagpur.
1750, September 25	Sadashivrao captures Sangola from the Pratinidhi, and enacts constitutional regulations.
1750, October 29	Tarabai returns to Satara.
1750, Nov. 17	Ramraja returns to Satara.
1750, Nov. 22	Ramraja placed under Tarabai's confinement.
1751, early months	Peshwa goes into Karnatak ; Tarabai's activities against Peshwa.
1751, July 16	Tarabai puts to death Anandrao Jadhav and other guards of Satara.
1752, Sep. 14	Reconciliation effected between Peshwa and Tarabai at Jejuri.
1760, December 18	Sambhaji of Kolhapur dies.
1761, June 23	Peshwa Nanasaheb dies.
1761, Dec. 9	Tarabai dies.
1762, Sep. 22	Jijabai adopts Shivaji.
1763, March 23	Ramraja formally crowned.
1773, February 17	Jijabai dies.

CHAPTER XIII

THE MONARCHY IN ECLIPSE

[1750—1761]

1 Ramraja installed.
2 Constitutional Revolution at Sangola.
3 Ramraja confined.
4 Tarabai reconciled.
5 Sambhaji of Kolhapur.
6 The Peshwa's objectives and weaknesses.

1. Ramraja installed.—Ramraja, the successor chosen by Shahu, was an utter stranger to the Maratha nation. Tarabai declared him to be the posthumous son of her son Shivaji born of the latter's wife Bhavanibai. According to her story, he was born at Panhala and was secretly removed to several other places for fear that Sambhaji of Kolhapur and his Rani Jijabai might resort to some foul play against the child's life. Ramraja's sister Daryabai Nimbalkar lived at Pangaon six miles south of Barsi, to whom the youth after some wanderings, came to be entrusted for being brought up. He thus lived his first two years at Panhala then about 16 years at Bavda or Gagangad and then for five years he resided at Pangaon. He was about 23 years old at his accession.

After the cremation rites of Shahu and Sakwarbai had been performed, an official deputation from Satara headed by Bapuji Khanderao Chitnis, brought Ramraja to Satara from his retreat at Pangaon along with his sister Daryabai Nimbalkar. Arrived at Vaduth on the Krishna on 26th December, he called on Tarabai the same afternoon in the temple of Shakunteshvar. The next day, 27th December the Peshwa along with the sardars and officials called on Ramraja and made their obeisance to him by offering nazars. Tarabai convinced the Maratha sardars of the genuineness of Ramraja's birth by eating food with him out of the same dish: and the youth was unquestionably accepted as Tarabai's real grandson.

On Thursday 4th January 1750, Paush Shukla, 1, Shak 1671, Ramraja left his quarters outside, passed through the gaily decorated city in a procession, and ascended the throne at Shahunagar late in the afternoon. The new king married two wives on 8th February, Tukabai (Shirke) and Sagunabai daughter of Baranji Mohite.[1] As the presence of the Pratinidhi was essential for the coronation and as Jagjivan Pratinidhi was in confinement, Bhavanrao, son of Krishnaji Pant of Vishalgad, was brought to Satara and made Pratinidhi by Tarabai. Bhagvantrao Amatya was also invited to Satara on that occasion and was given the robes of his office. Bhagvantrao was mainly instrumental in supporting Ramraja's succession.

The tutelage in which Tarabai constantly kept Ramraja was too irksome for him. From the beginning she severely controlled all his actions, stopped him from associating with the Peshwa with a view to maintaining her own importance in the administration ; and destroying the latter's overweening influence. For a time she conducted this game secretly trying to gather power in her own hands and allowing no chance to Ramraja either to obtain experience or wield authority independently. As she was then about seventy-five years of age, the best interests of the Maratha State would have been served only by allowing the new king to work in unison with the Peshwa. Ramraja was naturally inclined to support the Peshwa as against his grand-mother, but this conduct enraged the lady all the more, so that they soon became bitter opponents of each other. Tarabai began to hate and openly abuse him, which exasperated him still further. Purandare writes in February 1750, "If the Raja would live alone with her for any length of time, he is sure to keep her in confinement of his own accord." Matters, however, shaped just the other way. In a few months time, Tarabai arrested Ramraja at the Satara fort and kept him a close prisoner.

All the while the Peshwa watched the situation quietly and soon made up his mind to transfer all the administration to Poona, thus leaving the Chhatrapati and his grandmother free to do what they liked at Satara. Chimnaji Narayan Sachiv and the Pratinidhi's Mutalik Yamaji Shivdev were Tarabai's chief supporters and obstructed any move on the part of the Peshwa. Early in March fell the death anniversary of Tara-

1. *Nana Roz.* I. 125, 136 ; *Itihas Sangraha* P. D. p. 3.

bai's husband,[2] which used to be performed at Sinhgad where he had died; so under the pretence of being present at the ceremony, Tarabai left Satara and took up her abode at that fort, starting fresh intrigues against the Peshwa there.

From 26th December 1749 to 18th April 1750 the Peshwa stayed at Satara doing his utmost to sustain the new Chhatrapati's power and get him into a proper trim to carry out his duties in the best interests of the State. During this period the minister found himself so much entangled in the domestic concerns of the royal house, that he could not attend to the external affairs of a momentous character. He, therefore, sent his trusted agents to Raghuji Bhosle and invited him to Satara with the utmost expedition as the fittest person of responsible position for handling the situation. The latter arrived there about the beginning of April and the two surveyed the situation together for a week or two. The Peshwa then asked Raghuji to stay at Satara and use his best endeavours to put Ramraja in the proper way to discharge his duties. Raghuji stayed on at Satara till 8th July and the Peshwa went to Poona on 18th April, where his presence was needed for the thread ceremony of his son Vishvasrao and the marriage of Sadashivrao who had recently lost his first wife. The Peshwa writes to Dikshit, "I have now been at Satara for seven months. Constant bickerings are going on with the new Chhatrapati. He is entirely nerveless unable to make up his mind and act on his own initiative. I wonder if you can suggest some means by which I can secure the master's good will and have freedom for myself to attend to the pressing matters of the State."

Thus an impasse arose in the Chhatrapati's affairs at Satara and when Tarabai would not find Ramraja pliable for her purpose, she damned him for good, declaring that he was an impostor and not a true son of his father, though she herself had formerly called him legitimate. What Ramraja must have felt at such a crushing blow, had better be imagined. There were a large number of respectable Maratha gentlemen and families, scrupulous about their pure heredity and its preservation, who felt extreme mortification at this open repudiation of

---

2 फाल्गुन व० ९=3 March 1700.

Ramraja by Tarabai. Burhanji Mohite[3] a highly respected Maratha grandee, who had long lived with Raghuji Bhosle at Nagpur and who had just married his daughter to Ramraja, felt highly offended at this turn of events. "Hundreds of Maratha nobles assembled at Burhanji's house and started a sitting-in strike of starving themselves to death. They showered reproaches upon the old grand mama, saying "It was she who asked us to give our daughters in marriage to this king ; and now she declares he is not a true son of his father. What a shameful development ! You, Burhanji, must first kill us and then kill these newly married girls." Matters thus assumed a grave outlook. Military guards were called out to keep the peace. "Burhanji Bawa is proceeding to extremities and will end his life in a day or two." When such a situation developed at Satara the Peshwa left the place and went to Poona, unable to find a way for solving the social trouble which developed so unexpectedly at the capital of Shahunagar within a short time of the pious monarch's death.

2. *Constitutional revolution at Sangola.*—The Peshwa then made a pressing request to Tarabai to visit Poona. She agreed, left Sinhgad and reached Poona in June. Her partizans Bhagvantrao Amatya and Chimnaji Narayan Sachiv were also present. The Peshwa sent a request to the Maharaja at Satara to come to Poona. He arrived in August and all the assembled leaders of opinion and thought had full discussions together over the situation. Raghuji Bhosle, and Sar-lashkar Somavanshi were there, as also Sindia and Holkar from the north. Sadashivrao Bhau, Ramchandra Bawa, Mahadoba Purandare, Sakharam Bapu, then a rising diplomat of the Peshwa's party, these and others sat together for days and weeks and had heart to heart talks. The Peshwa tried his best to come to a kind of a working compromise, so that the administration should run smoothly and a rapid expansion of the Maratha power could be assured. Such a conference was indeed unique in Maratha history both in weight and variety of views. Here then the Peshwa took the final resolu-

3. Burhanji's one sister was the late Rani Sagunabai of Shahu and the second was the wife of Raghuji Bhosle, mother of Mudhoji.

tion of removing all official work from Satara to Poona, leaving the Chhatrapati and Tarabai to themselves at Satara. The Peshwa firmly urged upon the attention of the assemblage that in the interest of the State, the executive power must remain in his own hands and that he would not tolerate any interference with the administration from the Pratinidhi, or the Sachiv or any one else. For Sinhgad belonged to the Sachiv and afforded a centre for intrigue against the Peshwa. So he categorically demanded possession of that fort from the Sachiv. The Chhatrapati gave his written sanction to this proposal, causing further exasperation to Tarabai. The Sachiv as he refused to hand over the fort, was at once arrested (14th June), and a party of troops was despatched to take possession of the fort forcibly. It surrendered on 6 July. The Sachiv was set free and allowed to go home on 24th July,[4] after receiving sufficient compensation for the loss.

This was a critical moment for the Maratha raj. All India was having her eyes on Poona, eager to see in what manner the crisis created by Shahu's death was going to end. The Peshwa determined to have full power. Raghuji Bhosle heartily supported him and departed for his domain of Nagpur on 8th September, after arriving at a concerted settlement for the future administration of the Maratha State.

Like the Sachiv the Pratinidhi too was known to be a partizan of Tarabai. Personally Dadoba Pratinidhi possessed little capacity, but his Mutalik Yamaji Shivdev was clever and intriguing. Dadoba had been confined on the fort of Purandar and owned the important territory between Karhad and Pandharpur bordering on the east of Satara, and affording a convenient region from which the Mutalik could work mischief against the Peshwa. Sangola near Pandharpur was a small fortified post belonging to the Pratinidhi, which the Peshwa now demanded from him, as he had done Sinhgad from the Sachiv. The Peshwa brought both the Pratinidhi and the Mutalik for his grand conference of Poona and there dictated to them the terms on which he said he would set them free. If they hesitated, the Peshwa threatened them with dismissal from their hereditary posts. As soon as Raghuji left for Nagpur,

4. Nana Saheb Roz. 1. 43; P. D. 6. 63.

the Peshwa despatched Sadashivrao Bhau and Ramchandra Baba with an adequate armed force and Ramraja himself at their head to take possession of Sangola from Yamaji Shivdev. The latter resisted and waged a short struggle of two weeks; but being overpowered by the Peshwa's artillery, Yamaji delivered Sangola into Sadashivrao's hands on the Dassara day, 25th September. The neighbouring place of Mangalvedha was also reduced and assigned to the trusted Patwardhans for future defence. Thus the Pratinidhi's opposition was disarmed.

Sangola has become famous for the settlement that was drawn up there under orders of the Chhatrapati for the future regulation of the Maratha State. The scheme was conceived in Ramchandra Baba's head and executed by Sadashivrao's arm. A complete revolution was thus silently effected transferring all power from the Chhatrapati to the Peshwa. Within nine months of Shahu's death the Chhatrapati became a creature in the Peshwa's hands. The following is the substance of these new regulations. The system of the eight ministers had already fallen into disuse and the Prime Minister (the Peshwa) had begun to wield supreme power since the last years of Shahu. The only other ministers that now existed were the Pratinidhi, the Sachiv and the Senapati. The other four of Shivaji's system had already dwindled into insignificance. The Sachiv became perfectly innocuous hereafter. In order to deprive the Pratinidhi of any power of mischief, Bhavanrao was now brought to Sangola and formally installed as Pratinidhi by the Chhatrapati. Yamaji Shivdev having waged a war against the Peshwa fell from power and his nephew Vasudev Anant was made the Pratinidhi's Mutalik, as being more amenable to the Peshwa. The Senapati Yashvantrao Dabhade had proved incompetent on account of his incurable vices. So he was given a cash allowance for maintenance, and the Subah of Gujarat was divided half and half between the Gaikwad and the Peshwa.

Babuji Naik Joshi was another thorn in the Peshwa's side, as he claimed all power in the Karnatak. He was deprived of all such pretensions in the future, and the management of the Subah of Karnatak was taken over by the Peshwa.

Ramraja's position at Satara was also defined. Govindrao Chitnis was made the Maharaja's principal manager with his nephew Bapuji Khanderao as the military captain and Trimbak Sadashiv alias Nana Purandare as the Peshwa's representative helping him in keeping order. Yashvantrao Potnis and Devrao Lapate were to be the Chhatrapati's personal companions and advisers. Many other minor appointments were also made at Sangola which need not be detailed. Ramraja's sister Daryabai was expecting some substantial reward for her share in jockeying the Maharaja into the throne. Her husband Nimbaji Naik Nimbalkar was made Sar-lashkar, in the place of Appaji Somawanshi who was removed. Fatesinh Bhosle's affairs were falling into mismanagement. Trimbak Hari Patwardhan, one of the Peshwa's trusted dependents, was appointed as the principal manager of Fatesinh Bhosle at Akalkot.

Thus Bhau Saheb and Ramchandra Baba acting together with a strong hand quickly put an end to the intolerable situation which had developed, and evolved a fresh order of things under the sanction of the Chhatrapati. This willing co-operation and complete accord with the Peshwa's policy on the part of Ramraja was highly resented by Tarabai. For, after all the fountain head of power was the Chhatrapati, so Tarabai decided to keep him under her control. With an intent to thwart the Peshwa she left Poona about the middle of October and after visiting Shambhu Mahadev reached Satara on 29th October, organizing her own party and an armed force during the interval. From Poona she wrote to Shekh Mira, the guardian of fort Satara to store ample supplies and prepare for its defence. On arrival she compelled all officers and guards of the fort to swear allegiance and obedience to her personally. Some were won over by money and some by other inducements. She carried the two queens of Ramraja and his valuables from the palace below up into the fort. Ramraja was at Sangola during October and parting from Sadashivrao early in November and paying a visit to Shambhu Mahadev on the way, reached Satara on 17th November, taking up residence in his palace in the city. He was fully tutored by Sadashivrao to assert his power and control the activities of his grandmother from his capital. But this he could not do.

3. **Ramraja confined.**—On the 22nd November was the Champa-Shasthi day on which the family deity of the Bhosles was worshipped. Though previously warned, the Maharaja unguardedly went up to the fort for the sacred function, hoping to disarm all suspicions of the old lady. But at the very first meeting which they had in private, Tarabai strongly remonstrated with him against his lending support to the Peshwa and advised him to be guided by herself alone. Ramraja did not relish the advice and when in the afternoon he started on his horse along with his two Ranis in palkies to go down to the city, the gatekeepers who had received previous intimation, put him under arrest, and took him to Tarabai who kept him closely confined. Bapuji Chitnis and others below on learning this development, tried their best to release him, but once the gates were closed against all outsiders, the prisoner could not be freed without a regular siege and bombardment by artillery.

The fort of Satara being strongly defended, it enabled Tarabai to assert her power at once by issuing commands and taking the administration into her own hands. She brought to her presence, Dadoba Pratinidhi, and the Mutalik brothers Antaji and Yamaji Shivdev with the latter's son Gamaji, who helped her with men and money from the adjoining districts. The Peshwa kept cool, showed no irritation but adopted a wonderfully submissive attitude. He wrote to Purandare, "I have not the least desire to stand in opposition to the lady sovereign, our master and protector. You must solicit her pleasure and impress it on her how our enemies would take advantage, when evil reports reach the distant Delhi. You must also find out whether the confinement of the Chhatrapati is a mere show or harmful to him and how far the two are likely to collude against us. I should be informed about the persons in their confidence and their opponents. What is the attitude of Daryabai in this affair?" Purandare replied to this as follows: "Ramraja is being strictly guarded by Tarabai's men. He sends me piteous appeals to get him released." The Peshwa asked Purandare to persuade Tarabai to adopt a softer attitude. "If she persists in keeping the king a close prisoner and conducts the administration herself, the whole Maratha raj suffers disgrace in public. How is it possible for Her Highness to supervise from her snug perch on the fort political operations ranging over a wide area from Delhi to Rameshwar. It is not impossible for me at once to revert her to her former confinement, but I refrain from such a drastic measure, remembering that we are the Chhatrapati's servants through three generations. Any coercive steps by me will appear like a rebellion against the master. This I wish to avoid at any cost. I can easily put the families of the fort-guards under confinement and harassment so as to punish them for their treachery. I can also besiege the fort and prevent any communication with outside. But I desist. You must in sweet language persuade the lady to the right course. Please assure the King of our extreme concern for his welfare. Tell him to submit to Her Highness' wishes for a time. Assure Her Highness also that whatever she does I shall always remain her most obedient servant. You must quietly manage to win over the King completely to our views. You must on no account seek favour either from the priests or the guards in the employ of Tarabai."

These soft words on the part of the Peshwa were misunderstood by the lady and only served to stiffen her hostile attitude. Months passed in wrangling and wordy exchanges. There was another weighty reason why the Peshwa was reluctant to use harsh measures against the lady. A great stir occurred at this time in the Karnatak. Nasir Jang had led a strong expedition into that region during the closing months of 1750, which compelled the Peshwa to proceed to that quarter personally. So he did not want two major tasks on his hands simultaneously.

While Ramraja was a strictly-guarded prisoner in the fort, all his belongings, jewellery, plate and other valuables were in the palace below. The Peshwa ordered all these to be carefully collected, listed and kept secure at Purandar with a view both that Tarabai should not appropriate them and also to restore them to the King when time came, to prevent the calumny that would perhaps attach to the Peshwa's name that he had deprived the King of all his valuables.[5]

5. *Purandare Daftar* Part I 225-364 gives graphic details of Ramraja's affairs; P. D. 6. 147-153; Raj. 6. 273, 553.

In January 1751 the Peshwa and his cousin Sadashivrao started for the Karnatak to watch Nasir Jang's movements, keeping for the management of the Satara affairs a sufficient force under trusted agents. Purandare continued sending the Peshwa frequent reports from Satara, proposing certain alternative measures, such as using force against Tarabai so as to reduce her to submission, or leaving her alone and conducting the administration as best as possible, or bringing in Sambhaji from Kolhapur as a counterblast to the power both of Tarabai and Ramraja. The Peshwa patiently waited for a better turn of events and took no stern measures during his absence.

4. Tarabai reconciled.—The opinion of the Maratha nation unanimously condemned Tarabai's high-handed action in keeping the Chhatrapati, their master and sovereign, in confinement. In the course of time her hatred towards Ramraja grew so violent that in angry moments she began to use cruel and filthy language towards him. She at every moment declared that the raja was no son of her son Shivaji and that he was an impostor. This was felt by him as the most cutting stroke. For whatever the facts may be, Ramraja personally knew nothing about his birth and was not responsible for the reproaches his grandmother heaped upon him. She alone was the author of his fate in having brought him out of oblivion. After Shahu's death all moral checks on her behaviour vanished and she became violent and uncontrollable. In the meantime her ally Damaji Gaikwad along with the Dabhades came thundering against the Peshwa and ravaging his territory. He was, however, checked near Satara and finally humbled. This defeat of Damaji proved the ruin of all the lady's plans and measures, but it also served to incense her still more. Anandrao Jadhav, the Keeper of the Satara fort was put to death (16 July 1751) only because he had tried to obtain news of Ramraja's situation. Many guards and servants were similarly put to death or made to suffer indescribable hardships. As she found Dadoba Pratinidhi incapable of managing her affairs, she promised the Pratinidhi's post to Babuji Naik Joshi, thereby causing an unnecessary open war between Dadoba and Babuji. She started a low intrigue with the Nizam's Court, offering the Peshwaship to his minister Ramdas-

pant. It is difficult to understand how in all this she was serving the Maratha State. But the Peshwa with patience and fortitude gradually overcame all opposition and so thwarted the lady in all directions, that she found after a year's vain struggle that she had no course left except to make peace with the Peshwa and strike the best bargain possible with him. In June 1751, she sent her two agents Chinto Anant and Moro Shivdev, to negotiate terms of peace with the Peshwa who first demanded the release of Ramraja. Although this was not fully accomplished, Tarabai yielded so far as to come down from the fort along with Ramraja and to take up her residence in the town below. Later on she went and visited the Peshwa at Poona; but she violently opposed any idea of releasing Ramraja or of entrusting any power to him. Ultimately the Peshwa having practically obtained a free hand in the administration, despatched both the king and his grandmother back to Satara under a strong and able trusted commander Trimbakrao Pethe. He was to keep a strict control over both. A patched up peace in which both the parties understood each other's game was thus brought about in the month of September 1751; so that when the Nizam invaded the Peshwa's territory during the closing months of that year, Tarabai deputed Dadoba Pratinidhi to join and help the Peshwa. The Peshwa thankfully sent back the Pratinidhi as he had no troops and replied adroitly that the lady's blessings alone would enable him to ward off the danger created by the Nizam."[6] As Tarabai deprived Dadoba of his office of the Pratinidhi and gave it to Babuji Naik, both Dadoba and his Mutalik Yamaji became friendly to the Peshwa, in opposition to Tarabai.[7]

The reconciliation between Tarabai and the Peshwa was later confirmed on oaths which they both took in the presence of the deity of Jejuri on 14th September 1752. It was at this meeting that Tarabai solemnly declared that Ramraja was not the true son of his father, that his advent had brought disgrace on the Chhatrapati's house; that he should, therefore, be removed and Sambhaji of Kolhapur placed on the throne at Satara.[8]

6. Raj. 6. 235. 256; *Shahu Roz.* 115.

7. *Shahu Roz.* 234, 243, 244; P. D. 6. 213, 215; *Patre Yadi* 114.

8. Raj. 6. 257; *Treaties and Engagements* p. 46; *Itihas Sangraha* P. D. p. 7, No. 8.

20

A written agreement between Tarabai and the Peshwa took place at Jejuri in which the following words occur. "This Raja is false. Every one knows this. But he should not be killed. He should be treated as an illegitimate son like Fatesinh Bawa or Yesaji Kusaji. He should be supplied with the requirements of life; if necessary he should be kept confined but not killed." As years rolled on, Tarabai came to be fully reconciled to the Peshwa and during the last four years of her life there existed perfect amity between them. She witnessed the national disaster of Panipat on 14th January 1761 and died ten months later at Satara on 9th December 1761 (=Thursday 11 Jamadilaval).

Ramraja, however, had a most miserable life during Tarabai's usurpation of power. He continued in confinement till her death. Thereafter the Peshwa Madhaorao I formally crowned Ramraja at Shahunagar on 23rd March 1763.[9] Since then his lot became much improved although he was not allowed to assert himself as Chhatrapati, a role for which he possessed neither the training nor the capacity.

It is difficult to see how Tarabai in all her struggles could have improved the lot of the Maratha State by an inveterate opposition to the Peshwa. It is creditable to the Peshwa that he showed wonderful coolness under extreme provocation and took no drastic action against the old and revered lady, on whose account he lost three precious years of his valuable time, which he all along ardently desired to utilize in north India. The consequence was the mismanagement, dissensions and blunders which presaged the disaster of Panipat. It is a pity that a capable woman like Tarabai, who had in her younger days achieved signal success in the war against Aurangzeb, should find her after life altogether wasted. Thirty-six years of that life were spent in confinement either at Panhala or Satara. In her extreme old age she tried her hand after Shahu's death, with what result we have seen above.

5. Sambhaji of Kolhapur.—To conclude the story of the Chhatrapati's house a word is necessary to recount the

9. *Shahu Roz.* 99.

destiny of the other branch, that of Kolhapur. The Peshwa's effort to unite the two branches of Satara and Kolhapur proved of no avail. Sambhaji of Kolhapur had no special capacity for managing his concerns, which were better handled by his adroit queen Jijabai. The Peshwa kept amicable relations with him to the last. The management of his state fell into disrepute ; and his officials and subjects remained always discontented. No new conquests were made nor any capable servants reared up. Sambhaji died on 18th December 1760 without leaving any heir to the gadi after him. This afforded the Peshwa the desired opportunity to confiscate the Kolhapur State and annex it to Satara. Such a result would most likely have taken place if at that very time the Peshwa's position had not grown precarious owing to the disaster of Panipat which took place within a month of Sambhaji's death. In this connection writes Jijabai on 20th January 1761 : " It is highly to be regretted that the Pradhanpant, instead of offering condolences on the death of my revered husband, has sent troops under Hari Ram and Visaji Narayan to confiscate the State. Our friendship of long standing has thus been well rewarded ! But you must explain to Raghunathrao that we four Ranis of the late Maharaja are alive, one of whom Kusabai has advanced in pregnancy some months. The Peshwa has broken his solemnly given word. What more can I say ? "

Jijabai wrote letters to several persons and gave out the false report that her co-wife Rani Kusabai was enceinte. She also circulated further false news that the queen had given birth to a son on 25th May 1761. She wrote this news to Nanasaheb and Gopikabai also. Shortly after the Peshwa died on 23rd June. Nana Purandare went to Satara to meet Tarabai and arrange about the Kolhapur succession in consultation with her. But the report of a son having been born was after full inquiry found to be false, and it was admitted later by Jijabai herself in a personal meeting with the Peshwa Madhaorao, who, then in serious danger about his own position, did not invite further trouble on account of this Kolhapur succession ; so he allowed Jijabai to adopt any eligible boy and make him the Chhatrapati of Kolhapur. She thus adopted on the Dassara day of 1762 (September 27) a boy from the Khanwat branch and named him Shivaji. Jijabai continued to conduct the affairs of that State till her death on 17th February 1773.

6. **The Peshwa's objectives and weaknesses.**—The second half of the Peshwa Balajirao's regime (or the years 1749-61) has for various reasons become memorable in the history of India. It was during this period that the British power leaped up above the Indian horizon to stand later against the Marathas in the contest for the sovereignty of India. When the new Chhatrapati was installed on the throne at Satara, the Peshwa set before himself three main objectives, to humble the Nizam, to subjugate the Karnatak region, and to assert Maratha influence at the Court of Delhi. The intransigence of Tarabai and the incapacity of Ramraja led the Peshwa in the best interests of the Maratha State to remove all the administrative departments to Poona, where he had at hand three capable individuals, his own cousin Sadashivrao, a fearless executive officer, Ramchandra Baba Sukhtankar, a financer and diplomat of high order, and Mahadoba Purandare a selfless and foresighted servant of the Maratha State, by all of whom he was loyally served.

After the death of Shahu a sad state of disorder and misgovernment overtook the regions between Satara and Poona. Thefts, robberies, murders became so common that life and property were for a time quite unsafe. These were obviously the results of Tarabai's wanton interference with the administration ; and these disorders came to be accentuated when the Chhatrapati himself came to be lodged in strict confinement, having no property of his own and fearing momentary danger to his life. The confusion in the Chhatrapati's house quickly reacted upon the general populace outside. The only drastic remedy would have been to put the old lady in confinement as during the time of Shahu and to restore the Chhatrapati to his position. But the Peshwa declined to take such a step, and thereby became estranged from Mahadoba Purandare.[10]

It was a trying circumstance for the Peshwa that when

10. *Purandare Daftar* 1. 224, 225, 267-275, 345, 354 ; *Purandare Diary* pp. 71, 81, 83 ; P. D. 23, 43 ; *Patre Yadi* 103.

Tarabai took up a hostile attitude he should have been severely estranged from Mahadoba Purandare. Sadashivrao and Ramchandra Baba executed some bold and quick measures at Sangola and saved the situation. But this the Peshwa felt as an encroachment on his own powers. He bitterly resented Sadashivrao's action at Sangola and the two cousins were nearly on the point of an open rupture. In this situation Mahadoba quietly withdrew from all office work and retired to his home at Saswad, thus easing the tension so far as lay in his power.

Sadashivrao, however, took a different line of action, being encouraged and financially helped by Ramchandra Baba. He demanded from the Peshwa full power to conduct the administration, not approving the lenient method adopted by the latter. The Peshwa refused to surrender his power on any account. Sadashivrao thereupon threatened to resign and seek service under Sambhaji Raja of Kolhapur, who had written to him, offering him the post of his Peshwa with a jagir of five thousand along with the possession of three important forts Bhimgad, Pargad and Vallabhgad, all on the border of Kolhapur and Belgaum.[11] Happily the dispute was soon reconciled and nothing untoward happened in consequence. This was in the closing months of 1750, when Sadashivrao met the Peshwa after his expedition to Sangola.

In contrast with his father Bajirao, the Peshwa Balajirao suffered from one serious drawback. He was no soldier and could not personally conduct military campaigns. To meet this defect he often had to depend upon others thereby exposing himself to great risks. The Sindias and the Holkars became overbearing and practically independent. The Peshwa, therefore, reared new young men of his own caste and confidence such as Trimbakrao Pethe, Gopalrao Patwardhan, Visaji Krishna Binivale, Balavantrao Mehendale and others. But none of these could he sent to the north, so as to exercise control over the two powerful chiefs Sindia and Holkar. Ramchandra Baba being the richest public servant at the time, was a power by himself. He amassed a large fortune in the capacity of the Peshwa's agent, controlling and supervising the

11. *Purandare Diary* p. 60 ; *Patre Yadi* 72.

affairs of the Sindias. Jayappa became disgusted with Ramchandra Baba's greed and compelled the Peshwa to recall him to the south, just about the time that Shahu died. The Baba gave several lacs to Sadashivrao and guided him in his execution of the Sangola settlement. Ramchandra Baba died at Poona on 4th October 1754. He built a house in Poona which is said to have had seven storeys, the first of its kind then.

CHRONOLOGY

CHAPTER XIV

1750, November 22	Umabai Dabhade meets Peshwa at Alandi.
1750, December 5	Nasir Jang murdered.
1751, January 31	Muzaffar Jang murdered.
1751, January 31	Peshwa and Sadashivrao proceed to the Karnatak.
1751, Jan.-March	Damaji Gaikwad's raid upon the Peshwa's territories.
1751, February 18	Peshwa's forces suffer defeat at Bahadarpura in Khandesh.
1751, March 10	Damaji near Poona.
1751, March 15	Damaji defeated near the Venya.
1751, March 21-30	Light actions near Satara between Damaji and the Peshwa's troops.
1751, March 29	Peshwa at Pangal.
1751, April 12	Peshwa leaves for Satara.
1751, April 24	Peshwa reaches Satara, demands from Damaji half share of Gujarat.
1751, April 30	Peshwa raids Damaji's camp and makes him prisoner.
1751, May 11	Damaji kept in confinement at Poona.
1751, May 22	Peshwa reaches Poona.
1751, October 22	Raghunathrao starts for Gujarat.
1751, November 14	Damaji removed to Lohgad.
1752, March 30	Damaji agrees to cede half Gujarat.
1752, June 23	Damaji highly honoured at Poona.
1753, April 25	Ahmadabad captured but again lost.
1753, November 23	Umabai Dabhade dies.
1754, May 18	Yashvantrao Dabhade dies.
1757, October 11	Ahmadabad recaptured.
1759, March 4	Surat taken by the English.
1803	Broach conquered by the English.

CHAPTER XIV

DAMAJI GAIKWAD IN GUJARAT [1749—1759]

1. Damaji's onslaught upon the Peshwa.
2. The Peshwa hits back.
3. The Peshwa scores.
4. Ahmadabad captured.
5. Surat and Broach.

1. Damaji's onslaught upon the Peshwa.—The years 1750 and 1751 proved exceptionally stirring for Maharashtra and the Deccan in general. A severe struggle for power started between the Peshwa and Tarabai and a similar domestic trouble engrossed the neighbouring State of Haidarabad. Nasir Jang and Muzaffar Jang invaded the Karnatak and both were murdered in quick succession, the first on 5th December 1750, and the second on 31st January following. This was an opportunity for the Peshwa to interfere in the affairs of that State and assert his supremacy over it. With this intention he and his cousin Sadashivrao left Poona early in January with large forces to subjugate the southern regions. Fatesinh and Raghuji Bhosle joined them on their way.

In the meantime a dispute was long going on between the Peshwa on the one side and the Dabhade and the Gaikwad on the other. The Peshwa claimed a half share in the territory of Gujarat, a claim which the two vehemently resisted. After the Pratinidhi and the Sachiv, it was now the turn of the Senapati an old member of the Ashta Pradhans, to be humbled. Dabhade's house was divided against itself, and while Damaji Gaikwad was not particularly anxious to support either of them, he considered it advantageous to side with them in the resistance they jointly offered to the Peshwa's demand for a half share in Gujarat. During the rainy season of 1750 when the grand assemblage met at Poona, the Peshwa pressed Umabai Dabhade to accede to his demand. She in her extremity approached Tarabai against him. The two ladies started concerted measures to put down the Peshwa and raised a cry that the Chhatrapati's Raj was usurped by the Brahmans. They wrote strong appeals on this subject to most of the Maratha sardars and induced Damaji to head their cause. Umabai sent her agent Yado Mahadev to plead her case before the Peshwa : but having failed in his mission, Yado Mahadev returned without even accepting the customary hospitality from the Peshwa. Thereupon Umabai herself met the Peshwa at Alandi on 22nd November and finding that he would not relent in his demand, both Umabai and her daughter-in-law Ambikabai signed under compulsion a written consent agreeing to give up the half share of Gujarat.

This proved the beginning of the trouble. Tarabai and Umabai perfected their plans. The former obtained control of the Chhatrapati at Satara and invited Damaji Gaikwad to march upon Poona, as soon as the Peshwa had left that place on his Karnatak expedition early in January 1751. Thus during the next three months a severe commotion raged through Maharashtra owing to Damaji's irruption.

In addition to the usual skirmishes and plundering raids, there were two severe actions between the Gaikwad's and the Peshwa's troops, one at Bahadarpura in Khandesh on 18th February and the other on the Venya river near Satara on 15th March. In the first action Damaji defeated the Peshwa's army ; but in the second he sustained a severe set back. The Peshwa learnt of this great commotion when he was on the Krishna near Raichur and repaired to Satara hastily, where he arrived on 24th April. On 30th April he attacked Damaji's camp near Satara, plundered it completely and took Damaji captive. This short summary of the affair requires an elaboration.

The Peshwa had stationed in Baglan some of his trusted officers to oppose Damaji who had about 15000 troops with him. Hari Damodar Nevalkar, an ancestor of the future Rani of Jhansi, was the first to venture alone against Damaji. Balvantrao Mehendale, Bapuji Bhimrao and Mahipatrao Kavde hurried into Khandesh from Poona as soon as reports reached them of Damaji's devastating invasion. On the banks of the Tapti stood the two opposing forces, the Gaikwad's on the northern and the Peshwa's on the southern. For some time none dared to attack the other. Damaji then crossed over, attacked the Peshwa's troops at Bahadarpura, about ten miles from Amalner and routed them after a stiff fight. Damaji captured the elephant with the Peshwa's standard and secured a large amount of booty. The Gaikwad thereupon marched upon Poona devastating the territory on his way. From Talegaon came Dabhade and joined him. On March 10th the Gaikwad reached Nimbgaon Davdi. Trimbakrao Pethe came out of Poona to oppose him.

Poona fell into the throes of a scare. Government property was removed to Sinhgad and the residents of the city ran away with their valuables and other belongings. When the veteran Pilaji Jadhav learnt that the Gaikwad was going to devastate Poona, he came out of his post at Wadi, saw Damaji and induced him to desist from any aggression upon the innocent city. Some of the Peshwa's well-wishers also saw Damaji and thus reported their talk. " I saw Damaji and gave him the revered mother's letter (Radhabai's). He read it but gave no answer. I then spoke to him a few words of conciliation, when he said, " This is no time for friendship. You must leave my camp. I am come to wed and am seeking brides ; but there is time yet for the ceremony." He used such a haughty language and added, "The revered mother has fled to Sinhgad, where was then the need for her to write to me ? I know you have come to get news. Take away what you have seen. Tell the mother we have erected the welcome arch : your troops must pull it down." I then returned. Damaji has arranged his armies in five divisions, and is proceeding towards Satara." Pilaji Jadhav again wrote to him not to go against Satara and if he did, he would come to grief adding, " If you trust me, I will bring about a peaceful settlement between you and the Peshwa." Damaji replied, " I have given my sacred word to Tarabai which I cannot violate. Gamaji the Mutaliq, has come to me with Tarabai's letter." It is this insolent language of Damaji which irritated the Peshwa so severely in his future dealings with him.

For a time Damaji doubtless created a strong sensation. Tarabai collected a force of Mavlas to co-operate with Damaji. But Trimbak Sadashiv alias Nana Purandare left Satara with his force and joined the Poona army near Jejuri. Many other sardars came quickly and swelled the Peshwa's army.

Damaji proceeded straight upon Satara and pitched his camp at Varye and Mhasve on the river Venya. The Poona troops soon arrived and the Peshwa's camp was formed at Vaduth on the left bank of the Krishna about ten miles east. On 13th March Nana Purandare rashly attacked Damaji's camp, but being routed fell back upon Limb. But this was only a short-lived joy. Mehendale, Pethe and other valiant young commanders who were behind at Vaduth, made a concerted furious attack on Damaji on 15th March and gained a complete victory, capturing a large quantity of stores and belongings. Damaji and the Dabhade saved what they could and took shelter in the Mahar-dara Valley west of the town. This battle of the Venya decided the fate of the campaign. Again on March 21 Damaji organised his resources with some small help rendered by Tarabai. A light action took place with no decisive result.

The Peshwa's camp was now moved to the river Venya, where formerly Damaji's troops had taken post. Dabhade's plight became most miserable. He had no money and no supplies. He had to be content with what little Damaji chose to spare for him. Another action took place on 30th March on the plain of Pawai, in which the Gaikwad again sustained a defeat. His two sons and son-in-law took shelter with Tarabai in the fort.

2. The Peshwa hits back.—The news of the battle of the Venya on 15th March reached the Peshwa on the 29th at Nizam-konda near Panagal in the vicinity of the confluence of the rivers Krishna and Tungabhadra. He there made a grand demonstration of his power having been joined by most of the Maratha worthies including Ramchandra Jadhav, Udaji Chavan, Murarrao Ghorpade (with his four brothers), Fatesinh and Raghuji Bhosle. Had not the Gaikwad's affair called him away suddenly to Satara, he would have made short work of the Nizam's power then utterly disconcerted by the murders of Nasir Jang and Muzaffar Jang and the absence of a powerful personality to organize the resources of the Haidarabad State. Such a personality soon appeared in the French General Bussy. The mere demonstration of the Peshwa's power was enough to make the whole region from Haidarabad

to Trichinopoly submit to Maratha domination and quickly pay the tribute.

The Peshwa gave a grand entertainment to the Maratha assemblage, honoured them with gifts, and enlisted their sympathies for the course he was then following to root out the enemies of the Maratha power. Leaving Sadashivrao to complete the operations of this expedition, the Peshwa himself returned by the shortest route to Satara. On 12th April he writes, "Having effected a beneficial peace with the Haidarabad authorities, I am returning expeditiously to Satara; Raghuji Bhosle was willing to accompany me; but as he had other pressing work at Chanda Devgad and as there was no longer any need for me of his help, I allowed him to depart for his province." Within twelve days the Peshwa reached Satara on 24th April and found that Gaikwad was practically besieged by his troops, so that no supplies could reach him from outside.

But at the same time the Peshwa rightly concluded that the best way to master the situation at Satara was to gain ascendency at the Nizam's court; and this he had done before reaching Satara. "Where could I stand," he writes to Purandare, "if by chance I had lost my position in these quarters? Fortunately I have gained more than I had expected; and you must be in no hurry to conclude the affair of Satara. Try to keep up the stale-mate and remain on the defensive, till I arrive on the scene. When we meet we shall see how best to deal with the situation."[1]

On arrival in the camp on the Venya the Peshwa at once launched a severe offensive against the Gaikwad. Within a day or two Damaji found his position untenable and applied for terms. A personal conference was found necessary. The Peshwa sent his own agents Satvoji Jadhav, Nana Purandare, and Ramchandra Baba to fetch Damaji. He came along with Dabhade, talked to the Peshwa and returned to his camp. Thereupon he was asked to come and take up his residence near the Peshwa's quarters. He complied and fixed his post on the right or the southern bank of the Venya, the Peshwa being on the left side. The latter immediately made a stern demand for the half share of Gujarat. Damaji replied,

1. *Purandare Daftar* 1. 333-343.

"Gujarat belongs to Umabai Dabhade. I am only her servant. She has to decide the point." Damaji thereupon saw Umabai, explained to her the Peshwa's demand and resigned his own position as the agent of the Dabhades by delivering the seals and insignia of his office. Early in the morning of 30th April the Peshwa during the course of these negotiations suddenly attacked Damaji's quarters, when he was not ready to fight and was actually having his bath, being perfectly at ease under the solemn assurance he had received from the Peshwa against treachery.

Damaji called upon his followers to offer no resistance and allow the Peshwa's men to perpetrate what they willed. Vithal Shivdev plundered the Gaikwad's camp and carried his two brothers Khanderao and Jaysinh prisoners to the Peshwa. Manaji Paygude similarly captured Yashvantrao Dabhade and carried him to his own tent. Thereupon Damaji alone walked to the Peshwa's tent and offered himself for arrest, vehemently protesting against the flagrant breach of a sacred oath. The Peshwa put all the Gaikwad brothers together and kept them strongly guarded from outside communication. The Dabhades too were similarly placed together along with Umabai and when under such restraint, asked to cede half of Gujarat. They reluctantly signed their consent under compulsion and were on 11th May all despatched to Poona and kept confined in the house of Avji Kavde, under strict guards. They were to be released after they had actually handed over the districts in Gujarat demanded by the Peshwa. Two of Damaji's sons Fatesinh and Manaji remained in the Satara fort with Tarabai. The Peshwa's conduct in arresting Damaji against his plighted word was widely condemned at the time. But it must be remembered that Damaji himself had provoked the Peshwa's wrath by his wanton invasion of Poona, when the Peshwa was absent in the Karnatak.

After sending away the Dabhades and the Gaikwads to Poona, the Peshwa remained behind at Satara, negotiating his further course with Tarabai. But she declined to come down from the fort or deliver over Ramraja! The Peshwa wisely abandoned all coercive measures against her, stationed a strong force to watch her at Satara and himself returned to Poona on 22nd May. He very well knew that it was no easy matter to reduce Satara to submission, as the fort was well provisioned to stand a long siege. As with the capture of the Dabhades and the Gaikwads, the main support of Tarabai was gone, her own devoted followers also realized that hers was then a lost cause. The Peshwa hereafter abandoned her to her fate.

Thus both Tarabai and Ramraja at once lost all power and influence. But Damaji and the Dabhade, though well guarded at Poona did not give up their intrigues. They secretly carried on plans with Tarabai at Satara. When this was discovered, their confinement was made extremely rigorous from about 19th July onwards. On 14th November they were removed from Poona to the fort of Lohgad along with Ramchandra Basavant, Damaji's helpmate.

3. The Peshwa scores.— In the meantime the Peshwa sent Vithal Shivdev into Gujarat to take possession of the districts of Damaji, constituting the Peshwa's half share. A little later on 22 October Raghunathrao Dada was also despatched to Gujarat to complete the work. With him went two sons of Damaji, Khanderao and Sayaji. In the meantime Ramchandra Basavant escaped from Lohgad, went to Songad in Gujarat and started trouble against the Peshwa. Things went on in this way for some months when ultimately Damaji finding there was no use resisting the Peshwa's demand, agreed to the following terms on 30th March 1752 and was then released with all his relations and allowed to proceed to Gujarat :—

(1) Dabhade's claim to Gujarat was entirely abandoned;

(2) Damaji Gaikwad was to be the sole Maratha representative there with the title of Sena-Khas-Khel;

(3) He at once ceded half the territory and agreed to yield a similar half share of all that would hereafter come to be conquered;

(4) He agreed to pay a fine of Rs. 15 lacs to the Peshwa; and

(5) He likewise agreed to serve the Peshwa loyally hereafter with ten thousand troops wherever and whenever he would be called upon to do so.

This agreement was later confirmed in writing by Tarabai also. Thus this question of the Peshwa's claim to a half share in Gujarat, first put forth in 1726 came to be finally settled after a quarter of a century, and the Peshwa's authority as the supreme manager of the Maratha State was formally acknowledged by Damaji in the same way as Raghuji Bhosle had done in the case of Nagpur and as Sindia, Holkar and others were doing in Malwa and Bundelkhand. Raghunathrao was accompanied by Sakharam Bapu a competent rising diplomat, and together they executed the terms of the agreement on the spot in Gujarat, took possession of the districts allotted to the Peshwa's share and returned in May. Damaji himself so loyally carried out the stipulations that upon his visit to Poona on 23rd June 1752, he was highly honoured and cordially received, the Peshwa himself going a long distance in advance to meet him.[2] The outcome of this visit was an agreed plan to capture Ahmadabad, the capital of Gujarat which was still held by a representative of the decaying Mughal power.

It did not take long for the Peshwa to settle with Dabhade, who had to accept under compulsion the terms offered to him, and get reconciled to the fate that had come upon him. Umabai grew old and wearied and the Peshwa did his best to relieve her distress. She was brought to Poona from Talegaon for treatment in September 1753 and there she died on 28th November following. Her son Yashvantrao died the next year on 18th May 1754 near Miraj on his way back from the Karnatak where he had accompanied the Peshwa. Yashvantrao's son Trimbakrao II became the next Senapati,.which now remained only a nominal title. This Trimbakrao died in 1766 near Verul. The descendents of the Dabhade Senapati are still living at Talegaon on the scanty remains of their ancestral estates.

4. **Ahmadabad captured.**—Damaji Gaikwad and the Peshwa having been fully reconciled, they jointly undertook the task of conquering Ahmadabad which was indeed the capital city of Gujarat. Raghunathrao was appointed by the Peshwa to proceed to Gujarat for that venture. He left in January 1753 and having been joined by Damaji in Khandesh came directly upon Ahmadabad and besieged the city. Jawanmard Khan Babi and his helpmate Kamal-ud-din Khan tried their utmost to defend the city. They were overpowered and

2. Raj. Vol. 3. 393, 395; *Purandare Diary* p. 79.

surrendered the town to Raghunathrao on 25th April 1753, including the whole territory of Kathiawad, right up to Dwarka. The famous shrine of Krishna at this place came into Maratha possession and so continues till now.

The affair of Ahmadabad did not end here. It was recaptured by the Mussalman Nawabs of Palanpur and Cambay early in 1757. But the Peshwa took prompt measures, and the place was again secured on 11th October 1757. Ahmadabad thereafter continued to be a Maratha possession, with half shares for the Peshwa and the Gaikwad, until during the last Anglo-Maratha war it fell into the hands of the British on 1st December 1817.

5. Surat and Broach.—Another important town of Gujarat was Surat, with a long and chequered history of its own; while the British traders of the East India Company had gradually established their control over this excellent harbour on the west coast, it formed an important possession of the Mughal Empire and as such had attracted the cupidity of Shivaji long ago. Aurangzeb, however, cared for it only as an embarking station for Muslim pilgrims going to and returning from Mecca; and for this purpose he entrusted its management to the Siddi of Janjira as an expert naval commander. Thus Surat was being governed from Janjira by one of their naval chiefs.

In the times of the Peshwa Nana Saheb, the governor of Surat was Siddi Masud, an enemy of the Marathas, doing his utmost to defend the place against any attack by the latter. He secured the support of the British traders, who used to be well armed in naval defence. There was in addition a Mughal governor whose rule was nominal. Thus there was a keen rivalry going on for years between the four powers, for the possession of this lucrative naval post, the Marathas, the Siddi, the Mughal Governor Miya Achhan and the British traders. These last had just asserted their power by the destruction of Tulaji Angria and the capture of Gheria or Vijayadurg in 1756. The British tried to take possession of Surat by every contrivance they could think of. They concluded a treaty between these four powers, which on that account is termed Chauthia, on 4th March 1759. By this means they

21

first gained the friendship of the Marathas and put down Siddi Masud. Then they managed to obtain a *firman* of the Emperor of Delhi on 1st December 1759, granting them the governorship of the place so that the local Mughal Governor Miya Achhan lost all power. At this very time the Marathas became crippled by the disaster of Panipat, which gave a fresh start to British ambitions, by removing the only powerful competitor from the contest for the possession of Surat. In due course the English confirmed their hold on Surat and that port was finally lost to the Marathas.[3]

The Siddi of Surat had all along in the past been the best friend of the British, but the moment their interests clashed, the British removed him unceremoniously by bringing from Delhi a fresh *firman* against the Siddi. Broach was captured later by Mahadji Sindia during the first Maratha war and lost by Daulatrao in the war of 1803. Cambay alone managed to eke out its own controlled existence under its Nawab on a par with the Gaikwad's State of Baroda.

Such has been the chequered history of the four important towns and harbours which command the fertile territory of Gujarat.

CHRONOLOGY

CHAPTER XV

1720, Feb. 8	Bussy born.
1748, May 21	Nizam-ul-mulk dies aged 77.
1750, December 5	Nasir Jang murdered.
1750, December	Muzaffar Jung declared Nawab at Pondicherry.
1751, January 7	Muzaffar Jang leaves Pondicherry.
1751, January 31	Muzaffar Jang killed : Salabat Jang proclaimed by Bussy.
1751, February	Peshwa at Pangal, arranging to bring Ghazi-uddin from Delhi.
1751, March 23	Terms of peace arranged between Peshwa and Salabat Jang ; Ramdaspant's secret intrigue against the Peshwa.
1751, April 22	Ramdaspant seizes Peshwa's treasure near Aurangabad.
1751, Monsoon	Janoji Nimbalkar negotiates peace in Poona.
1751, November 15	Bussy starts offensive against the Peshwa.
1751, November 20	Battle of Parner, Chimnaji Bapuji killed.
1751, November 21	Surprise raid upon the Peshwa at the river Kukdi during a night of eclipse.
1751, November 27	Battle of Malthan, Mughals defeated.
1751, December 2	Fort Trimbak captured by the Peshwa.
1751, December	Raghuji Bhosle ravages Nizam's territory.
1752, January 6	Treaty concluded at Singwa, fort Trimbak restored to the Nizam.
1752, April	Ghazi-ud-din leaves Delhi for the south.
1752, April 7	Ramdaspant murdered.
1752, June 3	Chanda Saheb murdered.
1752, September 28	Ghazi-ud-din arrives near Aurangabad.
1752, October 16	Ghazi-ud-din killed by poison.
1752, November 24	Treaty of Bhalki ; Baglan and part of Berar come into Maratha possession.
1752, November	Muzaffar Khan Gardi comes into the Peshwa's employ.

1753, January 8	Peshwa starts on his first expedition to the Karnatak.
1753, March 20	Holi Honnur captured.
1753, May 14	Dharwar captured.
1753, June	Peshwa visits Kolhapur on his way to Poona.
1754	The Peshwa's second expedition up to Harihar.
1754, October 24	The Peshwa starts on his 3rd expedition to Bednur.
1754, November	The shrine of Trimbakeshwar restored by the Peshwa, Masjid pulled down.
1755, early months	Muzaffar Khan quarrels with Purandare, quits Peshwa's service and rebels at Savanur.
1756, March	Peshwa appears before Savanur.
1756, March 12	Muzaffar Khan makes a sally upon the Marathas.
1756, April	Severe fighting before Savanur.
1756, May 18	Savanur surrendered; Muzaffar Khan escapes; Murarrao Ghorpade agrees to serve the Peshwa.
1756, May 18	Salabat Jang dismisses Bussy.
1756, June-Oct.	Bussy's heroic stand against Salabat Jang at Char Minar.
1756, July	The Peshwa returns victorious to Poona.
1756, November 16	Bussy reinstated in service by Salabat Jang.
1757, January 1	Peshwa's expedition to Shrirangapattan.
1757, May	Peshwa receives tribute from Mysore and returns to Poona.
1757	Nizam Ali employs Ibrahim Khan Gardi.
1757	Shah Nawaz Khan takes possession of Daulatabad.
1757, Monsoon	Nizam Ali starts aggression against the Marathas.
1757, August 27	The Peshwa moves from Poona against Aurangabad.
1757, September 24	Nawab of Kadappa falls fighting against Balavantrao Mehendale; Kadappa captured.
1757, November	Hostilities start between Nizam Ali and the Marathas round Aurangabad.
1757, Dec. 12-16	Severe fighting before Sindkhed.

1757, December 17	Nizam Ali acknowledges defeat and requests terms of peace.
1757, December 29	Treaty of peace ratified at Sakharkhedla.
1758-1760	East coast region reduced by the Marathas.
1758	Salabat Jang dismisses Shah Nawaz Khan and appoints Haidar Jang his minister.
1758, May 11	Haidar Jang, Shah Nawaz Khan and his sons murdered.
1758, June 18	Bussy leaves Haidarabad finally, at the call of his superior, Lally.
1759, October	Nizam Ali dismisses Ibrahim Khan Gardi, who immediately accepts Peshwa's service.
1759, October 28	Muzaffar Khan attempts Sadashivrao's life and is executed.
1759, November 9	Fort Ahmadnagar secured by the Peshwa through Kavi Jang.
1759, December	War opens between Peshwa and Nizam.
1760, January	Marathas attack Nizam Ali near Udgir.
1760, January 22	Bussy taken prisoner in the battle of Wandewash and sent to Europe.
1760, January 26	A stiff action near Udgir, in which the Mughals are completely routed.
1760, February 3	Treaty of Udgir, rigorous terms imposed upon Nizam Ali.
1762, July 7	Salabat Jang kept under confinement by Nizam Ali.
1763, September 16	Salabat Jang put to death.
1783, March 17	Bussy once more returns to India.
1785, January 7	Bussy dies in India.

CHAPTER XV

THE MARATHA-NIZAM STRUGGLE

[1751—1761]

1. Bussy on the scene.
2. Maratha-Nizam war of 1751-52.
3. Use of artillery, Muzaffar Khan.
4. Fall of Savanur, end of Muzaffar Khan.
5. The Karnatak task unfinished.
6. Bussy at Char Minar.
7. The Nizam's defeat at Sindkhed.
8. Horrid murders
9. Battle of Udgir

1. *Bussy on the scene.*—Asaf Jah's expedition in the Karnatak and capture of Trichinopoly in 1743 proved his last great achievement; thereafter he fast declined in health and died at Burhanpur on 21 May 1748 at the age of 77. Before his death he prepared a document, in which among other things, he gave a strong warning to his son to keep on friendly terms with the Marathas and avoid hostilities with them. He expressed sentiments of amity towards the Peshwa. For a few years before his death he studiously avoided giving any irritation to the Marathas. But his son Nasir Jang being of a restless temperament tried to take advantage of his father's death by launching hostilities against the Marathas.[1] Nasir Jang also tried to intervene in the affairs of Delhi, but circumstances soon compelled him to check his ambitions both in the north and the south. The Peshwa had no small share in putting a curb on the aggressive moves which Nasir Jang attempted.

Muzaffar Jang a son of Asaf Jah's daughter, and Chandasaheb made a common cause against Nasir Jang, and by securing the support of the French of Pondicherry, tried to strengthen their position in the Karnatak. Nasir Jang realizing the danger from this quarter, secured several allies including the British merchants of Fort St. George and with huge forces descended into the Karnatak in 1750. The two armies came to oppose each other in the vicinity of Arcot. On December 5, 1750,

---

1. Raj. 3. 372; Raj. 6. 185, 186; P. D. 23-25; *Hingne Daftar* I—34, 38, 40.

Nasir Jang was suddenly murdered by his Pathan allies, who had proved faithless and who then raised Muzaffar Jang to the masnad. Muzaffar Jang proceeded to Pondicherry and was there acclaimed by Dupleix as the head of the Nizam's State. Accepting a strong contingent of French forces commanded by the rising Bussy, (b. 8th February 1720), Muzaffar Jang left Pondicherry on 7th January 1751 to proceed to his capital in the Deccan. After leaving Arcot as he was moving towards Kadappa, an unexpected encounter took place between the several Pathans and the French auxiliaries in the plain of Rakhoti (Lakki-reddi-palli) about twenty five miles south of Kadappa, wherein Muzaffar Jang was on January 31 suddenly killed with a bullet shot by the Pathan aggressors. Bussy disclosed a rare presence of mind on this critical occasion, proclaimed Salabat Jang as the rightful Nawab and marched on with him towards Haidarabad.[2] Bussy was guided in these measures by a clever Brahman diplomat Ramdaspant, who had been in Nasir Jang's employ, and whom Bussy now won over. Dupleix gave him the title Raja Raghunathdas. Bussy's Muslim secretary and interpreter Haidar Jang, a versatile and clever diplomat well-versed in French also rendered him faithful service. With the help of these two, Bussy saved the position of the Haidarabad State with consummate ability, and soon made himself indispensable. Ramdaspant was made the Diwan of Salabat Jang.

These changes in the fortunes of the Asaf Jahi State attracted the Peshwa's attention and created in him a desire to make the best use of them for the advantage of the Maratha power. Although the Peshwa was at the time involved in serious trouble with Tarabai, he managed to leave Poona early in 1751 and proceeded towards Aurangabad, subjugating the north Godavari region on the way. But as soon as he learned that Muzaffar Jang was killed and that Salabat Jang was coming towards Haidarabad, the Peshwa quickly turned southward to oppose them, arranging in the meantime to bring the late Asaf Jah's eldest son Ghazi-ud-din from Delhi to claim his father's possessions in the Deccan as the legitimate and rightful heir. But considering it dangerous to oppose Salabat

2. P. D. 25. 104, 109, 110.

Jang and involve himself in a fight with the well-trained French troops and their able commander Bussy, he managed to effect a peaceful understanding with Salabat Jang by engaging the sympathies of Janoji Nimbalkar a powerful Maratha chief in the Nizam's service. At the end of February the Peshwa halted at Panagal, whence he conducted negotiations with Bussy and Salabat Jang who were encamped about fifteen miles further south. Bussy was not then well conversant with the trends of Deccan politics, nor was he anxious to open a war against the Peshwa, as he was not then in full control of the military situation, so that he readily closed in with the Maratha offer of peace. It took two weeks for the negotiations to be completed and a settlement acceptable to both the parties to be arrived at. On 23rd March 1751 the Peshwa writes, "We have concluded a friendly arrangement with Salabat Jang," who agreed to pay 17 lacs to the Peshwa in order to purchase his non-intervention in the succession dispute, of which two lacs were paid in cash, and the rest was guaranteed by the bankers. The Peshwa cancelled his previous orders for occupying the Khandesh territory of the Nizam between Aurangabad and Burhanpur, on receiving a payment of three lacs more on that account.

Saiyad Lashkar Khan and Shah Nawaz Khan were two hereditary officers of Salabat Jang who had ably served Asaf Jah and who still continued to wield influence and power. The Peshwa managed to win over these nobles and tried through them to establish his ascendancy in the Nizam's counsels. Bussy, under Dupleix's instructions, was guided by Ramdaspant, in addition to his own secretary Haidar Jang. While the Peshwa's agents at the Nizam's court highly humoured Ramdaspant, he was secretly intriguing with Tarabai at Satara to oust the Peshwa from his position and secure it for himself or for some one of his relations. This was the game then being played by the two parties.

In the meantime Bussy was not long in studying and gathering into his hands the threads of Deccan politics, preparing for an eventual struggle, should that become necessary in order to put down the aggression of the Peshwa, who was fast occupying the forts of the Nasik district belonging to the

Nizam, and who in addition was persuading Ghazi-ud-din the eldest son of Asaf Jah to come to the Deccan and assert his claim to his father's dominions, thereby upsetting the arrangement Bussy had effected in favour of Salabat Jang.

2. Maratha-Nizam war of 1751-52.—Although Bussy and his advisers conciliated the Peshwa for the time being, in their hearts they decided to humble his pride. Ramdaspant was in this respect the moving spirit of the Nizam's Court. In spoken words he purposely disarmed all suspicions of the Maratha agents and news-reporters. The Peshwa returned to Satara from Panagal and Salabat Jang too moved on to his capital. On 22nd April, Ramdaspant captured and appropriated in the vicinity of Aurangabad a treasure of 5 lacs which was coming for the Peshwa from the north, thus committing a wanton breach of friendly understanding. When an explanation was demanded, such trifling excuses were made that they irritated the Peshwa all the more. Bussy and Salabat Jang prepared for war if Ghazi-ud-din would come to claim the possession of the State. But as the Peshwa was to be kept off his guard, Bussy and Ramdaspant deputed Janoji Nimbalkar to Poona for three months pretending to conduct negotiations of peace so as to be able to take the Peshwa by surprise in a sudden attack. But the Peshwa understood the game, refused to walk into the trap and prepared to meet the contingency.

Within a few months Bussy managed through strict discipline and incessant vigilance, to set the affairs of Salabat Jang on a sound basis. He selected for his camp a convenient spot in a corner of the town of Aurangabad and there fortified his position well. He quickly trained large fresh troops, paid them handsomely and regularly, and thus attained exceptional military efficiency unknown to the indigenous armies. His rigorous discipline all round began to have a telling effect upon the administration, and even Salabat Jang himself began to quake before him, so that the machinations of the other state officials were all put an end to. For his expenses Bussy obtained possession of some of the finest districts in the north-east, which became known as the Northern Sarkars and which came to be entirely managed by French agency

The expected war with the Marathas broke out in November, 1751. The Peshwa had already left Poona and marched towards Ahmadnagar in October. On 15th November Bussy left Aurangabad and after crossing the Godavari began ravaging the Maratha territories. The Peshwa took to guerilla tactics, burnt and desolated his own villages so as to starve the enemy whose main strength lay in his artillery, the reach of which the Marathas carefully avoided. Bussy ardently desired to blow away Poona with his guns : but he could hardly proceed so far. On 20th November a fairly stiff action was fought near Parner, in which one of the Peshwa's valiant officers, Chimnaji Bapuji was killed and Shamsher Bahadur's mare was wounded with a spear. The next evening November 21, while the Peshwa was engaged in his religious performances due to a lunar eclipse on the river Kukadi, artillery shots suddenly falling in, created a consternation ; the Peshwa ran away to save his life and his materials of worship were seized by the Muslims. On 27th November a bloody action took place near Malthan resulting in a severe defeat of Saiyad Lashkar Khan who lost a great deal in plunder. This battle is called the battle of the Ghod river. The neighbouring villages of Shikrapur and Talegaon (Dhamdhera) were plundered and destroyed by the Muslims. Raghuji Bhosle at this time came and joined the Peshwa after capturing many important places between Aurangabad and the Godavari. The Mughals then retired to Pedgaon or Bahadurgad, being hotly pursued by the Marathas during the march.

Nearly two months of such desultory warfare convinced Bussy that he was not strong enough to resist the Maratha tactics of a running fight and suggested the patching up of a peace in order to gain time. Envoys sat down at Singwa near Pargaon. The Peshwa had seized fort Trimbak, which Salabat Jang insisted on getting back. The Peshwa yielded and a restoration of status quo was agreed to on both sides on 6th January 1752, known as the treaty of Singwa. Konher Trimbak Ekbote was rewarded with the title of Phakde for distinguished service in this short war.

These operations did not however, decide the dispute of the two States finally or remove the cause of friction, viz., who was to be the deciding authority in the politics of the Deccan.

Bussy's advent in support of the Asaf Jahi State, doubtless irritated the Peshwa who now urgently invited Ghazi-ud-din from Delhi. The Khan left Delhi in April 1752 accompanied by Sindia and Holkar and reached Aurangabad on 28th September. But even before his actual arrival the very news of Ghazi-ud-din having left Delhi filled Salabat Jang with consternation, as a civil war between the two brothers became imminent; and with the advice of Bussy he left Aurangabad in order to establish himself far away at Haidarabad. Bussy's troops had not received their pay for some time and raised a dreadful clamour on the way. While they were camping at Bhalki about 40 miles east of Tulzapur, a mutiny broke out, in which the troops attacked Ramdaspant, their paymaster and killed him (7th April 1752). The other two prominent officials Saiyad Lashkhar Khan and Shah Nawaz Khan were already estranged from Bussy, as the latter was too overbearing and rough in his treatment of them. The Peshwa at once tried to seize this opportunity and asked Sindia and Holkar to bring Ghaziud-din on the scene as quickly as possible, and himself started in August to meet him in the vicinity of Aurangabad. Bussy and Salabat Jang too retraced their steps to that city.

The Peshwa and Ghazi-ud-din met early in October and concerted their plans, but before they could be executed, Ghazi-ud-din met with his death suddenly by poison at a dinner to which he was invited by Nizam Ali's mother (16th October 1752). So the whole project at once toppled down and things reverted to their former state. A large force of the Marathas with most of their leading commanders now assembled near Aurangabad and tried to surround Salabat Jang and force him into obedience. He and Bussy took their departure for Haidarabad and were followed by the Marathas harassing the Mughal rear. When he arrived near Bhalki he found himself completely surrounded by the Marathas who had guns with them on this occasion. Bussy had not his full forces with him, not being prepared for such an eventuality. For four days the Marathas so harassed their enemies that they lost large numbers from starvation and the Maratha artillery. Salabat Jang requested terms through the medium of Bussy. The Marathas insisted that they would accept nothing less than what Ghazi-ud-din had conceded to them. That condition was accepted and the treaty of Bhalki was the result. It was cemented by a formal exchange of visits and gifts of dresses and presents on 24th November 1752. The main part of this treaty of Bhalki was the cession of the whole western half of Berar between the rivers Godavari and the Tapti, by the Nizam to the Marathas. This also included the whole of Baglan and Khandesh. This demarcation of the Nizam's territory has practically existed to the present day. Before the treaty of Bhalki the Nizam claimed all the territory east of the Sahyadri range. Nasik, Trimbak[3] and all the important forts in that region thus passed into Maratha hands, and were soon put in an efficient state of management and government. Thus the liberation of a large part of Maratha homeland from the Mughal yoke was no small gain.

After the treaty was concluded the Peshwa and Bussy had many cordial visits and full talks. The former pressed the latter to accept his service, which he wisely declined. Bussy no longer remained an enemy of the Marathas.

---

3. This fort has a significant history for the Marathas, deserving mention. The Peshwa as dearly loved the north-Poona territory of the Nasik district as the southern region upto Satara. This was considered the heart of Maharashtra first liberated by Shivaji from Muslim yoke. Nasik and fort Trimbak were holy places where crowds of Hindu pilgrims flocked in from different parts of the country. Aurangzeb captured these places merely out of his fanatic policy, pulled down the ancient shrine of Trimbakeshwar and renamed Nasik as Gulchhanabad. Shahu and the Peshwa were keen upon getting these holy places back into Hindu possession. In fact Shahu had specially mentioned fort Trimbak in the demands of Swarajya he preferred through Balaji Vishvanath to Saiyad Husein Ali in 1718. Bajirao did not succeed in getting the places back. Sadashivrao Bhau succeeded in it through his trusted daring commandant Trimbak Suryaji, who captured the fort on 2nd December 1751. Nasik also was occupied and here the Peshwa rapidly erected palaces and temples. Though fort Trimbak was temporarily given back to Muslim control, it was recaptured by the Marathas within two years, the Musjid was pulled down and the original temple restored. Nana and Bhau paid their first ceremonial visit to this temple of Trimbakeshwar in November 1754. Several minor forts in the vicinity such as Karnala, Tringalwadi, Bitinga and others came at the same time into Maratha possession. Shivaji's birthplace fort Shivner was taken a little later in 1756.

3. **Use of artillery, Muzaffar Khan.**—One important lesson which deeply impressed the Peshwa and particularly his cousin Sadashivrao, who had acted as his leading commander during this war, was the supreme advantage of artillery and disciplined troops in Indian warfare when opposed to the traditional Maratha tactics. Bussy was now the chief exponent of the new European method of warfare, but neither Sadashivrao nor the Peshwa's son Vishvasrao ventured to work with Bussy; they contented themselves with borrowing the services of Bussy's Indian lieutenants like Muzaffar Khan or Ibrahim Khan whose troops' name Garde (Fr.), came to be corrupted into *Gardi* i.e. disciplined infantry trained on the western model in the use of artillery with absolute uniformity of dress and arms. The Peshwa discussed the subject with Bussy during their meeting at Bhalki, and engaged the services of Muzaffar Khan on a combined salary of Rs. 55,000 a month for himself and a corps of two thousand infantry and a thousand cavalry, with a park of guns. It was Malharrao Holkar who first tried the skill and efficiency of Muzaffar Khan and recommended him to the Peshwa. Unfortunately this man, although highly capable, proved extremely dangerous, as in an emergency he selfishly made bargains for personal gain rather than loyally execute the duty he had agreed to perform. Sadashivrao Bhau's stern character could not tolerate this trait of the Khan and the two became open enemies.

The political situation of India was fast changing. A war had begun between England and France in Europe, known as the Seven Years War (1756-1763), which produced serious repercussions in India. From Bhalki the Peshwa directed his steps to the Karnatak. During the next five years he led yearly expeditions into that region. The first is termed the expedition of Shrirangapattan 1753, January 8, to June 19. The reader is aware of the war that was waged in the region of Arcot between Muhammad Ali and Chanda Saheb for the Nawabship of Arcot in which Dupleix and Clive figured prominently. Chanda Saheb's murder on 3rd June 1752 proved a blow to Dupleix's diplomacy and ended the French supremacy in the Karnatak. In 1753 the Peshwa went directly from Bhalki to Shrirangapattan where he took up his station. On 20th March Bhausaheb captured the fort of Holi Honnur standing at the junction of the rivers Tunga and Bhadra. They turned back and captured Dharwar on 14th May. Thence on the way to Poona they halted at Kolhapur and were cordially received by Raja Sambhaji and his queen Jijabai, who gave Bhausaheb the forts of Bhimgad, Pargad, Vallabhgad and Kalanidhi along with the district of Khanapur, in fulfilment of an engagement which had been contracted earlier.

After the rains the Peshwa decided to proceed again to the Karnatak to complete his work of the previous year. During 1754 Bagalkot, Anjani, Harihar and Mundalgi were captured after severe fighting at each place and the Peshwa returned to Poona for the rains. This was his second regular expedition.

The next expedition of the Peshwa is termed that of Bednur. Leaving Poona on October 24, 1754, Nana Saheb and Bhau Saheb went to the western Karnatak and despatched Mahadoba Purandare to Bednur along with Muzaffar Khan Gardi. Purandare and the Khan came to loggerheads on a matter of discipline. It was discovered that the Khan did not entertain the stipulated quota of troops and ammunition and Mahadoba demanded a muster to which the Khan objected. Hot words ensued, when the Khan in extreme irritation walked away from the Maratha camp and sought service with the Raja of Shrirangapattan. He revolted openly against the Peshwa and organised a strong opposition to him. The Raja of Shrirangapattan was by no means friendly to the Peshwa, being unwilling to pay the tribute that the latter had demanded. The Nawab of Savanur was equally averse to accepting Maratha control and resisted the payment. Muzaffar Khan taking advantage of the Peshwa's difficulties made a common cause with his enemies and soon became a danger. The Peshwa returned to Poona, secured the friendship of Salabat Jang and Bussy, and planned a grand joint expedition to the south in order to counteract the menace created by Muzaffar Khan in that quarter.[4]

4. Fall of Savanur, end of Muzaffar Khan.—The years 1755 and 1756 proved a period of extreme anxiety to the

---

4. *Gwalior Phalke* 3. 295.

Peshwa. His brother Raghunathrao was in the north during the previous year and had achieved no marked success. Tulaji Angria proved most obnoxious and severe measures had to be employed to put him down. In order to make up for his weakness in naval warfare, the Peshwa effected a contract with the British borrowing naval help from Bombay, a step which eventually proved disastrous to the Maratha interests. At this very moment Jayappa Sinde came to be inextricably involved in a contest with his Rathod enemies in Marwar. The Peshwa possessed a strong nerve and made preparations for the capture of Savanur, whose Nawab had sheltered the rebel Muzaffar Khan and committed aggression. In order to strengthen his position, the Peshwa specially called to his side from the north Malharrao Holkar and his able lieutenant Shetyaji Kharade, and also Vithal Shivdev Vinchurkar: Janoji and Mudhoji Bhosle of Nagpur also joined him at his invitation. Murarrao Ghorpade unfortunately deserted the Peshwa and made common cause with the Nawab of Savanur, adding to the gravity of the Maratha situation.

The Peshwa arrived before Savanur at the beginning of March 1756 when serious operations were at once launched and constant fighting continued for two months. Salabat Jang and Bussy arrived very late and brought little substantial help.

The Nawab and Muzaffar Khan ably defended the place. On March 12 the garrison made a desperate sally in which a fearful slaughter of Muzaffar Khan's Gardis took place. The Khan had openly boasted of his invincible powers and defied the combined might of the Peshwa and Bussy. The Peshwa demanded from the Nawab the surrender of Muzaffar Khan, which was refused. During the month of May the strong walls and unrivalled defences of Savanur collapsed before the heavy fire directed by Bussy. Muzaffar Khan realizing that the place could no longer hold out, ran away to save his life and the Nawab surrendered Savanur to the Peshwa on 18th May, the first public demonstration in the south of the efficacy of western artillery, intently watched by friends and foes alike.

In this battle of Savanur both sides fought with utmost tenacity. Many Maratha commanders received serious wounds. Baba Phadnis (father of Nana) who was present in the camp writes, " The Nawab humbly sued for terms. Eleven lacs of tribute was agreed upon. The Nawab had no cash to pay : he ceded for half the amount half of his districts, Bankapur, Misrikot, Kundgol and Hubli. After finishing the affair of Savanur, the Peshwa and Salabat Jang proceeded together beyond the Tungabhadra when Bednur agreed to a tribute of 12 lacs. Similarly, the chiefs of Chitradurg, Raidurg and Harpanhalli came and paid tribute. Sondha agreed to pay 8 lacs. Mardangad and Basavapattan also came into the Peshwa's possession. After stationing Gopalrao Patwardhan and Raste in the Karnatak the Peshwa returned to Poona in July." Thus the southern frontier of the Maratha State now extended from the Krishna to the Tungabhadra river.[5]

After the fall of Savanur Murarrao represented to the Peshwa, " If you treat me with the importance and respect due to my position, I am prepared to serve you loyally, otherwise I shall give up all work and remain a silent private man." The Peshwa assured him of his sympathy and respect as an honoured member of the Maratha State saying, " If you serve the State loyally and enthusiastically, we shall highly promote your interests." He agreed to serve the Peshwa in future with all his heart, bringing his contingent of four thousand troops, and returned to his quarters at Gooty.

In this Savanur adventure Muzaffar Khan lost his reputation for good. When the Nawab expelled him on 19th March he sought temporary shelter with Ramchandra Jadhav, one of the Nizam's chiefs. Most of his followers deserted him for want of pay. The Peshwa alone against Sadashivrao's strong protest employed personal agents to induce the Khan to come back to his original post. The Khan had purchased ammunition from Goa for use at Savanur for which he owed a large sum to the Portuguese. His subordinates deserted him. Thus reduced to extreme beggary he readily complied with the offer of the Peshwa, conveyed through Shetyaji Kharade. The Peshwa paid him 25,000 rupees cash to meet his immediate needs, and the Khan once more joined service at Poona about the Dassara time of 1756.

The Khan was hereafter employed in reducing the difficult forts of north Konkan and was studiously excluded from

---

5. P. D. 28. 140, 182, 183, 185, Raj. 3. 472, 473, 479, 481.

any important campaign or foreign war which could afford him an opportunity to profit by collusion with the enemies of the Peshwa. But even in the reduction of forts he harassed innocent people and squeezed money, so it became increasingly difficult to manage him. Muzaffar Khan bore bitter hatred towards Bhau Saheb, and when the latter entertained the services of Ibrahim Khan, a rival Gardi commander, Muzaffar Khan sought to wreak his revenge. On the evening of 28th October 1759 as Bhau Saheb was transacting his routine business in his tent at the Garpir of Poona, the Khan's son-in-law Haidar Khan suddenly stabbed Bhau Saheb in the back. Fortunately the wound though severe did not prove fatal. An immediate inquiry was made and eight culprits including Muzaffar Khan and his son-in-law were blown away from guns on October 30.

5. **The Karnatak task unfinished.**—It would be convenient to conclude here the Peshwa's further dealings in the southern regions. During 1757 he himself once more marched into Karnatak. Leaving Poona on 1st January he and Sadashivrao reached Shrirangapattan collecting tributes on the way. Both Murarrao Ghorpade and Muzaffar Khan were present with the Peshwa. It was the latter's intention to take possession of that important capital town, so as to end the old Mysore Kingdom. During the siege of the town a chance gun-shot shattered the golden pinnacle of the famous shrine of Shrirangam. This was considered an evil omen and gave rise to mutual negotiations. The Raja and his minister agreed to pay a tribute of 32 lacs, of which only five were paid in cash and for the remaining, 14 valuable districts were given in mortgage. The Peshwa returned in May after leaving Balavantrao Mehendale as his deputy to finish the remaining work of the expedition, and captured the strong post of Shira on his way back.

After 1757 the Peshwa did not personally command an expedition in the south. Hereafter his lieutenants completed what remained to be executed. During the last three years the limits of the Maratha dominion covered the whole of the Kanarese region, comprising the present Mysore State stretching from the Kaveri river continuously upto the eastern coast.

When the Peshwa first started his work, the Maratha State was bounded in the south roughly by a line running from the mouths of the Krishna in the east to Goa in the west. In the actual conquest of the territory beyond this line, the work of Gopalrao Patwardhan, Balavantrao Mehendale, Visaji Krishna, Raste and Panse between 1757 and 1760 much exceeded the Peshwa's own gains between 1753 to 1757. The disaster of Panipat gave Haidar Ali the opportunity of his life to wrest back these conquests and practically to undo all the previous Maratha achievements.

Maratha ambitions in the Karnatak aimed mainly at the subjugation of the four Nawabs of Aurangzeb's days, viz., those of Shira, Savanur, Karnool and Kadappa. The fifth, namely, the Nawab of Arcot was saved from Maratha aggression by his support from the British. Shira and Savanur were reduced by the Peshwa himself. Kadappa, which claimed the districts of Kolar, Hoskot and Balapur once forming the Jagir of Shahji Raje, was subjugated by the prowess of Balavantrao Mehendale. Abdul Majid Khan the Nawab of Kadappa was a man of valour and resources. In the fierce engagement fought between Sidhout and Kadappa on 24th September 1757, the Khan was killed along with four hundred of his men. The same night Kadappa was captured. Thereafter Visaji Krishna directed his attention to Bednur, but before it could be subjugated, Visaji was called away suddenly to Poona. Haidar Ali as a commander of the Mysore army attained prominence at this very time and resisted Maratha aggression stoutly. He was an enterprising, skilful soldier, understood the art of war as no one else of his time did, and trained his armies in western discipline so thoroughly that he soon became irresistible in the south. Gopalrao Patwardhan worked hard to capture Mysore, but was called away to Poona in the midst of his operations. In the meantime Visaji Krishna reduced Ongole, Nellore, Sarwapilli, Kalahasti, and other posts along the east coast near the mouth of the Krishna river. The Maratha armies completed their conquest by a holy bath in the eastern seas. The Nawab of Karnool yielded to Maratha demands without resistance.

6. Bussy at Char Minar.—Here we must revert to

the story of the Peshwa's relations with Nawab Salabat Jang of Haidarabad, resuming the thread of the time from the peace of Bhalki in December 1752. Bussy was called upon to face the machinations of the two old and able servants of the State Saiyad Lashkar Khan and Shah Nawaz Khan, who became greatly jealous of his power and control of the administration, giving rise to murder and secret plots at the Nizam's Court to which ultimately Salabat Jang fell a prey.

While Bussy had been reducing Savanur in the summer of 1756, his master Salabat Jang wishing to be rid of this overbearing and grasping servant, sent him on 18th May, an order that he had been dismissed from service. This was the result of the serious alarm which Indian powers began to feel at the increasing domination which the English and the French began to exercise through their superior military organization. As soon as the Peshwa learnt of Bussy's dismissal, he offered to engage him in his own service and to all appearances this was agreed to by both the parties. But Bussy was a master tactician, intent upon impressing the Indian powers with a premonition that hereafter the Europeans were to be the masters in India. Bussy quietly said yes to every request that was made to him and asked for passports to proceed to Masulipatan after a few days stay at Haidarabad to collect his effects. The Peshwa even gave him his own escort on the way. With his whole following Bussy reached Haidarabad in June and took up his residence at the grand old edifice known as the Char Minar in the centre of the town, where he so fortified himself by means of his powerful artillery that he could not be dislodged. Salabat Jang came soon after with all his forces, but could make no effect upon Bussy's position during a stiff contest that raged for four months. In the end Salabat Jang was completely humbled and gave a written agreement to Bussy on 16 November reinstating him in his former position. After arranging his affairs in Haidarabad, Bussy left for Masulipatan to manage the lucrative districts he had obtained in the Northern Sarkars, for the expenses of his army. He returned to Haidarabad in September 1757.[6] Had not the fortunes of

6. The incident of the battle of the Char Minar has been eloquently described by many Indian and European writers. Its revolutionary character deserves to be well understood. See P. D. 25. 167.

the French so thoroughly waned during the Seven Years' War, it is clear that Bussy could never have been dislodged from the Nizam's State.

7. **The Nizam's defeat at Sindkhed.**—What with his grasping French auxiliary Bussy, and what with the increasing power of the Peshwa in his neighbourhood, Salabat Jang's position began rapidly to grow weaker. The lesson taught by Bussy at the Char Minar did not fail to impress the Peshwa also. He openly demanded from Salabat Jang all the north Godavari region under a threat of resorting to arms. Bussy was then away and Shah Nawaz Khan did not resist the Peshwa's demand. This was too much for the spirited brother of Salabat Jang Nizam Ali to bear. Guided by a clever Hindu diplomat Vithal Sundar, Nazim Ali enlisted the services of another of Bussy's captains Ibrahim Khan (later of Panipat fame). The Khan brought with him 2,500 trained infantry and fifteen guns on an annual payment of one lac. Shah Nawaz Khan, feeling nervous about his own safety when Nizam Ali thus began to assert himself, took prompt possession of Fort Daulatabad, removed there his family and valuables, and prepared to defend himself there in case of necessity, following the example of Bussy at the Char Minar.

Thus the two courts of Poona and Aurangabad occupied themselves during the monsoon of 1757 in preparing for another trial of arms. The Peshwa gave the command of the impending campaign to his eldest son Vishvasrao, a promising lad of fifteen, in order to afford him experience for his future position in the State. Dattaji and Jankoji Sindia who had just returned from their Marwar entanglement, were asked to train Vishvasrao under them and conduct the expedition to a successful issue. Damaji Gaikwad and other chiefs joined the army in due course. The Maratha forces left Poona on 27 August in the direction of Aurangabad, the Peshwa and Sadashivrao halting on the Godavari to watch the operations beyond. Aurangabad was the main objective for the Marathas to reduce and for the Nizam to defend. Hostilities began in November. Nizam Ali was put in charge of the campaign by Salabat Jang. Bussy was then absent on the east coast.

As the Marathas were marching upon Aurangabad, they

received news that Ramchandra Jadhav a powerful Maratha commander in the Nizam's service was coming rapidly from Bhalki to remove the threat to the capital. In order to prevent Jadhav attacking the Peshwa's army before Aurangabad, Dattaji learning that Ramchandra Jadhav was at Sindkhed quickly moved upon that place and at once invested it. These surprizingly quick movements were most effective. The small rampart of Sindkhed was not likely to hold out long. Nizam Ali with Ibrahim Khan Gardi at once marched from Aurangabad to Sindkhed, in the wake of Dattaji's men to relieve the pressure upon Jadhav, which increased every moment when swarming Marathas quickly gathered from various directions. A fierce struggle between the two opponents raged for nearly a month round that small place. Nizam Ali and Ibrahim Khan effected a junction with Jadhav and tried to break out all in a body through the Maratha cordon on 12th December under the shelter of their powerful artillery. A fierce battle was fought continuously for four days at the gate of Sindkhed, when Nagoji Mane a supporter of Jadhav was killed along with many of his followers. On 16th December darkness set in towards evening and the combatants parted. Victory remained with the Marathas.

The next few days decided the fate of the campaign. Hordes of Maratha cavalry came sweeping upon the Nizam's forces. On 17th December Nizam Ali acknowledging defeat sent Vithal Sundar to the Maratha camp begging for terms. Peace was concluded by the Nizam ceding to the Peshwa territory worth 25 lacs along with fort Naldurg. Ceremonial visits by the two principals at Sakharkhedla ratified and confirmed the treaty on 29th December 1757.[7] Once more the unity of Maratha ranks under the Peshwa's direction was plainly exhibited to the Indian world, finally closing the rift that Tarabai's activities had created.

The forces of disruption became now too apparent in the counsels of the State reared by Asaf Jah. Bussy had kept studiously aloof at Haidarabad during the late Maratha-Muslim struggle. After the war was over, he left for Aurangabad there to pay his respects to his master. On the way he

7. P. D. 25. 183, 184.

paid a cordial visit to the Peshwa and held an exchange of views on the general situation. He then arrived at Aurangabad and visited Salabat Jang with the utmost humility. He also paid a formal visit to Nizam Ali, being extremely careful to guard against any treacherous design on that chief's part. Shah Nawaz Khan fell into disfavour, and was dismissed from the Chief Minister's position by Salabat Jang, who appointed to that post, on the advice of Bussy, the latter's confidential secretary Haidar Jang. Thus at one stroke Bussy's voice again became powerful, a result most highly resented by Nizam Ali.

8. Horrid murders.—Salabat Jang began to quail before Bussy, under whose advice Nizam Ali was appointed to the government of Haidarabad, so that he might be safely kept at a distance. Haidar Jang immediately on coming to office, took possession of fort Daulatabad and removed from that place all partizans of Shah Nawaz Khan, keeping that Khan a closely watched prisoner. It became apparent that Bussy contemplated the same design against Nizam Ali also. Haidar Jang called on Nizam Ali and delivered him a message that Bussy wanted him immediately for a conference. Nizam Ali apprehending danger to his person answered that he would call on Bussy the next day. Haidar Jang insisted that he must go at once. This threatening tone roused Nizam Ali's suspicions and drawing the small dagger he carried in his hand, he immediately thrust it into Haidar Jang's body, killing him instantly. Vithal Sundar who was near cut off Haidar Jang's head and escaped along with Nizam Ali to safe quarters.

As soon as the news of this outrage became public, Basalat Jang collected a few of his Maratha followers, went and informed Bussy of what had happened. Bussy frantic with rage immediately despatched his subordinate Lachhman Dubash with instructions to kill Shah Nawaz Khan and his sons under the apprehension that they were the instigators of Haidar Jang's murder. This man went straight to the Khan's quarters, and murdered him with his two sons and another man Mir Muhammad Husain. Thus the 11th of May 1758 proved a day of wanton murders. Fortunately for Nizam Ali, Bussy was just then removed from the scene. War was raging furiously between the French and the British on the east coast. The French Governor Count Lally immediately recalled Bussy, who received the orders on 18th June and left immediately with all his French followers, leaving Salabat Jang to the mercy of his brother. Bussy fought in the battle of Wandewash in January 1760, was taken prisoner by the British and sent to Europe, only to return to India twenty years later in 1783 and to die here in 1785 at the age of 61.

After Bussy's departure affairs took a rapid turn for the worse in the Nizam's State. Basalat Jang and Nizam Ali quarrelled over the power to manage the administration as Salabat Jang was a mere figure-head, playing into the hands of his powerful ministers. During the war on the east coast, Captain Forde of the British East India Company marched into the Northern Sarkars and captured those districts for themselves : neither Basalat Jang nor Nizam Ali could prevent this. The latter demanded from Salabat Jang the sole management of affairs : but Salabat Jang was afraid of his own life being attempted by Nizam Ali's Gardis headed by Ibrahim Khan. He therefore stipulated that he would entrust him with all powers provided he dismissed Ibrahim Khan from his service. This he agreed to do. Ibrahim Khan was dismissed by Nizam Ali in October 1759 and the latter was given full powers of administration by Salabat Jang. When Sadashivrao at Poona learnt of Ibrahim Khan's dismissal, he at once engaged him in his employ, having already fully satisfied himself about the latter's honesty and capacity. This was the reason that provoked Muzaffar Khan to attempt Bhau's life as has been mentioned above.

9. Battle of Udgir.—Nizam Ali highly resented the aggression which the Peshwa, now armed with efficient artillery, commenced against the Haidarabad State, particularly by seizing Ahmadnagar, Daulatabad, Burhanpur and Bijapur all renowned capitals and relics of old Muslim glory. On 9th November 1759 Kavi Jang, the keeper of Ahmadnagar surrendered the place to the Peshwa on receiving a handsome reward in money and jagir. This led at once to a fresh outbreak of hostilities between the two neighbours. The Maratha forces led by Sadashivrao and Vishvasrao moved east from

Poona and descended upon the Nizam's territories in January 1760. Fighting commenced on the 20th of that month consisting of artillery and cavalry actions in the vicinity of Udgir a few miles north of Bidar. On 3rd February a stiff action was fought in which the Asaf Jahi forces were so completely routed that Nizam Ali sent ambassadors seeking terms. He agreed to surrender to the Peshwa territory worth sixty lacs together with the four Muslim capitals already mentioned. The treaty was concluded on 11th February and all the stipulated places came into Maratha possession within the next two months. The glory of this victory was, however, suddenly marred by the growing Maratha reverses in north India inflicted by the Pathan ruler of Afghanistan, Ahmad Shah Abdali. Sadashivrao was at once called upon to proceed to the north, before he was able to get the terms agreed to by the Nizam executed. The stunning blow that the Marathas a year after received at Panipat saved the Nizam's State from complete collapse. Salabat Jang could not hold his own against Nizam Ali, who first put him into confinement on 7th July 1762, and later put him to death on 16th September 1763.

CHRONOLOGY

CHAPTER XVI

1754	British move to put down Tulaji Angria.
1755, February 14	Raghuji Bhosle dies.
1755, March 10	Maratha-British agreement for putting down Tulaji.
1755, March 29	Captain James attacks Suvarnadurg.
1755, April 12	Suvarnadurg surrendered, land attacks on all sides upon the Angrian territory by Peshwa's men.
1756, February 7	Admiral Watson's fleet leaves Bombay.
1756, February 14	Vijayadurg surrendered after Angrian navy had been burnt down ; Tulaji surrendered and sent to Poona ; his mother and children submitted to Watson.
1756, June 28	Phonda vainly attacked by the Portuguese, Count Alva killed.
1756, July 20	Peshwa's protest against British possession of Vijayadurg.
1756, August 1	British mission to Poona.
1756, October 12	British-Peshwa agreement reached, Bankot ceded in lieu of Vijayadurg.
1757, March	Janoji Bhosle succeeds to the Nagpur state.
1758, September 23	Manaji Angria dies.
1758, Nov-Feb. 1759	Peshwa tours the regions of the west coast.
1759, January 28	Underi captured.
1759, February 21	Kansa alias Padamdurg captured.
1759, August	Price's mission to Poona.
1759, October 23	Price's mission returns.
1760	Clive in England for Indian problems.
1760, October 23	Rajkot of Revdanda pulled down.
1766	Tulaji's two sons Raghuji and Sambhaji, escape to Bombay.
1786	Tulaji Angria dies.

CHAPTER XVI

TWO INCORRIGIBLE CHIEFS

[1755—1760]

1 The Nagpur succession.
2 Tulaji Angria defiant.
3 Fall of Vijayadurg.
4 The Peshwa's protest.
5 Did the Peshwa destroy the Maratha navy?
6 Manaji and Raghuji Angria.

1. **The Nagpur succession.**—The Bhosles of Nagpur and the Angrias of Kolaba were the two incorrigible chiefs whom the Peshwa with all his patience and diplomacy found it hard to reduce to obedience in his effort at unifying the Maratha State. It is now time to describe the Peshwa's dealings with them. Raghuji Bhosle's relations with the Peshwa have been amply detailed in the foregoing narrative. Shrewd and alert as both were, they fully realized the advantage of preserving amity with each other and fully co-operating in measures of mutual benefit. Raghuji long suffered from a stomach complaint and was almost bed-ridden during the last two or three years of his life. Raghuji not only made his name in the conquest of Bengal, but he also exhibited great heroism in subjugating the Gonds and creating the Nagpur State as a distinct entity in which he stands quite on a par with Malharrao Holkar or any of the Sindias. He colonized Nagpur and other cities with Maharashtrian elements and made his State a strong and wealthy base by training a large band of devoted co-workers in war and diplomacy.

After having effected the conquest of Orissa and arrived at a final understanding with Nawab Aliwardi Khan in 1751, Raghuji led a peaceful life and did not concern himself with the various important projects and expeditions which the Peshwa restlessly carried out in the Karnatak region. Baburao Konher Kolhatkar was his intimate adviser who co-operated with Janoji, Raghuji's ablest son, in transacting current business pertaining to his rule of Nagpur. Raghuji died on 14th February 1755, when six wives and seven hand-maids are said to have immolated themselves on his funeral pyre. He willed that Janoji should become the Senasaheb-Subah after him. Of his four sons Janoji and Sabaji were born of the younger wife, and Mudhoji and Bimbaji of the elder one. The first two were fairly brave and capable men.

Janoji though born of the younger mother was older in age than Mudhoji, who was the offspring of the elder queen, which gave rise to a complicated dispute about the succession and considerably weakened the position of that principality. Disregarding the injunction of his father, Mudhoji claimed the position of Senasaheb Subah and wrote letters to Janoji with an address proper only to a younger brother. The dispute was referred to the Peshwa, who coveted a large amount for the succession fee. Janoji's adviser Devajipant Chorghode went to Poona and obtained the Peshwa's decision in his master's favour by promising to pay two and a half lacs as nazar. The Peshwa was at the moment proceeding to Savanur and invited both the brothers to join him. They complied and attended, with the result that the question of succession to the Nagpur estate came to be abnormally postponed. At last a conference was held on the Godavari in March 1757 and it divided the estate in two parts, Janoji was declared the Senasaheb Subah, and Mudhoji was asked to rule at Chanda with the title of Sena-dhurandhar. The Peshwa ratified this decision after exacting a present of 20 lacs from the four brothers.[1] For a time the Bhosle brothers worked together and helped the Peshwa in his attack upon the Nizam at Sindkhed. But the domestic dissensions of the four brothers never came to an end, and as a result the Nagpur State fast declined in power and prestige.

2. **Tulaji Angria defiant.**—The Angrias and their navy were the guardians of the western sea-board of the Maratha State. During Shahu's lifetime the Peshwa could not exercise full powers in restraining the disobedient sardars. For the

1. Khare 1. 11; Raj. 3. 188, 193, 464-468, 514, 556, 557; *Patre Yadi* 153-155; P. D. 20. 75; Ait. Pat. 96. See *Nagpur Bakhar* also. A vast literature has been published on the history of Nagpur to which the student is referred.

safety of the Maratha raj, as well as for restraining the aggression of the western powers, the west coast had to be carefully guarded from danger, and in this respect Tulaji Angria's hostility to the Peshwa soon became intolerable. In addition to the internal disputes of Indian powers, the French and the English trading companies now directly interfered in Indian politics. Bengal and Madras they largely seized and it became the Peshwa's duty to guard the west coast from a similar fate. It was necessary for him to have the Maratha navy entirely under his control.

The southern portion of the west coast was at this time controlled by Tulaji Angria who had his residence at Vijayadurg, and the northern portion by Ramaji Mahadev, the Peshwa's governor of Kalyan, both strong and singular personalities, who during the last several years contracted bitter hatred towards each other. The Peshwa in the midst of his other serious pre-occupations, did not personally deal with the Angrias but left every affair in that region in the hands of this Ramajipant, thereby only adding fuel to the fire. The Portuguese of Goa who had lost Bassein in 1739, were trying their level best to get back their possession and readily joined every opponent of the Peshwas. The Savant of Wadi was a protege of the Peshwa and was brought to extremities both by Tulaji and the Portuguese. During 1751 Tarabai then bitterly opposing the Peshwa, instigated both the Portuguese and Tulaji Angria and promised the former the return of their territory of Bassein, if they would put down the Peshwa. It became the Peshwa's policy therefore in this difficult situation, to prevent an alliance of the Portuguese of Goa and the English of Bombay. The Peshwa for some time was trying his utmost to gain the friendship of the English who bitterly hated Tulaji and gradually accepted the Peshwa's overtures. The British, intent solely on self-interest with no more love for the Peshwa than for Tulaji, proposed to join the Peshwa in putting down Tulaji. War was going on between the French and the English on the east coast. The Peshwa agreed that he would not help the French on the east coast if the English did not help Tulaji on the west. The Peshwa's only object in this proposal was to bring Tulaji under his control and prevent him from combining with the enemies of the Maratha

State. It was no part of the Peshwa's programme to destroy the Maratha navy owned by the Angria. Tulaji's own irascible temper aggravated the situation. He was possessed by an inordinate hatred for the Peshwa and particularly for Ramaji Mahadev the Peshwa's agent on the spot. He did not fall in with the Peshwa in executing the responsibilities of the Maratha State as a whole. He never showed the least inclination to come to terms with the Peshwa. Otherwise the latter would have gladly utilised his services and promoted the interests of such a valiant naval commander as Tulaji.

To preserve amicable relations with the Peshwa and prevent him from joining the French was the main plank of the British policy at Bombay after the fall of Bassein into Maratha hands. When severe tension grew between Ramaji Mahadev and Tulaji, the former by way of a counterpoise secured the good graces of the Bombay Council, in order to exercise control over both the Angrias and the Siddis of Janjira. During 1754 when the Peshwa was busy with the affairs of the Karnatak, Ramajipant had several talks with the Bombay Governor Bourchier and agreed to engage the services of the Bombay navy for putting down Tulaji Angria.[2]

The Peshwa's letters of 8 and 11 February and 8 March 1755 were placed before his Council by Governor Bourchier on 10th March 1755, and the following terms were finally agreed upon between the British and Ramajipant on 19th March :—

1. That both the Maratha and the British navy should be under the complete control of the latter ;

2. Whatever ships would be captured from the Angrias should be divided half and half between the two ;

3. That after Tulaji was overcome, the Marathas should cede to the British Bankot and its fort Himmatgad (afterwards named Fort Victoria) together with five villages in that neighbourhood ;

4. That the British should prevent any succour going to Tulaji through the sea ;

5. Whatever treasure, ammunition, guns or supplies would be captured or found in the forts and places belonging to the Marathas, should be equally shared ;

2. Forrest's *Maratha series*, War with the Angrias.

6. If the British and the Marathas should jointly attack Manaji Angria, the island of Khanderi should be ceded to the British.

These terms were sanctioned by the Peshwa and the war began.

3. **Fall of Vijayadurg.**—As the season of 1755 was advanced when the treaty was concluded, it was decided first to attack Suvarnadurg, the fort of Harnai, reserving the capture of Vijayadurg for the next fair season. Captain William James was appointed by the Bombay Council to lead the naval expedition and was accompanied by Ramajipant. They left the Bombay harbour on 22nd March and were joined by the Maratha naval ships outside the fort of Chaul. On 29th the joint navy fired on the Angria's ships in the harbour of Suvarnadurg. The latter ran away and escaped. On 2nd April gun-fire was opened upon the fort. On the 3rd an explosion took place in the fort in which the store of Angria's ammunition was burnt up. The next day 4th April, some of Angria's men came to Ramajipant with a white flag and the attackers landed in the fort, which surrendered on the 12th. Javji Gauli and Khandoji Mankar supported the operations from the land on behalf of the Peshwa. Shamsher Bahadur and Dinkar Mahadev were two other commanders whom the Peshwa nominated for conducting land operations against Tulaji. They descended through the Amba pass upon Angria's fort of Ratnagiri late in May and invested it on the landward side; but they could not take the fort without naval co-operation, which the advent of the monsoon prevented. That place was captured next year on 18th February 1756. A little before this Anjanvel and Govalkot were also taken from Tulaji's possession on 14th January of the same year by the Peshwa's men.

But the main objective of the campaign was to reduce Tulaji's seat of fort Vijayadurg or Gheria, as it used to be called after a village in the vicinity named Girye. How Tulaji remained so utterly indifferent or careless till the last moment is a mystery. He was perhaps over confident of defending the place against any odds and made no move. For two years the attack was being discussed and throughout 1755 most of his outlying posts were falling into the Peshwa's hands one after another and yet Tulaji did not stir. He managed to secure from Goa some slight Portuguese help of about 500 men. Rudraji Dhulap an Angrian lieutenant was worsted losing a large number of his own men and some of the Portuguese who had accompanied him.

In the month of October 1755 some troops under Capt. Clive and a naval force under Admiral Watson arrived from England at Madras. At that very moment, Madras received a demand for military help from Bombay to act against Tulaji Angria. The Madras authorities readily complied with the request of Bombay and despatched the forces both of Clive and Watson to Bombay. Governor Bourchier ordered these to proceed against Vijayadurg with definite instructions (1) that Tulaji should be brought to Bombay after the fall of his fort of Vijayadurg; (2) that the Bombay force should co-operate with the Peshwa's in capturing the other forts and places of Angria; (3) that until Bankot and its territory were actually delivered into British hands, Vijayadurg should not be restored to the Peshwa's possession; (4) that an effort should be made to secure such other places and harbours as would be considered beneficial to British interests; (5) that Tulaji was a very wicked man and his word should not be trusted. "He has for long destroyed many of our vessels and put us to the annual loss of 3 or 4 lacs for the last so many years. He should on no account be given up to the Peshwa; for he may again become free and molest us as before."

On 7th February 1756 fourteen British ships of war with a force of 800 English troops and a thousand Indians, left Bombay under Clive and Watson, all by the sea-route. It was expected that the war would continue long and stiff, but on the 7th day after leaving Bombay, Vijayadurg fell into British hands. Watson reported on 14th February, "We arrived before Vijayadurg on 11th and learnt that Tulaji was negotiating for terms with the Peshwa. "In order to prevent him from gaining time for negotiations, I at once called upon him to deliver the fort to us. On the 12th we started firing upon the fort. At four in the afternoon, a chance shot falling upon one of Angria's ships set fire to all his ships large and small about 70 in all, and they all were quickly burnt to ashes. On the

13th a few of our men landed; and prevented any of the Peshwa's men getting into the fort. Capt. Forde with 60 men entered the fort in the afternoon and planted the British flag on the top-mast. This morning all our men had an easy access into the fort. Ramajipant is coming to meet me today when I will demand the delivery of Tulaji Angria. We suffered no material losses."

As the British ships were sailing to Vijayadurg, about forty or fifty ships of the Peshwa joined them on the way. The land forces of the Poona Government were camping in tents on the east of the main fort. Tulaji was not prepared for the sudden rush that took place. He was expecting the arrival of the British naval ships since November and as none had made their appearance for over three months, he remained off his guard. As soon as he saw the ships, Tulaji ran into the Maratha camp to see Ramajipant, who did not pay much attention to what he had to say. Tulaji well knew how he was hated by the British. He then commenced firing upon the British ships from the fort, but almost at the start all his ships were suddenly set on fire and, to his utter dismay, immediately burnt down. The first thing Clive did was to enter the fort and take possession of all valuables. The Peshwa's men also rushed towards the fort, but Captain Forde stood at the gate with a drawn sword in hand, threatening to cut down whosoever should venture to step forth. Thus mortified, the Marathas returned to their camp. The British found in the fort 250 guns, ten lacs of rupees in cash, six brass mortars and about four thousand £ worth of goods and valuables.

Immediately on the arrival of the British ships in the harbour Ramajipant visited Admiral Watson on his flag-ship and mentioned that Tulaji was seeking peace terms. Watson answered, "I have no orders for making peace: but if you desire, let Tulaji come to me on my ship. If he does not come at once, I will fire on the fort." But Tulaji could not make up his mind. Then the British fired, burnt the ships of Angria and took possession of the fort. Tulaji surrendered to Khandoji Mankar and was securely guarded by the Peshwa's men. The next day Ramajipant again visited Watson on his ship, when the latter demanded the delivery of Tulaji. Ramaji replied that he would not hand over Tulaji unless he had written orders from his master. Ramajipant made a demand for the possession of the fort. Watson replied he had no orders but would hoist the Peshwa's flag along with his own. He would not allow the entry of Maratha troops into the fort if Tulaji was not delivered to him. The British dug up the fort for hoarded wealth, and obtained considerable amounts which they distributed to their men. As the Peshwa was absent at Savanur, no final solution could be found to dissolve the differences about the possession of the fort and disposal of Tulaji.

Edward Ives a surgeon on Watson's ship has left a journal of his travels and given some pertinent details about the affair of Vijayadurg. He mentions that when the British entered the fort, not more than 20 on their side were found dead or wounded. Tulaji had three days before left the fort having stationed his wife's brother in charge. The British found in the fort Tulaji's two wives and two sons. Watson went into the fort and took a kindly interest in them. They all with tears in their eyes bowed to the ground before him as Watson entered, and the Admiral assured them of safety and care on his part. Tulaji's aged mother was much moved by this assurance and replied "Now we are without protection,—no father, and no children. One six year old son of Tulaji held Watson's hand and said, "You are now my father." These words touched Watson's heart too. The British discovered in the fort in addition to the above family of Tulaji, ten English and three Dutch men imprisoned by Tulaji. They were all set at liberty."

The English obviously behaved contrary to the terms agreed upon by keeping possession of the fort, and appropriating all valuables and demanding the person of Tulaji. As soon as the British navy arrived at Vijayadurg, Tulaji in terror started negotiations with Ramajipant. The English construed this as a breach of agreement on the part of the Marathas in conducting negotiations for peace without the knowledge of the other allied party, and alone attacked the fort and prevented the Marathas from entering it. But the main fact is clear that it was the Peshwa who for putting down Tulaji sought the naval co-operation of the British. The British had not started the war against Tulaji on their own account. If the Marathas had not already hemmed in Tulaji by land over a length of more than two hundred miles, Tulaji could not have been so easily subdued. The British discovered that the harbour of Vijayadurg was a valuable base for their navy and proposed to keep it themselves exchanging it for Bankot and its fort Himmatgad. Ramajipant went to the extreme length of protest short of open hostilities, and bided his time until the Peshwa's return to Poona from Savanur. In fact the British tried to grab Vijayadurg and establish their sway over the west coast just as they had done on the east coast in Madras and Bengal. Indeed as Bombay was not then well developed, the British considered Vijayadurg as a most suitable port for the expansion of their power.

4. The Peshwa's protest.—The Peshwa arrived at Poona on 20th July 1756 and the next day he addressed a strong letter to the Governor in which he condemned the British action of keeping possession of the fort of Vijayadurg for which alone he had called in the British help. He demanded its immediate surrender if their amicable relations were to be preserved in the future. " If you do not act up, the future will lie in God's hands", added the Peshwa. A clear threat which could not be easily ignored.

To this the Governor made a mild reply on 1st August and promised to hand over the place as soon as the monson was over, when his ships could bring back the garrison, offering at the same time to send his two agents to Poona, Thomas Wyfield and John Spencer for a personal adjustment of the outstanding points arising out of the affair. The East India Co. at that moment had already a war on hand both in Bengal and Madras and were not prepared for an additional trouble on the west coast. Hence they readily yielded to the Peshwa's demand and staged a climb down.

The Portuguese tried to make capital out of the Peshwa's difficulties by attacking the Maratha post on Phonda, south of Goa on 28th June 1756. It was bravely defended by the Maratha garrison, and the Portuguese Governor Count de Alva was killed, losing ten guns and arms to the Marathas.

The British envoy from Bombay arrived at Poona and a fresh treaty was then drawn up on 12th October mainly stipulating that Bankot and ten villages should be ceded to the English in lieu of Vijayadurg. Govind Shivram Khasgivale at once proceeded to Vijayadurg and took possession of the fort on behalf of the Peshwa. Tulaji remained a closely watched prisoner in the hands of the Peshwa, along with his mother, wives and two sons Raghuji and Sambhaji confined in various forts from time to time. These sons escaped from their confinement in 1766 to Bombay, but the British did not give them shelter in their settlement. Raghuji then went to Haidar Ali and remained there long. Tulaji died as a prisoner in fort Wandan in 1786.[3]

5. **Did the Peshwa destroy the Maratha navy?**—Historians like Rajwade and others have scathingly criticised the Peshwa for having destroyed the Maratha navy by accepting British help for that purpose. Here it must be observed that on some important points the critics have proceeded on wrong assumptions. The Peshwa was intent on putting down the recalcitrant and defiant Tulaji Angria who obeyed no law and recognised no authority. The Peshwa had no grudge against the Angrian navy at all. The navy was burnt down by the Peshwa's allies the British. Once a war is on, it was difficult to regulate the destruction. After Tulaji was removed, the Peshwa did appoint another naval officer Dhulap in his place. Nor could the Peshwa conceive that he was doing damage to the Maratha State by removing Angria. He had already humbled Damaji Gaikwad and silenced Dabhade and Tarabai. The Peshwa did not remove Tulaji's brother Manaji who preserved his position at Kolaba. To defend the west coast properly by taking possession of the important points and harbours of Suvarnadurg, Anjanvel, Ratnagiri and Vijayadurg, was the principal aim of the Peshwa for which he called in British aid. But even in this point, it may be asked why did he neglect the obvious political dictum, on no account to call in an enemy to help one's cause. Here is the crux of the problem. The agreement for British

3. This Angrian episode synchronized with important happenings on the east coast, the Anglo-French war, the affair of Suraj-ud-Daula and Bussy's bold stand against the Nizam at Char Minar.

help was contracted early in 1755, when the British were not considered as unfriendly to the Marathas. The Seven Years War had not yet started. Bussy a French officer was already a friend to the Peshwa. These Western settlers, the French, the Dutch and the British, were working in India for over a century as peaceful traders, and their territorial ambitions were not disclosed till the grant of the Diwani to Clive by the Emperor in 1765.[4] In ascribing to the Peshwa an unpardonable fatal indiscretion, it seems we anticipate history, and powerful as the Peshwa certainly was during the late fifties, he had no reason to suspect that he could not control the action of the British power in Bombay.

One must also note the Peshwa's subsequent dealings with the British. He had set his heart upon subjugating the Siddi of Janjira and the Nawab of Surat, who received British support to the detriment of the Maratha State. So after Tulaji had been removed, the Peshwa turned his attention to Janjira and Surat and requested British help for that purpose in 1758. There were other points of friction between the two nations for the settlement of which British envoys were sent to Poona in August 1759, headed by Price.[5] Price arrived in Poona on 7th September and left it for Bombay on 23rd October 1759. Visits and discussions took place through Govind Shivram, but no decisive result came about, as on the point of the conquest of either Surat or Janjira, the British would not offer any support to the Peshwa. In fact they took possession of Surat themselves about this time. Price's journal forms an interesting study.

6. **Manaji and Raghuji Angria.**—With the death of Manaji Angria on 23rd September 1758, the element of disunion in the Angrian family was removed. Manaji's death

4. We well know that it was after the affair of Plassey that Clive began to formulate his dream of Indian conquest and he proceeded to England in February 1760 to personally discuss the matter with the British Prime Minister Earl Chatham; but Chatham did not support him, did not even care to meet him. Dupleix had certainly worked in that direction for a little while, but had failed and been recalled in disgrace.

5. Full account in Forest's *Maratha series.*

materially damaged the Peshwa's cherished ambition of subjugating the Siddi of Janjira, as he had zealously co-operated with the Peshwa in that task a few months before. Manaji left 14 sons, ten legitimate and four illegitimate. Raghuji the eldest and the most capable of them all, was invested with both the hereditary titles of Sarkhel and Wazarat-Mab. This Raghuji kept up a steadfast friendship for the Peshwa's house. After Manaji's death the Peshwa spent four long months November 1758 to February 1759 in touring and personally inspecting the position of the west coast with a view to organizing an expedition against the Siddi. Raghuji's youthful valour succeeded in capturing the Siddi's strong out-post of Underi on 28th January 1759 and the fort of Kansa or Padmadurg near Murud about three miles from Janjira itself on 21st February following. Underi was named Jayadurg. Janjira itself would have fallen into Maratha hands in a short time had not Sadashivrao Bhau been suddenly called to the north. Soon after on 13th October 1760 the Peshwa pulled down fort Rajkot of Chaul and the grand Masjid in it. Chaul a Portuguese possession, had long been in the Maratha hands, but the strong ramparts and the Muslim mosque formed a perpetual nuisance to the Hindu inhabitants of the place and were completely razed to the ground.[6]

6. *Patre Yadi* 182; P. D. 24. 261, 262, 265.

CHRONOLOGY

CHAPTER XVII

The Wazirs of Delhi :

1748 May – 13th May 1753, Safdar Jang.
1753 May 13 – 31st May 1754, Intizam-ud-daula.
1754 June 2 – 1759 November 29, Ghazi-ud-din Imad-ul-mulk.

1724,	Ahmad Shah Abdali born.
1737	Ahmad Shah Abdali takes service under Nadir Shah.
1739,	Ahmad Shah accompanies Nadir Shah in his expedition to Delhi.
1745, July 1	Zakaria Khan, Governor of the Punjab dies.
1747, June 19	Nadir Shah assassinated ; Ahmad Shah Abdali becomes King of Kabul.
1748, January 20	Abdali captures Lahore and advances towards Delhi.
1748, March 21	Abdali defeated at Manupur by Shahzada Ahmad ; Wazir Qamruddin Khan killed.
1748	Mir Mannu appointed Governor of the Punjab.
1748, April 25	Emperor Muhammad Shah dies at Delhi.
1748, April 28	Ahmad Shah proclaimed Emperor with Safdar Jang as Wazir.
1749, early months	Pathans of the Doab rise against the Wazir Safdar Jang.
" " "	Abdali invades the Punjab and returns on Mir Mannu agreeing to pay him annual tribute.
1750, August 3	The Doab Pathans start war upon the Wazir; Ahmad Khan Bangash attacks the Wazir's camp at Farrukhabad ; Navalrai the Wazir's commander killed.

1750, September 12	Battle of Kasganj, Safdar Jang himself wounded. The Pathans invest Allahabad; Wazir courts Maratha help from Poona.
1751, January	Sindia and Holkar met by Wazir's agents at Kotah : conditions of help agreed to.
1751, February 21	Safdar Jang leaves Delhi for the defence of Allahabad.
1751, March 2	Safdar Jang meets Jayappa and Malharrao and engages their services.
1751, March 20	Battle of Qadirganj : the Marathas rout Bangash : a bitter struggle follows.
1751, April 28	Battle near Farrukhabad, ten thousand Pathans cut down, Ahmad Khan Bangash's power extinguished : the Pathans led by Najib Khan invite Abdali from Kabul to their help.
1751, December	Abdali starts from Kabul for India.
1752, February	Through Maratha mediation, a treaty concluded at Lucknow closing the Pathan-Wazir war.
1752, March 15	Abdali captures Lahore.
1752, March 23	Mir Mannu submits and agrees to Abdali's terms.
1752, April 12	Safdar Jang makes a solemn agreement with the Maratha Sardars for the defence of the Emperor.
1752, April 23	The Emperor on the other hand ratifies Mir Mannu's arrangement with Abdali and the last returns to his country from Lahore.
1752, April 23	Sindia and Holkar reach Delhi and demand execution of their agreement.
1752, May 14	Sindia and Holkar leave for the Deccan with Ghazi-ud-din as required by the Peshwa.
1752, August 27	Khoja Javid Khan murdered by the Wazir.
1753, February 13	Abdali's agents arrive at Delhi demanding tribute.
1753, Mar. 26-Nov. 7	Civil war in Delhi. Surajmal supports the Wazir. Najib Khan appears on the scene to protect the Emperor against Safdar Jang.

1753, May 13	The Emperor dismisses Safdar Jang from Wazirship.
1753, June 14	Battle of Talkatora, Gosavi Rajendra Gir killed.
1753, August 19	Another battle, Safdar Jang defeated; the Emperor summons the Marathas to his help. The Peshwa despatches Raghunathrao to the north.
1753, September	A battle takes place resulting in heavy loss to Safdar Jang.
1753, November 7	War closed by a formal treaty between the Emperor and Safdar Jang. The latter withdraws to his Subah of Lucknow.
1754, October 17	Safdar Jang dies.

CHAPTER XVII

MARATHA ENTANGLEMENTS IN DELHI

[1750—1753]

1. Abdali and the Punjab, the start.—We have now to take up the threads of Maratha affairs in north India since the death of Raja Shahu and explain how a bitter struggle arose between the Pathan King of Afghanistan, Ahmad Shah Abdali and the Marathas of the Deccan, who contested for supremacy at the Court of Delhi. It was a long drawn drama with its tragic close at Panipat (January 1761).

Between 1741 and 1748 Balaji Bajirao had led four important expeditions personally into northern India, and kept a vigilant eye on the doings of his agents acting in his name in that distant field. But unfortunately his preoccupations in the south during the next eleven years after the death of Shahu, proved too engrossing to allow him time even to pay a single visit to the north. The affairs in that quarter came to be left entirely to Malharrao Holkar and the Sindia brothers, with the Hingnes at Delhi in charge of Maratha diplomacy, Govindpant Bundele in Bundelkhand and the Doab as a civil officer, and Antaji Mankeshwar as commandant of the small Maratha contingent in Delhi. The Peshwa's younger brother Raghunathrao was indeed sent twice to the north, but he proved too weak and incompetent for the heavy task.

Nadir Shah was assassinated on 19th June 1747 and his power and kingdom were usurped by his capable lieutenant Ahmad Shah Abdali. Born in 1724, Ahmad had enlisted in Nadir Shah's service at the age of 13 and accompanied that monarch into India in his famous expedition of 1739. He had gained in Nadir Shah's service the most valuable experience of leading armed forces into distant lands, and developed a greed of conquest, and more than once distinguished himself for valour, love of adventure and statesmanship. Within a few months of Nadir Shah's death he organized his rule at Kabul with the help of another able soldier and diplomat Shah Wali Khan, whom he appointed his minister. Shah Pasand Khan was another captain of ability whose services he secured, so that these three names became famous in future Indian history. Nadir Shah's immense wealth fell into Ahmad Shah's possession and enormously increased his power. These Pathan soldiers of fortune had close correspondence with their Indian brethren the Rohillas and the Bangashes, from whom they constantly acquired information of the conditions in India particularly of the Mughal Court. Thus Ahmad Shah early in his career conceived the plan of enriching his poor resources by draining away the wealth of India and particularly that of the Punjab, which he coveted as an outpost dominating the politics of Delhi. He never entertained the idea of obtaining for himself the crown of the Indian Empire. The Punjab alone being contiguous to his home in Afghanistan, he dearly prized as a paying adjunct of his western dominion.

The Punjab has been since ancient days the highway for any adventurer coming into this country, and its protection has ever formed the most troublesome problem for the imperial rulers of India. The moment the Indian hold on the Punjab became loose, foreign adventurers like Babar and Nadir Shah found it easy to invade India and establish power therein.

During Muhammad Shah's rule Zakaria Khan governed the Punjab for long with conspicuous ability. He died on 1st July 1745, leaving two sons Yahiya Khan and Shah Nawaz Khan, between whom a dispute immediately started for the succession. Qamr-ud-din Khan, the Wazir of the Emperor and his able son Mir Mannu supported the claim of Yahiya Khan, who was the Wazir's son-in-law and who ran to Delhi, for protection after his father's death. The younger brother Shah Nawaz Khan had an able assistant named Adina Beg, who sought the help of Shah Abdali and invited him to invade the Punjab. Abdali readily accepted the offer and led an expedition into this country in January 1748. He captured Lahore on January 20 and after completing his military preparations, proceeded further on towards Delhi during the next month. Emperor Muhammad Shah was at this time ailing, but he sent his son Shahzada Ahmad with the Wazir and other grandees like Safdar Jang, the Mir Bakhshi, and Ishwari Sinh of Jaipur with large forces and plentiful treasure. A stiff action between the imperial troops and those of Abdali took place at Manupur ten miles northward of Sarhind on 21st March, in which the Afghan Shah was completely routed; but at the beginning of the action a chance shot killed the Wazir Qamr-ud-din Khan.[1]

The Shah immediately returned to his country after conciliating Mir Mannu the Governor of the Punjab. The battle of Manupur proved the last victory won by the imperialists. The Emperor Muhammad Shah died at Delhi on 25th April, the news of which reached Shahzada Ahmad at Panipat on 28th and he at once proclaimed himself Emperor, acting on the advice of Safdar Jang, whom he appointed his Wazir, along with the charge he already held of the Subahs of Allahabad and Oudh. At this time all the Deccan had been lost to Delhi being owned partly by the Marathas and partly by the dynasty of Asaf Jah. Bengal, Bihar and Orissa had been already subjected to the Maratha Chauth. The Subah of Agra was usurped by the Jats under Surajmal. The Rajput rajas already acted as independent chiefs. The only territory that remained in the Emperor's direct charge was the north-western lands between Delhi and Attock, and parts of the Doab.

Next year (1749) when the Indian Pathans rose against the Wazir, the Shah Abdali entered the Punjab in the cold season. Mir Mannu opposed him near Wazirabad, but discovering that no help would come from Delhi, he saved himself by agreeing to pay Abdali the annual revenue of the four northern districts of the Punjab together with a cash nazar of Rupees ten thousand. As the summer advanced the Shah returned home with the acquisition he had gained.

2. The Pathan war, Safdar Jang seeks Maratha help.—Soon afterwards there arose dissensions in the Emperor Ahmad Shah's counsels. His mother Udham Bai and the eunuch Javid Khan intrigued against the Wazir and usurped all power,

1. P. D. 2. 9; *Patre Yadi* 65.

controlling the Emperor who remained immersed in the pursuit of pleasure to the detriment of the State, so that the Wazir Safdar Jang soon discovered that he had no authority to act. He could not prevail upon the Emperor to start personally with forces to defend the Punjab and prevent further invasions by Ahmad Shah Abdali. At the end of November 1748 Safdar Jang discovered a plot for attempting his life by means of an explosion of gunpowder as he entered the palace gate. The Emperor wishing to deprive Safdar Jang of his Wazirship, invited Nasir Jang from the Deccan for this purpose. The latter started for Delhi in March 1749. In this extremity Safdar Jang tried through the Hingnes, the Maratha agents at Delhi, to secure the Peshwa's help in maintaining his position. Upon this the Peshwa at once asked Sindia and Holkar to march southward and prevent Nasir Jang from crossing the Narmada for Delhi. Safdar Jang collected armies in Delhi and tried to maintain his position even by force against the Emperor, who got so frightened at the Wazir's move that he at once wrote an autograph letter to Nasir Jang to return to the Deccan and not to proceed to Delhi. Nasir Jang, therefore, was compelled to return from the Narmada in May. But Safdar Jang's position did not materially improve. On the contrary the Jats, the Rohillas and the Pathans of the Doab made a common cause against him and started an open aggression on his territory.

These Indian Pathans were the hereditary foes of the Mughals and dreamt of putting an end to the latter's rule in India. Having communications with the trans-frontier Pathans, they now began to assert their power. They were fanatics of the Sunni persuasion and bitterly hated the Shia Wazir, who had waged an unceasing war against them in the past, during the time of Muhammad Shah. The Rohillas had their seat at Barelli and the Bangash at Farrukhabad. While Safdar Jang was occupied at Delhi during 1750, his camp near Farrukhabad was suddenly attacked on the night of 3 August by Ahmad Khan Bangash, known in history as the lame Pathan. The Wazir's general Navalrai was killed and his whole camp was plundered. This was a grave disaster for the Wazir who had already been weakened at Delhi. The Pathans gathered their forces to the number of 60 thousand and marched into the Wazir's possessions. Safdar Jang prepared to meet the danger and urgently called in the help of the Jats and the Marathas under Sindia and Holkar, who had gone to the south to support the Peshwa at the accession of Ramraja and who were given leave by the Peshwa in July 1750 to proceed to the north.

Before the Maratha help arrived, Safdar Jang and his Pathan antagonists had fought a severe action at Kasgunj near Farrukhabad in the Doab on 12th September 1750. Here the Wazir again sustained a severe defeat, himself being wounded and carried away unconscious from the battlefield. This news reached Delhi and totally extinguished his waning prestige and the power, which he had for two years wielded at the capital. The Pathans after their victory marched straight upon Lucknow and for a time it was felt that all was lost for Safdar Jang. After plundering Lucknow the Pathans fell upon Allahabad and invested that fort, besides taking possession of Jaunpur and Ghazipur.

Safdar Jang feeling sorely distressed sought counsel with his shrewd wife Sadr-un-nisa Begam and some personal friends. They all with a united voice advised an alliance with the Marathas on any terms they would ask. Sindia and Holkar were nearing Kotah early in 1751; Safdar Jang sent his personal agents Raja Ramanarayan and Jugul Kishore, inviting them with all speed to run to his help. He himself left Delhi on 21st February and marched towards the east to relieve the pressure of the Pathans upon Allahabad. On the way he had a meeting with Jayappa Sindia and Malharrao Holkar on 2nd March and engaged to enlist their help on payment of Rs. 25 thousand per day. This was indeed a grave undertaking for the Marathas. The real antipathy was between the Emperor and the Pathans. The latter now dreamed of restoring the pre-Mughal Pathan Empire of Delhi as in the days of the Khiljis and the Tughlaks. They invited Ahmad Shah Abdali from the north-west and aimed a decisive blow at the Mughal Empire.

Writes Dr. Shrivastava, "The Ruhela and the Bangash Pathans were in treacherous alliance with the Abdali invader of Afghanistan. The history of the next ten years clearly demonstrates that Ahmad Shah Abdali swooped down the plains of northern India every time that his brother Pathans in Hindustan were hard-pressed by their enemies, not only to rescue them but also to help them in the realization of their dream, the Pathan supremacy over India. The Turani nobles of Delhi were the sworn enemies of the Wazir and were in secret sympathy with the Pathan rebels. Hence Safdar Jang could either allow the Pathans to usurp the Mughal supremacy and his own provinces of Oudh and Allahabad together with his office, or crush them with the help of the Marathas. He had to make a choice between two evils, a foreign invader assisted by enemies at home, or the Marathas who for years past had been distinctly loyal and been his own friends since 1747. One cannot accuse Safdar Jang of recourse to the humiliating expedient of calling in the Marathas."[2]

The Wazir in his extreme danger also engaged the support of the Jats on a promise of Rs. 15 thousand a day, similar to his stipulation with the Marathas.

In response to their undertaking, twenty thousand efficient Maratha troops entered the Doab and immediately routed the Bangash army under Shadil Khan at Kadirganj near Etawa on 20 March. This reverse immediately compelled Ahmad Khan Bangash to raise the siege of Allahabad and run to the defence of his capital of Farrukhabad. A very bitter struggle then ensued between the Marathas and the Pathans on the banks of the Ganges in that quarter. In the mean time two Rohilla leaders Sadulla Khan and Bahadur Khan with large forces came swiftly to the rescue of the Bangash. Gangadhar Yashvant of Holkar's party and Jawahir Sinh Jat advanced against these with fury and suddenness, and a heavy engagement was fought on 28th April in which ten thousand Rohillas were cut down along with their leader Bahadur Khan; Sadulla Khan saved his life by taking to flight. A large amount of plunder and a number of prisoners were secured by the Marathas.

At these occurrences Ahmad Khan Bangash completely lost heart and along with most of his followers decamped in the night. Several of his men were drowned in the river. The

2. *The First two Nawabs of Oudh*, p. 177; *Patre Yadi* 83.

Pathan camp was plundered and a large amount of booty was secured by the Wazir. Writes Govindpant Bundele, "The Pathans attempted the restoration of their rule at Delhi; and failing this, they wished to coerce the Emperor so far as to secure for themselves the posts of the Wazir and the Mir Bakhshi, so doing away with Safdar Jang's power. Ahmad Khan met the fate he deserved on the banks of the Ganges. If he had not been so routed, the Marathas would have lost all their labours and acquisitions of former years. The most faithless of all Pathans, Turai Khan had joined Ahmad Khan Bangash and was killed with all his followers." Thus it will be seen that at this critical juncture, it is the Marathas who saved the situation for the Empire. When the news of this Maratha victory over the Pathans reached Poona, a wave of enthusiastic joy spread throughout Maharashtra. The Peshwa offered his heartiest congratulations to the Sardars. Dattaji Sindia distinguished himself in this campaign of the Doab for the first time.[3]

3. **The Maratha objective.**—The object of the Marathas in all these undertakings was religious as well as political. They particularly intended to get the holy places of Prayag and Kashi back into Hindu possession. On 18th June 1751 a Maratha agent writes, "Malharrao has pitched his monsoon camp in the Doab. He intended to pull down the grand Masjid built by Aurangzeb at Benares and restore the original temple of Kashi-Vishveshwar. The Brahmans of Kashi feel extremely terrified at such a move, for they realize the Muslim strength in these places. What the holy Ganges and the Protector Vishveshwar can ordain will come true. The Brahmans are going to send a strong appeal to the Peshwa against any such attempt by his Sardars."

The Wazir-Pathan war was resumed after the rains. Instead of attempting conciliation, the Wazir disclosed a spirit of vengeance against the Pathans. The latter burnt their own lands and houses and resorted to the northern jungles and urgently invited Ahmad Shah Abdali to India. At this moment they obtained a unique leader, the famous Najib-ud-

3. Raj. 3. 160, 383, 384, 397; Raj. 6. 222; *Patre Yadi* 79, 82, 83.

daula, a bitter enemy of the Marathas and by no means friendly to the Emperor. He twisted the plain facts of the situation and took up the cry of "religion in danger," in order to denounce both the Marathas and their supporter Safdar Jang. The cry appealed to the common Muslim sentiment and helped to weaken the Maratha position. It was never obviously the intention of the Marathas to attack Islam or to convert Muslims to their faith. They were seeking only political power and through it religious freedom.

Towards the end of 1751 Abdali appeared again in the Punjab and the Emperor quaked in Delhi. He invited Safdar Jang to the capital to save the situation. The Wazir understood the danger, and extricating himself from the pursuit of the Pathans in which he was engaged, ran to Delhi. But before his arrival, the Emperor had sent his agents to Abdali, and agreed to give up the Punjab to him. Nor was the Wazir in a position to oppose the Abdali in a pitched battle. Sindia and Holkar were his allies. They had exhorted him in view of this fresh danger to conclude a peace with his Indian Pathans on reasonable terms through the medium of Gangadhar Yashvant, so that he (the Wazir) could devote his sole attention to the danger from the Shah of Afghanistan. In February 1752 the Wazir signed the treaty of Lucknow. By this treaty the Marathas obtained in lieu of their expenses and dues a large territory in the Doab, which henceforth they held right upto 1803 when Lord Lake conquered it from Sindia. The Peshwa's aim all along was not to seize the territory of others, but only to levy contributions in return for the protection he extended to them and to release the holy places from Muslim control. Muslim sentiment, however, proved too strong in this respect. The Muslim possession of the Hindu places was a matter of long standing prestige of conquest. Even Safdar Jang, otherwise so friendly to the Marathas and his son Shuja-ud-Daula, proved most unbending on this point of surrendering the holy places of the Hindus; and although they dared not give a flat refusal, knowing the strength of the Marathas, they usually bided their time by putting forth paltry excuses for not granting demand. At the present day the question has only an academic interest.

4. **The Punjab ceded to Abdali.**—In the meantime Najib Khan the leader of the Indian Pathans, smarting from the defeat he had to sustain at the hands of Safdar Jang aided by the Marathas, urged the Abdali Shah again to invade India to put down their enemy Safdar Jang and his usurping Maratha auxiliaries. In response to this invitation Ahmad Shah left Kabul in December 1751 and marched without opposition right up to the vicinity of Lahore. Mir Mannu continued sending urgent appeals both to the Emperor and to the Wazir for help. He resisted the Abdali Shah as long as possible, but finding himself worsted in an encounter near Lahore on 15th March 1752, he went to the Shah and in a personal visit effected an agreement to deliver up the two Subahs of Lahore and Multan to him (23rd March 1752).

The news of Abdali's return to the Punjab threw the Emperor and the city of Delhi into consternation. The Emperor sent angry summons to his Wazir to repair at once to the capital with the allied Maratha contingents. Safdar Jang received the call at Lucknow on 27th March and at once went and saw Sindia and Holkar at Kanauj as they were on the point of leaving for the Deccan. He effected with them a formal agreement for obtaining Maratha help in support of the Emperor's cause and ratified it on 12th April 1752 with solemn oaths and royal seals, the Wazir acting on behalf of the Emperor. The agreement contained the following material terms :—

(1) That the Peshwa should defend the Emperor from his internal enemies like the Pathans, the Rajputs or other rebels, and from external foes like the Afghan king Abdali.

(2) That the Emperor should pay 50 lacs to the Marathas for their help, of which 30 lacs was to be on account of Abdali and 20 lacs on account of internal foes like the Pathans.

(3) That in addition the Peshwa was given the right to levy Chauth from the Punjab, Sindh and the Doab.

(4) That the Peshwa be granted the Subahdarships of Agra and Ajmere, which he should administer on the traditional lines of Mughal rule.

(5) That if the Peshwa could not come personally to

serve the Emperor, he should depute his sardars for the purpose.[4]

To put this contract into execution Safdar Jang with Sindia and Holkar immediately went to Delhi, where they found on arrival that the agreement contracted with Abdali by Mir Mannu had been already ratified by the Emperor under his own signature on 23rd April. Kalandar Khan, Abdali Shah's agent had come to Delhi for the purpose, and as the Wazir had not arrived, the Emperor concluded the agreement in order to prevent Abdali from coming upon Delhi. The Shah returned home from Lahore immediately on the agreement being ratified. The Marathas were thus foiled in their first chance of expelling Abdali from the Indian soil. The sardars had come to Delhi for the purpose of proceeding towards the Punjab.

It is difficult to say why Safdar Jang delayed so long in reaching Delhi. His negotiations with the Marathas took time. The Wazir's enemies attributed the delay to the secret satisfaction that he felt at the Emperor being indirectly humbled. Although the Abdali Shah had returned home, Safdar Jang having come to Delhi was anxious at once to march into the Punjab and ensure its defence against the Pathan's further encroachment. The Emperor, however, would not support the Wazir, being terribly afraid of the latter's rising power. He refused to ratify the agreement made by him with the Marathas. The Maratha troops remained forcibly in Delhi and would not move away unless they received the promised 50 lacs. The presence of large armies in Delhi soon became troublesome to the populace, as in the absence of payment they freely plundered whatever they could lay their hands on. At this very moment came a call from the Peshwa for Sindia and Holkar to immediately repair to the south with Ghazi-ud-din. This proved a welcome solution of the immediate difficulty. Sindia and Holkar offered to go to the Deccan if the Emperor would grant the Subahdarship of the Deccan to Ghazi-ud-din, displacing Salabat Jang. Ghazi-ud-din was to pay a Nazarana of 30 lacs to the Emperor for his being confirmed : this amount was to

4. Raj. Vol. 1. 1 : Raj. 6. *Purandare Diary* p. 82 ; *Kotah Daftar* Vol. 1. 86.

be paid to the Marathas in part payment of the amount they had been promised. Thus the plan being settled, Ghazi-ud-din and the sardars left Delhi on 14th May and proceeded to the Deccan. We have already seen the sequel.

5. **Civil war in Delhi.**—Matters, however, grew worse between the Emperor and the Wazir. They became so suspicious of each other that they would not freely meet but considered themselves in danger of life from each other. Khoja Javid Khan, (Nawab Bahadur) with the Emperor's mother Udhambai the principal evil genius whom the Wazir would not tolerate, exercised all the imperial power. The Wazir managed to get rid of this Khoja by foul play. Inviting the Khoja to a dinner, he had him assassinated on 27th August 1752. This terrified the Emperor all the more so that the two became mortal enemies of each other. The Emperor realized that he was a mere prisoner in the Wazir's hands. Abdali was quick to discern the situation and sent his agent to Delhi demanding the yearly tribute of 50 lacs stipulated in the last year's agreement. The agent arrived at Delhi on 13th February 1753 and the Wazir with difficulty managed to send him back with some partial payment. The Wazir realizing his danger sent urgent calls to the Peshwa for armed help being quickly sent to him. The Emperor's mother Udhambai was a lady of great talent. She organized a strong opposition to Safdar Jang and moved the Emperor to fight him and remove him from his Wazirship. Intizam-ud-daula, son of Qamr-ud-din Khan was the Mir Bakhshi. and he joined Udhambai's scheme as also did Mir Shahab-ud-din, alias Ghazi-ud-din the younger. Antaji Mankeshwar commanded a small Maratha contingent at Delhi, and the Maratha envoys, the Hingne brothers, were approached by both the parties, the Emperor's and the Wazir's to support their respective cause.[5]

Antaji's graphic letter gives a vivid idea of life and conditions prevailing at this time at Delhi. He purposely wrote a clear description to the Peshwa and asked that either he himself or Sadashivrao Bhau should at once visit Delhi and personally resolve the Maratha entanglements, which, if allowed

5. *Aiti. Patravyavahar*. 89.

to drift, would surely bring about disaster. It is a pity the warning was not heeded. The Peshwa dispatched to Delhi his incompetent brother Raghunathrao, who made the confusion worse confounded, as the sequel will show. In the meantime the small but daring commander Antaji and a greedy ambassador like Hingne were called upon to deal with the grave situation at the capital as best they could. Everybody perceived that a civil war was about to rage in the capital, between the Emperor and his Wazir and Antaji's help was eagerly courted by both. Both offered him heavy bribes. Antaji recklessly agreed to support the Emperor, on condition that the two Subahs of Oudh and Allahabad, which had been held by the Wazir, should be given up to the Marathas.

At last open war broke out between the two principals at Delhi and continued for nearly eight months from 26th March to 7th November 1753. It is not necessary to describe it here in full detail. During the early phase of it, from 26th March to 8th May, there was hardly any actual fighting, as the Wazir though prepared to fight was long wavering whether he should resign his post and withdraw to his dominion of Lucknow. The second phase began on 9th May when Surajmal Jat arrived on the scene to support the Wazir, and the two chiefs besieged the Emperor in the fort and tried to capture his person by bombarding the palace. The slow progress of the war was brought to a sudden close by the unexpected arrival on the scene of Najib Khan Rohilla, a determined enemy of the Wazir : and although a time-server all along, his appearance to support the cause of the Emperor gave a decisive turn to the war. Fortunately the war did not extend beyond ten or twenty miles round Delhi.

On 13th May the Emperor dismissed Safdar Jang from his Wazirship and appointed Intizam-ud-daula in his place. Soon after the younger Ghazi-ud-din Imad-ul-mulk, then only 16 years old, resourceful though wicked, joined the Emperor. On 14th June a severe action took place at Talkatora in which Rajendra Gir Gosavi, a loyal supporter of Safdar Jang lost his life. Another pitched battle was fought on 19th August in which Safdar Jang lost his ground and began gradually to withdraw towards his own country. In the meantime the Emperor and Ghazi-ud-din wrote pressing letters to the Peshwa, to Sindia and to Holkar, to come with all speed to support the Emperor, offering one crore of rupees and the two Subahs of Oudh and Allahabad in return for their help.

As soon as the Peshwa received this call, he despatched Raghunathrao along with Sindia and Holkar from Poona. But before they could reach Delhi the war was over and there remained no need for Maratha troops in the north. The war had exhausted both parties. The Emperor invited Madho Sinh from Jaipur, who arrived and negotiated peace. The last action was fought near Barapula in which Safdar Jang lost heavily; he sent his agent to the Emperor asking pardon and praying that he should be allowed to retire to his two Subahs, renouncing all claim to the Wazirship. Wazi: Intizam-ud-daula. Udhambai, Madho Sinh and Surajmal all worked in their own ways in effecting a settlement between the two parties. A formal grant of his two Subahs was made to Safdar Jang, thus cancelling the promise already made to Antaji Mankeshwar. The treaty was finally concluded on 7th November 1753. Surajmal was pardoned by the Emperor for having joined in the war against him. Safdar Jang departed with all speed to Lucknow, thoroughly worn out by the trouble of war and the anxiety for his situation. He died within a year, on 17th October 1754 and was succeeded in the Subahdarship by his son Shuja-ud-daula, who figured prominently in the history of north India for the next twenty years.

CHRONOLOGY

CHAPTER XVIII

1749, June 10	Abhay Sinh of Marwar dies; his brother Bakht Sinh usurps the raj.
1752, June	Abhay Singh's son Ram Sinh seeks Jayappa Sindia's support to gain his kingdom.
1752, September 21	Bakht Sinh dies and is succeeded by his son Ajit Sinh.
1753, October 5	Raghunathrao crosses the Narmada for Delhi to set northern affairs right.
1753, November 3	Mir Mannu dies at Lahore; his wife Mughlani Begam seizes power.
1753, November 21	Khanderao Holkar at Delhi.
1753, December 17	Ram Sinh meets Raghunathrao and Jayappa at Jaipur and courts their help.
1753, December 17	Raghunathrao at the invitation of Ghazi-ud-din attacks the Jat Raja.
1754, January	Raghunâthrao invests Kumbher: the siege continues for 4 months.
1754, March 17	Khanderao Holkar killed; Malharrao swears vengeance against the Jat.
1754, May	Jayappa mediates peace with the Jat.
1754, May 17	The Emperor moves to Sikandarabad.
1754, May 18	Maratha armies leave Kumbher; Ghazi-ud-din and Raghunathrao fall upon Delhi.
1754, May 26	Imperial ladies plundered by Holkar's Pindaries.
1754, May 31	Emperor grants Ghazi-ud-din's demands.
1754, June 2	Ghazi-ud-din becomes Wazir; he deposes the Emperor and places Alamgir II on the throne.
1754, June 23	Jayappa Sindia goes to Marwar to support Ram Sinh.

1754, August 6	Jayappa at Merta.
1754, September 15	Jayappa routs Ajit Sinh at Merta—the latter flees to Nagore.
1754, October 25	Imperial *farman* issued granting districts in the Doab and the collection of pilgrim taxes by Marathas at Gaya and Kurukshetra.
1754, December	Raghunathrao enters the Rohilla country.
1755, Jan.-Feb.	Raghunathrao's pilgrimage to Garhmukteshwar.
1755, February 21	Jayappa captures Ajmere.
1755, March 3	Raghunathrao at Pushkar.
1755, April	Raghunathrao at Gwalior and thence he returns to Poona in August.
1755, July 25	Jayappa Sindia murdered at Nagore.
1755, October 16	Battle of Didwana in which Ajit Sinh's ally Anirudh Sinh is routed.
1756, January	Ajit Sinh visits Dattaji and begs for terms.
1756, February 7	Ghazi-ud-din at Sarhind; appoints Adina Beg to the Punjab and carries Mughlani Begam to Delhi.
1756, February	Malika Zamani and Najib Khan invite Abdali from Kabul to put down Ghazi-ud-din and the Marathas.
1756, October	Abdali's agent Kalandar Khan at Delhi demanding tribute.
1756, November	Peshwa despatches Raghunathrao to the relief of Delhi.
1756, December	Jahan Khan and Taimur Shah, defeat Adina Beg at Lahore and proceed to Delhi.
1757, January 5	Jahan Khan at Sarhind, followed soon after by Abdali. Mughlani Begam discloses to Abdali secret hoards of wealth at Delhi.
1757, January 28	Abdali enters Delhi.
1757, February	Abdali sacks and plunders Delhi with the help of Najib Khan.

1757, February 22	Abdali sends his generals towards Mathura.
1757, March 3	Abdali himself leaves Delhi for Mathura. The Jat Raja defies him.
1757, March 5—12	Week of the holi festival; Mathura subjected to untold atrocities; four thousand naked Gosavis fall fighting, having massacred a vast number of the Muslims.
1757, March	Cholera harasses Abdali's forces.
1757, April 1	Abdali leaves Delhi for Kabul, and rightly serves Mughlani Begam on the way.
1757, April	Abdali pulls down the Golden Temple of the Sikhs.
1759, December	Antaji Mankeshwar arrested and sent to Poona on charges of embezzlement.
1772, September 3	Ram Sinh of Marwar dies

Peshwa Raghunathrao

CHAPTER XVIII

MARATHA MISCONDUCT, ABDALI'S GRIP TIGHTENS

[1754—1757]

1 Raghunathrao before Kumbher.
2 The Emperor murdered.
3 Raghunathrao's mismanagement.
4 The Rathor War, murder of Jayappa.
5 Abdali invited.
6 Atrocities in Delhi.
7 Abdali's triumphant return.

1. **Raghunathrao before Kumbher.**—At Poona the course of events was not all running smooth. The Peshwa's plan of installing a friendly Ghazi-ud-din on the seat of the Nizam, fell through on account of that grandee's sudden murder. Sindia and Holkar had both been estranged in that transaction, as they had gained nothing for all the troubles and labours they had so long undergone. Jayappa Sindia and Malharrao Holkar, were openly hostile to each other. The Peshwa had fixed his attention long since on the conquest of the Karnatak : as he was no soldier himself, he always needed to have by his side some reliable person who could discharge efficiently the duties of a general. Such a person was his cousin Sadashivrao Bhau, who possessed both a stern and valiant character, but whose independent and unyielding temperament the Peshwa always feared. So when during the monsoon of 1753 urgent calls came to the Peshwa from Delhi, he made a choice which in the end proved fatal. He knew his brother Raghunath then 18 years old, was not capable of controlling difficult situations and divergent elements. But the recent conquest of Ahmadabad was to his credit, and the Peshwa deputed him to proceed to the north with Sindia and Holkar ; and himself marched into the Karnatak with Sadashivrao Bhau. The author of the latter's bakhar thus criticizes this move :—

"While Balajirao's reputation as a ruler was rising like the second moon in the Maratha State, his evil stars committed him to a wrong step in that he deputed Raghunathrao to gain his first experience in the north." This proved a fatal step.[1]

At this time Raghunathrao had with him most of the rising stars of the next generation, Sakharam Bapu, Chinto Vithal, Mahipatrao Chitnis, Shamsher Bahadur, Trimbakrao Pethe, Ramchandra Ganesh, Krishnarao Kale, Naro Shankar, Vithal Shivdev and Babuji Naik. They crossed the Narmada on 5th October 1753, and proceeding straight via Indore and Ujjain through the Mukundara pass, reached Jaipur in December having collected arrears of tribute on the way and overawed the Rajput chiefs. Govindpant Bundele joined the expedition from Bundelkhand.

There was hardly any particular objective for the Marathas at this time. The war for which they were so urgently invited had been closed, and now the presence of the large Maratha armies in the north was considered quite a nuisance, as they had to exact their subsistence from the inoffensive and hapless populace. In such circumstances unexpected hostilities with the Jat Raja of Bharatpur arose and were blindly welcomed by the Maratha leaders, as nothing better was then before them to occupy their energies. Surajmal Jat a valiant and powerful chief, ruled at Bharatpur possessing Kumbher and other fortified posts as strong bases. He had been the prominent supporter of Safdar Jang in the late civil war, and, although formally pardoned by the Emperor, was an object of bitter hatred to the Delhi Court and to the wicked Ghazi-ud-din the second, who now determined to punish him for his audacity. The Marathas had been recently granted the subahs of Agra and Ajmere in which they intended to establish their actual hold. The Subah of Agra was an object of greed to Surajmal, as it lay contiguous to his own possessions of Bharatpur and Mathura. The Subah of Ajmere was equally prized by the Raja of Marwar and excited the cupidity of Jayappa Sindia.

Malharrao Holkar sent his son Khanderao and his trusted lieutenant Gangadhar Tatya to Delhi to meet Ghazi-ud-din

---

[1] " बाळाजीपंत प्रधान बाजेच्या चंद्राप्रमाणें चढते केलें तें राज्य करीत असतां. पुढें विनाशकाले येणार भविष्य आलें, तेव्हां कलह लागण्यास कारण झालें कीं रघुनाथराव प्रथम स्वारीस हिंदुस्थानांत पाठविले." भा० ब० पृ. ४

and arrange plans for the campaign. They reached Delhi on 21st November and decided to conduct a war against the Jat raja. The Emperor not wishing to part with the Subah of Agra tried to conciliate Khanderao Holkar with presents and audiences; but the latter under the advice of Ghazi-ud-din spurned the Emperor's wishes and rejecting the presents returned to his father in January 1754, and hostilities were immediately opened against the Jat, by laying siege to Kumbher where the raja defended himself. Surajmal went to the farthest limit of conciliation in trying to avoid a war. For this purpose he sent his trusted Brahman minister Ruparam Kothari to purchase Maratha friendship offering to pay 40 lacs as the price of peace. Raghunathrao haughtily demanded one crore, upon which the Jat raja returned a small packet of gunpowder and shots in answer. Kumbher was at once invested and a bitter conflict lasted for full four months, January 20 to May 18, 1754. During the operations a chance shot killed Khanderao Holkar on 17th March, causing bitter grief to his father in his old age.[2]

In his agony Malharrao swore terrible vengeance against the Jats and would accept no compromise. Feelings ran high on both sides. Rani Kishori alias Hassia, the shrewd wife of Surajmal, whose advice he always sought in any difficulty, was well posted with the details of the severe estrangement existing between Malharrao and Jayappa. She won over the latter with gifts and friendly approaches. Jayappa agreed to use his influence and get Raghunathrao to raise the siege. The Jats defended Kumbher so valiantly that the Marathas had no prospect of victory. Malharrao felt extreme mortification at not being able to fulfil his solemn vow. Jayappa insisted that the best course was to come to an understanding with the Jat and end the futile fight, as Kumbher could not be reduced without long range guns which the Emperor possessed but

2. He was cut off in the prime of his life at the age of 30 and his wife the famous Ahalya Bai became a widow. She bore him one son Malrao who later died in 1767. Khanderao had other wives; three of these and seven maids burnt themselves alive on his funeral pyre. Ahalya Bai alone lived at the intense solicitation of her father-in-law Malharrao. Khanderao was certainly brave but was inordinately addicted to drink and dissipation. *Phalke series*, Gwalior 3. 205.

which he refused to lend. Under these circumstances a peace was concluded upon the Jat raja agreeing to pay 30 lacs in three yearly instalments and the Maratha armies left Kumbher on 18th May. Raghunathrao reaped failure.

2. **The Emperor murdered.**—Ghazi-ud-din was now the most powerful person controlling the affairs of the Emperor, whom he bitterly hated. He had failed to send the guns to Kumbher, and with the help of the Marathas Ghazi-ud-din prepared to vent his wrath on him. The Emperor now began to repent that he had exchanged Safdar Jang for Ghazi-ud-din. The latter's troops had received no pay for long, and as the Emperor would not give him funds, he besieged the palace and starved the inmates. Thereafter he crossed the Jumna and plundered several cities of the Doab. Intizam-ud-daula, the nominal Wazir could not help his master or stop Ghazi-ud-din's mischief. In order to obtain some relief Intizam-ud-daula carried the Emperor to Sikandarabad,[3] under pretext of a hunt, there to concert measures for securing help from the Rajput princes, the Jats and even from Safdar Jang. He removed the imperial zanana and their valuables to the same place, which he meant to fortify by bringing over the long range guns of Delhi.

Ghazi-ud-din watched these movements closely and with the help of Malharrao Holkar prepared to overpower the Emperor. The latter reached Sikandarabad on 17th May and the very next day the Maratha-Jat war was closed. Malharrao and Ghazi-ud-din marched together to Mathura with a view to falling upon Delhi, bringing out another Shahzada and deposing Ahmad Shah. This news reached the Emperor on 25th May at Sikandarabad and he became unnerved, and with his mother Udhambai and his favourite Begam Inayatpuri, started at night hurriedly to return to Delhi and entrench himself in the palace.

As soon as the Emperor's departure became known to Malika Zamani and other members of the harem (more than 350 all told), they hurriedly loaded their valuables on their

3. Sikandarabad is now in the district of Bulandshahar about 30 miles south of Delhi and 25 miles east of the Jamuna.

elephants and started in a long train for Delhi. The Maratha troops were not far off. They got news of these ladies escaping with their jewels and suddenly fell upon them, on the dark night of 26th May. The ladies were made prisoners and stripped of all their valuables and belongings: the camp of Sikandarabad was plundered of every useful article. When Ghazi-ud-din and Malharrao learned of this outrage on the imperial zanana, they felt ashamed. Malika Zamani called Malharrao to her presence and censured him. He slapped his own face in the Queen's presence and tried to plead his innocence saying that it was the work of the plundering Pindaries attached to the army. Malharrao caught hold of a few culprits and cut off their heads in her presence. He then collected all the ladies and their goods together and sent them two lacs for their expenses. Although the imperial jewellery was restored, a large stock of the Sikandarabad camp, 500 guns, tents, equippage and gold and silver trappings fell into Maratha hands. Ghazi-ud-din himself met Malika Zamani on 28th, fell prostrate before her and asked pardon.

But while these sad misfortunes were happening in the Doab, a big tragedy was being acted by Ghazi-ud-din and Malharrao near Delhi. Malharrao made some heavy demands upon the Emperor and himself followed to make them good. On 31st May the Emperor gave a written consent to all those demands. The Marathas began to plunder the outskirts of the city. On 1st June the Emperor removed Intizam-ud-daula from the Wazirship and appointed Ghazi-ud-din in his place. The next day a grand Darbar was held in which Ghazi-ud-din declared that Ahmad Shah was unfit to rule, brought out Azz-ud-daula, a grandson of Bahadur Shah, and placed him on the throne, giving him the name of Alamgir II. Ahmad Shah and Udhambai were made prisoners and kept confined. A few days later they were blinded and put to death. Such was the fate ordained for weaklings if they occupied imperial thrones.

Raghunathrao, Jayappa and other leaders soon after arrived at Delhi. Ghazi-ud-din promised them 82 lacs for their help in this grand revolution: what a contrast with the wise policy which Shahu Raja had followed throughout his long reign! The Maratha name and character henceforth received an indelible stigma.

3. **Raghunathrao's mismanagement.**—Let us now see what Raghunathrao did as the Peshwa's representative in the north. The new Emperor Alamgir II was now fifty years old, having been born on 6th June 1699. He had spent all his life within the prison walls of the palace and never breathed the free atmosphere of the outside world. He was intensely devoted to his religion after the manner of the great ancestor whose title he now adopted. He entrusted to the Maratha agents (the Hingnes) the work of collecting taxes on pilgrims at Gaya and Kurukshetra, which used to be formerly done by Muslims. A *farman* to this effect was issued on 25th October 1754. The Emperor wished to give over the management of the two holy places Prayag and Benares to the Marathas, but he was powerless in this respect as the places were owned by Safdar Jang. Although strict in religious observances, Alamgir's habits were licentious enough and he knew no moderation. He directed his lustful eyes on the youthful ladies of the imperial zanana.

Nor did the Emperor possess the nerve to exercise power independently in any affair. Whenever any one approached him with a complaint, he simply pointed to his Wazir. His aim in accepting the imperial dignity was simply to gratify his greed. He had a large family and needed funds for their maintenance and dignity. He had five sons, one daughter, in addition to the six sons of his brother, besides grand-sons and a great-grand-son. Each of these members had a stipend of 30,000 rupees yearly on paper. How to meet this huge expense was his first problem.

As regards the Wazir Ghazi-ud-din, he was certainly of all the imperial Wazirs the most selfish and unscrupulous ; and he lacked vision and a broad outlook. He utilised his talents in a time-serving policy, trying to gain his own ends. He inherited a large fortune from his father, more than a crore as was then reported. He had his own trained army numbering twelve thousand. But he could not gain the loyalty or devotion of his followers. All things considered, his master the new Emperor was ever ready to support him but the Wazir failed to earn his good will. No other Wazir witnessed such confusion, such lack of order and such poverty at the capital and outside, as happened to prevail during his six years of power. His own troops were always in want, never receiving their pay regularly. They tore the clothes off his person and dragged him through the streets of Panipat with such indignity as no other Wazir had ever before experienced. He promised enormous amounts to the Marathas for their help, but never fulfilled his word, so that they would not leave the capital until they received their dues. He would at one moment court the friendship of Najib Khan, at another seek favour from Abdali, but with none did he remain firm and true to his word. When ultimately he murdered the Emperor Alamgir in cold blood in 1759, he lost the confidence of all.[4]

It was with such a Wazir that Raghunathrao was called upon to deal immediately after the new Emperor was placed on the throne in June 1754. For full five months Raghunathrao remained moving near the capital trying in vain to obtain funds from the Wazir and the Emperor ; his huge forces consumed practically all that was available. He ultimately found his position so unbearable that in December he left Delhi and moved into the country of the Rohillas beyond the Jamuna. There he spent two months having holy baths and making pilgrimages to places like Garhmukteshwar. He could get no funds even here. He recrossed the Jamna and went into Rajputana for collecting tribute and after visiting Kannod, Narnol, Sambhar and other places, reached Pushkar on 3rd March 1755, accompanied by Malharrao Holkar.

At this time Jayappa Sindia was engaged in operations against Bijaysinh of Marwar. As Raghunathrao had nothing else to occupy him, he offered to join Jayappa : but the latter so strongly resented any interference in a task which he was handling with complete freedom and valour, that he sent a gentle hint to Raghunathrao not to come to Marwar. Raghunath, thus discomfited visited Gwalior which had just been captured by Vithal Shivdev, and finally returned to Poona at the call of the Peshwa.[5] It will thus be realized that Raghunathrao during his long expedition of nearly two years, September 1753 to August 1755, did nothing important which any

4. Thereafter there was no place where he could safely pass his remaining long life. Later on the Peshwas had pity on his misfortunes and gave him some lands in Bundelkhand where he with difficulty maintained himself till his death in 1802.

5. *Phalke series*, Gwalior 3. 284, 289 &c.

subordinate of his could not have done. Govindpant Bundele conveyed to the Peshwa plain sentiments disapproving Raghunathrao's ways and declaring that unless either the Peshwa himself or Sadashivrao came to the north, the lost ground could not be regained.

But the worst legacy that Raghunathrao left behind was the open hostility that he allowed to prevail between Antaji Mankeshvar, the Maratha commandant at Delhi and the Hingne brothers, the diplomatic representatives of the Peshwa at the Imperial Court. He could not reconcile these two chiefs any more than he could the other two, Sindia and Holkar. The origin of such disputes was in the greed of money. Whenever Maratha help was called for, it was the resident ambassador of the Marathas that was first approached, and he in his turn consulted the resident commandant. Hingne was the ambassador and Antaji the commander and each of them tried to utilise the occasion to improve his own monetary prospects. Hingnes also conducted a lucrative banking business, having branches in several outside places. Antaji's corruption and falsification of accounts became so notorious that the Peshwa issued orders to Sindia in 1759 to have him arrested and sent to Poona for trial. He arrived at Poona just at the time that Bhau Saheb was starting for the Panipat campaign ; and the latter had no leisure at the moment to examine the charges against Antaji. He was taken to the north along with the large Maratha armies and dearly paid by his death at Panipat for all his sins.

4. **The Rathor war, murder of Jayappa.**— Just as Malharrao Holkar after the death of Sawai Jaysinh obtained an excuse for interfering in the succession dispute of Jaipur, so now came the turn of Jayappa Sindia to interfere in the affairs of Marwar, when its ruler Abhay Sinh died on 10th June 1749, leaving a son Ram Sinh, not a very capable man, who expected to succeed to his father's throne, but who was set aside by the more valiant and warlike Bakht Sinh, brother of Abhay Sinh. The aggrieved Ram Sinh sought the support of Jayappa Sindia, who had looked for an opening to obtain ascendancy over the Rajput States and levy contributions. Jayappa assured Ram Sinh that he would take up his cause and help him to secure his father's throne as soon as he be-

came free from other pressing calls. In 1752 Jayappa when on his way to the Deccan escorting Ghazi-ud-din the elder from Delhi (June), made an attempt to help Ram Sinh to the throne; but Jayappa had with him only a small contingent at the time which was easily routed by Bakht Sinh. He was in a hurry to proceed to the south and could not then afford to go to Marwar. During the year 1753 when both Sindia and Holkar accompanied Raghunathrao to the north, Ram Sinh met them near Jaipur and reminded Sindia of his promise to help him to the throne. Raghunathrao agreed to depute Sindia for that purpose as soon as the affair of the war against the Jats at Kumbher would be settled. That affair occupied the Marathas for five months in 1754, and in June of that year Jayappa left for Marwar from Delhi accompanied by Ram Sinh. In the meantime Bakht Sinh had died (21st September 1752) and his young and energetic son Bijay Sinh had succeeded to the rulership of Marwar. Bijay Sinh had stationed himself at Ajmere which Jayappa invested, when the former considering Ajmere unsuited for carrying on prolonged hostilities, fell back upon Merta, about 40 miles northwest. Jayappa immediately followed Bijay Sinh to Merta in August and in a stiff action inflicted a severe defeat on the Rathors on 15th September 1754. Thereupon Bijay Sinh fell back still further north to Nagore another fortified place about 70 miles from Merta. Jayappa pursued him to Nagore and invested that place immediately. This siege of Nagore lasted long for nearly a year and now acquired a unique importance owing to the bitter fighting that raged round it between the Rathors and the Marathas. For a time it became a life and death struggle in that far away corner of sandy desert, where both water and food were scarce. Sindia in the meantime captured Ajmere on 21st February 1755 and expected that Bijay Sinh would submit. But the Rathor King was a man of resources and did not give up the struggle, although he all along kept up the show of negotiating for terms by frequently sending his agents into the Maratha camp. The Marathas got possession of most of the important posts of Marwar, including Jalor in the far south where the accumulated treasures of Bijay Sinh had been secreted, which now fell into Maratha hands. Even Jodhpur was attacked and there remained little hope for the Rathors to continue the struggle.

Nagore alone held out, as mines proved ineffective in the sandy foundations of the fort.

With the increase of the summer heat of 1755 the feelings of the combatants at Nagore also ran high, and Bijay Sinh looked out for some stratagem by which he could make short work of his redoubtable antagonist. The Rathor envoys were often coming and going from the fort of Nagore to Sindia's camp on the Peacock-lake (Taus-sar) about 7 miles distant, for negotiating peace terms. The talks were protracted over months and the party used to be accompanied by large numbers of clerks, accountants and servants. No foul play was suspected by the Marathas. On the morning of Friday 25th July, 1755, the Jodhpur Vakil Bijay Bharati Gosavi, accompanied by Rajsinh Chauhan and Jagneshwar, two of his helpmates, and a number of menials, some of whom were dressed like the Marathas, visited Jayappa's camp and held long discussions with him over the terms. The discussions were held in a tent in the middle of the open square of his camp, where the cavalry horses were tied in long rows. About 11 o'clock in the morning Jayappa's bath was ready, which he finished as usual openly seated on a wooden stool. Suddenly two beggars who had been picking up horse-grain in the compound ran at Jayappa, as he was drying his hair with a towel, and stabbed him, wounding him mortally, so that in an hour he died.[6]

A great hue and cry was at once raised. The ambassadors and the members of their party were cut to pieces by the infuriated Marathas. Before expiring, Jayappa gave full instructions to his brother Dattaji and son Jankoji for avenging the wrong without being in the least disheartened by his death. Thus fell a valiant Maratha soldier, a victim to the foul play of the Rajputs. Rawat Jait Sinh Sisodia an Udaipur representative residing with Jayappa, who happened to be present at the discussion, was innocently

6. These assailants had come in the party of the envoys dressed as beggars and watched for a suitable opportunity to get at Jayappa. It was a prearranged and deliberate attempt, not brought about by a sudden provocation produced by the insolence of Jayappa's language as is alleged by later writers. *Phalke series*, Gwalior 3. 320.

killed in the confusion, as every Rajput was considered succour.

Dattaji and Jankoji rose to the occasion and nothing daunted conducted the war all the more vigorously, having received speedy reinforcements from the various Maratha captains who were on duty at different places. Antaji Mankeshwar a daring soldier immediately started from Bundelkhand and successfully prevented Madho Sinh of Jaipur and other Rajput parties from reaching Nagore for Bijay Sinh's a suspect.[7]

Party-feeling between Sindia and Holkar ran so high that there were reports that Jayappa's murder was secretly instigated by Holkar. There is absolutely no proof on this point. But the Peshwa well knew the position of affairs and quickly recalled Malharrao to the south for conducting the war upon Savanur and left a free hand for the Sindia's party to close the Marwar operations with honour and advantage and vindicate the prestige of Maratha arms.

Jayappa's murder, however, did not avail Bijay Sinh in any way. He was soon brought to his knees mainly by the Sindian arms, although he tried to organize a formidable coalition of northern powers, including the Emperor, his Wazir, Najib-ud-daula, the Rohilla Pathans and others, in order to put down the Marathas. But such a heroic plan was beyond the powers of the Rathor prince. Madho Sinh of Jaipur despatched Anirudh Sinh with a strong force ; but he was routed in a pitched battle at Didwana on 16th October 1755; and he soon begged for terms. By the end of the year Bijay Sinh's position became so untenable that submission to Sindia's mercy was his only way of escape. He paid Dattaji a personal visit in January 1756 and agreed to the terms that were imposed. Dattaji too had learnt a bitter lesson and showed wise

7. Rajput accounts give a slightly different version of Jayappa's murder, declaring that it was not deliberately plotted in advance, that during the acrimonious discussion, hot words came to be exchanged and Jayappa uttered such insolent and foul language towards the accredited ambassadors, that in the heat of the moment they struck him down in an excited atmosphere. But the presence of armed and disguised assassins in the party of the ambassadors is a complete refutation of the defence put forth by Tod and the Vamsh-Bhaskar.

moderation. Bijay Sinh agreed to pay a fine of 50 lacs, ceded Ajmere and Jalor, and gave his cousin Ram Sinh a half share of his kingdom. Dattaji kept possession of Ajmere and had it strongly garrisoned for defence. He gave away Jalor to Ram Sinh ; but the latter continued to be unfortunate throughout life and died in distress on 3rd September 1772.

Thus after completing the requirements of a long and disastrous campaign Dattaji and Jankoji left Nagore, came to Ujjain in June and immediately proceeded to Poona. The Peshwa paid them a condolence visit in October at Chambargonda. Malharrao too came there for a visit, but Dattaji declined to receive him. The gulf between Sindia and Holkar widened.

5. **Abdali invited.**—Abdali's invasion of 1752 wrought almost as great a havoc upon India as that of Nadir Shah had done twelve years ago. Mir Mannu the Mughal Governor of the Punjab died on 3rd November 1753 and the affairs of the Punjab fell into extreme mismanagement. The principle of hereditary service then prevalent in India, ruined the State. The Emperor instead of at once appointing a capable man to hold the Punjab and guard the frontier securely, allowed Mir Mannu's widow Mughlani Begam to hold her husband's post in the name of an infant son who also died the following year. The Punjab now formed a part of the Afghan Kingdom with its Governor deriving his real power from the Shah of Kabul and not from the Emperor of Delhi. Mughlani Begam in order to retain her infant son in office looked to the Durani Shah for support. Ghazi-ud-din learning of the confusion at Lahore, started with a large force to make his own gain. He reached Sarhind on 7th February 1756 where Adina Beg, a competent Governor of the Doab, came and met him. Ghazi-ud-din sent him to Lahore, captured Mughlani Begam, the widow of the late Subahdar and her young daughter Umda Begam, with all her accumulated treasure and carried them to Delhi, after entrusting to Adina Beg the government of the Punjab. This Mughlani Begam was a woman of loose character, intriguing, and meddlesome, gaining her selfish ends by any unscrupulous means. When later on Abdali came to India she managed to gain his confidence and bring about the

ruin of Ghazi-ud-din who had wronged her, thereby affecting Maratha interests in no small measure.

Malika Zamani and other princely ladies of the Mughal harem came to experience actual starvation through the new Wazir's default of payment. He turned a deaf ear to their incessant pleadings, so that they in despair sent for Najib-ud-daula and held a long consultation with him about the situation. They all agreed that the Wazir was a creature of the Marathas, who had grasped all power, and that the only means of ousting the Marathas was to call Abdali to India. Thereupon Najib-ud-daula acting in the name of the ladies sent urgent and pathetic appeals to Abdali to come immediately to this land. Najib sent his own brother Sultan Khan to meet the Shah at Kabul and bring him with a sufficient force. Mughlani Begam, ousted from her power in the Punjab, wrote to the Shah, " I am ruined by the treachery of Indian chiefs. Goods and cash worth crores lie buried to my knowledge in the palace of my late father-in-law, Wazir Qamrud-din Khan, besides heaps of gold and silver stored inside the ceiling. If you invade India this time, the Indian Empire with all its riches will fall into your hands."[7a]

Abdali, however, did not want a war on his hands; and desiring to settle matters amicably he sent his envoy Kalandar Khan to Delhi in October 1756. But Ghazi-ud-din paid no attention to him. So the Shah arrived at Peshawar in November and sent his son Taimur Shah and his general Jahan Khan ahead to capture Lahore. Adina Beg was defeated in a fight and retired, and the Afghans came on conquering and plundering the territory right up to the banks of the Satlaj. On 5th January the Abdali's general Jahan Khan reached Sarhind without the least opposition. When such a state of weakness at Delhi was reported to the Shah at Peshawar, he himself left the place and came by quick marches right towards Delhi. The news of Abdali's sudden advance threw the people of Delhi into extreme consternation. The well-to-do gentry of the city went into the country with their valuables. Many retreated to Mathura thinking themselves safe at that holy

7a Excellent inside glimpses can be gathered from Hari Ram Gupta's recent fascinating publication "*Later Mughal History of the Punjab.*"

place. The Maratha commander Antaji Mankeshwar who was then near Gwalior, was summoned to repair to Delhi quickly. He came immediately with his band of five thousand troops. Woeful was the suffering of those who had left their homes at Delhi. They were robbed by the Jats and wild bandits on the way. The Wazir Ghazi-ud-din was powerless to cope with the situation. He visited Mughlani Begam and humiliated himself before her, to induce her to meet the Shah on the way and arrange for his return on payment of a heavy fine. Upon this Abdali's envoys came to the Wazir on 14th January asking for two crores and all the territory between the Indus and the Satlaj as the price of his return. In the meantime Najib-ud-daula joined Jahan Khan, the commander of Abdali's advance troops at Panipat.

The wicked Mughlani Begam began to play a double game. As the messenger of the Wazir arrived on a mission of mediation, she attained importance, got ready access to Abdali's counsels and managed to gain her own ends by supplying to the Afghan Shah all kinds of useful and valuable information about the Delhi government and its weakness. He too did not omit to humour her by showing extreme favour to her in order to profit by the information she disclosed of hoarded wealth. She knew men and affairs of Delhi intimately and disclosed full details to the Shah, including the plans and intrigues of the officials, the bankers and wealthy inhabitants and their secret treasures. The Shah was shrewd enough. To gain his own ends he treated her with affectionate favour, calling her his own daughter, and conferring on her the title of Sultan Mirza, as if she were his son. He bestowed on her as jagir the districts of the Jalandar Doab and Kashmir, and also obtained from her full details of the married and unmarried beauties of the Mughal palace and of the outside gentry including Hindus. This was indeed a selfish game of the Shah who arranged his further plans of squeezing wealth on the information he thus obtained.

6. **Atrocities in Delhi.**—When news actually arrrived that Abdali was nearing Delhi, the Emperor's Wazir on the 19th January left his palace alone with four servants and saw Abdali's Wazir Shah Wali Khan at his residence. The next day Shah Wali Khan took Ghazi-ud-din to the Shah's audience.

The Shah scolded Ghazi-ud-din for his incapacity and mismanagement and demanded one crore for confirming him in his post. Ghazi-ud-din replied, he had not even one lac, how could he think of a crore? Abdali next made his formal entry into Delhi on 28th January 1757 and had the Khutba read in his own name. He had with him a force of about 50 thousand troops, of which thirty thousand had come from Afghanistan, and about twenty thousand were new levies made in India.

The Abdali Shah now started a reign of terror inflicting all kinds of atrocities on the unfortunate residents not only of Delhi but of Mathura and other towns within about a hundred miles radius from the capital. The harrowing accounts of these atrocities are a most painful reading. How much wealth Abdali accumulated it is difficult to say: possibly he himself had no correct idea of it. In addition to what he might have carried away for his own State, most of his followers freely appropriated, whatever they could lay their hands on. A reporter writes "Most peoples' houses in Delhi were dug up to find hidden treasures. He sent his son escorted by ten thousand troops back to his country with loaded animals of accumulated treasure, choice horses, elephants, camels. People left their homes in huge crowds running for shelter to different localities. The territory round Delhi is now quite desolate. Mathura and Agra have also suffered the same fate. About 20 thousand Marathas and 15 thousand Jats are ready preparing for a conflict. The whole town of Delhi is occupied by the Pathan troops, each one of whom now owns a house occupying it as its real master. Many men have been killed; many women have been ravished; several committed suicide; others drowned themselves to avoid dishonour. All the imperial princesses that were discovered, have been married forcibly to these foreign invaders; every Hindu lady of handsome features was hunted out and taken into some Muslim harem. Najib Khan is appointed to govern the city. Abdali married the Wazir Ghazi-ud-din in his own presence to Umda Begam, daughter of Mughlani. Every house in the city was searched; every individual was examined for his belongings. Every householder was served with a written order to disclose his wealth. Those who resisted suffered terrible hardships. People brought out for sale whatever they possessed, but found no buyers. Several took poison and put an end to their lives. Minute details were supplied to the Shah by Mughlani Begam."

Antaji Mankeshwar did what he could to oppose the Shah Abdali's forces and sent full reports to the Peshwa. The news of the threat from Kabul had been very early received, and the Peshwa had not delayed a moment in despatching Raghunathrao and Holkar to Delhi in November 1756, that is, Abdali from Kabul and Raghunathrao from Poona started just about the same time and should have in the ordinary course faced each other near Delhi, as that city was almost equi-distant from the two bases. If Raghunathrao had moved as rapidly as Abdali did, the danger would have been warded off, at least much lessened. The Peshwa could not send back the Sindias as they had just arrived home after an arduous campaign in Marwar. Holkar probably was not inclined to face Abdali. It was the duty of Raghunathrao to go to Delhi expeditiously for the relief of the Emperor whom the Marathas had agreed to protect against all foreign danger. The Sikhs of the Punjab were Abdali's enemies, so that a strong Maratha force at or near Delhi would have prevented much of the plunder and atrocities that he committed.[8]

7. **Abdali's triumphant return.**—Having devastated Delhi for a month and drained out of it as much wealth as he could, the Abdali Shah on 22nd February 1757 sent some of his fanatical generals in different detachments to Mathura and other southern towns sweeping both the banks of the Jumuna. He gave clear orders to his men that "Mathura and other places are holy cities of the Hindus. It is your sacred duty to kill as many non-Muslims as you can and make heaps of their severed heads," promising that he would pay them Rs. 5 for each head. Mathura had no fortifications and fell an easy victim to the enemy's ferocious swords. Several houses were burnt down, idols in the temples were broken to pieces and trampled under feet. During the week of the spring festival of the Hindus, (5th to 12th March), the Afghans squirted the blood spray to imitate Hindu gaiety. They plundered Mathura, Brindavan and Gokul and filled the roads literally

8. P. D. 21. 104, 105, 107, 108.

with corpses. For days together the roads were impassable. Several thousand Hindus were cut down, Jahan Khan alone being responsible for slaying three thousand *Bairagis* and pilgrims.

Abdali himself moved from Delhi on 3rd March and advanced as far south as Mathura. He threatened the strong places of the Jat Raja, Dig, Kumbher and others. The Raja kept a watchful attitude, remaining on the defensive. He did not visit the Afghan King but sent his agents to negotiate a fine, at the same time preparing to oppose him if the occasion required it. This threatening demeanour of the Jat deterred Abdali. The Raja was saved from any loss or injury.

This successful defiance of Abdali by the Jat Raja is sufficiently eloquent, to prove that if Raghunathrao had advanced quickly, much of the havoc could have been prevented. When the Pathans came against Gokul under Abdali himself, four thousand naked Gosavis of that place came to oppose them and fought with such valour that several thousand of his followers were killed. This bitter experience was enough to make Abdali turn his back upon India. He sent Jahan Khan to Agra where also the same cruelties were perpetrated during a fortnight's siege of that place.

It was now the end of March and the summer of India with its extreme heat set in. The waters of the Jumuna had practically dried up and what little remained became foul with the decaying corpses; the only source of drinking water for the people being thus contaminated, a terrible epidemic of cholera started in the ranks of Abdali, nearly 200 deaths taking place daily. He wisely retraced his steps on 24th March from Gokul and after reaching Delhi quickly, did not stay there more than a day. He reinstated the Emperor Alamgir on the throne with all his former dignity, appointed Ghazi-ud-din as his Wazir and Najib-ud-daula his Mir Bakhshi and on April 1st departed for his native country. Reports declared that he carried away 12 crores of wealth altogether, of which he acquired 4 crores from the single house of the ex-Wazir Khan Khanan Intizam-ud-daula and one crore from Ghazi-ud-din. He carried away as well Muhammad Shah's daughter and other ladies from the imperial harem. They raised a terrible wail of grief and cries at such banishment for life. Abdali stationed Taimur Shah and Jahan Khan at Lahore for the protection of the Punjab and quickly returned to Kabul.

Mughlani Begam, however, got her deserts fully. Having obtained from her whatever he needed for his purpose, Abdali threw her over and had no time to attend to her solicitations. She followed him with resentment and angry cries up to the Chenab. But in the new government which Abdali established at Lahore, he made no provision for this grasping lady. His son Taimur Shah was married to the Emperor Alamgir's daughter Muhammadi Begam and given the charge of the Punjab; and when Mughlani found that she received no commission, no reward, not even the promised jagir, she became wild and showered filthy abuses upon the invader. She had nothing in hand to live upon and began to beg at Lahore from door to door. Once she went to the Wazir Shah Wali's tent asking redress but received such a severe caning in return that her mental condition can better be imagined. In Lahore where she had enjoyed only a little while before honours and position in her husband Mir Mannu's days, she had now to suffer such indignity as cannot be described in words."[9]

9. Maratha history is not concerned with the subsequent life of the Begam. She settled at Jammu and had little scope for interfering in politics. She died in 1779. Her life is fully recorded in Persian by her personal servant Miskin (one copy in the possession of Sir J. N. Sarkar), which supplies personal information on the political intrigues of the north west.

CHRONOLOGY

CHAPTER XIX

1756, October	Raghunathrao leaves Poona and Abdali Kabul, for Delhi.
1757, February 14	Raghunathrao at Indore.
1757, April	Abdali leaves Delhi for Kabul.
1757, May	Raghunathrao at Agra where Najib Khan submits his terms.
1757, August	Raghunathrao takes charge of Delhi ; Najib Khan is captured, but Malharrao saves him from being confined.
1757, September 6	Najib Khan leaves Delhi : the Doab is secured by the Marathas.
1757, October 22	Raghunathrao starts from Delhi for Lahore.
1758, January	Raghunathrao at Kunjpura.
1758, March 8	Raghunathrao reaches Sarhind, and captures it : Governor Abdus-samad Khan submits.
1758, March	Taimur Shah and Jahan Khan are expelled from Lahore by the Marathas.
1758, April 11	Raghunathrao takes up residence in Lahore.
1758, May	After arranging to hold the Punjab Raghunathrao starts for return to Poona.
1758, June 5	Raghunathrao at Kurukshetra.
1758, July	Tukoji Holkar and Sabaji Sindia subjugate the whole of the Punjab and plant the Maratha banner on the fort of Attock.
1758, August	Raghunathrao and Holkar marching through Rajputana, meet Jankoji and Dattaji Sindia returning to the north near Kotah instruct them to guard the Punjab properly.
1758, August 19	Jankoji and Malharrao meet near Kotah.
1758, September 16	Adina Beg dies ; Raghunathrao reaches Poona.
1758, December	Holkar and Gangadhar Yashvant meet the Peshwa in Poona. They immediately return to the north. Dattaji and Jankoji at Delhi.

M. H. II—26

1759, February 1	Sindias leave Delhi for the Punjab.
1759, March	Ali Gauhar and Shuja-ud-daula march upon Patna but are turned back by Clive and Knox.
1759, April	Dattaji appoints Sabaji Sindia at Lahore to hold the Punjab.
1759, May	Dattaji returns from Lahore.
1759, June 1	Dattaji crosses the Jamna into the Doab.
1759, June	Najib Khan pays an abortive visit to Dattaji. He agrees to construct a bridge at Shukratal.
1759, July	Dattaji pitches his camp near Shukratal.
1759, September 15	Dattaji attacks Najib Khan but fails.
1759, October 21	Govindpant Bundele crosses the Ganges and harasses the Rohillas.
1759, October	Abdali takes possession of Lahore.
1759, November 8	Sabaji driven from Lahore reaches Dattaji's camp near Shukratal.
1759, November 30	Ghazi-ud-din murders the Emperor, the ex-Wazir and four others.
1759, December 3	Abdali comes on thundering from Lahore.
1759, December 11	Dattaji hurriedly marches towards Delhi.
1759, December 18	Dattaji crosses the Jumuna at Kunjapura
1759, December 24	A severe action takes place at Thaneshvar between Dattaji and Abdali.
1759, December 31	The two opponents face each other near Barari Ghat with the river Jamuna between.
1760, January 6	Dattaji sends away his baggage and non-combatants and prepares to face Abdali boldly.
1760, January 10	Dattaji falls fighting at Barari Ghat and Jankoji is wounded: their army falls back upon Kotputli. Abdali takes possession of Delhi.
1760, January 13	Malharrao Holkar in Rajputana learns the news of Dattaji's fall.
1760, February 5	Malharrao Holkar joins the Sindias.
1760, Feb.—March	Running fight between the Marathas and the Afghans: the latter prove too strong.

CHAPTER XIX

ABDALI'S TRIUMPHANT ADVANCE

[1759—1760]

1 Raghunathrao at Delhi. 2 The Marathas reach Attock. 3 Failure to restrain Najib Khan. 4 Dattaji locked at Shukratal. 5 Dattaji falls at Barari Ghat.

1. Raghunathrao at Delhi.—It has already been mentioned that it was never the intention of Shah Abdali of Kabul to gain the crown of Delhi and rule India. He scrupulously avoided entanglements and commitments in Indian affairs. His only purpose was to hold the Punjab if possible up to the river Satlaj, and assure himself of a steady income to meet the expenses of his large army and the administration of his poor country. If Najib Khan, Malika Zamani, and other anti-Maratha elements had not played a hostile part, there was every possibility of matters being settled amicably between the Marathas and the Afghan King. Whenever there appeared a chance for such rapprochement, Najib Khan intentionally came in the way and prevented an understanding with the Marathas.

From Attock to the Bay of Bengal stretches a vast plain of enormous extent unimpeded by any natural obstacles except the numerous rivers all easily fordable in the dry season, and unless some special arrangement was made at Attock or Lahore to hold a strong enemy in check, any conqueror from beyond the Indus valley could easily sweep down the whole north Indian region, as had been exemplified times without number ever since the day of Alexander. The Wazir and the Marathas failed to make proper provision in this respect. Raghunathrao left Poona in October 1756 and should have reached Delhi in time to face Abdali and compel him to return. But moving slowly and having no strength to enforce his own judgment, he reached Indore on 14th February 1757, when Abdali had sent out parties against Mathura. Raghunathrao and Malharrao occupied themselves in exacting tributes from the

Rajput thereby contracting their ill-will, and reached Agra in May, where Ghazi-ud-din welcomed them with all his heart. In the absence of Abdali, Najib Khan felt terribly afraid of Maratha vengeance and proposing the following terms of submission, thus wrote to Malharrao :

1. I am your son, not deserving chastisement at your hands. I am ready to hand over Delhi to your possession and walk away to my own lands beyond the Jamuna.

2. If you so desire, I am quite ready to bring about a permanent understanding between you and the Shah Abdali and fix up the demarcation of the spheres between you two.

3. I am prepared to keep my son Zabeta Khan with a party of seven thousand armed followers in your camp, as my hostage, by way of guarantee for the due performance of my undertaking.

4. If with all this you are bent upon waging a war against me, I am ready to accept the challenge, placing my faith in God and His decision.[1]

This was a reasonable proposal and should have been readily accepted. But Najib Khan had made himself so odious to the Emperor that the latter preferred Ghazi-ud-din to him. The Marathas entered the Doab and soon captured not only all the territory up to Saharanpur, but easily took possession of Delhi itself in August, after a fortnight's struggle. Najib Khan was captured with all his friends and followers by Vithal Shivdev, who for that achievement was rewarded by the Emperor with dresses and ornaments and given the title of Umdat-ul-mulk and a jagir near Nasik, which his family still holds.

1. P. D. 2. 77. See also Nuruddin Hussain's *Life of Najib-ud-daula* translated by Sir J. N. Sarkar (Marathi version in *Ait. Patrav.* No. 447). Dr. Shrivastav in his life of Shuja-ud-daula (I) writes (p. 30 and 53) :— "Determined to revive the long forgotten days of Aurangzeb, the Qazi of the town of Benares rallied a party of fanatical Muslims and demolished on 2nd September 1755 the renovated temple of Vishveshwar situated in a corner of the Alamgiri mosque. Upon this the Peshwa asked Shuja to hand over the holy city to the Marathas. He prepared a sanad to that effect and made it over to the Maratha agent Gopalrao Ganesh. But Raghunathrao broke off the negotiations with Shuja." P. D. 21. 124; 27. 165.

Najib Khan's character was well-known to every Maratha and even every Muslim in the north. He had all along been the chief source of mischief for the Marathas, and had early in the year himself participated in the atrocities inflicted upon the Hindus of Mathura, Agra and other places and in the terrible desecration of Hindu shrines. It was, therefore, highly necessary to keep him permanently secured, preferably in a distant southern fort after the fashion of Chanda Saheb at Satara. Every Maratha of Delhi and the north advised such a course to Raghunathrao. But Najib wormed himself into Malharrao's bosom. He made piteous appeals to him, that if he were saved from death or indignity he would serve the Maratha cause with all his heart. Malharrao was moved ; the author of *Siyar-ul-mutakherin says,* Holkar received large bribes from Najib Khan and earnestly pleaded with Raghunathrao to release the Khan and utilise his services to strengthen the Maratha hold not only over Delhi and the surrounding regions but also through him and the Pathans of the lower Doab, over the eastern lands of Benares and beyond. The prospect was indeed alluring. Raghunathrao could not resist Holkar, and yielding to his entreaties, allowed Najib to depart unscathed to his home on a verbal promise never more to interfere with the concerns of Delhi and to surrender all his fortified posts in the Doab to the Marathas. The serpent's tail was merely trodden upon. On 6th September Najib left Delhi for his patrimony.

Najib Khan having been removed, Raghunathrao formally installed the Emperor on the throne, confirmed Ghazi-ud-din in the Wazirship and appointed Ahmad Khan Bangash Mir Bakhshi. He then despatched parties to take possession of the Doab and himself proceeded to Garh-mukteshvar apparently to settle the government of the territory surrendered by Najib Khan, but really to take a holy bath in the Ganges and purify his soul by a visit to the numerous sacred spots and scenes reminiscent of the ancient epic days. Renko Anaji and other Maratha captains secured Saharanpur after driving away Najib's deputy Qutb Shah, and proceeded up to the foot of the Himalayas driving Najib Khan to his original home beyond the Ganges. Raghunath wrote to the Peshwa glowing accounts about these achievements. He boasted of having established Maratha supremacy throughout north India from the Satlaj to the environs of Benares and proposed that he would soon release the Punjab from Abdali's possession. Not a few discerning Maratha agents in the north brought to Raghunathrao's notice the weakness of these arrangements, but the chief was so hypnotised by Holkar that he turned a deaf ear to them. Antaji Mankeshvar, the Hingnes, Govindpant Bundele, Gopalrao Barve, and others like them were all more or less corrupt, carrying on nefarious transactions to satisfy their selfish greed or private pique. After spending four months in arranging the affairs of Delhi where Antaji Mankeshvar and Krishnarao Kale were stationed, Raghunathrao left for the Punjab on 22nd October, the Dassara day, accompanied by Malharrao. They reached Kunjpura in January, accepted submission from its commandant Najabat Khan in February 1758 and reached Sarhind on 8th March.

2. **The Marathas reach Attock.**—Here the Marathas for the first time came into contact with the Sikhs who had been bitter enemies of the Pathans of the trans-frontier regions, and who had the ambition of creating an independent Punjab as their motherland. During the ten years 1755-65 there appeared three powerful leaders of the Sikhs, Jasasinh Ahluwalia, the founder of the present State of Kapurthala, Alasinh Jat (Ala Jat of the Maratha papers) founder of Patiala, and Jasasinh Ramgadia, who all successfully fought and resisted the aggression of Ahmad Shah Abdali, whom they hated more than they did the Marathas. During 1757 Ahmad Shah Abdali after demolishing the Hindu shrines of Mathura, pulled down on his way back through the Punjab the golden temple of the Sikhs at Amritsar and filled up with earth the sacred lake in front of it. But no sooner did the Afghan King turn his back, than the Sikhs rebuilt the temple and restored the lake which we see to this day. Abdali had left his son Taimur Shah and his general Jahan Khan at Lahore for the government of the province with a fairly large army of occupation. At Sarhind Raghunathrao discussed the question whether he should proceed to Lahore or turn back without caring to subjugate the Punjab, which the Sikhs were disputing with the Pathans. But the Emperor and Ghazi-ud-din were anxious to

recover the Punjab, and Adina Beg the Mughal Governor of the Jalandar Doab between the Satlaj and the Bias, was already waging a relentless war against the Pathans with the help of the Sikhs and encouraged R'rao in that project. This appeared in a way a mad venture particularly as the Marathas thereby lengthened their line of communication with their base at Poona, while they had no means of holding a territory extending to the Indus. This would have been possible if the Maratha position at Delhi had been made perfectly secure as against their antagonists Najib Khan and Malika Zamani.

Ever since the invasion of Nadir Shah, the Punjab had been the land of constant contention between various forces and so subject to plunder and devastation that the residents had developed a sort of resigned mentality bowing to the inevitable. Raghunathrao laid siege to Sarhind, which had a garrison of ten thousand Pathan troops commanded by Abdussamad Khan. The Khan was wounded and made his submission to the Marathas, agreeing to serve them in the same way that he had done Abdali before. In this fight of Sarhind Ala Sinh Jat joined the Marathas to expel the Pathans. At this moment Taimur Shah and Jahan Khan were already being harassed at Lahore by Adina Beg and now, learning that the Marathas after capturing Sarhind were coming in strong bodies against them, the two Afghan chiefs evacuated Lahore and fled to their native land with as much wealth and goods as they could carry. They were hotly pursued by the Marathas, and had to leave all their equipage and belongings on the river Chinab as they could not carry them away with safety and these were easily secured by the Marathas. They then gave up the pursuit of the retiring Afghans and returned to Lahore.[2] Raghunathrao reached Lahore on 11th April and was right royally entertained with joyful illuminations by Adina Beg and others in the Mughal palace of Shalemar. This was the Maratha New year's Day of the Bahudhanya Shaka.

The territory between the Satlaj and Attock was in those days distributed for administrative purposes into three divisions, the southern, the middle and the northern, with their

2. Letter of Hari Bhide, P. D. 27. 218.

capitals at Multan, Lahore and Srinagar. When Raghunathrao with his valiant bands was so enthusiastically welcomed at Lahore and Prince Taimur and Jahan Khan had returned precipitately in great discomfiture, Abdali became almost hopeless of recovering that land, particularly as the Sikhs were his worst enemies. From subsequent events one is apt to ridicule this as an audacious venture of the Marathas trying to hold such an extensive country from Poona. But the conditions of 1758 did not warrant any such fears. Abdali was then finding extreme difficulty even in holding his own. In 1758 he was threatened by the Persians from the west; his own nephew Abdur Rahman rose against him and went to Poona seeking the Peshwa's support in regaining his inheritance. The three Sikh chiefs mentioned above were brave leaders and allies commanding a considerable following of the best soldiers in Asia.

At Lahore, therefore, Raghunathrao and his advisers found the situation easy and favourable. Abdussamad Khan who was a prisoner in Maratha hands, with characteristic double-dealing offered to undertake the defence of the frontier against Abdali on behalf of the Marathas. From Poona the Peshwa despatched Abdur Rahman with all haste to Lahore with instructions to Raghunath to make the best use of him in the scheme he was now executing. Raghunathrao, therefore, consigned the trans-Indus regions of Peshawar to these two Muslim agents, Abdur Rahman and Abdussamad Khan, posting them at Peshawar, with a considerable body of troops. They were asked to capture the territory of Kabul and Kandahar which had formerly been parts of the Indian sphere of the Mughal Empire and which had been lost since the days of Muhammad Shah. This meant a complete extinction of Ahmad Shah Abdali, a man of supreme resourcefulness and capacity in which he equalled or excelled even Nadir Shah. Herein lay the hidden danger, which no one then could gauge or foresee. After all it is the personal factor that predominates in human affairs and that cannot be predetermined.

Tukoji Holkar, Sabaji Sindia, Renko Anaji, Rayaji Sakhadev, Gopalrao Barve, and other captains were asked to hold the Punjab for a few months before Dattaji Sindia could arrive and make some permanent arrangement. Dattaji was then at Poona and momentarily expected to come to the Punjab. Obviously the weakest link in the chain was that no strong Maratha leader of prestige was associated with Abdussamad Khan to guard and hold Peshawar, the trans-Indus gateway of India in the north-west. The Peshwa sent distinct orders to station Holkar at Lahore. As Dattaji was shortly expected, the provisional arrangement was hoped by Raghunathrao and Holkar to last a few months without disturbance. But well posted with all Indian details as Abdali was, he struck at this very weak point, utilised Najib Khan and killed Dattaji. One can never leave things to chance. The responsibility for these consequences comes home to Holkar.[3]

Raghunathrao and Holkar left for the Deccan towards the end of May 1758 having on the way performed their religious ceremonies on 5th June at Kurukshetra. The other party of Abdur Rahman and Abdussamad with Tukoji Holkar and Sabaji Sindia left for the frontier and about July planted the Maratha standard on Attock and established revenue administration in that extreme north-western region. Adina Beg accepted the responsibility of paying 75 lacs to the Marathas by way of income from the newly conquered territories of the Punjab. The revenue management was entrusted to Sadiq Beg and his Hindu banker Lakshmi Narayan. All Maharashtra felt electrified with the proud performance of Raghunathrao and his bands having reached the extreme frontier of India and bathed their horses in the Indus.[4] It is, however, true that the Maratha possession of these distant regions did not last long, perhaps half a year. Adina Beg's death on 16th September 1758 gave the first signal of the impending danger; and later on Abdali during the summer of 1759 was able to recover from his internal troubles. He retook Peshawar in August and shortly after marched into the Punjab. But be-

3. *Phalke series*. Gwalior 3. 92, 376 and 112.

4. Sir Jadunath in his *Fall of the Mughal Empire* II, p. 76 wrongly asserts on the strength of P. D. 27. 218 that the Marathas never went beyond the Chinab river. But Chandrachud Vol. 1. 49 and another part of it printed later at Gwalior by Dongre No. 4. (two important papers) clearly prove that the Marathas captured Attock and for a time collected taxes and administered the districts right up to the Indus. Akhbarats and other sources support this conclusion.

fore we take up the narrative of 1759, we must first conclude the story of the return journey of Raghunathrao and his party in a false hope that all was well on the frontier.

3. **Failure to restrain Najib Khan.**—All friends of the Maratha cause sent urgent and pathetic appeals to Raghunathrao not to think of returning to the Deccan quickly, but to canton at or near Delhi in order to give stability to the arrangements just made, and to exercise a check upon evil-doers and inspire confidence among those who like the Pathans of the Doab were vacillating. In fact Raghunathrao received strong appeals from various quarters that he should stay on till at least Dattaji Sindia or some other responsible leader should arrive on the spot. But Raghunathrao played into the hands of Malharrao Holkar, who was deluded by the mischievous Najib Khan's assurance that all was well and that he would see to it that Abdali did not return. While he was making these professions, Najib was actively intriguing with that monarch to come to India and save the Muslim interests from Maratha aggression. Even this double dealing of Najib Khan was plainly reported to Raghunathrao by several responsible agents, but he turned a deaf ear to all such suggestions and directly set out in haste from Karnal on his homeward journey without visiting Delhi on the way.[5] He should have at least clearly reported these protests to the Peshwa before going back.

As Malharrao was anxious to collect tribute from the Rajputs, the two marched separately through Rajputana to Malwa. On the way they accosted first Jankoji Sindia and then Dattaji both proceeding to the north. These two had not started from the south together. Jankoji left Poona in February 1758 and Dattaji in May after having celebrated his own marriage with Bhagirathibai in March. Jankoji reached Ujjain in March and after spending a couple of months there proceeded to Kotah, where in July he met Raghunathrao then on his return home. In this visit they fully discussed matters of moment and the general situation at Delhi and in the Punjab.

5. A vast number of letters speak this sad tale, which the student should carefully note. P. D. 2. 88, 89; P. D. 21. 156-158; P. D. 27. 150, 156, 226, 229. *Bhau Sahib Bakhar* is most eloquent and records facts from authentic sources.

Raghunathrao strongly impressed on Jankoji's mind how Malharrao obstructed any action being taken against Najib Khan, who required to be checked in time and prevented from creating mischief. How utterly foolish was it to expect Jankoji to do what he as a master had failed to effect! Raghunathrao begged Jankoji, "You must do me this one favour, never mind even if it cost a crore or vast armies, viz., you must restrain this Najib Khan finally. Malharrao considers Najib as his adopted son. He has many such sons to look after. Najib is terribly wicked and will surely ruin the Maratha prospects."

In a few days, on 19th August, Jankoji saw Malharrao himself returning. He tried to avoid a personal meeting after his experiences of Nagore and the murder of Jayappa; but Gangoba Tatya brought about an interview between them. After all Najib Khan was not restrained. He did the mischief for which the Marathas had to suffer in the end.[6] Dattaji reached Ujjain in June and in a short time met Raghunathrao and Malharrao returning from the north. The same talks were held between them as with Jankoji.

Raghunathrao reached Poona on 16th September and in his own way communicated a full tale to the Peshwa of what he had been able to accomplish in the north, particularly how, owing to Malharrao's interference Najib Khan was left at large. The Peshwa at once detected the lurking danger and sent for Malharrao to Poona in all haste for a personal explanation. Unfortunately Malharrao then was seriously ill at Indore during October and November. He sent Gangadhar Yashvant on to Poona to explain matters and himself followed in December. In January the Peshwa directed Malharrao immediately to repair to the north and support the Sindias. This Malharrao failed to do, why it is not possible now to determine. He spent one full year (1759) doing nothing important, mostly in Rajputana, from whence he hastened to Delhi on 13th January 1760 after learning at Jaipur that Dattaji had fallen at Barari Ghat on the 10th of that month.

4. **Dattaji locked at Shukratal.**—We shall now narrate

6. See P. D. 2. 94. 21. 162; Kotah Daftar 1. 183, 190. Note the strong words used by Marathi writers in describing Najib Khan.

how the mistakes of Raghunathrao and Malharrao and incidentally of the Peshwa brought about the ruin of Dattaji Sindia. In November 1758, Dattaji and Jankoji met at Rewari and proceeded to handle the situation of Delhi with which they had no occasion till then to be conversant, nor a first hand acquaintance particularly with the character of Holkar's proteges Ghazi-ud-din and Najib Khan. This meant that they were called upon single-handed to execute the commitments which had been already made, viz. to restrain Najib Khan, provide for the defence of the Punjab, release the Hindu holy places from Muslim control, and acquire funds to the extent of a crore or two for paying off the Peshwa's debts. The last item required the extension of Maratha power on the east up to Patna. These were the grand tasks entrusted by the Peshwa to the Sindias and solemnly accepted by them, in colossal ignorance of the circumstances.

When the Sindias arrived at Delhi, Vithal Shivdev was near Saharanpur seizing the Rohilla possessions. Najib Khan had then collected a large force and was openly defying the Marathas. Arriving at Delhi in December the Sindias were compelled to waste three precious months in arranging the affairs of the Emperor and the Wazir, in which they had to act with unprecedented sternness. The Emperor's son and heir apparent Ali Gauhar, later known as Shah Alam II, had left Delhi the previous year and was trying to take possession of the eastern territories of Bihar and Bengal, which had now been practically seized by the English East India Company. He invaded Patna in conjunction with the Nawab Shuja-ud-daula of Lucknow in March 1759 but was turned back by Clive's troops under Col. Knox.

Dattaji found Ghazi-ud-din utterly worthless for the execution of any useful plan, so that the former paid no attention to him and managed matters independently. He sent his forces to capture Najib Khan but failed. He, therefore, decided first to settle the affairs of the Punjab and then start operations against Najib. With this object he left Delhi on 1st February 1759 and proceeded to the Satlaj where Sadiq Beg and Adina Beg's widow and son met him. In consultation with them and with the other advisers he posted Sabaji Sindia at Lahore for the protection of the Punjab as Sabaji had already subjugated the territory right up to the Indus. The Peshwa had suggested the name of Naro Shankar for the sole charge of the Punjab and Dattaji also accepted the suggestion, but Naro Shankar was not very enthusiastic on the point and would not accept the commission without express written orders from the Peshwa. Dattaji did indeed realize the necessity of a first class Maratha sardar being permanently posted to Lahore: but this he thought could be later done by the Peshwa himself. Dattaji could not personally remain in Lahore as he had other momentous affairs on hand. There was then no news of any threat from Abdali and things were quiet beyond the frontier.

After making the best arrangements he could, Dattaji returned from the Punjab in May, crossed the Jamna into the Doab on 1st June and set himself to overcoming Najib Khan. Dattaji was accompanied by Govindpant Bundele, a steady and conciliatory man who had direct intimate dealings with Najib Khan and the other Rohilla Pathans. Many advised Dattaji to ignore Najib Khan and push on. But this was neither advisable nor possible, as Najib Khan at large was the greatest mischief-maker of the day. In the meantime Najib too, with deep treachery at heart, professed readiness to perform whatever Dattaji would ask him to do. A personal visit was arranged between them through the mediation of Govindpant. But the visit proved abortive. Najib Khan came all alone into Dattaji's tent, but before talks could be started, some of his followers rushed in and carried Najib Khan away forcibly, under the supposition that his life was in danger. Whether the whole plan was a prearranged ruse or not cannot be ascertained. Thereafter negotiations began through agents. Najib Khan agreed to help Dattaji in carrying all his troops across the Ganges by means of a bridge of boats which he agreed to construct; and with this understanding both proceeded to Shukratal,[7] a place suited to the construction of a bridge, as the river bed there was full of small islets, and the mud banks sufficiently high. It proved a fatal step for Dattaji to have tried to conciliate Najib Khan. He could easily have

7. Shukratal on the western bank of the Ganges, 40 miles south of Hardwar, and 16 miles east of the railway station Muzaffarnagar. Beyond the river lay Najib's own residence Najibabad about 20 miles to the east.

been attacked and captured, but on the advice of many experienced men on the spot, Dattaji decided to utilise Najib's services as was suggested by Malharrao. Najib Khan had said when coming out of Dattaji's tent, "the looks of these Marathas appear wicked : they cannot be trusted." Jaitsinh Gujar, a zamindar of Shukratal and the environs, was entrusted with the task of constructing the bridge, as he was considered an expert. Najib Khan reached Shukratal at once, while Dattaji followed slowly, to allow time for the construction of the bridge. But the monsoon arrived, the river rose in floods and Najib Khan urged that the operations of the bridge could not be pushed on. Dattaji finished his holy baths on the way at Garhmukteshvar and pushing on encamped at Mirapur about a couple of miles from Najib's camp, which was pitched in a huge bend of the river.

Heavy rains had made the whole place muddy and movement was impossible. Najib utilised this circumstance to his best advantage. He was fully conversant with the situation and the surroundings, the range of rain, the country paths and the prominent people, to which Dattaji was an utter stranger. Najib Khan sent his secret personal agents to Shuja-ud-daula, to Hafiz Rahmat and the other Pathans and also to distant Afghanistan inviting Ahmad Shah Abdali quickly to India and giving him all possible details of the situation at Delhi and Shukratal and of the Sindia's position. Thus he organized a formidable coalition against the Marathas with such secrecy that Dattaji soon became perplexed. Najib Khan represented to Shuja that to allow Dattaji passage to the east was suicidal, as he would soon wrest from Shuja his two Subahs of Oudh and Allahabad. If on the contrary he would help Najib in his distress and join the Muslim combination, Shuja could become Wazir and restore the prestige of the Mughal Empire. But Shuja knew Najib better than Dattaji, and did not at all put trust in the professions of one who was known to be so unfaithful. Besides in religious matters the Shia Shuja was no friend of the Sunni Najib. However, the only object which Shuja wished to secure was to resist by all possible means the cession of Prayag and Benares to the Marathas. That was indeed a sentimental point, but the surrender of these two places would spell disaster to Muslim prestige throughout

India. With this view Shuja sent his two Gosavi captains with about ten thousand men to the Ganges opposite Shukratal to help Najib Khan and safeguard his own position.

In the meantime Najib Khan entrenched himself at Shukratal so formidably that the Marathas could not easily attack him. He collected troops and within a couple of months as the bridge became ready, instead of its serving Dattaji's purpose, it became a most convenient channel for Najib Khan himself to bring in supplies and maintain communication with the Pathans beyond. Before the end of August Dattaji saw through Najib's game clearly and began counter measures to defeat it. On 15th September Dattaji made a sudden attack on Najib Khan's camp, but it failed, the Marathas lost some men and retired at nightfall. Thereafter skirmishes occurred for nearly two months, but on account of the broken terrain Dattaji could not close with his opponent ; ignorant ot the latter's schemes he persisted in his efforts, never suspecting that Shah Abdali of Kabul would come upon him suddenly from the north-west. In order to cut off Najib Khan's supplies and support from beyond the river, Dattaji despatched Govindpant Bundele on 21st October with ten thousand troops via Hardwar where there was a ford. The Pant went straight against Najibabad plundering and burning on the way, but was repulsed by Hafiz Rahmat and Dunde Khan who rapidly came upon him in response to Najib's call. Govindpant was forced to beat a hurried retreat. Anupgir Gosavi too crossed the river by the bridge and joined Najib Khan at Shukratal by the end of October. Dattaji besieged the camp of Najib Khan at once. With an efficient army under him and many devoted followers, Dattaji never till the last moment felt daunted.

Early in 1759 Shah Abdali was reported to be in extreme peril, but he soon recovered his position and was agitated in his mind to learn that the Punjab for which he had toiled for the past several years had been lost to the Marathas, that his son and Jahan Khan had returned after suffering a terrible defeat, and lost their valuables and a large number of fighting men, that the Marathas had planted their flag on Attock and that a rival to him had appeared at Peshawar, in the person of his own cousin Abdur Rahman, with Maratha support. Fully informed of

Dattaji's position at Shukratal the Abdali Shah immediately organized his forces, despatched Jahan Khan with a sufficient army to take possession of Lahore in July 1759, just at the moment when Dattaji was persuading Najib Khan to build for him a bridge of boats on the Ganges. The Shah himself took post in Peshawar and stood ready to support Jahan Khan who had advanced into the Punjab. It has already been mentioned that no permanent arrangement had been made by the Peshwa for holding the Punjab. Sabaji Sindia was merely a temporary caretaker, with only slight forces at his command, with which he certainly could not defend a territory extending over more than 300 miles. Short work was done of the many scattered Maratha parties in the outposts of the province and Jahan Khan appeared before Lahore in August. Sabaji maintained his position with great valour and strength, inflicted a crushing defeat upon Jahan Khan, who was severely wounded and lost his son in the action. Jahan Khan's return to Peshawar in discomfiture so roused the fury of the Shah that he immediately came upon Lahore, with all his strength. Sabaji Sindia could not oppose him and retreated in extreme consternation reaching Dattaji's camp at Shukratal on 8th November to tell the sad tale that the Punjab had been lost, that many Marathas in different places had been cut down to the number of about one thousand, that most of the survivors had lost all their belongings and were helplessly fleeing about to save their lives from the merciless Afghans.

In this dangerous predicament the heroic Dattaji was not at all daunted. He possessed wonderful courage but did not unfortunately combine it with prudence and circumspection. Instead of at once falling back upon Delhi and calling in sufficient aid from different quarters, he attempted alone to oppose the full force of the Afghan King, who was advancing with the fury of a tempest. Dattaji clung to his position at Shukratal for more than a month even after the arrival of Sabaji Sindia and tried to force Najib Khan into surrender.[8] This proved an impossible task, Najib Khan continued freely getting supplies and men in large numbers from across the Ganges and the news of Abdali's rapid advance heartened Muslim resistance.

8. See *Phalke series* 3. 190.

Another evil effect of Abdali's advance was that the Wazir became entirely unnerved. He was in extreme fear of life and suspected that the Emperor would give him up and join the Afghan King. So being out of his wits he had the Emperor Alamgir II murdered on 30th November 1759 along with the former Wazir Intizam-ud-daula and four minor persons, having taken the party out under the pretence of paying a visit to a Muhammadan saint who had arrived in the vicinity. He thereupon raised to the throne a princeling and gave him the name of Shah Jahan Sani. When Ali Gauhar learnt of his father's murder in Bihar he declared himself Emperor on 22nd December, 1759.

5. Dattaji falls at Barari Ghat.—The news of this diabolical crime reached Abdali at Sarhind on the third day, and so enraged him that he at once proceeded to Delhi to punish the wicked wrongdoer, although he had originally formed no intention this time of proceeding beyond Sarhind. The Marathas had absolutely no hand in the murder, but their general support to Ghazi-ud-din made them responsible for the miserable fate of the Emperor. The whole course of events from now on to the battle of Panipat, took an entirely different turn, rousing feelings of anger and revenge.

The Peshwa in Poona hardly knew anything about this development. Holkar roved in Rajputana dealing with trivial matters and acted criminally in not running to save the situation in the Punjab, brought about by Najib Khan and Ghazi-ud-din, both helped by Holkar from the beginning.

As Abdali came rapidly marching upon him in the first week of December, Dattaji was compelled to give up his attempt against Najib Khan. He hurriedly broke up his camp and left Shukratal on 11th December to face Abdali beyond the Jamuna, which he crossed on the 18th, and arriving at Kunjpura he learned that about 40 thousand Afghans under Taimur Shah had reached Ambala. It was quite rash on his part to proceed alone against Abdali's full force, but retreat was a word which Dattaji never knew, and he at once divided his forces into two parties, the light one of twenty-five thousand he led himself against the advancing enemy and the other consisting of heavy baggage, artillery and the camp fol-

M. H. II—27

lowers, were sent back to Delhi under Govindpant Bundele. On 24th December he met the Afghans near Sthaneshwar and had a stiff encounter with them for a couple of hours, in which the two parties remained equally balanced. Dattaji lost about four hundred of his men but held the ground.

Evidently Abdali avoided an open encounter with Dattaji at this time and waited to be joined by the Rohillas so that he could attack the enemy with success. Therefore Abdali crossed the Jamuna the same night at Buriaghat[9] and proceeded towards Saharanpur, where Najib Khan joined him. Thereafter the combined armies marched along the eastern bank of the Jamuna towards Delhi. Dattaji at once turned back to save the capital, moving by the opposite bank of that river. By the end of December the two opponents stood parted by the river facing each other some ten miles north of Delhi, Abdali taking his position at Luni and Dattaji at what was known then as Barari-ghat. Ghazi-ud-din, now thoroughly terrified, was assured of safety by Dattaji, who asked him to organize the defence of capital by all means.

Dattaji was advised by many well-wishers to fall back from Delhi, join Holkar, obtain further reinforcements and then oppose Abdali with a sure chance of success; but he declined to follow such a defeatist course : losing Delhi meant, in his opinion, the loss of so many years of labour and success. He considered himself quite able to hold his own and save Delhi until succours arrived, for which he had sent urgent demands. Malharrao was expected every moment, and why he did not at once move north from Jaipur is a mystery, which can be explained only on the supposition that he wished to benefit himself by the sacrifice of Sindia. Dattaji had about him, devoted veteran men of his own, besides Naro Shankar and Bundele. Dattaji cared rather to prevent the harm and atrocities sure to happen to Delhi in case he gave the place up to Abdali's vengeance.

On 6th January Dattaji sent away all his camp followers, non-combatants and heavy baggage to Rewari, and prepared to encounter Abdali if he should venture to attack Delhi, remaining entirely on the defensive until Holkar should arrive,

9. Buriaghat is about 130 miles north of Bararighat.

and guarding the fords of the river with strict vigilance. It was the height of the cold season in north India. Dattaji did not expect a direct attack either on Delhi or on his camp at Bararighat. The river at this place was divided into two streams of scanty water enclosing between them something like an island overgrown with tall reeds which could easily conceal men and horses. Abdali sent Najib Khan to attempt a crossing at this place on the morning of Thursday, 10th January 1760. The Rohillas came on camels and small elephants with only two light guns on each, all hidden by the tall reeds. Sabaji Sinde was guarding the ghat and resisted the attackers with his few men, after reporting the attack to Dattaji. The latter without knowing either the exact numbers or the concealed guns of the enemy, proceeded rashly to protect the ford with a handful of men wearing only swords and not equipped with any firearms. A deadly combat ensued in the dried bed of the river and Jankoji soon after came up and joined in, but a chance bullet struck Dattaji dead and another wounded Jankoji making him unconscious. The loss on the Maratha side was by no means heavy, certainly less than a 1,000. But the death of Dattaji created a panic and severely damped the Maratha spirit. The army at once dispersed, everybody running to save himself in whatever way seemed possible. Dattaji's head was cut off by Kutb Shah, the reputed Guru of Najib Khan, and presented to the Shah Abdali. Jankoji was removed hurriedly by his followers, who all ran south to Kotputli, in Jaipur State, about 28 miles north-west of Alwar. Here Malharrao Holkar joined the fugitives on 15th January. Najib Khan immediately after raided Dattaji's camp and carried away some plunder and a few Muslim prisoners such as Sadiq Beg's children, Lakshmi Narayan, (Adina Beg's manager), and others, who could not save themselves otherwise. Dattaji's headless body was duly cremated by his followers.

This terrible news spread all over India like wild fire. Sabaji Sindia who was in charge of the Barari Ghat ford, ran and joined the camp at Kotputli. Poor Ghazi-ud-din sought the shelter of the Jat Rajah. Abdali immediately took possession of Delhi and appointed Yakub Ali Khan as its Governor. He was in great straits regarding money. He had a large army to maintain and Delhi had nothing to offer, having been completely sacked by him two years before. Najib Khan could not pay him anything but begged the Shah to stay on and not to depart immediately, otherwise, he argued, the Marathas would return and destroy him in no time. At his request Abdali sent insistent demands for funds to Shuja-ud-daula, Surajmal Jat, and Madho Sinh Raja of Jaipur; but all returned a negative answer, urging they had no funds to spare. The Jat indeed made a very bold reply. "You must first drive the Marathas away from Delhi, assure us that you are the master there, and then we shall be your willing vassals." Abdali was not inclined to remain as the Emperor of India. He had his best interests centred in Afghanistan. The Peshwa in the south was preparing a powerful expedition for the relief of Delhi, with which the Abdali Shah was not at all inclined to entangle himself. Ali Gauhar had already declared himself Emperor and was waiting at Allahabad for a favourable turn of events, which would enable him to proceed to Delhi and secure the throne.

At Kotputli the funeral ceremonies of Dattaji were performed, and the party moved back to Sabalgad on the Chambal where in February Dattaji's wife Bhagirathibai gave birth to a son. Malharrao Holkar comforted them all as an elderly guardian. They then began measures for recovering their lost position and driving away the invader by employing guerilla tactics in which Holkar was an adept. On 24th January a campaign was commenced. Abdali was watching the Maratha movements, having advanced parties of his men to prevent any Maratha move against Delhi, which he did not leave for some time. During February and March skirmishes took place between the Afghan parties and Holkar's bodies. The latter while plundering in the Doab suffered a severe defeat near Sikandarabad on 4th March. Full accounts of these occurrences quickly reached the Peshwa at Poona with a united demand that unless a strong and efficient artillery and some commander of outstanding merit appeared in the north, to conduct operations against the Durani Shah, it was not possible to drive him away and recover the lost position.

CHRONOLOGY

CHAPTER XX

1760, February 13	News of Dattaji's death reaches the Peshwa.
1760, March 7-14	Meeting of leaders at Patdur : Bhau Saheb nominated to lead a well prepared expedition to Delhi with Ibrahim Khan's artillery.
1760, March 14	Bhau Saheb starts from Patdur.
1760, April 12	Bhau Saheb reaches the Narmada.
1760, May 31	Bhau Saheb reaches Gwalior.
1760, June 27	Sardars meet Bhau Saheb near Agra : also Surajmal Jat. Abdali encamps near Aligarh.
1760, July 13	River Gambhir crossed by Bhau.
1760, July 16	Bhau Saheb reaches Mathura.
1760, July 18	Shuja joins Abdali in his camp.
1760, August 2	Delhi taken from Abdali's possession.
1760, August	Abdali moves his camp to the Jamuna opposite Delhi : negotiations conducted for peace.
1760, Aug.-Sept.	Food scarcity in Maratha camp.
1760, October 7	Bhau Saheb leaves Delhi for Kunjpura.
1760, October 10	Shah Alam proclaimed Emperor.
1760, October 17	Kunjpura captured: Qutb Shah put to death.
1760, October 25	Abdali crosses over at Bagpat to the right side of the Jamuna.
1760, October 28	Abdali halts at Sonpat.
1760, October 31	Bhau Saheb returns and forms his camp at Panipat.
1760, November 4	The two parties face to face at Panipat.
1760, Nov. 19 and 22	Light actions take place.
1760, December 7	A severe battle, Balavantrao Mahendale killed.
1760, December 17	Govindpant Bundele killed in a surprise attack. Abdali's position highly satisfactory.

CHAPTER XX

FROM PATDUR TO PANIPAT

[1760 March-December]

1. **Bhau Saheb's advance to Delhi.**—The news of Dattaji's death at Barari Ghat reached the Peshwa at Ahmadnagar on 13th February, 33 days after the event. He at once called back Bhau Saheb from Udgir with all his troops in order to concert measures for avenging Sindia's death. Patdur near Jalna was chosen as the place where they could all conveniently meet and whence the armies could proceed direct to the north without delay. The news from Delhi certainly staggered the Peshwa and his advisers, but did not damp their spirits. The Maratha State had just reached the zenith of its power, it had ample resources in men and money, and during the last 25 years a large number of capable young leaders had been trained to discharge both military and civil functions efficiently. The whole service was never better manned than at this moment. A loud cry therefore arose from all quarters at once for fully equipped armies being hurried to Delhi in order to drive away the invader. It took Bhau Saheb a week or two to close his operations and effect a favourable peace with the Nizam, although he could not owing to this trouble in the north exact the fullest reparations as he had all along intended. The Nizam too on getting news of the changed military situation in north India, demurred to fulfil the promises which he had made under pressure of arms. The Peshwa, Bhau Saheb, Raghunathrao and other leaders and diplomats all met at Patdur on 7th March 1760 and deliberated upon future measures night and day for a whole week. A free discussion took place among responsible leaders and every detail of past mistakes and shortcomings and future possibilities came under a scathing scrutiny and thorough

investigation. Sindia and Holkar were the only leaders who were absent from this conference. The gist of the discussion was the disclosure of the mismanagement and disorder that largely figured in the two expeditions of Raghunathrao, who was found to be incapable of exercising power or controlling subordinates and punishing them properly for dereliction. Hingne, Antaji Mankeshwar, Bundele and so many others required checks by a supervising master which Raghunathrao failed to exercise. A woeful mismanagement of his accounts also became all too plain. These matters which used to be publicly talked of and discussed before now, came up for a searching criticism at this conference. The result was a startling revelation to the Peshwa. A strong man clever with the pen and the sword, possessing experience of warfare and diplomacy, one who could create order out of chaos, was now needed; and everybody pointed to Bhau Saheb as the right leader to handle the situation in the north. It till now had been the Peshwa's settled intention to nominate Raghunathrao again to go to the north. But a different resolution was taken at Patdur : the die was cast.

Sadashivrao who had developed after his great uncle Bajirao I, was nominated to command the expedition which was hurriedly organized. Most of the young and old soldiers and diplomats were immediately told off for that duty. Sadashivrao was asked to take the Peshwa's eldest son Vishvasrao a lad of 18 with him, both by way of giving him an invaluable training for the future Peshwaship and also as a convenient check upon the former's impetuosity. The whole plan was arranged deliberately by the Peshwa going into every detail of the past and selecting the present personnel. Nothing was left to chance or extraneous influences. Damaji Gaikwad, Yeshvantrao Pawar, Naro Shankar, Vithal Shivdev, Antaji Mankeshwar, Balavantrao Mehendale, and the young Nana Phadnis, then not yet twenty and only five months older than the Peshwa's son Vishvasrao, these with thirty thousand select and well armed troops with the best military equipment and the finest artillery, the best horses and the choicest elephants were placed under the command of Bhau Saheb. This force in due course increased on the way as it proceeded, through allies joining in and fresh enlistments made.

The brave and faithful Ibrahim Khan Gardi with his efficient park of artillery made a valuable addition to Bhau Saheb's equipment. It must, however, be remembered that although the Maratha assemblage at Panipat numbered about 2 lacs of souls, quite two-thirds of these were non-combatants, being personal servants, clerks, shopkeepers, and other non-descript people. Bhau Saheb left Patdur on 14th March 1760 and exactly after ten months later on 14th January 1761, met his fate at Panipat. Raghunathrao was asked to remain watching the mischievous activities of the Nizam in the Deccan.

It was expected that the Shah Abdali would as usual march back to his country in summer, and in that case most of the Rajput and other powerful chiefs would readily join the Maratha standard. But this did not prove true. Abdali stayed on in India and most of the northern potentates did not venture to incur his displeasure by joining the Marathas: indeed several remained simply watching the game, waiting ultimately to throw in their lot with the successful party. Yet another disappointment was in store for Bhau Saheb. He expected to reach the Doab in about two months and to attack the Afghans at once in summer by crossing the Jamuna in boats' He therefore asked Govindpant Bundele to keep ready for this purpose a large number of boats. But the whole project fell through as the Marathas were unavoidably detained for over a month in crossing the small river Gambhira beyond the Chambal, both of which were in untimely flood that year on account of early rains.

Bhau Saheb reached the Narmada on 12th April, crossed at Handia and proceeded straight north via Sihore and Sironj, without visiting Bhopal or Bhilsa. By the end of May he reached Gwalior, but thereafter took more than a month to cover the short distance of 70 miles to Agra. On 16th July he was at Mathura.

While nearing Agra he met first Malharrao Holkar near Dholpur and Jankoji Sindia a little later, in the last week of June. Surajmal Jat who was already at war with Abdali, came and joined Bhau Saheb, cordially offering presents and dresses. He only stipulated that as his country lay in the main route of the Maratha army, no damage should be done to it, that no tribute should be demanded, that he would willingly serve the Marathas with a contingent of ten thousand troops and give shelter to their ladies and non-combatants. Bhau Saheb readily accepted these conditions and issued strict instructions to his men that the Jat territory should in no way be molested.

As soon as reports arrived of Bhau Saheb having left the Deccan with a large army, Najib Khan begged the Shah to remain in India for the hot season and thus preserve the work that had been so far accomplished. Najib agreed to defray the Shah's expenses. Ultimately the Shah yielded and pitched his camp at Ramgarh which he had recently captured from the Jat and named as Aligarh, and himself with a party of followers took up his residence at Anupshahar on the Ganges about 40 miles away.

In July the Jamuna was found unfordable and no means could be obtained for the Maratha artillery to cross over so as to get at the enemy and finish the contest quickly. Heavy rains prevented all movement. It was, therefore, decided to advance to Delhi and capture the capital from Abdali's agent, Yakub Ali Khan. He was easily overcome, and was allowed to return to his master's camp if he surrendered the town. Delhi was taken after a slight bombardment of the fort; and Bhau Saheb and the whole party of Maratha chiefs made their formal entry into the capital on 2nd August 1760. The Abdali Shah sent out parties for the succour of the capital but the Jamuna proved an impassable barrier. The possession of Delhi by the Marathas at once changed the aspect of the war. The centre of political activity and imperial transactions, now came back to Delhi from the hands of Abdali, who for a time had wielded all power. The Marathas were now in high spirits and confident of driving out the Pathan invaders from India.

2. **Shuja-ud-daula joins Abdali.**—Shuja-ud-daula of Oudh was then a very powerful potentate with a large army and ample funds, whose support was likely to turn the scale in this war. Both Bhau Saheb and Abdali tried their best to win him over. The former despatched his agent to Lucknow first from Gwalior and again Naro Shankar and Ramaji Anant, both influential and well-known to Shuja almost agreed to join the Marathas. They were his father's friends

and he had no regard for the profession of Najib Khan whom he hated, both as a Sunni and as a treacherous time-server. When this inclination of Shuja was revealed to Abdali, he became extremely anxious and deputed Najib Khan to go to Shuja personally and win him over. He quickly proceeded towards Shuja's quarters, kept an armed force at Kanauj and crossed over to Mehdi Ganj where he met that chief for a short time and so overwhelmed him with arguments of common interests and professions of fidelity that Shuja had to yield. He soon prepared his forces, marched with them into the Doab and was cordially received on 18th July in their camp at Anupshahar both by Najib Khan and the Abdali Shah.

This stroke proved a great blow to the Maratha cause. For if Shuja had remained on the side of the Marathas, there was every chance of the Afghan Shah returning in discomfiture. It must, however, be said to Shuja's credit that he all along exerted his best influence to bring about a lasting peace between the two antagonists and to prevent a recourse to arms, which even Abdali was anxious to avoid. Another loss to the Maratha cause was the sudden desertion and departure of Surajmal Jat from Delhi back to his capital Bharatpur. The Jat Raja had never agreed to serve the Maratha cause beyond his own jurisdiction. He had agreed to do what he could within his own territory. As soon as Delhi was captured, Surajmal demanded that he should be put in charge of its government. This Bhau Saheb for obvious reasons could not do. Delhi essentially belonged to the Emperor now. Shah Alam, who was at Allahabad and Shuja-ud-daula who aspired to the Wazirship would never allow the Jat ruler to be the guardian of that capital town. All other alleged reasons for Surajmal's desertion of Bhau Saheb are on historical scrutiny untenable and false.

3. Negotiations for peace.—For two months and a quarter from August to October, Sadashivrao with his whole following of over a hundred thousand souls, stayed at Delhi and practically consumed the entire food supply of the city and its surroundings, so that in a short time the Marathas began to suffer for want of funds and provisions. No supplies could come from outside. Govindpant could not send funds from

the Doab, which yielded him little; Bhau Saheb ordered treasure from Poona, which did not arrive. Negotiations which had been going on with the Shah for settling terms of peace and for the latter's return to his country, did not prove successful, and in a short time Bhau Saheb began to feel the pinch. Bapuji Ballal (Phadke) wrote from the Maratha camp on 15th September, " it is yet a month for the floods of the Jamuna to subside and the river to become fordable : peace does not seem to be in sight : our troops are starving : our horses no longer know what gram is. The army is losing its morale, no funds can be obtained. The prospect appears extremely gloomy." Nana Phadnis wrote to his uncle Baburao about the same time, " After the capture of Delhi by Bhau Saheb, Shah Abdali moved his quarters from Anupshahar to the side of the Jamuna opposite the city. He has secured all the boats. We clearly see his army from our side of the river. Shuja is engaged in mediating terms of peace but he cannot be trusted. We are quite strong, but hunger is staring us in the face. If the water goes down in a month's time, there is likelihood of the two armies coming to close grips. One good thing is that there is perfect harmony in our counsels. Bhau Saheb is sure to carry things to success." Bhau Saheb himself wrote the following letter to the Peshwa explaining the whole position clearly :—

" We arrived at Delhi with the sardars and took possession of the city. The Shah Abdali with Shuja and Najib Khan has moved to a spot on the opposite side. The river is still in flood. Shuja and Najib Khan have suggested certain terms for a peaceful return of the Shah. They have proposed that the Punjab be ceded to the Afghans with Sarhind as the boundary between the two spheres, that he should take charge of Delhi, appoint Shuja as the Wazir and Najib Khan as the Mir Bakhshi. These are the terms that the Shah Abdali offers. We have urged that the Maratha influence should extend to Attock and that we shall take charge of Delhi and the Emperor, although we shall make such appointments to the high posts as will make no material change from the past. Unless a mid-way between these two extremes is found out, it seems the negotiations will break down. If the river had not been an impediment, we should have come to grips with the enemy long ago. We will not accept any dictation of terms.

Both the sardars Sindia and Holkar are loyal and contented. There is perfect harmony in our counsels civil and military. Our serious trouble is our low food supply. No loan is available as bankers have closed their operations on account of the serious conflict that is raging. The Shah Abdali is in high spirits, having gained signal victories over the two sardars. Our present position is doubtless grave. We shall try every means to secure a negotiated peace and avoid recourse to arms. If it comes to fighting, we shall acquit ourselves with credit and determination. If His Highness the Peshwa recovers his health, we shall have gained all that we desire."

These three authoritative pronouncements explain the situation clearly and at the same time set at rest various controversies and questions that have gathered about the subject, such as reports of severe disagreement between Sadashivrao and Holkar, that Bhau Saheb's irascible and haughty temper alienated his subordinates leading ultimately to the final disaster, that he haughtily discarded the terms offered by Abdali, and so on. He himself admits the gravity of his situation due to want of supplies and funds. He came from the south with the avowed purpose of opposing the Afghans openly and putting an end to the constant disorder and confusion which had raged at Delhi for years. There was certainly a crop of rumours and bazaar reports spreading at the time throughout the country, which have partly survived to the present time. But these should be discarded in preference to the original and authoritative statements quoted above. Bhau Saheb was a strong man, but not at all vainglorious and overbearing as some writers would make him. Malharrao Holkar had a genuine difference of opinion on the point of military tactics. He was not used to artillery warfare and was out and out an advocate of the guerilla system. But such differences of opinion cannot be construed as disloyalty. Bhau Saheb had come with an efficient artillery to match the Abdali's, managed by a competent and loyal Muslim officer Ibrahim Khan to whom Bhau Saheb was solemnly pledged, that he would not resort to a running and harassing warfare to which heavy artillery was not suited. That is why the vast plain of Panipat was later selected as the field of operations. Holkar had shielded Najib Khan in the past, but that no longer formed a ground of debate at the present moment. Malharrao too had lost the spirit of his youth, and the infirmities of age were having their effect on him. If he, therefore, looked upon Bhau Saheb and the other youngsters as raw youths, void of experience and circumspection, a certain amount of latitude may be allowed for Holkar to hold such views, so common to old men in all ages.

The prolonged stay at Delhi began to tell severely upon the Maratha position. Bhau did not obtain funds at Delhi. His monthly expense amounted to about five and a half lacs of rupees : and this amount went on increasing as prices and the time advanced ; so that during the ten months that Bhau Saheb was in the north, he may be said roughly to have required nearly a total of eighty lacs, of which he obtained about 23 lacs in the north from various sources. He obtained in coin about nine lacs from the silver ceiling of the Diwan-i-Khas, which had been partly dismantled by Ghazi-ud-din before, and of which the remaining portion was now utilized by Bhau Saheb in his extreme need of funds. Later on he acquired about 7 lacs out of the plunder of Kunjpura. The balance had to be made up either by loans or by a supply from the south, which did not arrive.[1]

Nor must one forget that in this respect the Shah Abdali too was in no better position. He too had come to extreme distress, having received only ten lacs from Najib Khan since his arrival. He stayed in India for a full year and a half from October 1759 to March 1761 : and this time he obtained little by plunder. His army was nearly as large as that of the Marathas, although the Rohillas and Shuja-ud-daula, his principal allies defrayed their own expenses. The trans-Jamuna region had for long been severely taxed and stripped of all its wealth. There was often an angry exchange of hot words between the Shah and Najib-ud-daula. The former was so hard pressed and dissatisfied with the Indian situation that he considered it the best policy to arrive at a peaceful understanding with the Marathas and return to his country without damaging his prestige. Sadashivrao thus wrote to Govindpant on

1. P. D. 2. 130, 131, P. D. 27. 255-258. *Purandare Daftar* Vol. I, No. 389. Sir Jadunath clearly explains the financial position of Bhau Saheb on page 263 of his *Fall of the Mughal Empire*, Vol. 2.

2nd September, "Naro Shankar has been entrusted with the command of Delhi. The Shah Abdali, the Rohillas and Shuja-ud-daula are conducting negotiations of peace with us, but knowing that these would be protracted and that it is harmful to remain here idle, we have decided to advance to Kunjpura, thus drawing the enemy to the north and relieving the pressure upon Delhi ; you will in the case be free along with Gopalrao Ganesh to move into the Doab and devastate the Rohilla country."[2]

Najib Khan was not slow in counteracting this move of the Maratha leader. He circulated false rumours that Vishvasrao was made the Emperor, that money was coined in his name by tearing down the silver ceiling of the Audience-Hall. He also violently opposed every move on either side for coming to a peaceful understanding. Shah Abdali was not at all anxious to hold and occupy Delhi : and Najib Khan rightly feared that if the capital city remained in Maratha possession, he would have to endure the utmost vengeance at the hands of the Marathas after the Afghan monarch had returned to his country. Sadashivrao had deputed his ambassadors Kashiraj and Bhavani Shankar to Shuja for negotiating terms of peace and Shuja's agent Devidatta was living with Sadashivrao for the same purpose. But the conflicting interests of the various parties and Najib's obduracy obstructed every attempt to adjust matters. Najib Khan wanted to crush the Marathas finally. Shuja aspired to the Wazirship and objected to any Pathans wielding power at Delhi. The Shah himself desired to secure an honourable retreat to his country, remaining content with the possession of the Punjab only. When Dattaji fell at Barari Ghat, the Marathas retreated to the Chambal and gave up Delhi, which was exactly midway between Sarhind and the Chambal, a distance of 320 miles. If Bhau Saheb had agreed to cede the Punjab and make the Satlaj the boundary line between the two claimants, a negotiated peace was quite possible.

4. **Kunjpura captured.**—On 7th October Bhau Saheb left Delhi for Kunjpura, a distance of 78 miles, while 78 miles

2. Raj. Vol. 6. 404.

further north was Sarhind. Bhau Saheb went on from Delhi, minutely examining the fords of the Jamuna, and as none was discovered, he made no arrangement for guarding against the eventuality of the Shah crossing over to his side. Sonpat 36 miles from Delhi and Panipat another 20 miles beyond were passed by Bhau Saheb. Kunjpura lay 22 miles further north on the right bank of the river Jamuna, an outpost strongly guarded by the Shah Abdali's partizans and plentifully stocked with provisions and ammunition as a mid-way base for his return. Having travelled two stages from Delhi, Sadashivrao discovered the mischievous report Najib Khan had circulated and at once arranged for a public ceremonial and declaration at Delhi, proclaiming Shah Alam as the Emperor and appointing in his absence his son Jawan Bakht as his regent (Vali-Ahad) and minting fresh coins in that Emperor's name, (10 October 1760.)

Advance parties of Sindia, Holkar and Vithal Shivdev arrived before Kunjpura on 16th October and called upon Najabat Khan, the keeper of the place to surrender. He refused and a severe bombardment by Ibrahim Khan proved effective. Abdussamad Khan and Mian Qutb Shah who were posted at Sarhind ran to the help of Kunjpura and even Abdali sent large succours from the east bank of the Jamuna to that place. But before any effective resistance could be made, the place was captured the very next day, 17th October, Damaji Gaikwad rushing with his valiant parties through the breaches made by the heavy guns in the huge stone walls. Nearly ten thousand Afghans were killed or wounded in the action. Abdussamad Khan was killed and Qutb Shah and Najabat Khan secured alive. Najabat Khan died of his wounds, his son Dilir Khan escaped, while Qutb Shah was put to death by Bhau Saheb in retaliation for his having cut off Dattaji Sindia's head at Barari Ghat a few months before. Qutb Shah's severed head was paraded through the Maratha ranks.

The capture of Kunjpura marked the highest triumph of the Maratha power. For the present the needs of the Maratha army were more than met. Two lacs maunds of wheat, ten and a half lacs in rupees and another ten lacs worth of arms, ammunition and valuables were secured, including some five guns and three thousand horses. The Zaver elephant of

Dattaji Sindia which had been carried away at his fall now came back to Maratha possession. Much plunder besides this was appropriated by the various members of the Maratha army. Two days after this happened to be the Dassara day, Sunday 19th October, which was celebrated with the greatest pomp and triumph, such as was never witnessed by any Maratha before or after. A grand Darbar was held at which actual gold was presented to Vishvasrao, instead of the customary leaves of the Apta tree.

The loss of Kunjpura was deeply felt by the Shah Abdali and excited in his heart bitter animosity towards the Marathas, thus rousing supreme anger and hatred in the Pathan breasts, and hereafter changing the essential character of the struggle, by adding an element of ferocity to what was a mere trial of strength before. The bitterness thus started continued long after Panipat and is even now disclosed in the partisan writings. Abdali at once addressed his soldiers in animated tones, saying, "My men, how do you endure this open affront given us by the Kafir Marathas? Don't you feel impelled to inflict upon them adequate retribution? You must now be ready to sacrifice all, even your lives, in the grave trial that is awaiting us."

In this agonising mood Abdali moved slowly along the left bank of the Jamuna from opposite Delhi to the north, carefully looking out for a ford and utilising local men in effecting a crossing with his whole army and guns on to the other side, in order to get at the Marathas for a close combat. About 20 miles north of Delhi he reached Baghpat on the east bank of the river, where after four days inspection he decided to cross the river on October 25. It was a daring experiment which might as well have proved disastrous. But Abdali had gained uncommon experience in crossing numerous rivers and streams during his long previous career throughout Central Asia and India, so that he could fully gauge the possibilities of a succesful fording. His followers hesitated, when after a devout prayer to Allah, he untied the girth of his horse and rushed into the stream followed by an equally enthusiastic train. The water level had now considerably subsided and the horses could get across swimming part of the way where the water was deep. Within three days, he carried across without being detected, his whole army and heavy artillery on the backs of elephants and camels. This dexterous move is highly extolled by all writers as a rare feat of generalship.

5. **Face to face at Panipat.**—On 28th October 1760 Abdali started north in search of the Marathas along the right bank of the Jamuna, and after a journey of 7 miles reached Sonpat. Bhau Saheb received this news of Abdali's crossing over on the 28th while he was proceeding northward having left Kunjpura on October 25 with a view to replenishing his supplies and crossing the Jamuna on to the other side to get into contact with Abdali. He also meant to gain the friendship of the Sikhs if possible. But rejoicing that Abdali had himself come over and was now within his easy reach, Bhau Saheb immediately retraced his steps and arrived at Panipat within five miles of Abdali's advance troops. The two forces sighted each other towards the end of October, when the advance parties of the two combatants had slight skirmishes. Bhau's original plan was to encounter Abdali before he had time to organize his troops in battle array and even during the act of crossing if possible. But by the time he arrived at Panipat, he found the Shah well prepared for a combat, and realized that the determined stand of the Afghans and their perfect order were not to be trifled with. Bhau Saheb could not easily rout them and find his way back to Delhi, unmolested.

He, therefore, decided on the advice of Ibrahim Khan Gardi to entrench himself on the plain with the town of Panipat north of him, and remain on the defensive until the other party got weakened by starvation, so as to combine guerilla tactics with the use of trained infantry and artillery. He was encumbered with a large number of non-combatants and some ladies ; these now formed a drag on him consuming his supplies and requiring protection. If Bhau had only the fighting force with him, he would have easily fought his way through the enemy's ranks. But this did not now seem possible, and in order to save them he created a defensive camp, of tents and huts, about 6 miles in length from east to west and about 2 miles deep north to south. He dug a large trench round this camp about 25 yards broad and 6 yards deep[3] ; and the heaps of earth thus brought up formed a huge wall upon which guns were mounted. The Abdali Shah too formed a permanent camp facing the Marathas, about three miles to their south with the village of Sonpat behind. He fortified his position with trenches and wood defences made of felled trees. In this way the passage home of the two antagonists came to be blocked against each other. None could escape without annihilating the other. On 4th November Bhau Saheb wrote to Govindpant, "We are now face to face with the enemy and have prepared ourselves for an encounter, having pitched our camp on the plain of Panipat. Abdali's way home is completely blocked by us. Every day we capture his camels, horses and oxen in large numbers. Now the Doab is freely open to you. You must bring treasure and supplies from your district and deliver them at Patpatganj opposite the south corner of the city of Delhi, whence we shall manage to take them. You must stop any treasure and supplies reaching Abdali from the Doab. The Jat Raja is quite friendly and will in no way obstruct you. Now is the time for you to do your utmost." On 5th November Krishna Joshi, one of Bhau Saheb's retinue, wrote from Panipat a full account of Bhau Saheb's position, in which he said, "Bhau Saheb has returned to Phanipath from Kunjpura, and daily skirmishes are occurring between the two opponents. The Muslims fear our strong artillery. No corn now reaches the Abdali's camp, where there prevails extreme scarcity. If he within the next three or four days advances against us, he will be annihilated by our guns. Our camp has plentiful supplies which can be had very cheap. There are good auguries all round and our men are in high spirit. Abdali, Najib Khan and Shuja will now meet with their ruin within a week. The Shah, although a general of standing and experience, is now so humiliated that he dare not advance all these days. His road to his country is blocked ; and he has no hope of success in a fight and, cannot afford to remain idle where he is for want of food." This was the condition of affairs in the first week of November, and the Marathas could then have attacked Abdali with success. Why Bhau Saheb

---

[3] पन्नास हात रुंद व बारा हात खोल., भाऊसा० बखर.

waited thereafter for the two long months of November and December is a mystery which cannot be satisfactorily explained. But the accounts presented by the two invaluable compilations, Bhau Saheb's *Kaifiyat* and his *Bakhar* give the whole story lucidly, and doubtless they bear marks of having been compiled from original documents, which are now not forthcoming. The *Kaifiyat* is very accurate and the *bakhar* an enlarged edition of it, quoting long passages exactly as they are in the former.

In a few days, however, the position came to be reversed. Abdali moved his camp quite close to the bank of the Jamuna, although at first he was a few miles away from it. This gave his camp not only a plentiful supply of water, but made his communication easy with the region of the Doab which was in Najib Khan's possession and from which he arranged to obtain plentiful supplies. The Doab was essentially a Muslim-ruled country, and as feelings ran high at the time, Govindpant or any of the Maratha officials could obtain no supplies for delivery into the Maratha camp. There was a strong anti-Hindu feeling and it was with difficulty that Govind Ballal held his position round about Etawa. In a few days the Shah Abdali posted strong guards all round the Maratha camp and prevented any supplies reaching it. He cut off Maratha communications towards the south with Delhi and Rajputana, and the east beyond the Jamuna. The way north towards Kunjpura was for a time open, but Kunjpura was soon retaken by Abdali and all Maratha communication stopped on that side. The west was a thorny uncultivated country, full of brambles and jungle. For two months no news reached the Deccan from Panipat.

After the first week of November Abdali's position began to improve daily, and in proportion that of Bhau Saheb began to deteriorate. He could not get supplies from any quarter. Abdali slowly gathered into his hands all the points that first appeared to be an advantage to Bhau. But the latter's courage was undaunted, against which was matched the superior generalship of the Abdali Shah, who had seen fighting throughout his life.

The field of Kurukshetra stretching down to Panipat is a wide plain, battles on which from uncounted ages, have decided the fate of India and now yet another momentous decision was to be reached on that battle-scarred plain. The moment arrived for Bhau Saheb to grapple with the Abdali troops, for which he had been longing ever since he left the Deccan.

From 1st November 1760 to 14th January 1761 for full two and a half months, the Marathas remained entrenched in their camp and lost whatever chance they at first had of achieving success, every day that passed making their position worse. They gradually lost heart and despaired of victory. During these two and a half months light skirmishing was going on constantly between the two armies, but three or four stiff actions also took place. Once on 19th November Ibrahim Khan's brother Fath Khan Gardi executed a secret night raid upon Abdali's camp, dragging light guns by the hand : but he was easily repulsed and returned discomfited. Three days after in the afternoon of 22nd November, the Durrani Wazir was detected by Sindia's men reconnoitering a well near the Maratha camp, and he was immediately attacked by Jankoji Sindia with fury. Nearly all the Wazir's party was cut down and he was hotly pursued right up to the Durrani camp. In this encounter Sindia showed unexampled impetuosity, but could not win all the success his efforts deserved on account of the failure of the Peshwa's troops to render him timely support. A thousand Rohillas were killed and a few of their guns were captured by the Marathas. Darkness set in and the combatants parted, otherwise greater havoc would have been inflicted upon the Afghans.

All this while Bhau Saheb and the other leaders were constantly urging Naro Shankar at Delhi and Govind Ballal in the Doab to do their utmost to send supplies and cash to Panipat and relieve their misery. But the Durranis were so watchful and alert that they successfully prevented any article or cash reaching the camp at Panipat. Another serious encounter occurred about a fortnight after the one described above, on 7th December, when Najib Khan without permission from the Shah and acting on his own responsibility, made a precipitate attack on a party of the Marathas who were manœuvring their guns in certain positions. The small party was severely handled and pressed back right to the ditch by Najib

Khan. But the latter's presence being noticed, huge Maratha parties came upon him like lightning. More than three thousand Rohillas were mown down by the guns of Ibrahim Khan and the swords of the Huzrat under Balavantrao Mehendale. But a chance shot killed this brave young leader of promise and marred the value of the success the Marathas had attained. That night Balavantrao's wife became Sati. The death of this hero spread a heavy gloom throughout the camp. The slide down of the Maratha hopes definitely began from this moment.

Govindpant in the lower Doab was, however, fully apprized of the state of things prevailing at Panipat and strove hard to collect supplies and cash from the region east of Delhi, and tried to forward them to the beleaguered camp. He made a large stock of things gathered from Sikandarabad and other places, and his parties were moving within ten to twenty miles of Shahdara (opposite Delhi), Ghaziabad and Jalalabad. The agents employed by Najib Khan watched these operations of the Pant and communicated the news of their activities to the Rohilla chief. He at once despatched Atai Khan and Karimdad Khan with a party of some five thousand fresh troops that had just arrived from Afghanistan. These troops crossed the Jamuna and moved rapidly in search of the Maratha foraging parties. On the evening of 16th December they came upon a small party of Naro Shankar's men, and cut them all down. The country around was all hostile to the Marathas and burning for revenge against their fearful depredations in the past. The next morning, 17th December, the Afghans started again and came across a Maratha party at Ghaziabad, who were all similarly cut down. Thence they rode about ten miles north-east to Jalalabad where they found Govindpant himself, who not suspecting any sudden attack by the enemy, was engaged in saying his prayers and preparing his meal, with only a small party of personal servants. As soon as they were attacked, they mounted their ponies and ran to save their lives in different directions. They were hotly pursued and a bullet shot brought the Pant down from his horse. The Muslims closed upon him, cut off his head and carried it to the Shah in triumph. Abdali paraded the head in his camp and sent it as a present to Bhau Saheb. Govindpant's son Balaji was with his father, but was saved by his servants. Thus perished an old and faithful servant of the Peshwas who had for thirty years laboured hard to keep the Maratha flag aloft in Bundelkhand and the Doab. Essentially a non-military man, proficient in accounts and revenue matters, he happened to be the only prominent Maratha in the north at the time of Bhau Saheb's expedition. Naturally, therefore, Bhau Saheb called upon him to execute many responsible functions and duties, which he was unable to perform owing to the disurbed condition of the regions in which he worked. His descendants still live at Saugor.

The Marathas were now faced with terrible starvation brought about by a complete stoppage of food supplies from outside. As the high price of food exhausted the money in Bhau Saheb's treasury, he with Sindia and Holkar erected three separate mints in the camp and melted down all the men's and women's gold and silver ornaments, thus producing a quantity of fresh rupees stamped with the words *Bhaushahi*, *Jankushahi*, and *Malharshahi*. But this money did not last for more than two weeks.

Still neither side was willing to attack the other. For two months they had tried to obtain a superiority in light cavalry actions. It was clear that so long as the main armies chose to remain stationary, the force whose light cavalry held the command of the open country would starve the other force out. In this game the Shah Abdali ultimately succeeded in getting the Marathas in his strong grip. Bhau Saheb ever since his start from the Deccan had placed his main confidence in the infantry corps of Ibrahim Khan and they had so far given a very good account of themselves. The idea of remaining entrenched at Panipat was a result of this confidence. The Marathas were rendered unassailable so long as they remained within their entrenchments. Bhau Saheb waited long in this entrenched position expecting Abdali to attack him, as he was sure of victory in the event of such an attack. Abdali saw through Bhau Saheb's game and studiously avoided an open attack upon the Maratha camp, hoping to get the victory when the Maratha army would be forced to come out through sheer starvation. Bhau's letters to Bundele are full of rage and railing for the latter's failure to goad the Abdali Shah into an attack upon the Maratha camp.

When thus reduced to extremity, Bhau made, so says Nuruddin Husain Khan, a last moment attempt to negotiate peace with the Afghan monarch, and offered to pay him a heavy fine for being allowed to withdraw from the contest and retire safely to the south. But, as before, Najib Khan persuaded the Shah to reject the proposal and welcome an opportunity to slay the infidels in a holy war. Indeed Najib Khan was instrumental in bringing about the Maratha ruin, proving thereby the character that Hafiz Rahimat had given him.[4]

4. "Najib Khan is a vulgar upstart, who had first entered his master's service as a poor infantry-man, but now has risen to be the dictator of Delhi and the Prime Minister of the Abdali Shah for Indian affairs."

CHRONOLOGY

CHAPTER XXI

1760, December 27	The Peshwa at Paithan.
1760, Dec. 31	The Peshwa leaves for the north.
1761, January 4	Parashar Dadaji's treasure surprised.
1761, January 4	Bhau Saheb in extremity : attempt to obtain terms for escape fail.
1761, January 12	Bhausaheb takes the resolution to move the whole camp in a square.
1761, January 14	The final combat ; death of Vishvasrao causes debacle ; a fearful massacre follows.
1761, January 15	Abdali prays at Ali Kalandar's Darga at Panipat.
1761, January 16	Abdali leaves for Delhi.
1761, January 18	Abdali holds a consultation with the Maratha agent Hingne ; the Peshwa crosses the Narmada.
1761, January 24	News of disaster reaches Peshwa at Bhilsa.
1761, January 29	Abdali enters Delhi and deputes Yakub Ali, to meet the Peshwa in Malwa.
1761, February 10	Abdali's agent Gulraj meets the Peshwa in Malwa with presents from Abdali.
1761, March 20	Abdali leaves Delhi for Kabul and the Peshwa for Poona from Pachhor.
1761, April 6	The Peshwa passes through Indore.
1761, May 16	The Peshwa at Toka ; is weighed.
1761, June 5	The Peshwa reaches Poona.
1761, June 12	The Peshwa takes residence at Parvati.
1761, June 23	The Peshwa dies.
1772, April 14	Abdali dies at Kabul.
1783, August 16	Bhau Saheb's wife Parvatibai dies.

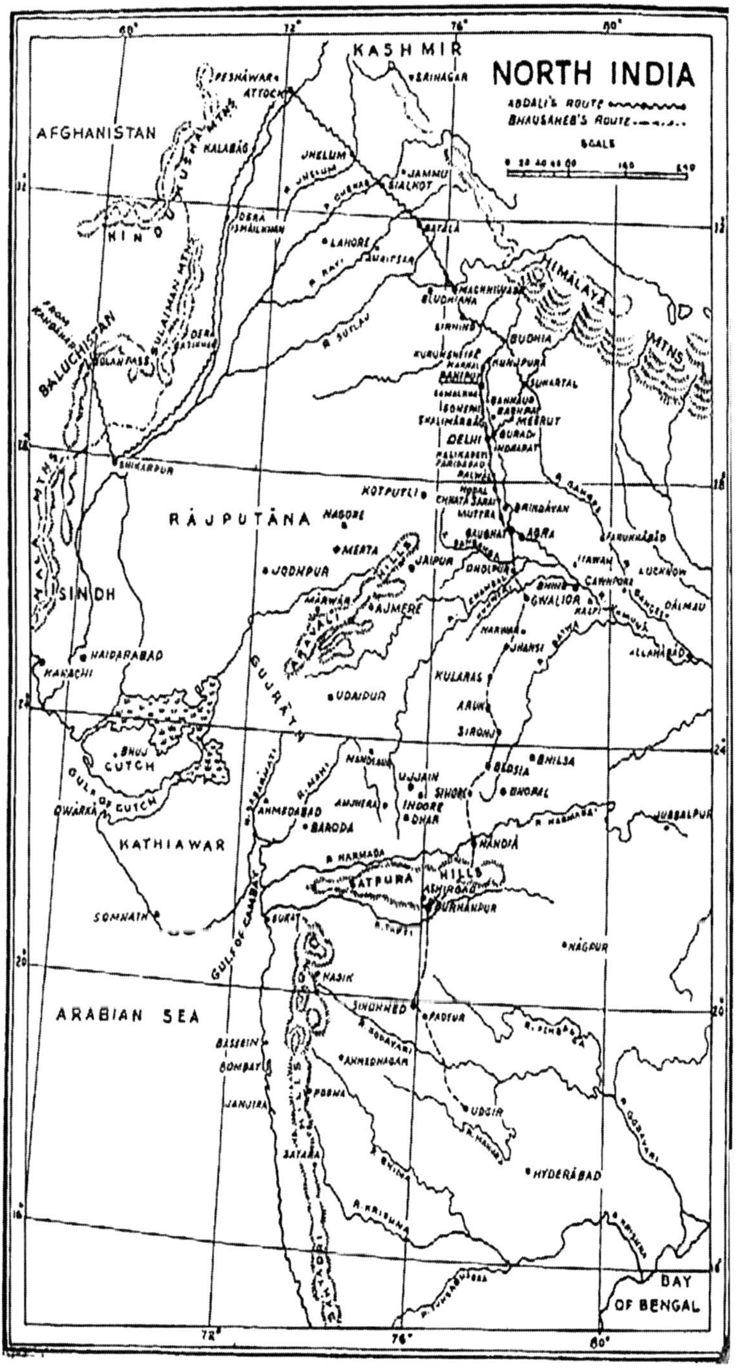
NORTH INDIA
ABDALI'S ROUTE
BHAUSAHEB'S ROUTE
SCALE
KASHMIR
AFGHANISTAN
BALUCHISTAN
SULAIMAN MTNS
RĀJPUTĀNA
SINDH
GUJRĀT
KATHIAWAR
CUTCH
GULF OF CUTCH
GULF OF CAMBAY
ARABIAN SEA
BAY OF BENGAL
HIMALAYA MTNS
SATPURA HILLS
ARAVALI HILLS
PESHĀWAR
ATTOCK
KALABĀG
JHELUM
SRINAGAR
JAMMU
SIALKOT
LAHORE
AMRITSAR
BATĀLA
MACHHIWARA
LUDHIANA
SIRHIND
BUDHIA
KUNJPURA
SUKARTAL
MEERUT
DELHI
SHIKARPUR
KOTPUTLI
NAGORE
MERTA
JODHPUR
JAIPUR
AJMERE
AGRA
BRINDĀVAN
DHOLPUR
GWALIOR
FARUKHĀBĀD
LUCKNOW
CAWNPORE
DALMAU
ALLAHĀBĀD
JHANSI
KULARAS
SIRONJ
BHILSA
BHOPAL
HAIDARABAD
KARACHI
BHUJ
DWARKA
SOMNATH
UDAIPUR
AHMEDABAD
BARODA
UJJAIN
INDORE
DHAR
JUBBALPUR
NANDIA
BURHANPUR
SURAT
NAGPUR
NASIK
SINDKHED
BASSEIN
BOMBAY
JANJIRA
AHMEDNAGAR
POONA
SATARA
UDGIR
HYDERĀBAD
R. NARMADA
R. TAPTI
R. GODAVARI
R. KRISHNA
R. BHIMA
R. GANGES
R. SUTLAJ
R. RAVI
R. CHENAB
R. JHELUM
72°
76°
80°

CHAPTER XXI

THE TRAGIC CLOSE AT PANIPAT

[1761]

1. Cup full to the brim.—Govind Pant's death and the manner in which it was compassed, roused both rage and despondency in all Maratha breasts; and hereafter from 21st December to 14th January increasing misery fell upon the Maratha camp and all hope of relief was lost. Another mishap came soon after the death of Govind Pant. He had collected about four and a half lacs of cash and sent it to Naro Shankar to be despatched to Bhau Saheb, who had deputed a special agent to Delhi for that purpose. A little over a lac reached the Maratha camp on 21st December : the remaining 3 lacs were entrusted to Parashar Dadaji, a young captain in Holkar's service. A party of picked horsemen each carrying Rs. 500 left Delhi early in January making secret marches by night. Being unware of the changed location of the Afghan camp[1] they, in the darkness and cold of the last night of their march, stumbled into the circle of the piquets of the enemy on the south-western or Delhi side of the route. They were at once detected and all put to death, except a few who escaped. This happened on 4th January. Their leader Parashar Dadaji returned to Delhi on the 6th. Bhau Saheb tried to hold on bravely and kept up the spirits of the inmates of the camp now entirely dependent on him. All his efforts to obtain supplies of grain or cash proved fruitless. The small city of Panipat was denuded of every thing, food, timber, grass and gardens, for supplying the crying need of the Marathas ; the populace of that city were mostly

1. Kotah papers 1. 222.

Muslims and altogether hostile, as they were dispossessed of all their belongings. Thus the whole camp found starvation and death staring it in the face. The only course now open to the Marathas was either unconditional surrender or a last desperate effort to fight their way through the enemy's ranks. After prolonged deliberation, the latter course was approved and accepted. But Bhau Saheb continued his efforts through his agents with Shuja to obtain terms on which they could secure their release from the dreadful situation.

By this time it was known that the Peshwa had left Poona and was coming to the north with large forces. But while he was growing anxious about the condition of affairs in the north, he had absolutely no news for long, as all letters and despatches were intercepted by the enemy. He had left Poona in October and was slowly raising money, men and supplies both by way of a check over the Nizam and also to meet the probable requirements of the army in the north. He took a second wife, a young girl of nine near Paithan and celebrated the ceremony on 27th December. It is wrong to suggest that he took to amorous pleasure with a second wife and neglected to succour his cousin.[2] He was already fast declining in health and Sadashivrao was extremely anxious on his account. Nor is it right to hold that Bhau Saheb delayed his final attack under the impression that the Peshwa would soon arrive and in that case they could crush the Muslims between the two Maratha armies. Bhau Saheb was in no need of additional troops. His difficulty was about feeding his men and keeping open his line of communication. So the mystery of Bhau Saheb waiting for two and a half months before he delivered his final attack, cannot be satisfactorily explained.

Abdali's allies, however, became very impatient and urged him to no longer delay the final assault on the enemy. His only reply was, "My duty is that of a general, and let me be full master in this. You can take care of your politics as you wish, but do not interfere with my military plans." He was always alert and constantly on the move. He had a small red

2. In this connection a fanciful suggestion has been put forth by Mr. Shejvalkar in his recent work on Panipat that the Peshwa took this second wife as a cure for his fast failing health! (See P. 120).

tent pitched in advance of his camp to which he regularly came every morning for his prayers and for his breakfast, and spent the whole day in moving round the entire camp, inspecting the arrangements, giving instructions and tightening his hold on the Marathas. He never rode less than 30 miles a day. He reserved a special guard of 5 thousand troops to go round the whole camp and keep a strict look out for the slightest remissness in his army or any activity of the enemy. He asked Shuja and the other allies to enjoy sound sleep and rest as usual, without worrying themselves about the war.

Conditions in the Maratha camp grew desperate with the passage of time. Many Maratha groups, who in search of food moved out of the camp, were cut down by the enemy patrols. Starvation and death loomed large before every body's eyes. Animals died in large numbers and the consequent stench became most obnoxious. Young and old, leaders and men all urged Bhau Saheb that it was no use waiting any longer, that they would rather die fighting with the enemy than perish through starvation in the camp. All gathered and took full counsel together. There was the annual Sankrant day on 10th January, which they celebrated as best they could, eating away the last stock that they possessed. The next three days were spent in discussing the arrangements for a final dash ; assigning duties and giving full instructions on the various points of the ensuing combat. By the advice of Ibrahim Khan, the whole force was to move slowly on in a square formation, all the four sides of which were to be protected by heavy artillery. The ladies and non-combatants were to be put in the centre, and the whole mass was to move in a block under the protection of Ibrahim Khan's cannon. One serious defect of this arrangement was that it could be easily disturbed by the slightest tactics of the enemy, as actually happened.

Having completed his final dispositions for the morrow and issued full instructions to his subordinates, Bhau Saheb, if Kashiraj is to be believed, made during that fateful night a last minute effort by addressing a note to Kashiraj, saying, " the cup is full to the brim : not a drop more can it contain. Please let me have a final reply on the adjustment of the dispute." Early in the morning of the 14th Kashiraj presented the note to Shuja who directed Kashiraj to go and show it to the Shah. By the time the Shah came to know of it, the Marathas were already seen moving against the Durrani Camp. Still Abdali replied, "Wait for a day and we shall think how to end the affair." But by this time the fighting had nearly commenced.

2. **Position of the Parties in the field.**—At last the fatal 14th January arrived for Bhau Saheb to get into close grips with the Abdali Shah, for which he had been longing ever since he left the Deccan. The Shah did not take long to realize, when on that early morning he reconnoitred the huge mass of the whole Maratha camp moving in a block towards him, that it was no longer to be one of the light actions which he was having during the last two months. He at once prepared his whole army for a final issue and quickly arranged his line of battle with judicious calculation for reaping the highest advantage. In arranging his men he used his best discretion, assigning suitable positions and duties to his various captains and allies. Of his total of sixty thousand, nearly half was foreign and half Indian, the major portion consisting of cavalry with a small admixture of infantry. He placed Barkhurdar Khan and Amir Beg on his extreme right wing keeping next to their left the Ruhelas of Hafiz Rahmat and those of the Bangash Nawab. Thereafter in his line came his camel swivels and his own Kabuli infantry. Next to these came the central command of the Wazir Shah Vali Khan in whom he had the highest confidence. To the left of the Wazir was posted Shuja-ud-daula leading his own contingent, closely joined on his left by Najib Khan's party. The extreme left of the line was made up by Shah Pasand Khan along with the Shah's own slave squadrons and his personal body-guards, the last two having been kept behind in reserve to be moved as necessity would demand. It would here be noticed how the Ruhelas, the Bangash contingent and Najib Khan's men were purposely wedged in between the Shah's own foreign troops, as he was suspicious of the loyalty of his Indian allies. He himself remained behind the whole line, directing the operations and repairing any weak points that would develop when the action came to be joined.

As the Marathas moving in a square formation approached the long and well arranged Afghan line facing them, their original plan of mass movement could not be carried out. Failing to force a passage for moving on, Bhau Saheb precipitately reformed his men in a long line similar to that of the enemy so as to fight them out and obtain a passage through, the main object being to effect an escape rather than annihilate his opponents. This tactical and sudden change created a sort of confusion among Maratha ranks, causing extreme annoyance to Ibrahim Khan, as his plan came to be entirely upset.[3] The Khan, however, quietly accepted the situation and tried to do the best he could under the circumstances. When Bhau Saheb prolonged his force in a line, he gave his extreme left wing to the care of Ibrahim Khan and his heavy artillery, with Damaji Gaikwad next to him for the Khan's support. Bhau Saheb himself took his station in the centre with his devoted Huzrat troops, with which he faced the Afghan Wazir. Antaji Mankeshwar, Pilaji Jadhav's son Satvoji and some minor chiefs were posted towards Bhau Saheb's right, the extreme end in the line being specially strengthened by the veteran fighters of Yashvantrao Pawar, Jankoji Sinde and Malharrao Holkar. Bhau Saheb could not keep any portion in reserve, as the whole camp was intended to force a passage through the Afghan ranks. With this disposition Bhau Saheb attempted to rush through the enemy's ranks with his entire army.

Before describing the actual nature of the titanic struggle that now followed, some salient points regarding the position of the two parties deserve to be noticed. Although the two forces and particularly that of the Marathas, were large on account of the vast numbers of the non-combatants, the strength of the actual fighting calibre has now been ascertained to be sixty thousand Muslims and forty-five thousand Marathas. The latter were certainly weakened by starvation and the loss of animals. In this respect the Afghans were in high and buoyant spirits. In generalship also, the superiority of Abdali was obvious, as Bhau Saheb with all his enthusiasm was inferior to the Shah in the military handling of a battle-field. Bhau Saheb had from the beginning a great faith in his powerful artillery of more than two hundred pieces, and in its effective use by his

3. The last night's plan of square formation was given up. रात्रीच चौबुर्जीचा मनसुबा राहिला. भा० ब०

trusted commandant Ibrahim Khan. But this itself proved rather a handicap in the predicament that had developed. The heavy guns took time to be brought into proper position, while the Maratha army was on the move. Otherwise this heavy arm of the Maratha force could have done great execution. On this occasion Ibrahim Khan's long range cannon overshot their objective and could be easily silenced, when the two sides came close together. The Shah on the other hand had no heavy guns of the Maratha type : he had instead an efficient set of about two thousand light guns, camel-borne swivels, which could inflict severe havoc upon the dense mass of the Maratha ranks at short range. These light-guns of the Afghan Shah were handled each by two expert gunners riding one camel. Besides, this whole corps was kept in reserve by the Shah for a last moment execution, after the Marathas had exhausted themselves in the early stages of the combat. In addition to this light artillery the Shah kept in reserve a select force of six thousand Kazalbash of his personal body-guard, with fine young horses freshly imported from the north-west. The members of this Kazalbash corps regarded themselves as the Shah's faithful slaves, receiving special treatment in food and dress. It is these two bodies of carefully reserved men which decided the issue.

Another handicap from which the Marathas suffered arose out of the difference in the dress of the two combatants. The Marathas of the south wore their plain shirts, while the Afghans dwelling in the cold mountains of their native land were protected with a thick woollen or leather waist-coat ; most of the higher men wore besides a plaited armour of iron upon which the swords and spears of the Marathas could hardly make any impression. The Abdali Shah kept his eye steadily upon the slightest move of his opponents and promptly corrected every trifling short-coming in his ranks. He allowed the Marathas to spend themselves in an initial dash, himself standing on the defensive during this stage. He patiently waited till the Marathas became completely exhausted and then brought into action at the right moment not only his reserve but also some of those who had run away and hidden themselves in the rear ranks.

Bhau Saheb's original plan of forcing out a passage required a careful combination between his three arms, artillery, infantry and cavalry. Such a combination could not be preserved in the combat as it actually developed. The Maratha units neither understood, nor had a mind to follow accurately the instructions that were issued to them on the basis of the plan advised by Ibrahim Khan.

3. The combat.—The action was joined at about nine in the morning and continued unabated till nearly three in the afternoon. In their first rage the Marathas fought vigorously and committed great havoc upon the Afghan soldiery. The Maratha left and right wings and the centre maintained a grim struggle for the first few hours. The Gardi-Ruhela duel, Bhau's clash against the Wazir Shah Vali and the Sindia-Holkar sweep from the Maratha right against Najib Khan and Shah Pasand, brought out the determined valour of the Marathas and inflicted great destruction upon their opponents. The Afghan position was saved only by the timely succours which that Shah rendered wherever he discovered danger threatening. Ibrahim Khan furiously attacked the right wing of the Shah and killed Atai Khan with some three thousand men of his corps, making the Shah for a moment nervous about the issue. He, however, immediately pushed up his reserves and recovered his position. Ibrahim Khan's infantry corps was outnumbered, surrounded and annihilated, his heavy guns entirely silent during the mixed combat at close quarters.

The fight in the centre, however, was likewise tenacious and dreadful on account of the presence there of the Maratha Commander and the Peshwa's son. Before the determined onslaught of Bhau Saheb the Durrani centre of Shah Vali Khan completely broke down. When Shuja perceived the sad plight of the Wazir, he sent Kashiraj to ascertain the facts. The latter found Shah Vali Khan sitting on the ground, beating his forehead in agony and trying to rally his flying followers piteously crying, "Where are you running away my friends : Kabul is far off ; you can't reach it by running away." When the Shah came to know his Wazir's dangerous situation, he immediately detached fresh troops for his relief and had all the fleeing men called back on pain of cutting them down. About thirteen thousand troops that had withdrawn from the battle were thus thrown into the combat at two o'clock in the afternoon. Till that hour Bhau Saheb, Vishvasrao, Ibrahim Khan, Yashvantrao Pawar, Jankoji Sindia, Antaji Mankeshwar and the rest had done their best and their attack had developed furiously. The enemy was yielding ground and the Marathas appeared almost within an inch of winning. The combat on the right of the Maratha line was equally stiff, with Jankoji Sindia boldly engaging Shah Pasand Khan and Najib Khan's Rohilas, who suffered heavily.

The Maratha troops who had been marching from the early dawn and strenuously fighting for over five hours without food and water, now began to show signs of exhaustion. Abdali chose this moment to throw in his reserves of ten thousand men into the battle. These reserves turned the scales decisively against the Marathas ; and their destruction was completed by the Afghan squadron of 1500 camel swivels, which wheeled round in three batches of 500 each, doing immense damage at close range. In the midst of such a terrific fight a stray bullet from a *Zamburak* struck Vishvasrao dead on his horse *Dilpak* a little before three in the afternoon. This proved the sign for the rot to set in. Bhau Saheb not bearing to see the sight of his dead nephew, placed him on an elephant and rushed headlong with his personal guards into the Afghan ranks until he quickly disappeared. This last half-hour witnessed a frightful carnage round the Peshwa's flag. According to the Hindu scriptures suffering death on the battle field bestows merit on the warrior. From this point of view the Marathas certainly attained it by their supreme sacrifice at this last moment. The disappearance of Bhau Saheb at once created a panic, and before four in the afternoon of that short January day, a general flight commenced with the debacle consequent upon such an occasion. A small proportion of the common fighters and some of their leaders such as Malharrao Holkar, Damaji Gaikwad, Vithal Shivdeo and a few others made their way safely out of the holocaust, when they realized that the day was lost. But the major portion of that vast army with their families and camp followers perished by the cold steel of the pitiless Afghans. The field was littered with the dead and the wounded of the helpless non-combatants, stragglers, bazaarmen, clerks, accountants and others. Several ran back to the camp where there was none to protect them and where the Afghans cut down as many as they could in the early waning moon-light of the 8th night of the bright half of Poush. The carnage continued the next day also. A few of the Marathas escaped towards Delhi, Rajputana and the country of the Jats. The Jat Raja and his Rani Kishori took the utmost care of these fugitives providing them with food, clothes, and residence and comforting them in their unspeakable suffering.

The battle-field was examined the next day by Anupgir Gosavi and Kashiraj under instructions from Shuja-ud-daula. They discovered 32 large heaps of corpses, which when counted numbered 28 thousand. Countless corpses were besides found strewn on that vast plain, and the nooks of the jungles around. About 35 thousand were taken prisoners and slaughtered in cold blood by the heartless Durranis. About 8 thousand Maratha refugees and four hundred of the officers took shelter in Shuja-ud-daula's camp. The latter besides generously affording them all the protection he could, despatched them under a strong escort to Surajmal's dominion financing their journey from his own purse. The huge trench of Panipat was equally full of dead bodies, and several wounded men succumbed to their wounds in the extreme cold of the night. It is estimated that nearly 75 thousand Marathas were killed in this huge slaughter and some 22 thousand saved their lives by paying ransom.

Ibrahim Khan Gardi and Jankoji Sindia were captured wounded and subsequently put to death. Not much plunder could be secured by the enemy beyond some horses and the camp equipage in Panipat. The dead bodies of Vishvasrao and Bhau Saheb were recovered, properly recognized and given the due rites by Anupgir Gosavi, Kashiraj and others, for which concession Shuja pleaded with the Shah personally and paid the Abdali a consideration of three lacs. Bhau Saheb's head was recovered from a Durrani trooper by the exertions of the Nawab and was burnt a day later. Kashiraj himself wrote letters to this effect to the Peshwa. Bhau Saheb's wife Parvatibai returned safe to Gwalior and joined the Peshwa near Bhilsa.

The Afghan monarch Ahmad Shah commemorated his triumph by paying a visit the next day to the shrine of the Muslim saint Ali Kalandar in the Panipat village, wearing a gorgeous dress and jewels including the Koh-i-noor and offered devout prayers for the great victory he had won. Thereafter he struck his camp and started for Delhi where he arrived in three days, and camped outside the city. On 29th January he made a formal entry into the city and took up his residence in the halls once occupied by Shah Jahan and his successors, holding court in the Diwan-i-Khas after the fashion of the Mughal Emperors. But on account of various troubles he had no peace at heart and departed for his native country on 20th March.

The victor himself wrote the following account of this battle to Raja Madho Sinh[4] :—

"The flame of fighting blazed up and raged on all sides. The enemy too distinguished themselves and fought so well, that it was beyond the capacity of other races. Gradually the fighting passed from the exchange of cannon and rocketfire to the discharge of muskets, from which it proceeded to the stage of combat with swords, daggers and knives. They grasped each other by the neck. Those dauntless bloodshedders (the Marathas) did not fall short in fighting and doing glorious deeds. Suddenly the breeze of victory began to blow and as willed by the Divine Lord the wretched Deccanis suffered utter defeat. Vishwasrao and the Bhau who had been fighting in front of my Wazir were slain and many other Sardars also on their side fell. Ibrahim Khan Gardi and his brother were captured wounded. Bapu Pandit (Hingne) was taken prisoner. Forty to fifty thousand troopers and infantry men of the enemy became as grass before our pitiless swords. It is not known whether Malhar and Janko have been slain or what else has happened to them. All the enemy's artillery, elephants and property have been seized by my men."[5]

4. The victor's plight, conciliating the Peshwa.— During his residence of two months at the capital, Shah Abdali confirmed the arrangement that Bhau Saheb had made, by de-

4. Sir Jadunath Sarkar, *Modern Review*, May 1946. Here Abdali definitely says that Sadashivrao was slain : so all theories about the future pretender being the real Sadashivrao must be set at rest finally.

5. Graphic descriptions of this bloody battle have come down from the pen of many writers. Kashiraj's bakhar and the short autobiography of Nana Phadnis can be read with advantage.

claring Shah Alam Emperor, his son Jawan Bakht then at Delhi acting as the heir. He appointed Najib Khan to the post of Mir Bakhshi and entrusted the management of the Empire's affairs jointly to him and Jawan Bakht. He refused to appoint Shuja-ud-daula as the Wazir, a reward which he was ardently expecting from the Shah for the valuable part he had played as an ally in the recent struggle. Shuja felt this as a bitter humiliation and left abruptly for Lucknow on 7th March. This indeed in no way affected the Shah as he hardly cared now for the politics of India. He was now faced with an open mutiny of his own Afghan troops, who had received no pay for the last 18 months of their sojourn in India. They had expected to go back rich and wealthy by the acquisition of Indian spoil, but this could not be, as they had little or no plunder this time. They had not received even their pay. Their maintenance alone cost the Shah as much as the Marathas or about a crore of Rupees per annum. The Maratha camp at Panipat was plundered, but hardly any thing valuable was found there as the Marathas had sold every bit of whatever could fetch them food. The Shah himself lived in a gorgeous palace at Delhi apparently unconcerned about his return, while his troops were longing to go home fearing that as the Marathas were expected to return headed by the Peshwa, another war would be inflicted on them. When the pressure of the clamour became severe, the Shah asked Najib Khan to procure money to pay his troops, as the Khan was now the sole custodian of the imperial affairs. Najib Khan urged his utter helplessness in the matter of funds, and said he had already given away all that he could possibly procure. He suggested that Surajmal Jat should be attacked and made to yield treasure of which he possessed plenty. It meant another war, and the Afghan troops declared they would not move unless they received their past wages. The Shah could find no way out of the difficulty and decided upon returning home. He left Delhi on 20th March and reached Afghanistan in May.

After studying the movements and arrangements made by the Shah Abdali, let us review his attitude as it affected the Marathas. The grand victory of the Afghans and the crushing defeat inflicted by them upon the Marathas, availed the victor but little. He never coveted the crown of Delhi. His only anxiety was to hold the rich province of the Punjab in order to relieve the needs of his poor country, without undergoing the risk of interfering with the affairs of Delhi or the rights of the Marathas in that sphere. Had it not been for the personal animosity of Najib Khan towards the Marathas, the dreadful struggle of Panipat would not have occurred at all. But having gone the length of a stiff and costly war with the Marathas, the Shah was now anxious to close the bitterness that had been roused, and to ensure in future that the Marathas should not molest him so far as the Punjab was concerned. And when he learned at Delhi that the Peshwa himself had arrived as far as Gwalior with large forces, and that the war might be renewed any moment now under conditions very adverse to him, with his own troops in open rebellion, he became impatient to arrive at an understanding with the Peshwa which the Maratha agent Hingne had already offered to bring about immediately on the Shah's arrival at Delhi. Bapuji Mahadev was sent for with this object within four days of the battle of Panipat; he writes, "I met the Shah through his Wazir Shah Vali Khan, and explained to him that the Peshwa had no ill-feeling towards him, that he should safely march back to his country, and that he (Hingne) would undertake to effect a lasting peace between them. The Shah readily agreed to this proposal and at once asked Yakub Ali Khan to proceed to Gwalior and bring about a treaty of peace personally with the Peshwa. The Shah gave his solemn consent to the proposal and then decided to return to his country. When he reached Lahore, he again sent pressing instructions to Yakub Ali Khan not to delay the subject of a lasting peace."[6]

Had the Peshwa been in his normal health mentally, a treaty could have been at once arranged: but even here the trouble arose partly through Najib Khan, who was now exposed to the vengeance of the Marathas, and partly through the stunning blow which the whole Maratha nation and their northern policy had received on the fatal 14th January. Several precious months were wasted in gathering the actual facts, even as regards the fate of Bhau Saheb himself. For a time no Maratha general dared to come to Delhi and meet the Afghan monarch. If Malharrao Holkar and Naro Shankar had remained at Delhi or come back as soon as Hingne called them, the peace negotiations would not have been delayed. On 23rd March the Peshwa wrote to Hingne, " I am enclosing my replies to the letters received from the Shah Abdali and his Wazir Shah Vali Khan and delivered here by their agent Gulraj. I am now deputing Anwarulla Khan and Hussain Muhammad Khan to negotiate peace with the Shah. I have authorized Malharrao Holkar to conclude the subject. You must now deal directly with Holkar and accept his decision. I want you to take full counsel with these two advisers, Anwarullah and Hussain Muhammad, and continue to keep me informed of the progress of the negotiations. Where is the Shah Abdali now? Has Ghazi-ud-din interviewed him? Please write all details."

The Peshwa repeated the same query on 6th April to Hingne and asked, "Who is now the Padshah at Delhi, who is the Wazir, why has Abdali left so abruptly, what are now the designs of Ghazi-ud-din and the rest?" The Peshwa added, " Malharrao Holkar is now at Gwalior with large forces and will attend to our concerns in north India."

Early in May 1761 Gangadhar Yashvant on behalf of Holkar reported to the Peshwa, "before departing for his homeland, the Shah gave definite instructions in the presence of Hingne, to Shuja-ud-daula and his Ruhela allies, that he had effected a lasting peace with the Peshwa and that they all should respect the latter's authority, which course alone would benefit them most." The Peshwa cordially accepted the Shah's proposal of deputing Yakub Ali to Poona with Hingne for fixing up the definite terms of a lasting peace.[6]

This subject of peace came to be unavoidably delayed for nearly two years. The Peshwa himself died in June, giving rise to the unfortunate domestic dissension between the new Peshwa Madhavrao and his uncle Raghunathrao. One point is thus as clear as day light that the field of Panipat, however dreadful to the Marathas on account of the heavy death roll, decided nothing finally and only maintained the status quo ante so far as the Delhi politics was concerned.[7] Abdali himself thus wrote to the Peshwa, " There is no real reason why there

6. *Hingne Papers* I. 202, 205, 207, 210.
7. P. D. 2. 103, 146 and 21. 202.

should exist any ill-feeling between you and us ; true, you have lost your son and brother in the unfortunate fight : but it was entirely provoked by Bhau Saheb and we could not act otherwise than we did in self-defence. However, we are deeply sorry for these losses. We readily leave to you the subject of the imperial management of Delhi, provided you allow us to hold the Punjab up to the river Satlaj, and support Shah Alam as the Emperor. You must forget the regrettable events that have taken place and entertain a lasting friendship towards us, which we are anxiously soliciting."[8]

With such gestures and letters breathing a genuine spirit of conciliation and good will, the Abdali Shah sent his agent Gulraj to the Peshwa accompanied by the customary dresses. Gulraj met the Peshwa in Malwa on 10th February 1761 and Gangadhar Chandrachud was commissioned to proceed to Delhi and adjust matters. Thus a considerable delay ensued, and the treaty of peace took nearly two years to be finally concluded, although the essential points had been discussed and determined before 20th March i.e., the day on which both Abdali and the Peshwa left their respective stations for their homes. There was another strong reason for Abdali to come to an immediate understanding with the Peshwa. The Sikhs had grown powerful in the Punjab and violently resisted Abdali's claim to that province. After Panipat the Shah Abdali had to come to the Punjab year after year and to return each time in discomfiture after being molested and repulsed by the Sikhs. Ahmad Shah lost his health and vigour in the vain attempt to conquer the Punjab, and the last few years of his life were for him sad and inactive. He suffered from a carbuncle which put an end to his life on 14th April 1772, at the age of 48.

In the mean time Abdali's agents Gulraj and Anand Ram had arrived in Poona, and the Peshwa Madhavrao I put the final shape in February 1763 to a treaty of peace and good will. The Peshwa sent dresses and a handsome elephant to the Shah from Poona, thus finally effacing the sad memories of the fatal day of Panipat.[9]

8. *History of the Sikhs* by Dr. Hari Ram Gupta ; Sarkar's *Fall of the Mughal Empire* II, p. 379.

9. Madhavrao Roznishi, 1. 1, 6, 7 ; *Aitihasik Tipne*, 1. 56.

5. **The Peshwa breaks down in Bundelkhand.**—Here we must go back and review the movements of the Peshwa during the four months from October 1760 onwards, when his son and cousin were being hard-pressed at Panipat. He had received no news of any adverse occurrences in the north and was quite at ease as regards the affairs in that quarter, having provided everything that was needed for Sadashivrao's expedition. As usual he left Poona at the Dassara time and prepared to march to the north for completing the political settlement in that quarter, after Abdali had been expelled, as was fully expected. The last letter that he received from Bhau Saheb was dated 14 November, when the two opponents had just confronted each other at Panipat and a decision was momentarily expected. So without the least concern the Peshwa moved leisurely to Ahmadnagar and spent two months on the Godavari, but having received no news of the northern affairs he was getting increasingly anxious every day about the fate of his armies and wrote to several persons asking for news. Suspecting some mishap he hurriedly left his quarters on the last day of 1760, with his brother Raghunathrao and another large army led by the two Bhosle brothers, Gopalrao Patwardhan, Sadashiv Ramchandra, Yamaji Shivdev and others. On 9th January he sent back Raghunathrao to watch the Nizam. On 18th January the Peshwa entered Malwa and at once wrote to Bhau Saheb asking him to hold the Abdali Shah until he himself arrived, when they could easily crush him between the two armies. While in wait at Bhilsa for tidings, he intercepted a banker's private messenger on 24th January, who was the bearer of a letter which indicated by metaphors relating to jewellery, that something serious had happened to the Maratha host. Among other enigmatical expressions there were these words: "two pearls dissolved, twenty-five gold mohurs have been lost, and of the silver and copper the total cannot be cast up." In due course further details reached him, telling how the Marathas having been cooped up in the entrenchment at Panipat were nearly starved and clamorously rushed forth to fight and were ridden down by the superior weight of the Afghan army. The Peshwa retired to his tent literally with a broken heart, unable to endure the grief. Gradually news filtered to him daily as streams of ill-fated men gradually returned in distress, but no

one giving full and satisfactory details as to what had actually happened.[10]

For over a month a dreadful suspense prevailed in the Peshwa's mind and in that of his followers. It was only in February when he met Nana Purandare on his return from Panipat that the Peshwa could get some reliable and tangible details of the fate that had overcome the Maratha army on 14th January. The death of his son and the complete destruction of his huge splendid army plunged the Peshwa for a long time into terrible grief, and the uncertainty was heightened by the reports that Bhau Saheb and Jankoji were returning wounded. It took at least two months more to prove the falsity of these reports; but all the same it diverted the Peshwa's attention to the immediate inquiry about the fate of those who were supposed to be still alive. The shock itself proved too much for the frail and declining constitution of the Peshwa already stricken down by an incurable malady; and the idea of his proceeding towards Delhi had to be given up. It was unfortunate that Malharrao and Naro Shankar left Delhi in a panic. Had they taken their stand at the capital, the Peshwa would have joined them and could have restored Maratha power at Delhi, having brought about a friendly understanding with the retiring Shah Abdali. The Peshwa proceeded north from Bhilsa on 7th February and reached Pachhor about 32 miles further. Here he made a long stay, and after full deliberation retraced his steps to the south on 22nd March and passed through Indore on 6th April. The two months that the Peshwa spent near Bhilsa and Sironj were not wasted. Maratha power and prestige were quickly re-established in Malwa, Bundelkhand and the Doab. Although the Peshwa himself was overcome with sorrow and affliction, there were men and captains about him, who did their best in restoring the Maratha rule which had been shaken for a few months. The panic-stricken leaders, Malharrao Holkar, Naro Shankar, the Pawars and others who had left Delhi, without making a bold stand, were severely dealt with, all their possessions being confiscated for a few months, and later restored to their holders as soon as normal conditions began to reappear. Malharrao Holkar took the lead promptly

10. *Raj.* 3. 210; *Khare* 1. 26.

in restoring the lost Maratha prestige. The leading Rajput prince at this time was Madho Sinh of Jaipur. Malharrao sternly demanded the arrears of tribute, which the Rajah refused to pay and prepared to resist by a recourse to arms. Malharrao took up the challenge readily and in a sanguinary action at Mangrol, 20 miles north east of Kotah, which lasted for two full days, 29th and 30th November 1761, Madho Sinh was completely humbled. This one instance dispelled all rumours of the Maratha power having vanished from north India. By this timely stroke Malharrao regained his former glow of prestige in Maratha politics, lost by his precipitate flight from the field of Panipat.

6. Review of the disaster.—It is now over 180 years since the third battle of Panipat was fought by the Marathas and it has made a permanent mark in the history of India. Patient and critical enquiry is still being persistently carried on by writers and students each trying in his own way to assign praise and blame. Let us here take a short dispassionate review of the whole struggle which proved so fatal to the Marathas at Panipat, and properly assess the responsibility for that momentous result.

Such an important affair as this national disaster could not have remained without a formal inquiry. It stands to reason to suppose that the Peshwa Madhavrao I got a full and formal report prepared about the event dealing both with its antecedent and remote as well as immediate causes.[11] These

11. The two valuable documents known as Bhau Saheb's Kaifiyat and Bhau Saheb's Bakhar are possibly the result of such an enquiry instituted for the edification of the future administrators. These two tracts practically summarize all the salient features eloquently expressed for the appreciation of an average reader. They are evidently based on original materials. Holkar and Naro Shankar were punished by the dying Peshwa himself for their dereliction. History is often blind and cruel towards the authors of a lost cause, and the victors usually win their case in public estimation. Recent research has brought to light a large quantity of literature in Marathi and Persian particularly the three volumes 2, 21 and 27 of the P. D. Selections and the *Purandare Daftar* volume 1, the excellent Persian accounts of Kashiraj and Nuruddin Hussain, letters in Rajwade Volumes 1 and 6, along with the clear reasoned analysis presented by Sir Jadunath Sarkar in his *Fall of the Mughal Empire*. Volume 2. These will be found of immense help in elucidating the subject.

have been already made clear in the preceding pages.

Maratha affairs in the north came to be mishandled by Raghunathrao, who could not compose the growing differences between the two leading chiefs Sindia and Holkar.[12] Sadashivrao was mainly sent to set right past abuses, a task which he quickly and effectively executed. He was doubtless the fittest leader that the Maratha nation then possessed. He was respected and feared, and possessed unflinching courage. He was certainly often obstinate and hot-tempered, but these drawbacks were the result of a genuine desire to serve his nation. He had never before gone to the north, but this point he soon made up by constant inquiry and labour. Compared with his Afghan opponent, he must be reckoned inferior in generalship being seven years junior to the Shah Abdali, who had possessed matchless experience of warfare in central Asia, having received his training under Nadir Shah, the Napoleon of Asia, dealing with varied characters and situations, overcoming obstacles of flooded rivers, difficult mountains and human eccentricities. This is well illustrated by the cool and patient manner in which Abdali managed every detail of this campaign, and the way in which he soon dexterously turned a critical situation against his opponents. He took possession of the Jamuna and assured for his army plentiful supplies from the country beyond, having cleverly succeeded in besieging the Marathas in their entrenched camp.

Malharrao Holkar and others had suggested to Bhau Saheb to keep the women and the non-combatants behind somewhere near the Chambal or near Mathura : the rejection of this precaution proved disastrous. He encumbered himself with an unnecessarily large number of non-combatants at least three times that of the actual fighters. If he had not been so hard pressed to feed this large number, the starvation would not have been so acute.

We can here thus summarise the main causes of the Maratha disaster at Panipat : (1) Raghunathrao's failure to main-

12. The Peshwa himself never went to the north after the death of Shahu. He could easily have gone there during 1759, when there was no major issue in the Deccan to occupy his attention.

tain order and discipline among Maratha agents in the north; (2) the failure of Holkar to restrain Najib Khan from doing mischief; (3) the Peshwa's failure to go to the north and adjust matters when it was yet time to mend them. These were the antecedent causes. The immediate causes were (4) the failure of Bhau Saheb with Dattaji Sindia's example before his eyes, to keep women and non-combatants behind at Bharatpur or even at Delhi at the time when he left that place to advance upon Kunjpura; (5) as soon as the two armies came face to face about the last day of October, Bhau Saheb should have at once attacked Abdali and maintained communications with his base at Delhi. He wasted two and a half months on the defensive in a besieged camp until starvation compelled him to make the last desperate effort for escape. But we have now no means of knowing why Bhau Saheb waited so long. (6) And the last culminating point was reached, when Bhau Saheb finding Vishvasrao killed, rushed headlong into the fight, perhaps under the impression, "after me the deluge." (7) One serious handicap from which the Marathas suffered may be noticed in passing. The strength of the Maratha fighter was in his horse. It was his horse that gave the strength of mobility to the Maratha army. Bhau Saheb commanded at Panipat a large body of the finest troops that ever went out from the south. But during the months of starvation in his besieged camp, most of the horses died, compelling all troopers to play the role of infantry for which they were not trained. This drawback could not be remedied.

One school of critics argue that the Marathas lost the day at Panipat because they gave up their traditional method of guerilla warfare. But such a view has no basis in fact. It is doubtless true that it was this method which enabled the Maratha nation in the last century to rise above others. But this warfare was suited only to the hilly regions of the Deccan plateau; it could not be effective in the vast plains of northern India, where not a single natural barrier exists from the Indus to the Bay of Bengal. Nor were the Marathas at home in these foreign regions, the inhabitants of which were not only strangers but positively hostile to them. To obviate these defects Bhau Saheb equipped himself with an efficient artillery, with which he reduced Delhi and Kunjpura.

The situation so changed on the last day at Panipat that the same artillery proved an encumbrance.

7. **Significance of the disaster.**—It is a popular mistake of long standing to suppose that the third battle of Panipat destroyed the Maratha power in the north or that it essentially shook the Maratha Empire of India. Notwithstanding the terrible losses in man power suffered on that field by the Marathas, the disaster decided nothing. In fact it pushed forward in the distant sequel two prominent members of the dominant race, Nana Phadnis and Mahadji Sindia, both miraculously escaping death on that fatal day, who resuscitated that power to its former glory. Not long after the battle of Panipat the Maratha power began to prosper again as before and continued to do so for forty years, until the death of Mahadji Sindia or until British supremacy was established early in the 19th century by the second Maratha War (1803). The first set back the Maratha power received was by the premature death of their greatest Peshwa Madhavrao, which enabled the British power to come forward so easily on the stage of history and dispute Indian supremacy with the Marathas for a quarter of a century. The disaster of Panipat was indeed like a natural visitation destroying life, but leading to no decisive political consequences. To maintain that the disaster of Panipat put an end to the dreams of supremacy cherished by the Marathas, is to misunderstand the situation as recorded in contemporary documents. The truth is correctly stated by a learned scholar who asserts that,

"The fall of the Angrias (1756) and the disaster of Panipat (1761) freed the British from the thraldom of insidious neighbours and hastened their rise."[13] This is indeed the indirect but important consequence of the Maratha disaster. Instead of this event crushing Maratha aspirations for good, it certainly gave them a new strength and a fresh vigor in their efforts to establish supremacy over the Indian continent. Their mettle was severely tested and found to be as vigorous as ever before. In the midst of the extreme misery and distress of the beleaguered camp, there was absolutely no sign of panic or re-

13. Gerson da Cunha's *Origin of Bombay.*

volt, no wail of despair or defeat. Bhau's courage inspired every soul to supreme exertion, and even after the final rout, people wrote and spoke of the event as if they were heroes. The Marathas have been a practical people possessing a temperament which never was overenthused under victory or crushed under disasters. Writes Maj. Evans Bell, "The battle of Panipat was a triumph and a glory for the Marathas. They fought in the cause of "India for the Indians," while the great Muhammadan Princes of Delhi, of Oudh and the Deccan stood aside, intriguing and trimming. And though the Marathas were defeated, the victorious Afghans retired and never again interfered in the affairs of India."

It is significant that while the two combatants, the Marathas and the Muslims, were locked in a deadly combat on the field of ancient Kurukshetra, Clive the first founder of the British Empire in India, was on his way to England to explain the feasibility of his dreams of an Indian empire to the Great Commoner Lord Chatham, then the Prime Minister. Panipat indirectly ushered in a new participant in the struggle for Indian supremacy. This is indeed the direct outcome of that historical event, which on that account marks a turning point in the history of India.

Oppressed by the Wazir Ghazi-ud-din's vulgar ambition and relentless ferocity, the Crown Prince Ali Gauhar was compelled to flee from Delhi in May 1758 and seek safety in exile. The Wazir's foolish measures brought down on his head and on his Maratha confederates the wrathful invasion of Ahmad Shah Abdali, and led to the prolonged contest between the two for the mastery of the Punjab and the paramountcy over Hindustan. It finally culminated in the Maratha rout at Panipat two years later. This absorbing contest made it impossible for the Wazir and his Maratha allies to take note of the political revolution that had come over Bengal by the battle of Plassey and its sequel. The English merchants were thus enabled to make a successful bid for the position of King-makers in Bengal and Bihar, and to use the power thus acquired to cleverly throw their net of supremacy over the whole land. The ignorant and mutually quarrelling Indian chiefs failed to realize the significance of these British activities and the meaning of their political and territorial ambition. Ali Gauhar, Shuja-ud-daula,

Surajmal, Ghazi-ud-din, Najib Khan, Raghunathrao, Malharrao Holkar, each and all unaccustomed to take long views, could not appreciate the trend of the epoch-making events that were happening in Bengal and in the Karnatak. They all wasted their energies in personal squabbles at Delhi.

The battle of Panipat was fought on 14th January 1761. The very next day the Mughal Emperor Shah Alam in his effort to recover Bengal sustained a severe defeat on the river Son at the hands of the British forces led by Major Carnac. Shah Alam's French officers were taken prisoners and he had to throw himself on the British protection. The day after this event, that is on the 16th January, Pondicherry, the rival of Madras, fell into British hands, thereby smashing the French power in India. These three days proved momentous in determining the future fate of this country. The Peshwa sank to his grave under the blow of Panipat, and for a few years the British had no rival on the horizon. The tone of their behaviour and correspondence markedly changed from the days of the Peshwa Bajirao I to those of Madhavrao, as the missions of Gordon and Price amply testify. The rise of Haidar Ali in the South was also the direct result of the Maratha rout at Panipat.

If these broad political issues of the Indian situation are kept out of sight, Panipat in itself brought to the Marathas a unique experience in politics and war, and heightened their national pride and sentiment, as nothing else could have done. The disaster instead of damping their spirits, made them shine higher as, when a nation is on the path of advancement and progress, such ups and downs are inevitable. Such valiant soldiers as Dattaji, Jankoji, Ibrahim Khan, Sadashivrao and Vishvasrao did not die in vain. They left their mark on the fortunes of their nation and prepared it for a greater effort such as the young Peshwa Madhavrao actually put forth. Out of death cometh life, is only too true. Although one generation, the older one, was cut off, the younger generation soon rose to take its place and perform the nation's service as before. The disaster was felt as personal by almost every home in Maharashtra, and every soul was stirred by it to rise to the nation's calls.

8. **The Peshwa's last days.**—In view of his ruined health it was decided that the Peshwa should return to Poona. He left Pachhor on 22nd March and after crossing the Narmada and the Tapti, performed his father's death anniversary rites at Toka on the Godavari on 16th May. At the Narmada he fainted and was luckily saved from drowning. Here he was weighed and found to be 4568 tolas or about 114 lbs., while six years before his weight was 178 lbs.[14] As his son Narayanrao had an attack of small-pox, the boy with his mother was left behind and the Peshwa reached Poona about 5th June. Here Purushottamrao Patwardhan remained in attendance and managed to humour him. His once robust body had now become extremely emaciated; his memory faltered; his temper had become irritable so that his friends and advisers dreaded to appear before him and avoided all talk with him. He unwittingly gave out state secrets to those who came to see him. On 12th June he left the Shaniwar palace and took his lodgings in a house on the Parvati hill, where he expired in the early part of the night of Tuesday 23rd June. The funeral took place at the new wooden bridge.[15] After the funeral rites were over, Madhavrao received the Peshwa's robes from the Chhatrapati at Satara on 17th July.

Balajirao had two wives Gopikabai and Radhabai. By the former he had three sons Vishwasrao, who died at Panipat, Madhavrao who succeeded him, and Narayanrao who succeeded Madhavrao came to be murdered. Sadashivrao's wife Parvatibai returned safe from the battlefield of Panipat and died on 16th August 1783.

9. **Balaji Rao's character.**—Peshwa Balajirao was certainly more fortunate than his father and grandfather in both his surroundings and the instruments which came ready to his hand. The political performance of the first four Peshwas is rightly considered unique in Indian history, inasmuch as they not only rapidly expanded the limits

---

14. Nana Phadnis in his autobiography gives interesting details of the Peshwa's health as he was with him part of the way.

15. Raj. Vol. 6. 416; P. D. 18. 163. *Purandare Daftar*, Vol. I; Chitnis bakhar of Ramraja.

of the Maratha Empire far beyond the dreams of those who valiantly fought the war of Independence against Aurangzeb, but they certainly gave to Maharashtra and the territories they subjugated outside, a humane and benign rule in severe contrast with the rapacity and anarchy that set in after that Emperor's death. The main credit for establishing a sagacious and healthy administration over vast territories goes to this third Peshwa, whose solid and useful work conducted with patient toil for years unfortunately came to be clouded by the sad and sudden end which closed his all too short career. With all his faults and failures we can certainly accept in substance the judgment pronounced about him by discriminating writers.

One contemporary opinion runs thus : " Balajipant Nana secured the affection of the great Chhatrapati Shahu and promoted in the service of the State all those who had been selected and raised to high positions by his father and uncle. He encouraged talent wherever he detected it, and bestowed titles, gifts and honours upon those who exhibited valour and capacity. With a heart disposed towards public welfare, he manned the services with highly qualified individuals. Sardars and people undertook adventures and carried out grand conquests. His sweet, conciliatory and forgiving ways conquered the hearts even of his enemies. His conquests extended from Rameshwar to Indra-Prasta. Nana Saheb and Bhau Saheb were both incarnations of divine qualities."[16]

So long as the benign hand of Shahu was at his back, Nana Saheb succeeded in holding together several discordant elements, but after the death of that monarch, he was confronted with serious political complications arising one after another, and thereafter his weakness of character and consequent failures became glaring. After Shahu's death he removed the Maratha administration from Satara to Poona, thereby incurring the charge of usurpation against his master the Chhatrapati. In the northern affairs he could not compose the differences between the chiefs Holkar and Sindia and allowed them a free hand against the Rajputs, who thus became estranged. He did not take steps to set right the mismanagement created in that sphere by his bro-

16. Peshwa bakhar in Raj., Vol. 4 and the bakhar of Bhau Saheb.

ther Raghunathrao. For crushing Tulaji Angria, this Peshwa called in the help of the British who soon proved too strong for him. He lost control of affairs towards the end of his career, and died in a demented state deeply mourning the deaths of Vishvasrao and Bhausaheb.

Balajirao was a man of refined taste, fond of leading a luxurious life and enjoying splendour and the fine arts. During his regime the social life of Maharashtra underwent great changes in various directions. The Maratha camp life rapidly lost its original rudeness and simplicity, and fashioned itself on the enervating splendour of the imperial court. It is difficult to estimate correctly the financial position of the Maratha State under him. The public debt is reckoned by one authority to have been about 17 lacs at the time of the Peshwa's death ; other students have calculated it at about a crore of Rupees. But fifty lacs will not be an unreasonable figure, by no means discreditable to his administration. The Peshwa was an expert in accounts and penmanship, and exercised strict control over receipts and expenditure. Public servants were trained in a special institution of the Secretariat called the *Phad*, where Nana Phadnis himself received his training.

The Peshwa used persuasive methods both in diplomacy and war rather than force. It is wrong to charge him with a predilection for his own caste. He treated all castes equally and laid down the principle of equal treatment and impartial patronage for all. Nevertheless as the Peshwas were intimate with their Brahman relations and friends, it is quite true that the latter received much, though not exclusive attention and encouragement. With all the stortcomings and mistakes of his rule, Balajirao will certainly be remembered as one of the four great Peshwas. who extended Maratha rule practically throughout India.

Sir Richard Temple thus summarises Balajirao's character : "Balaji's character was formed on the same lines as that of his father, and his disposition moved in the same direction. But though a man of skilful address, of influence in counsel and of ability in the field, he was inferior to his father both as a soldier and as a politician. He well knew how to utilise the talents of those about him, and some of his greatest successes were won for him by his lieutenants. Still he was ever to the front, organizing or supervising and he saw the Maratha power attain its zenith. It was under him that the Maratha cavalry fully one hundred thousand strong could truly boast that they had slaked their thirst in every stream that flowed between Cape Comorin and the Himalayas. But he did not take, perhaps he was not capable of taking, any steps for rendering this widely extended dominion advantageous to the people. He allowed Maratha rule to continue to be what it had been from the first, more an organization of plunder than a system of administration. Personally he was unscrupulous in this respect, morally inferior to his father and grand father."[17]

Grant Duff's opinion is more balanced : "Balaji Bajirao was one of those princes whose good fortune originating in causes anterior to their time, obtained in consequence of national prosperity, a higher degree of celebrity than they may fully merit. He was a man of considerable political sagacity, of polished manners and of great address. The territory under the immediate care of the Peshwa had been in a progressive state of improvement. Balajirao appointed fixed Mamlatdars or Subahdars each of whom had charge of several districts. They held absolute charge of the police, the revenue and the civil and criminal judicature and in most cases had power of life and death. The commencement of a better system of administration particularly for Maharashtra is ascribed to Ramchandra Baba Shenwee and after his death Sadashivrao improved on his suggestions. A Shastree of respectability named Balkrishna Gadgil was appointed head of the Poona Nyayadhishi or court of justice, and the police was much invigorated at the capital. Under the Government of Balajirao, Panchayats, the ordinary tribunals of civil justice began to improve. The Maratha dominion attained its greatest extent under Balajirao's administration and most of the principal Brahman families can only date their rise from that period. In short the condition of the whole population was in his time improved and the Maratha peasantry sensible of the comparative amelioration which they began to enjoy, have ever since blessed the days of Nana Saheb Peshwa."[18]

17. Oriental Experience, P. 392.
18. Volume 2, P. 157.

Kincaid adds some interesting touches :—"Of all his cities Balaji loved Poona best. He spent vast sums in attracting to it learned scholars, devout Brahmans and famous poets. He encouraged trade, built fountains, improved roads and created fresh peths or quarters. Sadashiv Peth and Narayan Peth are still populous and fashionable. He greatly improved the lake at Katraj and planted innumerable trees on the roads to Theur, Alandi and Ganeshkhind. But the monument that today most vividly recalls to the visitor's mind this magnificent prince is the Parvati Hill. Before Balaji's time a tiny temple to Parvati crowned its summit and the shrine had acquired the reputation of curing sick people. Once Gopikabai suffering from a sore heel, went to see the hill Goddess and was cured. Her husband to show his gratitude erected the noble temple now known as Deva-deveshwar. After Shahu's death Balaji placed in it the *Padukas* or sandals of Shahu and thus the hill became a monument of the Maratha king. In the plain to the south the Peshwa gave great feasts and distributed charity, while to the north he built another temple on the hill to the God Vishnu and on the 11th of every month he went regularly to worship at the Vishnu's shrine. Indeed he so loved the hill that he built a palace there and when he felt death coming near, it was to the Parvati Hill he went to die. The fame of Balaji Peshwa resounded from the Indus river to the southern seas."[19]

19. *History of the Mar. People*, Volume III, pp. 76-77.

CHRONOLOGY

CHAPTER XXII

1745, February 16	Madhavrao born.
1753, Dec. 9	Madhavrao married to Ramabai.
1761, July 6	Nizam Ali deposes Salabat Jang, appoints Vithal Sundar his minister.
1761, July 20	Madhavrao receives robes of Peshwaship.
1761, Sept. 29	Malharrao Holkar's wife Gautamabai dies.
1761, Nov. 29-30	Holkar routs Madhosinh at Mangrol.
1761, Nov.	Nizam Ali's aggression upon Poona ; Toka and other holy places ravaged ; Shrigonda dug up.
1761, Dec. 8	Nizam Ali occupies Chas and comes to Uruli where he is routed.
1762, January 5	Raghunathrao makes peace with Nizam Ali.
1762, January 7	Madhavrao proceeds to Karnatak.
1762, March	Malharrao Holkar arrives from Malwa.
1762, June	Madhavrao entrusts Miraj to the Patwardhans.
1762, July	Poona Court torn by factions.
1762, August 22	Raghunathrao flees to Wadgaon.
1762, Sept.-Oct.	Raghunathrao at Vinchur, prepares to oppose Madhavrao : Nizam Ali and Janoji Bhosle join him.
1762, November 7	Indecisive action on the Ghod river.
1762, Nov. 12	Madhavrao being defeated at Alegaon submits to Raghunathrao and is confined. A memorable assemblage of Maratha Chiefs.
1762, Nov. 21	Raghunathrao restores to Nizam Ali all the territory ceded by him at Udgir ; he makes fresh appointments to offices.
1762, Dec. 6	Raghunathrao leaves Alegaon for Satara.
1762, Dec.	Raghunathrao makes Ramchandra Jadhav Senapati and his own infant son Pratinidhi.
1762, Dec. 29	Raghunathrao invests Miraj : Mahadji Sindia and Damaji Gaikwad join him.

1763, February 3	Miraj surrendered.
1763, February 9	Nizam Ali and Janoji Bhosle meet at Gulbarga; Vithal Sundar and Gamaji Yamaji join the confederacy.
1763, March	Raghunathrao and the Maratha Chiefs form a union to oppose the hostile confederacy.
1763, March 10	Raghunathrao comes upon Aurangabad : Holkar joins him ; Ramchandra Jadhav arrested ; war started upon Nizam Ali.
1763, April-June	Mutual territory between Burhanpur and Haiderabad ravaged : Poona sacked and burnt.
1763, May 10	The Marathas at Medak near Haidarabad.
1763, Aug. 9	Maratha armies at Majalgaum.
1763, August 10	Battle of Rakshasbhuvan : Vithal Sundar killed ; Nizam's army annihilated.
1763, Sept. 1	The Peshwa crosses the Godavari and threatens Nizam Ali.
1763, Sept. 9	Salabat Jang beheaded by Nizam Ali.
1763, Sept. 23	Treaty of Aurangabad ; the Peshwa gets back all the restored territory.
1763, October	Madhavrao returns victorious to Poona and resumes authority.
1763, October 26	Mahadji Sindia meets the Peshwa on the Godavari; Raghunathrao repairs to Nasik.

Peshwa Madhavrao I

CHAPTER XXII

MADHAVRAO COMES INTO HIS OWN

[1761—1763]

1. **Nizam Ali's Attack upon Poona.**—It had generally been agreed before the death of Nanasaheb Peshwa that his son Madhavrao, then sixteen years of age, should succeed him in the Peshwaship and conduct the administration under the guidance of his uncle Raghunathrao. Another person of the young Peshwa's family who sought to guide his counsels, was his mother Gopikabai, a self-assertive lady, who had witnessed the march of events in the State since the days of the great Bajirao.

Raghunathrao was of a weak and vacillating nature, self-indulgent and shamelessly sensual ; his past mismanagement of the affairs of north India was a proof of his unfitness for the arduous task of guiding the State at this critical moment. He was, however, so vain-glorious as to boast that if he had been in command at Panipat, he would have won the day. It is no wonder that he now attempted to obtain the Peshwaship for himself and immediately addressed letters to the Emperor and to Shuja-ud-daula outlining his plans and seeking their support. But these dreams of Raghunathrao were doomed to failure, as not a single person in the administration would support his nomination to the Peshwaship in supercession of young Madhavrao's claim. He had to fall in reluctantly with the general sentiment. Madhavrao proceeded to Satara, as soon as the obsequies of the dead Peshwa were over, and on 20th July received the robes of office at the hands of the Chhatrapati. This proved an ominous start and foreboded stormy weather ahead. Raghunathrao had to remain sullenly content with the position of a mere adviser having no real power. A letter of 6th July written within a fortnight of the late Peshwa's death, recorded that "difficult times are ahead. Sakharam Bapu and Baburao Phadnis are conducting the provisional administration".

If Raghunathrao had honestly accepted his trust and willingly co-operated with his nephew, the general atmosphere and the political situation were indeed favourable to such a course. The defeat at Panipat and the terrible carnage that followed it, rankled deep in the heart of the nation and made them forget their petty differences and close their ranks. They were only too anxious to wipe out the ignominy of the defeat and avenge the deaths of their leaders and relatives. A wise and resolute leader would have at once directed this spirit of willing sacrifice and selfless service of the nation into fruitful channels. The departure of Abdali to his country after expressing a sincere desire to gain the Peshwa's friendship, had left the northern field completely open. But Raghunathrao's attitude from the beginning was averse to any patriotic move for undoing the results of Panipat. A strong selfless leadership was not to be expected from such a feeble-minded egotistical man, who found himself in the position of a guardian of a young prince. He selfishly directed his efforts to an internecine struggle with his nephew, which ultimately ruined both him and his country.

A newsletter says, "Upon reaching Poona Raghunathrao began to ignore the young Peshwa and conduct every matter of administration himself. But Madhavrao was not to be so easily silenced." Thus arose an unpleasant position in which the Peshwa's mother and her partizans ranged themselves in a strong party opposing R'rao's measures, a development which was soon reported to the Nizam's Court, giving it an opportunity to profit at the expense of the Marathas. At this time Nizam Ali had attained predominance in the counsels of Salabat Jang and started forcibly to recapture the rich districts of the Raichur Doab which had been ceded to the Marathas by the treaty of Udgir. To counter this move Madhavrao and R'rao proposed an attack upon Aurangabad; in their sore need of funds they melted personal ornaments and the gold and silver vessels of household use to mint money. They also sent urgent calls to Damaji Gaikwad and Malharrao Holkar to come to Poona with all expedition, as they were the only two leaders who had escaped safely from the disaster of Panipat, and who were experienced elders whose word carried weight. Malharrao was, however, prevented by circumstances from leaving his station in Malwa. He was charged with the duty of preserving Maratha prestige in north India and arranging the treaty of peace with Abdali. His wife Gautamabai died at Indore on 29th September 1761 and the mourning and funeral rites occupied Malharrao's attention for a time. He had a war on his hand against Madhosinh of Jaipur and while engaged in the operations he received wounds in the battle of Mangrol (29 November), which kept him confined to bed. It was only in March 1762 that Malharrao could reach Poona.

The disgrace of Udgir gnawed at Nizam Ali's heart, and as soon as the rains were over, he marched directly upon Poona at the head of a powerful army of sixty thousand men, with a determined intention to capture the nerve-centre of the Maratha power and to prostrate it permanently. Fire and desolation marked the trail of Nizam Ali's invading forces. By destroying Toka and Pravara-Sangam, two great centres of Hindu religious sanctity, in November, he added fierce fanaticism to his political aims. He dug up Sindia's palaces at Shrigonda for obtaining hidden treasure. The menace so quickly approached Poona, that it then created a scare, in consequence of which the Peshwa's family and some of the general populace removed themselves for safety to Lohgad, Purandar, Sinhagad and other places.

At this trying moment Madhavrao and his uncle sent urgent calls to Janoji Bhosle and other Sardars to join the Peshwa's standard, so that a force of about seventy thousand was assembled by the end of October. With this army they at once moved to oppose the enemy and bring him to submission. Avoiding a general action, they harassed the progress of the enemy at every turn, and wore down his spirit in several skirmishes which took place at Ahmadnagar, Shrigonda, Hivre and Bhuleshvar on the enemy's route towards Poona. On 8th December Nizam Ali occupied Chas, 20 miles north of Poona and pushed on to Uruli less than one day's march from that capital. Here his advance was halted. His devastation of the places of sanctity had already estranged his Maratha subordinates and sedition was being successfully employed in his ranks. Ramchandra Jadhav and Mir Mughal, Nizam Ali's brother, deserted him and came over to the Peshwa. This defection in his forces created a serious situation for Nizam Ali, who came to be practically surrounded at Uruli and was compelled to beg for terms to secure his retreat.

At this time the selfish Raghunathrao, who then guided the affairs on behalf of the minor Peshwa, showed undeserved mercy and closed with Nizam Ali's offer " to surrender territory worth forty lacs." The Peshwa wrote to his mother on 5 January 1762, " We had humbled Nizam Ali and completely overwhelmed him, when he made overtures for peace through his brother and Ramchandra Jadhav, who had already joined us." The precipitate conclusion of peace by Raghunathrao was highly resented by most of the prominent leaders assembled on the occasion, such as Gopalrao Patwardhan, Trimbakrao Pethe, Babuji Naik, Janoji Bhosle and others, who considered it a splendid opportunity of humbling the troublesome Nizam Ali. The atmosphere in the Maratha camp became surcharged with suspicion and completely destroyed whatever cordiality had at first existed between the Peshwa and his uncle. Raghunathrao was openly accused of harbouring illwill towards his nephew and of securing the good will of Nizam Ali, as a potential ally in a future contest for the Peshwaship, which the uncle was then secretly planning to secure. Gopikabai and the Patwardhans openly accused R'rao's Diwan Sakharam Bapu, as the author of a secret understanding between Nizam Ali and Raghunathrao.

2. **Civil War, the Peshwa defeated.**—A few months after his return to Haidarabad Nizam Ali deposed his brother Salabat Jang (6 July 1762), keeping him under his restraint and usurped the sole power on the advice of Vithal Sundar, whom he now appointed his Divan.[1]

1. Vithal Sundar Parashurami, a clever diplomat brought up by Ramdaspant during the early rule of Salabat Jang identified himself with the fortunes of Nizam Ali and was rewarded by him with the title of Raja Pratapwant. He was a Deshastha Brahman of the same caste as Sakharam Bapu, and for a time played an important part in the fortunes of Haidarabad.

Madhavrao all along watched the course of events with a keen and intelligent interest, and soon obtained full insight into the problems affecting the Maratha State and the capacities of the various agents that handled them. It was quickly discovered by many that here was a master who possessed a judgment of his own and a determination to execute it fearlessly. On the day after the conclusion of peace at Uruli, he writes to his mother, "Dada Saheb declares his intention of retiring from worldly affairs and devoting the rest of his life to worship and prayers. Sakharampant also declines to continue in office, resenting the factious intrigues of the Konknastha clique. I am soliciting Dada Saheb not to withdraw and I do respectfully seek his advice." Trimbakrao Pethe a capable person of standing and experience, held long and open discussions with Raghunathrao on the present troubles and thus reported the outcome to Gopikabai from his camp at Uruli. "Dada Saheb is altogether unfit for the high responsibility of managing the affairs during the Peshwa's minority. It is well-known how he had mishandled the situation in the north and added to the financial burden of the State. I cannot put my trust in his word. Babuji Naik and some others would not like to serve if Sakharam continues in office. Dada Saheb requires sixty or seventy lacs a year to meet his personal expenses. Whence can all this money be obtained? During Nana Saheb's regime Dada Saheb always returned from his campaigns with heavy debts and the Peshwa quietly put up with the loss. But now who can exercise a salutary check on his action? Unrestrained he would simply wreck the administration. Now the relations between him and Rao Saheb (Madhavrao) are severely strained. Every one in this huge camp has become sullen, brooding over the dismal consequences which are sure to follow."

Nor was R'rao himself slow in expressing similar threats of retirement to Gopikabai. He writes, "I have no desire to run the State; Sakharam Bapu and I have decided to retire and entrust the conduct of affairs to Rao Saheb and Baburao Phadnis. I am a simple soul, unused to diplomatic ways. I unguardedly give out what comes uppermost in my mind and find myself ever misunderstood. I have lost all interest in the State." These protestations, however, lacked sincerity and were designed to conceal his evil intentions. Gopikabai in order to avoid an open rupture used her good offices to effect a compromise, and directed that Sakharam Bapu should withdraw, leaving the management of affairs to Trimbakrao Pethe and Baburao Phadnis acting under orders of R'rao. This obviously meant that the two Karbharis were to act as a check upon Raghunathrao's freedom, and it pleased no party. He chafed under the restraint placed over his free action by subordinates, who had been thrust on him and whom he disliked. He took Bapu's retirement as a personal affront. On the other hand the two Karbharis, Pethe and Phadnis, felt themselves insecure in their position and responsibility.

Under such a tension the affairs of the State began to languish. The Peshwa and his uncle left Uruli on 7th January with their forces for the Karnatak to save their possessions from the growing encroachments of Haidar Ali of Mysore during the last two years. On the way the differences between the two assumed such proportions, that from Chikodi on the Krishna, the uncle returned to Poona in resentment. Madhavrao alone proceeded with Trimbakrao Pethe towards the Tungabhadra, reporting to his mother the severe breach of amity with which R'rao had returned and asking her to keep a vigilant eye over his movements. Malharrao Holkar had arrived from Malwa at Wafgaon (Nasik) in March at an urgent call from R'rao and caused serious anxiety to the Peshwa, as he (Holkar) was an avowed partizan of his uncle.

Madhavrao seeing the turn of events began to strengthen his own party, and on his march southward put Govind Hari Patwardhan in possession of the fort of Miraj, a safe position for retreat in case of trouble. Govind Hari and his son Gopalrao were the moving spirits in the young Peshwa's counsels and the transfer of Miraj into their hands alarmed R'rao in no small measure. Govind Hari lost no time in strengthening the fortifications of Miraj and preparing by force of arms to prevent any attempt to remove him. At the end of the hot season the Peshwa returned to Poona with a fair supply of funds and materials of war.

The months from June onward in that year (1762) witnessed an abnormal agitation at Poona as the ill-feeling that was brewing between the two parties for some time past now flared up afresh. Discussion, mediation, arbitration and other methods of conciliating R'rao were in vain tried openly and privately, in full Darbars and in personal meetings. But R'rao's restless ambition to gather supreme power in his own hand and to conduct the State affairs himself unfettered, made him reject all efforts to effect a reconciliation. Gopikabai, Madhavrao, Trimbakrao, all spoke out their minds freely ; only Sakharam Bapu continued to speak in such an ambiguous and involved manner that no definite formula could be evolved.

Madhavrao anxious to live in amity with his uncle pleaded for his cooperation on bended knees. But his appeals fell on deaf ears : Malharrao Holkar also arrived at Poona and participated in the discussions. At the end of a month's vacillation, R'rao came forth with an open demand for a separate jagir yielding an annual income of ten lacs in addition to five important forts. The Peshwa could not tolerate such a rival power and stoutly opposed the demand. Under such a tension a report went out that the Peshwa contemplated the seizure of his uncle and keeping him in confinement. Alarmed by such fears Raghunathrao suddenly left Poona on 22nd August, and went to the nearby village of Wadgoan, where the Peshwa and his mother immediately followed him inviting him to return. Outwardly signifying compliance with these importunities, Raghunathrao suddenly decamped with a few followers and by way of Koregaon and Ahmadnagar, reached Vinchur near Nasik, where Sakharam Bapu had secured the support of Vithal Shivdev. Here soon arrived Aba Purandare, Naro Shankar Raja Bahadur, and Bahiro Anant, partizans of Raghunathrao and these in concert prepared to fight the Peshwa's party, having secretly arranged to secure the support of Janoji Bhosle and Nizam Ali. Soon the signal went round and a considerable force of some fifty thousand including the Nizam's contingent, became ready to march upon Poona.

Madhavrao and his advisers, realizing that Raghunathrao was not a man to scruple to go to any length, at once prepared to accept the challenge and decide the issue by an open contest. For a time quite a race went on for securing adherents by exchange of oaths, while negotiations for a peaceful solution continued to the last minute, in which Ram Shastri,

Krishnarao Parasnis, Gangadhar Bhat Karve and other respectable mediators tried their utmost. There indeed was a large number of disinterested persons fully loyal to the State, who found themselves perplexed as to which party they should join, having been approached by both. Gopikabai's brother Malharrao Raste, e.g., joined the uncle's party, while Anandrao and the other brothers remained faithful to Madhavrao.

The Peshwa left Poona to meet the forces of his uncle; and the rival armies faced each other on 7th November on the river Ghod, which flows in a south-easterly direction about 30 miles from Poona. A desperate action was fought on that afternoon; and the evening darkness separated the combatants without any decisive result.

The Peshwa thereupon moved his camp from the banks of the Ghod river to Alegaon about 15 miles further south, near the northern bank of the Bhima. Here R'rao's forces now joined by his friend Nizam Ali soon came in pursuit and suddenly fell upon the Peshwa on 12 November; the latter not being ready suffered a severe reverse. Unwilling to protract this civil strife, the young Peshwa made up his mind to surrender. He fearlessly rode into the uncle's camp and delivered to him both his power and person. Malharrao Holkar acted as the mediator and brought about peace between them. Madhavrao completely humbled himself before his uncle, placing the latter's shoes on his own head. Raghunathrao reciprocated the kindly sentiments in apparent sincerity, declaring that he did not covet power or prestige. But he was bent upon wreaking his vengeance upon some of the Peshwa's ardent supporters, particularly Gopalrao Patwardhan, Trimbakrao Pethe and Baburao Phadnis. The two latter were sheltered at Baramati by Babuji Naik; Gopalrao proceeded to join his father at Miraj and like a soldier prepared there to resist Raghunathrao.

3. **The assemblage of Alegaon.**—In the midst of such a dreadful contest Alegaon presented a unique spectacle of two opposing armies now amalgamated in a huge camp numbering over a lac of men, with most of the prominent Maratha leaders and diplomats present. The presence of these worthies for some days of November 1762, lent a lurid colour to this gigantic assemblage, partaking along with Nizam Ali in a solemn con-

clave for settling the domestic dispute of the Peshwa's household. Indeed the recent disaster of Panipat paled into insignificance before the immediate problem of reconciling the present conflicting interests.

On 21 November the Peshwa and his uncle entertained Nizam Ali at a dinner and exchanged civilities. On 23rd Vithal Sundar, the Diwan of Nizam Ali was similarly treated. Having come so courteously to support Raghunathrao in his sore need, must not the ally be properly rewarded? Murad Khan one of Nizam Ali's officials acted as the intermediary, through whom secret negotiations were conducted with Raghunathrao. The territory of sixty lacs surrendered at Udgir was demanded, and Raghunathrao agreed to return the major portion, together with the fort of Daulatabad, which was now given back into the charge of Murad Khan. Ramchandra Jadhav came over into Maratha service on condition that the Senapati's post lost by his father Chandrasen should be given to him. After these agreements were effected, Nizam Ali departed for his capital. Janoji Bhosle doubtless aspired to be the Chhatrapati, a move certainly initiated by Raghunathrao. But for the moment it was dropped and Janoji was given leave to depart after some discussion of the subject.

Raghunathrao thus tried his best at Alegaon to make his position as secure as possible against future trouble from his nephew. He placed strict restraint upon Madhavrao's person with a guard of 2,000 men to watch him. The activities of Gopikabai at Poona were similarly controlled by placing a strict guard at the Shaniwar palace where she resided. But this was not enough to make Raghunathrao's position perfectly safe. He must have about him such persons for immediate duties as possessed unquestioned loyalty to him. Trimbakrao Pethe and Baburao Phadnis were removed from their offices. Sakharam Bapu was appointed the chief executive officer with a rich jagir for his expenses and the fort of Sinhagad for a secure residence. Nilkanthrao Purandare another partizan was similarly given the fort of Purandar. The Phadnis family were the hereditary pursers of the Peshwa's house. They were deprived of that office and Chinto Vithal Rairikar, Raghunathrao's confidential secretary, was made the Phadnis. Malharrao Holkar was given leave to return to his work at Wafgaon, but

Raghunathrao particularly kept by his side Damaji Gaikwad for the expedition to Satara and Miraj, which he now planned to secure, in order to punish the Patwardhans and their partizans and control the Chhatrapati.

Having effected these changes Raghunathrao left Alegaon on 6th December in full force and spent about a week at Satara, ensuring Ramraja's support. Dabhade was at this time deprived of the office of Senapati, which now was conferred upon Ramchandra Jadhav, and that of the Nyayadhish upon Vithal Shivdeo, with the provision of a jagir in each case. The office of the Pratinidhi could not be so easily disposed of. The Pratinidhi's Mutalik, Gamaji Yamaji was a powerful man, a relation of Vithal Sundar, now in league with Gopalrao Patwardhan. Raghunathrao cut the knot by appointing his own infant son Bhaskarrao to that office with Naro Shankar to perform the active duties. This ridiculous change soon provided the spark for an explosion. The infant Bhaskarrao died within three months of his elevation to the dignity, and his deputy Naro Shankar succeeded to the post. These uncalled for changes roused a general discontent throughout the land, which was voiced by the Brahman community in an open letter of protest to Raghunathrao. They pointed out that he was ruining the State by seeking the help of the Nizam, said that it was sad to keep the Peshwa's mother under detention and that several devoted servants had to flee the country for safety. The Brahmans roundly ascribed the trouble to Raghunathrao's evil genius Sakharam Bapu.

But these admonitions could not turn Raghunathrao from his guilty ambition. He considered the Patwardhans at Miraj as the chief offenders, and called upon them to surrender that place. Govind Hari defiantly replied he would not evacuate Miraj, unless he was recompensed for the huge expenses that he had incurred in raising troops for the Peshwa and strengthening the defences of Miraj. This insolent defiance of his commands drew on the Patwardhans the full weight of R'rao's wrath. From Satara he marched upon Miraj and with a mighty horde of forty thousand laid siege to it on 29th December. Govind Hari stoutly defended the place and his son Gopalrao harassed the besiegers from outside. Raghunathrao sent a detachment under Nilakanthrao Purandare to chastise

Gopalrao, who was defeated near Jamkhindi, and ran for shelter to Nizam Ali. The siege of Miraj was hard pressed and Govind Hari after negotiating for terms surrendered it on 3rd February (1763).

From Miraj R'rao moved southward to put down the aggression of Haidar Ali, but before he had proceeded far, reports reached him of a coalition being formed between Nizam Ali and Janoji Bhosle with the host of malcontents like the Patwardhans and the Pratinidhi, who had been deprived of their patrimony and dignity. The moving spirits of this coalition were the Nizam's Diwan Vithal Sundar and the Pratinidhi's deputy Sadashiv Yamaji, familiarly known as Gamaji. Agents quickly moved from all these chiefs to different places. Janoji Bhosle required little persuasion to fall in with Nizam Ali's views. They met at Gulbarga on 9th February and formed a definite pact for seizing the Peshwa's lands and sharing the spoils. They organised their forces and arranged a definite plan of campaign. Gamaji undertook to lead an army against Satara, seize the person of the Chhatrapati, and instal Janoji in his place. Janoji and Nizam Ali together directed the operations and moved in hot haste against the Peshwa's territories. Nizam Ali sent his arrogant demands to the Peshwa, calling upon him to deliver all the territory and forts lying east of the Bhima river, restore the jagirs of those who had been unjustly deprived of them, and accept his own nominee as his Diwan and be guided by his advice in all concerns of the Maratha State.

4. **Maratha-Nizam hostilities.**—The situation thus became one of the gravest danger to the Maratha State, threatening its entire independence. The treasury of Poona was empty, the army already depleted by desertions, lacked equipment. Such a critical moment, however, served to unite the divergent elements and the common danger induced the various parties in the Peshwa's Darbar to lay aside their differences and join in repelling the hostile combination. Madhavrao wrote pathetic letters to his mother, describing the state of affairs and the need of a joint effort, which both his uncle and Sakharam Bapu now wholeheartedly undertook to lead. They had about 50 thousand men under their command but lacked the means to

face the enemy's powerful artillery in an open action. Avoiding a close engagement, they decided to wear out the enemy by laying waste his territory and keeping him on the run. In a revengeful temper R'rao turned from Miraj north towards Aurangabad. As the combined armies of Janoji and Nizam Ali moved along the Bhima ravaging the Peshwa's territory, the Marathas similarly began to ravage the Nizam's territory, and early in March attacked Aurangabad, but failed in making any effect upon the town which was stoutly defended by Murad Khan. In order to save the city, Murad Khan paid 2 lacs. Malharrao Holkar joined the Peshwa's army near Aurangabad on 10th March, and the whole body started with great impetuosity towards Malkapur devastating the Bhosle's territory.

Ramchandra Jadhav whom R'rao had induced to desert the Mughal service, proved rather a clog than a help. This Jadhav like his father bore an inveterate enmity to the Peshwas; and now as the Maratha forces were camping near Aurangabad, he made a secret attempt on R'rao's life, which fortunately failed of effect. He had before this plundered the territory of Satara and desecrated the shrine of Pandharpur, an act which made him more odious than a real Muslim. R'rao at once arrested Jadhav and kept him closely confined during the period of hostility.[2]

For full five months from 10th March to 10th August, the two combatants occupied themselves in wearing each other out, destroying each other's territories and seeking some advantageous position for an action where a decision could be obtained. While the Mughals ravaged the Maratha country between Nasik and Satara, the Peshwa's forces retaliated by a similar process between Malkapur in the north and Haidarabad in the south. When the Marathas entered the Bhosla's possessions in Berar, Nizam Ali came on their heels. But the Marathas giving him the slip and avoiding an action, fled southwards to Sholapur and Naldurg. Nizam Ali then changed his tactics, finding it futile to pursue the nimble Maratha horse with his heavy train of artillery. In order to draw the

2. When peace was concluded in September Jadhav was restored to Nizam's service, but was never fully pardoned. Nizam Ali had him murdered in 1770.

Marathas back, he entered Maharashtra about the middle of April when the Marathas were plundering in the vicinity of Yadgir and Bedar. Vithal Sundar's nephew Vinayakdas ravaged the rich towns of Nasik, Junnar and Sangamner. Nizam Ali himself turned his attention to Poona, and Gamaji marched southwards devastating Satara. They carried fire and sword into the countryside and met with little opposition.

Poona shared a dreadful fate by a major portion of it being completely burnt down. Gopikabai had left the city and taken shelter at Sinhagad with her little son Narayanrao and jewellery and valuables. Most of the Poona gentry ran for safety to different places and forts. The idols of the temples on the Parvati hill were broken and desecrated. Naro Appaji had paid a huge ransom to Nizam Ali to purchase the safety of the town, but lost the amount into the bargain. Gopikabai bitterly felt the conduct of Gopalrao Patwardhan and held him responsible for the fate of the Peshwa's capital. But Gopalrao was now a helpless spectator, unable to prevent mischief to Maratha interests. Indeed he keenly watched for an opportunity to come back to his allegiance after issuing unscathed from the invidious position he found himself in.

5. The decision of Rakshasbhuvan.—The Peshwa and his uncle after despoiling Naldurg on 10th April, Udgir on 23rd April and Medak on 10th May, arrived before Haidarabad, where they learned of the spoliation their capital had suffered at the hands of the enemy. The Peshwa wrote to his mother on 5th June, "We have retraced our steps from Bhaganagar and reached the banks of the Krishna, looking out for a suitable opportunity when we can avenge the cruel fate the enemy has inflicted upon Poona." On the same date Raghunathrao also wrote to Gopikabai expressing his indignation against Nizam Ali. He was so impatient to close in with the enemy that it was with difficulty that Malharrao Holkar, Sakharam Bapu and other chiefs restrained him for a time, until the enemy was isolated by the separation of his new allies Janoji Bhosle, Gopalrao Patwardhan, Piraji Nimbalkar, Dhaygude, the Pratinidhi and others, who had to be weaned away from Nizam Ali's side. For this purpose secret negotiations were now undertaken. Govind Shivram was sent to Gopalrao and

Sakharam Bapu to Janoji Bhosle, with offers of restoring them to their jagirs, if they would desert Nizam Ali and resume their former loyalties. All these deserters had practically gained nothing and lost much by their new alliance. Janoji realized that he had little prospect of getting the Chhatrapati's throne, while on the other hand, the Peshwa threatened him with being replaced by Mudhoji at Nagpur. His province of Berar had been overrun and plundered. At the Peshwa's summons Mahadji Sindia marched from Ujjain to attack the northern parts of the Bhosle's territory. Inducement was offered to Nizam Ali's brother Basalat Jang and he came over to the Peshwa's side. So did Piraji Nimbalkar a subordinate chief of Janoji Bhosle.

These negotiations continued throughout July. Nizam Ali then saw his position deteriorating and began to look for a place of safety where he could escape a sudden Maratha attack. Early in June the Peshwa's army turned back homeward from Bedar, cautiously feeling its way for a position from which it could overcome the enemy marching in its direction.

By the time the two armies had come near enough, Nizam Ali's allies began to desert him, one by one, giving out as an excuse that they were returning home for the monsoon. This large scale defection so unnerved Nizam Ali that he countermanded his original movement and began a retreat to Aurangabad as the best place for safety during the wet weather. Janoji Bhosle was still in the Mughal camp, and sent news of his change of plan to the Peshwa, advising an attack before the enemy crossed the Godavari. The Peshwa began a hot pursuit of the retreating enemy, reaching Bid on 5th August. On the 9th the Marathas arrived at Majalgaon, where the report came that Janoji and the Pratinidhi had separated from the Mughal army, and that Nizam Ali with a few followers, had hurriedly crossed the flooded Godavari, leaving behind at Rakshasbhuvan his main army and the artillery under the command of Vithal Sundar, who were to have crossed over the next day. Naro Shankar and Sakharam Bapu were away arranging Janoji Bhosle's desertion, and although the Peshwa's army was feeling the strain of long marches for several days, it was decided to attack the enemy at once without allowing him time to escape across the flooded river. It was the dark night of the last day of Ashad with pouring rain and lightning flashes making movement difficult. Orders were circulated to begin the march long in advance of day-light, so that swarms of light Maratha troops swept down upon the unwary Mughals a little after sunrise on the 10th.

The Nizam's artillery opened upon the Maratha vanguard when a stray rocket struck a tumbril containing shells and caused a loud explosion. Taking prompt advantage of the confusion thus caused, Aba Purandare and Vinchurkar drove in the enemy's outposts and rushed towards the main body, while a strong column under Raghunathrao himself closed in. Vithal Sundar immediately formed his men and furiously pushed back the advancing Marathas. He quickly overcame and surrounded R'rao seated on his elephant. At this critical moment, young Madhavrao rushed in from the rear driving Vithal Sundar and his column back towards the river, and relieving his uncle from imminent capture, a feat in which Mahadaji Shitole attained special distinction. Vithal Sundar with several other prominent chiefs either fell fighting or were captured, so that within two hours the Marathas gained a complete victory. The Peshwa himself wrote to his mother the following account immediately after the action.

" Learning the dispersed condition of the enemy's army we closed upon them this morning. After a short but severe engagement at close grips, we gained a decisive victory. Vithal Sundar's severed head was brought in. His nephew Vinayakdas, and Gopaldas the raja of Kandhar were killed. Murad Khan and sixteen chiefs are taken prisoners. About eight thousand of the enemy's troops and four thousand trained infantry were slaughtered. Fifteen elephants, twenty-five pieces of cannon, and a large number of animals and quantities of material were secured. Shahji Supekar, Sadashiv Ramchandra and some others of our service who had deserted to the enemy, saved their lives by flight. The river saved Nizam Ali from a similar fate."

The severed head of his able minister Vithal Sundar was sent to Nizam Ali, who remained a helpless spectator on the other side, mourning the slaughter of his fine army. Fearing that the Marathas would now cross the river and attack him, he asked Murad Khan, a prisoner in Maratha hands to seek terms of peace. The whole large and rich territory between the river Manjra and Aurangabad worth about a crore of rupees was demanded, but this demand could not be at once pressed home owing to the flooded river. Nearly a month was lost in a useless wait, in which Nizam Ali could organize a defence of his position. During this interval, Janoji Bhosle, Gopalrao and others made their submission to the Peshwa and were restored to favour. They took no part in the actual fighting of the 10th August; the Peshwa by this conduct purposely impressed it upon them that he did not much care for their co-operation in humbling Nizam Ali and was himself able to enforce his power upon all. Some three weeks were wasted before this victory could be pressed to advantage.

On 1st September Malharrao Holkar and Janoji Bhosle crossed the Godavari, followed soon after by the entire Maratha army and marched upon Aurangabad. After some stray warfare and continued negotiation, a treaty was concluded on 25 September by which the Nizam surrendered to the Peshwa territory worth 82 lacs, that is, all that had been already secured at Udgir four years before, but which the self-seeking R'rao had given back at Uruli and Alegaon. This treaty is known as the treaty of Aurangabad.

Thus ended the Maratha-Nizam contest which had continued intermittently for over two years from June 1761 to September 1763. Several efforts were made by the successors of Asaf Jah to cripple the aggressive Marathas: and now came forth the spirited Nizam Ali to avenge the set-backs of Salabat Jang's regime, taking advantage of the internal troubles of the Peshwa's house; and once more the Marathas proved their superiority over the Mughals.

The battle of Rakshasbhuvan was won mainly through Madhavrao's own initiative and energy exhibited throughout the campaign. Not only did he manoeuvre the initial stages cleverly through his uncle, but even on the day of the battle it was due to his careful planning and disposition of the troops at every stage that the day was won. Never before had such terrible losses been inflicted upon the Nizam. Madhavrao on this occasion proved his capacity in war as well as in the management of the general administration, thus winning the applause of his people and mastery over the hearts of friends and foes alike.

The victory of Rakshasbhuvan had repercussions throughout India. It proved that the disaster of Panipat had not crushed the Maratha power and that they still possessed the vibrant energy which had carried their banners to the far corners of India, and that they were still a power to be feared and respected. The more immediate effect of this victory was the assertion of his power by the young Peshwa, both over his uncle and his partizans. He proved his worth by dint of his own inherent strength in controlling and ruling the vast Maratha State. By contrast his uncle's levity and want of decision came to be clearly exposed. He could no longer hold his able nephew in thraldom or tutelage. Madhavrao during these two years gained the most valuable experience of his life, both in war and diplomacy, by controlling divergent elements, and by leading his nation to its former prestige. The generation that Panipat had destroyed, was again thus quickly replaced by another no less worthy. Rakshasbhuvan proved the beginning of this national revival.

But Raghunathrao's profession of a wish to retire was by no means sincere : he was all along thinking of the best way of getting mastery over his nephew, to whom he soon after repeated his demand of a jagir worth nine lacs and five important forts. Sakharam Bapu also was uneasy and skulking and expressed his wish to retire from service, Madhavrao well knowing what mischief the two were capable of, flattered them for their vast knowledge and experience, and told them how their presence about him was essential for conducting the administration. With this object he hereafter kept Sakharam Bapu near his person to advise him on matters of moment, but gave him no particular office or independent voice. Bapu understood the Peshwa's game, but could not find a way to obstruct it openly. From Aurangabad, the Peshwa returned to Poona and his uncle to Nasik to perform his devotions at Trimbakeshwar, with Govind Shivram and Trimbakrao Pethe placed by the Peshwa as his own personal agents in attendance on him.

Plenty of miscellaneous work arising out of the recent war kept Madhavrao fully occupied nearly up to the end of October in the vicinity of Aurangabad. Mahadji Sindia, who had been equally involved in domestic dissensions, came from Ujjain at the pressing invitation of the Peshwa, met him at the crossing of the Godavari on 26th October during his return journey to Poona; and by his ready obedience and willing service at once earned the good opinion of the Peshwa. Nana Phadnis and his cousin Moroba were restored to their former offices which they had lost during the short regency of R'rao. The young Peshwa and his equally young coadjutors, Nana and Mahadji, both having miraculously escaped death at Panipat, now formed a trio upon whom the future destiny of the Maratha nation so vitally depended.

CHRONOLOGY

CHAPTER XXIII

1761, Oct.	Govind Shivram's abortive mission to Bombay for British help.
1763, Novr.	Kedarji Sindia entrusted with Sindian estate by Raghunathrao.
1764, Febr.	The Peshwa starts for Karnatak.
1764, April	Haidar Ali marches upon Savanur.
1764, May	Battle of Rettehalli ; Haidar routed.
1764, May	Mahadji Sindia flees to Ujjain in anger against Raghunathrao.
1764, June	The Peshwa forms his monsoon camp in the Karnatak.
1764, July	Surprise attack upon Gopalrao Patwardhan.
1764, Oct.	Raghunathrao leaves Nasik for Karnatak.
1764, Oct. 23	Battle of Baxar : the British inflict defeat upon the Emperor and his allies.
1764, Novr. 6	Peshwa captures Dharwar after two months siege. Sadashivrao Bhau's pretender appears.
1765, Jan. 25	Fort Malwan captured by the British.
1765, Jan. 27	Raghunathrao joins the Peshwa near Savanur.
1765, Mar 30	Treaty of peace with Haidar Ali at Anantapur.
1765, May 3	Malharrao Holkar routed by Fletcher near Kara, escapes to Kalpi.
1765, June	The Peshwa returns to Poona from Karnatak.
1765, Aug. 4	The Pretender examined by Holkar at Sultanpur. He escapes, is pursued and brought to Poona.
1765, Oct 15	The Pretender tried by a council of 26 and imprisoned for life.
1765, Ending months.	Janoji Bhosle and Nizam Ali at war.

1766, Jan.	The Peshwa joined by the Nizam's forces marches against Bhosle. He submits and accepts the treaty of Daryapur.
1766, Feb 5-15	Peshwa and Nizam Ali fraternizing in a friendly visit, cement cordial relations.
1766, March	Babuji Naik humbled.
1767, Nov. 19	Mostyn's mission to Poona and Brome's to Nasik.
1768 Feb. 27	Mostyn and Brome return to Bombay.
1772, Oct. 13	Mostyn arrives at Poona as British Agent.

CHAPTER XXIII

THE PESHWA ASSERTS HIMSELF

[1763—1767]

1 Offensive against Haiderali.
2 The Kolis of Purandar.
3 Peace with Haidar Ali.
4 March against Janoji Bhosle.
5 Friendship with Nizam Ali.
6 Babuji Naik humbled.
7 The Pretender, Sadashivrao Bhau.
8 Mahadji Sindia's rise.
9 The British menace.

1. Offensive against Haidar Ali.—Madhavrao's Peshwaship lasted eleven years and four months, from 20 July 1761 to 18 November 1772, the first two years of which were a period of tutelage as we have already seen. During his last year he was entirely bed-ridden, so that it was only for about eight years that he actively controlled the management of affairs and marked his personal stamp on the administration. His activities may be arranged under four main heads, viz. :—

1. His Karnatak expeditions for putting down Haidarali;
2. His relations with Nizam Ali ;
3. His struggle first against his own uncle and then against the Bhosles of Nagpur ; and lastly
4. The revival of Maratha power in the north.

There are of course other minor episodes intermixed with these : but if these four heads are kept steadily in view, it would be easier to study the complexities of this Peshwa's situation and estimate at their true value his powers as a great ruler. He gave a distinct promise of attaining to the position of the supreme arbiter of India's destinies in competition with the two contemporary British statesmen Clive and Warren Hastings. It would be convenient to take up for narration the Karnatak expedition first. But before doing so we must review the general situation of Indian politics, which forced itself on the Peshwa's attention and induced him to prefer this one task to others more or less equally urgent.

It was generally believed that the Maratha power had suffered its death-blow by its severe rout at Panipat: and this sentiment was aggravated by the domestic dispute in the Peshwa's family, immediately after his accession. But a new hope arose when the young Peshwa proved his capacity at Rakshasbhuvan by putting down Nizam Ali and his unholy alliance with Maratha deserters. Both the south and the north claimed the Peshwa's attention equally, when he found himself free during the closing months of the year 1763. While Haidar Ali pushed back the Maratha power from the Tungabhadra to almost the banks of the Krishna, the situation in the north threatened to be no less alarming. Najib Khan Rohilla who was then managing the affairs of Delhi was having an uneasy time with the Jats, the Sikhs and the Abdali king of Afghanistan. The Emperor Shah Alam II and the Wazir Shuja-ud-daula in their attempt to regain the lost ground in Bihar in conjunction with Mir Qasim, were repelled by the rising British power, now an additional factor for the Marathas to deal with. During 1763 when the Peshwa was locked up in a life and death struggle with the Nizam, Haidar Ali conquered Bednur, established his hold upon the Nawabs of Savanur, Karnool and Kadappa, who had long ago been subjugated by the Marathas. Haidar Ali seized likewise the territory of Murarrao Ghorpade, so that Haidar's threat came nearer home and could not be overlooked. The Peshwa's sore need was money so that after full deliberation, he for the present deferred the northern task to a future date, and decided early in 1764 to undertake an expedition to the south for punishing Haidar Ali and putting an end to his aggression.

To collect a sufficient army and equip it with arms occupied the Peshwa's time in January, and it was not before February that he was able to cross the Krishna. During the Peshwa's journey to the south Haidar Ali was busy making his preparations to resist the Maratha advance. He sought Nizam Ali's co-operation but did not succeed in obtaining anything from him beyond hollow promises. Leaving Bednur in April Haidar Ali marched to the vicinity of Savanur where he prepared to meet the advancing Marathas in an open engagement. The Nawab of that place had long since accepted Maratha over-lordship, and the advance of Haidar's troops threatened his very existence. This meant an open call to the Peshwa to save his vassal from imminent danger. Gopalrao Patwardhan was immediately detached with two thousand select troops in advance to hold up Haidar's march and defend the Nawab.

The Peshwa invited Murarrao Ghorpade, won him over to his cause and secured his aid in the forthcoming contest with Haidar Ali. The ensuing struggle indeed put to the test the respective capacities for war and organization of the two combatants, both active, tenacious and daring. There were skirmishes, moves and counter-moves. In May, Haidar Ali who had been lured out of his strong position at Rattehalli, was surrounded and severely defeated. Losing a thousand men on the field, he retired to Anavati in the forests of Karwar. The season was fast advancing, the campaign so far had proved inconclusive; the Peshwa, therefore, decided to stay on and finish his task during the ensuing cold season. This decision was highly welcomed and heartened the Maratha ranks for a supreme effort. Murarrao joined the Peshwa in May and was rewarded for his services by the conferment of the office of the Senapati of the Satara Raja. Formal documents of this appointment were executed next year (20 September 1765). This office had just fallen vacant on account of Ramachandra Jadhav's dismissal for misconduct.

The temporary lull in the operations caused by the monsoon was utilised for advancing preparations and making dispositions of troops to bring the enemy quickly to his knees. The region between Dharwar and Savanur formed the main theatre of the campaign. In the month of July Haidar planned a secret night attack against Gopalrao who was defending Savanur, but the latter having received a timely warning through his spies, remained on the alert and the enemy's design came to nought. The Peshwa at once reinforced Gopalrao and directed his own attention to the capture of Dharwar, a strong and well defended fort, the principal station commanding the northern region of the Karnatak. Haidar's commandant Fazl Ali Khan stoutly defended the post for two months, at the end of which he surrendered the place to the Peshwa on 6 November on a promise of his personal safety.

This quick success at once raised the spirits of the Marathas, and with the close of the rains the offensive was resumed against the enemy. On 1st December a decisive action was fought at Jadi Anwati, a little to the south of Savanur, where Haidar had pitched his main camp which was suddenly attacked by the Marathas. Haidar Ali was completely routed, and 1200 of his men were slain. He took shelter in the neighbouring thick woods and thus saved himself from complete annihilation. In his action of Anwati Murarrao Ghorpade figured conspicuously. After this encounter Haidar Ali never ventured to come to close grips with the Marathas, but retracing his steps remained hidden in the thick jungles of Bednore and continued desultory warfare, prolonging the contest and thereby wearing out his opponents, till the setting in of the rains. During the interval he continued negotiations to end the war for the time being. Haidar Ali was indeed well posted with the situation at Poona and the differences that had arisen between the Peshwa and his uncle. Circumstances again conspired to give him an opportunity to secure favourable terms. How such a consummation came about can be explained by reference to Raghunathrao's activities at Nasik, which often marred the success of many of the Peshwa's plans.

2. **The Kolis of Purandar.**—It has already been explained how Raghunathrao pretended to retire from worldly concerns and took up his residence at Nasik, when the Peshwa started on his expedition against Haidar Ali early in 1764. Madhavrao tried his best to keep him pleased by writing respectful letters, reporting to him the progress of the war and often seeking his advice on state matters. As the Peshwa was away from the capital, he had asked the uncle by way of giving him occupation to supervise the affairs of Poona. During the summer of 1764 the Koli guards of the fort of Purandar, who had long been hereditary servants, revolted against Nilakanth Aba Purandare in whose possession the fort lay. Purandare punished them with dismissal with the result that they all in a body took forcible charge of the fort in the absence of Aba who was then with R'rao at Nasik. Raghunathrao coveting the fort for himself as a place of refuge, played a trick upon the Peshwa, wrongly charging him with having secretly instigated the Kolis to rise. The incident roused a storm of indignation among the partizans of the two

principals, and revived the atmosphere of suspicion and acerbity which had happily been laid at rest the year before.

The Peshwa explained the affair to his uncle disavowing any sinister intention on his part and repudiating incitement from him in the rising. In itself the incident was trivial, but it is now clearly proved that the uncle selfishly turned it to the Peshwa's disadvantage, declaring it to be a deliberate attempt by the Peshwa to undermine the uncle's power. The latter called Nana Phadnis from Poona to Nasik and asked him to work there under his direct supervision. This Nana could not agree to do and matters came to such a pass at Nasik that R'rao threatened to create trouble for the Peshwa. Nana Phadnis reported to the Peshwa these affairs and his own inability to conduct the current administration at Poona. This sudden crisis caused severe annoyance to the Peshwa in the Karnatak. Fearing that his uncle would again revolt and commence his former intrigues, Madhavrao invited him to his camp to advise him on the operations against Haidar Ali. Even for this R'rao proposed his terms through Govind Shivram which the Peshwa accepted ; and he left Nasik in October 1764 and moving in a lordly leisurely fashion, emphasizing his importance on the way, reached the Peshwa's camp near Savanur on 27 January following.

3. **Peace with Haidar Ali.**—The arrival of R'rao on the scene, at once gave a new turn to the war. The Peshwa, the Patwardhans, Murarrao, the Nawab of Savanur were all in high spirits, vigorously prosecuting the war and hoping to impose such terms on the enemy as to finish him finally by recovering the whole territory usurped by Haidar, and restoring the Raja of Mysore to his former position. Haidar's agents were in the Maratha camp discussing terms of a lasting peace; these negotiations R'rao now took into his own hands and so managed them as to impose a curb on the increasing power and popularity of the Peshwa. Like Nizam Ali, Haidar Ali also was the declared opponent of the Marathas in the south, whom R'rao managed to spare as an eventual counterpoise, if the Peshwa should prove too strong for him. So on one pretext or another R'rao proposed to close the operations by giving easy

M. H. II—32

terms to Haidar Ali. The Peshwa could not offend his uncle, and the plan of humbling Haidar Ali completely had to be given up for the present. A treaty was ratified on 30th March through Haidar's representative, Mir Faizulla. The terms agreed to were :—

(1) that Haidar Ali pays 30 lacs cash for expenses;

(2) cedes all the territory to the north of the Tungabhadra, and

(3) leaves Murarrao Ghorpade and the Nawab of Savanur unmolested as Maratha vassals."

This treaty is known as the treaty of Anantapur. Thus once more Raghunathrao was responsible for saving a declared enemy of the Marathas, who was on the point of being wiped out within a month or two. How this result reacted upon the future Maratha fortunes history has recorded. For the present the Peshwa stationed Gopalrao, Murarrao and the Rastes with adequate forces under them to defend the acquired territory and returned to Poona in June, visiting several holy shrines on the way, and collecting arrears of tribute.

4. **March against Janoji Bhosle.**—While Madhavrao was trying to restore the lost ground in the south, affairs developed in the north greatly to the detriment of the Marathas. Without anticipating events, we must know what main problems engrossed the Peshwa's attention in the south. As has been mentioned before, the British now came forth to contest Indian supremacy with the Marathas, whose temporary eclipse in the north afforded a valuable opportunity to the East India Company. While Madhavrao was overcoming the Nizam at Rakshasbhuvan, the British managed to drive away the legitimate Nawab Mir Qasim from Bengal. Again, while the Peshwa was occupied in reducing Dharwar, the British won their grand victory of Baxar (October 23, 1764) over the combined power of three Muslim potentates the Emperor, the Wazir and the subahdar, and established their sway over the vast territory of eastern India from Allahabad to the Bay of Bengal. This was bitterly resented by the Peshwa, as a direct challenge to Maratha supremacy in the north. Malharrao Holkar tried to dislodge the British from the Doab in the early months of 1765, but was compelled to retire after sustaining a

severe defeat.[1] The Peshwa discussed this development with his uncle at Poona during the rains of 1765 and begged him at once to proceed to the north, as the most experienced Maratha captain then alive and retrieve the lost prestige. Raghunathrao started from the Deccan as usual after the Dassara season.

At this moment a frightful struggle was raging in Berar between Nizam Ali and the Bhosles of Nagpur, both of whom had appealed to the Peshwa for help, in consonance with the understanding that had been arrived at when the treaty of Aurangabad was concluded two years ago. The Peshwa always apprehended that a combination between his uncle, the Bhosle and the Nizam would gravely menace his position, and determined to utilise the occasion to reduce the overgrown power of the Bhosle and draw the Nizam closer to him. The Bhosle, a member of the Maratha State, was often disloyal to the Peshwa, being in the habit of intriguing with the Peshwa's enemies. Janoji's atrocities during the summer of 1763 in the devastation of Poona and other places, the Peshwa had neither forgotten nor forgiven, and now came an occasion to teach him a lesson by putting down his treachery. Madhavrao gave his uncle only a vague general outline but did not disclose his line of action, nor his inner motives as to which side he was going to espouse, and asked his uncle to join him at the Godavari directly from Nasik. The Bhosle and Raghunathrao hardly expected that the Peshwa would make friends with Nizam Ali and manage to foil their secret intrigues.[2] At the Godavari Nizam Ali's forces joined the Peshwa by previous arrangement, and the two marched against Bhosle and within a month reduced him to such sore straits, that he humbled himself abjectly before the Peshwa at Daryapur near Amraoti, at the end of January 1766. Janoji ceded to the Peshwa territory yielding 24 lacs out of the 32 lacs worth he had received two years before as appeasement before the action of Rakshasbhuvan. He now solemnly agreed to join the Peshwa whenever called upon to do so in future expeditions. Raghunathrao was thus made a helpless witness of Janoji's humiliation.

---

1. This severe disaster the veteran Holkar took so much to heart that he deteriorated in health and died a year later (20 May 1766).

2. See Ait. Pat. 106 dated 25th November 1765.

5. **Friendship with Nizam Ali.**—On his way back the Peshwa added to his success another diplomatic victory by bringing about a most successful and cordial meeting with Nizam Ali near Kurumkhed (Dist. Umarkhed) in south Berar. It was a deliberate step taken by secret previous arrangement, without giving an inkling of it to his jealous uncle. This clever diplomacy turned a traditional enemy into a potential friend, thereby closing old sores which had marked the Maratha-Nizam relations from Palkhed to Rakshasbhuvan (1763). To make Nizam Ali innocuous for some time if not a cordial friend, was no small achievement and this new policy was not quite heartily endorsed by the so called wise-acres of the day steeped in selfish intrigue. The meeting of the two potentates, Madhavrao and Nizam Ali took place at Manrath and Takli on the Godavari and lasted for ten days from 5th February with a lavish display of cordiality, ceremonials, dinners, presents and sports, all without a trace of suspicion between the two camps. Public Darbars and private talks were conspicuous. To the Hindu and the Muslim alike the sight was strikingly amazing, the like of which had hardly ever been witnessed before. Nizam Ali probably ten years senior in age was highly impressed with the young Peshwa's independence of thought and policy; and the cordial friendship thus established lasted right up to the days of Kharda (1795), and was proudly recalled by the former chief in his future dealings. When Raghunathrao on his way to the north learned the full account of this unique visit, his equanimity was highly disturbed and he wrote uneasy letters to his agents.[3] Indeed it was this high regard of Nizam Ali for the Peshwa, which induced him to espouse the Barbhai's cause against Raghunathrao after Narayanrao's murder.

Madhavrao was thus the first bold builder of a new era of honest dealings in politics, discarding the traditional intrigue and dissembling in dealing with friends and foes alike. Many instances of this fresh departure of open and frank diplomacy are available in the short career of this independent Peshwa. In all his transactions one notices a pleasant ring and a refreshing change to a courageous innovation.

3. P. D. 20. 165, 166, 167, 172, 174.

6. **Babuji Naik humbled.**—Babuji Naik Joshi of Baramati was an old hereditary servant who had looked upon the rise of the Peshwas with a jealous eye. He was an eye-sore to the late Peshwa. During recent days he sided with Gopikabai's party and served Madhavrao pretty loyally. But he was often whimsical and extremely fickle minded. During the Peshwa's expedition into the Karnatak the year before, he was discovered to have conducted an intrigue with Haidar Ali. The matter was investigated and the Naik was exposed. But he did not repent and continued to offer pinpricks to the Peshwa often opposing his commands. He possessed two strong forts, Sholapur and Wandan, where he fortified himself and stored his valuables. The Peshwa could not trust his loyalty and ordered that the two forts be taken out of his possession. The Naik resisted the Peshwa's demand and refused to surrender the forts. Ramchandra Ganesh the Peshwa's captain attacked the forts and took them away forcibly (1766 March). The Naik remained sulking in his jagir at Baramati, but dared no longer stand in opposition to the Peshwa. Babuji was in many ways a singular personality bound in relationship with the Peshwa's house. He witnessed the regimes of six consecutive rulers.

7. **The Pretender, *Sadashivrao Bhau*.**—In between many important affairs of State, the Peshwa had always on hand not a few matters of a secondary nature but exasperating enough for the time being. One such subject that for long attracted serious notice in Maharashtra, was the crop of impostors that the disaster of Panipat gave rise to. Of many well-known persons that perished on that field the bodies were never fully recognised and properly cremated. Sadashivrao Bhau and Jankoji Sinde were long reported missing, although the immediate household of the Peshwa knew the truth of their death through their trusted agents. An impostor personating the dead Sadashivrao, continued to cause trouble and sensation in the Deccan for a number of years. A Kanoja Brahman named Sukhlal appeared in Bundelkhand near Chhatrapur towards the end of 1761 and was declared to be Bhau Saheb by a few minor Maratha officials in that quarter such as Ganesh Sambhaji, Vishwasrao Lakshman Raja Bahadur, and others. He

soon collected a large following and roamed about exacting tribute and levying contributions. For the first few years his activities were confined to north India. During 1764 he crossed the Narmada and appeared in Maharashtra. On 14 January 1765 Madhavrao issued orders for making an enquiry and ascertaining the truth or falsity of the man. Accordingly Malharrao Holkar held a council of enquiry at Sultanpur on 12 August 1765, examined Sukhlal and declared that he was not the real Bhau Saheb. Then Sukhlal ran away and started fresh trouble. Hari Damodar Nevalkar and his son Raghunath Hari, ancestors of the Rani of Jhansi, pursued the pretender, captured his person and sent him to Poona for punishment. There again several prominent persons of Poona separately examined the man and declared him an impostor. He was then publicly exhibited for a whole day in the Budhwar square of the city. On 15 October 1765 Ramshastri and a large number of officials again examined him in front of the deity of the Parvati temple. Here he confessed his guilt, gave out his whole previous history and was punished with life imprisonment.[4]

Jankoji Sindia also was similarly impersonated and the offender was properly punished.

8. *Mahadji Sindia's rise.*—Mahadji Sindia having been occupied with his elder brothers in his early life, has received hardly any special mention in existing papers. Out of the large family of Ranoji Sindia, Mahadji was the only son who escaped death in the nation's cause, and lived long enough to be the main support of the Maratha State. Born probably about the year 1727 he was mostly employed in various Maratha transactions in north India, and was wounded in the leg and picked up unconscious by a passing water-carrier, Rana Khan by name, on the fatal day of Panipat. He came from Malwa to the Deccan in December 1762 and joined the Peshwa in the siege of Miraj, when the question of his succession to the Sindian estate had not been yet decided. A large amount of succession fee called Nazarana was demanded, which

4. He was at first kept at fort Ahmadnagar and thereafter at other places. He escaped from fort Ratnagiri in 1776 and after some commotion was apprehended and put to death.

he could not pay and Raghunathrao out of spite for his nephew, appointed Kedarji and later Manaji Sindia to inherit the estates of that family. The widowed ladies of that family created no small trouble for Mahadji. In a letter dated 8 July 1767 Mahadji complains bitterly that his own mother Chimabai had no means of livelihood and that she had to contract heavy debts to sustain herself and knew not how to repay them.

During 1763 and 1764 Raghunathrao and the Peshwa sanctioned conflicting arrangements for the Sindian succession. Mahadji was out of favour with Raghunathrao, although he studiously avoided taking sides in the domestic dispute of the Peshwa's house. During the summer of 1764 when the Peshwa was absent in the Karnatak, Mahadji returned to Ujjain without obtaining formal leave of Raghunathrao, who at once issued orders to have him arrested. But Mahadji was not the man to be so easily coerced. He opposed his pursuers boldly and after reaching Malwa safely, at once took the management of his patrimony in his own hands, without caring to acknowledge Manaji or Kedarji, the nominees sanctioned by Raghunathrao. When Kedarji was summoned by Raghunathrao to his presence, he made this bold reply. "The revered Mahadji Bawa is already performing loyal service here. To him you should address whatever commands you wish to issue. I am entirely obedient to his wishes. We shall both serve you loyally." When Raghunathrao thus failed to detach Kedarji from Mahadji, he nominated another Sindia Manaji as the head of the family instead. Manaji was the grandson of that Sabaji Sindia who had carried the Maratha arms to Attock and who was also a member of the same family. During all these years Mahadji did his best to sustain the Maratha interests in Malwa and Rajputana. He carefully husbanded his scanty resources and strengthened his military position by entertaining a regularly paid force of troops and collecting a band of devoted followers about him. One of his lieutenants Ragho Ram Page writes on 17 August, 1765, "Here Mahadji has about him a band of devoted comrades ready to sacrifice their lives for him. All are of one mind, imbued with a spirit of loyal service to the Peshwa in exact imitation of the devoted sacrifice of his eminent brothers before him.

Thus the period of some eight years from 1761 to the end of 1768 marks the tutelage of Mahadji's life, and in the beginning of 1769 he emerges as a man of destiny on the pages of history.

9. **The British Menace.**—The President of the Bombay Council while giving instructions to Thomas Mostyn whom he nominated his ambassador to Poona, wrote, on 16 November 1767, "The growing power of the Marathas is a subject much to be lamented and has not failed to attract our attention as well as that of the Presidencies of Madras and Fort William."[5] In fact much more did Madhavrao lament and apprehend the growing power of the British during the latter part of his short regime. Both looked upon each other as the most potential enemies of the future: and Madhavrao was all along keenly alive to the fast increasing danger. The British had already planted their power in Madras and Bengal, and now deplored that they could not make a similar headway in the west! During 1761 when Nizam Ali threatened an attack upon Poona, R'rao sent his agent Govind Shivram to Bombay asking for military aid. Govind Shivram returned with certain stipulations upon which the British agreed to lend a military contingent. Thereupon Raghunathrao sent counter proposals with Baji Gangadhar; but as the British demanded in return for such help the cession of Bassein and the whole of the island of Salsette, Raghunathrao found this unacceptable and wrote a biting reply to Bombay that Bassein could never be parted with. The danger of the Nizam's invasion had already passed and the British aid was no longer needed.

A little later when the Peshwa undertook operations against Haidar Ali, the Bombay authorities tried immediately to profit by the contest. They were very eager to possess the coastal regions bordering the islands of Bombay, which supplied them with their daily needs of provisions and fuel, which they studiously watched for an opportunity to seize. A wanton aggression was committed by them on 25 January 1765 by capturing the fort of Malvan belonging to the Chhatrapati of Kolhapur and naming it Fort Augustus.

5. Forrest, *Maratha Series*, page 141.

This incident spread alarm throughout Maharashtra about the British objective in India, of which Madhavrao was not slow in taking notice. Indeed hereafter he counted this western power as his enemy number one, and in his own way slowly prepared to meet them. His friendship with Nizam Ali was the first step to that end. His uncle and the Bhosles of Nagpur were the weakest links in this connection, being most likely to yield to any temptation offered by the British. Hence the stern measures that Madhavrao had to take against them. Haidar Ali of Mysore was an antagonist whom the British equally hated and feared, so that when in 1767 war started between them, the Bombay President sent an embassy to Poona headed by Thomas Mostyn to seek an alliance with the Peshwa's Government. The mission left Bombay on 19 November and reached Poona on 29th. Mostyn had an assistant named Brome who visited Raghunathrao at Nasik. Although the members of the mission were most civilly treated at the Maratha Court, they obtained no material results, as their real intentions had become too naked to the Maratha Government to be ignored, and the party returned to Bombay in great disappointment on 27 February 1768. The only gain they made was the valuable information they gathered about the acute dissension then raging between the Peshwa and his uncle. Brome's overtures to Raghunathrao will be referred to later. After dealing with his uncle, the Peshwa slowly prepared to meet the British menace, so that the Bombay authorities once more posted Mostyn at the court of Poona, where he arrived on 13 October 1772, a short while before the Peshwa's death. Mostyn continued there to the end of 1774 and witnessed the affair of Narayanrao's murder.

CHRONOLOGY

CHAPTER XXIV

1761, Nov. 29-30	Battle of Mangrol, Malharrao Holkar defeats Madhosinh.
1762-67	Abdali's efforts to regain the Punjab thwarted by the Sikhs.
1763, July	Battles of Katwa and Gheria, Mir Qasim routed by the British.
1764, May 3	Battle near Patna, Shuja-ud-daula and Mir Qasim defeated.
1764, Oct. 23	Battle of Baxar, Hector Munro inflicts crushing defeat upon the Emperor, the Wazir and Mir Qasim.
1765, February	Malharrao Holkar effects peace between Jawahir Sinh Jat and Najib-ud-daula.
1765, March 30	Shuja meets Holkar at Anupshahr and obtains his help against the British.
1765, May 3	Holkar severely beaten by Fletcher near Kara.
1765, May 3	Clive arrives at Calcutta.
1765, June 24	Clive leaves Calcutta for the northern scene.
1765, July	Clive reaches Allahabad.
1765, August 2	Clive arranges a treaty with Shuja-ud-daula.
1765, August 12	Clive receives the grant of Diwani from the Emperor.
1765, Sept.	Clive returns to Calcutta.
1766, Feb.	Raghunathrao starts on his northern expedition.
1766, May 20	Malharrao Holkar dies.
1766, June	Raghunathrao invests Gohad.
1767, Jan. 2	Raghunathrao negotiates peace with the Rana of Gohad.
1767, Feb.	Raghunathrao leaves Gohad for the south.
1767, March 27	Malrao Holkar dies.
1767, April	Ahalyabai defies Raghunathrao's threat.
1767, Dec. 21	Madhosinh of Jaipur dies.

1768	Mahadji obtains his family rights and headship.
1769, Ending months	Maratha forces proceed north.
1770, April 5	Battle of Govardhan, Nawal Sinh Jat routed; Marathas take possession of Agra and Mathura.
1770, April 5	Najib-ud-daula offers submission but starts his old game.
1770, April 5	Maratha forces enter the Doab against the Bangash Nawab and encamp at Ramghat.
1770, August 23	Balavant Sinh of Benares dies.
1770, Sept. 8	Treaty of peace with the Jats.
1770, Oct. 31	Najib-ud-daula dies; his son Zabeta Khan confined but released by Holkar.
1770, Dec. 15	Marathas capture Etawa and march on Farrukhabad, whose Nawab restores Maratha territories.
1770, Dec.	British oppose Maratha schemes through Mirza Najaf Khan; Emperor seeks Maratha protection.
1771, Feb. 10	Mahadji takes possession of Delhi and places Jawan Bakht on the throne.
1771, April 12	Emperor leaves Allahabad for Delhi.
1771, July 11	Ahmad Kh. Bangash dies.
1771, July 26	The Emperor reaches Farrukhabad.
1771, Nov. 18	The Emperor reaches Anupshahr; Mahadji meets him.
1772, Jan. 6	The Emperor enters Delhi and occupies his throne.
1772, Feb.	The Emperor and the Marathas march in pursuit of Zabeta Khan.
1772, March 4	Mahadji captures Shukratal.
1772, April 14	Ahmad Shah Abdali dies at Kabul.
1772, April 14	Najibabad captured; and spoils of Panipat recovered by the Marathas.
1772, Monsoon	Mahadji and Visaji Krishna arrange affairs of Delhi.
1772, Nov. 18	The Peshwa dies at Poona.

CHAPTER XXIV

MARATHA AMBITIONS COMPLETED IN THE NORTH

[1761—1772]

1 Maratha set back in North India.
2 Malharrao Holkar worsted.
3 Clive and the Diwani.
4 Raghunathrao before Gohad.
5 Expedition of Ramchandra Ganesh and its results.
6 British opposition to Maratha plans.
7 The Emperor restored to Delhi.

1. **Maratha set back in North India.**—Writes Dr. Dighe,—"The consequences of the Maratha disaster of Panipat did not long remain concealed from friends or foes alike. Maratha dominant position in Hindustan was no longer tenable. So long as Marathas could not support their authority by armed might, the northern potentates were not going to respect their commands. Maratha dominion in the north,—Delhi, Agra, Doab, Bundelkhand, Malwa—became aflame with revolt of petty rulers, rising of local militias and disturbances of hill-tribes, and the next few years witnessed the shrinking of Maratha frontiers and withdrawing of their rule to the south of the Chambal.

"Ahmad Shah Abdali the victor of Panipat was hardly in a better plight. The year 1761-62 proved that this best Asiatic general of his age could win battles but not the subsequent dominion. He failed to reap the harvest of his amazing successes. His vision was bound by the narrow limits of his mountainous homeland of Afghanistan with the Punjab if he could possibly annex that province. Hence when his soldiers mutinied for arrears of pay and pressed for immediate return, the Shah Abdali retraced his steps and marched back to his country throwing back his life's chance. His withdrawal from the scene of his recent successes let loose pent up forces, brought new personalities on the stage and effected such a change in the situation that the Shah no longer remained the master of it."[1] His advance through the Punjab was so successfully held up by the Sikhs, that he gradually lost all that he had gained during ten years of hard fighting. Between 1762 and 1767 he struggled manfully to put down the Sikhs but was beaten in the end. He had by then lost both his health and vigour, sank into inertia and died rather a miserable death a few months before the Peshwa Madhavrao.

Among northern opponents of the Marathas the Rajputs were the most powerful with Madhosinh of Jaipur at their head; but Malharrao Holkar soon succeeded in putting them down. Madhosinh and his confederates sustained a severe defeat at the hands of Holkar at Mangrol near Kota on 29th and 30th November 1761, and could no longer stand in opposition to the Marathas. Holkar was, however, called away to the south and Mahadji Sindia was for long crippled by not being at once recognized as the heir to his ancestral estates. It therefore took several years for the Maratha power to regain its pre-Panipat position in the north. The natural result of this Maratha deterioration was the easy ascendancy which the British acquired in Bengal and Bihar, where the three legitimate owners, the Emperor, the Wazir of Oudh and the Nawab of Bengal, were quickly put down during the three years following Panipat. Neither the Bhosles of Nagpur nor the Peshwa offered the least resistance to this British aggression. For young Madhavrao on gathering the reins of Government in his hands after his victory at Rakshasbhuvan (August 1763), the aggression of Haidar Ali became the most pressing problem and he was compelled to leave the northern affairs to Sindia and Holkar. Sindia, however, was for some years disabled from taking a bold action by Raghunathrao interfering in the succession dispute of the Sindian fief and declaring Mahadji a rebel.

The Emperor Shah Alam lived then at Allahabad, enjoying the hospitality of the Wazir, while the British managed the revenues of Bengal and Bihar on behalf of the Nawab. The deposed Mir Qasim had tried in vain to resist the British pretensions, but his fall left the entire field open to British ambition. If it suited their purpose, they openly interfered in the concerns of the Indian powers, but if it did not, they put

1. Allahabad History, *Peshwa Madhaorao.*

forth the cogent and plausible excuse that they must refer the matter to their home authorities for orders, which meant a delay of years. Even in India they never neglected to support one power against another. They professed to act in the name of the Emperor, when they meant to put down the Nawabs of Bengal and Oudh. The successes they gained at Plassey and Baxar drove them from one height to another. Their position was peculiarly safe in comparison with the Indian powers they had to deal with. If they found their move disadvantageous, they could easily retrace their steps and offer the plea of orders from home. Indian powers once involved in an affair could have no choice but to reap the fruit of their action.

Mir Qasim whom the British themselves had raised to the Nawabship, soon became odious to them, when he began to assert his legitimate rights. The two became open enemies and went to war. Mir Qasim was defeated in two successive actions at Katwa and Gheria in July 1763 with the result that the British made Mir Jafar the Nawab a second time. Mir Qasim thereupon secured the aid of Shuja-ud-daula, and the two under the direction of the Emperor made a bold effort for regaining the lost provinces of Bihar and Bengal. In this venture they secured the co-operation of the Marathas and renewed hostilities against the British. The latter took up the challenge. Major Carnac advanced upon the combined armies of the confederates. On 3rd May 1764 a battle was fought near Patna in which the allies suffered a defeat. But no decision was reached: the two armies remained camping in Bihar during the monsoon and as soon as the rains were over, they came for a final action, which was fought at Baxar on 23rd October 1764. Maj. Hector Munro utterly routed the three potentates and compelled them to fall back upon Benares with their hopes of recovering their eastern possessions finally extinguished. The Emperor submitted to the dictates of the British and sought their protection.

Thus the battle of Baxar completed the process begun at Plassey seven years before. The Bhosles of Nagpore were for long demanding the Chauth as overlords of the province. To them Mir Qasim had long been appealing for support. But Janoji neglected this important responsibility and busied himself with destroying the Peshwa's capital of Poona in alliance with Nizam Ali. The result was that the British could easily establish their permanent sway on the two rich eastern provinces of India.

When the two rivals, the Marathas and the Afghans, retired from the Indian contest, there was a kind of vacuum in the centre. But nature abhors vacuum. New forces rushed in to seize the central authority vacated by the two powerful antagonists. Najib Khan Rohilla assumed supreme authority in Delhi, which was challenged by the Jat of Bharatpur, who had now gained strength. Both the chiefs solicited Maratha help: and Malharrao Holkar was asked to handle the situation. This Maratha chief looked upon Najib Khan as his adopted son and had no mind to support the Jat. After some fighting Malharrao patched up a treaty of peace between Najib Khan and the Jat ruler Jawahirsinh and became free to answer a more urgent call.

2. **Malharrao Holkar worsted.**—After Baxar the English ardently tried to capture Mir Qasim and punish him severely for the bloody massacre he had perpetrated of Ellis and other Englishmen at Patna. But Shuja protected Mir Qasim from British vengeance. Thereupon Major Fletcher marched against Shuja and chased him right up to Allahabad, taking possession of that chief's strategic post of Chunar, which formed the base for any conqueror descending upon Bihar from the north. The British also took the precaution of declaring that they were acting on behalf of the Emperor, whose territories they professed to protect against his treacherous servants Shuja and Mir Qasim. The proclamation which they issued at this time is an amusing piece of political chicanery.[2]

The English having captured Allahabad now began their march upon Lucknow the capital of Shuja. In his extreme peril that Prince learnt that the two Maratha captains Malharrao Holkar and Mahadji Sindia had been near Agra, negotiating the terms of peace between Najib and the Jat. As Holkar's force was already in the Doab, Shuja turned to that chief for aid. Writes Holkar on 30th March 1765, "I have arrived at Anupshahr where Shuja-ud-daula came and met me. I have

2. *Persian Calendar* 1. 2609.

agreed to lend him my armed aid and with this purpose am now proceeding towards the Ganges."

Thus Shuja and Malharrao joined their forces to which Ghazi-ud-din the ex-Wazir brought his own quota also. Major Fletcher who was keenly watching these movements marched upon them from Allahabad. The two opposing armies came face to face on the plain of Kora : Malharrao Holkar with his guerilla tactics at first severely harassed Fletcher. But the latter brought his excellent artillery rapidly into action on 3rd May and compelled Holkar to retire to Kalpi for safety. Says a Maratha newswriter, "the English possessed a powerful artillery, before which our men were unable to stand firm and took to flight. Malharrao has reached Kalpi in great distress." The guerilla warfare of the Marathas came to be doomed.[3]

At the moment of Holkar's reverse Mahadji Sindia was near Kota in Rajputana and ran immediately to that veteran's support. But as the affair had been finished, he could do little to retrieve the position. He wrote to the Peshwa on 10th August, "Holkar is at Datia, where I am going to meet him and with his co-operation I am anxious to undertake some grand projects." Most of the Indian politicians and potentates of the day watched the change with anxious dismay. Shuja-ud-daula in his perplexity asked for advice from Ahmad Khan Bangash. The latter told him, "Don't entertain the false hope that others would come and fight your battles. If you have the nerve, stand forth boldly against the English, even if you perish thereby. If you have not such a daring in you, you must go unhesitatingly to the English General and quietly accept whatever terms he imposes upon you." Shuja acted up to this latter course.[4]

3. Clive and the Diwani.—Politics in north India assumed a rapid change in the autumn of 1765. The Emperor grew most impatient to reach Delhi and occupy his throne. All India breathlessly watched whether the victorious English would halt at Allahabad or proceed to convey the Emperor to the imperial capital. At this moment there arrived on the

3. Khare 575 ; P. D. 29. 90, 98.
4. Dr. Shrivastav, *Shuja-ud-daula* II, p. 2.

Indian scene the great architect of the British Empire, Clive, now in the capacity of the Governor of Bengal with full powers to handle the situation. The English nation had already come out victorious in the Seven years' war (1763) and acquired unrivalled supremacy on the sea. Clive had keenly observed contemporary events and possessed unsurpassed knowledge of the political complexities of India. He landed at Calcutta on 3rd May, the very day that Fletcher inflicted the signal defeat upon Holkar. He correctly gauged how bitterly every Indian potentate resented British aggression, and with a resolve to disarm all hostility Clive left Calcutta on 25th June for the theatre of war. He reached Allahabad at the end of July.

Clive, separately interviewed the various persons concerned and fixed his line of action. He met the Emperor and obtained from him for the East India Company the office of the Diwani of the three provinces of Bengal, Bihar and Orissa, that is, the exclusive power to collect the revenues and dispose of them, without the responsibility for the provincial administration and without the appearance of complete annexation. Clive put this in a solemn document and had it sanctioned by the Emperor. He similarly dealt with Shuja-ud-daula and the Nawab of Bengal and bound them in separate treaties, which formed the basis upon which the future Empire was to be gradually built up. This was indeed a clever stroke of policy quickly executed within the first week of August[5] by which the British rulers obtained the substance of power without accepting the administrative management. The Emperor, the suzerain authority, the Wazir of Oudh and the Nawab of Bengal, who were the links of an indivisible chain, the central master and provincial servants in the traditional Mughal hierarchy, came to be permanently separated under the scheme of Clive, having nothing to do with one another and at the same time unable to stand independently on one's own resources without the Company's armed help for their sustenance.

Clive spent about a month in quieting the ruffled feelings of the various parties and impressed upon them that a new era

5. The agreement with Najmud-daula of Bengal was effected in July: that with Shuja is dated 2nd August and the grant of Diwani is dated 12th August.

of peace and good-will had taken the place of that of a ruinous war. He recognized the power of the Emperor himself, but removed the two Nawabs from his control. As the former was impatient to go to Delhi, Clive assured him that this would be accomplished as soon as circumstances permitted. Raghunathrao appeared on the scene only a few months after these important transactions, but he hardly understood the significance of the changes and concerned himself with the usual old routine of internal politics.

Having accomplished an enormous amount of diplomatic work, Clive returned to Calcutta in September. A Maratha agent at Allahabad thus reported on Clive's performance, "the whole of Bengal from the sea coast up to Benares has become English, with no impediment between. Those who were hostile have become their creatures." Thus the scheme of the conquest of Bengal upon which the Peshwa Balajirao had set his heart, was executed by a foreign power.

4. **Raghunathrao before Gohad.**—The powerful Jat Raja Surajmal perished at the height of his greatness in fight against Najib Khan on 25th December 1763. His chief Queen Hansia alias Rani Kishori adopted Jawahirsinh as her son, who succeeded Surajmal and continued his vigorous career defying all his three opponents, the Mughals, the Marathas and the raja of Jaipur. The Marathas recovered their position in a few years and appeared on the northern scene in 1766 headed by R'rao who, as we have already seen, parted company from the Peshwa at Kolhapur in February, and taking Janoji Bhosle with him reached Jhansi in April, where Sindia and Holkar joined him. The Jat Rana of Gohad backed by the powerful arm of Jawahirsinh formed at this time a strong anti-Maratha coalition, which R'rao found it necessary to put down. As plans were being formed for the reduction of Gohad, Malharrao Holkar died near Alampur on 20th May, creating an additional problem about the succession. As R'rao's arrival heartened Maratha friends, ambassadors arrived from the Emperor asking him to stand against the English and undo what Clive had accomplished the year before to the detriment of the Muslim powers. But R'rao did not agree to the task and contented himself with sending diplomatic missions to the various Indian

powers and also one to the British at Calcutta for negotiating a common agreement.[6] Gohad was besieged but no progress was made for several months, as the trans-Chambal Jats strongly supported the Rana of Gohad, and R'rao soon found it difficult to extricate himself from an awkward job. Holkar and Gaikwad two prominent Maratha captains left him in disgust as their troops had received no pay for several months and were on the point of revolt. Several surprise attacks launched against Gohad ended in failure. The situation was saved by the mediation of Mahadji Sindia, who arranged an accommodation with the Rana on 2nd January 1767. He agreed to pay a fine of 15 lacs and the siege was raised.

Raghunathrao then proceeded in the direction of Dholpur to meet the Jat Jawahirsinh. He was in severe distress for want of money and was operating almost in a vacuum. Just then news arrived that Ahmad Shah Abdali had appeared in the Punjab and the two parties became anxious to avoid hostilities. Jat envoys met R'rao in his camp and communicated to him their master's readiness to pay him some nazar and serve under him when necessary. The proposal was accepted and Jawahir was invited to a personal interview. But the latter suspected treachery and went away without meeting the Maratha generalissimo. A temporary truce was concluded, the Jat agreeing to pay the balance of the subsidy promised to Holkar the year before, and accepting a small jagir southwest of Bharatpur. Raghunathrao was compelled to retrace his steps to the south, in great embarrassment for money, without accomplishing any tangible results during one and a half years of his much trumpeted expedition. In March 1767 he arrived in south Malwa and learning that Ahalyabai's son Malrao had died on the 27th of that month, decided to improve the occasion to his own selfish advantage, by seizing the hoarded wealth of that pious lady, on the pretext that the Holkar State was now heirless and deserved to be confiscated.

The spirited daughter-in-law of Malharrao Holkar who had given his very best to the Peshwa's house, was not to be easily cowed down. When Raghunathrao under the evil advice of Gangadhar Chandrachud and Chinto Vithal ordered an

6. *Persian Calendar* 2. 78, 145, 207.

attack upon Indore, none of his followers would obey him. Ahalyabai prepared to defend Indore against the wanton aggression and received full sympathy in her resolve from all the Maratha captains in R'rao's camp. He felt extreme irritation at such a discomfiture and saved his face by himself offering to call upon Ahalyabai for a condolence visit without any armed following. The question of choosing an heir for the State of Indore was referred by the lady to the Peshwa at Poona, and the uncle could not override it. He hurried back to Nasik in summer utterly crest-fallen with no face to confront the Peshwa.

This failure of R'rao had a disastrous effect upon the Maratha prestige in the north. The Jat Raja Jawahirsinh, finding that the Maratha armies had retired, invaded Bundelkhand during the autumn of 1767 and quickly effected the conquest of all the Maratha possessions in that region right up to Kalpi, whose guardian Balaji Govind Kher was powerless to oppose him. By October practically the whole of Bundelkhand was lost and it became now the first concern of the Peshwa at Poona to put down the Jats if Maratha power had to be saved in the north. A mere accident came to rescue the Maratha position at this time. Jawahirsinh was attacked by the Raja of Jaipur and was severely defeated at Maondha near Narnol on the Jat frontier on 14th December 1767. Jawahir's stormy career came to a tragic end soon after, when in July 1768 he was suddenly cut down by a favourite soldier whom he had disgraced.

5. Expedition of Ramchandra Ganesh, its results.—Madhavrao was all along anxious to rectify the Maratha position in the northern sphere and was able for the first time to make necessary preparations during the monsoon of 1768 after he had disposed of his uncle. But a few more months were lost in settling the rebellion of Janoji Bhosle by the treaty of Kankapur in March 1769. Then the Maratha armies under two able commanders Ramchandra Ganesh and Visaji Krishna began their march towards the north. Mahadji Sindia and Tukoji Holkar had preceded them by a few months.

The Emperor at Allahabad, sulking under British restraint, felt encouraged by this Maratha advent and promised to pay

50 lacs if the Marathas would put down the Jat rebels. Madhosinh, the Raja of Jaipur, who had for several years dominated the politics of north India, died on 21st December 1767, leaving behind him a chaotic legacy. His successor Pratap Sinh now joined the Marathas and so did the Nawab of Bhopal.

Madhavrao's orders to his commanders were to proceed straight to Delhi and take possession of the capital. But the Jat State opposed the Maratha advance in the region of Agra. Torn by dissensions that State had lost its former cohesion and could no longer present a formidable barrier. The fratricidal war between Nawalsinh and Ranjitsinh had reduced the strength of the Jats and invited foreign intervention. Ranjitsinh courted Maratha aid and with these allies defeated Nawalsinh in a closely fought action at Govardhan on 5th April 1770. This spectacular victory over the Jats produced immediate results. The Marathas occupied Agra and Mathura, and Najib Khan who held the imperial capital opened negotiations and offered his co-operation in recovering the old Maratha possessions beyond the Jamuna. Accordingly the Maratha armies crossed that river near Mathura in April 1770, and entered the territory of Ahmad Khan Bangash of Farrukhabad. The Marathas established their camp at Ramghat near the Ganges on the advice of Najib Khan, who now began to play the same old tactics that he had employed at Shukratal eleven years before, the only factor against him now being that there was no Abdali to back him from beyond the Indus. Ahmad Khan Bangash had his camp on the other side of the Ganges and kept up a secret understanding with Najib Khan in order to bring about Maratha ruin. For a time the Marathas found themselves in a critical position at Ramghat, having been completely surrounded by hostile Pathan elements. Being informed of this situation of his armies, the Peshwa immediately prepared to despatch from the south another strong force for their relief. Happily, however, the Maratha captains had grown wiser by past experience, and with clever tactics managed to save their situation on the Ganges by slowly retiring to safer positions on the Jamuna. Just at this moment of crisis, Najib Khan died on 31st October 1770 on his way to his home at Najibabad, thereby greatly relieving Maratha anxieties. His son Zabeta Khan inherited his father's power and property.

The Peshwa on learning of the safety of his armies in the north, gave up the idea of sending relief to them.

The Bangash Nawab failed to grasp the import of the clever tactics which the Maratha commander had followed in planning a temporary withdrawal and effecting a complete separation between the two Pathan wings, the Bangash and the Rohilla. Ramchandra, as soon as he learnt that Najib Khan was dead, placed Zabeta Khan, who was then in the Maratha camp, in detention. But Tukoji Holkar true to the traditions of Malharrao, managed to save Zabeta Khan by secretly removing him away and setting him free from his confinement.

As soon as Zabeta Khan became free, he repaired to the Emperor and wrested the office of Mir Bakshi from him. With this additional authority he marched against Ramchandrapant in the Doab. The rains were over by this time, the Maratha strategy was perfect. Ramchandra and Mahadji acted in full co-operation and completely overcame the forces of the Bangash and the Rohillas. They captured Etawa and marched on Farrukhabad on 15th December 1770. Ahmad Khan now in a subdued mood, begged for life, ceding to the Marathas all the territory that they had possessed before the day of Panipat. Ahmad Khan felt this mortification so severely that he died in grief on 11th July 1771. The former Maratha position was completely retrieved.

How keenly Madhavrao watched and how anxiously he directed the operations of this northern expedition, is found clearly explained in a recent find of a letter addressed by him on 21st December 1770 to his commandants Ramchandra Ganesh and Visaji Krishna.[7] He writes,—

"It is now over twenty months since you were asked to proceed to the north with a force numbering some fifty thousand led by picked captains. Never since the celebrated expedition of Bhau Saheb to Panipat had such a large force advanced to that region. You were invested with full powers and asked to reduce the Jat and other rulers who had thrown off their allegiance to our government and to impress upon the Rajputs, the Sikhs and the Abdali king that the Maratha rule

---

7. *Ait Sankirna Sak*. 7 p. 42.

had again been as vigorously restored in north India as before. Full confidence was reposed in your capacity and valour to achieve these objects, and thereby to bring in a plentiful supply of money contributions. The two experienced chiefs of the houses of Sindia and Holkar, the main props of our State, were purposely associated with you in your present undertaking.

" It seems, however, that you have not all been working in full co-operation. Holkar and Sindia are openly at loggerheads and you two are not working in perfect union either. Fortunately you have obtained a grand victory over the Jat raja, but in the end little substantial benefit has resulted from that victory. You have also had consultations with Shuja-ud-daula, but have not succeeded in taking from him the possession of the two holy places, Benares and Prayag, a longstanding claim which you should have obtained. Your dealings with the Rohillas have yielded no better results, although the death of the wicked Najib-ud-daula offered you a most favourable opportunity of obtaining satisfaction for all the past wrongs. You can now easily take possession of Delhi and give the Wazirship to Shuja and not to Ghazi-ud-din who has lost all credit. You must control Najib's son Zabeta Khan without doing him any harm or indignity. In fact, you have now a golden opportunity before you and you must turn it to the best advantage. This is possible only if you all act in perfect concert. You all well know how disunity and self-seeking have ruined our interests in the past. You must realize that each one's personal interest is best served by working for the united good of all. Rest assured that your master the Peshwa will amply reward your individual merit."

6. **British opposition to Maratha Plans.**—During all these events the antagonism between the two leading Maratha sardars, Sindia and Holkar, continued to hamper Maratha operations, with no master on the spot to control their activities. Neither Ramchandra Ganesh nor Visaji Krishna could dictate orders to these powerful hereditary chiefs : but for a time these two Brahman commanders and Mahadji brought severe pressure upon Tukoji and compelled him to give up Zabeta Khan whom he had sheltered. The Jats who had been humbled early

in the year, were negotiating for peace. A treaty was signed on 8th September 1770, by which Nawalsinh agreed to pay 65 lacs by way of expenses to the Marathas ; and his brother Ranjitsinh gave up his claim to the Jat Kingship, receiving for his maintenance a jagir worth twenty lacs. In this way the two wars, the one with the Jats and the other with the Rohillas and the Pathans, came to a successful close, thereby clearing the ground for the settlement of the Emperor's position. So long as these neighbouring powers of Delhi were hostile, no headway could be made with the central plan of restoring Maratha influence at the capital.

Readers may be aware that for some years, the Emperor Shah Alam's affairs were managed by his chief adviser Mirza Najaf Khan, who was a protege of the British and, being in their pay, opposed any plan of the Emperor to trust his fortunes to Maratha management, in preference to the British protection which he was enjoying at Allahabad. Another strong supporter of the British cause was Balavant Sinh, the Raja of Benares, whose death on 23rd August 1770 removed the last obstacle to the establishment of Maratha influence at the imperial Court. The British always dreaded a combination of northern powers under Maratha hegemony, and had since the day of Plassey made it the main object of their policy to oppose such a combination. Mir Qasim and the Nawab of Bengal also worked strongly against their British antagonists. As the Emperor would be the central figure of any hostile combination, the British held him tightly in their grip at Allahabad. None understood these currents and cross-currents of the political situation better than the Emperor himself. Twelve years had passed since the murder of his father and yet he, a homeless wanderer all the time, was no nearer the goal of his ambition. He had amply judged what benefits he could expect from his British protectors, and what faith he could place in their sweet professions. Now as the Marathas appeared on the northern scene, swiftly restoring their lost prestige, the Emperor called upon his British patrons either to advance and oppose the Maratha aggression openly, or allow him freely to choose his own way. Mere soothing promises had been too much for him to bear with patience. He would no longer be satisfied with specious promises and demanded immediate action, not advice. He said he was no Emperor without the possession of Delhi.

So when the Maratha forces were camping in the Doab in 1770, Shuja-ud-daula visited Ramchandra Ganesh on behalf of the Emperor. On 10th August the Emperor himself wrote to Ramchandrapant, "we are glad to receive your assurance that the strictest harmony exists between you and our brother the Wazir Shuja-ud-daula and your promise to outrival the Wazir and the English in serving the interests of our Empire. We have full faith in your loyalty and attachment. If you act as you profess, we will also look upon you as graciously." The Emperor wrote similar letters to the other Maratha leaders and to the Peshwa also, showing how impatient he had become to reach the capital under their protection.

7. **The Emperor restored to Delhi.**— The Emperor's mother Zenat Mahal also urged him to the same course, viz., to accept Maratha protection. He deputed Mirza Najaf Khan to meet the Maratha generals and arrange the details. In order to put pressure on Shah Alam, Sindia threatened to raise another Emperor to the throne and make Ghazi-ud-din then living in the Maratha camp the Wazir. This threat had immediate effect. Early in 1771 Mahadji directed his attention to the capture of Delhi, which was then held by Zabeta Khan. Sindia advanced with his forces and took possession of the capital on 10th February. He placed Jawan Bakht (Shah Alam's son) on the throne and offered him nazar. The occupation of Delhi proved highly beneficial to the Maratha cause. On 12th February Shah Alam ratified a formal agreement with the Maratha agents and left Allahabad on Friday 12th April on his journey for Delhi. He reached Farrukhabad on 26th July and halted there for some time arranging his affairs for his eventual position. On 16th November he reached Anupshahr, where Mahadji Sindia came and made his obeisance. Thence they travelled together to Delhi and made a formal entry into the capital on 6th January 1772 (n.s.). The Marathas thus regained the position which Sadashivrao Bhau had lost by the disaster of Panipat. The Peshwa on hearing of

this development communicated some pertinent reflections to his general in the north :

"I quite appreciate the value of a performance which the English desisted from undertaking. I should, however, like to know what amount of money and territory the Emperor has given you. You have now been out there for three saesons. The Emperor has attained his cherished object, but I don't see what you have gained. Our men have shed their blood, in return for which you must acquire money and territory proportionate to the sacrifice. Have you at least freed the holy places of Kashi and Prayag from Muslim control ? You must likewise recover the cost of the troops employed and the debts our Government have incurred in this venture. The English if they had been so minded, did certainly possess the strength to place the Emperor on his ancestral throne : but as their power is mainly based on the sea, they declined to go a long way inland without a corresponding advantage. Now, you must remember never to allow the English to make a lodgment at Delhi. If they once obtain a footing, they can never be dislodged. Of all the European nations, the English are certainly the strongest. They have seized strategic points and have formed a ring round the Indian continent, from Calcutta to Surat." These prophetic words of the Peshwa exhibit his grasp of the political situation of this country and his impatience to prevent their further aggression.[8]

The Emperor was thus firmly seated on his hereditary throne, and as Zabeta Khan was now the only person who was capable of doing mischief towards the Marathas, Mahadji and Visaji Krishna with the Emperor at their head, marched against him in the Doab in February 1772, and subdued all his territory of Rohilkhand. Again did Zabeta Khan entrench himself at Shukratal, which Mahadji captured on 4th March. The Khan eccaped in the darkness of the night to the territory of Bijnor. He was hotly pursued right up to Najibabad, known then by the name of Patthargad, or stone fort, which also the Marathas captured in April, along with Zabeta Khan's family. He then escaped to the northern jungles. At this time Mahadji avenged the wrongs and atrocities that the traitor Najib had

8. *Kaifiyats and Yadis*, p. 159.

formerly inflicted upon the Sindian house. The Rohilla's tomb was opened and his remains scattered. Whatever was found existing from the spoils taken at Panipat was recovered, including, as the report goes, even some Maratha women. Immense booty was obtained including horses, elephants, guns and valuables. Mahadji ever after felt a legitimate pride as an avenger of past injuries. The Rohillas were a race celebrated for valour, but not a single member of that race would come forth boldly to stand in opposition to the Marathas at this time. Zabeta Khan thereupon sought shelter with the Jats and the Sikhs. The news of these successes reached Poona in May and gladdened the dying Peshwa's heart. The Maratha forces returned to the capital for the rains.

It was no small comfort to the Peshwa to feel that he was after all able to wipe off fully the disgrace of Panipat and to restore Maratha power to a position which his three great ancestors had toiled to build up. Zabeta Khan alone remained as a disturbing factor in the sphere of Delhi. The Emperor too out of selfish motives would not allow him to be crushed. Shah Alam was perhaps the most faithless and intriguing person known to Indian history, and proved a perennial problem for Mahadji to handle. He alone, however, served him to the last and did his best to save his life and dignity in the most dangerous situations. Nor was Shuja-ud daula happy at the rising tide of Maratha fortunes, and instead of joining the Marathas in resisting British aggression, became the foremost Indian chief in planting British supremacy in India.[9]

It is not necessary to emphasize the weakness of the Maratha character as evidenced by the divided counsel existing in the Maratha camp during the momentous expedition that has just been described. There was no controlling voice of a respected master on the spot, and it is no wonder if divergent views prevailed in questions of war and policy. Holkar never gave

9. History amply records how Indian liberties were bartered away mainly by the four Muslim potentates of Oudh, Murshidabad, Arcot and Haidarabad. Not a single Hindu joined in this unholy game until the end of the eighteenth century, when, at the advent of Wellesley, there remained not a single Hindu leader to resist the onward march of the British power.

up his old game of shielding the Rohilla chiefs and exasperated Mahadji beyond measure. Visaji Krishna's sane and conciliatory attitude alone saved the situation. He befriended Zabeta Khan and restored his family to him on payment of a ransom. The Emperor continued to practise his treachery and managed secretly to bring about a wanton attack upon the Maratha camp at Delhi on 18th December 1772. The attack miserably failed of effect and the Emperor was compelled to make abject submission. But before the imperial administration at Delhi and in the north could settle down to normal conditions, the Peshwa was dead at Poona, and his brother the next Peshwa came to be sadly murdered, which led to the withdrawal of the Maratha forces then in the north.

CHRONOLOGY

CHAPTER XXV

1764-67	Friction between the Peshwa and Raghunathrao reaches a climax.
1766, Nov.	Peshwa proceeds to Karnatak.
1767, January	The Peshwa holds a surprise inspection of his forces.
1767, February	The Peshwa captures Shira ; extends protection to the Rani of Bednur.
1767, May	The Peshwa hurriedly closes Karnatak operations and returns to Poona.
1767, June	Raghunathrao returns discomfited to Nasik and begins preparations for a conflict with the Peshwa.
1767, Sept.	They two meet at Anandvalli.
1767, Oct. 13	An agreement reached between them.
1767, closing months	Raghunathrao starts fresh intrigues.
1767-69	Haidar Ali regains lost ground in the Karnatak.
1768, early months	The Peshwa and Raghunathrao prepare for war.
1768, April 19	Raghunathrao adopts a son, Amritrao.
1768, May	The Peshwa advances against his uncle near Nasik.
1768, June 10	Battle of Dhodap ; Raghunathrao routed, captured and confined at Poona.
1768, Aug. 18	Damaji Gaikwad dies.
1768, Sept.	Janoji Bhosle rises against the Peshwa.
1768, Dec.	The Peshwa restrains Damaji Gaikwad's sons.
1769, January	The Peshwa joined by the Nizam's forces marches upon Nagpur ; the Bhosle brothers ravage the Peshwa's territory.
1769, March	Janoji surrounded ; he opens negotiations for peace.
1769, March 23	Treaty of Kanakapur arranged.
1769, April 18-24	Ceremonial visits of Peshwa & Bhosle.

1769, ending months.	Expedition sent to north India.
1770, Jan.	The Peshwa in the Karnatak.
1770, Feb.	Nizam Ali and Murarrao join the Peshwa.
1770, April 30	Fort Nijgal captured : Narayanrao wounded.
1770, May	Illness compels Peshwa to return from Karnatak.
1770, Oct. 19	Fort Gurrumkonda captured by Pethe.
1770, Dec.	The Peshwa starts for Karnatak, but is compelled to return, leaving the war to Trimbakrao Pethe to complete.
1771, Jan. 17	Gopalrao Patwardhan dies.
1771, March 8	Pethe's great victory over Haidar Ali at Moti Talav, (i.e. Chinkurali)
1772, March	The ailing Peshwa brings Raghunathrao to his presence and entrusts Narayanrao to his care.
1772, May 18	Janoji Bhosle dies after his visit to the Peshwa.
1772, June	Trimbakrao recalled from the Karnatak.
1772, Oct. 6	Raghunathrao escapes from confinement, but is secured.

CHAPTER XXV

INTERNAL AFFAIRS OF THE STATE

[1765—1772]

1 Raghunathrao's demand for partition.
2 Raghunathrao finally overcome.
3 Bhosle brought to obedience.
4 Damaji Gaikwad's death.
5 War with Haidar Ali renewed. (1767-1772).

1. ***Raghunathrao's demand for partition.***—Since the Peshwa's success at Rakshasbhuvan Raghunathrao had been realizing that he was eclipsed by his nephew's increasing prestige and moral greatness. He could only make a theatrical exhibition of his inherent weakness, which the fulsome flattery of his immediate comrades like Chinto Vithal served only to enhance. Raghunathrao's wife Anandibai was probably too young at the time to advise him for better or worse. The Peshwa did his utmost to keep him contented and got out of him whatever good work he was capable of. The Peshwa's mother Gopikabai, sick of the constant turmoil, followed the same course and went to live in the neighbourhood of Nasik, seeking peace in pious contemplation. A report from Raghunathrao's quarters says, "Chinto Vithal is Dada's sole adviser. Some of Holkar's party have joined here and keep him in humour. A motley has assembled, each one with a selfish motive, with little regard for the interests of the State. The Shrimant is extremely fickle-minded. Every wise counsel from sane persons is misrepresented to him. He expressed his desire to solemnly make the vow of fire-worship (*agnihotra*). Preparations were quickly made; all the earthwork and brickwork for the altars were completed; and just at the moment when the ceremony was to start, Dada suddenly declared, 'I can't stand this wearisome job' and threw all the brick constructions into the Godavari. Priests had been brought from long distances in palanquins with bearers supplied for all; and now when they had all assembled, they have been dismissed. Chinto Vithal is bent upon ruining the

M. H. II—34

Maratha State." This little incident well illustrates the whimsical nature of Raghunathrao.

More than once during the recent years did Madhavrao personally and in writing, remonstrate with his uncle, strongly complaining that his sardars flagrantly disobeyed his commands and sought refuge with his uncle and obtained protection. This undermined the Peshwa's authority and could not be tolerated in the wider interests of the State. These remonstrances fell on deaf ears, and the Peshwa found himself thwarted at every step on account of the dual authority operating in the administration. He placed all his cards openly on the table; but Raghunathrao shifted his ground, and every minute succumbed to tale-bearers who distorted every word and action of the Peshwa.[1]

In his letters to his uncle's adherents, the Peshwa particularly urged that all owed loyal service to the State; the uncle asked for partition, which would reduce its strength and invite its enemies to fall upon it. He would therefore not be a party to any such division. He would rather surrender his Peshwaship and place himself at his uncle's service.

The situation reached its climax at Poona in the autumn of 1765, when the two chiefs came together face to face and held acrimonious discussions for over a month. Madhavrao explained his policy to Raghunathrao's confidant Chinto Vithal : "Ours is a large State which deserves to be sustained by all, small or great. Dada Saheb however demands a partition. I cannot be a party to such a foolish measure. The age-long practice has been that full responsibility is centred in one person, exercising undivided control over all members. He is to provide for all according to his best judgment. Dada Saheb's demand amounts to setting aside this time-honoured practice. He asks for the possession of Gujarat for himself and a number of forts to be placed under his exclusive management. This is certainly not the way to preserve the State intact. I am quite willing to withdraw entirely from public affairs and take up my residence in a far away corner. But I will not allow the State to be thus partitioned. Let Dada-

1. For instance the affair of Naro Krishna may be studied in P. D. 19, 52; *Patreyadi* 211, 213; Raj. 13, 84.

Saheb alone exercise the supreme power. I shall be content to do what little I can if he requires it of me. This in my opinion is the only solution of our present troubles."

A number of letters of this type speak clearly how the two parties were disposed to each other. After a good deal of deliberation Raghunathrao agreed to undertake an independent task on his own exclusive responsibility unhampered by the Peshwa, and the demand for partition was for the time shelved. In February 1766 Raghunathrao proceeded to the north and the Peshwa returned to Poona after a friendly meeting with Nizam Ali. How Raghunathrao mismanaged this northern enterprise has been already described.

2. **Raghunathrao finally overcome.**—After his dismal failure in his contest with the Rana of Gohad, Raghunathrao returned discomfited to Nasik in June 1767, violently chafing at heart and throwing the blame of his failure upon his nephew. Once more the old fissure reappeared in a dreadful form, straining their mutual relations and making them so suspicious of each other, that they would not openly meet together. Bent upon putting the dispute to the arbitration of the sword, Raghunathrao began to raise troops and make war-like preparations at Nasik.

During the past two years the Peshwa's high character and capacity had been amply exhibited, in severe contrast to the low reputation of his uncle. Everybody well understood the merits of the domestic dispute. Raghunathrao's nefarious activities filled the Peshwa's Court with alarm. The various sardars and leaders were approached by both for armed help. Keepers of forts began to be seduced. While a large number of public servants were neutral at heart, their loyalties came now to be divided. There was an all round commotion in the country as preparations grew apace for an armed conflict. Madhavrao removed Sakharam Bapu from office, on account of his dubious loyalty and appointed Moroba Phadnis as his immediate secretary. The Peshwa showed great forbearance and commenced negotiations with his uncle through Govind Shivram, whom he deputed to meet the uncle and adjust their differences on some reasonable basis. But Govind Shivram failed in his mission, and the Peshwa specially selected Sakharam Bapu and sent him to Raghunathrao to negotiate a peaceful solution and avoid extremities. Sakharam Bapu enjoyed Raghunathrao's confidence and arranged a personal meeting of the two chiefs. As a last resort the Peshwa left the capital to meet his uncle and decide the dispute in person. Large forces accompanied them both and the atmosphere became surcharged with suspicion; for a long while a personal meeting between them became impossible. When the Peshwa was at Rahuri nearly half way between Nasik and Poona, Chinto Vithal arrived from Dada to negotiate an understanding; after a good deal of discussion and reference backwards and forwards, the uncle and the nephew met near Chandore on 12th September and proceeded together to Anandvalli by easy marches.

The Peshwa was now bent upon seeking a final issue of the conflict and directly demanded complete surrender from Raghunathrao or an appeal to the decision of arms. He purposely assumed a stern and uncompromising attitude and abandoned the fruitless formalities of the previous years. This sudden change in the Peshwa's attitude could not be mistaken, and Raghunathrao climbed down in his pretensions. Thereupon numerous drafts and proposals were committed to paper, the one procrastinating, the other pressing for decision. When thus forced to decide, Raghunathrao spoke out, "You are the Peshwa and the master. I have no concern with your administration." He agreed to retire on condition that his debts of 25 lacs incurred in the northern expedition were paid off and a suitable maintenance was provided, enabling him to lead a life of resignation at some holy place. Though it was a heavy responsibility, the Peshwa, anxious to close the affair finally in a peaceful manner, agreed to the demand, asking in turn the delivery of the forts of Ahmadnagar, Ashirgad, Shivner and Satara then held by Raghunathrao. He likewise agreed to assign a jagir of ten lacs for the latter's maintenance. This arrangement was ratified on the Dassara day (3 October, 1767), and dresses were exchanged in apparent reconciliation. After spending a few days at Anandvalli, the Peshwa and his uncle parted company.

This agreement proved only a temporary truce. By it Raghunathrao lost the high position and influence he had so long wielded in the State, a humiliation which stung him severely. He immediately started his former intrigues with Nizam Ali, Haidar Ali, Damaji Gaikwad, Janoji Bhosle and others, upon whose attachment he had long counted. At this time the British mission under Mostyn arrived in Poona : Mostyn's assistant Brome visited Raghunathrao at Nasik, had several interviews with him (from 19 December 1767), and promised him British help if he would take up arms against the Peshwa. When Madhavrao learned of these activities of his uncle, he felt extremely annoyed and regretted very much that he had not once for all dealt severely with the latter last September and finished him at a stroke. He again called up his forces and marched in the direction of Nasik. Damaji Gaikwad and Holkar's Dewan Gangoba Tatya openly espoused Raghunathrao's cause ; while Tukoji Holkar chose to remain neutral, but Mahadji Sindia came and joined the Peshwa.

Raghunathrao had no male issue and he in order to lend colour to his cause, formally adopted on 19th April a boy from a different family and named him Amrịtrao. This meant that Raghunathrao had reverted to his former demand of a half share in the Peshwa's dominion. This was an emphatic challenge to the Peshwa. Raghunathrao's plan was to put off the campaign to a more suitable time after the rains : but the Peshwa refused to let him choose his own convenience. In May he rapidly moved in Raghunathrao's direction giving him no chance to escape. The latter was found camping below fort Dhodap. When he heard of the approach of the Peshwa's army, he lost his nerve and hastily took shelter in that hill fort, thus shattering the popular belief of his intrepidity as a soldier. Gopalrao Patwardhan and other lieutenants of the Peshwa dashed against Raghunathrao's army and made a clean sweep of it on 10th June. From among Raghunathrao's adherents Chinto Vithal was captured wounded and his brother Moropant was killed. Sadashiv Ramchandra saved his life by flight. Much booty in horses, elephants and material was secured. The Peshwa now demanded his uncle's unconditional surrender. The latter had no alternative. He came down and surrendered his person and the fort. He was immediately made prisoner, taken to Poona and kept closely confined in the palace. It will thus be seen that this unseemly contest lasted intermittently for full seven years from June 1761 to

June 1768; and the trouble and anxiety of it contributed to the break down in the Peshwa's health more than any other cause.

Instead of following the Muslim practice of doing short work with opponents, the Peshwa behaved with unexampled generosity to his uncle. He was given all personal comforts and facilities during his confinement. Raghunathrao, however, did not take his defeat manfully. Trivial complaints constantly poured out from him, to enforce which he resorted to fasting and other methods of self-torture. Reports came that he performed sunworship and incantations in order to encompass the ruin of the Peshwa. He maintained a large useless establishment of Pandits, musicians, Haridasas, in addition to a large body of servants and retainers along with a number of concubines. All this was intended to spite the Peshwa by compelling him to bear the enormous expense. Raghunathrao's ambition in life was to shine forth as the legitimate Peshwa, which he could not fulfil during Madhavrao's regime. When after three years of confinement the latter felt his end was near in March 1772, he sent for his uncle, begged him most earnestly to forget the past and take care of his young brother Narayanrao after he was gone. But this tragic and solemn appeal failed to create in Raghunathrao any lasting sentiment either of duty or of affection. He did not scruple to create fresh trouble for the Peshwa and disturb his peace in death. On 6th October 1772, that is, six weeks before the Peshwa's death, Raghunathrao effected his escape from the Poona palace, and began to collect troops in order to seize the Peshwaship. He was immediately pursued, captured once more at Tulapur, and sent back to confinement.

The Maratha State had fallen on evil times. The Chhatrapati's house collapsed after Shahu's death. The Peshwa's house was about to suffer a similar fate after the third Peshwa's death. Fortunately his son Madhavrao came to its rescue, although he had to waste years of precious life in overcoming the mischief in his own family. This domestic feud did not fail to affect the other members of the State, viz., Sindia, Holkar, Gaikwad and Bhosle, who were now its four main props, and whom the same evil contagion affected in a greater or less degree. The first two have been incidentally dealt with in the foregoing narrative. The last two deserve a special mention. We shall first deal with the Bhosle of Nagpur.

3. **Bhosle brought to obedience.**—This family from the beginning showed an unwillingness to submit to the Peshwa's authority and never realized that under the political circumstances of the times, they could not maintain their own individual existence without the support of the central Government. They were ever ready to take advantage of the Peshwa's difficulties and could not be depended upon in a case of emergency, a tendency which the spirited Peshwa was not going to tolerate. In the year 1766 Janoji Bhosle was humbled after a short campaign and was let off lightly on account of Raghunathrao's intercession on his behalf. Janoji, however, succumbed to the wicked advice of his minister Dewajipant and started his old game of intriguing against the Peshwa and violated the agreement contracted in 1766. Some two years passed and the Peshwa after disposing of his uncle at the battle of Dhodap in June 1768, decided to teach a severe lesson to Janoji who had coquetted with the Peshwa's enemies. Madhavrao sent for the Nagpur minister Dewajipant for a personal visit at Poona. The latter refused to obey the summons and avoided a meeting with the Peshwa, but at the same time conducted informal intrigues with Raghunathrao and the British detrimental to the Peshwa's authority. On 21st September Madhavrao wrote to Janoji, "Your agent Chimnaji Rukmangad has come and offered an explanation on your behalf, but I want Dewajipant here at once for settling our dispute." He again wrote a month later calling upon both Janoji and his minister peremptorily to come and meet him. When this stern warning fell upon deaf ears, the Peshwa at once opened hostilities against Bhosle and marched upon his territory through Berar and threatened to capture Nagpur itself. Dewajipant realized the peril he was running into and came to meet the Peshwa in Berar. He was at once put under arrest, a step which irritated Janoji all the more.

The Peshwa had organized a strong expedition under Ramchandra Ganesh to be despatched to the north. He now diverted these forces and ordered that general to fall upon Nagpur, and ravage the Bhosle's territory. Gopalrao Patwardhan who had been asked to move into the Karnatak was immediately recalled and an all round offensive opened against the Bhosle brothers. In response to the Peshwa's request for military help, Nizam Ali despatched his forces under his minister Ruknud-daula with Ramchandra Jadhav supporting him. Thus reinforced the Peshwa began aggressive movements in the Bhosle raja's territory and captured the fort of Amner without much effort. He did not thus take long to seize the Bhosle possessions of Berar right up to the river Wardha. Early in January 1769 the Peshwa marched upon Nagpur and Ramchandra Ganesh reduced Bhandara. A severe action was fought on 10th January at Panchgavan near Akola, in which Narahar Ballal Risbud an able commander of the Bhosles was killed.[2]

All this while Diwakar Pandit from his confinement in the Maratha camp managed to conduct intrigues with his master, communicating to him vital information and directing plans and measures for overcoming the Peshwa. Acting on this advice Janoji who had formed his base at Chanda and being unable to meet the Peshwa's strength with his small force, had adopted guerilla tactics, gave out that he would march upon Poona, liberate Raghunathrao and instal him in the Peshwa's seat. He crossed the Godavari and began mercilessly ravaging the territories of his opponents. Madhavrao was compelled to give up his objective of reducing Chanda and hurriedly despatched Ramchandra Ganesh and Gopalrao Patwardhan in pursuit of Janoji to prevent him from reaching Poona. For three or four days during February Poona was in great alarm and confusion on account of the false reports spread by Janoji. The Peshwa took prompt measures for counteracting these reports and relieving the people of unnecessary fears.

Janoji was hardly able to make good his words. After crossing the Godavari, he began plundering the Nizam's possessions in the vicinity of Bhalki and Medak. But he was closely pursued by Ramchandra Ganesh and Gopalrao, and was so harassed that his troops had actually to starve during a vexatious running fight which continued over long distances through-

2. P. D. 20. 200-210 and 224.

out the month of March. Janoji came gradually to be surrounded in the region of the middle Godavari and was compelled to save himself by seeking shelter in the forests of Chinur situated in the Andhra country. Writes Haripant Phadke on 13th March, "The Peshwa arrived yesterday at Kanakapur on the north bank of the Godavari. Janoji is hiding in the jungles of Chinur about 60 miles eastwards. Gopalrao is at Brahmeshwar." At this stage Janoji's brother Mudhoji joined the Peshwa, realizing that the former was now in a helpless situation. The exhaustion of both the parties induced them to seek a termination of their hostilities by coming to a mutual accommodation. Gopalrao acted as the mediator. The Peshwa addressed a conciliatory appeal to Janoji expounding the brilliant prospect of a joint national endeavour, and inviting him to a personal interview. The Peshwa's magnanimous offer did not fail to evoke a graceful response from Bhosle, as they both came to realize the wisdom of serving the Maratha State, forgetting the past and sincerely co-operating for the national interest. The Peshwa gave his sacred word in the name of his revered father and his family deity, that he would wholeheartedly and sincerely exert himself in promoting the highest good of the State. The Peshwa sent his emissaries to fetch Janoji, and when he arrived he was welcomed at some distance on 18th April by Moroba Phadnis and Haripant Phadke on behalf of the Peshwa. On 24th April the Peshwa and Bhosle met in a grand ceremony of enthusiastic reception near Mehkar and held cordial discussions, in which Nizam Ali's representative Rukn-ud-daula fully participated.[4]

A treaty of mutual friendship was then drawn up and was ratified at Kanakapur or Brahmeshwar, places opposite to each other at the confluence of the two rivers the Godavari and the Manjra, where the two camps moved during the interval for convenience of food and water. The document contains 19 articles written in the form of demands and replies and amounting in substance to an agreement by Janoji, that he and his house would ever implicitly

4. P. D. S. 20. 257, 258, 263, 264, 268-270, 274, 278. *Ait. Patravyavahar* 116-119.

obey the Peshwa as the head of the Maratha State; that he would not increase the prescribed number of his army; that he would serve the Peshwa with five thousand troops whenever and wherever called upon to do so; that he would pay a tribute of 5 lacs yearly; and that he would conduct no intrigue against the State with any foreign power.[5]

It was discovered during these long drawn transactions that the root cause of the Peshwa-Bhosle trouble was the mischief created by Dewajipant, who was declared to be an undesirable character unworthy of trust. The Peshwa convinced Janoji how dangerous it was to keep him in his service. Janoji at the instance of the Peshwa kept the Pandit closely confined. All this happy result however came to be nullified when the Peshwa and Janoji were both dead. Diwakar Pandit was set free and resumed his old intrigues to the detriment of the Maratha State. History records how he played into the hands of Warren Hastings.

This war of short duration between the Peshwa and the Bhosles of Nagpur and its happy termination mark the signal triumph of this Peshwa's policy at once stern and conciliatory, which brought into closer union several disaffected members of the Maratha State. An attempt was for the first time made to define clearly the relations between the Central power and its feudatory members. The treaty of Kanakapur marks a distinct departure from the previous policy of appeasement and corruption. The Peshwa reached this consummation by slow stages, in which he first made his neighbour Nizam Ali a friend and disarmed his uncle's power of mischief.

4. **Damaji Gaikwad's death.**—The Gaikwads of Baroda, the Bhosles of Nagpur, the Sindias and the Holkars were now left as the four principal subordinate vassals, upon whom the Peshwa depended for the defence of the Maratha State, so that the history of these four houses also forms an important part of this Peshwa's distinguished administration. Of all these Damaji Gaikwad was the most shrewd and circumspect, avoiding both the extremes—either strong attach-

---

5. Ait. Patr. 117-119.

ment to the Peshwa or open defiance. The test of his loyalty came when a fierce war raged between the Peshwa and his uncle during 1768. Damaji mainly devoted his energies to consolidating his power in Gujarat, extending his boundaries up to Palanpur in the north, and Dwarka in the west, and carefully avoiding participation in the domestic dispute of the Peshwa's house. He had long worked under R'rao and been associated with him in many campaigns, so that it was difficult for Damaji to disobey Raghunathrao when called upon to help him. But during 1767 and 1768 Damaji was in declining health and shrewdly avoided taking sides in the civil war. He had toiled for forty years and greatly helped in extending and resuscitating the fortunes of the Maratha State in Gujarat and Kathiawad. Damaji died at Baroda on 18th August 1768, leaving four sons Sayaji, Govindrao, Fatesinh and Manaji who all took part in the subsequent history of the Marathas. The usual succession disputes started between these brothers, and thereby weakened their position. On 21st December 1768, Madhavrao addressed this stern rebuke to Fatesinh. "It is reported you are quarrelling with your brothers and on that account damaging the interests of your possessions and estate. We cannot tolerate any disturbances of this kind and have sent Appaji Ganesh with orders to take charge of the state, and conduct the administration independently of you. Please hand over the management to him and repair immediately to Poona for whatever representation you may have to make. Govindrao is already here and in the presence of you all we shall decide your dispute; and our decision will be binding upon you all. No excuse will be accepted. It is our duty to decide who is fit and who is unfit among you all. We won't allow any mischief to be created. If you have any regard for your interest, you must implicitly obey this summons and act without hesitation. If you disobey you will have to suffer heavily. Please take heed and act."

This eloquent letter illustrates the Peshwa's passion for doing impartial justice to the members of the State and his desire to enforce his commands. During the war with Raghunathrao Damaji had sent his son Govindrao with a contingent to help him. For this delinquency the Peshwa imposed a fine of 23 lacs on Govindrao and appointed him Damaji's successor on payment of a nazarana of 27 lacs in addition. Thus Madhavrao was the only Peshwa who understood the weakness of the Maratha constitution and who exerted himself to the utmost to remedy the evil.

5. War with Haidar Ali renewed (1767-1772).—The Peshwa had returned to Poona during the monsoon of 1765 after re-establishing Maratha sway over the region between the Krishna and the Tungabhadra. During the mid-sixties of the eighteenth century the Marathas, the British, the Nizam and Haidar Ali were the four powers contending amongst themselves for sway over peninsular India, some trying to form alliances with another in order to get the better of the others. Madhavrao was anxious first to finish Haidar Ali before attending to the English aggression in the north. During 1766 he made friends with Nizam Ali so as to prevent him from joining either his uncle or Haidar Ali. Towards the end of 1766 he first despatched Gopalrao Patwardhan to the Karnatak and himself followed him soon after by the eastern route, capturing Surapur, Raichur and Mudgal. Thereupon he exacted tributes from the chiefs of Kanakgiri, Advani, Bellari, Karnool, Chitradurg, Devdurg and Raidurg, and prepared to march against Shrirangapattan, the principal seat of Haidar Ali. The Peshwa was in high spirits at this time with a number of able diplomats and generals helping him. While camping at Devdurg in January 1767 he held an unexpected inspection of the number of troops and their equipment belonging to the chiefs serving in the campaign. After the inquiry he severely punished the delinquents with the result that thereafter complete discipline prevailed in his camp without any room for irregularity or fraud. In February the Peshwa captured the strong fort of Shira from Haidar Ali's possession. Nizam Ali and his son came and joined the Peshwa here against Haidar Ali. The Nawab of Shira and Mir Reza, one of Haidar Ali's principal chiefs, came over to the Maratha service.

On 4th March the fort of Madgiri was captured in one day, a performance which very much impressed the enemy. The Rani of Bednur and her son who were Haidar's prisoners in this fort, were liberated and sent to Poona for protection.

Now only two places, Shrirangapattan and Bednur remained in Haidar Ali's possession to which the Peshwa next directed his attention. This move so paralysed Haidar, that he sent his agents humbly seeking terms and agreeing to surrender all the territory in the Karnatak that the previous Peshwa Nanasaheb had possessed. About this time Raghunathrao, highly discomfited in his northern expedition, again started trouble at Poona which obliged the Peshwa to return, accepting the terms offered by Haidar Ali, instead of finishing him completely. While the Peshwa was in the Karnatak the British Government of Madras made overtures to him for his co-operation against Haidar Ali and sent their agent Lt. Tod to arrange a friendly treaty. But knowing how dangerous it was to take foreign help for putting down one's enemy, the Peshwa wisely rejected the British offer. Tod thus reported to his superiors, "I blush when I think the degree of contempt I was treated with considering my station and those I represented. Nevertheless I kept my temper and showed as little sign of disgust as possible." Madhavrao concluded a separate peace with Haidar Ali and went to Poona, having established a high position for Maratha arms and prestige in the minds of his rivals.[6]

During the next two years the Peshwa, as has been explained before, was involved in wars first against his uncle and then against Janoji Bhosle, so that he had no leisure to direct his attention to Haidar Ali till the closing months of 1769. This interval (1767-69) enabled Haidar Ali to recover much of the lost ground and resume authority over some of the chiefs who had previously become Maratha tributaries. He had humbled Murarrao Ghorpade and the Nawab of Savanur. The Peshwa was therefore required to begin over again all the work that had been previously accomplished. He stationed Gopalrao Patwardhan for the protection of Savanur and himself marched straight against Shrirangapattan. Haidar Ali remained under cover of the forests of Bednur, resorting to the same old tactics as in the previous years. Nizam Ali and Murarrao Ghorpade both joined the Peshwa in February 1770, as also most of the other Palegars. The fort of Bahirogad covering Bangalore, and those of Devraidurg and Kolar were captured.

6. *Haidar Ali* by N. K. Sinha, p. 107.

On 30th April while fort Nijgal was being stormed, the Peshwa's brother Narayanrao received a wound in his hand, fortunately not very serious. After all the Peshwa's strenuous effort, he could not accomplish much as the season was advanced, and the premonitions of his fatal malady compelled him once more to retrace his steps to Poona, leaving further operations to Trimbakrao Pethe.

Towards the end of 1770 the Peshwa again started for the Karnatak, but was compelled by his severe ailment to turn back from Miraj. For two years from the summer of 1770 his commander Pethe accomplished much of the remaining work in the Karnatak, with the co-operation of the Patwardhans. During the rains of 1770 Haidar Ali suffered several reverses at the hands of Pethe. Heavy artillery was supplied by the Peshwa from Poona, along with fresh contingents of troops. Towards the end of 1770 Gopalrao Patwardhan who had been ailing for some time under the severe strain of years, became seriously ill and handing over the charge of the operations to his brother Vamanrao, returned home. He died at Miraj on 17th January 1771, deeply mourned by the whole nation.

Trimbakrao relentlessly pressed the campaign against Haidar and inflicted upon him a crushing defeat in a battle near Shrirangapattan on 5th March 1771, which is known as the battle of Chinkurli or the Moti Talav. Several thousand of the enemy's troops were slain and a large booty of animals and materials secured. Haidar Ali escaped with his life in disguise during the darkness of the night. Pethe at once followed him to Shrirangapattan, but the place was impregnable and no impression could be made against it for a long time. The rainy season of 1771 arrived and the Marathas, encamped at Moti Talav, continued operations in various directions, inflicting severe reverses upon the enemy at many different places. But Haidar Ali too went on tenaciously opposing the Marathas and holding his ground with courage and fortitude. It was a difficult job for Trimbakrao. For three years continuously the Maratha troops had been out on field service, wearied by constant campaigning and now extremely impatient to go home. In the mean time alarming news arrived of the increasing illness of the Peshwa at Poona, which depressed every body.

Haidar Ali too was no less wearied and his only hope now lay in the report of the Peshwa's severe illness threatening his life. For some months he was negotiating with Pethe for terms : and when the latter received peremptory summons to return to Poona, he made the best bargain he could, concluded a treaty with Haidar, and returned in June 1772. Haidar Ali agreed to pay a fine of 31 lacs in cash and surrender a large part of the territory south of the Tungabhadra. That he could not finally destroy Haidar Ali's overgrown power, was the only regret that preyed on the dying Peshwa's mind at the end of his short but eventful career.

CHRONOLOGY

CHAPTER XXVI

1770, early	First appearance of a wasting intestinal disease in the Peshwa.
1770, autumn	Sakharam Bapu asked to conduct administration and initiate Narayanrao in it.
1770,	Special rites performed for the Peshwa's cure.
1770, Dec.	The Peshwa weighed against gold.
1771, April	Gopikabai meets the Peshwa at Poona.
1771, Aug. 28	The Peshwa conveys a warning to Narayanrao to be of good conduct.
1771, August	The Peshwa receives treatment from three experts of Poona, Goa and Jaipur.
1771.	The Peshwa at Katore on the Godavari and at Sidhtek for change.
1772, Summer	The Peshwa takes up his residence at Theur.
1772, Sept. 30	The Peshwa gives his last directions.
1772, Nov. 18	8 o'clock morning, of Kartik Krishna 8, the Peshwa expires, Ramabai becomes Sati.
1788, Aug. 8	Gopikabai dies at Gangapur.

M. H. II--35

CHAPTER XXVI

TRAGIC END

[1772]

1 The Peshwa's incurable malady.
2 His last will.
3 Peaceful death.
4 The wife and the mother.
5 Character of the Peshwa.
6 Foreign eulogy.
7 Anecdotes.

1. The Peshwa's incurable malady.—What a tremendous strain must have been caused by the momentous events described above on the body and the mind of a boy called upon at the age of sixteen to manage the concerns of a far flung Empire in its hour of the greatest peril. A tall lean but muscular figure, fair and commanding in appearance, soon lost all its original vigour, particularly when it was discovered that an insidious wasting disease had housed itself in his frame unnoticed. For some time the patient fought the malady with his inborn courage and continued his usual hard work. Towards the end of 1770 he proceeded from Poona bent on completing his work in the Karnatak, but he so quickly broke down on the way, that he had to return from Miraj and yield himself to proper treatment. Thus his last two years were spent in seeking health, now at Katore on the Godavari, then at Sidhtek, and lastly at Theur in the vicinity of Poona.

There was then no scientific treatment of tuberculosis, a disease called by the ancients Raj-Yakshma or the prince of diseases. In his case it was of the intestinal variety as can be ascertained from the unbearable pain in the stomach, which often made the Peshwa cry out for a dagger to open his bowels with. The lungs and the chest were intact. The Peshwa did not take long to realise that his end was approaching, but happily lived long enough to learn that splendid victories in the north had crowned his all too short a career and that Haidar Naik in the south had also been humbled though not crushed in the summer of 1772. The Mughal Emperor had again come under Maratha protection early in that year and been restored to his seat at Delhi, in opposition to the British plans, thereby exhibiting to the world that the batle of Panipat had not made a final decision. The various members of the Maratha confederacy had all been completely restored to the Peshwa's allegiance, so that it became a legitimate boast of the Maratha nation that obedience and harmony were never more in evidence in the Maratha State than at this period. The Bhosles of Nagpur, the Gaikwads of Baroda, the Ghorpades of Gootty, the Pratinidhi and Babuji Naik were mercilessly corrected. The arch-intriguer Gangoba, Holkar's Diwan, was made an example of; Tukoji Holkar, Ahalyabai, Mahadji Sindia became attached to the Peshwa as never before. The restraint put on the Peshwa's uncle Raghunathrao, checked the factious tendency among others as well. Dada's supporters Chinto Vithal, Sadashiv Ramchandra, Sakharam Hari learnt the lesson of their lives. Even men like Haripant Phadke and Nana Phadnis, the most confidential and trusted secretaries of the Peshwa, stood in the greatest awe of their master.[1]

The veteran Sakharam Bapu shrank from playing his evil pranks. In the autumn of 1770 when work accumulated with which the Peshwa's failing strength could not cope, he called upon Sakharam Bapu to dispose of the routine work and initiate Narayanrao into the administration. Brahmans were employed at different shrines to recite prayers and solicit divine favour for restoring the Peshwa's health. His mother Gopikabai suggested certain sanctified rites, which were punctiliously carried out by Nana Phadnis under his own personal supervision. When returning from Miraj to Poona the Peshwa was weighed against gold on the bank of the Krishna; he was also again weighed at Katore on the Godavari and the metal was distributed in charity to the poor. Janoji Bhosle who had recently made his submission expressed great concern on account of the Peshwa's ailment; he specially came to Poona during

---

1. Gangadhar Tatya had to suffer confinement for three years for evading payment of heavy ransom of thirty lacs laid on him for having been the main instigator of Raghunathrao's rebellion. He was severely caned in open Darbar, a treatment unbecoming for the head of a state in the opinion of some, but which doubtless served to strike terror into every heart.

the summer of 1772, personally to plead with him to soften the rigour of his uncle's confinement, lest, as was then believed, the prisoner should practise evil rites for hampering the Peshwa's recovery.[2]

While the Peshwa was seriously laid up at Poona, his mother too became very ill at Nasik and desired to proceed to Benares to end her life at that holy place. But the lady was persuaded to abandon her intention, as she was unable to bear the strain. The Peshwa wished to meet her ; she could not come to Poona, nor could the Peshwa be taken to Nasik in his precarious state of health.[3] Narayanrao used to be in close attendance upon the Peshwa, but the latter was not entirely satisfied with the way he behaved. This boy was fanciful, easily excitable, and inclined to disregard elderly folks and advisers. It is recorded in a paper dated 28th August 1771 that the Peshwa administered some strong advice to Narayanrao, on various matters. The severity of the admonition discloses the Peshwa's extreme dissatisfaction with the young lad's character.

The Peshwa was placed under expert treatment. Of the physicians who treated the patient in his last days at least three names are available. One was Baba Vaidya of Poona ; there was a European physician probably from Goa; and there was one north Indian celebrity named Ganga Vishnu hailing from Jaipur who treated the Peshwa for some two years.

2. The last will.—After the summer months of 1772, the Peshwa visibly grew worse and all hopes of recovery began to be given up. He strongly desired to end his life in the presence of his family deity Ganesh, and was therefore removed to the famous shrine at Thcur where permission was granted to all and sundry to come and see him. Here he sent for his uncle Raghunathrao along with Narayanrao and the principal officers, and in their presence executed what has been called his last will, which is dated 30th September 1772, and which thus runs in substance :—

1. "All my debts should be paid even by using, if neces-

2. Janoji died at Tulzapur immediately after on 16th May 1772.

3. It is recorded that Gopikabai saw him at Poona for a few days in April 1771.

sary, my private purse in the possession of Guruji (Mahadaji Ballal) ;

2. The system of farming the revenues is found oppressive to the ryots : it should be modified after a careful enquiry.

3. The two holy places Prayag and Benares should be released from Muslim control. This was the ardent desire of my sires and now is the time to carry it out.

4. My mother's desire to perform the pilgrimage of Benares should be fulfilled as soon as convenient.

5. The obsequies of Bhau Saheb should be performed next February, whether aunt Parwatibai becomes sati or not.

6. The annuities assigned to the worthy Brahmans of Benares should be regularly paid and continued in heredity.

7. Dinners in connection with my funeral rites should be served to two lacs of Brahmans each with half an anna for *dakshana*.

8. Dadasaheb should have five lacs of jagir assigned for his maintenance in order to keep him contented.

9. The charities of the Shravan month should be continued as long as the administration brings in at least 5 lacs of revenue yearly."

The responsible officers swore in the presence of Ganapati that they would execute all these wishes.

3. **Peaceful death.**—The religious turn of the Peshwa's mind and his desire to render justice to all are evident in this paper. Thereupon knowing that his end was near, he called to his presence nearly every body of importance and spoke to them, taking his final leave in great composure of mind and peaceful satisfaction of duty done. His wife Ramabai mostly lived at Poona and occasionally visited her husband's death-bed like a pious and devoted wife. She performed severe austerities for his recovery. The malady often caused the patient excruciating pain and moments of agony, in which he loudly groaned calling upon his attendants to put him to death. In its last stage he abhorred the very sight of food, but when he abstained from eating anything, the people round him would not eat. For their sake he would force himself to take a light diet. To the last moment he was keen and conscious and as stern as ever, so that even in that weak condition people hardly

dared to approach him. Sakharam Bapu and Nana Phadnis kept him constant company during his last days, and were enjoined to conduct the affairs of the State after him, making Narayanrao the Peshwa. In face of the cruel untimely death which he knew was fast approaching, with scarcely the strength to move his limbs in bed, he uttered not a single sigh of disappointment or sorrow. The thought that he had fulfilled his life's task cheered him to the last. He invited Ramshastri to his presence as also the other worthies of his court and spoke parting words to each and all. To the last moment he retained his senses, and expired at 8'clock in the morning of Wednesday Kartik Krishna 8th, 18th November 1772.

4. The wife and the mother.—The Peshwa's wife Ramabai showed equal fortitude by immolating herself on the funeral pyre of her husband. She walked in procession in the midst of funeral music and the beating of drums for the distance of about half a mile from the temple to the river, where the cremation was to take place. Reaching the burning ghat at the edge of the water, she stood boldly and cheerfully on the holy stone (*Dharma-shila*) in front of her husband's lifeless form, gave away in charity all the ornaments she was wearing, entrusted Narayanrao to the care of Dada Saheb, and with a serene countenance gave her blessings to all the assemblage. A small stone memorial erected in her pious memory stands today to remind the curious visitor of the blessed life of this loving pair, who departed in close company never to be parted in after life, Ramā and Mādhav, as the people believed, the very incarnation of Lord Krishna and his consort Lakshmi.

Ramābai, daughter of Ramchandra Ballal Joshi of Miraj, was married on 9th December 1753 when she was six or seven years old and departed life at the age of twenty-six. She was handsome, strong and healthy. She bore her husband no children. She was a devoted wife always in awe of her husband and never interfered in concerns outside the palace. She often visited the holy places in the Deccan.

Madhavrao's mother Gopikabai was also a typical woman, strong-willed, shrewd and experienced from having watched the rising course of the Maratha State since the days of her renowned father-in-law. Madhavrao, it would seem, had taken more after his mother than his father. During the first year or two of her son's Peshwaship she directed the affairs of State and offered advice on questions of moment. But when she came to realize that her interference bred a factious spirit at the court, she retired completely from Poona and took up her permanent residence at Gangapur near Nasik on the Godavari. Here she passed all her remaining life in prayer and worship till her death in 1788. She had an annuity of Rs. 12,000 assigned for her expenses. Though the mother and the son did not often meet, they exchanged frequent and regular correspondence which breathes intense affection and mutual regard. Madhavrao reported to his mother mostly in his own hand in Balbodh script every little affair of importance, not only of personal health but also those of a political character, battles, treaties, behaviour of officers and relatives. He freely sought her advice on critical occasions but never accepted it against his own judgment. Once she recommended that transit duties be remitted in the district of Nasik, as there was famine and grain scarcity. But the Peshwa did not accept the recommendation, urging that if he allowed remittance in one district, he would have to do the same in all others. Gopikabai was at least ten years older than Raghunathrao, who feared and respected her outwardly, although she spurned him for his wicked and selfish ways.

5. **Character of the Peshwa.**—Of all the Peshwas Madhavrao stands by common consent as the greatest in point of character. He possessed all those qualities which a good ruler ought to have,—thorough honesty, love of impartial justice, quick despatch, concern for the welfare of the people committed to his charge, and an independent judgment, formed after full enquiry, upon which he acted without fear or favour. If one takes into account that he was only sixteen when called upon to manage the complex affairs of a widely spread Empire, and that within some eleven years, of which many were wasted in an unnecessary civil war and in fighting a consuming disease, he carried to completion the main objects of his three eminent predecessors, then only can one form a correct estimate of his powers. Indeed, he stands as an outstanding figure in Maratha history and as a brilliant ornament to his nation. He

possessed the statesmanship of Balaji Vishvanath, a valour second only to that of Bajirao, and a sternness which his father lacked. He wiped off the disgrace which the Maratha nation had suffered on account of the disaster at Panipat, and restored the Maratha fortunes to such a glory that it is rightly claimed that the premature death of this young Peshwa was a greater blow to the Maratha State than the disaster of Panipat. The great historian Grant Duff has justly emphazised the same view by saying, that "the plains of Panipat were not more fatal to the Maratha Empire than the early end of this excellent prince."

When the battle of Panipat carried away the three leading members of the Peshwa's house, Bhau Saheb, Vishvasrao, and Nana Saheb soon after the first two, it was commonly believed that the Maratha State would soon collapse. But Madhavrao in a short time managed to raise a new generation of capable leaders to take the place of those that had perished, and he raised the State to such a height of glory that if luckily he had been spared a few years more, there was every chance of the dream of a Maratha Empire for India conceived and fostered by Shivaji, Bajirao and others, coming true. Maratha supremacy never meant extinction of the Muslim or other nationalities. It only meant that supreme political power would rest with the Marathas. The Marathas claimed religious freedom for themselves and for all those who inhabited this vast continent. They did not suppress the Mughal Emperor of Delhi : they helped him to regain his lost throne and to maintain his rights and authority. They only claimed to guide his political counsels.

But the preeminent service of Madhavrao consisted not so much in his achievements and conquests, either in the south or in the north, as in the general improvement of the moral tone of the Maratha administration to which hardly any of his predecessors had attended. Corruption was severely rooted out, the revenue system was so reformed as to conduce to the welfare and prosperity of the people. The judiciary began to function efficiently under the management of the eminent judge Ram Shastri. Complaints came to be speedily noticed and wrong-doers rightly punished. Many vexatious taxes and imposts were removed. Definite rules and conditions of service were framed and promulgated for the jagirdars and their military equipment.[4] The whole administrative staff of officials came to be purged of various evil practices that had become rampant. The system of *Veth* or exaction of forced labour from lower classes, was entirely abolished, and every kind of service came to be paid for in cash. The very name of this Peshwa came to be held in awe by the rulers and the ruled in and out of the Maratha State. Agencies were employed to gather secret news by which reports of evil practices reached him, so that even his immediate servants used to be in great fear of the Peshwa's punishment. Quite a new generation of honest and efficient officials, clerks, accountants, supervisers, revenue collectors, military suppliers, came to be reared up. Leaders and commanders of military corps shed their proverbial lethargy and became alert and obedient. The want of efficient artillery was keenly observed by this Peshwa, and he organized a special branch for the manufacture of fire-arms and ammunition. Indeed, this was one of the most important subjects which the Peshwa personally supervised and continuously toiled to improve.

Madhavrao was not only an administrator but by experience quickly became an efficient commander of large armies as well. He often exhibited unexampled valour and skill in strategy. He was certainly an autocrat of the type that was then common all over the world, but he was benevolent and selfless like his contemporaries in Europe. He devoted his whole life to the service of his people.

The mere mention of a few outstanding names among his immediate and trustworthy subordinates, is enough to convince us how this Peshwa reared up a new race of men and purified the corrupt system of administration, raising it to a high level. Ram Shastri, Govind Shivram Tatya, Naro Appaji, Mahadaji Ballal Guruji, Trimbakrao Pethe, Gopalrao Patwardhan, Ramchandra Ganesh, Visaji Krishna, Nana Phadnis and his cousin Moroba, Haripant Phadke and his brothers, are some of the celebrities of Madhavrao's creation. These names are to this

4. Madhavrao's Diary by Vad. Vol. I, pp. 306-365, P. D. Vol. 39.

day remembered as almost household words in Maharashtra. It is these men that worked to preserve the Maratha State in the chaotic situation which overtook it after this Peshwa's death. There is also a number of names of the opposite type who were severely dealt with and ultimately reclaimed. The Pratinidhis, Janoji Bhosle and his brothers and his minister Dewajipant, Chinto Vithal, the Chandrachud family, Babuji Naik, Murarrao Ghorpade, Naro Shankar, Sadashiv Ramchandra, all these learnt a new and salutary lesson. Ram Shastri was to Madhavrao more than what Ramdas was to Shivaji. He was a real guru and the final referee in all matters of a mundane nature; even outside his department of justice. He along with Govindpant Tatya and Guruji formed a trio which was respected and feared by high and low alike for their pure and upright character. Most of the sardars, Mahadji Sindia, Tukoji Holkar, Ahalyabai, Damaji Gaikwad and his sons, the large family of the Patwardhans, these and others became devoted and obedient servants of the Maratha State. The net revenue of that State at the time of this Peshwa's death has been variously calculated and may be reliably put down at about ten crores of rupees annually in the coin of those days.

The trials and hardships to which Madhavrao was exposed since the very start of his short career, compelled him to detect the most vulnerable spot in the Maratha body politic. The Maratha State since Shahu's days had developed not as a strong unitary Government but as a confederation of states loosely held together under the central authority. In this confederacy the rights, duties and responsibilities of the feudatories had never been clearly defined or rigidly enforced. Madhavrao inherited this unfortunate legacy and found to his cost that the jagirdars either openly defied the central authority or joined the enemies of the State. With the help of competent confidential advisers he gradually succeeded in checking the evil by punishing the wrongdoers and creating solidarity and a workable unity in the Government. This significant achievement becomes plain not only in his wars and administrative measures, but even in the jealousy, which his growing power excited in the minds of the British. On 10th March 1771 the Madras Council wrote,—"From the present conduct of the Marathas both in the north and in the south and from the genius, spirit and ambition of Madhavrao we are inclined to suspect that their designs are not confined to the mere collection of Chauth, but extend to the subjugation of the whole peninsula."[5]

6. **Foreign eulogy.**—Sir Richard Temple, by no means an admirer of things eastern, records the following eloquent testimony about the character of this Peshwa.

"In some of the characters just depicted there has been found virtue of the secondary type, energy, courage, enthusiasm, patriotism and the like; but in none of them is to be seen virtue of the purer, nobler, loftier quality. In Madhavrao there is virtue of the best stamp. In trying moments he evinced not only presence of mind but also a proud consciousness that by him an example should be set to all around. He chose ministers with discrimination, some of whom justified his choice by their subsequent achievements. He enforced strictness in the service of the state and strove to procure honesty so far as that was procurable in a corrupt age. If an instance occurred of bad faith in high places, he would denounce it with a frankness surprising to those who lived in evil times. Though obliged to keep the uncle out of positions which afforded opportunities of doing harm, yet he showed the utmost consideration towards his relative. When two of his officers during a siege wanted to fight a duel over a quarrel, he told them, instead to scale the deadly breach, promising to decree in favour of the disputant who should first plant the national flag upon the rampart. His care extended to the fiscal, the judicial, and the general departments. All men in his day knew that the head of the state was personally master of the work, was the friend of the oppressed and the foe of the oppressor, and was choosing agents who would carry out his beneficent orders. His thoughtfulness and considerateness were untiring and were often shown in a signal or graceful manner. For instance, he conferred benefits upon the descendants of the cavalry leader Santaji Ghorpade, who had been assassinated by Shivaji's son and successor, in order that such tardy justice as might be possible after the lapse of a generation, should be done. All

5. Dr. Sinha's *Haidar Ali*, p. 157.

the while he was engaged in war and politics. He had to hold his own against the Nizam of the Deccan ; to drive back Hydar Ali of Mysore, to retrieve that disaster at Panipat which had grieved his father to death. While greatly superior to his predecessors as a civil ruler, he was not inferior to them as a warlike commander. His lieutenants were just retrieving the Panipat disaster, when his own health, always delicate, gave way. Anticipating death, he adjured his uncle to protect the next Peshwa, who would be a boy to avert disunion from the reigning family and save the empire from distraction. What reply he received we know not: at all events he was allowed to die in hope ; we shall soon see how cruelly the hope was belied. True to the habits of his race, he retired to a rural village not far from Poona, and died quietly in the 28th year of his age ; and that village is to this day regarded by the Marathas as one of the most classic spots in their historic land. His childless widow, to whom he was devotedly attached, burnt herself with his corpse, to satisfy her grief as well as to obey the behests of her religion. This is an instance of those who are virtuous in their joint life and to whom death brings no separation.

That Madhavrao, a Hindu Prince, should have done so much in so brief a life as his, under such disadvantages and despite such temptations that, before being cut off, in the heyday of his career, he should have evinced such capacity as this, not only in affairs susceptible of management by youthful genius, but also in matters ordinarily demanding the experience of ripe years, is truly astonishing. Indeed, he is for ever to be revered as the model prince, 'the flos regum' and as one of the finest characters that the Hindu nationality has ever produced."[6]

Writes Kincaid, "Threatened both by domestic and foreign enemies, Madhavrao triumphed signally over all. Yet his triumph had brought him no rest. Victorious over his foes he had spent his years in tireless labour to better the condition of his people. Every department was quickened by his supervision, his industry and his example. His secret intelligence was faultless ; and no matter how remote the officer guilty of

6. Oriental Experience, pp. 393-396.

acts of tyranny, he rarely escaped punishment. The Peshwa's armies went well-equipped on service for the entire military organization was under his direct control. Quick to anger, he was no less quick to forgive. And the only fault that the harshest critic can find in this admirable ruler is, that he shortened a life precious to his people by his arduous and unceasing toil."

7. **Anecdotes.**—Maharashtra still loves to repeat a number of anecdotes and reminiscences illustrating the high moral character of this Peshwa, which are doubtless substantially true and give an accurate picture of his personality. When Madhavrao like a pious Brahman, at first began to devote much of his time to prayer and ritual, Ram Shastri sternly rebuked him for neglecting his secular duties and advised him to repair to Benares to spend his life there, if he were inclined to be so sanctimonious. The Peshwa quietly and thankfully took the hint and dropped his priestly role. He doubtless possessed an irritable temper, but that only disclosed his aversion for injustice and wrong and his impatience to correct blemishes. On that account he soon came to be feared and obeyed.

When he found that death was near, he set about destroying the accumulated store of secret state papers, referring to the low intrigues of his officials and servants. Sakharam Bapu learning what the Peshwa was doing, approached him and humbly remonstrated against this procedure. The Peshwa unable to move from his bed, asked Bapu to hand him a certain packet from the adjoining chest. When Bapu brought the bundle out, the Peshwa asked him to open it, read the contents and tell him whether he should destroy or keep it. To his amazement Bapu discovered that the papers in that bundle referred to his own secret intrigues and plots of a criminal nature deserving punishment. The Peshwa had in his possession those proofs of Bapu's guilt, but had never let him know what accusations had reached him through various channels.

Madhavrao's attention to details excites our admiration. He inquires about the construction of unauthorized buildings in Poona. He scrutinizes the lists showing the number and pay of his attendants. From the Karnatak he inquires how

Nana Phadnis was behaving in Poona, like a master or a servant.[7] He wishes to be informed of the arrangements for supplying fodder to the cattle attached from Babuji Naik's establishment at Baramati. His daily accounts contain references to very small items of expenditure such as Rs. 1-8 for lamp oil supplied to clerks. He personally chooses dresses and presents to be given to Nizam Ali and his suite or to an envoy from Goa or to Ghazi-ud-din. He minutely examines cases of embezzlement. There used to be much corruption among inspecting officers sent out to examine the military equipment of the jagirdars and sardars, the number and quality of their men and horses, their saddles and arms and accoutrements. The inspectors when bribed certified that there were no deficiencies. When complaints were received, the Peshwa sent his own trusted agents such as Guruji, Nana Phadnis, Naro Appaji to detect frauds. When these special agents arrived for inspection, the whole official staff was in consternation and quaked for the heavy punishments that awaited them. It would thus appear that this Peshwa's rule was far above that of his contemporaries in rooting out official corruption and venality.

The Peshwa would not allow the ryots to be molested on any account. He paid compensation to them when they suffered losses from the march of troops. During his tours he personally inquired into the people's grievances and removed the iniquities that he noticed. Remission of revenue was granted when there were political disturbances or failure of rain. A Kotwal's duties and the rules which should guide him in his management of the towns, are found clearly set down in various documents issued by the Peshwa, and now reproduced in the Peshwa's Diaries.

This Peshwa's death ushers in a new phase in Maratha history which will form the subject of my concluding volume.

---

7. P. D. 39. 64. This masterly letter illustrates the Peshwa's character vividly.

INDEX

N.B.—Some topics of general interest are given under the individuals concerned.

M. H. II—36

NEW HISTORY
OF
THE MARATHAS

NEW HISTORY
OF
THE MARATHAS

VOLUME I

SHIVAJI &. HIS LINE

[1600-1707]

BY

GOVIND SAKHARAM SARDESAI

GYAN

ISBN : 978-81-212-1570-1(Set)

ISBN : 978-81-212-1571-8 Vol.1 (HB)

First Published, 1946

Published, 2018

Published by

Gyan Publishing House
5, Ansari Road
Daryaganj, New Delhi-110002
Phone: 011-47034999, 9811692060
www.gyanbooks.com
E-mail: books@gyanbooks.com

Printed at: G. Print Process, Delhi.

To the Memory of

Sayaji Rao Gaekwad

Sena-Khaskhel Samsher Bahadur,

Grand Commander of the Star of India,

Maharaja of Baroda

[1875-1939]

to whom I have given all my life's years of Service, and who had led my young steps into the pleasant path of History.

G. S. Sardesai

PREFACE

The great historian of the Rise of the Dutch Republic has truly remarked : "The spectacle of a brave nation, inspired by the soul of one great man and rising against an overwhelming despotism, will always speak to the heart from generation to generation." This hope has inspired me to write my book. And there is a special need in the present condition of India why we should know and ponder on such a history. Maratha history is no longer the cherished treasure of a single community or province ; it should prove a source of inspiration, wisdom and warning to all India.

The character and achievements of Shivaji and the Peshwas have left a permanent mark on the history of India. They form the most recent example of our genius for nation-making of which we today may well be proud. Of all the diverse races inhabiting the Indian Continent, each gifted with a peculiar trait of its own, the Marathas alone can claim to have made a distinct contribution to the political fortunes of this land by daring to establish Indian self-rule throughout the country, although measured by the length of time their construction proved too short-lived. For over half a century the politics of India were directed from Satara or Poona. The Maratha Government, with all its faults, inspired the people under its rule with a living sense of unity and co-operation without which no self-rule is attainable. It thus provided free scope for the energies of all classes of the people, each according to its natural bent. This is a political lesson which India sorely needs today. If the true function of history is to impart wisdom of the past for the benefit of the present, to warn a nation in the days of prosperity against the hidden dangers of creeping deterioration, as also to stimulate its courage and call forth its recuperative energy in times of adversity,—then India cannot afford to ignore the lessons which Maratha history has left behind in its short but eventful career. The inspiring careers of Shivaji and Baji Rao I, the daring planning and earnest execution of Madhav Rao I and Mahadji Sindia, contrasted with the vices and follies of Raghunath Rao Dada and Baji Rao II, convey a moral which modern India will be the wiser for laying to its heart.

Unfortunately, however, no worthy narrative of Maratha achievements and failures has yet been written by weaving together all the fascinating and colourful material which the patient industry and critical acumen of modern scholars have made available to us. The subject still waits for scientific investigation by a trained mind endowed also with the constructive vision of a true historian. By far the largest proportion of the original sources exists in Marathi only, and they cannot reach workers ignorant of that language. On the other hand indigenous writers in Maharashtra are often handicapped by their ignorance of Persian, French and sometimes English also, and their want of access to essential books and manuscript records in these foreign languages ; for we should never forget that the history of India in the eighteenth century is made up of the varying strands of the European and Indian powers struggling for dominion in this vast land, and each of them has left records of its transactions written in its native tongue, which cannot be left out of account.

The historical ancestors of the Marathas such as the Mauryas, the Guptas, the Yadavas, the Parmars and others who had wielded the sceptre in this land at different times, have left very scanty records of their reigns. What remains to remind us of their times consists of a few cryptic inscriptions, fanciful eulogies (*prashasti*) of court poets, and a few old coins or stray notices of foreign travellers. No full and documented history can be built in such poverty of materials. But as the Maratha rule best known to us, happens to be a very modern phenomenon, there are available in the Marathi language the most valuable materials in the form of state-papers, news-reports, diplomatic despatches, legal decisions, diaries, chronologies, land-grants, official and private correspondence, military regulations, budgets and accounts. The enormous volume of these records can be judged from the fact that at a rough estimate they extend over a hundred thousand printed pages. This is a proud heritage of Maharashtra unshared by any other province of India.

The first history of the Marathas worthy of the name was published by Captain James Grant Duff in three volumes as far back as 1826. Since then a vast amount of original material unknown to him has come to light. Historical research in our country has made phenomenal progress during the present century, with the effect of profoundly altering the objective of historical treatment. Besides fresh points of view are being forced on us by deep social changes bringing on a new mental outlook and by the advancing tide of research and criticism in this field as in others. As Goethe observes :

"History must from time to time be re-written, not because many new facts have been discovered, but because new aspects come into view, because the participant in the progress of an age is led to standpoints from which the past can be reviewed and judged in a novel manner."

My second justification for attempting this task can be best stated in the words of Professor Goldwin Smith : "Each nation in the main writes its own history best ; it best knows its own land, its own institutions, the relative importance of its own events, the characters of its own great men. Each nation has also its peculiarities of view, its prejudices, its self-love, which require to be corrected by the impartial or even hostile view of others."

An extreme form of national pride had hitherto kept our modern Maratha historical workers back from using the English language, which is the only medium that can reach all parts of India and also make their researches available to the civilized world in general. The most glaring example of this mental attitude was the great explorer and life-long devotee of the muse of history in Maharashtra, the late Vishwanath Kashinath Rajwade. Had he and other workers of his school published the results of their investigations in English, instead of exclusively in Marathi, they would have reached students of history all over India and enabled Maratha history to become a fruitful subject of higher study and criticism in our Indian Universities, and thus speeded up a healthy advance in our knowledge of this subject. Rajwade's scholarly dissertations on various historical topics, his illuminating discussions of problems of philology, grammar and religion as also the researches of the Poona Itihas Samshodhak Mandal, have for this reason remained a sealed book to all other provinces of India and indeed to the rest of the non-Marathi world.

I started my study of Maratha history forty years ago, and embodied the result in a work completed in nine volumes written in the Marathi language and entitled *The Marathi Riyasat.* In it I tried to bring together the scattered, disarranged and uncalendared (even unlisted) mass of historical data and opinions found in that tongue and, after comparing them with available materials in other languages, to construct a compact critical study of the rise and fall of the modern Maratha State. My work too like Rajwade's, remained unknown to the world ignorant of my native language. The present *New History of the Marathas,* to be completed in three volumes (the whole now ready in manuscript), is the first attempt to present a fresh and full treatment of Maratha history in English, embodying the results of the latest research. It is not a translation of my *Marathi Riyasat*; nor does it pretend to be a work of the ideal merits as described above. Indeed no one individual, unless he has the encyclopaedic mind of a Gibbon, can do full justice to the subject, which requires rather the co-operative effort of a syndicate of scholars. In the absence of the hope of any such ideal combination, this book is offered to the public in full consciousness of its imperfections. If it provokes further study and thought in any corner of the great republic of letters, I shall be happy. And I shall be happier still if after a look at my book, some better gifted scholar is tempted to advance this subject, handle the enormous mass of materials and produce the long sighed for masterly History of the Marathas.

One word more of apology is needed from me. The Marathas have long been misjudged by their rivals and adversaries and painted in blackest colours both during and after the period of their downfall, as if they had no single good point to their credit. This attitude became confirmed in popular mind owing to the first flush and glow of the foreign conquest. But more than a century has elapsed since the Maratha State was extinguished, a sufficiently long period for the dust of passion to settle down and enable us to form a sober and rational judgment and to justly appraise the virtues and defects of that race. It is still a difficult task for a Maratha writer to paint his people's history on a canvas with colours that truly represent facts and avoid prejudices. In the following narrative I aspire to produce a true apologia (*Kaifiat*) of the Maratha people and place it before the impartial public. It is mostly made up of the utterances of the great figures who dominated the historic stage during the two centuries of our rise and fall.

A studied attempt has been made to weave into the narrative ample citations from original authorities. This appeared to be the only way of making the reader acquainted with the pith and essence of the Marathi papers. So far as possible the sources have been indicated in the foot-notes, though, it must be admitted, the materials are so varied and extensive that it is not possible to quote chapter and verse evidence in every case. As a supplementary attempt the reader's attention may be invited to the author's "Main Currents of Maratha History" published a few years ago. In it have been discussed some of the outstanding and debatable questions arising out of the past life of the Maratha people.

My grateful thanks are due to the numerous scholars and publishers of original materials on which this work is mainly based. I cannot adequately acknowledge the debt I owe to my valued friend Sir Jadunath Sarkar for his patient revision of my manuscript, to him a labour of love, the worth of which those only can estimate who are acquainted with his extraordinary erudition and his rare critical acumen. I am equally indebted to Dr. V. G. Dighe, my constant companion and collaborator in all historical work during the last seventeen years without whose unstinted help I could never have completed my onerous undertaking. I am inscribing this work to the sacred memory of my first great inspirer the late Sayaji Rao Gaikwad of Baroda, whose grandson the present Maharaja Pratapsinh Rao continues to take the same interest in my historical labours.

The publisher and I highly regret that the abnormal conditions of life prevailing in the country now for years have not only delayed the publication of this work, but prevented us from executing our cherished desire of putting in maps, illustrations and other essentials of study adequately. We can only hope to make up the deficiency in the succeeding volumes.

Kamshet
Dt. Poona, 31st Oct. 1946 — G. S. SARDESAI

CONTENTS

CORRECTION

Page 27, line 3 bottom	read समा	for मसा
Page 62, line 20	read operations	for operation
Page 69, line 8, first para	read gold	for good
Page 79, line 4 of 4th Section	read An	for As

Page 149, Section 5, "Bijapuri activities, Baji Ghorpade crushed".

Page 180, last line	read "20 November"	
Page 210, line 2 of second para.	read advisers	for guru
Page 211, line 9 of Section 2	read "weighed"	for "weighted
Page 232, line 8	read three thousand	for 30000
Page 267, line 5	read subjugated	for subjected

Page 269, foot note 6 is given on next page.

CHRONOLOGY

CHAPTER I

(*Most of the dates are merely approximate.*)

B.C. 73 — A.D. 218	Sātavāhanas rule over Mahārāshtra : Bhaja, Karla and other caves excavated.
A.C. 550 — 753	Early Chālukya dynasty.
608 — 642	Chālukya ruler Satyāshraya Pulakeshi.
634	The country of Mahārāshtra officially defined.
750 — 975	Rāshtrakuta rule.
800 — 1000	Early Marathi writers.
884 — 959	Rājashekhar, great poet in Mahārāshtri.
975 — 1189	Later Chālukyas.
1187 — 1294	The dynasty of the Yādavas.
1153 — 1276	Chakradhar, founder of the Mānabhāv sect.
1276	Chakradhar and Hemādri meet their death.
1290	Saint Jnaneshwar wrote his great work.
1310	Muslim subjugation of peninsular India completed.
1323	Pratāparudra of Warangal captured by Md. Tughlak.
1325	Muhammad Tughlak makes Deogiri his capital.
1336 April 18	Harihar crowned King of Vijayanagar.
1347	Ala-ud-din Hasan Shah founds the Bahmani kingdom.
c. 1350	Saint Nāmdev flourishes.
1565 Jan. 22	Battle of Talikot ; Vijaynagar destroyed.
1548 — 1599	Saint Eknāth.
c. 1600	Rise of the Bhosles to prominence.
1607 — 1650	Saint Tukārām.

CHAPTER I

EARLY BEGINNINGS

[Up to 1600 A.C.]

1. Origin of the Marathas.
2. The Marathi language.
3. Political Background of Maharashtra.
4. Rise of the Manabhav sect.
5. Manabhav literature.
6. Deaths of Chakradhar and Hemadri.
7. Successful revolt against Musl: ns.
8. Saints and writers of Maharashtra.
9. Maratha character.
10. The present day Marathas.
11. The Maratha country pulsation.

1. Origin of the Marathas.—The latest census has computed two and a half crores of persons to be the Marāthi-speaking population of India, and most of them inhabit that portion of the country which has been known by the ancient name Mahārāshtra, 'the great nation of the Rathas, Rathikas or Rashtrikas', famous from the days of yore for valour and energy. In the literature of the early Christian centuries the words *Mahārāshtra, Mahārāshtrika* and *Mahārāshtri* (the last being the name of one of the Prakrit languages) occur in copious frequency. *Mahārathi* (masculine) and *Mahārathini* (feminine) are words in the Karla cave and other inscriptions of the Sātavāhana period. Varāhamihira, a famous astronomer of the sixth century, uses the word Mahārāshtras, which later came to be corrupted into Mahrāttā or Marāthā. Rājashekhar, a Sanskrit author of the 9th century, uses the word Marahatti in the feminine gender. The word occurs in various forms in all subsequent literatures of India.[1]

Mahārāshtra, as its plain meaning shows, is a great Rāshtra or nation formed by a race of men who in ancient times were probably known as Ratthas, some of whom came to be styled Mahāratthas or great Ratthas. The land which they occupied also came to be called after them, that is, the

1. Several hypotheses have been put forth by different *scholars* on the origin of the word *Maratha.*

country of great men. Their language too was first known as Mahārāshtri, a Prakrit dialect whose range was originally much wider than that of the present Marāthi, its later derivative. The large tract of western India known to this day as Mahārāshtra, extended from the Arabian sea on the west to the Satpura mountains in the north, and comprised the modern tracts of Konkan, Khandesh, Berar, part of the Central Provinces, the British Deccan and about a third of the Nizam's dominions, the whole being known as Marātha-vādā.

The land south of the river Narmada was called by the Aryan settlers as Dakshināpatha and included the Dandakāranya which was so named from the vast forest that stretched southwards from the Tapti to the Godavari. During the early centuries of the Christian era Mahārāshtra consisted of three distinct portions, *viz.* the first, Vidarbha or Berar ; the second, Asmaka or the Godavari basin (later known as Seuna Desh) ; and the third Kuntala, that is the valley of the river Krishnā. It also embraced the western coastal region known as Aparānta or Konkan, stretching from Daman in the north to Goa or even Karwar in the south. Thus, the lands between the Narmada and the upper Krishna practically formed the main Mahārāshtra country in which first the Prakrit Mahārāshtri and later its derivative Marathi, was spoken and which linguistically and geographically is one solid homogeneous block, although at present cut up into several disjointed political areas.[2]

Thus Mahārāshtra proper where the Marathi language prevails, can be understood with almost exact accuracy as a right-angled triangle, of which one side is represented by the western coast line from Daman to Karwar and the other from

2. The Aihole inscription of the famous Chalukya monarch Satyāshraya Pulakeshi dated the Christian year 634 (556 Shaka), accurately mentions the extent of Mahārāshtra, as containing three portions, altogether comprising 99,000 villages. The three parts probably are Vidarbha (including Asmaka), Kuntala, and Aparanta. अगमदधिपतित्वं यो महाराष्ट्रकाणां, नवनवतिसहस्रग्रामभाजां त्रयाणाम् ॥

Subsequent to the date of this inscription ample testimony is available confirming this description of Mahārāshtra, but the exact number of villages in it and its accurate demarcation are still open questions.

Daman straight east to Nagpur and Gondia, practically along the river Tapti. The hypotenuse of this triangle would be an irregular line joining Gondia to Karwar and touching in its course the towns of Belgaum, Sholapur and Bidar. The North Khandesh territory lying between the rivers Tapti and Narmada is indeed a border land of essentially Mahārāshtrian character. In the daily religious rites of the Maratha people this demarcation of Mahārāshtra is still being commonly repeated.[3]

The people of this land were known in early ages as Ratthas, Mahāratthas or Rāshtrakutas, who had long since earned great distinction for wealth, valour and political power. An image of a Mahā-rattha warrior is to be seen to this day in the Nane-Ghat caves near Junnar, which were carved by the Andhra rulers about the first century of the Christian era. The present Marathi tongue is the direct descendant of the literary Prakrit *Mahārāshtri*, the language of Mahārāshtra.

These ancient Ratthas came to be divided into and known by the names of several sub-tribes or families, such as the Sātavāhanas, the Bhojas, the Mauryas, the Kadambas, the Silāharas, the Yādavas, the Chālukyas, the Rāshtrakutas, etc., some of whom established in this region powerful kingdoms of their own, patronized arts and literature and produced many great rulers of outstanding merit. Their cultural achievements are perpetuated to this day by the unique execution and grandeur of the caves of Bhaja and Karla, of Ellora, Ajanta and Elephanta, and the temples and sculptures in which this land of Mahārāshtra so fully abounds. These Ratthas or Mahāratthas must have been a hardy race in whose character the best traits of the Aryan settlers from the north were blended with the best characteristics of the indigenous stock of western India.

2. **The Marathi language.**—The Aryan settlers when they first entered this vast Indian continent brought with them their ancient Vedic culture and their highly refined tongue Sanskrit, which in due course imparted its polish to the origi-

3. "गोदावर्याः उत्तरे or दक्षिणे तीरे or कृष्णावेण्योः उत्तरे तीरे'

nal dialects which used to be spoken in the various wild recesses of the land. These local speeches came to be styled under the common denomination "Prakrit", meaning the natural and unartificial dialects used by the common folk as distinguished from Sanskrit, which was the refined medium employed by learned priests, poets and authors in their works. These Prakrit speeches came to be classified, according to their regional character or religious importance, into five or six main divisions each with a literature and a grammar of its own, viz. Mahārāshtri, Pāli or Māgadhi, Ardha-Māgadhi, Sauraseni and Paisachi, not to speak of Tamil and other primary Dravidian tongues which prevailed in the southern peninsula. Of all these mediæval languages, Mahārāshtri was the most highly cultivated and at one time it was most widely used in popular speech and literature, right from the borders of Malwa and Rajputana in the north to the banks of the Krishna and the Tungabhadra in the south. Buddhist literature mostly exists in Pāli and Jain literature in Ardha-Māgadhi, while Sauraseni prevailed in the region round about Mathura, the land of the Saurasenas, and Paisachi had its hold in the north-west, *i.e.*, in the western Punjab and beyond. All these Prakrit languages have been freely employed by classical writers like Kalidas and others in the dramas that they produced, Sanskrit being spoken by the higher characters and the Prakrits by the females, servants and lower classes. It is clear that by about 500 B.C. Sanskrit had gone out of use as a spoken language and the Prakrits had taken its place in popular parlance. The most important of these Prakrits was doubtless Mahārāshtri in which there exists a copious literature, consisting of several well-known works of high merit, such as *Sapta-Shati, Setubandha, Gauda Vaho* and *Karpura-Manjari*, etc. The first of these, that is, *Sapta-Shati*, is a famous anthology of 700 verses selected from different writers by King Hala of the Sātavāhana dynasty, who flourished about the first century after Christ. This *Sapta-Shati* contains the names of mountains, rivers and towns of Mahārāshtra, many of which are still extant. Grammarians specifying rules for the various Prakrits mainly depend upon Mahārāshtri for their illustrations. The word Mahārāshtri came to be corrupted into Marhati or as it was latterly called, Marathi. Rajashekhar, a learned Mahārāshtra poet, who is known to have lived from 884 to 959 A.C., has written several Sanskrit and Prakrit works, *Ramayana*, *Bala-Bharata*, *Viddha-Shala-Bhanjika*, *Karpura-Manjari*, etc., and his Prakrit works in point of style mark the borderland between the outgoing Mahārāshtri and the incoming Marathi.

If one were to trace the linguistic development of India through ancient times, one might roughly put down Vedic Sanskrit to be the spoken speech of the early Aryans until about 500 B.C.; Mahārāshtri and the other Prakrits were in vogue for about a thousand years from 500 B.C. to 500 A.C., after which Marathi and other modern Indian languages gradually began to take shape; and Marathi became the language of the court and learned writers from about 800-1000 A.C. onwards. *Bhāvārtha-Dīpika*, a commentary on the *Bhagavadgita* by the first great writer in Marathi, Jnaneshwar, is the earliest celebrated work in Marathi, having been completed in the year 1290 A.C. during the reign of King Ramachandra Yadav of Devgiri, only four years before he was attacked and his kingdom destroyed by the Muslim conqueror Ala-ud-din Khilji. Jnaneshwar concludes his work with these words, "I have thus decorated the Goddess of *Gita* with this country ornament."[4] Side by side with the use of the Prakrits and Marathi, the use of classical Sanskrit was never abandoned as the literary tongue *par excellence*. Learned scholars always preferred to write in Sanskrit.

One may be curious to know what are the oldest existing compositions in Marathi. Curiously enough, the oldest writing[5] in Marathi comes from the Mysore State, being dated 983 A.C. A few inscriptions in old Marathi have been found in different places, such as Palasdev (1157 A.C.), Ter (1184 A.C.), Parel (A.C. 1180), another at Patan in Khandesh (A.C. 1206) and one at Pandharpur (A.C. 1273). Some stray pages of *Panchatantra* translated from Sanskrit into old Marathi and

4. शके बाराशें बारोत्तरें । तैं टीका केली ज्ञानेश्वरें ।
केलें ज्ञानदेवें गीते । देशीकार लेणें ।

5. श्रीचामुंडराएं करवियले= "Executed by Chamund Rai" is an inscription near the left-foot of the statue of Gomateshwar at Sravana-Bel-gola about 60 miles north-west of Mysore.

an astronomical treatise by Shripati called *Ratnamālā* are known to be the earliest extant compositions in Marathi. Mukundrāja preceded Jnaneshwar by about a hundred years and wrote his work *Viveka-Sindhu* in Marathi, although the present manuscripts give a modernized form of it. The Mahanubhav literature of the last quarter of the thirteenth century is also available for the study of old Marathi. While, therefore, we are sure that modern Marathi began to take a definite shape about 1200 A.C., the writing, the forms and structure now available to us, belong to a much later period.

It was Jnanadev's boast to have transplanted the best thoughts of the Sanskrit language into the popular Marathi. He bestows the highest eulogy on Marathi and declares it to be in no way inferior to the polished Sanskrit. What height the Marathi language and the Maratha people had then attained can well be imagined from the following eloquent words of Jnanadev. "There rules," says he, "Shri Ramachandra, the magnificent scion of the Yadav dynasty, the supporter of all arts, a monarch who rules justly."[6]

Since the days of Jnaneshwar a regular succession of saints and poets began to appear rapidly and to enrich the Marathi language in increasing volume and grandeur, till the advent of the great Maratha hero Shivaji. A people is thus inseparably connected with its land and language.

3. Political background of Maharashtra.—How was this land of the 'great nation' ruled in bygone ages? The earliest glimpse we obtain in this connection refers to Chandra-

6. तेथ यदुवंश विलास । जो सकल कला निवास !
न्यायातें पोषी क्षितीश । श्रीरामचंद्र ॥

This compliment paid by the great author to King Ramadeva need not be interpreted as an accurate historical statement. It was rather the formal expression of a poet's reverence towards the ruling sovereign.

About Marathi Jnaneshwar says —

मूळ ग्रंथीच्चिया संस्कृता— । वरी मराठी नीट पाहतां ।
अभिप्राय मानिलिया चित्ता । कवण भूमि ते न चोजवे ॥
माझा मऱ्हाठाचि बोल कौतुकें । परी अमृतातें ही पैजा जिंके ।
ऐसीं अक्षरेंचि रसिकें । मेळवीन ॥

gupta Maurya, an Indian warrior contemporary with Alexander the Great, who had established his sway over Mahārāshtra. Chandragupta's grandson Ashoka took the cue from his grandfather and extended his Empire to the east and the south. Throughout this Indian continent his numerous edicts have been discovered, which prove that great monarch's zeal for the spiritual amelioration of his people and his enthusiasm for the spread of the teachings of Lord Buddha. Thereafter during the early centuries of the Christian era, Mahārāshtra was ruled for about 300 years (B.C. 73 to A.C. 218) by a dynasty of rulers known as Āndhra or Sātavāhana whose capital city was Pratisthān or Paithan, situated on the river Godavari, then a renowned seat of learning, culture and commercial activity. Some of the Puranas enthusiastically describe the conquests and achievements of these Sātavāhana rulers, after whom the present Shaka era has been named. The Sātavāhanas attained a high degree of civilization which is disclosed by the wonderful caves of Nasik, Karla, Bhaja, and Kanheri, as well as by a number of coins and inscriptions which have been discovered, belonging to that dynasty.

The several clans of the ancient Ratthas, among whom may be included the Rāshtrakutas, the Bānas, etc., exercised influence at different places under the Sātavāhanas, although they were then too weak to assert any organized political power. During the 4th and 5th centuries the Gupta Emperors of northern India now and then extended their influence over rulers of the Deccan such as the Vakatakas, Kalachuris and Kadambas, but it is doubtful if the Guptas actually ruled over any portions of these Deccan lands. At the beginning of the sixth century, however, a new dynasty of the Chālukyas appeared on the scene and gave this land a succession of wise and strong rulers for more than a century and a half. They ruled from Badami, now a town in the district of Bijapur. Satyāshraya pulakeshi, the most famous ruler of this Chālukya dynasty,[7] who reigned from 608—642 A.C., successfully repelled an attack of the Emperor Harsha and strongly guarded the northern boundary of Mahārāshtra at the river Narmada. The Chinese traveller Yuan Chwang visited Pulakeshi's court

7. See note 2 on page 12.

and has left an illuminating account of that ruler's policy and achievements, and of the Maratha people as well. The Chālukyas worshipped the God Shiva and assumed grand titles significant of their power and fame.

The Chālukyas were succeeded by another powerful dynasty, the Rāshtrakutas, who ruled Mahārāshtra for a period of 225 years from about 750 to 975 A.C., the longest on record for any southern Hindu dynasty to hold sway. It is a most important epoch in the history of the Deccan, when both the Karnatak and Mahārāshtra were welded into one political entity. Most of the rulers were able men ; in a line of 14 kings only 3 were found to be inefficient. Jainism, Hinduism and Buddhism lived side by side in this land in perfect harmony under these Rāshtrakuta rulers.

Krishna I of this dynasty was a great builder who caused to be excavated out of solid rock the celebrated Kailas temple of Ellora, a magnificent specimen of Hindu art and a veritable wonder of the world. The name Rāshtrakuta was in local parlance changed into Rathod a clan-name later assumed by the proud rulers of the Jodhpur State. This dynasty had its main capital at Mānyakhet (Malkhed) with minor capitals, such as Chandrapur (Chandwad), Lattatur (Latur), etc. at different times. However clever and valiant might have been these Rāshtrakuta rulers, they altogether neglected the naval defence of their country, in which the Arabs of the west seemed to excel at this period.

It was the later Chālukyas again who gave a death-blow to the Rāshtrakuta power and ruled Mahārāshtra for some two hundred years from 975 to 1189 A.C. from their capitals of Mānyakhet and Kalyani near Bidar. They produced some ten brilliant rulers of outstanding merit. Tribhuvanmalla Vikramāditya VI was the greatest monarch of this dynasty, and he founded an era named after himself. His prime minister Vijnaneshwar, the author of the *Mitāksharā*, is still held in high esteem as an eminent jurist of Hindu Law.

After the later Chālukyas, Mahārāshtra came to be ruled by another powerful dynasty, the Yādavas, a clan from north India who had been striving in ages past to wield power and influence at different places. They wrested the sceptre from the Chālukyas and ruled for over a hundred years from 1187 to 1294 from their famous capital Deogiri, which the Muslims later named Daulatabad. Four eminent Yādava rulers, Singhana, Krishnadeva, Mahādeva and Rāmadeva became celebrated in the history of the Deccan for having patronized art and literature, the signs of which are amply visible to this day. The great mathematician Bhāskarācharya, the Yādava minister Hemādri, a versatile writer and inventor of many practical arts, and Hemādri's right-hand helpmate the scholarly Bopadeva, are all names among many others, still cherished in Maratha memory with peculiar reverence.

Hemādri holds an important place in the history of Mahārāshtra. He was in many respects far ahead of his times. He was not only a learned scholar, but also a minister (*Shrikaraṇadhipa*) of the Yādava rulers possessing great powers of organization and a wide outlook directed to the many-sided improvement of the people inhabiting the Yādava dominion. With the help of a number of scholars he promulgated a huge compendium of religious observances, entitled *Chaturvarga-Chintamani*. He also produced works on medicine, introduced a code of private and official etiquette and of forms of address in private and public correspondence. He changed the Devnāgari script so as to suit a fast running hand by joining the letters, a mode which is known as Modi and which has long been current in Mahārāshtra.[8] A special art of constructing houses and temples with hewn stones piled one upon another without the use of cement or mortar, was invented by Hemādri and came to be widely adopted throughout Mahārāshtra. The grain Bajri as a cheap food-stuff of plentiful yield, is said to have been first introduced by Hemādri. To his great work *Chaturvarga-Chintamani* he has added an illuminating supplement entitled *Yādav-Prashasti* in which he has immortalized the history of the Yādava rulers ending with Mahādeva Yādava.

4. **Rise of the Manabhav sect.**—With the changes of dynasties, Mahārāshtra preserved its political freedom for some two hundred years more than its sister provinces in the

8. The oldest paper now available in this script dates about half a century after Hemādri.

north. Here foreign conquest was never dreamt of and no provision against it was considered necessary. About 1000 A.C. the Muslims began to knock at the gates of India, and by the end of the twelfth century Delhi passed into their hands, ushering in a new political experience for the warring indigenous princes of this vast country. It required a hundred years more for the shock to reach Mahārāshtra from Delhi. During the last quarter of the thirteenth century between about 1270 and 1295 when Jnaneshwar was penning the eulogy of Rāmachandra Yādava, a sudden collapse came, which requires to be explained on the basis of recent historical research. A dim light in the midst of complete darkness is perhaps to be found in the rise of the Mānabhāv sect and the conflict it provoked in the religious sphere. Let us see what the Mānabhāv revolution effected in the spheres of religion, society and politics of the period.

The word Mānabhāv is a corruption of the Sanskrit original *Mahānubhāva*, meaning great respectability. The Mānabhāv sect, also known as Jayakrishna or Achyuta, is an important body of free-thinkers advocating a distinct departure from the traditional Vedānta system of religion formulated by Shankarāchārya. Indeed, from about the eleventh century onwards, as in earlier times, there has been a peculiar upheaval in Indian religion and society, giving rise from time to time to a number of divergent sects, such as the Vaishnavas, the Shaivas, the Lingayats, the Nath-panthis and Warkaries of the Pandharpur movement. During the thirteenth century a learned Nagar Brahman from the district of Broach in Gujarat named Haripāldev migrated to Ridhpur near Amraoti in Berar, and there under the inspiration of a learned saint named Govind Prabhu started preaching doctrines of a revolt against some of the absurdities of current orthodoxy.

This Haripāldev, newly named Chakradhar by his guru, toured through Mahārāshtra and by his earnest oratory and forceful reasoning, collected round himself a large number of disciples, mostly learned Brahmans from different places. He possessed a wonderful mastery over the Marathi language and explained through its medium the best thoughts in the Upanishads and other old philosophical works, exposing the incongruities that existed between the real ideals and the actual practice of the Hindus of his time. Chakradhar soon came to be worshipped and respected by large masses of people as the very incarnation of God wherever he went. Thus a new sect came into existence, although Chakradhar himself never avowed that he was preaching a new religion. He is credited with an abnormally long life of more than a century, 1153 to 1276 A.C., which he spent in passionate preaching and enforcing rigid discipline upon his followers in every minute detail of conduct and worship. He did not confine his activities to Mahārāshtra only, but travelled over wide regions outside, extending roughly from the river Krishna in the south to the bank of the Indus in the north, a unique performance in the history of religious movements. Chakradhar's successes extended even beyond the Indus to Peshawar and on to Kabul, where his followers read and recited the sacred texts in the language.

Chakradhar concentrated his teaching upon the worship of Krishna, emphasising dualism in contravention to the then existing *Advait* system as enunciated by Shankarāchārya and adopted for centuries by the common masses and rulers of the Yādava dynasty. The main points on which this new teaching differed from the old can be thus summarized : (1) Chakradhar did not accept the sanctity of the Vedas as the ultimate authority, (2) he denounced the artificial divisions of caste and (3) the adoration of the numerous gods, their forms and incarnations. (4) He also rejected the pollution by touch in any shape or form, upholding all human beings as equal in sanctity. He also enforced a strict vegetarian diet and allowed no sensual excesses unlike the Shāktas and Tāntrikas. The Mānabhāvs have two distinct orders, the householders and the recluses. The latter admit even women to the status of religious celibates ; the former live much the same social life as the common mass of their brother Hindus, and can be hardly distinguished by any special conduct at this day.

5. **Manabhav literature.**—But it is more in the literary sphere than in the religious, that the Mānabhāvs have rendered their greatest service, which is not yet widely nor ade-

quately recognised. They rigidly prohibited the use of Sanskrit either in common prayer or in their literary works. They adopted pure Marathi as the only channel of expression holding it to be as sacred as Sanskrit and, like our popular Mahārāshtra saints, made available to the common folk the highest philosophical thought of the old Sanskrit works. They were the first to create Marathi proto-types of the various forms, constructions and styles of classical writers, their Samhitas, Sutras, Bhāshyas and even the metres of the Sanskrit verse, both of the *Aksaragana* and the *Mātrāgana* systems. The Mānabhāv scholars were the first to write elegant Marathi prose, unlike the Sanskrit writers who preferred the metrical form. This Mānabhāv prose is of the blank verse type.

Chakradhar himself never wrote any work of his own. He had a large number of gifted disciples all passionately devoted to him and whole-heartedly co-operating with him in his attack on orthodoxy. Every act and incident of his life, as also every utterance of his, were properly recorded and later arranged in two important works,—the first containing his sermons and utterances is termed *Siddhanta-Sutra-path*[9] and has become the sacred book of the sect which the followers read and recite. The other, recording his acts and incidents, is called *Lilacharitra*.[10] In order to preserve the sanctity of the text of these works, they were purposely written in thirteen different code-scripts according to as many sub-divisions, which prevented their being tampered with by ignorant readers. These two form the sacred scriptures of the Mānabhāv sect and are the compositions of Mahindra Bhatt Vyās, a learned scholar, who was helped in his task by half a dozen other scholars of equal calibre. One noticeable peculiarity of these works is that exact dates and places are mentioned in most cases for the occurrences that are narrated, and this fact materially helps the student of history. The use of the code scripts has preserved the original language from any manipulation or interpolation by subsequent scribes, so that in the Mānabhāv works we find today the very words, phrases and forms of the day of their composition, without the modernization which has

9. सिद्धान्तसूत्रपाठ. 10. लीलाचरित्र.

vitiated the contents and form of the writings of our other Mahārāshtra saints like Jnaneshwar and Eknāth.

Other works of high literary merit came to be written in quick succession by Mānabhāv writers on the model of the old poetical compositions of the Sanskrit Kavyas: the following seven of these are held in great esteem—

1. *Rukmini-Swayamvara* by Narendra Borikar;

2 & 3. *Shishupāla Vadha* and *Uddhav-gita* by Bhāskarbhatt;

4. *Vatsalā-Harana* by Dāmodar Pandit;

5 to 7. *Riddhipur Varnan, Jnana-bodh* and *Sahyādri-Varnan* are three descriptive narrations.

The first of these *Rukmini-Swayamvara* is contemporary with the *Jnaneshwari*: the others belong to a little later period. All are in the common *ovi* metre and can take a high rank for their literary merit. Not a few women have figured among their authors. These Mānabhāv compositions long remained unnoticed by the scholarly world probably on account of the strange antipathy that Hindu orthodoxy entertained towards that sect. How and why such antipathy arose is a riddle which deserves to be satisfactorily solved.

6. Deaths of Chakradhar and Hemadri.—The propagation of the Mānabhāv doctrines appears to have had an intimate relation with and was certainly a contributory cause of the sudden fall of the Yādavas of Deogiri, the very heart of the region, where Chakradhar first began his fanatical activities by openly preaching against orthodox beliefs and practices. He was doubtless a contemporary of the great Hemādri, the *Shrikaranādhipa* of the powerful king Mahādeva Yādava (A.C. 1260-1271), so that Hemādri and Chakradhar are found acting on the stage of mediæval history, both learned and possessing extraordinary capacity for organization and using their utmost powers, the one upholding the orthodox system and the other preaching a revolt. It would appear that Hemādri purposely promulgated his comprehensive code of religious observances (the *Chaturvarga-Chintamani*) consisting of four large books or parts, (1) the *Vratakhanda* or vows, (2) the

Dāna-khanda or charities, (3) the *Tirtha-khanda* or pilgrimages, and (4) the *Moksha-khanda* or salvation, with several supplements (*Parishesha-khanda*) emphasizing the worship of various deities, of the manes and ancestors, the daily and seasonal duties with penances for failure. Hemādri completed this work during the regime of Mahādeva Yādava, who was succeeded by his nephew Rāmachandra in 1271. Rāmachandra obtained the crown by cruelly putting to death Mahādev's son Aman, and confirmed Hemādri in his post. It is well-known that these Yādava rulers traced their descent from Shrikrishna and were his ardent devotees, just as were Chakradhar and his followers, who on that account were freely admitted into the palace and harem of Deogiri in a brotherhood of common worship, a result which the minister Hemādri highly resented and opposed with all the powers he possessed.

Recent research based on the evidence of the Mānabhāv writings throws a lurid light on the manner in which both Chakradhar and Hemādri met with their deaths.[11] A certain manuscript of the *Lilā-Charitra*, written shortly after 1276 (and not yet published) mentions that Hemādri with the help of his own priests and those of the Yādava rulers discovered the whereabouts of Chakradhar, sent his troops after him and had him killed in 1276 at Khokargaon (near Pāthardi, District Ahmadnagar). When this event came to be reported to Rāmdev, he was filled with wrath against Hemādri and soon after put him to a cruel death in retaliation for Chakradhar's death. This conclusion is indirectly corroborated by some verses in the *Mahikāvati bakhar* published by Rajawade.[12]

This story may be true or false, but the reason of the sudden fall of king Rāmachandra Yādava may be looked for in the weak and vicious character of his rule (notwithstanding his eulogy by Jnaneshwar) aggravated by religious disputes distracting the king's attention from preparations for defence

11. A large amount of literature of inscriptions and *prashastis* is available on the life and work of Hemādri, but there is no mention how he came by his death. See K. A. Padhye's *Life of Hemādri*, wherein are reproduced all the inscriptions and *Prashastis* in full.

12. Page 81, verses 54 and 55. See Prof. V. B. Kolte's paper in the *Nagpur University Journal*, December, 1941.

against attacks from outside. Disorder and neglect certainly appear to have facilitated Ala-ud-din's sudden and successful attack upon Deogiri in 1294, probably incited thereto by Mānabhāv agents imparting secret information to the conqueror about the weakness of Yādava rule.

But here we must first turn to the strong Hindu reaction which the rapid Muslim conquest provoked in the southern lands of this continent.

7. **Successful revolt against the Muslims.**—Towards the end of the 10th century of the Christian era a new race of conquerors from beyond the Himālayas began to knock at the gates of India. The task was begun by that consummate Turkish general Mahmud of Ghazni and completed by an equally tenacious conqueror known to history as Muhammad of Ghor. Within two hundred years, the whole of northern India was reduced. A hundred more years passed and the Muslims undertook the subjugation of the Deccan by crossing the Narmada for the first time.

There were at the time, in the south, four or five important Hindu Kingdoms which the Muslims reduced within less than a quarter of a century. Ala-ud-din Khilji attacked Deogiri in 1294 and forced its ruler Rāmdev Rao into submission. Malik Kafur, Ala-ud-din's Lieutenant, overran and destroyed the Kākatiya kingdom of Warangal[13] in 1309, and the Hoysala kingdom of Dwārasamudra in 1310. Immediately after these successes he overran the Chola and Pandya kingdoms of the extreme south and planted the green banner of Islam on the southernmost point of India. Thus Ala-ud-din Khilji before his death could boast of having subjugated the whole of the Indian Continent. His son Mubarak Khilji and thereafter the stern Tughlak Sultan Muhammad, extinguished the last vestiges of Hindu power in the south ; and this Tughlak ruler in order to hold the lately conquered territory in perfect submission, in 1325 transferred his capital to Deogiri, which he named Daulatabad, and for some years after he took up his residence here in the south. Thus the Muslim conquest of

13. Old name *Ekashila-Nagari* or *Varnakula*, hence the present name.

India appeared to be complete by the year 1326. In this way all the work of the great builders from Chandragupta Maurya to Rāmdev Rao of Deogiri and of Pratāprudra of Warangal, covering a period of some sixteen and a half centuries, was undone within less than a quarter of a century, an extraordinary phenomenon, for which no parallel can be found in the history of the world.

There had been foreign conquerors in India before ; and they had all been quickly absorbed and assimilated in the body of Hindu society. But these new Turkish fanatics were of an entirely different type. They were not content with the acquisition of mere political power. They descended upon the plains of Hindustan not as mere conquerors and plunderers, but as crusading warriors bent upon spreading their holy faith in the land of the infidels. When they overthrew the Hindu kingdoms of the north and established themselves in the land, they set about systematically to force their religion upon the people, to desecrate the Hindu temples and their magnificent edifices, to break down the idols, mutilate statues and works of art, disfigure stone inscriptions beyond recognition. Out of the material obtained by such wanton destruction, they erected prayer-houses for the use of the Faithful. In order to stamp out heathenism and gather the Indian people within the fold of Islam, these ruthless vandals prohibited the public exercise of the Hindu religion and subjected its devotees to disabilities and penal laws. The Hindus were not allowed to dress well, live well or appear prosperous. Vexatious taxes were imposed upon them and their seats of learning were destroyed.

North India is a huge plain with hardly any natural impediment or stronghold to withstand hardy and determined soldiers sweeping from Attock down to the Bay of Bengal. The Hindus of this vast region internally divided and disorganised as they were, offered little or no resistance to their Turkish oppressors. They meekly submitted to all the ill-treatment that was inflicted upon them, and betrayed a strange incapacity to offer a combined opposition in defence of their land and religion. But the Hindus of the south, particularly the stern Kāpālika and Shaiva sects, the Mānabhāvas and the Lingayats inhabiting the lands of Kampli, near Anagondi and

Warangal, were not slow to react and resist the Muslim aggression. How this revolt was successfully organised forms an instructive study.

Warangal was the capital of Telangana, the coastal region between the Godavari and the Krishna, and for centuries it was ruled by a dynasty of the Kakatiyas. It was first attacked in 1303 by Ala-ud-din's general Malik Fakhruddin Juna, who later figured as the notorious Sultan Muhammad Tughlak of Delhi. He was routed with heavy loss by the valiant ruler Pratāprudra Kakatiya, who then became an eyesore to the Muslim conquerors. Years passed. The Khiljis were succeeded by the Tughlaks, who sent a strong expedition against Warangal in 1321. For two years the struggle continued unabated. Pratāprudra was overcome and captured alive. He was being taken to Delhi as a trophy of the war, when, finding the insult too bitter to bear, he put an end to his life in 1323. This sad end of their valiant leader roused the people as nothing else would have done.[14]

After a year's time Muhammad Tughlak became the Sultan of Delhi and at once removed his capital to Deogiri (1325) ; and from his seat in that strong fort he started measures to put down the rising opposition of the Hindus. The fall of Warangal had spread the infection of revolt to the neighbouring region of Kampli on the Tungabhadra, where another brave Hindu warrior Kāmnāth, inflicted crushing defeats upon the forces sent against him by the Sultan from Deogiri. Exasperated by this disgraceful reverse, the Sultan sent another and more powerful expedition for the conquest of Kampli in 1327. Kampildeva finding resistance hopeless, prepared a huge fire and along with all his women folk burnt

14. For this and the following narrative N. Venkataramanayya's *The Early Muslim Expansion In South India* (Madras Univ. Publication, 1942), is the main authority. On p. 188 occurs this evidence on the foundation of Vijayanagar.—

स एव खलु माधवो वसुमतीं चतुःसागरी-
मसाकलितमेखलां नयति बुक्कराजं युधः ।
तमन्वजनि सायणस्तमनु भोजनाथश्वता-
वुभावुदयमाश्रितावचलमत्र विश्वेश्वरं ॥

himself alive in it in order to escape the disgrace of falling into the enemy's hands. A large number of prisoners was however captured and carried in chains to the Sultan, whose joy at this success was unbounded. He returned to Delhi with his booty and prisoners. Among these latter were two brothers, Harihar and Bukka, who had formerly served as ministers at Kampli and helped Pratāprudra of Warangal. The Sultan knew their worth, converted them to Islam and used them well with a view to employing them in the event of any Hindu revolt in the south. These spirited brothers had witnessed the changing fortunes of the Hindus ever since the fall of the Yādavas and secretly nursed in their hearts a feeling of revenge, and they waited for a suitable opportunity.

Sultan Muhammad Tughlak soon found himself involved in serious troubles as much in the north as in the south, but he was not a bit inclined to relent in his resolve to put down the Hindu Kafirs. During 1330 and 1331, one Kapayyā Nāyak of Warangal and another Somdevrāj of Kampli rose against the Sultan, put the Muslim governors to flight and asserted independence in their respective localities. The news reached the Sultan at Delhi. He held a council of war with his advisers and decided upon their suggestion to employ the services of the two brothers Harihar and Bukka, now Muslim converts and as such expected to do their best to uphold their adopted faith in the same manner as their predecessor Malik Kafur had done. The two brothers accepted the mission readily and fully provided with men and materials soon appeared before Kampli.

How wide-spread and bitter was the Hindu feeling of revolt at this time can be gathered from the conspicuous part which the Shankarāchārya Mādhav Vidyāranya, the learned and influential head of the Shringeri Math, played by taking the lead in politics for putting down Muslim aggression. Mādhavācharya and his two equally competent brothers, Sāyannā and Bhojanāth held deliberations with the two heroes Harihar and Bukka, persuaded them to renounce their newly-accepted faith and after bringing them back to the Hindu fold by means of certain penances, made them lead the whole movement to a successful issue. Thus were politics and religion put to the highest test in the nation's cause. The example proved highly rousing. The Sultan's plans were entirely foiled. The holy Guru Mādhavācharya took up his residence at Anagondi where the two brothers Harihar Rai and Bukka Rai paid him due reverence. A fresh plan was conceived in mutual consultation for founding the seat of a new Hindu Empire at the bend of the river Tungabhadra, just opposite Anagondi. This was the origin of Vijayanagar which rapidly grew into a well-protected, wealthy and powerful city. In this new capital the two brothers were crowned kings on 18 April 1336. Muhammad Tughlak had the mortification to lose his southern provinces for good.

This newly created Empire of Vijayanagar gradually increased in power and extent and for more than two hundred years stemmed the tide of Muslim conquest in the south. Although thereafter Vijayanagar was itself destroyed by the combined power of the Muslim rulers in the famous battle of Talikot (January 22, 1565), the various local powers that survived, were never crushed altogether, but continued to drag on a submerged existence in different localities right up to the British conquest of India. Historically, however, this experiment of Vijayanagar served as a source of power and inspiration to the genius of Shivaji, since his father Shahji had his life's activities concentrated upon the region of Bangalore, Kampli and Kanakgiri, and, we may be sure, that Shivaji took his cue from the example of Harihar and Bukka, of personal valour joined to the spiritual power of the Shankarāchārya. It is well known, that Shivaji closely followed this model and revered his gurus Tukārām and Rāmdās. The causes of this Hindu rebellion against Muhammad Tughlak, as later of Shivaji's against Aurangzeb, were, it should be noted, more cultural than political; the Hindus always attached greater importance to the preservation of their religion than to political freedom. Herein lies the importance to Maratha history of the Hindu revolt which led to the foundation of Vijayanagar.

8. Saints and writers of Maharashtra.—As a reaction to Muslim aggression in India, the spirit of revolt rapidly spread throughout the land and paralysed all the energy of Muhammad Tughlak. Mahārāshtra was not slow to follow in the footsteps of Vijayanagar, but here the revolt took a different shape. Husain Zafar Khan, a trusted commandant whom the Tughlak Sultan despatched to quell the rebellions in the south, himself assumed the lead of the rebels, and declared his own independence at Gulburga, assuming the royal title of Ala-ud-din Bahman Shah and founded in 1347 what came to be known in history as the Bahamani Kingdom. This Muslim ruler was shrewd enough to realize that it was no use exasperating the Hindus by interfering with their religion. They readily accepted his new tolerant rule though alien in faith. During the next two hundred years this Bahamani Kingdom, like its sister of Vijayanagar, went on flourishing side by side, although between them a spirit of rivalry and mutual aggression continued all the time. Towards the end of the fifteenth century, the Bahamani Kingdom broke up into five separate branches, of which three, namely those of Bijapur, Ahmadnagar and Golkonda became fairly powerful after absorbing the other two of Bidar and Berar. These three have become known to history as the Adil Shahi, Nizam Shahi, and Qutb Shahi, from the names of their respective founders. We are not here concerned with the internal administration of the original Bahamani kingdom or of its later branches, except in so far as they contributed to the Maratha rise.

As the founder of the Maratha kingdom had his home near the western ghats, his fortunes came to be mainly connected with only the Nizamshah of Ahmadnagar and the Adilshah of Bijapur. Although the five combined Muslim rulers dealt a death blow to the Hindu kingdom of Vijaynagar, they did not succeed in subjugating the more southernly territories of that Hindu power. The general policy of these Deccani rulers was of tolerance towards the Hindus, as they had become wiser by the fate which the intolerant Khiljis and Tughlaks had to suffer on account of their extreme hatred towards the main populace over whom they ruled. In all essentials the Bahamani rulers and the Sultans of the offshoot kingdoms, depended upon the Hindus for their own existence and studiously refrained from injuring Hindu sentiment. The hilly regions of the west remained practically unconquered. The Muslim character of the rulers was confined only to their personal religion and did not affect their subjects. Writes Ranade, "These nominal Muhammadan rulers were virtually controlled both in the civil and military departments by Maratha statesmen and Maratha warriors. The hill-forts near the Ghats and the country thereabout, were in the hands of Maratha captains, who were nominally dependent upon these Muhammadan sovereigns." Indeed, if Muhammad Adilshah of Bijapur, who came to the throne in 1627 and who completely reversed the tolerant policy of his father Ibrahim Adilshah, a ruler of exceptional impartiality who had been revered as Jagat-Guru by the Hindus themselves, had not resumed the old practice of desecrating Hindu temples and plundering their wealth, it is probable that Shivaji would not have undertaken to found an independent Maratha Kingdom. Under the advice of his minister Mustafa Khan, Muhammad Adilshah promulgated fresh regulations[15] for putting down the Hindu religion and thus invited the extreme wrath of prominent Marathas of the day. The conversion of Bajaji Nimbalkar of Phaltan to the Muslim faith is an evidence of this changed policy of Bijapur which impelled Shivaji to make a fresh bold move.

The Hindus in general—the Maratha forming no exception—have during historic times cared more for their religion than for political power. When the Ghaznivides and the Ghoris, the Khiljis and the Tughlaks practised fearful persecution in religious matters, they provoked opposition and revolt. The great Emperor Akbar wisely changed this policy and thereby strengthened his empire. Akbar's policy was reversed by Aurangzeb and this generated the Maratha movement for independence, a repetition of the same experiment that had led to the foundation of Vijayanagar. This vein of rebellious sentiment runs through the vast Marathi literature of the three or four centuries that followed the extinction of the Yādavās of Deogiri; from the time of Mukundraj and Jnaneshwar to that of Tukārām and Rāmdās, the whole range of Marathi literature accurately reflects the workings of the

15. See Regulations of Md. Adilshah, Nos. 21, 44, 48, 51 and 53 in Parasnis' *Itihas-Sangraha, Aitihasik Sphuta Lekh* 2-7.

popular mind. Viewed in this light the teachings of these saints are clearly marked by three successive schools of thought, first that of Jnaneshwar and Nāmdev (13th and 14th centuries), the second Eknāth and Tukārām (15th and 16th centuries), and the third of Rāmdās (17th century), the last being contemporary of Shivaji himself. These saints and writers were mostly men of learning and experience, having widely travelled on pilgrimages throughout India on foot, and gained first-hand information of local occurrences which they often actually witnessed. They can be likened to our present day newspaper reporters. They delivered orations and held *Harikirtans* which were avidly listened to, and which supplied the spiritual background to the political aims of workers like Shivaji.

There are two particular services which these writers have rendered to society. The old precious store of learning and philosophy which till then had been confined only to Sanskrit and was consequently unintelligible to the masses, was rendered by them into various popular and attractive forms of Marathi verse, often set to musical tunes; and secondly, they made an ardent and piteous appeal to God Almighty through their favourite deity to intervene on behalf of the oppressed peoples and bring them relief from Muslim persecution. The well-known story of Dāmāji Pant, a revenue collector of the Bedar district, is a typical instance in which he miraculously escaped the wrath of his master for having distributed gratis government stores of corn, through the actual intervention of the Vithoba of Pandharpur.[16] A studied effort was made by some of the saints towards reconciling the two conflicting faiths in mutual recognition of the essential unity of Rāma and Rahim, of Vithobā and Allāh. The warring sects of the Hindus themselves, the Shaivas and the Vaishnavas were reconciled in a symbolized installation of Vithobā at Pandharpur.[17] Tukārām

16. The story refers to a devastating famine which occurred in Mahārāshtra for seven long years from 1396 A.C., which is still remembered as Durgādi.

17. "It cannot be doubted," writes S. M. Edwardes, "that the remarkable movement which centres so largely about the God Vithobā and Pandharpur, embraced persons of various castes and elevated to sainthood

represented the Pandharpur movement of passionate prayer of complete non-violence and patient resignation to the Divine Will. "The pulsation of a new national life began to stir throughout the land and was accompanied in the popular belief by the revolt of the Hindu pantheon against the tyrannous deity of the Muslim."[18]

The rapid change in the structure of the Marathi language itself bears unmistakable evidence to the political domination secured by the Muslim conquerors. While the great work of Jnaneshwar contains not a single Arabic or Persian word, Eknāth's writings exhibit a very large percentage of those foreign words imposed on Marathi. When Shivaji came forth boldly to oppose Muslim aggression and renovate Hindu religion and culture, he promulgated his own Sanskrit code of official terms, replacing the Persian ones of the court language of the foreigners. The change back to Sanskrit became quickly effective during Maratha rule.

But there is another class of writings which tried to account for this new agitation in Mahārāshtrian life. They consist of early *bakhars* and *prashastis* (introductions) attached to Sanskrit works. Most of the *bakhars* of Shivaji, Hanmante's introduction to the *Rājavyavahār Kosh*, Gāgābhatt's foreword to the *Kāyastha-Dharma-Pradip* composed by him, and the *Bhatta-Vansha-Kāvya*, the elaborate exposition of Parmānand's *Shiva-Bhārat* (two long chapters), some of the Hindi works of poets Bhushan and Lal Kavi, an anonymous poem purporting to be Shivaji's letter to Jaya-Sinh, all these particularly treat the subject of the rise of Shivaji, but explain it in a different manner. They describe the Earth as personified, unable to bear the atrocities of the Mlechhas towards gods, brahmans and cows, and seeking relief from the god Brahmā, who in his turn appeals to Shankar, Vishnu or the goddess Bhavāni, and ultimately these gods heeded the solemn prayer of the Earth and agreed to undertake a fresh incarnation for redressing the prevailing wrongs, and thus is Shivaji described to have been born. This is the orthodox explanation

---

representatives of even the lowest castes in Mahārāshtra" (Intr. Grant Duff's *History*, p. lxxiii).

18. Introduction to *Maratha Ballads* by Acworth.

of the rise of Shivaji recorded before the days of the present epoch of historical research.[19]

9. **Peculiarities of the Maratha race.**—M. G. Ranade, the author of *Rise of the Maratha Power*, has propounded two important questions which a student of Maratha history has to solve. They are: (1) Why was the first successful attempt to throw off the Muhammadan yoke made in western India, and (2) what are the circumstances in the nature of the country, and the habits and institutions of the people inhabiting it, which favoured such an attempt and rewarded it with success? The veteran administrator and erudite scholar Sir Richard Temple has supplied an answer to these questions.[20] He says:—"The Marathas have always formed a separate nation and still regard themselves as such. They possess plain features, short stature, a small but wiry frame. Their eyes are bright and piercing and under excitement will gleam with passion. Though not powerful physically as compared with the northern races of the Punjab and Oudh, they have much activity and an unsurpassed endurance. Born and bred in and near the western Ghat mountains and their numerous tributary ranges, they have all the qualities of mountaineers. Among their native hills they have at all times evinced desperate courage. Away from the hills they do not display remarkable valour except under the discipline supplied by able leaders of other races. They never of themselves show an

19. For instance I may quote a few lines—

देवदेव रिपवो वसुंधरां । पीडयन्ति यवना भृशातुरं । तत्कुरुष्व जगतीसमीहितं । म्लेच्छवर्गमधुना शृणीहि तं ॥ त्वं शाहपृथ्वीपतिवीरपत्न्यां । अस्यां समासाद्य मनुष्यजन्म । म्लेच्छापहत्या सुखमारचय्य । भूमेः पुनः स्थापय वर्णधर्मान् ॥ औरंगजेबयवनाधिपभीत-विप्रत्राणाय यः परिगृहीतनवावतारः ॥

Trans.—Sire, these Muslims, the enemies of the gods, are severely oppressing the Earth; therefore you must rescue her from her agony by killing them at once. You must take your birth in a human form from this lady (Jija Bai), the wife of the brave Shahji, and bring about the happiness of the earth, by killing the Mlechhas and restoring the spiritual bliss of the people.

So the god Vishnu took a fresh incarnation in order to protect the Brahmans who had been terrorized by the Yavan Emperor Aurangzeb.

20. *Oriental Experience*, p. 339.

aptitude for organization, but when so organized, they are reckoned among best soldiers. After the fall of the Maratha Empire, they have betaken themselves mainly to cultivation and to the carrying business connected with agriculture.

"The Maratha peasantry possess manly fortitude under suffering and misfortune. Though patient and good-tempered in the main, they have a latent warmth of temper and if oppressed beyond a certain endurable limit, they will fiercely turn and rend their tormentors. Cruelty is also an element in their character. Traditions of plunder have been handed down to them from early times and many of them retain the predatory instincts of their forefathers. The neighbourhood of dense forests, steep hill-sides and fastnesses hard of access, offers extraordinary facilities for the display of valour and the preservation of liberty. They work hard in the fields and possess a fund of domestic virtue. The Marathas are born equestrians and sportsmen. As a rule they are not moderate in living and are not infrequently addicted to intemperance. They often feel proud of their low origin even after attaining greatness. The Sindhias boasted of having been the slipper-bearers of the Peshvas."

Writes Yuan Chwang in the middle of the 7th century—

"The manners of the Marathas are simple and honest. They are proud and reserved. If any one is kind to them he may be sure of their gratitude, but if any one injures them, they will take their revenge and risk their life to wipe out dishonour. If any one in distress appeals to them, they will leave aside all thoughts of self in their anxiety to help. Even if they have an insult to avenge, they never fail to warn their enemy. In battle if they pursue the fugitives, they always spare all who surrender. These men love study and there are many heretics among them." These traits of the Maratha character are found even to-day.

10. The present day Marathas.—Thus from the Mauryas to the Yādavas there stretched a period of fifteen centuries, during which many great races and families came, settled and ruled in Mahārāshtra, only a few of whom have been prominently mentioned here. But there were certainly a large number of others, who, like the Kadambas of Banavasi, or the Silaharas of Kolhapur, Karhad and Thana, or the Vakatakas of Berar, the Kakatiyas of Warangal and the Ballals of Sagar, cannot all be here minutely enumerated, though they undoubtedly entered into the composition of the present-day Maratha nation at one time or another of our past history. Conquest and rule formed the sole occupation of these races and families. The conquerors often took for their wives maidens from the defeated races, thus giving rise to a free mixture of blood. The present day Maratha race boasts of including at least 96 separate families of whom several were long considered to be of very noble blood such as the Mauryas, the Sendrakas, the Rathods, the Silaharas, the Yadavas, etc., each with its high traditions of past valour and glory. The physical and mental powers of the present-day Marathas are a proof of the laws of heredity.

The rise of the Marathas under Shivaji is a problem which has been thoroughly analysed and reviewed by different writers in recent times. The Marathas as a people doubtless possessed in their vein high blood and noble tradition derived through ages from their royal ancestors such as the Mauryas, the Rāshtrakutas, the Chālukyas and the Yādavas, not to mention the more recent additions to the original stock by the arrivals from time to time of north Indian Rajput tribes such as the Paramars (the present day Pawars), the Solankis, the Bhosles, the Ghorpades, the Mohites, the Mahadiks, the Gujars, the Shirkes, the Sawants, the Ghatges, the Manes, the Dafles, the various Deshmukhs of the Mawals, several of whom adopted new surnames, in some cases from the places they occupied in the Deccan and from other sources. The Nimbalkars of Phaltan, for instance, are indeed the Paramars of Dhar who, after being expelled by Muslim conquerors from their habitation in Malwa, at first took their residence at Nimbalak in the Deccan and received their present name from that village. The Bhosles similarly are believed to have migrated from Rajputana and settled near Verul in the vicinity of Daulatabad. Shivaji's mother came from the Jadhao family, doubtless descendants of the ruling Yādavas of Deogiri, who continued to drag on a subdued existence in the region once ruled by their royal ancestors. The Ghorpades are indeed a branch of the Bhosles who acquired that surname from one of their ancestors capturing a fort by climbing up a rampart on a rope tied to an aguana (*i.e.* Ghorpad). The several Deshmukhs of the Maval valleys such as the Jedhes, the Bandals, the Khopdes, the Pasalkars, the Silimkars and so on, acquired their present surnames when they came into and colonized those regions west of Poona, and figured prominently as early associates of Shivaji.

11. **The Maratha country in pulsation.**—To quote Temple,[21] "The Maratha country is strategically important as well as highly picturesque. Much of it lies in the bosom or near the skirts of the Ghat mountains. The vapours from the Arabian Sea are propelled by the south-west monsoon against the mountain tops of the Sahyadri range and produce an abundance of regular rainfall giving rise to luxuriant vegetation and the spectacle of numerous cascades tumbling down the perpendicular flanks of the mountains.

"The mountains stand in the midst of a fertile and populous country. On both sides of them are rich valleys, cultivated plains, numerous villages and large towns. Thus insurgents or warriors had here a complete military base with sources whence supplies could be drawn and with strongholds for organising power or for securing refuge. This hill country has been regarded by strategists as one of the strongest in India in a military sense. It extends over nearly 500 miles from north to south and has numerous fortresses which are virtually impregnable when resolutely defended. Several of these are surrounded with historic tradition. In former times there was no road worthy of the name across these mountains. No means of passage existed for wheeled traffic save steep rugged pathways for footmen and pack animals. It is this range of the Western Ghats which enabled the Marathas to rise against their Muhammadan conquerors, to reassert their nationality against the whole power of the Mughals and to establish in its place an Empire of their own. It should be remembered that the principal power, the widest sovereignty which the

21. *Oriental Experience*, p. 345.

British overthrew in India was that of the Marathas. It was against them that the British had their stiffest and sanguinary actions.

"The political importance of these western mountains is indeed striking. Firstly, they nourish a resolute, enduring, daring almost audacious spirit among their inhabitants. Secondly, they offer strongholds and fastnesses to which these inhabitants can resort whenever they are pressed by an enemy. In fact they long and successfully defied the attempts of the Muslim rulers of Bijapur and Ahmadnagar to subdue them; and thirdly, they lie between fertile countries, consequently, the men of the hills can make rapid raids for plundering or marauding purposes, just as the eagle swoops from its eyrie upon the quarry. After these sudden descents they can rapidly carry off plunder, treasure and the like to the hills, and once they are there, it is difficult to approach them." Innumerable instances have occurred in Maratha history in which the agents of Government removed their valuables and womenfolk to these mountain fastnesses and thus prevented them from falling into the enemy's hands. Indeed, the possession of these strongholds has often formed a subject of bitter strife between various Maratha clans. It is thus that these regions became the cradle of greatness, power and Empire for the Marathas.

It will be clear from the foregoing analysis of the condition of Mahārāshtra and its people that it was never completely subjugated by the Muslim conquerors. The prevalent system of village autonomy ensured the peoples' freedom in point of justice and police. The various landlords enjoyed practical independence for ages. The physical character of the country and the mental cast of its people, were entirely different from those of the other parts of India. The people of Mahārāshtra always possessed a spirit of revolt and independence and only needed some capable leader to organise them. It has often been a moot question in historical disquisition, whether it is the sudden advent of a qualified leader that moulds the character of a people and exacts national service from them; or whether it is the circumstances and the situation of a people which bring forth the sort of leader they need. We cannot categorically maintain either the one view or the other. Very often there is partial truth in both. Carlyle says, "a hero is both the creature and the creator of the times he lives in." Revolutions do not invariably become successful because there are bound to be a large number of favourable and adverse factors in any situation.

The rise of the Bhosles to power will be the theme of the next chapter. In addition to the several causes which facilitated and hastened that rise, one can doubtless notice in the ancestry of Shivaji the two traditions of royalty and independence, one handed down to him through his mother, who entertained a vivid memory of the glory of the royal rule of her Yādav ancestors; and the other reaching him through his father Shahji, who had taken his cue for his life's exploits from the theatre of the old Vijayanagar Empire, the traditions of which could not have yet become totally lost to memory. The Bahamani kingdom although Muslim in character, was not able to destroy or obliterate these old lingering traditions; the actual sway of the Vijayanagar Empire over Mahārāshtra, over, for instance, Karhad, Sangameshwar, Prabhavali and other places is still preserved in the anecdotes of Dado Narasinh and the colonization effected by the black and the white Khojas.[22] Shivaji's father performed his life's work in the old Vijayanagar territories as the sequel will show.

22. These anecdotes refer to the colonization and government of the western regions by the Hindu and Muslim rulers of Vijayanagar, Bedar, and the Silahar Kings of Karhad and Kolhapur. The details of these transactions are scattered over many sources among which may be mentioned *Shiva-Charitra-Sahitya*, Vol. I, No. 2; the *Sardesai Bakhar* in the history of that family, vol. 1, pages 49-53; Raj. vol. 8, letters 1 and 2; Rajwade Introduction, p. 418; *Rise of the Maratha Power*, p. 33, etc.

CHRONOLOGY

CHAPTER II

1552	Maloji Bhosle born.
1592	Shah Jahan born.
1594 March 15	Shahji Bhosle born.
1594	Death of Burhan Nizam Shah : Mughals invade the Deccan.
1597	Death of Babaji Bhosle.
1599	Akbar marches into the Deccan.
1599—1631	Murtaza Nizam S. rules from Deogiri.
1600	Defence of Ahmadnagar by Chand Bibi.
1600 Aug. 19	Ahmadnagar falls : King Bahadur Shah taken prisoner.
1605	Death of Akbar : accession of Jahangir.
1605 Nov. 5	Shahji married to Jija Bai.
1608	Jahangir begins conquest of Deccan.
1609	Malik Ambar's son Fath Khan married at Bijapur.
1616 Feb. 4	Battle of Roshangaon, Ambar routed.
1616 Oct. 16	Khurram moves from Ajmere against Malik Ambar.
1617 Oct. 12	Jahangir takes up residence at Mandu.
1616 Nov. 10	Khurram returns victorious to his father at Mandu.
1619	Sambhaji born to Shahji and Jija Bai.
1620	Death of Maloji Bhosle.
1621 April 4	Shah Jahan reaches Burhanpur to punish M. Ambar.
1622 March 24	Shah Jahan returns north after receiving Malik Ambar's submission.
1624 November	Battle of Bhatavdi, Ambar inflicts defeat upon the Mughals.
1625	Shahji quits Ambar : joins Bijapur.
1626 May 14	Malik Ambar dies : Fath Khan becomes minister.
1626 October	Shahzada Parwiz dies.

1627 April 6	Birth of Shivaji.
1627 Sept. 12	Ibrahim Adil Shah dies : Muhammad Shah succeeds.
1627 Oct. 29	Death of Emperor Jahangir.
1628	Fath Khan imprisoned by Nizam Shah.
1628	Shahji returns to Nizamshahi service.
1628 Feb. 4	Shah Jahan becomes Emperor.
1629 July 25	Lukji Jadhavrao with sons and grandson murdered by Nizam Shah.
1629 Dec. 3	Shah Jahan leaves Agra for the south.
1630—1631	Dreadful famine in the Deccan.
1630 Nov.—March 1632	Shahji accepts Mughal service.
1630	Adilshahi general Murar Jagdeo burns Poona.
1631 Jan. 18	Fath Khan released and reinstated by Nizam Shah.
1631 March	Fath Khan murders Nizam Shah and submits to the Mughals.
1631 June 7	Death of Mumtaz Mahal, cor[illegible] of Shah Jahan, at Burhanpur.
1631 June 10	Khan Jahan Lodi dies fighting.
1632 March	Shah Jahan leaves for Agra.
1633 June 7	Mahabat Khan captures Daulatabad.
1633 Sept.	Shahji installs a new Nizamshahi prince at Pemgiri.
1633 Sept. 23	Shahji and Murar Jagdeo unite against the Mughals.
1634 Oct. 26	Mahabat Khan dies.
1635 Sept. 29	Shah Jahan leaves Agra for Deccan.
1636 Jan.	Shah Jahan reaches Daulatabad and proclaims extinction of the Nizam-Shahi Sultanate.
1636 May 6	Shah Jahan concludes treaty with Bijapur and sets out for Agra.
1636 Aug. 17	Shahji besieged in fort Mahuli.
1636 Oct.	Shahji capitulates to the Mughals and departs for Bijapur.

CHAPTER II

SHAHJI THE RISING SUN

(From Roshangaon to Mahuli—1614-1636)

1. Survey of the situation.
2. The family of the Bhosles.
3. Battle of Roshangaon.
4. Shahji's marriage, Shivaji born.
5. Battle of Bhatavadi.
7. Shah Jahan's march against Nizam Shah.
6. Rebellion of Khan Jahan Lodi.
8. Shahji's bold stand.
9. Moral of the two figures.

1. Survey of the situation, 1605.—The political situation of Mahārāshtra towards the end of the sixteenth century must be borne in mind if we are to understand the rise of the Bhosles to royal power. The great Emperor Akbar after consolidating his Empire in North India decided to subjugate the region south of the Narmada, but found that task not quite so easy as his earlier conquests. Three Emperors in succession had to expend their might before they could make a small headway in the Deccan.

The death of Burhan Nizam Shah of Ahmadnagar in 1594 gave rise to murders and intrigues in rapid succession and the confusion that ensued in the fortunes of that state was taken advantage of by Akbar, who at once sent an army for its conquest. At this critical hour the famous Chand Bibi stood forth boldly, organised a strong opposition, and heroically defended Ahmadnagar for some years. Eventually about the middle of 1599 Akbar himself marched southwards at the invitation of his trusted general Abul Fazl and occupied Burhanpur without opposition. His son Daniyal and the Khan Khanan were charged with the duty of taking Ahmadnagar at a time when internal dissensions precluded the effective defence of the place, and Chand Bibi the only capable leader was either murdered or constrained to take poison by her own servants. The town was stormed without much difficulty in August 1600 and formally surrendered on the 19th of that month. The young King Bahadur Shah and his family paid the penalty for their crime of independence by life-long imprisonment in the fortress of Gwalior. At this moment of success Akbar received the news of his son Salim being in open rebellion and was compelled to return hastily to the north.[1] Thereafter his fortunes rapidly declined and he died in 1605 without leaving a worthy successor.

The history of the Marathas would possibly have taken a different turn if Akbar had been succeeded by a more competent ruler than the slothful, easy-going, pleasure-seeking Jahangir. This trait of his character paved the way for the Maratha ambitions, which came to be fostered, although for his own ends, by the astute Malik Ambar, an Abyssinian Muslim in origin, who when young had been made a slave and brought to India by a merchant of Baghdad and sold to Chengiz Khan a minister of the Sultans of Ahmadnagar. The latter detected Ambar's capacity and trained him for the service of the Nizamshahi State. In a short time he became a power in the Deccan and set at defiance all Emperor Jahangir's efforts for over fifteen years. He practically re-made the history of the Deccan for that period with the help of many Maratha captains. The Abyssinian emigrants here gained opportunities unequalled elsewhere for displaying their rare capacity for sea-faring, land warfare, management of men and civil administration. They were no longer household slaves and palace eunuchs as in the north, but regents of kingdoms, generalissimos of armies, admirals of fleets, viceroys of provinces.

Undaunted by the loss of Ahmadnagar, Malik Ambar selected Parenda, Junnar and Daulatabad in succession as temporary seats of safety for the new Sultan Murtaza Nizam Shah (1599-1631) and himself conducted the administration with consummate skill both in war and diplomacy, attending at the same time to the welfare of the subjects. He at last kept the Shah secure in the difficult fort of Daulatabad and established a separate city for administrative purposes at Khadki in the vicinity of that fort. This city was afterwards named Aurangabad when Aurangzeb became his father's viceroy in the Deccan in 1636.

1. *Akbar* by Vincent Smith, p. 277.

The various Maratha clans of the Deccan were dragging on their obscure existence in the service of one or other of the three Muslim potentates of the Deccan with hardly any idea at the time of asserting their independence. Among them the Jadhavs with their seat at Sindkhed in the vicinity of Daulatabad were then powerful in the service of the Nizam Shah. The Bhosles were at first comparatively insignificant. Maloji Bhosle the grandfather of Shivaji had to content himself by serving as a petty horseman in the employ of the Jadhavs. The cousins of the Bhosles, *viz.* the Ghorpades, served the Adil Shah of Bijapur, enjoying a small jagir at Mudhol. The clan of the Morés enjoyed almost royal power and influence in the hilly regions west of Satara, while rendering nominal service to Bijapur.

Jahangir resumed his father's policy of subjugating the Deccan in 1608 and the war thus started continued practically till 1636 when Shah Jahan ultimately succeeded in putting an end to the existence of the Nizamshahi Kingdom. It was during the course of this long war that Maloji and Shahji Bhosle rose to prominence as helpmates of Malik Ambar. The period bristles with the names of captains on the two sides and with stirring incidents of a varying character. Fortunately two independent sources, Fuzuni Astarabadi's Persian account of Malik Ambar and the Sanskrit narrative of Parmanand named the *Shiva Bhārat*, help us to determine the main story of this struggle with tolerable accuracy.

How Malik Ambar with his scanty resources resisted for fifteen years the power of the Mughal Emperor backed by his wealth and enormous resources and directed by the best generals and competent Shahazadas like Parwiz and Khurram, has become a problem in the history of the art of war. Ambar boldly opposed the Mughals by adapting his tactics to the geographical conditions of the southern regions and by developing a particular method of fighting the enemy, which is known as guerilla warfare and which Shivaji later used with such effect against his opponents.

2. The family of the Bhosles.—The family of Shivaji claimed descent from the Sisodia Ranas of Udepur, but its name *Bhosle* has not been satisfactorily accounted for. There is no doubt that the ancestors of several present day Maratha families, as has been shown in the first chapter, migrated from the north and settled in Mahārāshtra, representing to this day the Rajput or Kshatriya blood. One tradition says that after the capture of the fort of Chitod by Ala-ud-din Khilji early in the fourteenth century (1303), a member of the ruling family of the Ranas, named Sajjan Sinh or Sujan Sinh escaped from the miseries of foreign conquest and wandered into the southern regions in search of employment during the troubled reign of Muhammad Tughlak. Sajjan Sinh died about 1350 and his fifth descendant Ugrasen had two sons Karna Sinh and Shubha Krishna. Karna Sinh's son Bhimsinh received from the Bahmani Sultan the title of "Raja Ghorpade Bahadur," with a jagir of 84 villages at Mudhol where the family still rules. Bhim Sinh's descendants thus came to be known as Ghorpades who have now extensive branches at different places in Mahārāstra. Shubha Krishna's descendants are known as Bhosles and form a younger branch of the original family.[2]

A grandson of this Shubha Krishna was one Bābāji Bhosle who died in 1597. Babaji had two sons, Māloji (born in 1552) and Vithoji. Maloji, his son Shahji and Shahji's son Shivaji are the three persons most intimately concerned with the events which form the subject of our present study. These Bhosles purchased the headship or *patilki* of Verul near Daulatabad and some other villages in the region of the rivers Godavari and Bhima and maintained themselves by managing their landed property and by military service under the Nizam-

2. The descent of the Bhosle family from the Ranas of Udepur has not been authentically proved. It is supported by copies (not originals) of some Persian firmans in the possession of the Rāja of Mudhol. But some scholars consider them spurious. The question of the origin of the Bhosles came for investigation at the time of Shivaji's coronation when the rites due to a Kshatriya were denied to him. In this connection the student can study with advantage Shivaji's circular letter dated 28th January 1677, printed by Kulkarni in No. 3 of his "*Old Historical Documents*", p. 41. Some consider the name Bhosle as a corruption of the word Hoysal, a family which ruled at Dwara Samudra. But these Hoysals are known to have been a branch of the Yadavas. As Jija Bai came from the Yadava family, she could not have contracted marital connection with another Yadava family.

shahi rulers. On the whole the members of the Bhosle family appear enterprizing, resourceful and self-reliant, men of strong will and pride, never submitting to an insult. Their family was numerous and always mutually helpful.[3]

Māloji and Vithoji possessed huge and strong bodies, too heavy, it is said, for the Deccani pony to carry. They were the *patils* of Verul (Ellora) a village near Daulatabad, and enlisted as guards in the service of Lukhji Jādhavrao the baron of Sindkhed, in the vicinity of Daulatabad which became the capital of the Nizamshahi State after Ahmadnagar had been lost. Lukhji, a descendant of the dethroned royal family of Deogiri, was at this time a noble of the first rank in the service of the Nizam Shah, wielding influence in the politics of the Deccan. The Bhosle brothers found employment as troopers under Lukhji Jadhav and at the same time managed their old landed property at Verul and other villages.

The river Narmada has formed the main boundary between the northern and southern halves of this Indian continent. The first important post which the conquering armies from the north after crossing this river must secure in order to confirm their footing in the south, is Burhanpur on the river Tapti and its covering fort Ashirgad. The next advance is to the region of Daulatabad, Ellora and Aurangabad, about a hundred miles south of Burhanpur. Some 75 miles further south stands Ahmadnagar the main key for any northern conqueror to possess for holding the south. Burhanpur, Aurangabad and Ahmadnagar thus form the principal chain of posts and the region of bitter contest round which converges the present story of the Mughal advance and the Maratha resistance.

3. **Battle of Roshangaon.**—Malik Ambar possessed a keen perception and a rare capacity for organization. He made friends with the ruler of Bijapur, the wise Ibrahim Adil

3. In contemporary writing their names are mentioned not singly but with the honourable word "Rāje" added after them, as Maloji Raje, Kheloji Raje, Vithoji Raje, etc. But this word Raje does not necessarily signify kingship. It was a commnon practice with most Maratha clans to add the word Rāje after their individual names. The practice is still kept up.

Shah, who celebrated in his capital, under his own personal direction and at his own expense, the marriage ceremony of Malik Ambar's son Fath Khan in 1609, that is, just about the time that Jahangir's forces marched from Agra against Ahmadnagar. Malik Ambar improved the Nizam-Shahi state in various ways. His genius perhaps appears pre-eminent in so administering the Nizamshahi territories as to make the peasantry his best support. Ambar's land revenue assessment scheme earned for him a unique reputation and became a model for succeeding rulers to copy. Agriculture and industry were so fostered by him in the state that the country became prosperous and brought in a regular income. Although he was a Muslim, his rule came to be much appreciated and respected by the Hindus; it was so entirely free from any religious persecution, that the Hindus became his best friends.

It is not necessary here to discuss in detail the various expeditions sent by Jahangir to the Deccan and the measures adopted by Malik Ambar to thwart them. In 1608 Jahangir appointed to the government of the Deccan Abdur Rahim Khan-Khanan, a great and valiant noble of his Court, son of the famous Bairam Khan of Akbar's days. When this general who had long served in the Deccan before, arrived on the spot with large forces, Malik Ambar assumed a most submissive attitude and by agreeing to the terms imposed, avoided open war and gained time for preparation. The Emperor, however, became impatient and sent large reinforcements under his son Parwiz along with several veteran generals. He later recalled Khan-Khanan, and appointed in his place his son Shah-Nawaz Khan. These two—Parwiz and Shah-Nawaz—brought the vigour of their youth into action and started all-round operations which continued for three or four years before a decision was reached.

On behalf of the Nizam Shah, Malik Ambar organized his armies to oppose the Mughals in the vicinity of Jalna. Along with his Muslim commanders he had under him "Jadu Rao, Babaji Kante, Bhosle, Udaram Brahman of Mahur and other nobles of the Maratha race". Profuse seduction was practised on both sides. Prince Parwiz and Shah-Nawaz Khan offered inducements to some of Nizamshahi commanders so that " Adam Khan Habshi, Yaqut Khan, Jadu Rao, Bābāji Kante and Udaram Brahman deserted their master and accepted the Mughal service." At last the battle was joined on 4th February 1616 at Roshangaon in a bend of the river Dudhna about 10 miles west of Jalna, when a crushing defeat was inflicted upon the troops led by Ambar.[4] Malik Ambar fled for life and saved himself by taking shelter in the impregnable fort of Daulatabad. Shah-Nawaz razed to the ground Malik Ambar's new capital Khadki and carried away enormous plunder to Burhanpur.

Shahzada Parwiz had already been recalled and even the success achieved by Shah-Nawaz Khan did not avail the Mughals much. For, as soon as the Mughal troops retired, Malik Ambar resumed his former game and soon recaptured all the territory that had been recently wrested from him. When the intelligence of this fresh advance on the part of Malik Ambar reached Jahangir, he reappointed Khan-Khanan as Governor of the Deccan and himself marched at once from Agra to Ajmere and thence despatched his third son Khurram with a large force against Malik Ambar. Khurram left Ajmere on 16 October 1616, and was joined at the ford of the Narmada by Khan-Khanan, Mahabat Khan, Khan Jahan and other renowned Mughal generals who were already working in the Deccan. In order to support this grand effort, the Emperor himself left Ajmere on 10th November 1616 and took up his residence at Mandu to be nearer the field of activities.

Khurram at once started vigorous action. He sent his envoys to Bijapur demanding help and co-operation from the Adil Shah. Malik Ambar and the Adil Shah had not now the heart to offer any opposition to this formidable advance of the Mughals. They both sent costly presents to the Prince and agreed without the least demur to deliver over Burhanpur, Aurangabad and Ahmadnagar. Malik Ambar per-

4. See Sir Jadunath's Malik Ambar, Ind. Hist. Quar., 1933-4. It is clear that Lukhji Jadhavrao deserted to the Mughals for the first time before the battle of Roshangaon; although he came back to his allegiance now and again, he continued his vacillating conduct to the last and thus came to be murdered in 1629. The Bhosle who fought for Malik Ambar at Roshangaon must have been Maloji.

sonally waited upon the Shahzada and delivered the keys of the various forts and the territory of Balaghat, *i.e.* the region of Berar. Khurram felt highly gratified with this easy victory for which he had not been required to fire a single shot or unsheath a single sword. Convinced that his task had been fully accomplished, he consigned the protection of the newly conquered territories to his two trusted generals Khan-Khanan and his son Shah-Nawaz Khan and returned in triumph to his father's presence at Mandu, (12 October 1617). Jahangir was so highly pleased with Khurram's quick performance and with the numerous costly presents he had brought with him, that he bestowed on him special honours and the grand title Shah Jahan, by which he came to be known thereafter. Khan Jahan Lodi, Udaram, and possibly Lukhji Jadhav and other officials from the Deccan came and paid their homage to the Emperor at Mandu. Convinced that the Deccan had been finally subjugated, the Emperor proceeded to Ahmedabad.[5]

But all this apparent victory was a hollow show adroitly got up by Malik Ambar. He immediately started his former aggression, this time with greater vigour than ever before. He first enlisted the support of both the Adil Shah and the Kutb Shah, explaining to them how it was essential in their own interest to form a confederacy against the common danger. They made vast preparations for a concerted plan to drive the Mughal forces back beyond the Narmada. In a short time they harassed the Mughal Governor Khan-Khanan at Burhanpur so severely that he sent piteous appeals to the Emperor for further provisions and help. Malik Ambar's advanced parties even crossed the Narmada and entered Malwa. An interval of nearly three years since Shah Jahan's achievement had wrought important changes in Jahangir's fortunes. Excesses had shattered his health. Serious plots were started at his court for seizing the imperial power. There was open jealousy on this account between Nur Jahan and Shah Jahan. The

5. The British Ambassador Sir Thomas Roe arrived at Agra in January 1616 and travelled with the Emperor to Ajmere, Mandu and Ahmedabad. He left for England in August 1618. He has recorded some graphic details of the Mughal Court pertaining to this period and the Emperor's efforts to conquer the Deccan.

Emperor lost all his former vigour and nerve and became unfit to control his affairs. His only answer to Khan-Khanan's piteous appeals was to once more request Shah Jahan to go to the Deccan and put down Malik Ambar's rebellion.[6]

Shah Jahan reached Burhanpur on 4th April 1621, at once pursued Malik Ambar with vigour and expedition and drove him back beyond the Godavari. The campaign was fought throughout the year. Malik Ambar finding himself unable to cope with the situation, once more made submission to the Prince and agreed to give up the territory that he had seized. This time Shah Jahan's attention was riveted more upon the political developments at his father's court than upon the conquest of the Deccan. He gave easy terms to Malik Ambar, retraced his steps in haste to Burhanpur, encompassed the end of his rival and brother Khusru, and left that place for the north on 24th March 1622. The next five years of Jahangir's life were full of convulsion, intrigue, and plots for power in which Nur Jahan and Shah Jahan were mainly involved. It is necessary for a student fully to grasp the intricacies of the situation of the Mughal Empire during these five years, at the end of which Jahangir died and Shah Jahan succeeded him. It is these intricacies that gave the Marathas their coveted chance.

4. **Shahji's marriage, Shivaji born**—This period of five years (1622-27) is full of stirring incidents and extreme unrest throughout India in which two great figures, Shah Jahan in the north and Shahji in the south, gradually emerge on the stage of history. Shah Jahan was born in 1592 and Shahji two years later on 15th March 1594. Their deaths similarly took place within a short interval of each other, in 1666 and 1664 respectively; the former lived for 74 years and the latter 70. They opposed each other in the Deccan for some eight years (1628—1636), when Shah Jahan came down in pursuit of Khan Jahan Lodi and with the intention of finishing the Kingdom of Ahmadnagar, which Shahji did his best to save with all his skill. Shah Jahan's career is well-known to history,

6. The student should note the intrigues at the Imperial court at this time and Shah Jahan's fears about his brother Khusru.

but as Shahji's is obscure, it is necessary to give first a few facts of his ancestry and domestic history, which are also connected with the life of Shivaji.

It has already been mentioned that Lukhji Jadhavrao, a descendant of the Yadav kings of Deogiri, was a powerful noble, holding lands and high military commands under the Nizamshahi rulers. The Bhosles were also a large family, comparatively poorer, possessing only a few villages in Patilship between Daulatabad and Poona. Tradition says that Māloji Bhosle took service under Lukhji Jadhav and used to stand guard at the gate of his palace. Once during the spring festival (*holi*) Jadhavrao invited Māloji and other subordinates for the usual ceremony of playing with red powder and dye. Māloji took with him his little son Shahji to the assemblage. Lukhji Jadhav had a daughter named Jija Bai, of nearly the same age as Shahji and seated her by his side. When during the ceremony the guests began to work the dye-syringes, the two children also amused themselves in the pastime. The comic sight impelled Jadhavrao to utter a casual remark, "How now, would not these two form a handsome pair?" Maloji heard the words, and at once in a loud voice called upon the assembly to bear witness that Jadhavrao had publicly betrothed his daughter to Shahji. Jadhavrao vehemently repudiated the construction put upon the words uttered in jest, and considered Maloji's position too far below his own to warrant a family connection between master and servant. Thus a quarrel began between these two families, and Māloji quitted Jadhavrao's service to seek his fortune elsewhere, so as to rise to a position in which he could demand Jadhavrao's daughter in marriage for his son. He soon managed to amass some wealth and enhance his reputation, so as to figure prominently in higher circles. He repaired the old dilapidated temple of Ghrishneshwar at Verul and built a large tank at the shrine of Shambhu Mahadev near Satara and thus removed the scarcity of water at the place from which the large crowds of pilgrims had so severely suffered. Māloji was doubtless a man of resourceful and independent spirit.[7] He succeeded in

7. Highly eulogistic accounts appear to have been recorded in Sanskrit about the exploits of Māloji and Shahji, after Shivaji's reputation

winning over the Nizam Shah probably through Malik Ambar, to sanction the match which Jadhavrao had spurned at. The Sultan of Ahmadnagar recognized the worth of Maloji's services in the struggle against the Mughal Emperor and bestowed on him a small jagir consisting of the districts of Poona and Supa, so that he became more of a peer to Jadhavrao. He then openly demanded the latter's daughter in marriage for his son and the ceremony took place at Sindkhed on 5th November 1605 (Margashirsha 5 of the bright half). Of this marriage was born Shivaji many years later.

The time of Shahji's marriage with Jija Bai coincided with the death of Akbar and the accession of Jahangir to the Mughal throne. The subsequent events connected with Jahangir's efforts to subjugate the Deccan have already been narrated. When Lukhji Jadhavrao deserted his master Nizam Shah and joined the Emperor's side, the loss was more than made up by Maloji's loyalty and attachment to Malik Ambar, whose methods of war and diplomacy proved for the Bhosles a veritable school of which the rising Shahji did not fail to take full advantage. Māloji died in 1620 and his mantle fell upon his son now 26 years old and worthy in every way. He soon became the right hand man of Malik Ambar.

Shahji's marriage with Jija Bai, however, did not prove a source of conjugal felicity. The desertion of Jija Bai's father to the Mughals only served to widen the gulf between the two families. Shahji later took a second wife from the Mohite family of Supa and Jija Bai came to be practically neglected by her husband. Parmananda, the author of *Shiva-Bharat*, says that Jija Bai bore six sons to Shahji of which only two Sambhāji and Shivāji grew up to manhood, the others dying in infancy.[8] Sambhaji is said to have been born in 1619 when Shahji was 25 years old.

had been fully established. Vide *Sanads and Letters*, pp. 211—215, and the unique Sanskrit composition known as Sambhaji's *dan-patra*. Paramananda follows in the same strain in his *Shiva-Bharat*.

8. तस्य तस्यामजायन्त पुत्राः षट् शुभदर्शनाः ।
तेषां मध्ये शंभुशिवौ द्वावेवान्वयवर्धनौ ॥

शि० भा० ८.२३.

When Māloji Bhosle died, his son Shahji inherited both his father's position and jagir. He had a younger brother, Sharifji, who was deeply attached to his person and cause. Together the two brothers pulled through weal and woe for many a long year.[9]. Maloji's brother Vithoji had eight sons, all strong and capable, who mostly followed Shahji's fortunes. Thus the large Bhosle family of young and energetic enthusiasts, possessing a spirit of valour and adventure and bent upon improving their fortune, proved a great national asset in the endeavours of Shahji to defend the Nizamshahi cause against Mughal aggression, particularly after the death of Malik Ambar.

5. **Battle of Bhatavadi.**—Shah Jahan, as has been already mentioned, left Burhanpur for the north in March 1622 and soon came to be involved in the war of succession which raged throughout India during the next five years and which threw into utter confusion the affairs of the Empire, thus supplying the welcome opportunity for Malik Ambar and Shahji to strengthen their position in the south. Shah Jahan turned a rebel and was vigorously pursued by Parwiz and Mahabat Khan. Lest Shah Jahan should join Malik Ambar and offer a formidable opposition, Jahangir directed Shahzada Parwiz to put down the combination. Malik Ambar accepted the challenge and resorting to his tactics of guerilla warfare managed to inflict a crushing defeat upon the combined force of the imperialists and the Adil Shah at the famous field of Bhatavdi, about ten miles east of Ahmadnagar. Graphic descriptions of this battle (date November 1624) are given by Paramanand and the Persian writers. The success was mainly due to Malik Ambar's superior tactics of long and patient manoeuvering for contriving an inescapable trap in which the Mughal and Bijapuri forces were caught. Thus this battle of Bhatavadi forms a landmark in the history of the Maratha rise, as Shahji's genius shone brilliantly on the occasion in support of Malik Ambar. He received the best lesson of his life in the art of overcoming a superior enemy through tactical methods. The full and

9. Their enmity towards the Jadhavs grew bitterer every day and resulted in many untoward scuffles of the type which Shakespeare has represented as occurring between the Montagues and the Capulets.

detailed description of this battle of Bhatavadi given by the author of the *Shiva-Bharat* deserves a careful study. Shahji was therein heartily supported by his brother Sharifji and by Vithoji's sons.[10]

This phenomenal success of Malik Ambar gave Shahji an importance and worth of which Malik Ambar soon became jealous. Relations between them became intolerable and Shahji to save his reputation quitted the service of the Nizam Shah and sought his fortune under the Adil Shah. This transfer appears to have taken place soon after the battle of Bhatavadi, some time in 1625. Shahji, however, retained his hold on his jagir of Poona, which was situated on the border-lands of the two kingdoms and proved a fruitful source of contention between them. Soon after Shahji's going into the service of Bijapur his second wife, Tukabai in 1630 gave birth to a son, named Ekoji, or Vyankoji in the popular language, who later founded the Maratha kingdom of Tanjore.

While Shahji was away at Bijapur, Malik Ambar died on 14th May 1626, with the result that the fortunes of Ahmadnagar began thereafter rapidly to decline. Its end was hastened by two other events of political importance, the death of the Emperor Jahangir on 29th October 1627 and the accession to power of his ablest son Shah Jahan on 4th February 1628. Ibrahim Adil Shah of Bijapur who had patronized Shahji at his court also died on 12th September 1627. Another event of equal importance to Maratha history was the birth of a son to Jija Bai and Shahji on 6th April 1627,[11] who was named Shivaji and who later founded the Maratha independence. The year 1627 is thus a turning point in the history of the Deccan. During that year Prince Shah Jahan, then a rebel against his father, lay in concealment in the vicinity of Junnar while his family was kept in hiding in the fort of Asheri near the port of Mahim on the west coast. It was only when he heard

10. About 20 names of Muslim generals and of more than a dozen Maratha captains are given by Parmanand in *Sh. Bh.* chap. 4 and most of the former are also mentioned by Fazuni Astarabadi. These two independent Persian and Sanskrit authorities confirming each other, enhance the value of the *Shiva-Bharat* as a work based on authentic sources.

11. Jedhe gives Shivaji's birth-date as 19th February 1630.

of his father's death in the Punjab that Shah Jahan left Junnar for the north, and secured the Mughal throne for himself, blinding his rival Shahryar.

6. **The rebellion of Khan Jahan Lodi.**— This Mughal grandee of first-rate eminence and power, became the immediate cause of a sudden turn in the politics of the Deccan. Khan Jahan was an able Afghan general and diplomat to whom Jahangir had entrusted the government of the Deccan. During Shah Jahan's rebellion, Lodi's position became delicate between the two powerful factions at the court. As governor of the Deccan he received conflicting orders and executed what he considered best. He was commanded to hunt out Shah Jahan from the Deccan ; but he was not sure of getting from the Emperor the timely support he needed for that purpose. He thus came to incur the bitterest displeasure of Shah Jahan and prepared for the evil day by appeasing the authorities of the Nizamshahi government. Hence much of Shah Jahan's achievement in the conquest of the Deccan now came to be nullified by Khan Jahan. Shah Jahan did not forgive Khan Jahan for having failed to support his cause, and made it his first concern after securing the throne to punish him severely for his sins of commission and omission.

At the beginning of his reign Shah Jahan was full of vigour and activity, and not the luxury-loving pacific monarch he developed into in his later years. During his father's regime he had repeatedly distinguished himself in his expeditions to the Deccan, the circumstances and situation of which he had thoroughly grasped. He well knew the policy of Malik Ambar and the power and influence of Shahji and the other Bhosles. He was personally acquainted with the geographical formation of the districts of Nasik, Junnar and north Konkan and the declining condition of the Kingdom of Ahmadnagar. The first subject that attracted his attention after his coronanation, was the subjugation of the Deccan, particularly the Nizamshahi state which had so long dragged on a precarious existence and which had successfully defied the might of both Akbar and Jahangir for a quarter of a century. Shah Jahan rightly judged that the troubles of the Deccan were the creation of Khan Jahan Lodi's mischievous policy and set himself to right them. It is this Mughal expansion in the south which first Shahji and later his son Shivaji undertook to resist. Shah Jahan, however, took nine years to accomplish the conquest of Ahmadnagar, contrary to his expectation of a short campaign.

When Shahzada Parviz who held the viceroyalty of Mughal Deccan, died in October 1626, Khan Jahan Lodi was appointed to that office, and he had under him an intrepid Afghan comrade, named Darya Khan. Khan Jahan had for some time felt it difficult to hold his position in the Deccan, as he was not supported from the headquarters during the last days of Jahangir, and found it expedient to appease the Nizamshahi authorities by ceding some of the conquered territories in order to avoid an open conflict for which he was not prepared. He restored the portion of Berar known as Balaghat to the Nizam Shah, receiving a cash payment of three lacs in return. This was the territory which Shah Jahan had himself conquered some years before from Malik Ambar.

When Shah Jahan came to the throne he confirmed Khan Jahan Lodi in his post and commanded him to take back the territory of Balaghat. This the Khan did not do his best to effect, and Shah Jahan called him to his presence to explain his conduct. During the visit the Khan conducted himself rather insolently, and fearing some severe punishment fled away to save his life. He was hotly pursued and having lost two sons and a son-in-law in an action on the river Chambal, he broke out in open revolt and sought protection with Murtaza Nizam Shah in the Deccan. The latter welcomed this powerful Mughal noble as a providential contrivance to save himself from the Mughal conqueror, gave him all the help he could afford and assigned him the district of Bid for his expenses. About this time the Nizam Shah kept his minister Fathkhan in confinement, called back Shahji from Bijapur to his service, and prepared for a stiff contest with the Emperor. He did not realize that the time of confusion and vacillation in the imperial council had ended with the last days of Jahangir, and that a new, strong and inflexible opponent was now on the throne of Delhi.

7. **Shah Jahan's march against Nizam Shah.**—Shah Jahan immediately realized the danger and personally undertook a strong offensive against the ruler of Ahmadnagar. He left Agra on 3rd December 1629 and after crossing the Narmada on the 12th February following, arranged his forces in separate divisions under able commanders and started a vigorous offensive with the double purpose of putting down Khan Jahan Lodi and subjugating the Kingdom of Ahmadnagar. He similarly threatened Adil Shah and obtained powerful armed aid from his state to co-operate with him. These Bijapuri contingents were commanded by Ranadulla Khan and Kanhoji Jedhe, Maratha Deshmukh of Kari. Against these formidable opponents on all sides, Khan Jahan Lodi and Shahji Bhosle could not hold out long. We are not here concerned with the fate of Khan Jahan. In the closing months of 1630 defeats were inflicted upon him. His stronghold of Bid was captured and the rebel with his helpmate Darya Khan became fugitive. They turned again to the north. An action took place near Sironj on 11th January 1631 in which Darya Khan was killed. Five months later, on 10th June, Khan Jahan too was killed near Kalinjar after fighting valiantly to save himself.

The history of the Jadhavs and the Bhosles is interrelated with the measures which Shah Jahan took in this southern invasion, which for various reasons did not promise him easy or early success. During the two years 1630-31 a terrible famine ravaged the southern lands. The monsoon failed for two successive years and no crop could be reared. The descriptions of this famine form a heart-rending story.[12] No road was safe and masses of hungry beggars fell upon the stocks of food-provisions meant for the Mughal army. So Shah Jahan found his task most difficult to accomplish. He, however, did his best to prosecute the war. He particularly started underhand intrigues in the councils of the Nizam Shah. Lukhji Jadhav had long ago deserted to the Mughals with all his family and troops. He was a powerful and trained

12. Elliot & Dowson, Vol. 7, p. 24 ; *Shiva Bharat* 8.53-55 ; Moreland. "From Akbar to Aurangzeb", p. 212 ; Thompson and Garratt, *Rise and Fulfilment*, p. 18.

captain, and now backed by the support of the Emperor, he proved to the Nizam Shah a perpetual thorn in his side acting from his seat at Sindkhed. Under the pretext of negotiating some important political move, the Nizam Shah called the whole brood of the Jadhav Captains for an interview in the fort of Daulatabad on 25th July 1629, and murdered most of them in cold blood. Shahji's father-in-law Lukhji, his sons Achloji and Raghuji and grandson Yashwantrao lost their lives in this unexpected treachery. Lukhji's brother Jagdevrao and son Bahadurji alone escaped to Sindhkhed. These wanton murders created a feeling of revulsion and disgust against the Nizam Shah, particularly among his Maratha followers; and even Shahji found his life unsafe. He had already received tempting calls from the Emperor to desert the Nizam Shah and go over to the Mughals. He thought it prudent, therefore, under the pressure of circumstances, to give up the rapidly declining fortunes of the Nizam Shah, and accepted a *Mansab* under Shah Jahan. For about a year and a half, from November 1630 to March 1632, Shahji served the Mughal cause. For this desertion the Bijapuri general Murar Jagdev burnt his residence at Poona.

In the meantime the murder of the Jadhavs proved disastrous to the Nizam Shah's cause. He restored to power his former minister Fath Khan; but the latter finding no escape out of the hopeless situation and hard-pressed by the imperialists, determined to seek his own selfish ends by sacrificing his master. He first put Murtaza Shah under confinement, placed his infant son Husain Shah on the throne, and conducted negotiations for his own submission to the Emperor. Soon after in March 1631, Murtaza Nizam Shah, who had so long suffered the agonies of varying fortune, came to be murdered. Fath Khan unable to hold out against the Emperor any longer, made his submission to him.

At this time Shah Jahan from his headquarters at Burhanpur while directing the various operations for prosecuting the war, had to suffer a domestic bereavement. His favourite queen Mumtaz Mahal who was with him, died at Burhanpur during child-birth on 7 June 1631 and her dead body was taken to Agra a few months later to be finally deposited in the famous

Taj Mahal. This personal loss and the prevailing famine caused to the Emperor a severe depression of spirits, and leaving the conduct of the campaign to his able general Mahabat Khan he returned to Agra in November 1632.

8. **Shahji's bold stand.**—As soon as Shah Jahan left for the north, Shahji found his position with the Mughals untenable. He deserted the Mughal cause and returned to the side of the Nizam Shah, determined to make one more heroic effort to resuscitate the falling fortune of that state under which he and his family had so long thrived. Mahabat Khan, however, won over Fath Khan and captured the fort of Daulatabad on 7 June 1633. Fath Khan and his master Husain Nizam Shah were secured and despatched to a Mughal prison.

But the fall of Daulatabad did not prove the end of the Nizamshahi State. At this critical moment Shahji stepped in boldly to maintain its existence. For him indeed it was a dangerous enterprise, to reconstruct an all but extinguished state and carry on a war unaided against the Emperor's might. Within only three months of the fall of Daulatabad Shahji selected Pemgiri or Bhimgad, a strong inaccessible fort of Ahmadnagar as the capital of the Nizamshahi State, placed there a young Nizamshahi prince on the throne (September 1633) and in his name carried on the administration as before. In this adventure Shahji managed to enlist the sympathies of the Adil Shah and his minister Murar Jagdev, who personally came to his help with fresh and well equipped armies. That a small Jagirdar like Shahji should dare to throw down an open challenge to Shah Jahan and invite his wrath upon his head, shows how self-confident and resourceful Shahji must have been. He quickly collected men and money and made preparations for a stubborn fight. Murar Jagdev joined him from Bijapur as is evidenced by the incident of Shahji contriving to weigh an elephant for a propitiatory rite which Murar Jagdev performed at the junction of the Bhima and the Indrayani on the occasion of a solar eclipse on 23 September 1633, when this Brahmin Vazir of Bijapur distributed in charity articles equal in weight to that of the elephant. In memory of this occurrence the village Nagargaon was renamed Tulāpur (the town of weighing), a name which it still bears.

In the hazardous step which Shahji had now taken, the training he had received under Malik Ambar in guerilla warfare, proved of immense advantage.

Mahabat Khan was extremely disturbed by this fresh move of Shahji. He had fondly believed that his task was over and that the credit of subjugating the Deccan was finally his. Shahji's bold stand embarrassed him so severely that he sent repeated requests to the Emperor for fresh troops and funds, and at the same time sent agents to Bijapur calling upon the Adil Shah to withdraw his help from Shahji. But Mahabat Khan did not succeed and was so cruelly rebuked by the Emperor that the veteran general, unable to bear the situation put an end to his life on 26 October 1634. Says Ranade :—

"The conditions of Ala-u-Din's invasion of 1316 were repeating themselves after three hundred years with a momentum which made resistance hopeless. The Hindus had then yielded to the avalanche which swept over the land. They had, however, learned wisdom under the hard discipline of subjection to foreign masters. They had been able to turn the edge of foreign conquest and even succeeded in taming the violence of the foreigners."[13]

But the task of Shahji was by no means easy. He soon found himself very hard-pressed in all directions. Some time before this, the Mughals, according to one tradition, succeeded in capturing Shahji's wife Jija Bai, but she cleverly managed to save the young Shivaji from capture by concealing him in an out of the way place when she received a secret warning that Mahaldar Khan the Mughal guardian of fort Trimbak, was on her track. This Khan was formerly an intimate friend of Shahji and his family, but now a servant of the Mughals. Jija Bai is said to have fallen into Mahaldar Khan's hands and remained confined for a time at the fort of Kondhana (Sinhgad) and was later released on payment of a ransom by her uncle. The details of this incident are nowhere fully recorded, but have been referred to by Grant Duff on the authority of an authentic paper which he had secured but which is now missing. This must have taken place before 1636.

13. *Rise of the Maratha Power*, pp. 43-44.

It has also been recorded that Shahji, when hard-pressed applied to the Portuguese Governor of Chaul (Revdanda) seeking shelter for his womenfolk and children there, in order to prevent them from falling into the hands of the Mughals. The Portuguese, however, had been recently so severely handled by Shah Jahan that they pleaded their inability to comply with Shahji's request, but suggested they could obtain for his family a safe retreat under the jurisdiction of the Siddis of Janjira. Any way these stray notices disclose how Shahji was situated in his life and death struggle.

Shah Jahan was fully roused to this new danger, and once more exhibited phenomenal activity by himself marching rapidly to the Deccan in 1635. He left Agra on 29th September, crossed the Narmada on 4th January 1636 and quickly reached Daulatabad. At this time he had with him his son Aurangzeb, now seventeen years old, Mirza Raja Jayasinh, Shaista Khan and other young and active generals, who later on figured so prominently during Shivaji's days. Immediately on his arrival Shah Jahan devised a consummate plan of operation for closing upon Shahji simultaneously from all directions, for which he assigned definite tasks to his various commanders. Aurangzeb at the centre was personally entrusted with the general execution of the measures determined upon. The Sultans of Bijapur and Golkonda were forced into cooperation with the Mughals under a threat of complete extinction.

Shahji had collected under him about 12,000 troops, mostly men disbanded after the fall of Daulatabad, and he now started raiding the Mughal territory as far south as Bedar and concentrated his main activity in the difficult regions of the north Konkan, himself moving between Junnar and Sangamner, with fort Mahuli as the headquarters of the puppet Nizam Shah. Shaista Khan captured fort Trimbak from Shahji and hunted him through Junnar and Sangamner as well. In his extremity Shahji placed the Nizam Shah in fort Mahuli, a few miles north of Kalyan, and began his last effort. The Bijapuris finding further resistance hopeless, accepted the terms that were offered to them by the Mughals and deserted Shahji. The Kutb Shahi court of Golkonda also was similarly coerced into submission, so that within a few months Shahji alone had to bear the whole brunt of this relentless war. Shah Jahan had won the greatest triumph of his life. After forty years of strife, the affairs of the Deccan came at last to be settled. The position of the Emperor was asserted throughout the land beyond challenge. On 6 May 1636 Shah Jahan sent to Adil Shah a solemn letter impressed with the vermillion impression of his palm, promising observance of the terms agreed upon, with an appeal to God and to the Prophet to be witnesses. An abstract of the treaty was engraved on a gold plate and delivered to Adil Shah.

This treaty sealed Shahji's fate. He came to be severely excluded, cut off from the outer world and hemmed in at fort Mahuli. He could not now hold out against the full might of the Emperor. Muhammad Adil Shah well knew the worth of Shahji and tried his best to save him from utter ruin. He sent a gentle hint to the Emperor that the latter's presence was no longer necessary in the Deccan, that the peaceful avocations of the people suffered from the constant movements of large armies ; that Shahji alone was no longer of sufficient consequence to detain the Emperor for the supervision of further operations and that Adil Shah undertook the responsibility of taking away from Shahji the five forts which he still held. Shah Jahan in his wisdom accepted this sound advice and after entrusting the remaining campaign to his general Khan Zaman, his son Aurangzeb and the Adil Shah, himself left Daulatabad on 11 July 1636 for Agra, after finishing the conquest of the Ahmadnagar kingdom. There now remained the two vassal kingdoms of Bijapur and Golkonda which dragged on their precarious existence for some fifty years more.

Within three months of the departure of Shah Jahan Shahji came to his last gasp. Ausa and Udgir which he had held were soon reduced. Khan Zaman joined by the Bijapuri troops under Ranadulla Khan and his lieutenant Kanhoji Jedhe, marched upon Junnar and a detachment arrived before Poona to seize Shahji's home. Shahji fled to the mountains of Kondhana and Torna, which the Mughals found it impossible to approach owing to the heavy rains that had started. As soon as the rains ceased, he was hunted out and finally resorted to fort Mahuli, which was difficult of access from outside. The Mughals soon arrived and sat down before the gates of that fort in August 1636, stopping all ingress and egress. Says the Jedhe Karina, "The fort of Pemgiri was too small, so Shahji removed the Sultan to Mahuli which was quickly invested by Khan Zaman and Ranadulla Khan. At this time Kanhoji Jedhe Ranadulla Khan's adviser kept secret communication with Shahji. When the provisions on the fort were exhausted, Shahji's men began to starve and he was compelled to seek terms. In October he offered through Ranadulla Khan to hand over the fort and the puppet Nizam Shahi prince on a promise that Shahji should agree to serve Bijapur and that in the Nizam-Shahi territory south of the river Godavari, which had fallen to the sphere of Bijapur, a jagir should be given to Shahji in payment of his services. This was reported to Bijapur and a written promise to that effect was received. The terms having been agreed to on both sides, Shahji handed over the fort of Mahuli to the Mughals and was honourably received by Ranadulla Khan in a personal meeting. Thereupon Shahji had a long cordial talk with Kanhoji Jedhe and his principal agent Dadaji Krishna Lohkare. Shahji said to Kanhoji, "You are a powerful Deshmukh of Maval; and I have secured this territory as my jagir. So you must help me in establishing my control thereon." Kanhoji replied, "I will serve you with all my heart if you obtain Ranadulla Khan's permission to this transfer of service." This was agreed to and Shahji left for Bijapur and entered the service of that state. Kanhoji Jedhe thereafter remained Shahji's helpmate. Shahji himself writes, "When I quitted Mahuli and hurried to Bijapur within the space of 20 days along with Ranadulla Khan, the Shah of Bijapur conferred on me a jagir of four lacs and commissioned me for the conquest of the Karnatak."[14]

It thus becomes clear how Shahji made the best of a bad bargain. By boldly standing forth to oppose the Mughal Emperor, he served the cause of the Deccan sultanates and earned their respect and goodwill as a champion of their liberties. Ranadulla Khan, the Adil Shah's favourite general exert-

14. Shivaji Souvenir, pp. 115-6; Jedhe Karina in Shiva Charitra-Pradip, p. 39.

ing great influence in his counsels, became Shahji's supporter and intimate friend. Kanhoji Jedhe, the Deshmukh of Kari, who was indispensable to Bijapur in keeping order in the western lands, did his utmost through Ranadulla Khan to shield Shahji from the Mughal wrath. The Adil Shah undertook the responsibility of seeing that Shahji created no mischief again in the Maval regions, from which Shah Jahan had finally expelled him. This clearly proves in what high estimation both Shah Jahan and the Adil Shah held Shahji. Thus the war that had devastated the land for nearly nine years came to a close in October 1636. Shah Jahan had no personal grudge against Shahji and wisely accepted the Adil Shah's guarantee for his good conduct. Shahji, however, cleverly managed to retain possession of his Jagir of Poona and left his wife Jija Bai and her guardian Dadaji Konddev to manage it on his behalf, himself being debarred from residing in it. The child Shivaji thus became a personal witness of these momentous events.

9. **Moral of the two figures.**—The courage and foresight with which Shahji defied the Mughal power for at least three years, dodging and deluding renowned Mughal generals, became a living example to his son Shivaji, teaching him how the weak could wear out the strong. Day in and day out during that long period, we can imagine, how the stirring incidents must have beeen narrated from mouth to mouth, how anxiously and breathlessly Jija Bai and the whole household with their numerous devoted followers must have awaited momentary news of every passing occurrence and how deeply they must have thought of their fate. Shahji's Court poet Jayaram Pandit has rightly hit upon the inner meaning of this great war by comparing Shahji and Shah Jahan together in the following Hindi[15] lines :—

15. जगदीश विरंञ्चिकु पुछत है कहो शिष्ट रची रखे कोन कहां।
कर जोरि कही जयराम विरंच्ये तिरलोक जहां के तहां॥
ससि वो रवि पूरब पश्चिम लों तुम सोय रहो सिरसिंधु महा।
अरु उत्तर दछन रछन को इत साहजु है उत साहिजहां॥
रा० मा० वि० चंपू—पृष्ठ २८०

The God Vishnu asks the Creator,—

" I am glad you have executed my commands and created the universe ; but I should like to know what provision you have made for its protection:"

The God Brahma replies:—

" Yes, I have taken measures for this purpose also, by appointing the Sun and the Moon to look after the concerns of the East and the West. Don't be anxious, pray, but go to sleep at ease in the milk-ocean."

Vishnu—" Yes, but what about the South and the North ? "

Brahma—" That too has been provided for. Raja Shahji is looking after the South and the Emperor Shah Jahan the North."

Just as Shivaji and Aurangzeb complement each other's history, so exactly do their fathers too, who were close contemporaries and who in their own way served their respective national interests. If history is no accident and has a sound basis in cause and effect, the twenty years period from Roshangaon to Mahuli, 1616-1636, establishes an unforgettable contact of these two personages, the one an Emperor and the other a King-maker, a contact which the difference in their worldly fortunes cannot affect.

CHRONOLOGY

CHAPTER III

1635	Shahji obtains a military commission from Adil Shah.
1635 — 1642	Venkatapati II rules at Penukonda.
1642 — 1673	Shriranga Rai III, the last of the Vijayanagar Emperors.
1636 Oct.	Shahji joins Bijapur service.
1637 Dec. 3	Randaula Khan and Shahji destroy Ikkeri.
1638 — 1640	Shira and the Western Karnatak reduced. Shahji establishes himself at Bangalore.
1640	Shivaji married to Sai Bai.
1640 — 1642	Shivaji's visit to his father at Bangalore.
1643	Death of Randaula Khan. Shahji and Shivaji visit Bijapur.
1644 August 1	Shahji in disgrace.
1645	Mustafa Khan captures Vellore.
1646 June 5	Mustafa Khan marches against Shrirang Rai.
1648 July 25	Shahji arrested at Jinji.
1648 Nov. 9	Mustafa Khan dies.
1648 Dec. 28	Jinji captured by Bijapur forces.
1649	Shahji confined at Bijapur.
1649 May 16	Shahji obtains release.
1651	Shahji at Kanakgiri.
1654	Shahji's son Sambhaji killed at Kanakgiri.
1656 Nov. 4	Muhammad Adil Shah dies.
1658 May 26	Shahji absolved from collusion with his son.
1662	Shahji visits Mahārāshtra, advises Shivaji to build Raigad.
1663 April	Adil Shah marches to Bankapur.
1664 Jan. 23	Death of Shahji near Basavapattan.

CHAPTER III

SHAHJI'S LATER CAREER.

(1636-1664.)

1. Shahji's work in Karnatak. 3. Shahji under disfavour.
2. Shahji possesses Bangalore. 4. Shahji's two sons in action.
5. Shahji's death.

1. Shahji's work in the Karnatak—About the entry of Shahji into the Bijapur service, the six-articled chronology remarks, "During Shak 1557 (1635), Shahji Raje obtained from the Adil Shah a command of twelve thousand horse with the provision of land for his expenses. This land included the Poona country, the management of which was entrusted by him to Dādāji Kondadev of Malthan. He made Poona the seat of his rule and started operations by drawing a good plough through the land, (in order to remove the evil effects of the plough drawn by asses a few years before under the orders of Murar Jagdev). Dādāji brought in cultivators to settle on the land and made it rent-free for the first five years. Shahji Raje left for Bijapur."[1] Shahji's later career is thus concerned with the affairs of the Karnatak.

The increasing Mughal pressure from the north awakened the rulers of Bijapur and Golkonda to the dangers into which they were likely to be thrown in the future and induced them to compensate themselves for their territorial losses by carrying out fresh expansions in the south. With this object the two States entered into a mutual compact for the conquest of the Karnatak in co-operation, the western portions going to Bijapur and the eastern ones to Golkonda. These southern regions formerly belonged to the great Empire of Vijaynagar which had been grievously humbled by the Muslim Powers

1. Shiv Ch. Pradip p. 70.

on the famous battle-field of Talikot or Rakshas Tagdi. After that decisive battle the victors plundered and burnt the great Hindu capital and within a couple of years thereafter it came to be practically deserted. The conquerors, however, made no headway beyond, nor did they actually bring under their control the vast peninsular lands from the west to the east coast. They returned to their capitals after plundering and devastating the Hindu capital. Hence those territories continued to be ruled by the various provincial branches of the old Vijaynagar government, mostly relatives of the royal and ministerial families, who established their independent rule at different places and carried out unceasing warfare at the expense of each other. It is not necessary for our purpose to detail the narrative of these political transactions.

The power and culture of the vast Vijaynagar dominions thus came to be preserved after Talikot by these various provincial members, who established their principalities at Penukonda, Vellore, Chandragiri, Shira, Ikkeri, Jinji, and other places. Their wealth and prosperity as well as their internal animosities excited the greed of the Muslim Courts of Bijapur and Golkonda. Muhammad Adil Shah, unlike his predecessor Ibrahim, was a fanatic in religious matters and being desirous of pulling down the Hindu temples and plundering their wealth for the glory of Islam, he despatched a strong expedition for the conquest of the Karnatak under his commander-in-chief Randaula Khan with Shahji under him. Muhammad Shah was guided in this policy by an equally fanatical minister Mustafa Khan, at whose instigation the famous Murar Jagdev had been murdered shortly before.

The survivors of the ruling family of Vijaynagar after the fall of their capital removed to Penukonda, where ruled in succession

1 Tirumal, the First, 1565—1583 ;
2 Srirang Rai, the Second, 1585—1595 ;
3 Venkatapati, the First, 1595—1614 ;
4 Ram Rai, 1614—1635 ;
5 Venkatapati, the Second, 1635—1642 ;
6 Srirang Rai, the Third, 1642—1673.

This last Venkatapati and his son Srirang Rai (the Third), happened to be the rulers when Shahji and Randaula Khan started on their expedition of conquest. Venkatapati and his son in vain tried to organize and unite the various provincial governors, now styled Nayaks, in order to make a bold stand against the Muslim forces. But none saw the wisdom of such a course. Some of them actually sought Muslim aid from Bijapur to adjust their internal disputes. At the time of Shahji's invasion Virabhadra Nayak ruled at Ikkeri, a decayed town now known as Sagar (Mysore State, Shimoga District) ; Keng Nayak ruled over Kongu near Coimbatore, Jagdev Rai at Kaveripattan, Kanthi Rav Naras Wodiyar at Shrirangapattan, Vijay Raghav at Tanjore, Tirumal Nayak at Madura, and Venkata Nayak at Jinji. These were the main chiefs who came in for a share in the misfortunes to which this Muslim expedition exposed the Karnatak. The time was quite opportune for a bold valiant Hindu leader appearing on the scene and organizing a united opposition ; but such a course was reserved for Mahārāshtra, not for the Karnatak, where the Muslims dealt separately with each chief and effected their purpose.

Shahji under Randaula Khan's command took part in three successive expeditions into the western Karnatak between 1637 and 1640. They usually started from Bijapur after the rains and returned there before the next monsoon. Their avowed aim was to enhance the glory of Islam by putting down the Hindus, desecrating their temples, and bringing their hoarded wealth to Bijapur. In the first expedition they started in 1637 *via* Dharwar and Laksmeshvar and came straight upon Ikkeri, then a wealthy capital city ruled by Virabhadra Nayak, son of Bhadrappa Nayak. Before the huge armed forces of Bijapur the stone ramparts of Ikkeri could not long hold out. After less than two months of siege Virabhadra was humbled and compelled to seek terms for submission. Ikkeri was captured and razed to the ground on December 3rd, 1637. Virappa surrendered half his territory and paid a fine of 18 lacs of Hons and removed himself to Nagar, now called Bednur. The poor peaceful citizens of a once prosperous kingdom either lost their lives or their homes. In order to preserve their honour Hindu women killed themselves by jumping into wells with their children. The whole territory was similarly ravaged and subjugated. It was the first experience which the peaceful populace of the south had of the havoc fire-arms could inflict.

The second expedition, that of 1638, penetrated still further east and south. This time Randaula Khan had under him another stern commander Afzul Khan, in addition to Shahji. The former was deputed against Shira whose master Kasturirang Nayak after a short resistance made his submission upon receiving a solemn promise on sacred oaths that his life would be spared. When, however, the Nayak came for a personal conference, Afzul Khan put him to death in cold blood and took possession of the city and all its wealth, thus establishing a reputation for treachery and violation of solemn oaths, a sample which remained impressed upon Shivaji's memory when he refused to believe the Khan's plighted word and paid him back for his treachery at their celebrated interview below Pratapgad in 1659.

While Afzul Khan was occupied with Shira, Shahji proceeded against Bangalore and captured that fort from its keeper Kemp Gauda. He found this place convenient for holding the southern territories, and was permanently posted there by Randaula Khan with the sanction of the Adil Shah. Hereafter Shahji made Bangalore his principal station, with a governor's court and insignia almost approaching that of independent royalty. He soon reduced Kanthi Rav Naras Wodiyar of Shrirangapattan to obedience.

A similar success crowned Randaula Khan's third expedition (1639-40) when Basawapattan was captured after putting down its ruler Keng Nayak. Tumkur, Balapur, Vellore, and several other places were quickly reduced and Randaula Khan returned in great glory to Bijapur. The Sultan was so highly gratified with the Khan's success that he himself went out of the capital a long way to welcome him at the river Krishna and held grand celebrations at Bijapur to commemorate the unprecedented triumph of three years' continuous effort in which all the Hindu potentates of the south had been overcome, large cities conquered, and enormous wealth amounting to more than 4 crores of Hons or 16 crores of rupees brought into Bijapur. With this pile of money several grand edifices were erected in Bijapur, such as the Dad-Mahal, the Gol-Gombaz and others.[2]

2. **Shahji's possession of Bangalore.**—In those days of difficult communication between the centre and the outlying provinces, it is no wonder that the local governors assumed almost royal splendour and independence of action. Shahji thus established his position at Bangalore with the airs of a great chief, for which he had already proved his worth. He spent most of his time henceforth at Bangalore and occasionally held his court at Kolar and Balapur also. For the military and administrative work which he had to execute in a foreign land, he transplanted many Brahman and Maratha families from Mahārāshtra and trained them as hereditary officials loyal to his cause. He introduced Marathi as the Court language into the Karnatak regions, and along with it the Mahārāshtra system of revenue and accounts. He held an open Court, wherein he entertained musicians, poets, writers and saints. Thus in a short time a miniature Mahārāshtra arose in the midst of the Kannad and Tamil lands, the effects of which have survived to this day through three centuries of change. Although the actual conquest of Tanjore was left to be accomplished by Shahji's worthy son Ekoji in 1675, the necessary preparations were all completed during the twenty five years of the former's regime. Shahji, however, always remained loyal to Bijapur. He remitted regular contributions of money to the Adil Shah and was so careful and guarded in his official dealings that he gave no cause for suspicion or complaint. The people of these southern lands looked upon Shahji's rule as almost a providential continuation of the old Vijayanagar tradition carried on in its essential spirit by a Hindu leader. His loyalty, however, came to be suspected for a while owing to extraneous causes as will be explained later.

In the meantime two of Shahji's sons were growing up with him and breathing the prevalent atmosphere. The elder Sambhaji now about twenty years of age was directly working

2. Vide Sarkar's *House of Shivaji*, p. 27; Dr. Saletore's paper on the fall of Ikkeri, H. R. C. 1939; Govind Vaidya's Kanthi Rav Naras Charitra, half yearly Journal, Mysore Univ. 1930, etc.

under his father. His second wife's son Ekoji was now about ten and fast coming into his own. The third son Shivaji lived with his mother in Maharashtra and was slowly building up his character in the independent surroundings of the western hills, untrammelled by any regulations of service or of any superior commands, although nominally he too was answerable both to his father and to the Sultan of Bijapur. He received the best training then available under the care of a loving mother and a wise guardian, and grew up manly and self-reliant. In 1640 his mother got him married to a girl from the Nimbalkar family of Phaltan, named Saibai. In the art of government, however, his direct contact with the neighbouring people of the turbulent Mawals on the one hand and his intimate pupilage under the consummate Dādāji Kondadev on the other, gave him some very unique experience of a revolutionary character. He thus started his own organization, military, civil and revenue, which could not long be concealed from the public gaze. His precocious and wild enterprizes reached Shahji's ears through the latter's agents at Bijapur. Shahji thought it necessary to restrain him and keep him on the traditional path of service and strict obedience to their Muslim sovereign. So Shahji, acting either on his own initiative or under gentle hints from Bijapur, called Shivaji to his presence along with Jija Bai, Dadaji and their personal staff. That he had to see his newly wedded daughter-in-law was given out as the plausible excuse. Though the actual date of the visit is nowhere recorded, it may be presumed that for about two years between 1640 and 1643, the party was away from Poona, mostly at Bangalore and a short while at Bijapur on the way back. What happened during this long visit, how their mutual relations were adjusted, what particular points of policy were evolved, we can surmise only by reading between the lines of stray and scrappy notices occurring in the *bakhars* and in the writings of poets like Jayaram and Parmanand, which have to be co-ordinated with the Persian accounts of the Muslim writers as well. As conjecture and imagination can alone become one's guide in solving these hazy but important questions, there is bound to be ample room for difference of opinion.[3]

3. A statement in a Peshwa's *bakhar* deserves to be noted and runs

Jija Bai during this visit to Bangalore possibly could not find ease and comfort in the surroundings of her husband's residence and contrived to spend most of her time in pilgrimages to the numerous famous Hindu shrines in the south. The Adil Shah was curious to know how matters were developing and invited Shahji with his whole family to Bijapur some time about 1643. In the summer of this year Shahji's friend and patron Randaula Khan died with the result that Shahji was left without a supporter at the Court.

So, some time during 1643, Shahji with his whole family went to Bijapur, and during his absence from Bangalore a strong revulsion against Muslim rule started in the Karnatak. In 1642, Venkatapati the 2nd, died and his son Srirang Rai, the last unfortunate relic of the decadent Vijaynagar glory, came to the throne, organized his resources at Vellore and tried to recall the slipping power into his hands. Shivappa Nayak of Bednur and the other local Nayaks rose simultaneously to undo the effects of the Muslim conquest. Muhammad Shah was thus faced with a difficult situation and to save the fruits of past labour organized a fresh expedition to go to the Karnatak and to put down the rebel elements. He entrusted the command of this fresh expedition to the fanatic Mustafa Khan who had long suspected Shahji to be disloyal at heart, and who was bent upon teaching him a lesson. In order to support the expedition with all his might the Shah himself followed and took up his residence at Bankapur. In this way fresh troubles came about in the Karnatak and soon involved Shahji in them. The *Pharman* of 1st August 1644 says that Shahji had been disgraced.[4]

Shivappa Nayak offered a bold opposition to the Muslims at Ikkeri and Sagar, but in a bloody action which ensued he was completely overcome. Mustafa returned victorious to Bijapur after reducing western Karnatak to obedience. But the young Srirang Rai was fast making headway and unless he

thus :—"Shahji actively executed the wicked policy undertaken by the Muslims to uproot the Hindu religion and make the whole country full of Muslims. This move of Shahji was highly resented by the Gods and a new defender was created." Raj. Vol. 4.

4. Shiv Ch. Sahitya, IV, p. 21.

was crushed the Muslim possession of the Karnatak was not free from danger. In order to put him down, therefore, another expedition was fitted out jointly by the Shahs of Bijapur and Golkonda under Mustafa Khan, who proceeded straight against Srirang Rai, captured his seat of Vellore, and returned in glory in 1646. Shahji, it seems, was not present in this expedition but remained at Bangalore watching the course of events.

3. **Shahji under disfavour.**—Srirang Rai organized his resources and soon recaptured Vellore. The news reached Bijapur and made the Shah furious. Shahji's enemies did not omit to add fuel to the fire. The negotiations that were being carried on between Srirang Rai and Shahji were an open secret. Insinuations reached the Shah's ears accusing Shahji of disloyalty by supporting Srirang Rai. This was just the moment when Shivaji in the west had captured Sinhgad and practically asserted his independence in the district of Poona. This could not be, so the Shah concluded, without his father's complicity. But to bring a powerful chief like Shahji to obedience or even to express distrust towards him was not an easy task. The Shah, therefore, organized an expedition in 1646 against Srirang Rai, gave the command to Mustafa Khan with secret instructions to arrest Shahji if he was found remiss in his duty or intriguing with the enemy. Mustafa was accompanied by Afzul Khan, Rustum-i-Zaman, son of Randaula Khan, and other nobles. The expedition left Bijapur on 5th June 1646 and travelling *via* Gadag and Lakshmeshvar reached Basawapattan in October, when Shahji and Asad Khan joined the main army with their contingents along with some of the local Palegars. Like a deluge the swollen forces rolled upon Vellore, when Srirang Rai and the Nayaks of the south sent offers of submission pleading for life and safety. Mustafa Khan kept a close watch on Srirang Rai's movements. The latter implored Shahji to mediate. Shahji broached the subject of peace to the Khan and proposed terms. But Mustafa Khan was not in a mood to show regard to Shahji's mediation, and pretending an appearance of outward friendship, allowed Shahji a long rope. Matters, however, rapidly came to a head. Srirang Rai decided on an open fight. A sanguinary action ensued in which he was worsted and he fled away to save his

life. Vellore fell again into Mustafa Khan's hands. Shahji too was for the time being saved from an open rupture with the Commander-in-Chief. Mustafa Khan returned to Bijapur once more in triumph. Srirang Rai dragged on a humbled existence for a good long time thereafter.

A general report was made to the Adil Shah that Shahji was not loyal at heart but secretly supported the Hindu faction to the best of his ability. The Shah was convinced that the various Hindu Palegars looked up to Shahji for a lead and that if he was not checked in time, it would be impossible for the Muslims to hold their sway in those southern regions.[5]

A similar position was already developing in Mahārāshtra also, so that both Sinhgad and Bangalore became danger signals for the ruler of Bijapur.

After long and anxious deliberation, another expedition left Bijapur early in 1648 commanded by Mustafa Khan, and this time it came straight from Vellore upon Jinji, then the storm-centre of Hindu revolt. Mustafa Khan was joined by the famous Mir Jumla on behalf of the Kutb Shah. How this nobleman's ambition created fresh complications is a point a careful student of contemporary history must take note of. Shahji tried to work his way through the factious maze towards increasing his own importance and in an unguarded moment offered to quit the Bijapur service and accept one under the Kutb-Shah. Mustafa Khan this time was bent upon sternly weeding out the treasonable elements that he knew to be infesting his own camp, and thereby made himself odious even to some of those who were working under him, such as Asad Khan, Shahji and Rustum-i-Zaman. Mustafa Khan concluded that Shahji was the sole origin of the trouble and with great wariness tried to create proof of his guilt. The Bijapur armies were then occupied in the siege of Jinji, for which the duties were severally assigned. In this connection Mustafa Khan had a fracas with Shahji upon some point of honour. Shahji thereupon threatened to withdraw altogether with his troops, unless he was at once paid in cash for the expenses. Mustafa Khan resented this insubordination, but pretending cordiality, formed

5. See *Shiva Bharat* 9.28-44.

a secret plot to have him arrested. Baji Ghorpade of Mudhol, a vassal of Bijapur and notoriously antagonistic to Shahji, was instigated by Mustafa Khan to make a sudden dash upon Shahji's residence in the dark hours of early morning when Shahji, after nightlong revelries, was sound asleep. The raid succeeded and Shahji was arrested in his bed at Jinji on 25th July 1648 along with his trusted helpmate Kanhoji Jedhe. Mustafa reported the affair to the Shah at Bijapur and asked for further orders.

Muhammad Adil Shah was at this time bed-ridden, having been weakened by an attack of paralysis, and well realizing the consequences of alienating a powerful Maratha captain of Shahji's status, ordered Mustafa Khan to send Shahji at once to the Court and despatched his own sober and trusted minister Muhammad Khan to take charge of the situation before Jinji in preference to the irascible Mustafa. The Shah also deputed Afzul Khan to take charge of Shahji and bring him to Court. But before the Vazir arrived on the scene, Mustafa Khan had died on 9th November 1648. Muhammad Khan continued the siege and captured Jinji on 28th December following, from its defender Rupa Nayak. Jinji's immense wealth hoarded through seven centuries of continuous rule by Rupa Nayak's ancestors, was loaded on 89 strong elephants and the caravan wended its way slowly to Bijapur under Afzul Khan's vigilant eye, along with the captive Shahji. The party arrived at their destination during the following summer months. Next year the Bijapur forces raided and plundered Tanjore, Madura and other important places ; and the Vazir Muhammad Khan returned to the capital after having completed the conquest of the whole of the Karnatak except Bangalore. Srirang Rai, however, was not finally crushed. The general impression at the Shah's Court was that this conquest would not have taken so long had Shahji not interfered by shielding the Hindu princes.

Two danger spots, however, remained for the Adil Shah to overcome, before he could feel his conquests safe. Bangalore in the south and Sinhgad in Mahārāshtra were strongly held by the two sons of Shahji and Jija Bai. How to reduce these two places became the paramount question of the moment for the Adil Shah. This question involved the fate of Shahji now a captive, who had just reached Bijapur. How was he to be dealt with ?

As soon as Shahji's person was secured, one army was despatched from Jinji to take possession of Bangalore, and another from Bijapur to retake Sinhgad and the sister fort of Purandar, both strongly held by Shivaji. At both these places long and sanguinary actions took place in which the two sons of Shahji gave such an account of their valour and capacity,[6] that the Sultan was no longer in doubt as to what he was to look for, if rigorous measures were to be adopted against Shahji. The father, a self-made and capable chief had proved his mettle against the Mughal Emperor Shah Jahan ; and now he was further strengthened by his two sons of equal or greater worth. It was no easy task to reduce such a power ful chieftain.

4. **Shahji's two sons in action**.—When Shivaji at Poona learnt that his father was in trouble at Bijapur, he at once applied to Shahzada Murad Bakhsh, then the Emperor's representative in the Deccan. As exchange of envoys and discussions on the question of Shahji's release followed. Murad Bakhsh wrote to say that he was returning to Delhi and would send the Emperor's orders as soon as he reached that place. At Bijapur the question of Shahji's release was for two months under agitation. He was entrusted to the care of Khan Ahmad, the Sar-Lashkar, a man inclined to effect an amicable settlement and not to adopt extreme measures. On behalf of the Shah Khan Ahmad proposed to Shahji that he should surrender Sinhgad and Bangalore and continue to serve the State as before. Shahji agreed to the compromise adding that neither he nor his sons were hostile towards the Shah: they needed fields for honourable work in life and sufficient support from the Bijapur Court. If they secured these, they would always render loyal service. This basis for a final reconciliation was agreed upon. Shahji gave his own autograph letters to his two sons calling upon them to give up Sinhgad and Bangalore respec-

6. An eloquent and detailed description of the two actions may be read in the pages of Parmanand's *Shiva-Bharat*, Chapters 13 and 14.

tively to the Adil-Shahi officers, and thus save his life. These orders were forwarded to the two sons, and Shahji was honourably set at liberty on 16 May 1649 after a detention of nearly ten months. Along with Shahji, his comrade in arms Kanhoji Jedhe was also released. Shahji was reinstated in his former position and honours, and was employed at Bijapur for a few years. Thereafter he was again asked to proceed to the Karnatak to complete the conquest of Tanjore and other districts. As soon as he was set at liberty, he asked Kanhoji Jedhe to go and help Shivaji in his efforts to settle the Poona regions. The parting message of Shahji to Kanhoji runs thus:—

"You have on my account suffered hardships of imprisonment and dishonour. I have now agreed to undertake the completion of the Karnatak business, provided I am given the Bangalore province and its revenues of 5 lacs Hons. You own hereditary lands in the Mawals and wield influence in those parts. You should hereafter go to your home, serve Shivaji and reduce to obedience those Deshmukhs who are still holding out. If either the Mughals or the Adilshahi authorities send armed forces to chastise Shivaji, you should fight them out and remain faithful to Shivaji's interests."[7]

Shahji returned to the Karnatak again and spent several years in the Raichur Doab making Kanakgiri his headquarters, and promoting the endeavours of his two sons for bettering their fortunes. Ekoji remained at Bangalore and Sambhaji joined his father at Kanakgiri. Bijapur and Golkonda came to open war in 1651 over the division of the recent conquests of Jinji and this indirectly helped Shahji and his sons. Shahji on behalf of Bijapur fought against Mir Jumla of Golkonda. The latter was worsted and had to pay 9 lacs of Hons to Shahji as the cost of war. From 1653 onward Shahji alone became the principal support of the Adil-Shahi State in the southern regions.

Kanakgiri in the region of the dilapidated Vijayanagar was then a place of historical importance full of old traditions of the fallen Hindu Empire. Here resided Sambhaji with his

7. This explains Shivaji's stand against Morays. Jedhe Shakavali. This precious chronology came from the family of Kanhoji Jedhe of Kari.

father and shared his labours. Here they realized the contrast of the former glory and the present misfortunes of the Hindus under Muslim rule. Sambhaji too like his younger brother Shivaji possessed an ample spirit of resistance. He had for his support several members of the learned and valiant Hanumante family, headed by Naropant the father of two capable sons Janardan and Raghunath. These are known to have played an important part in Shivaji's history. Appa Khan the Palegar of Kanakgiri raised the standard of revolt, with which Shahji and Sambhaji found themselves unable to cope. So in 1654 the Adil Shah sent Afzul Khan to their support. During the encounter that ensued, Sambhaji was killed, as was supposed, through the deliberate neglect of Afzul Khan to reinforce Sambhaji at a critical moment. The mother Jija Bai at any rate felt severe grudge against this arrogant Bijapuri general and later urged Shivaji to pay him back fully in his own coin in the struggle of 1659.

Shahji, while fully sympathising with the plans and movements of his son Shivaji in carving out an independent principality for himself, was shrewd enough not to involve himself in his son's affairs and remained a loyal servant of Bijapur to the last. This attitude was facilitated by the death of Muhammad Adil Shah on 4 November 1656 and the murder of his faithful minister Khan Muhammad a year later. The intrigues that ensued for power at Bijapur after the Shah's death and the aggression started against that State by Shahzada Aurangzeb, visibly weakened the Adil-Shahi power and considerably facilitated Shivaji's moves. At this time Shahji seems to have felt extreme irritation against the Bijapuri authorities and conveyed to them a threat of resignation and retirement from their service.[8]

Matters, however, seem to have been amicably composed and Shahji continued to the last a loyal servant of Bijapur, notwithstanding frequent reports of the father and the son colluding against the State. On 26 May 1658 "Maharaj Farzand Shahji Bhosle was informed by Ali Adil Shah that the offences of his son Shivaji would not be laid upon him;

8. *Shivaji Souvenir*, p. 115; *House of Shivaji*, p. 87.

that he should keep his mind composed regarding all matters and that the grace and the favours which he had enjoyed till then would be continued in the same measure and even more. No change or deprivation in his ranks and fiefs would be made."

After 1658 Shahji and his son Ekoji tried hard to conquer Tanjore from its ruling chief, but a powerful combination was formed by the local Nayaks which kept Shahji out. After the murder of Afzul Khan in 1659, Shivaji's power rapidly increased, and the Court of Bijapur in their danger employed Shahji in bringing about a reconciliation with Shivaji. In this connection Shahji once more returned to Mahārāshtra, spent some time in his son Shivaji's company, personally inspected his territories and suggested measures for their consolidation. Jija Bai too had then the happiness to be restored to the affections of her husband.

Thus Shahji about the year 1662 was purposely employed by Ali Adil Shah to mediate a peace with Shivaji. The father urged Shivaji not to molest Bijapur any more, as after all the Adil Shah had been all along their bread-giver, upon whose salt they had thrived. Shivaji agreed to commit no wanton aggression thereafter against Bijapur but to form a confederacy of the Deccan Powers against their common enemy the Mughal Emperor. Shivaji agreed to the suggestion and promised not to make any deliberate move against Bijapur, provided no wanton provocation was given to him.[9] Later for strategic reasons Shivaji had to capture the important fort of Panhala from Adilshahi possession in March 1673.

This visit of Shahji to his old jagir, the seat of his early career, is memorable in several ways. The father and the son had been separated for more than twelve years in which Shivaji had earned a great name for himself. Like a devout son and religious enthusiast he showed his father the utmost veneration in the old prescribed style, meeting him in advance in a temple outside and walking bare-footed alongside his father's palanquin. They freely talked and deliberated upon the present situation and future prospects. Shahji certainly

9. Letters quoted in *Shivadigvijay*, p. 330.

had unique personal experience of Deccan warfare for forty years and was responsible for a vast amount of useful instruction which Shivaji received from him in the arts of war, diplomacy and government.

As regards the Mughals, Shahji could not advise Shivaji in a dogmatic manner, but as Poona and Kalyan were then (1663) in Mughal hands, the urgent question that faced both the father and the son was where to make a permanent seat of his kingdom, where safety could be fully assured and of which Shivaji could not be easily dispossessed, as had happened in the case of Poona. They together executed a long tour of inspection practically between forts Trimbak and Rangna or roughly between Nasik and Belgaum and after a careful examination of the various possible sites, they together selected the extensive plateau of Rairi near Mahad, for the capital of the future Maratha Kingdom. The hill thus approved, fortifications and the necessary buildings were soon completed during the next few years, and Raigad figured as the Maratha capital. The choice has been more than justified by subsequent history.

5. **Shahji's death.**—After a full and frank association for several months together, the father and the son parted early in 1663, after which Shivaji executed his blow against Shaesta Khan at Poona followed by the daring raid upon Surat, which supplied funds for the embellishment of Raigad. As Shivaji and Jija Bai took up their first residence on the Rairi plateau after the former's return from Surat, their joy was suddenly marred by Shahji's death near Basavapattan from an accident in riding. During April 1663 Ali Adil Shah marched against Bankapur and urgently called to his presence his two commanders Bahlolkhan and Shahji. They arrived and were both kept under arrest. Shahji was, however, released within two days and sent against the Nayak of Bednur who had rebelled.[10] After accomplishing his commission within a few months, he started for Bangalore. While halting at Basavapattan on the way he heard of some game in the vicinity and rode out for a hunt of which he was very fond. While following an antelope his

10. English Records on Shivaji No. 67 of 20 July, 1663

horse's foot got entangled in a hole, bringing down both the horse and the rider, the latter dying instantly. This happened on Saturday 23 January 1664 and the news reached Shivaji at Raigad. The pious Jija Bai was stunned by the blow and wanted to become a sati. We have only to imagine Shivaji's feelings at such a prospect. He made piteous appeals to her and the mother yielded, keeping him company for ten more years on earth.

Besides Sambhaji and Shivaji, the sons of Jija Bai, and Ekoji, the son of Tukabai, Shahji had four illegitimate sons, Bhivji, Pratapji, Santaji and Raibhanji. Sambhaji who was killed at Kanakgiri left two sons, Surat-Singh and Umaji, descendants of both of whom survived long afterwards.

Shahji is rightly considered as the creator of Maratha culture and influence in the south. He transplanted many Mahārāshtrian families, of the Brahman, Maratha, and artizan classes whose descendants are still found in those parts. It was Shahji who fully demonstrated the possibility of weak peoples standing boldly against strong oppressors if they but unite and organize themselves. Clive and Dupleix are said to have discovered the secret of Indian conquest by a few organized regiments on the western model ; but a similar weapon of guerilla warfare was first developed a hundred years before them by Shahji himself. He became a king-maker in fact, and can in a full measure be called the real inspirer of Shivaji in creating the Maratha Swarajya. Shahji certainly imbibed the tradition and culture of Vijayanagar and transmitted them through his many-sided activities to the worthy representatives of his nation. After the extinction of Vijayanagar, Shahji was the first Hindu leader who could with rapid movements and local knowledge prove a match for the forces of Delhi or Bijapur.

CHRONOLOGY

CHAPTER IV

1627 April 6	Birth of Shivaji (on 19 Feb. 1630).
1633	Appointment of Dādāji Kondadeo to administer the Poona region.
1636 — 1647	Shivaji's residence at Poona ; 1647-1667 at Rajgad ; thereafter at Raigad.
1637 — 1647	Dādāji as Bijapuri Governor of fort Kondāna.
1640 — 1642	Shivaji's visit to Bangalore.
1643	Shivaji's visit to Bijapur.
1644	Organization of the 12 Mawal valleys.
1644 Aug.	Kondāna (Sinhagad) captured.
1645 March 30	Sacred vow to found *Hindwi Swarajya*
"	Official seal introduced by Shivaji ; offices created for his new government.
1646 — 1656	Muhammad Adil Shah lies ill.
1647 March 7	Dādāji Kondadeo dies ; Torna captured.
1648	Chakan and Fort Purandhar captured
1649	Sambhāji Mohite surprised ; battles of Shirval and Purandhar ; Musa Khan killed ; Fateh Khan routed.
1653	Swarajya completed ; started construction of the coastal fort of Vijayadurg.

CHAPTER IV

THE FIRST PHASE OF THE MOON

[1644—1653]

1. Shivaji's birth and training.
2. His guardian Dadaji.
3. The first coup.
4. Dream put into action.
5. Independence achieved.

1. Shivaji's birth and training.—Shivaji was born on 6th April 1627 in the fort of Shivner near Junnar, or as some recent sources assert, about 34½ months later on 19th February 1630.[1] Unfortunately sufficient evidence is not available to establish either of these two dates as absolutely correct. Jija Bai, Shivaji's mother, was in great distress during the early years of his life. The Emperor Shah Jahan invaded the Deccan and after a strenuous effort of eight years subjugated the whole of the old Nizamshahi Kingdom of Ahmadnagar which Shivaji's father Shahji had tried his best to save. For the first few years of his life Shivaji was a wanderer with no settled home. From Shivner where he was born he moved with his mother and occasionally with his father too from place to place as safety and convenience required. Where and how long he had to remain in such separation in his childhood cannot be ascertained. This only explains how he became inured to a life of danger and hardship ever since his birth. Shivner, Baizapur, Shivapur, and Shivapattan are some of the places, where, we can conjecture, Shivaji spent the first nine years of his life, before he came to have his own home at Poona. Nāro Trimal Hanmante and Gomāji Naik Pānasambal are known to have been his care-takers at this period.

The marital life of Jija Bai can by no means be called happy. We have seen how her wedding itself was a subject

1. In the following narrative I am using the first or the old date. It is not necessary here to discuss the merits and the evidence of these two dates. The greatness of Shivaji is in no way affected, whichever date is accepted.

of compulsion. The Bhosales and the Jadhavs are not known to have then been on very friendly terms. Indeed their pent up feuds used suddenly to burst into flame on trivial grounds as illustrated in the Khandagle elephant episode.[2] In the battle of Bhātavdi, Shahji won the day, and Jija Bai's father in the opposite camp had to save himself by flight. The Jadhavs certainly claimed a higher descent from the royal house of Deogiri ; while the Bhosles were not admitted to possess any such royal blood. Both Jija Bai and the child Shivaji proved to Shahji rather an encumbrance than a help, while the elder Sambhāji to some extent certainly was his father's useful lieutenant.

October 1636 saw Jija Bai restored to a settled peaceful life at Poona under the guardianship of Dādāji Konddev, who built for them a palace at Kasba, which was known as the Lāl Mahal. Here Shivaji lived with his mother from 1636 onward until they removed to Rajgad some time after Dādāji's death in 1647 (7th March). From Rajgad after his safe return from Agra Shivaji moved about 1667 to his new Capital Raigad where building work had been started in 1664.

It is these very hard knocks of his early days which proved highly beneficial to Shivaji in his later career. Adversity is the mother of resourcefulness and ingenuity, qualities, of which both Jija Bai and Shahji were living examples. Jija Bai, a truly Kshatriya lady full of varied memories of her royal ancestors of Deogiri and possessing a dauntless spirit of adventure and defiance chastened by years of suffering ever since her marriage, was to young Shivaji a veritable guardian angel. On her part all her future solace centred in his well-being and good fortune. Practically deserted by her husband, what hope could she have in life, unless this son grew up to be her sole prop ? Her high spirit could never let her accept any compromise on right principles. The father had defied with his small power the might of the Mughals for seven years. Why may not the son do at least as much, if not more ? Man can do what man has done.

The independent charge of his father's jagir at Poona

2. Sh. Bh. 3. 15—45.

proved of great advantage to Shivaji. In this small jagir all kinds of experiments could be quickly tried in the art of government, and valuable experience gained which could be later utilised on a wider scale when the time came. In Shivaji's helpless situation his mother naturally was his sole guide and mentor. She was a versatile woman, well-trained, according to the notions of those days, in traditional religion and mythology. The traditions of Rāmdeo Yādav, of Hemādri, of Jnāneshvar possessed for her a peculiar charm on account of the high moral tone and the free atmosphere of independence they breathed ; and her capacious mind invested them with a glow of the splendour of the indigenous Aryan culture as contrasted with Muslim vandalism and iconoclastic methods. The wanton cruelties of Ala-uddin Khilji and Muhammad Taghlak, the barbarities of Tamerlane, the *johars* perpetrated by the Rajput women of Chitod, ever rankled in Jija Bai's heart. Such a lady, we may be sure, taught her dear young son the need of a supreme effort for avenging wrong and achieving national regeneration.

Their secluded life in the hilly Maval country afforded plenty of out-door occupation and opportunities of adventure. Robberies, commotions, disorders were of common occurrence. The climate itself imposed constant exposure to rain, sun and cold, and other privations of various kinds. Riding, wrestling, spear-throwing, swordsmanship, swimming through torrential floods, in these and similar sports Shivaji developed a kind of wild comradeship both with man and nature ; soon his aimless wanderings were transformed into studied excursions for organizing defence and protection either against the neighbouring chiefs or petty local evil-doers.

Time and surroundings usually suggest to all creatures the means of defence against wanton aggression or of escape from dangerous situations. One very common method of defence of Shivaji's days was the art of disguise. It had then been carried to perfection. Most people, men and women, of those days studied the art as a necessity for the safety of life and valuables. A smattering knowledge of several languages, a handy provision of clothes and necessary tools, and above all, a ready wit, these were the normal essentials for a successful disguise. Shivaji in addition could dexterously imitate the voices of birds and beasts and knew a few words and sentences of several Indian languages picked up on purpose. His sense of hearing was particularly well developed. He could cover long distances on foot, without fatigue, quickly jumping over obstacles, was a consummate wrestler, and an accurate shot with a catapult or a match-lock. It would appear that he had traversed and thus knew intimately the hills and valleys, the passes and strongholds on both sides of the Sahyadri range between Nasik and Kolhapur and possibly much beyond. His walks and rambles were both intensive and deliberate, with his eyes and ears always alert, thus making him gain first-hand acquaintance with the sentiments of the people, their habits, occupations and resources, and impart to them in return his spirit of valour and defiance.

This training in activity between the years of ten and fifteen was supplemented by the teachings of his mother, his guardian Dādāji and his immediate personal staff in the spheres of moral development and administrative duties. The country atmosphere in which he grew up developed a healthy mind in a healthy body, and made him wary and buoyant in contrast with the indolent, corrupt and pleasure-seeking nobles and princelings at Muslim Courts. Shivaji was doubtless taught reading and writing, and he heard portions of the Mahābhārat and the Rāmāyan as expounded by the family preachers. In those days paper was scarce and only important transactions used to be committed to writing. Many letters have been discovered issued under Shivaji's name, but unmistakable and clear evidence is wanting to prove how much of them was penned by him. That does not mean that he was illiterate as some writers would have us believe. To attribute illiteracy to him on this account is entirely unreasonable and unwarranted. State papers in those days were drafted by secretaries and clerks and concluded by ministers. The signing of letters and papers by the master himself as is done now, was not the prevailing practice then. But adding a few words or lines in autograph was prevalent.

Harikirtan or what may be called devotional songs and

sermons by household preachers and celebrated saints like Tukārām, was then a very common means of general education and the training of the young and the old; and Shivaji lost no opportunity of profiting himself by such occasions. Hindu shrines and places of worship he punctiliously visited and took an intelligent concern in their working as a nation-building factor. A large number of his letters deal with the management and proper upkeep of shrines and religious establishments.[3] Of all concerns of life religion occupied his best thoughts and energies. He received his most useful education not through books on the present day model but in the wide school of experience, supplemented by such portions of old texts as relate to the common maxims of politics, morals and philosophy, *e.g.* parts of the *Rāmāyan, Mahābhārat,* some of the *Smritis,* probably portions of *Shukraniti* and *Chānākyaniti* and the lives of the saints. *Vidurniti* was possibly a favourite chapter selected from the *Mahābhārat.* It is said that the *Yuddha-Kand* or the War-chapter of the *Rāmāyan* was regularly read and expounded at night to all the garrisons of Shivaji's forts as part of their discipline.

2. **His guardian Dadaji.**—Another powerful factor in Shivaji's training was his guardian Dādāji Kondadev. The training he imparted in the practical business of government and the meticulous care he bestowed upon Shivaji's general well-being, are in a great measure responsible for what Shivaji afterwards grew to be. Dādāji was not a mere clerk or accountant but a noble character, a man of business, a keen observer of events and situations, a circumspect politician imbued with the prevalent spirit of love for his country, hatred towards foreign domination and religious persecution. He was much older than Shahji and had served the Bhosle family through thick and thin as their trusted friend and adviser. Dādāji rendered conspicuous service in relieving the distress of the ryots during the terrible famine of 1631-32 and resettling

3. On 25th May 1642 he thus wrote to the Deshpande of Rohida: "You have violated the arrangement effected for the worship and management of Raireshvar. You must at once come and answer for your unwarranted interference." (Raj. 15.266).

the Poona region after that devastation.[4] Dadaji was himself a Kulkarni of Malthan and looked after the adjoining villages of Hingni, Berdi, Deulgon and others, which belonged to the Bhosles. When Shivaji acquired the Jagir of Poona and Supa, Dādāji was entrusted with its management so as to make it yield a handsome income. This he did with great assiduity and attention. Papers of the decade 1637—1647 mention him as the accredited governor of fort Kondhana and the districts attached to it.[5]

This new post of Dādāji as manager of the Poona jagir was by no means a bed of roses. Murar Jagdev during the late war had devastated Poona and the surrounding country constituting Shahji's jagir. These Dādāji had to restore. Poona was then a Kasba town, *i.e.* a large village with a standing market of its own. In this market-place Dādāji built a commodious house for Shivaji, known as the Rangmahāl or the Lal-Mahal and procured for him costly clothes, jewelry and equipment, so that people might look upon him as their legitimate master and pay him due respect. The jagir extended from Junnar in the north to Wai in the south and included Chakan, Supa, Baramati and Indapur as the principal Talukas, the names of which are current to the present day. It was to be ruled from Sinhagad, a secure place centrally situated, the northern-most boundary of the jagir touching the forts of Shivner and Trimbak, which Shahji had been compelled to yield according to the terms of Shah Jahan's agreement. Shivapur at the foot of Kondhana was named after the young master where new extensive gardens and mango groves were laid out by Dādāji. The Shivapur mangoes are to this day considered a rarity in the Poona market. Jija Bai later founded a new town at the foot of fort Rajgad, and named it Shivpattan.

Jija Bai and Dādāji had Shivaji married to Sai Bai from the Nimbalkar family about the year 1640 : Shahji's mother Dipa Bai also had come from the same Nimbalkar family. By

4. One paper of December 1633 says, "Dādāji then came to be appointed the revenue officer of the district. He restored the lands to prosperity and compelled the Deshmukhs and the Kulkarnis to help cultivation by peopling the lands." (S. C. Sahitya 2.95-96.)

5. Raj. 17.7 and 18.7, 9, 19.

this time the affairs of the jagir had been put on a sound basis; the restoration of peace and order brought prosperity to the Bhosle estates which they had not known before. The finances improved along with the growth of protection and government. A well-organized force of undoubted loyalty was raised from among the local elements known as the Mavlas, who though ignorant and rugged, proved to be his most trusted and loyal followers, capable of any sacrifice that they were called upon to make. Indeed these hardy mountaineers of the Maval hills formed in his later organization the main stay of Shivaji's fighting machine. This native militia protected the jagir from robbery, molestation and disorder. The wild animals that infested the jungles of the jagir, damaged crops and created terrible havoc. Dadaji took special measures to put an end to this evil. Another beneficial measure adopted by Dādāji was to improve the yield of the land by encouraging agriculture and gardening in all possible ways. Says an old paper, "New crops were reared in every village; mango, tamarind, pomegranate, lemon came to be planted afresh. Of every ten new trees planted, one was given to the owner for his use, and only the remaining nine were taxed; one-third of the crop being taken by Government, and two-thirds left to the owner." This was the practice of Malik Ambar's days and was now universally adopted. Lands were measured and their ownership fixed, new lands reclaimed and irrigation by wells and canals attended to. In a short time the jagir attained a degree of prosperity unknown before. Increase in income became quickly apparent and could be utilized for further improvements.

Another measure of public benefit was the settlement of long-standing disputes through village Panchayats and other indigenous judicial bodies. Dādāji moved from place to place with his young master hearing causes and dealing out justice without favour or prejudice. In all these measures he particularly held up young Shivaji as the sole master and ruler of the people and every transaction was made in his name. This detailed work supplied Shivaji with an excellent opportunity for learning practical methods of government and gaining useful experience of public matters. Dādāji was a strict disciplinarian himself and never lax or remiss in exacting implicit obedience to his orders. He executed speedy and impartial justice. His name as a vigilant and unflinching administrator long survived his death, and fifty years later attracted the notice even of the Emperor Aurangzeb during his long stay in the Deccan. Thus the five or seven years of Shivaji's growing boyhood were most usefully spent.

3. **The first coup.**—While the father was certainly happy in the Karnatak over the glowing reports he received of the improvement of his jagir, a kind of restless anxiety touched his mind possibly through reports from Bijapur that his young son under the guidance of his spirited mother and the stern Dādāji Konddev, was developing an unpleasant attitude of defiance towards the ruling authorities. Shivaji organized his men, repaired and garrisoned the forts and supplied them with provisions, so that a compact growing centre of subversive activity had come into being. These growing portents could not be neglected by the Bijapur Court and a report of them must have been transmitted to Shahji at Bangalore with hints that the son and his establishment deserved to be carefully watched and kept under control, while it was not yet too late. At the same time reports of Shahji's activities in the distant south did not fail to reach Shivaji and Jija Bai's ears, particularly that phase of the Karnatak expedition, in which the Hindu religion was ruthlessly put down, lands devastated, shrines desecrated, idols broken, women's honour violated and all the accumulated wealth of centuries drained away. Was it not a shame that Shahji more than any one else, should be the instrument of destroying his own religion and enhancing the credit of the Muslim rulers and their faith ?[6]

Some time in 1640, Shivaji with his mother and guardian paid a visit to his father at Bangalore. Shahji was anxious to meet them after four years of separation and to see the

6. Though factual evidence to prove how the minds of responsible persons at Poona and Bangalore responded to and reacted on the reports of occurrences in those two places, is lacking, we have to read between the lines of what stray notices we get on paper.

newly-wedded wife of his son. So he sent for them and the whole family spent the next two years together.

Shahji was the loyal servant and supporter of a Muslim State. Bangalore and the surrounding country were full of the old Vijaynagar relics and traditions, which now came to be crushed with a high hand. There were shrewd diplomats and wise and far-sighted counsellors at Shahji's Court, who freely asked themselves questions like these as occasions arose : Was it not Shahji's duty to try and preserve this noble ancient culture and learning ? Why should he not at least protest strongly against these destructive actions of the Bijapur Government ? Why should he not at least refuse to execute them himself ? The boy Shivaji listened in childish surprise.

This anti-national trend of Shahji's service under Bijapur could not be relished by Jija Bai and Shivaji, who had begun actively to dream of salvation from the Muslim yoke, of creating a new state wherein political and religious freedom and toleration for all would reign supreme. The incompatibility of the views and future aims of the father and the son, soon became marked, and it was decided that Shivaji should return to his native country from Bangalore. But a call had come for them all from Bijapur to visit the Court and make their personal obeisance to their liege lord, thereby affirming their loyalty unmistakably. Towards the end of 1642 or the beginning of 1643 the whole family journeyed from Bangalore to Bijapur with their full camp and retinue.

Shahji appears to have accepted the force of the arguments of the opposition and thereafter tried actively to support the Hindu cause by helping Srirang Rai, the last representative of the old Vijaynagar Empire, and often remonstrating with effect against the devastating character of Mustafa Khan's policy.

A very late tradition tells us of young Shivaji's spirit at this time when he was summoned to the Bijapur Court. Would he not make his bow according to the punctilious Muslim prescription ? In the open Darbar he simply executed the ordinary form of Maratha salutation, respectable enough but not reaching the extreme point of the Muslim *sijda*, i.e. touching the floor with the fore-head. The father explained away the rudeness by urging the rustic boy's ignorance of court etiquette. Shahji, even if he had the wish, could not restrain the turbulent spirit of his son.

4. **Dream put into execution.**—Upon his return journey from Bangalore, the father supplied the son with a full equipage for an independent court. Parmanand says, "in a few days Shahji Raja gave leave to Shivaji to depart from Bangalore at an auspicious moment, supplying him with infantry, cavalry and elephants, also prominent ministers, renowned instructors, costly flags and insignia of royalty and with plentiful treasure."[7] Shyāmrao Nilkanth Peshwa, Bālkrinshnapant Muzumdar, Bālāji Hari *Majalsi* (or Sabhasad, *i.e.* member of Council), Raghunath Ballāl Korde, Sonopant Dabir, Raghunath Ballāl Atre Chitnis,—these and other officers trained under Shahji are said to have been told off for duty with Shivaji. When exactly these ministerial offices were created and appointments made to them, cannot be determined. They must have been gradually brought into employment, as Shivaji's new raj came into being.

Shivaji's and Dādāji's experiment of improving the land and the government of the jagir, roused a spirit of emulation and gave a new life to the Maval country. Young friends and playmates of the locality and surrounding regions began to flock round him to share his labours and render any sacrifice that might be demanded. In this way he began to gather around himself a band of young faithful comrades. His vision expanded; he began to dream of a new *swarajya* outside the limits of the original jagir but based upon it. He used to hold secret consultations with these comrades in arms, planning to capture forts, secure funds by daring attacks on private and public treasures, selecting suitable persons for particular jobs, employing spies to gather information about the strength of the garrisons of forts, about buried wealth, and the measures concerted by the Bijapur and other authorities to stop these activities. On broad, plain issues these young enthusiasts sought the advice and guidance of Dādāji Kondadev. Gomāji

7. *Shiv-Bharat*, 10.25-27.

Naik Panasambal, Yesāji Kank, Tānāji Malusre, Bāji Pāsalkar, and Bājirao Jedhe, son of Kānhoji Jedhe, became Shivaji's early helpmates. They possessed influence in different localities which they soon organized for the main objective.

Shivaji had a persuasive tongue. He addressed his comrades and brought home to them how the foreign Muslim rule inflicted hardships and wrongs upon their homeland and their religion. He narrated to them graphic stories of what he had seen and heard. Was it not their duty to avenge this wrong? Even an effort in that direction was laudable and necessary. "Why remain content with the gifts conferred by foreigners or with our paternal acquisitions only? We are Hindus: this whole country is ours, and yet it is occupied and held by the Muslims. They desecrate our temples, break our idols, plunder our wealth, convert our countrymen forcibly to their religion, kill cows openly; we will suffer this treatment no more. We possess strength in our arms. Let us draw the sword in defence of our sacred religion, liberate our native country and acquire new lands and wealth by our own effort. We are as brave and capable as our ancestors of yore. If we undertake this sacred task, God will surely help us. All human efforts are so helped. There is no such thing as good luck or ill-luck. We are the captains of our soil and the makers of our freedom."[8] These words appealed to every ardent mind and roused even those who were slothful and indolent.

An old paper contains the following statement: "Complete darkness prevails under Muslim rule. There is no inquiry, no justice. The officials do what they please. Violation of women's honour, murders and conversions of the Hindus, demolition of their shrines, cow-slaughter, and similar despicable atrocities prevail under that government." The Nizam Shah openly murdered Jija Bai's father, his brothers and sons. Bajāji Nimbalkar of Phaltan was forcibly converted to Islam. Countless instances could be quoted. The Hindus could not lead an honourable life. This is what moved Shivaji to righteous indignation. An intense feeling of revolt took possession of his mind. He at once set to work. He thought to himself,

8. Sabhāsad Chronicle. See also Raj. 15.3.

"One who is strong in his weapon has no difficulty and no fear."[9]

Soon a complete revolution in the people's ideology and outlook was the result of this young leader's activity. The former lethargy was rooted out. The dormant atmosphere of Mahārāshtra came to be galvanized. Everyone began to look about and think for himself. Some readily joined in this new rising, some perforce went into opposition, no one could remain indifferent or apathetic.

"Soon after returning from Bangalore to Poona, the twelve valleys of the Mavals were captured," is a cryptic but significant statement of the *bakhars*, now corroborated by a Persian *farmān* dated 1st August 1644. The *farmān* is a letter addressed by the Shah of Bijapur to Kānhoji Jedhe of Kari. It runs thus:—

"Shahji Bhosle has been disgraced and removed from the Court and it is now reported to us that his agent Dādāji Kondadev has commenced rebellious activities at fort Kondhana. In order to put him down and assert our rule over the territory, Khandoji and Bāji Ghorpade have been commissioned to proceed against him. You are, therefore, hereby commanded to join the Ghorpade with your full contingent and destroy that wicked rebel Dādāji and his supporters with all your might. Upon the successful execution of this task, you will be properly rewarded."[10]

The clearly dated explicit evidence contained in this paper removes all doubt about Shivaji's early activities and supplies us a definite starting point in his career. Since Shahji also has been mentioned as being already disgraced, we can definitely assert that the father Shahji was then looked upon by the Bijapur authorities as the author of the whole mischief. It is significant that the *farmān* mentions Dādāji as the agent in this mischief and that Shivaji's name nowhere occurs.

9. This is said by Rāmchandrapant in his Maratha Polity.

गांडीविनो मतमिदं कुतो दैन्यं कुतो भयम् ।

गांडीवी is a person wearing a weapon.

10. S. C. Sahitya 4, p. 21.

Although he was suspected, he was then too young to be separately noticed. In fact Shivaji's name begins to appear officially after Dādāji's death, or a year or so before that, in that famous letter of Shivaji to Dādāji Naras Prabhu about the oaths they had exchanged before Raireshvar in the summer of 1645. This position also leads one to conclude that Dādāji wholeheartedly supported the new movement of revolt against Muslim domination, and in every way encouraged Shivaji as the fittest instrument to lead the movement to success. It is also clear that the first fort captured by the rebels was Sinhagad and not Torna, which came into Shivaji's hands a year or two later. Nor did Torna possess the strategic importance of Sinhagad. Shivaji discovered hidden treasures at Torna, on which account it received prominence, as a divine dispensation of the goddess Bhavāni to help Shivaji's cause. For security of person and property, Sinhagad was long a necessary adjunct of Poona, which city being on a plain was ever vulnerable.

In 1644 Shahji fell into disgrace at the Bijapur Court probably for complicity in the revolt of Srirang Rai. So long as Randaula Khan was living, he could control Shahji's activities with tact and softness ; Randaula's death in 1643 altered the situation and brought trouble for both Shahji in the south and Dādāji at Poona. The affair of this first revolt of the Bhosles against the Bijapur authorities dragged on practically for five years from 1644 to 1649, occasionally assuming a formidable aspect as matters progressed. The Sultan Muhammad Shah was not able to control the situation and his failing health aggravated it and favoured the rebels. After the capture of Sinhagad in 1644, Shivaji commenced open aggression against Bijapur, of which further proof is supplied by another valuable document dated 30 March 1645, also a letter addressed by the Adil Shah to Kānhoji Jedhe, and his Deshpande Dādāji Naras Prabhu. It says :—"Shivaji Rāje has turned disloyal to the Shah inasmuch as he has organized troops of the Māvlas and having taken possession of fort Rohidā, has established his own garrison in it. He has also built a new fort and named it Rajgad and thus strengthened his position. You have openly joined him and pay him the revenue, instead of obeying our officer at Shirval. You give him insolent replies. This cannot be tolerated. Unless you at once resume your obedience to the Thanadar of Shirval, you will be put to death without mercy."

This letter clearly unfolds the early moves of Shivaji. After Sinhagad he took Rohidā, built Rajgad, and established his hold on that portion of the Maval, all within a few months, indeed an astounding performance. What was first started in secrecy, took now the form of an open challenge. Dādāji Naras Prabhu referred the letter to Shivaji and asked him what reply he was to make. Shivaji thereupon wrote to Dādāji Prabhu the following reply on 16 May 1645:—"The Shah is entirely misinformed. Neither you nor I have turned disloyal. Please see me with that letter immediately. You have no reason to feel distressed. Raireshvar, the divine master of your valley, inspires you and me alike and gives us success. He gives us power enough to establish *Hindawi-Swarajya*. We are mere instruments in divine hands. Come what may, we should stick to the secret oaths we have exchanged, as advised by Dādājipant, in the presence of Raireshvar. He wills it all. Don't lose courage."[11] Letters like this tell us definitely how Shivaji set out on his mission. As usually happens, he outwardly professed perfect loyalty to the Sultan and urged that the activities he undertook were entirely in self-defence and part of the Government's work, intended to put down lawlessness and disorder, as peace was highly essential for the development of this hilly country, which for centuries past had known no rule, no authority, no order and which now had begun to yield a good return.

Thus Shivaji pushed on without caring for consequences. He possessed a quick eye for judging men. He picked up suitable helpmates, promoted them according to their deserts and exacted great tasks from them. He roamed over the country minutely observing the capacities of the men and resources of the people. If a writer, he gave him a writer's job ! if a brave

11. The temple Raireshwar is near the Rairi hill and should not be confused with fort Rohida, which was later renamed Vichitragad and which has no Shankar temple. The two are five miles apart. The oaths took place on the Rairi hill near Kari, the seat of the Jedhes.

man, he was made a captain. He wrote letters, paid visits, contracted friendships often through marriage ties, persuaded, threatened, coerced and thus strengthened his party. People talked of him as a heaven-sent leader, one whom they must implicitly obey.

The voluminous writings of Rāmdās supply ample evidence of these early activities of Shivaji. They have prepared for us a stirring narration of how the people of Mahārāshtra began buzzing about, ready to sting in all directions. That narration is a piece of national history like what is enacted in all ages and climes by men of action or "heroes as kings" as Carlyle loved to call them. The storm was raised. Shivaji alone could ride it and reach the harbour safely. A new bright hope dawned on the land. The pious Jija Bai became the protecting angel for all. In fact nothing gave Shivaji such supreme joy in life as when he came and reported her amidst gleeful laughter the graphic details of his numerous adventures and received her cordial approval in return.

These activities of Shivaji could not be long kept secret. The officers and land-holders of the Bijapur Government soon came to know them and reported them to the headquarters. Fortunately for Shivaji as he started on his adventurous course, Sultan Muhammad Shah of Bijapur fell ill and for some time his life was despaired of. That is the real reason why no strong and immediate action could be taken against Shivaji. The Shah continued ill during the next ten years 1646-56, rapidly declining in health and strength, to the utter neglect of the State affairs.

The two sons of Jija Bai possessed a peculiar nerve and resourcefulness. What Shivaji did in Mahārāshtra, his elder brother Sambhāji imitated to some extent in the Karnatak. The Shah considered Shahji to be the principal author of the mischief and had him arrested as has been already noticed in an earlier chapter of this work. It can be noticed that Shahji's arrest caused no set-back in Shivaji's intrepid plans of establishing his independent kingdom. His small beginnings were potentially firm and he fully believed that the Shah dared not injure a single hair of his father's head. The result came out just as he expected.

In this connection Parmānand narrates an interesting incident, when Shivaji's father was arrested and threatened with death by the Shah at Bijapur in the summer of 1649, if the fort of Sinhagad captured by Shivaji were not at once restored. The father thereupon appealed to his son to give back the fort and save his life. Now Sinhagad was a precious possession on which Shivaji had lavished years of labour and expense, and which formed the main basis of his life's plan. He was not therefore inclined to give it up. His mother earnestly pleaded with him for the sake of her husband. The mother and the son disagreed and decided to abide by the advice of their wise counsellor Sonopant Dabir. Sonopant advised Shivaji to give up the fort, explaining the essentials of a political game to which Parmānand has devoted one long chapter of his work, urging that for a man of valour the whole world is wide open.[12]

5. **Independence achieved.**—From 1644 to 1674, from the capture of Sinhagad to Shivaji's coronation at Raigarh, is a period of three very convenient decades through which a student can review that great hero's life ; *viz.*, 1644-1653, 1654-1663, and 1664-1674. How these decades are distinctly marked and particularized will be explained later, but we must first set down the main incidents of the first decade, the end of which marked the first complete stage of Shivaji's journey. Some of the incidents of this first decade cannot unfortunately be accurately dated. We have already reviewed the affair of the Raireshvar temple where solemn oaths were secretly exchanged. Shortly thereafter Dādāji Kondadev died on 7 March 1647, having already given sufficient initiative to his young master and in peaceful contentment at the prospect of his success as a national hero. The event caused no break in Shivaji's plans, which had long ago been formed after full deliberation. Dādāji had played his part in setting Shivaji on his legs, who now came forth with renewed vigour and started open aggression against Bijapur. He easily captured Chakan and naming it Sangrāmdurg placed his own garrison there. His next move

12. सुविक्रान्तस्य नृपतेः सर्वमेव महीतलम् ॥ १६.४५.

was against Purandar the capture of which proved somewhat dramatic.

Shivaji's home at Poona was guarded by two strong sentinels, Sinhagad in the south-west and Purandar in the south-east. This latter fort was held for Bijapur by a Brahman officer named Nilo Nilakanth Sarnaik, a friend and neighbour of Shahji and his family. During the rains of 1648, fearing an invasion from Bijapur, Shivaji wrote to the Sarnaik begging for a shelter on the ridge below the fort during the inclement weather. The request was granted and Shivaji established a post at the foot of the fort. Soon after the festival of Divali arrived, on which day Shivaji and his mother were invited by the Sarnaik up to the fort for exchanging friendly greetings with his brothers who had already secretly approached Shivaji for a settlement of their family dispute. One night during the Divali, Shivaji arrested all the brothers in their beds and took possession of the fort for himself. The situation was fully discussed during the few following days, and the brothers were all set at liberty after having been bound by sacred oaths to hold the fort for Shivaji and remain loyal to him. In this way Shivaji managed to secure the fort without shedding a drop of blood in a manner which is illustrative of his singular skill in contrivance. The family of the Sarnaiks continued to serve the Maratha raj to the end of its days. Next year when Bijapuri armies came against Shivaji, Purandar proved to him of immense value. In vain the Bijapuri armies launched frequent attacks upon Shivaji from their camp at Shirval. He could easily turn them back from his strong position up the fort. In this fight Musa Khan was killed and Fateh Khan took to flight on being routed.[13] Thus both Sinhagad and Purandar have played an important part throughout Maratha history.

Supā was another important post not far from Poona, which was held by a rather uncongenial neighbour, Sambhāji Mohite, a staunch loyalist of Bijapur and in addition an unfriendly relation of Shivaji, as his sister Tuka Bai was the second wife of Shahji. Sambhāji Mohite, a hereditary noble of Bijapur, would not be persuaded to join Shivaji's move-

13. *Shiva Bharat*, Chap. 14.

ment nor enter his service. On the other hand, as he was likely to prove an obnoxious spy on Shivaji's activities, it was not possible for Shivaji to tolerate him in his immediate vicinity. Sambhāji possessed an armed force of some three hundred troops. One dark night Shivaji with a band of brave followers made a sudden raid upon Supā, surprized Sambhāji and his guards, plundered all his belongings, and took possession of Supā himself. Shivaji tried to explain his plan to Sambhāji and persuade him to join his movement, but as the proud man would not yield, Shivaji sent him under proper escort to his father at Bangalore and reported to him the measures he had taken. It is unfortunate that we have no record as to when exactly this affair took place. We can duly surmise that it must have been between 1649 and 1652.[14]

Thus Shivaji managed to secure his position in the territory roughly between the Bhimā and the Nirā, between Poona and Shirval, having strongly guarded the central posts of Chakan, Purandar, Supā and Bārāmati, all of which were quickly and easily subjugated without cost or bloodshed. In this way a small and compact independent kingdom soon came into existence. Shivaji was careful not to attempt expansion beyond his well regulated frontiers until he felt his power well established and fully organized in all the essentials required by good government. The goodwill of the people under him formed his main support. This sympathetic policy, this attention to the well-being of the people under him appealed to all, and at once made apparent the contrast of his beneficent and orderly rule to the Muslim disorder and confusion outside. For full seven years after Dādāji's death, Shivaji concentrated his energies in organizing his strength all round, making his rule acceptable to all. An independent rule means a compact, well-defined geographical unit with clear regulations and a proper gradation of officers. The motto of the official seal which Shivaji adopted for his plan is itself an evidence of his aim. It runs thus:—" This seal of Shiva, the Son of Shah, shines forth for the good (of the people). It is daily to increase like the

14. *Shiva Bharat*, Chap. 14; Raj. 20.47, pp. 70-71, mentions Sambhāji Mohite was arrested i.e. 1657. But the event seems to have been therein recorded long after it took place.

first phase of the moon and is going to be respected by the universe." Shivaji aptly compares the first stage of his pian to the first phase of the moon. These phases were to increase gradually and attain their fullness ! This seal is found impressed on all Shivaji's papers from 1645 onward.[15] His aims and objects could not have been better expressed than in this pithy sentence.

Like the official seal, the title Chhatrapati also appears to have been assumed long before his formal coronation in 1674, perhaps during this first constructive stage of his *swarajya.* The title was borrowed from the ancient Hindu works on polity and modelled on the traditional ideas of kingship. *Shukraniti, Manusmriti* and probably Chanakya's works appear to have been consulted by Shivaji's or his mother's agents. The Council of Eight Ministers, their ancient titles, and the name Chhatrapati were by no means new creations. There were ready forms and names in use during Hindu and Muslim rule and some of those were naturally adopted by Shivaji as time and convenience required. *Peshwa, Muzmudar, Dabir, Sarnobat, Surnis* are Persian Office-titles which were later converted by Shivaji into Sanskrit ones. Not only titles, but forms of letters and documents, the system of accounts, revenue terms, office insignia which had long been in vogue during Muslim domination were adopted wholesale often in Sanskrit equivalents,[16] and given the garb of the Aryan model.

Rājwāde maintained on the authority of some old papers, that the word Chhatrapati appeared to have been applied to Shivaji in 1648. Some pieces alleged to be of Sant Tukārām's composition are found addressed to Shivaji in which the word Chhatrapati is used. Tukārām died in 1650, and if the compositions are not spurious, one must conclude that Shivaji styled himself Chhatrapati as early as that date. There are

15. See *Patra Sar Sangraha.*

प्रतिपश्चंद्ररेखेव वर्धिष्णुर्विश्ववंदिता ।
शाहसूनोः शिवस्यैषा मुद्रा भद्राय राजते ।।

16. अखंडित लक्ष्मी आलंकृत राजमान्य, राजश्रिया विराजित and similar phrases are originally Persian forms translated into Sanskrit and Marathi.

obvious difficulties in determining these points. Few authentic original papers have survived. What we now possess are copies of old papers, in which the copyists have taken liberties with the original text or unconsciously inserted their own additions. A letter of 1653 and others of many of subsequent dates, have seals of Shivaji's *Peshwa Shyāmrājpant*[17] and other officials, the actual words of which prove that the first phase of a full *swarājya* with the King and the necessary Ministers, was doubtless completed and announced by the year 1653, and this fact is fully corroborated by Shivaji's own authentic letter addressed by him on 17 July 1653 to his Guru Siddheshwar-bhatt Brahme of Chākan, whom probably he had employed to make spiritual invocations in his hazardous undertakings. Shivaji writes in this letter, "Through the strength of your penance my desire of establishing a kingdom has been accomplished in full measure as originally planned. Therefore I am pleased to assign to you an annuity of a cash payment from the Junnar treasury of one hundred gold hons" (Rs. 300).[18] This is a definite statement and although the Kingdom mentioned in it may not be more than the patrimony of his jagir, one can conclude that Shivaji's *Swarajya* was fully completed by the year 1653. It had to be expanded by further effort, but the first stage was completed within ten years of the capture of Sinhagad.

Fort Vijayadurg is said to have been built in the Vijaya Shak *i.e.*, the Christian year 1653. If this be true, it becomes clear that Shivaji had during these quiet years made a complete tour of the Konkan districts west of the Sahyadris and realized the possibilities of a future expansion over these coastal regions in which the Europeans had established their trading factories. The English planted a factory at Rājāpur in 1648, the Dutch at Vingorla about the same time, the Portuguese had their ancient post at Chaul, with all of whom Shivaji established friendly contacts. He decided to make the west coast the base of his future kingdom and defend it with a navy of his own. He also explored the possibilities of a friendly

17. शिवनरपति हर्षनिधान । श्यामराज मतिमंत प्रधान
18. *Sanads and Letters*, p. 113.

understanding with the *Siddis* of Jangirā, the only Muslim element on the west coast between Kalyān and Sondhā. In this way his conception of a *swarajya* took a definite shape by the year 1653. During the first few years Shivaji acted as his father's deputy, but after the release of Shahji, Shivaji declared his own independence in his jagir.[19]

Parmānand gives a fitting tribute to the completion of this first stage of Shivaji's project. "The Mahārāshtra country," he writes, "then attained its literal significance, *viz.*, the great nation, on account of Shivaji's effort."[20] "The people of Mahārāshtra became rich and happy." We thus see how the first phase of the moon covered the first decade of Shivaji's undertaking since the seizure of Sinhagad was completed.

19. Raj. Vol. 17-19; *Patra Sar Sangraha*, 717-722. In these and other papers there is further evidence that Shivaji's administration was already completed. A judicial decision issued under Shivaji's government and bearing the date 21 March 1657, contains many signatories among whom occur Shyāmrāj Nilkanth Peshwā, Vāsudev Bālakrishna Muzumdār, Sonāji Vishvanāth Dabir, Bālkrishnapant and Nāropant Hanmante Dikshit, Mahādāji Shāmrāj Surnis, Nurbeg Sarnaubat, infantry, and Pantāji Gopināth Chitnis, with the last words, "under permission from the Huzur." It should be noted that in those days even petty jagirdars used to have officials under them called '*Chitnis*, *Muzumar*, *Peshwa*, *Surnis*, *Dabir*, etc. so the use of these by Shivaji does not signify his own creation. He adopted what was already available

20. महाराष्ट्रो जनपदः तदानीं तत्समाश्रयात् ।
अन्वर्थतामन्वगमत् समृद्धजनतान्वितः ॥ शि० भा० १०.३२.

CHRONOLOGY

CHAPTER V

1636 — 1644	Aurangzeb Governor of the Deccan : Aurangabad named after him.
1648	Death of Daulatrao Moray.
1649 — 1654	Afzal Khan Governor of Wai.
1653 Jan. — 1658 Feb.	Aurangzeb again Governor of the Deccan.
1655	Aurangzeb invades Golkonda.
1655 closing months	Shivaji's first attack on Jāvli.
1656 Jan. 26	Hanmantrao Moray killed and Jāvli captured.
	Mullah Ahmad surprised, Kalyan and Bhivandi sacked.
1656 May	Yashwant Rao Moray and brothers killed.
1656 Nov. 4	Death of Muhammad Adilshah.
,,	Aurangzeb launches attack upon Bijapur.
1657 April	Shivaji plunders Junnar and Ahmadnagar.
	Shivaji sends Sonopant Dabir as envoy to Aurangzeb.
1657	Shah Jahan taken ill.
1657 Oct.	Shivaji subjugates north Konkan : Kesari Sinh dies fighting at Prabalgad.
1658 Jan. 25	Aurangzeb leaves Aurangabad for Delhi. Shivaji builds Pratāpgad : appoints Moropant Peshwa : other ministries created : south Konkan and Rajapur raided : Bālāji Āvji employed as Chitnis : seizes territories of the Sidi.
1658 July 21	Aurangzeb becomes Emperor.
1659 March 5	Shivaji concludes a treaty of friendship with the Sāwant of Wadi : Bhavāni sword obtained.
1659 Aug. 16	Portuguese Viceroy reports Shivaji's complete possession of south Konkan.
1659 Sept.	Afzal Khan starts against Shivaji.
1659 Oct.	Afzal Khan encamps at Wai.

1659 Oct.	Shivaji takes up his residence at Pratāpgad.
1659 Nov. 10	Afzal Khan meets with his death.
1659 Nov. 11	Battle of Wai ; Bijapur army routed
1659 Nov. 28	Shivaji captures Panhāla.
1659 Dec. 28	Bijapur forces routed below Panhāla : Raibag and other towns sacked.
1660 Jan.	Shaista Khan arrives as Governor of the Deccan.
1660 Feb.	Shaista Khan takes possession of Poona.
1660 May	Panhāla besieged by Salabat Khan.
1660 June	English factors aid the besiegers of Panhāla.
1660 July 13	Shivaji escapes from Panhāla.
1660 July 14	Bāji Prabhu slain at Vishālgad.
1660 August	Shaista Khan captures Chākan.
,,	Shivaji despatches Sonopant Dabir to Shaista Khan.
1660 Sept. 22	Shivaji gives Panhāla back to Bijapur.
,,	Shivaji constructs Suvarnadurg.
1664	Shivaji constructs Sindhudurg.
1680	Shivaji constructs Kolaba.

CHAPTER V

RAPID PROGRESS

[1654—1660]

1. Short work with Morays.
2. Political situation of 1657.
3. North and South Konkon seized.
4. Administrative Measures.
5. Afzal Khan's End.
6. Panhala invested, Shivaji escapes.

1. Short work with the Morays.—How Shivaji's first achievement reacted upon the policy of Bijapur and upon that of the Mughal Emperor will be seen in the sequel. The next stages of his experiments in *swarajya* become sharper and brighter as years pass on. The second stage (1654-64) is made up of extraordinary incidents which converted him into a full-fledged hero of Mahārāshtra.

Shivaji henceforth undertook rapid expansion all round, steadily building up on the original foundation, but carefully avoiding conflict with powerful neighbours and removing internal opponents who showed jealousy for his rise. Most of the Deshmukhs of the Mavals gradually joined him and willingly accepted his lead. But there were some who had a long hereditary greatness to boast of, and whose devotion to Bijapur was too strong to make them respond to the national call. The Morays of Jāvli surnamed Chandrarāo at the western foot of the Mahābleshvar hill, were an ancient Deshmukh family of respectability and high Kshatriya pretensions, as a branch descended from the great Chandragupta Maurya, a claim which was denied to the Bhosles. The Morays were allied by family ties to most of the other Maval Deshmukhs and refused to join Shivaji's standard. It thus became the first necessity for Shivaji to disarm the hostility of the Morays, as obviously one sheath cannot hold two sharp swords. Shivaji for years meditated upon the least harmful way of dealing with this prickly thorn. For long he waited patiently and left no stone unturned to find a friendly solution for an increasingly irritating situation, which soon became aggravated by the appointment of Afzal Khan to the Governorship of Wai in the year 1649. The Khan was explicitly commissioned to put down Shivaji's growing power, and he lost no opportunity of encouraging the Morays to oppose Shivaji's moves.

The friction between Shivaji and the Morays started as early as 1648, when Daulatrao Moray, a man of prestige and standing died, leaving no accredited heir or capable successor to administer his estates. Daulatrao's widow adopted Yashvantrav, a younger member, and conducted affairs with the help of Hanumantrao Moray, a distant relation of the family. Determined to crush the defiance of the Morays Shivaji spent years in negotiation for a peaceful way to gain his object. There arose a sort of a triangular contest between the Morays, Shivaji, and Afzal Khan representing the power of Bijapur. About the year 1654 Afzal Khan came to be transferred from Wai to Kanakgiri, and the coveted opportunity arrived for Shivaji to reach a decision. He took into his confidence some of the Maval Deshmukhs, particularly Kānhoji Jedhe, Haibatrao Silimkar and other neighbours of the Morays, and sent a proposal to Jāvli demanding terms which the Morays refused to accept. Then with the contingents of these Deshmukhs he dispatched his commander Sambhāji Kāvaji with a small force threatening their residence. This first attempt proved ineffectual, when Shivaji sent another force under Raghunāth Ballāl Korde. A battle was fought near Javali in which Hanumantrao Moray was killed ; Yashvantrao fled for his life and took shelter in the fort of Rairi. Pratāp Rao Moray escaped to Bijapur for seeking the Adil Shah's help to oust Shivaji from Javli (26th January 1656). Shivaji himself at once proceeded to Jāvli, stayed there for two months, rehabilitating the house of the Morays and strengthening his hold upon the principality. In the meantime Yashvant Rao started serious trouble afresh from the hill-top of Rairi, a large and lofty plateau near Mahad, which belonged to the Morays. Shivaji sent troops and his agent Haibatrao Silimkar to Yashvant Rao demanding submission. After a long negotiation a meeting was arranged at the foot of Rairi in May. When the Morays came down to meet Shivaji, he killed the principal offender Yashvant Rao and carried his two sons Krishnaji and Baji as captives to Poona. Later on these two brothers also were detected conducting secret intrigues with Bijapur and were therefore put to death.

In this long and vexatious affair many have accused Shivaji of wanton treachery. The Morays could easily have saved themselves if they had had the wisdom to yield, as happened in the case of the Sarnaik of Purandar. The women and dependents of the Morays were most kindly looked after. The verdict pronounced in common parlance on the Moray affair says, " A dozen advisers gathered, and the state of the Chandrarais suffered a fall."[1] Out of a long tale of conflicting details only the main story is summarized above. Shivaji seized the domain with all its wealth and treasure accumulated through centuries of power. History will certainly pronounce an adverse judgment upon Shivaji's dealings with the Morays. The result, however, proved highly beneficial to his purpose, as the world came to know what to expect from him if an open opposition were offered to his plans and desires. Fort Wasota which belonged to the Morays soon fell into his hands. So all the twelve Mavals from Junnar to Wai came into Shivaji's possession.

When Jāvli was taken Shivaji erected a new fort to command the valley of the famous Pārghat and gave it the significant name of Pratāpgad. The work was executed by Moropant Pingle, whose father had served Shahji in the Karnatak and who himself had then come over to Shivaji's service. A new image of the goddess Bhavāni was installed in this fort, where Jija Bai often came to live. Moropant Pingle soon became Shivaji's right hand man and was made the Peshwa or Prime Minister when Shyāmrājpant died about 1658.

Jāvli marked the first grand link in a chain of achievements which cover the second decade of Shivaji's exploits and which brought him to the inescapable notice of the two great Powers then ruling in the Deccan, Bijapur and Delhi. A new personality representing the Mughal Empire had now come on the stage of history, Aurangzeb, the astute son of the declin-

1. मिळाले बारभाई, बुडाली चद्रराई ॥ See *Moray Bakhar*, *Shiva Bharat*, *Jedhe Shakhavali*, etc. Shivaji acted on the plan suggested by his father, see p. 78 above.

ing Shah Jahan, a bigot in religion, who soon became an inveterate enemy of Shivaji.

2. **Political situation of 1657.**—Nine years senior in age to Shivaji, Aurangzeb was born at Dohad on 24th October 1618 and shared his father's hardships and wanderings during his boyhood. As he grew up, he developed austere ways and a hardened heart, which marked his career throughout life. He witnessed the war which his father had waged in the Deccan and in which Shivaji's father came to be expelled from his homeland. When after the conquest of the Nizam-Shahi territories, Shah Jahan returned to the north, he appointed Aurangzeb his representative or Subahdar in the Deccan with a commission to settle the conquered territories. In this office he continued first for 8 years (1636-44), and again for five years from January 1653 to February 1658. During the break of the nine years between the two charges (1644-52), Aurangzeb was occupied with imperial wars on the north-west frontier, which did not touch the Marathas. During his first Viceroyalty of eight years, Aurangzeb was occupied in consolidating the Mughal power and creating an orderly government. But there is nothing noteworthy about his work or movement during this period. Shivaji was then young and no disturbance was expected from the Marathas. Aurangzeb was fond of hunting and selected for his official residence, in preference to the northern far away Burhanpur, the newly erected town of Khadki in the vicinity of Daulatabad, which had been founded by Malik Ambar, and named it after himself. This new town of Aurangabad was a more suitable place from which to watch the Maratha activities centering on Poona.

But the interval of eight years between 1644 and 1653 had seen great changes in the south, not less than six different individuals having governed the Deccan territories of the Mughal Empire, including such well known figures as Mirza Raja Jaysingh, Shahzada Murad Baksh, and Shaista Khan. None of these, however, left behind him any conspicuous mark of his rule. Shivaji was then mainly occupied in consolidating his paternal jagir without rousing Mughal opposition. It was about 1657 when Shivaji's vision began to expand beyond his father's jagir, that he attracted Aurangzeb's notice for the first time. When freed from the affairs of the Morays of Jāvli, Shivaji made his first open raid upon the Mughal territory in the summer of 1657, and plundered Junnar and Ahmadnagar. He simultaneously carried on an offensive movement against the Adil-Shahi possessions of north Konkan, by capturing Kalyan and Bhivandi. The Court of Bijapur was then involved in the wanton Mughal invasion which followed the death of Muhammad Adil Shah on 4 November 1656. A high road from Junnar to Kalyan then carried the inland trade of the Deccan plateau to the ports of Kalyan and Bassein on the west coast, then centres of wealth and traffic, which commanded the fertile region below the Ghats crossed by numerous navigable creeks. Shivaji considered the possession of this rich territory a highly advantageous adjunct to his jagir and one which could be easily defended from his base of Poona.

3. North and south Konkan seized.—Shivaji's clever spies were long employed in the surrounding country and he himself toured the Kalyan district in order to gauge the strength of its defences. During 1655 as Shivaji was launching his attack on Jāvli he received news that the Adil Shah of Bijapur being in sore need of money had called upon the Governor of Kalyan named Mulla Ahmad,[2] to personally convey all his accumulated revenue to Bijapur under a strong escort. Relays were laid on the route and local officials instructed to render help. Shivaji employed one party to make a sudden dash and carry away the treasure as it would pass by the route of Purandar, and another simultaneously to fall upon Kalyan itself. The plan proved eminently successful and the entire treasure was carried away safely and deposited in the strong vaults of Rajgad. While this sudden dash was being perpetrated near Poona, Shivaji's Peshwa Shyāmraj Nilakanth and his cousin Dādāji Bāpuji with a body of select troops surprized Kalyan itself, then denuded of all means of defence in the absence of the Governor. Another party of expert Mavalas

2. Sarkar's *House of Shivaji*, p. 65 and *The Leading Nobles of Bijapur*, p. 55.

led by Sakho Krishna Lohokare swooped down simultaneously upon the neighbouring post of Bhivandi. Shivaji planted strong garrisons both at Kalyan and Bhivandi and prepared to resist any reprisals by Bijapur. He then fortified the harbour of Kalyan and captured Māhuli and the other neighbouring forts to the south and north of Kalyan. Chaul, Tale, Ghosale, Rajmachi, Lohgad, Kangori, Tung-Tikonā, all these were quickly seized one after another and strongly fortified, so that within a year's time Shivaji's small estate came to be doubled in extent and more than doubled in point of value and resources. Thus towards the end of October 1657 the whole province of north Konkan came into Shivaji's possession. He lost no time in establishing a strong and beneficent rule therein, so as to make the people feel the happy effects of the change in comparison with the previous misrule. Shivaji appointed Ābāji Sondev as the first Governor of this Kalyan province. The Portuguese of Chaul felt serious alarm for their security on account of this new Maratha neighbour.

A widely current anecdote concerning this raid on Kalyan certainly created universal admiration for Shivaji's character and high morals. Mulla Ahmad the Bijapuri Governor of Kalyan had left his family behind, including his young and extremely handsome daughter-in-law who fell into Ābaji Sondev's hands. Ābāji considering that she would be an acceptable present for his young master, sent her properly escorted to Poona. But Shivaji who respected every woman's honour as his own mother's, remarked to the lady on arrival, "Oh how nice would it have been if my mother were as fair as you are," and at once sent her to her home with due apologies for her capture. At the same time he conveyed to Ābāji his stern sense of displeasure and circulated a severe warning to his officials against this wicked universal practice.

With the capture of Kalyan Shivaji's sway came to be exercised over a triangular tract the base of which was formed by the line of the sea-coast from Bassein to Rājāpur and the two sides running from these points and meeting at Indāpur. He reduced several forts in this region, among which was fort Prabalgad near Panvel, which was held by a Bijapuri captain named Kesari Sinh, who lost his life in the encounter. Thereupon Shivaji personally went up the fort and discovered at a certain spot a hidden treasure in large vessels full of *mohars*, *hons* and gold bars. Kesari Sinh's mother and two children were at the same time taken, hiding from fear of Shivaji. He, however, went to the lady, prostrated himself before her as if she were his own mother, gave her a Palki to ride in and sent her to her native residence at Deulgaon under his own escort. The dead bodies of Kesari Sinh and others who had fallen in defending the fort, were cremated with due rites and honours. Such treatment given to the vanquished foe spread to distant places Shivaji's fame as a benevolent ruler.

From the north Konkan district, Shivaji at once turned towards the south *via* Chiplun right on to Rājāpur and still further on as far as Sondhā, personally inspecting the country he traversed, and acquainting himself with its defensive and financial capacities. After finishing his tour he returned to his headquarters at Rajgad. He seems to have decided after this inspection that the west coast should form the most convenient base for his future operations. His eyesight was as keen as that of a hawk. He quickly discerned the value of situations, characters and objects and formed his plans as best suited for his purpose.

4. **Administrative measures.**—In his plan of conquest and expansion, Shivaji was particularly careful to make his rule agreeable and beneficial to the people who came under it, by means of equal and speedy justice, by fresh avenues of honourable work in life, and by relieving the miseries of the poor. Wanton plunder and exploitation were rigidly put down. He fully pressed into his service the available capacities of his people, which he had an almost inborn genius to detect. Writes his courtier Sabhāsad, "People are happy when they get wealth, the country can be held through a line of forts, and in this way is a kingdom built up. The best line for the defence of the Deccan lands is the Sahyadri range, the inhabitants of which are expert in climbing hills through torrents of rain, through dense forests and difficult passes. From amongst these Shivaji picked up his helpmates, Mavlas from the Deshmukhs and the Deshpandes, and raised them to positions of honour.

Through their local connections, Shivaji negotiated the capture of forts, sometimes by offering bribes or other inducements, at other times by taking advantage of existing dissensions among the defenders. More often, clever tactics were resorted to, as for instance, introducing into the forts his own men with heavy bundles of hay on their heads carried for sale, in which arms were secretly concealed. In this way many forts were easily secured and placed in charge of trusted keepers. The Maharaj was extremely kind to his men and solicitous of their welfare. People flocked to him in thousands. Honest workers were amply rewarded. Those that proved dishonest and treacherous were carefully weeded out and punished. Thus a strong contrast between the methods of his government and those of the Muslims, became quickly apparent. Under the latter rich men were openly plundered ; while Shivaji protected them from harm."

As the administrative work increased, new appointments were made. Nilo Sondev, brother of Ābāji the Governor of Kalyan, was made Muzmudar. Ānāji Datto was made Surnis or Sachiv. Gangu Mangāji was appointed Waqenavis ; Mānkoji Dahātonde the Surnobat of cavalry died and in his place was appointed Netāji Pālkar. But more than all, the services of a most faithful and capable Secretary Bālāji Āvji were obtained for the office of his Chitnis. Bālāji was indeed an acquisition. For now Shivaji had to depend for the prompt and proper transmission of his orders upon a trustworthy and devoted secretary. Such a one was found in Bālāji. His father Āvji Chitre and his brothers held high positions under the Siddis of Janjira on the west coast. The family came to be disgraced and severely punished by the Siddis on account of some supposed derelictions of duty. Āvji's brother was put to death and his wife Gul Bai and children ordered to be exiled to Maskat. Gul Bai proved a clever woman ; as she and her children sailed in a ship from Janjira proceeding to Maskat, she managed by bribing the Captain to be disembarked at the port of Rājāpur, where her brother Visāji Shankar, a respectable trader, purchased her and the children as slaves by paying to the Captain the amount he demanded for them. Gul Bai had three sons, Bālāji, a fairly grown up lad, and two younger ones Chimāji and Shyāmji. Bālāji wrote a nice hand and was brought up by his uncle and initiated into his business. The three brothers and their mother changed their names and lived in hiding at Rājāpur for fear of being discovered and ill-used by the Siddis. When Shivaji happened to visit Rājāpur about the year 1658 Bālāji contrived to meet him, related his troubles and begged to be saved from the Siddis' wrath. Shivaji readily agreed, being delighted to have an opportunity of serving the Hindu cause, and took the whole family under his protection. They amply repaid these favours by faithful service through generations.

Once the main principles of Shivaji's policy are fully grasped, no fair-minded critic can accuse him of wanton aggression against the Mussalmans as a class. To him both the Adil Shah and the Emperor of Delhi were exactly alike. To protect the Hindus in their own land and to secure them full liberty to practise their religion in the way they liked, were Shivaji's aims, and when these were opposed he exacted full retribution. But even in doing this, he exhausted all peaceful methods before coming to an open conflict. In the beginning he was absolutely friendly towards Aurangzeb. In fact during the early career of Shivaji Aurangzeb was an unknown quantity. Nobody could then foresee that he would become an Emperor and that he would be such a fanatic as to hunt down the Hindus and their religion in the way he did. He unnecessarily started aggression against Bijapur in 1656 and against Golkonda in 1657 and for the first time attracted notoriety for wanton interference in the affairs of the Deccan Sultanates. His character came to be thoroughly exposed next year (1658), when he imprisoned his father, deceived his brothers, snatched the throne for himself and perpetrated atrocities against his eldest brother Dara Shukoh. These events created a stir throughout the land, so that Shivaji later on considered it his duty to resist Aurangzeb's wicked policy with all the means he could collect, including the plunder of Surat. But up to 1656 at any rate, Shivaji's relations with Aurangzeb were by no means hostile. We must read and follow history chronologically without allowing later events to warp our judgment in dealing with earlier ones.

As soon as Aurangzeb led an expedition against Bijapur after Muhammad Adil Shah's death, Shivaji sent his foreign minister Sonopant to Aurangzeb offering to join the Mughals in their war against Bijapur, provided that he was allowed to acquire the territories of the Konkan with all the forts situated therein for his *swarajya*. Sonopant returned with a confirmation of his request and Shivaji at once invaded those lands. He gauged rightly that in the dissolution of Bijapur, the Marathas had a better claim to their homelands than the distant Mughals. Shivaji did not spare even the Mughal possessions of Junnar and Ahmadnagar so contiguous to Poona and so essentially Maratha in character. In 1657 he suddenly fell upon Junnar, his own birth-place, and carried away gold, jewellery and horses. His armies proceeded further on towards Ahmadnagar plundering the intervening country right up to the gate of that old capital. The strong garrison of Ahmadnagar happily saved the town itself. Aurangzeb took prompt measures to prevent fresh molestation on the part of Shivaji. Fearing further chastisement Shivaji sent his ambassador Krishnāji Bhāskar to Aurangzeb in order to explain away the past deeds and urge his claim to the Bijapur districts of north Konkan.

Fortunately for Shivaji Aurangzeb at this moment became extremely uneasy on account of the news he had received of his father having fallen dangerously ill. He hastily prepared to go to the north with all the troops he could collect and contest the throne. He kept the news of his father's illness a close secret and administered especially grave warning to the Bijapur authorities to restrain Shivaji with all their might, telling them if at all his services were considered needful, he should be employed in the distant field of the Karnatak like his father Shahji.

Aurangzeb left Aurangabad on 25 January 1658 and crowned himself Emperor at Delhi in the following July. Shah Jahan remained in confinement at the fort of Agra, which Aurangzeb did not visit during his father's life-time. When Shah Jahan died on 22 January 1666, Aurangzeb entered Agra and took his seat on the peacock-throne for the first time in the following May, when Shivaji paid him his famous visit.

As soon as Aurangzeb grasped the imperial power, he appointed his maternal uncle Shaista Khan, a trustworthy and valiant general, to the government of the Deccan, with special instructions to prevent Shivaji from doing mischief. Shaista Khan arrived at Aurangabad in January 1660. These events in the north and their dates in particular must be borne in mind if we are to follow Shivaji's doings in the south, after 1658.

We have already seen that during the latter part of 1657 and the whole of 1658, Shivaji was busy consolidating his position in north and south Konkan, exactly adjoining his paternal jagir above the Ghats which he had formed into an independent State. The Sahyadri range has many tortuous passes and valleys through which Shivaji kept up easy and safe communication from the upcountry to the coast. As these passes were not then very well-known nor used by large armies, Shivaji conducted his affairs without molestation from his enemies. The territory of north Konkan was then divided from that of south Konkan by the creek known as the Vashisthi river, which runs from Chiplun to Dabhol. The country north of this river right up to Bassein, formed part of the old kingdom of Ahmadnagar and was handed over to the Adil Shah by the treaty of 1636. The lands south of the Vashisthi river already belonged to Bijapur and formed part of a jagir assigned to Rustam-i-Zaman. Shivaji's growing prestige along the whole coast from Kalyan to Vingorla with Dabhol and Vijayadurg as fortified bases, excited the jealousy of this Rustam-i-Zaman and of the other powers such as the Siddis of Janjira and the European traders, with their factories on the coast.

The Siddis purchased Shivaji's friendship by handing over to him their posts of Tala, Ghosala and Rairi, of which Shivaji personally took possession during his southern tour early in 1658. Thereupon Shivaji visited the shrine of Hareshvar and proceeded to Rājāpur with a view to helping the Sāvant of Kudal whom Rustam-i-Zaman had attacked during the summer of 1658. This Sāvant was also a scion of the Bhosle family and in his extremity had appealed to Shivaji for help. Shivaji then personally toured the whole region of south Konkan and established his post at Rājāpur. Friendly negotiations took place between Shivaji and the Sāvant, whose envoy Pitāmbar Shenvi visited Shivaji and concluded with him a formal treaty of mutual friendship and help on 5th March 1659. The Sāvant from now onward practically remained a faithful ally of the Chhatrapatis, although their relations were occasionally disturbed by extraneous circumstances. During these negotiations Shivaji visited Kudal, where he purchased a fine sword of European make for 300 hons and named it the '*Bhavani*'. He successfully used it in many an encounter. It was with this sword that he killed Afzal Khan a few months later.[3]

This many-sided activity of Shivaji discloses his singular capacity. His vigilant eye roamed everywhere far and near. Early in his career he visualized the necessity of a strong navy with suitable bases for its location to protect his newly-formed kingdom. The first naval fort he built was Vijayadurg which was commenced in 1653, the next was Suvarnadurg constructed in 1660, Sindhudurg or Malvan came into being in 1664, and the last great naval post was Kolaba which he finished just before his death in 1680. It is obvious from this that Shivaji's naval effort was both earnest and continuous, and in his opinion the most valuable means of protecting and expanding his kingdom. Says Dr. Sen[4]:—

"The coast lines of the Konkan broken by many creeks offered excellent shelter for ships and the rocky islands near the coast presented invulnerable sites for naval strongholds. Once in secure possession of the Konkan, Shivaji early realized the necessity of a strong fighting fleet. The peace and prosperity of his *raj* demanded it. It was not his aim to secure the freedom of the seas against the world. He was quite content to share the sovereignty with his neighbours. On 16 August 1659 the Governor of Goa wrote to the King of Portugal, 'Shivaji has made himself master of the lands near Bassein and Chaul and built some ships of war at Bhivandi, Kalyan, and Panvel." The Mughal Emperors had criminally neglected this vital subject.

From the Konkan we must now turn our attention to the uplands.

3. It is still in the possession of his descendants at Satara.
4. *Military History of the Marathas*, p., 173 and on.

5. **Afzal Khan's end.**—How far Shivaji expected smooth-sailing in his efforts to build up an independent kingdom for the essentially Maratha lands it is difficult to say, but he certainly kept himself prepared for any eventuality. It was too much to expect the Court of Bijapur, however decadent, to relinquish possession of the Maratha territories which had been earned by centuries of heroic endeavour, without making an attempt to save them from this upstart. The Bijapur Government was now indeed in a sad plight, what with Mughal aggression and what with the sudden rise of Shivaji in his homeland. Muhammad Shah's queen Badi-sahiba was then managing the State affairs in the name of her young son Ali. Sometime ago Shahji was asked to restrain his son from encroaching upon the Adil-Shahi lands. He replied that he was not responsible for his son's conduct and that the Bijapur Government might take any steps it liked against him. The power of Bijapur was now practically collapsing, and even its Muslim nobles had turned disloyal. Shahji alone stood by his master during these critical times. This is clearly proved by a recently discovered *farman* addressed to Shahji on 27 May 1658, which states, "We are satisfied with your explanation that you cannot restrain your son and that you are not responsible for his acts. We have therefore restored to you all your jagir at Bangalore together with all the honours and titles which you formerly held."[1] This document also proves how powerless the Bijapur Government was against Shivaji's aggressions, which went on steadily increasing after Aurangzeb's departure from the Deccan; and none of the various other nobles of Bijapur would undertake the chastisement of Shivaji. Afzal Khan alone volunteered for that hazard.

Afzal Khan's name has often been mentioned before in connection with Shahji's affairs. He was reported to be an illegitimate son of the late Muhammad Shah, his mother having been a cook in the royal kitchen. He had distinguished himself in the Karnatak wars, but the Bijapur State had by now come to be dismembered, the Maratha lands being seized by Shivaji and the Karnatak lands by his father. It, therefore, became a matter of life and death for Bijapur to put

5. House of Shivaji, p. 87.

down Shivaji. Afzal Khan entertained a long-standing inveterate antipathy towards Shahji and his sons. The resources of Bijapur were, however, scanty and it was rightly felt that Shivaji could not be easily overcome in the difficult regions which he had occupied. The Bijapur Queen, therefore, secretly advised Afzal Khan to lull Shivaji's suspicions by pretending friendship or by any other method that could be employed in order to have him captured alive or dead. Afzal Khan hardly needed this reminder. His treacherous conduct towards Kasturirang Naik of Shira was notorious throughout the land. He, therefore, in his vanity readily accepted the task of humbling Shivaji by fair means or foul, reckless of the consequences.

After the conquest of Jāvli Shivaji was occupied in strengthening his position in the vicinity of Wāi. He had built Pratāpgad where he was supposed to have his main residence, treasure and stores. Afzal Khan too was intimately acquainted with the Wai district of which he had long been the governor. He started from Bijapur in September 1659 with a select army of twelve thousand and travelling *via* Pandharpur, the Mahadev Hills and Maladi, arrived at Rahimatpur and purposely behaved as a ruthless fanatic by desecrating Hindu temples and idols to give his expedition a stern and vengeful appearance. He particularly demolished the famous temples of Tulzāpur and Pandharpur out of spite for Shivaji. At Malavdi he wreaked his wrath against Bajāji Nimbālkar who had recently been reconverted to Hinduism at the instance of Shivaji and his mother.

Afzal Khan's movements were being closely watched by Shivaji from Rajgad. He soon decided to give him battle in the surroundings of Wāi and Jāvli, which were full of lofty hills and impenetrable valleys, and took up his residence along with his mother at Pratāpgad above the mountain pass of Parghat west of Mahabaleshvar. When the Khan learned that Shivaji was at Pratāpgad, he came straight against him to Wāi and there formed his camp in October, this place being about 16 miles due east of Pratāpgad, with the high plateau of Mahabaleshvar between. The Khan's vandalism and wanton atrocities had roused such strong feelings of hatred and wrath against him in the minds of the common people, that he lost all local sympathy and help. By the middle of October the two opponents stood facing each other, the one to the east at Wāi, the other to the west at Pratāpgad, each meditating upon the best means of overcoming the other.

The fort of Pratāpgad perched on an inaccessible narrow hill-top, was not at all suited for an open fight such as the Khan could offer, nor was it possible for him to move his large army in mass to the vicinity of that fort. Shivaji remained entirely on the defensive securely seated on the hill-top like an eagle watching for an opportunity to fall upon its prey. The Khan, on the other hand, was devising methods to draw out Shivaji from his perch for a personal meeting, with the object of getting his enemy under his clutches without recourse to an open fight. Thus a personal meeting became an inevitable objective for both of them. As Shivaji could not avoid it, how to make such a personal meeting successful became the serious thought both to Shivaji and the Khan each day that passed. In vain might the Khan keep his large army under harness for any length of time and produce no result, nor could Shivaji endure an interminable strain. Shivaji's ingenious brain alone could dissolve the situation ; no outside means was available.

As Shivaji remained entirely on the defensive and bided his time, it was Afzal Khan who became impatient to start talks for alluring Shivaji into a personal visit under the pretext of arranging an amicable settlement. For this he had to select a convenient agent, one who knew Shivaji and who would loyally help the Khan in bringing about a personal meeting. Krishnāji Bhāskar, the Kulkarni of Wāi, whose descendants are still living there, and who owed everything to the Bijapuri Government, was induced by Afzal Khan to take up the mission. He was asked to assure Shivaji of the Khan's high regard and great friendship for him and his family and bring him over to Wāi for a personal exchange of views. It was suggested that if Shivaji willingly offered to submit to the Shah's authority, he would be cordially received and highly promoted in the Adilshahi service like his father, that it was quite possible that his own ambitions and the interests of the Bijapur Government could be mutually adjusted to the satisfaction of both.

The Khan's game clearly was to inveigle Shivaji into the Muslim Camp, so that means could be easily found to detain him and carry him in chains to Bijapur, or encompass his ruin in some other way. The plan was quite transparent to a man of Shivaji's keenness, particularly as the Khan's views, his present professions and past conduct were matters of common knowledge.

So Krishnāji Pant came on a mission to meet Shivaji at Pratāpgad on behalf of the Khan and performed his part quite loyally and dexterously. Shivaji saw through the trap that was being laid for him. He, however, betrayed no impatience or acerbity on his part and professed cordial submission, expressing withal a filial reverence towards the Khan, whom he requested to extricate him (Shivaji) out of the awkward situation into which his reckless conduct had launched him. Shivaji, however, was in no hurry to push up the business, and thought it prudent to lengthen out the negotiations and professed his utter helplessness to cope with the Khan's preparations and his extreme fear of venturing into the Khan's camp.

Shivaji lavished the utmost attention and comfort on the Khan's ambassador Krishnāji Bhāskar and had long talks with him. He appealed to the Brahman's religious instinct to further the great work he had undertaken of Hindu revival, and asked for his help in defeating the plot of the Khan. Krishnāji, although convinced of Shivaji's noble intentions, stood firmly honest in his master's service. He had not fathomed the Khan's inner motives. He was well entertained at Pratāpgad and was persuaded to explain to the Khan that Shivaji confessed his inability to fight with such a large force, that he now repented of the follies he had committed, and that if the Khan would pardon him and spare his life, he would readily hand back all the territory he had seized. With these professions Krishnāji Bhāskar returned to Wāi accompanied by Shivaji's agent Pantāji Gopināth to explain matters fully and arrange details for a personal meeting of the two principals. Through this Pantāji Pant Shivaji cleverly turned the Khan's game against him. Pantāji urged, if the Khan's professions of amity and cordiality were honest, why should he not trust Shivaji as well and come fearlessly to meet him at Pratāpgad, where no troop movements were practicable for either party. Pantāji Gopināth was a devoted adherent of Shivaji, adept in discovering secrets by means of covert tactics and clever insinuations. With him was an expert spy of Shivaji named Vishvās Rao Nānāji, who, disguised as a fakir, roamed about the Khan's camp begging and praying and collected valuable information of the Bijapuri plans and arrangements. In this way frequent messages and messengers passed between Wāi and Pratāpgad, enabling Shivaji to gather full details of the situation and form suitable plans for overcoming his opponent.

The Khan was entirely lulled into the belief that he could easily gain his object without recourse to open fight. Most of the Deshmukhs in those parts were being led by Kānhoji Jedhe and turned hostile to Afzal Khan. The Khopde Deshmukh alone was unfriendly to Kānhoji, having openly sided with Afzal Khan and promised to him that he would manage to capture Shivaji alive.[5] Under these circumstances the Khan directed his efforts to inducing Shivaji somehow to come out. He spread out his troops through all the open spaces of the district with instructions to capture Shivaji if he ventured out. Shivaji was fully alive to these plans, being well posted with timely news of every move of his enemy. He stationed his own select bands in various secret recesses unobserved by the enemy and ready for any emergency. Pantāji Gopināth with his sweet tongue and animated asseverations managed to induce the Khan to come to the foot of the Pratāpgad fort for a meeting with Shivaji. The Khan was quite confident of his superior personal strength. Pantāji Pant assured the Khan that once they met, Shivaji would follow him wherever he was wanted. In this way a meeting was finally agreed upon in a situation and under conditions in which Shivaji became the master and the Khan the dupe.

Minutely observant as Shivaji was, he foresaw every possible contingency and prepared for it in advance. He selected the spot for the meeting, at the base of the rampart where now stands a splendid tomb built recently by the Nizam of Hyderabad. A highly ornamented and attractive bower of woodwork

5. Raj. 15.302.

was erected where the two were to meet and greet each other. Shivaji made lavish arrangements for the food and comfort of his guests. Only one path was cleared through the dense forest from the foot of the Parghat to go up to the place of the meeting. All other byepaths were made inpassable by putting in obstacles of felled trees. The Khan's people freely came, inspected the spot and convinced themselves that all was perfect. There was nothing to rouse suspicion. The Khan was to come fully armed and in his own palanquin with a personal following of 1500 bodyguards ; but even these could not all be accommodated at the hill-top. They remained scattered guarding the spot. Lest Shivaji might take fright and not come at all to the meeting, the Khan's party was reduced to the minimum with only two armed servants alongside of him. Even then the whole plan was obviously more dangerous to Shivaji than to the Khan, then about 20 years older than the former. Shivaji was to have no servant with him inside the tent and certainly no visible arms. The two Brahman ambassadors, Krishnāji Pant for the Khan and Pantāji Pant for Shivaji, were to be present for helping the initial introduction and the expected discussion.

That Shivaji was prepared for the worst is evident from the fact that he had made arrangements for his work being continued in a systematic manner, in case he was killed or taken away as a captive. Jaja Bai, Anāji Datto, and Bālāji Āvji remained in the fort above when Shivaji left it, walking down to meet his guest.[6]

Thursday 10th November 1659 (Margashirsha Shukla 7 of Shak 1581) was fixed for this eventful meeting. The time probably was the afternoon between three and four o'clock. During the morning Shivaji finished his daily worship of the Bhavāni, had his breakfast, put on his dress with an iron cuirass of chains under his coat, and a metal cap over his skull inside the turban, and a long white flowing robe over all with broad long sleeves which probably covered a short sword in one hand and tiger-claws[7] on the fingers of the other. When

6. The following message was delivered before parting : "We have taken up the challenge, (होड); God wills it. If it proves adverse for me, you should destroy the enemy without fear and protect the *rai*."

7. A scorpion-like weapon, बिचहू says Sambhāji in his *dānapatra*.

all was ready he received the blessings of his mother and started.

The Khan had already arrived and was in his seat, when Shivaji came in and was announced by Krishnāji Bhāskar. As Shivaji walked in, the Khan rose up and embraced him, tightly gripping him with his left arm and stabbing him with a dagger. Shivaji with perfect presence of mind thrust his short sword and the tiger-claws into the Khan's huge body, ripping open the bowels and bringing him instantly down to the ground. The whole affair was finished in a moment. The Khan's servants rushed forth to save their master, but were cut down by Shivaji's bodyguard. The two Brahman diplomats were dumb-founded. The body of the Khan was placed in the palanquin by the bearers, but as they started to carry it away, they were attacked and disabled. Shivaji's men severed the Khan's head, carried it up to the fort and exhibited it on a high mast from the topmost bastion. The preconcerted signal was at once given and the concealed Maratha soldiers rushed out from their holes, cutting every Bijapuri trooper that came in their way.

This in the main is the outline of what took place on this memorable occasion. There are ever so many details added in ballads and tradition as the result of the free play of popular fancy all over the country, that it is difficult to separate the grain from the chaff. The event has stirred Maratha hearts to their depths now for two hundred and fifty years.[8]

Those who have visited the locality with its dark winding paths up the hill can well realize the woe that befell the huge

8. Afzal Khan's ballad composed and sung by Ajnāndas has been printed, in which the author says he was sent for from Poona by Jija Bai to Pratāpgad and was ordered to sing the glorious achievement of her son. In those days this was the only means of publishing such events. Ajnāndas says he composed the ballad and so impressed Jija Bai and Shivaji with its recitation that they rewarded him with two lbs. of gold ingot and a horse. The piece stirs our heart even to-day and contains many details which may be taken as accurate. Any way this is the only extant record of that memorable incident. The writer has used the words "Chhatrapati" and "Maharaj" for Shivaji. He describes him as one out of whose tank all animals have their drink in peace. Religious fanaticism is attributed to Afzal Khan. A very readable English translation in verse is published by Acworth.

Bijapurian army scattered through the pathless valleys on that short November evening with the bright half-moon just glimmering and exposing the bewildered Muslims to the swords of the nimble Maratha soldiery rushing out of the woods to prevent their escape. The battle if it could be so called is known as the battle of Pratāpgad. Netāji Pālkar, Moropant Pingle, Kānhoji Jedhe and several others had their appointed places and assigned tasks, pre-arranged according to plan, which were accurately executed. Shivaji had given strict injunctions to all to spare those of the enemy who would willingly surrender, and avoid bloodshed as much as possible. On the next day Shivaji attacked the Khan's main camp at Wāi where his son Fazl Khan was in charge with probably more than half the original army. Fazl Khan was routed and saved his life by flight. Two other sons of Afzal Khan, Rustam-i-Zaman and several distinguished nobles were captured along with an amount of plunder in animals and valuables worth about 10 lacs in all.

This Afzal Khan episode once again proves the decline of the state of Bijapur. In the long run murder does not pay. Muhammad Gawān, Chānd Bibi, Lukhji Jādhav, Murār Jagdev and many others were murdered in cold blood under Muslim Governments. What good these murders availed, history has not been able to pronounce. Very recently in Bijapur itself the Vazir Khan-i-Muhammad and after him Bahlolkhan met the same fate at the hands of the Queen Dowagar Badi Sahiba. Shivaji abhorred wanton murders, and would not have killed Afzal Khan if he could have helped it. While it is perfectly true that he was prepared for any eventuality, he was forced to extreme measures in self-defence and would have gladly spared Afzal Khan if possible. It would have been the height of folly if he had gone to the meeting unprepared.

6. Panhala invested, Shivaji escapes.—Shivaji was perfectly aware that the death of Afzal Khan was only the beginning of a long-drawn struggle and that it was necessary for him to follow up his victory till the Bijapur ghost should be fully laid. He despatched Ānaji Datto with a large force and captured Panhālā, the capital of the western Adilshahi district, through negotiation on 28th November, that is, within 18 days of Afzal Khan's death. Panhālā and the surrounding district of Kolhāpur, Vasantgad, Khelnā, Rangnā and other minor forts quickly surrendered. At this time Shivaji named Khelnā Vishālgad. The district of Kolhāpur and the forts of Panhālā and Vishālgad had been long assigned to Rustam-i-Zaman as his charge. He was now joined by Fazl Khan who had escaped from Wāi after his father's death, and the two nobles came to oppose Shivaji at Panhālā. They were defeated on 28th December 1659 by Shivaji and were pursued almost to the gates of Bijapur. Netāji Pālkar and other generals of Shivaji plundered the towns of Raibag, Gadag and Laksmeshvar with the intervening country. By the end of January 1660 Shivaji was back at Rājgad with a huge amount of booty.

In his extremity the Adilshah called to his side Siddi Jauhar, his viceroy in charge of the province of Karnool and induced him to undertake the task of subjugating Shivaji and bringing him to submission. Siddi Jauhar was at this time given the title of Salabat Khan. Bāji Ghorpade, Rustam-i-Zaman, Fazl Khan and several others joined the Siddi and a large number of troops came against Panhālgad. The Siddi of Janjirā and the Sāvant of Wādi were induced to work against Shivaji simultaneously. Shivaji too prepared to face the enemy and took up his residence at Panhālgad with the object of personally directing the defence. The Bijapurians besieged the fort, giving rise to determined warfare on both sides for some time since May 1660. Kadtoji Gujar conducted the defence of Panhālā under Shivaji's direction, and the Sarnaubat, Netāji Pālkar, remained outside to harass the enemy and devastate his outlying territories so as to stop supplies and reinforcements reaching the besiegers.

Salabat Khan was a resourceful commander. He pressed the siege with vigour and contrived soon to make Shivaji's position perilous. Jija Bai at Rajgad learned that the siege of Panhāla was being hard-pressed against Shivāji and feeling extremely anxious about his safety, called Netāji Pālkar to her side and chided him for his indifference in the matter of relieving the siege of Panhālā. Parmānand has eloquently described Jija Bai's interview with Netāji, who assured her that all would be well.

Salabat Khan in the meantime approached the English factors of Rājāpur for ammunition and some English gunners, who could create havoc among the defenders of Panhāla. Revington, the Chief of the factory with his assistants Mingham and Gifford came with an efficient heavy gun and ammunition to the help of Salabat Khan. This European gunnery proved highly effective and made Shivāji's position altogether untenable. This wanton interference of the English merchants ol Rājāpur rightly gave offence to Shivaji and made him take tc reprisals with serious consequences for the English as will bt noticed later.

At this very moment when Shivaji was hard-pressed al Pānhālā, another serious danger appeared against him in th(north. Shaista Khan, the renowned Mughal Commander, wh(had been appointed Governor of the Deccan, arrived at Ahmad nagar. At the end of February 1660 he left Ahmadnagar an(established his hold on Poona and Bārāmati and pushed righ up to Shirval towards south in April, when Shivaji was sur rounded at Panhāla. Shaista Khan concluding that this wa the best opportunity for him to reduce Shivaji's northerı possessions and thereby to bring about his complete ruin, re traced his steps, occupied Poona in May taking up his residenc in Shivaji's palace of Lāl Mahāl. In August he wrested Chāka from its valiant Commander Phirangoji Narsālā. Shivaji thu found himself almost crushed between two huge grinders. Bu it is only at such critical moments that Shivaji's genius shon at its brightest and proved his mettle. At this time he sen his capable minister Sonopant Dabir to Shaista Khan beggin for terms of settlement and at any rate to soften the Khan' bitterness towards him. The Khan was almost inclined to abat his rigour towards Shivaji knowing very well how difficult i was for his troops to conduct a war in the difficult trac of the western hills. In the meantime the situation was reporteu to Aurangzeb, who urged Shaista Khan not to accept Shivaji's word but to prosecute the war relentlessly and destroy his power finally. For this purpose the Emperor ordered Jashwant Sinh from Gujarat to proceed against Shivaji's possessions and reinforce Shaista Khan. Shivaji well understood what he could have to expect from the Mughals in future, and for the moment concentrated his attention on the best way of removing the pressure against Panhhālā.

He opened negotiations with Salabat Khan and begged for terms for his submission. A provisional truce was arranged in order to allow a personal meeting and Salabat Khan temporarily stopped the siege-operations. In this situation, on the dark night of 13 July 1660 when heavy rain was falling, Shivaji escaped through a back gate of the fort and took flight to Vishālgad, accompanied by a small party of loyal followers led by a devoted servant, Bāji Prabhu Deshpande. His escape was quickly detected and a party of the enemy followed almost on his heels. By daybreak the pursuers came so close as almost to prevent Shivaji getting safely into the fort of Vishālgad. At that critical moment Bāji Prabhu occupied the narrow pass known as Ghod-Khind (horse-ravine) at the eastern entrance of Vishālgad and allowed his master time to get safely into it and himself stoutly resisted for hours the huge body of pursuers with his own small band, until they were all cut down to a man and Bāji Prabhu himself fell mortally wounded. He had, however, the satisfaction of learning before he expired that his master had reached the fort safely. This sacrifice of his own life by Bāji Prabhu is gratefully remembered to this day by the Maratha nation and is typical of the way in which Shivaji was served throughout his career. Needless to say that this sacrifice was profusely rewarded.[9]

This escape of Shivaji foiled the Bijapuri plans of capturing him. On 22nd September 1660 he gave up the fort of Panhālā formally to the Adil Shah and concluded peaceful relations with him so as to gain time to attend to the Mughal onslaught.

---

9. *Raj.* 15.363.

CHRONOLOGY

CHAPTER VI

1660	Ali Adil Shah II wrests power from Badi Sahiba.
1661 Jan.	Kartalb Khan humbled by Shivaji.
1661 Feb.	Shaista Khan captures Kalyan.
1661 March	Shivaji attacks Rājāpur, arrests 6 English factors.
1661 April 29	Shivaji expels Survé from Shringārpur ; conciliates that family later and also the Shirkes.
1661 May–1662 June	Badi Sahiba's pilgrimage to Mecca.
1662	Shahji reconciles Shivaji to Adil Shah.
1663 Jan. 17	The English factors of Rājāpur released.
1663 April 5	Night attack on Shaista Khan.
1663 April 6	Mughals attack Sinhagad.
1663 Summer	Adil Shah reaches Bankapur : opens war against Shivaji (1663-1664).
1663 Summer	Shivaji attacks pilgrim ships to Mecca : writes a strong remonstrance to Mughal officials.
1663 June	Shaista Khan retires to Aurangabad. Muazzam appointed Governor with Jashvant Sinh.
1663 Dec.	Shaista Khan leaves for Bengal.
1664 Jan. 1	Shivaji leaves Nasik for Surat.
1664 Jan. 8-9	Shivaji sacks and burns Surat.
1664 Jan 10	Shivaji leaves Surat for Raigad.
1664 Jan. 23	Death of Shahji.
1664 May	Shivaji at Kudal to defend the Sawant.
1664 Sept. 30	Mirza Raja Jay Sinh commissioned to proceed against Shivaji.
1605—1667	Mirza Raja Jay Sinh's Life-period.
1664 Novr.	Shivaji sacks Mudhol, kills Bāji Ghorpade.
1664 Novr. 25	Shivaji starts building the Sindhudurg castle and organizes a naval force.
1664 Dec.	Khawas Khan and Ekoji defeated near Khānāpur.

1664 Dec.	Shivaji plunders Hubli.
1665 Jan.	Shivaji captures Pondā : makes peace with the Sāwant.
1665 Jan. 19	Jay Sinh reaches Burhanpur.
1665 Feb. 8	Shivaji plunders the harbour of Basrur.
1665 Feb.	Shivaji at Gokarna.
1665 Feb.	Jay Sinh starts the offensive against Shivaji.
1665 March	Jay Sinh at Poona.
1665 March 30	Dilir Khan invests Purandhar.
1665 March 31	Jay Sinh encamps at Saswad.
1665 April 14	Dilir Khan captures Rudramal.
1665 April 14	Murār Bāji killed.
1665 May 20	Shivaji's envoy Raghunath Pandit meets Jay Sinh at Saswad.
1665 June 11	Shivaji visits Jay Sinh.
1665 June 13	Shivaji meets Dilir Khan.
1665 June 14	Shivaji concludes treaty with Jay Sinh.
1665 June 15	Shivaji surrenders Sinhagad and other forts.
1665 Sept. 5	Shivaji receives Imperial *farman.*
1665 Novr. 25	Jay Sinh opens operations against Bijapur, Shivaji joins in them.
1666 Jan. 16	Shivaji's unsuccessful effort to capture Panhāla.
1666 Jan.	Netāji Pālkar quits Shivaji's service and joins Bijapur.
1666 March 20	Netāji receives Imperial *Mansab* from Aurangzeb.

CHAPTER VI

UPS AND DOWNS

[1661 — 1665]

1. Kartalb Khan humbled.
2. English Factors confined.
3. Night raid on Shaista Khan.
4. Surat sacked.
5. Bijapuri activities ; Baji Ghorpade crushed.
6. Jay Sinh and Shivaji face to face.

1. Kartalb Khan humbled.—The Afzal Khan affair taught Shivaji how to deal with outside forces. Shaista Khan was now in Poona slowly putting restraints on Shivaji's freedom and did not hazard an immediate open war. For the capture of Chākan he had to pay a heavy price in a thousand valuable lives. Shivaji after escaping from Panhālā reached Vishālgad safely and thence quickly proceeded to Rājgad for taking measures to stop the terrific onslaught of Shaista Khan, who now directed his attention towards reducing Shivaji's power in north Konkan, which supplied him with his principal resources in money and provisions. With the object therefore of capturing Kalyan, Shaista Khan equipped a large army and despatched it under a valiant and trustworthy commander named Kartalb Khan accompanied by a brave Brahman warrior lady and her full contingent ; she was the wife of the old grandee Udārām of Basim, who had rendered distinguished service to Jahangir and Shah Jahan. Aurangzeb entertained a high regard for this lady and had conferred on her the title of Rai-Bagan (the tiger-princess).

Kartalb Khan left Poona in January 1661 and descended the western Ghats by what was known as Umbar-Khind at the foot of fort Lohgad, a little to the south of the present railway station of Lonavla, a difficult passage as the railway route itself shows by running through so many tunnels. The pass of Umbar-Khind was extremely narrow and about 8 miles in length, but more than 15 miles from the eastern plain to the western, and hardly allowed more than two men walking abreast. The path is steep and narrow and runs through a barren waterless tract with huge precipices on the two sides. Shivaji had studied the intricacies of the passage and being well informed by efficient spies, he tried to encompass the complete ruin of Kartalb's forces. His well trained parties of infantry remained hidden in secret recesses, ready to pounce upon the enemy at the given signal. The Mughals unsuspecting any untoward trouble, leisurely descended through the narrow pass in evident glee, encumbered with baggage, guns and ammunition. As soon as the whole force had been practically entrapped in the narrow defiles, the two entrances above and below came to be suddenly closed by Shivaji's men, so that the Mughals could neither turn back nor proceed on : and missiles of stone and bullets began to fall upon them from the adjoining rocks. Kartalb Khan found no way out, his men were dying of suffocation and thirst, so that he begged the Rai Bagan to intercede with Shivaji. The Marathā exacted a heavy fine and lo ! in a moment the path was left clear, so that the Mughals could wend their way back to Poona in utter discomfiture. Parmānand has described this episode of Umbar-Khind with graceful eloquence.[1]

As soon as Kartalb Khan was disposed of, Shivaji appointed Netāji Pālkar to look after the Mughals, and he himself rapidly moved against Rājāpur as much to wreak his vengeance upon the English factors for their wanton interference at the siege of Panhālā, as to further weaken the Bijapur power by seizing its territory of the south Konkan as well. Dābhol, Rājāpur and Kārwār were then wealthy ports thriving on foreign trade. Rustam-i-Zaman the nominal governor did not raise a finger for his master. Shivaji probably in the early months of 1661 conducted a regular raid through the Konkan territory, plundered Nizampur, put down the chief of Palwan near Dapoli, captured Dābhol from its owner surnamed Dalvi, worshipped at the shrine of Parshurām near Chiplun, proceeded to Sangameshvar, also a rich port then, and stationing there two of his trusted officers Tānāji Mālusre and Pilāji Nilakanth, himself suddenly appeared before Rājāpur.

Here he plundered the English factory and kept under restraint six of the East India Company's officials. He collected

1. Sh. Bh. Chapter 29.

a large plunder from Rājāpur and appointed his own administrators at the port, and also at Khārepātan about ten miles to the south. In the meantime receiving news that Surya Rao Surve, the Chief of Shringārpur near Sangameshvar had attacked Tānāji Mālsure and defeated him, Shivaji ran back from Rājāpur to Tānāji's succour. This Surve like the Moray of Javli had often intrigued against Shivaji ; the latter now determined to teach him a lesson. Shivaji came straight upon Shringārpur on 29 April. At his approach the Surve ran away to save his life, so that his principality stretching from Sangameshvar to Dapoli, fell into Shivaji's hand without a contest. Shivaji built new forts in this region for its protection. They were named Prachitgad, Palgad and Mandangad. Trimbak Bhaskar was appointed to administer this newly conquered territory.

The affairs of the Surves of Shringārpur used to be administered by another chief named Wāghoji Shirke (of Kutre) who was won over by Shivaji and gave his daughter Soyra Bai in marriage to the young hero. This was his second wife, taken no doubt for political motives in order to win the two great ancient Kshatriya families, the Surves and the Shirkes.[2] Thus the two powerful chiefs of south Konkan, the Shirkes of Kutre and the Surves of Shringārpur, were won over by Shivaji to his service, so that the whole west coast from Bassein to Malwan together with the inland territory stretching up to the Sahyadris came into Shivaji's possession. The lands east of the Sahyadri range were already in his possession from Junnar to fort Rangna, so that we now get a rough idea of the way in which Shivaji steadily consolidated his possessions,

2. The Chhatrapatis received many Shirke ladies into their house and married their own daughters to Shirkes, as this table will show :—

Wāghoji Shirke

Tanaji | Pilāji = Surve daughter | Soyrā Bai = Shivaji

Kānhoji

Sakwarbai = Shahu | Rānoji | Ganoji = Shivaji's daughter | Yesubai = Sambhāji having carved them out from the Bijapuri and the Mughal dominions.

2. **English Factors confined.**—It is necessary here to revert to the story of the English factors captured by Shivaji at Rājāpur. The friction between them had a previous history, without which the present scuffle cannot be properly explained. English factory records now published throw full light on the affair. When early in 1660 Shivaji's men came upon Dābhol, that port had in it three trading vessels belonging to Afzal Khan who had been cut down by Shivaji. Muhammad Sharif the Governor of Dabhol conveyed those ships quickly to Rājāpur at the request of Fazl Khan and delivered them for safety into the custody of the English factory, lest they should fall into Shivaji's hands. As Shivaji was at war with Bijapur, he sent his agent to Rājāpur to take possession of those ships of his enemy. The British would not give them over on the plea that Fazl Khan owed them large amounts, which they wanted to recover out of the property contained in those ships. When Shivaji arrived at Rājāpur, the Chief of the factory, Remington, for fear of being seized, ran for safety out to the sea, but Doroji succeeded in seizing the goods and detaining the second Officer Gifford (20 January 1660). At this stage Rustam-i-Zaman pleaded with Shivaji for restoring the goods and releasing Gifford. Shivaji agreed and the affair was for the moment closed.[3]

Then came the siege of Panhālgad, where the Rājāpur factors came to fight against Shivaji at the call of Siddi Jauhar Salabat Khan. Remington, Mingham, Gifford, and their interpreter Velji went to Panhālgad, supplied ammunition and opened a most damaging fire against the fort. Shivaji warned them that as traders they ought to remain neutral and not take sides in an internal war, and that since they had taken part in the war against him, they would have to suffer the conse-

3. It may be mentioned that in those days many private persons and rulers and chiefs also used to engage their capital in private trade on the sea, keeping their own ships and plying them to different lands, reaping enormous profits by such exchange of commodities. Even the Mughal Emperor and the Bahmani kings had their own ships working on the sea.

quences. They ridiculed this threat and exhibited their own flag at Panhālā in open defiance and fired some very destructive shots making Shivaji's position untenable. It was this wanton offence for which Shivaji was bent upon exacting full retribution.

Such a time was not long in coming. The English grenades were fired at Panhālā in July 1660, and Shivaji appeared at Rājāpur in the following March with the double object of punishing the English traders and bringing under his sway the whole of the southern Konkan, then belonging to Bijapur. On arrival at Rājāpur he invited the factors to pay him a visit, and they too out of curiosity, as if in utter ignorance of their conduct at Panhālā, called on him, when six of them Randolph Taylor, Richard Taylor, Gifford, Ferrand, Richard Napier, and Samuel Bernard were immediately put under restraint, their goods confiscated, and they themselves were removed to different places and confined, some at fort Songad near Mahād, and some at fort Wāsotā. Shivaji stationed a competent officer, Rāoji Somnāth, to manage the affairs of Rājāpur and look after the comforts of the six factors in confinement. In a few days Rāoji Somnāth informed the factors that they would be set at liberty and amply recompensed for their losses, if they would readily help Shivaji in his projected campaign against the Siddis of Janjira, but that if they refused, they would have to pay ransom for their release. The factors flatly rejected this offer. Many Muslim and Hindu traders and bankers of Rājāpur were similarly dealt with. Shivaji urged that he was in open war against Bijapur, and whoever opposed him would have to suffer the consequences.

Shivaji took particular care to supply the best available comforts to the factors whom he had kept in confinement. Their release was, however, long delayed owing mainly to their stiff and uncompromising attitude and partly to Shivaji's preoccupations also. They swore and threatened, committed self-abnegation, sent highly provocative and distorted accounts to their President at Surat, whom they requested to intercede with Shivaji, pay the fine and obtain their release. But the President refused to interfere in this affair as it had originated from their own unwarranted behaviour. In a letter dated 10th March 1662, the President chides them in the following terms:—

"How you came in prison you know very well. It was not for defending the Company's goods : it was for going to the siege of Pannella and tossing balls with a flag that was known to be the English. [Shivaji's action] was exactly as any other would doe, having power to revenge himself of such affronts. For merchants are not to sell their goods, when if of that nature as granadoes, to goe and shoote them off against an enemy ; for Merchants while trading in a strange country one may live quietly ; if not, medling, must looke for a requitall of their deserts. We must tell you plainly and none but what rehearsed is the cause of your imprisonment ; Mr. Revington himself having mentioned the commands of Shivaji not to sell any ; [these words] are cast in your teeth of being at Pannella castle because he would returne the injury as he hoped more to his satisfaction, if he could obtain money by this means."

The President confessed his inability to coerce Shivaji into obedience, and when the prisoners became convinced that they could not obtain release through any outside agency, they pleaded with Rāoji Somnāth for mercy. In the meantime Revington fell ill and obtained release for treatment. He reached Surat on 17 October 1661 and died there a year later. // On 17 January 1663 Rāoji Pandit came and carried the other captives to Rājāpur where they were released, when the following message under Shivaji's seal was read to them. " Let us forget the past. We had on hand a war with Bijapur for which funds were needed, and so Rājāpur had to suffer. We shall not repeat the affair." After this the English factors resumed their trade at Rājāpur. A writer in that factory informed the Surat President that "Shivaji's raid on Rājāpur cost it in plunder the amount of 24,000 Hons, the death of two persons and the detention of the factors for two years." The English merchants long continued to press Shivaji for reparation of the damage caused to them in the Rājāpur plunder, but he declined, being sure he had acted with perfect justice.

3. **Night raid on Shaista Khan.**—It has already been mentioned that while Shivaji had a stiff war on hand against Bijapur, Shaista Khan was pressing him severely from another direction. After the retreat of Kartalb Khan in February 1661, Shaista Khan immediately sent another large army into north

Konkan and wrested from Shivaji's hands Kalyan and its adjoining districts upto Pen. The next rainy season brought in a temporary cessation of hostilities ; but operations were soon resumed and Namdar Khan marched against Pen where Shivaji routed him in January 1662. During this whole year there was no large-scale open warfare, but Shaista Khan wove his coil round Shivaji and crippled him in the region round about Satara. For a time Shivaji felt completely nonplussed against the growing menace of the Mughals. Here was the Khan backed by the full resources of the Empire then at its zenith, and practically all the *swarajya* which Shivaji had so long built up had been overrun by the Mughals. The Khan occupied the very palace of Shivaji, his soldiers and spies roamed throughout the land hunting Shivaji out like a beast of prey beaten out of the jungle. For three long years now Shivaji struggled and chafed, and racked his brain severely for a solution.

But the genius of great men shines in such darkness. Some act of stern retribution must be done to the Khan personally, if an open fight was out of the question. After long thinking and deep planning Shivaji contrived his own ingenious device. He came to stay at Sinhgad in order to make a sudden dash upon the Khan's residence at Poona, which was his own palace, every detail of which was known to him. Shivaji sent two Brahman spies and collected whatever information could be obtained about the arrangements and disposition of the Mughal camp. He himself selected some four hundred clever and intrepid Mavlas, dressed them as Mughal soldiers and descended from Sinhgad on the afternoon of 5 April 1663, with a night of the 6th rising moon before him. Coming near the main gate of the camp in the early hours of the night they were admitted without suspicion, on declaring that they were a party of Mughal troops going in to relieve those who were already on duty. The Mughal armies were full of such new recruits. It was the month of Ramzan when the Khan and his household after breaking their day's fast retired before midnight. The moon set. While the camp and the Khan's quarters were enveloped in quiet and darkness with a few dim lights showing how the people were stationed and distributed at different points, Shivaji with about fifty men entered the house through a hole made in the weak kitchen-wall behind without noise. They made their way into the bed-rooms, cutting the cloth partitions through and slaughtering men and women in their beds. Shouts and cries arose and confusion overcame all. Having thus perpetrated terrible havoc, Shivaji and his party left hurriedly, some being cut down as they ran out, but most of them escaped safely back to Sinhgad. It was discovered later that the Khan himself was not among those that were killed. He escaped with the loss of his fore-fingers. One of his sons was killed along with one captain and six women. Two of his sons and eight maid-servants were wounded. Thus did Shivaji avenge himself upon Shaista Khan for having made him a homeless wanderer for three long years.[4]

Jashvant Sinh was close to the main Mughal camp, but did not raise a finger to save his chief. Early next morning the Mughals set out to make a furious attack against Sinhgad, but the guns on the fort played heavily against them. To besiege the fort and force Shivaji into submission was a long affair, not considered feasible as the rains were approaching. After this dreadful experience Shaista Khan considered Poona unsafe for his residence and retired to Aurangabad for the rains. Later in the year Jashvant Sinh tried to invest Sinhgad, but gave up the attempt as hopeless. This daring execution of the Maratha hero increased his prestige. He was considered the very incarnation of Satan, from whom no place was safe and for whom no feat was impossible. The whole country talked of it with astonishment and terror as a superhuman deed. The news reached Aurangzeb on 8th May and caused bitter humiliation and sorrow to his whole Court and family, as the Empire's premier peer was thus cunningly struck down by the devilish Maratha. Aurangzeb peremptorily transferred him to Bengal. The Khan left the Deccan on 1st December 1663 for his new province. Shivaji became a noted hero who had withstood two great powers with consummate stratagem. But more was yet to come.

4. **Surat Sacked.**—Shivaji was not the man to rest on his oars. His keen mind devised fresh blows at the Mughals.

4. Vide Shiva-C-Sahitya 5.12.

The night attack on Poona, however spectacular, did no material damage to the Emperor. During the rainy season of 1663 Shivaji's spies and agents were busy watching the northern Mughal territories between Poona and Burhanpur and picking out the weakest point for a fresh infliction, as open war had now broken out between them. He sent round a band of clever spies, obtained correct details of the Mughal dispositions far and near, and then made up his mind to strike at Surat and raise such a huge fire in the breast of the Emperor that his reputation would be for ever darkened, as the poet Bhushan puts it. The plan was kept a closely guarded secret. Nobody knew where Shivaji was going. He gave out that he was proceeding to the south, but actually moved towards the north.

We are now in the second decade of Shivaji's career. His rising moon grew continuously to fulness, every year bringing in fresh problems, new dangers, successful escapes, and additional glories in rapid succession. His restless mind always looked out for fresh adventures. The captain of his spies, Bahirji Naik after a strenuous tour brought him news about the wealth of distant Surat, the prosperous gateway of India, a port from which thousands of Muslim pilgrims embarked for Mecca and returned every year. Most of the seaborne trade of Mughal India passed through Surat, giving it an eminence even greater than that of Imperial Delhi. There lived at this port at least twenty merchants, both Hindu and Muslim, who could be assessed by crores and at least two or three who could be counted the richest in the world. One Mulla Abdul Jafar alone owned nineteen ships laden with costly goods.

Shivaji made up his mind. Would he succeed in an attack on such a place, at least two hundred miles away without good roads or easy means of communication ? The only highway to Surat lay through Burhanpur, which Shivaji must avoid. He had already established two military camps in the vicinity of Danda Rajpuri and Pen, with a view, as he gave out, to putting down the Siddi and the Portuguese. He established another camp near Nasik, all containing select men personally picked. With proper instructions issued in advance, portions of these specially prepared troops numbering about four thousand in all, started from their stations at an auspicious moment previously selected. Shivaji himself left Nasik about 1st January 1664 and his men marched through Mahuli, Kohaj, Jawhar and Ramnagar, all the detachments uniting at Gandevi, 28 miles south of Surat on Tuesday 5th January. The news of his approach reached Surat like a flash of lightning causing extreme terror and anxiety in every breast. Many people left the town with their families for safety outside.

Surat castle then had a fort-wall not very strong, while the town with the main populace and the business centre lay outside the walls. The Governor of the town was one Inayatulla Khan who had kept no troops for the protection of the town, although he drew cash allowance for their expense. From Gandevi Shivaji sent special agents in advance to inform the Governor and the merchants of his intended arrival and assuring them that he meant no harm to anybody, that he was at open war with the Emperor, for which he was in sore need of funds which he must obtain from those who traded under the Emperor's protection and who could pay.[5] For years, he urged, the Emperor had driven him out of his house at Poona and appropriated all his treasure and belongings. He expected from Surat a handsome amount, about 50 lacs which could be easily subscribed by the wealthy merchants of the town. Shivaji also addressed letters of similar import to the Governor and to some particular merchants asking for contributions and warning them of the consequences of a refusal. "Tomorrow," he said, "we shall be at Surat when you should pay me a visit and deliver the specified amount. If you fail to comply, we shall have to use severe methods of collecting money, such as plunder and arson, for which the responsibility will be yours." The Governor sent his agent with an impertinent reply, upon which Shivaji detained the messengers and himself arrived at 11 o'clock in the morning, the next day, Wednesday 6th January camping with his followers in a garden outside the Burhanpur gate.

No one took notice of Shivaji's warning and none came

5. The whole account is compiled from a number of sources now published and available., Factory Records, Foreign Biographies, Manucci, Dutch accounts and others.

out to meet him. Besides the Indian merchants in the town there were English and Dutch factories at the river wharf with their own fortified enclosures. But Shivaji had not come prepared with artillery to engage in an open warfare with the handful of foreign traders, who had plenty of goods but little of gold and silver. It is not right to argue that he was afraid of them and so did not molest them. The experience of Rājāpur was fresh in his memory. Indeed he was not in a position to fight even the Governor of Surat if he had chosen to defend the town or the fort. It was because the Governor in a panic ran to the fort for safety and left the town at the mercy of the Marathas, that the subsequent troubles occurred. Shivaji's move was an open challenge to the Emperor and a means of acquiring the sinews of the war that had been imposed on him.

Writes Thevenot: "All the town of Surat was plundered except the monastery of the Capuchins. The plunderers did no harm to the Convent. For the first day in the evening Father Ambrose, who was Superior of it, being moved with compassion for the poor Christians living in Surat, went to the Rājā and spoke in their favour, praying him not to suffer any violence to be done to them. Shivaji had a respect for the Father, took him into his protection, and granted what he had devised in favour of the Christians."[6]

On the day of his arrival Shivaji sent for some local merchants and employed his men to force out funds from them as far as possible by peaceful and persuasive methods. Some of the merchants were detained by him as prisoners. On Thursday 7 January the cowardly Inayat-ulla sent a young man to Shivaji with a pretended offer of peace. After a little conversation the young man approached closer to Shivaji saying that he had to communicate something in private and suddenly rushed forward to stab him with a concealed dagger that he had brought with him. A Maratha bodyguard struck off the assassin's hand, but the fellow hurled himself upon the Rājā. Shivaji's clothes were seen stained with blood. The guards wanted to start a general massacre of the townspeople and of the prisoners that had been assem-

6. Sen's Foreign Biographies, P. 179.

bled; but Shivaji sternly prohibited such a course and only cut off the hands of a few known culprits. If according to his own previous demand upon the Governor and the three principal merchants Haji Saiyad Beg, Bahirji Bohra, and Haji Kasim, they had personally come and negotiated for the amount of ransom in a reasonable mood, all the subsequent miseries could have been avoided. But the foul plot of the Governor to get Shivaji murdered, excited his spirit of revenge and then he ordered a general sack of the houses of the rich and setting fire to various localities. Throughout the 8th and the 9th of January this work of plunder and devastation continued with unabated fury; numerous houses were consumed by fire, and nearly two-thirds of the town destroyed. "The fire turned the night into day as during the day time; the smoke had turned day into night, rising so thick that it darkened the Sun like a great cloud." This description of the English chaplain is closely followed by the poet Bhusan in his poetic fastion.[7]

The Marathas broke open the doors of houses and chests and carried off as much booty as they could lay their hands on. No resistance was offered to this plunder and heaps of articles of all kinds were accumulated in front of Shivaji's camp. He made the best of his four days' run at the town but shrank from any wanton cruelty for extracting money.[8]

On Saturday the 9th of January Shivaji received news of a Mughal force coming rapidly for the rescue of the town, and next day he left the place as suddenly as he had arrived, carrying away nothing but gold and silver, pearls and diamonds, and precious ware of light weight and small size. Heaps of clothing and household articles that were collected were freely distributed to the townspeople as there was no time to open a sale for them. It is not possible to offer an accurate estimate of the value of the plunder he carried away, possibly Shivaji himself had never the time to make an exact calculation. But it must certainly have been above a crore of rupees, possibly double that amount. The plunder was carried straight to Raigad and was utilized in fortifying that capital of his future government. The giant water-fortress of

7. Vide Verse 201 of *Shiva-raj Bhushan Kavya*.
8. See Sarkar's Shivaji and his Times p. 100.

Sindhudurg at Malwan was also constructed out of this plunder nearly at the same time. The Mughal forces from Khandesh arrived before Surat a week after Shivaji had left it and found that place entirely defaced.[9]

5. Position of Bijapur, Baji Ghorpade.—About a week after Shivaji's return to Raigad he received the sad news of his father's sudden death near Basavapattan, south of the Tunga-Bhadrā river, on 23 January 1664 in an accident while out hunting. This incident necessitates a reference back to Shivaji's relations with Bijapur and the part played therein by his father. In September 1660 Shivaji gave the fort of Panhālā back to Bijapur and brought about a kind of truce with that State in order to direct his attention to Shaista Khan's aggressions. He also strengthened his hold upon Rājāpur and south Konkan, taking advantage of the struggle for power that was then going on between the young Ali Adil Shah and his mother the queen Badi-Sahiba. By the end of 1660 Ali seized the sole power and the queen marked her displeasure by going away on a pilgrimage to Mecca. She was away for a year from May 1661 to June 1662. During this interval Ali Adil Shah tried to befriend Shivaji by calling upon Shahji to act as a peace-maker. For two or three years since the affair of Afzal Khan, Shivaji had been openly at war with Bijapur as we have already seen. During this period the conduct of Shahji was not altogether free from suspicion. Outwardly he disclaimed any responsibility for his son's conduct, but at the same time he did not as readily help the Shah in suppressing the revolt of Shivaji. How could he ? He was as human as any father and son to-day. The noble enthusiasm of the son was rewarded with success and in comparison the father was pushed into the background. After all every successful revolutionary is a rebel at the start, and he becomes a legalized monarch only after a career full of perils and adventures.

The death of Shahji opened the third and last phase of Shivaji's guiding star. Upon the recall of Shaista Khan, the

9. सुरत बेसुरत 'Surat was denuded of all its glory' is the common description of this episode given by the *Bakhars*.

Emperor sent his son Shahzada Muazzam as Governor of the Deccan with Jashvant Sinh as his lieutenant. They were both lukewarm in taking any strong measures against Shivaji, who, however, allowed himself not a moment's rest. He and Netāji Pālkar fell like vultures upon the Mughal territories between Ahmadnagar and Aurangabad. Shivaji's navy too now began to molest the pilgrim ships proceeding to Mecca from Surat. Shivaji was supposed to be some supernatural being possessed of wings which carried him anywhere, having the power to make himself invisible and roam about wherever he liked without being observed. The English factors wrote, "Report has made Shivaji an airy body and added wings. Or else it would be impossible he could be at so many places at one and the same time. He is and ever was for a running banquet plundering and burning those towns which have neither defence nor guard. The Deccan is embroiled in civil wars, Shivaji reigns victoriously and uncontrolled. He is a terror to all the kings and princes round about, daily increasing in strength. He is nimble and active, imposing strange labour upon himself and exercises his chiefest men that he flies to and fro with incredible dexterity."

At this time (1664) Shivaji wrote a very strong letter to the officers and counsellors of the Emperor, in which he wrote, "You very well know what results have been achieved by the famous generals and able counsellors sent by the Emperor during the last three years for seizing my country and my forts. How is it you don't realize that this is an impossible task? Your officers are not ashamed of reporting entirely fictitious accounts. My home here is not like the towns of Kalyani and Bedar which could be easily assaulted and taken. My country has lofty hill-ranges two hundred leagues in length and forty in breadth and is well protected by sixty strong forts newly built. Afzal Khan came against me and perished helplessly. Your great Amir-ul-Umra Shaista Khan laboured hard for three years and went away in disgrace after suffering a terrible disaster. It is my duty to guard my land, and I will do it. Thank God, no invader of my beloved country has yet bloomed forth."[10]

10. House of Shivaji, by Sarkar, p. 98. For Bijapuri nobles see p. 55.

It has already been mentioned that Ali Adil Shah took back the fort of Panhālā from Shivaji. Early in 1663 the Shah started on an expedition into the Karnatak and took his station at Bankāpur, determined particularly to recover the territories of south Konkan, which Shivaji had seized and bring back to obedience the Sāvant of Wādi who had gone over to Shivaji's side. The presence of Adil Shah cowed the Sāvant as well as the Dutch factors of Vingorla and the Portuguese of Goa. This move was at once opposed by Shivaji who personally arrived at Kudal in May and threatened all those who had deserted him. The Dutch and the Portuguese readily purchased his goodwill by bringing in costly presents. Shivaji established a strong garrison in Kudāl and returned to Rajgad in June.

The Adil Shah could not bear this direct affront to his power. He concentrated his best effort upon recovering Kudāl and sent a large force under Ikhlas Khan to recover Kudal, and at the same time ordered his minister Khawas Khan to proceed with a well-equipped army from Bijapur to reinforce Ikhlas Khan. Bāji Ghorpade of Mudhol was at the same time ordered to proceed against Kudāl. Shivaji's half brother Ekoji from Tanjore also arrived on duty to oppose Shivaji and wrest Kudāl from his possession. This was indeed a formidable combination, the details of which were being constantly reported to Shivaji, as the concentration took months in being organized and executed. Shivaji was equal to the danger and boldly attacked the various confederates piecemeal. This was Adil Shah's last stroke against Shivaji.

Adil Shah's plans came to a head during the autumn of 1664, and Shivaji struck the first blow most unexpectedly in the month of November of that year by suddenly falling upon Mudhol the seat of his cousin and inveterate enemy Bāji Ghorpade, who was a staunch adherent of Adil Shah, deadly opposed to any move like that of Shivaji towards *swarajya*, and who, it should be noted, had taken the leading part in the arrest of Shahji before Jinji in 1648. This last incident was rankling in Shivaji's heart.

Shivaji's plan was to prevent Ghorpade from joining Khawas Khan in an attack upon Kudāl. Learning that Shivaji was rapidly coming upon Mudhol, Bāji Rāja left the place and boldly came out to meet him with his whole following. A sanguinary action ensued in which Bāji and several of his officers lost their lives. Shivaji then captured and plundered Mudhol and secured an amount of wealth that had been accumulated there through many prosperous years of peace. Shivaji had no time to lose, because he was anxious to dispose of his next opponent Khawas Khan, who had left Bijapur for Kudāl. Māloji Ghorpade the youngest son of Bāji was installed as the Chief of Mudhol,[11] and Shivaji immediately afterwards turned to the direction in which Khawas Khan was reported to be moving. The latter was suddenly attacked, about which the Dutch factors wrote, "Sivaji had gone to Khānāpur with the pick of his men to plunder it and that in doing so he had passed Khawas Khan's army within a mile without that lord's stirring.[12] The Khan got so severely wounded that he soon died and lost 200 men besides all the cash. Shivaji leisurely plundered Khānāpur, Hubli etc. and sent off the goods in due security.[13] Shivaji himself wrote about this encounter, "Thereupon Khawas Khan marched upon me, and I on my part answered his charge vigorously. A stiff battle ensued in which the enemy was completely routed and ran back to Bijapur after losing some brave commanders under him. I then turned to punish the Sāwant for his wanton desertion of my cause, plundered his territory and captured his forts and towns. As the Portuguese sheltered him I blew their fort of Ponda with gunpowder and captured it by sheer force. They negotiated for peace and gave me some guns. Pitāmbar Shenvai came to me as an envoy of peace to treat both for the Sāvant and the Portuguese. I annexed half the territory of the Sāvant and restored the other half to him. I

11. Years afterwards Shivaji thus wrote to Maloji, "it is to be regretted that your father forgetting all the good that my father had done him, sided with Mustafa Khan in capturing him. It was your father who gave over my father as a captive into Mustafa's hands, thus causing bitter enmity for years between your house and mine resulting in bloodshed. My people killed your father in a fight but now has arrived the occasion for rectifying the past mistakes." (Shivaji Souvenir P. 146).

12. This report of Khawas Khan's death was false. He long served Bijapur and came to be murdered on 20 Jan. 1676.

13. Dr. Balkrishna, Shivaji the Great, Vol. I, p. 533.

reminded him that he was a son of the Bhosles and ought to join me in saving our country and religion."[14]

During this war Shivaji's half-brother Ekoji came from Bangalore to serve the Bijapur cause. But after all, his strength was too small and Shivaji did not care to notice his reprehensible conduct, till after his own coronation ten years later. These unbrotherly pin-pricks he wisely reserved for future retribution. The Adil Shah, however, rewarded Ekoji for his services.[15]

Shivaji had already realized the advantages of a strong navy, with the help of which the European powers so weak on land made permanent settlements on the west coast and amassed untold wealth through foreign trade. To hold them in check he created a naval base of his own in the vicinity of the Dutch and the Portuguese settlements by erecting the wonderful fort of Sindhudurg on a difficult rock near Malwan. This costly work was commenced on 25 November 1664 and its completion was possible only on account of the vast accumulations Shivaji had made by seizing the wealth of many trading towns. The country acclaimed Shivaji's exploits and felt thankful that Providence had at last sent them a redeemer.

"War to pay for war" was Shivaji's principle of national rule, call it what you will, plunder, or robbery or in modern democratic parlance, a legalized war indemnity imposed by a victorious Government, or the Tonnage and Poundage of Hampden's days. Before the fort of Sindhudurg was ready, Shivaji built his ships in that harbour and ordered them about for asserting his power throughout the coastal regions. He personally led the first daring expedition southward. On the morning of 8th February 1665 he suddenly appeared in the harbour of Basrur as far south as the coast of Bednur, with a large group of ships totalling 85 of medium size and three men-of-war of a superior type. In one day he amassed a huge quantity of plunder from that port and returned to Karwar, devoutly worshipping on the way the Mahabaleshvar image at Shiva—Gokarn[16] on the Shivaratri day, and in the midst of

14. Shivaji Souvenir p. 144.
15. B. I. S. M. Q. 11, p. 47.
16. Kalidas mentions this shrine of Gokarn in Ragh. VIII. 33.

his rejoicing receiving the dreadful news of an attack on his dominions by Mirza Raja Jay Sinh, he hurried back by land to face the new danger. Such was the great hero's life, genius leading to success, success to wealth, that again to renewed dangers which he ultimately overcame with singular will power to reach a haven of safety. All his past year's work at Kudāl and his power over its ruler the Sāvant were entirely upset; the same Pitambar Shenvai going to Bijapur on behalf of the Sāvant, and effecting a fresh treaty with that Court for a coalition against Shivaji. The Sāvant needed one more severe lesson.

6. **Jay Sinh and Shivaji face to face.**—By his surprise attack on Surat Shivaji invited upon himself the full wrath of the Emperor. Aurangzeb recalled Muazzam and Jashvant Sinh and despatched a fresh expedition under Mirza Raja Jay Sinh with Dilir Khan to assist him and with full equipment to annihilate the growing power of Shivaji and to effect the final conquest of Bijapur. Jay Sinh and Dilir Khan were the ablest and most devoted of Aurangzeb's nobles and whole-heartedly undertook their mission. Jay Sinh had never known a reverse in his career. In 1617 when twelve years old he entered the Delhi Emperor's service and had since then distinguished himself in various imperial campaigns from Balkh in the north to Bijapur in the south, and from Kandahar in the west to Monghir in the east. During Shah Jahan's reign he had been rewarded practically on every annual birthday celebration for some victory gained by him. At the Emperor's Court Jay Sinh was on the same level of honour as the sons of the Emperor. He was no less adept in the art of diplomacy than in that of war, for which his coadjutor Dilir Khan was highly distinguished. In any serious danger threatening the Empire Jay Sinh alone was the Emperor's last resort. He possessed a sweet persuasive tongue, and could speak the three foreign languages Turki, Persian, and Urdu in addition to his own Rajasthani. He had now reached the age of sixty and had developed the statesman's sobriety and circumspection by long past experience. It was not, however, with a light heart that he accepted the present command, having before him the sad examples of Afzal Khan, Shaista Khan and Jashvant Sinh.

"The task I have undertaken allows me not a moment of ease and peace," are words found repeated in almost every letter that he now wrote to the Emperor.

It was on 30 September 1664, the occasion of Aurangzeb's birthday celebration, that Jay Sinh received the formal dress for this signal undertaking. In addition to Dilir Khan he took with him his son Kirat Sinh, Daud Khan Qureshi, along with several Rajput and Bundella princes. Nicholo Manucci accompanied him in charge of the artillery. Never had such a select force crossed into the Deccan before. Jay Sinh forded the Narmada on 9 January 1665, reached Burhanpur on 19th, and after spending a few days there in preparation, he arrived on 10 February, at Aurangabad and on 3rd March at Poona, which Jashvant Sinh immediately left on his return journey. At this time Shivaji, as we know, was on the Kanara coast.

Immediately on his arrival and even before it Jay Sinh took steps to prevent any kind of help reaching Shivaji from Bijapur. Indeed it was at the behest of the Emperor that the Adil Shah had been recently waging a war against Shivaji and that even the Sāvant of Kudāl had deserted the latter's cause. The Emperor had urged Jay Sinh to pursue Shivaji into the Konkan, a proposal which he stoutly resisted, knowing full well that those inaccessible hilly regions were most unsuited for the military operations of the army he was commanding or for any effective action against Shivaji. He, however, at once established his hold on the western uplands between Lohgad and Rajgad, and allowed no base to Shivaji in and round about Poona. He sent his envoys to the English at Bombay and the Portuguese at Goa, and invited their navies to co-operate in a war against the rebel. Jay Sinh also sent special Brahman agents to the various Poligars of the Karnatak. Afzal Khan's son Fazl Khan and the Nayak of Bednur joined Jay Sinh with their quota of troops. Jay Sinh also tried to weaken Shivaji's own following by offering bribes and alluring promises. At his request the Emperor invested him with full authority to order and execute anything he thought necessary in the interest of his heavy task. He had full control of the treasury without any interference from the Accounts and Audit officials. Knowing that the monsoon was due soon, Jay Sinh established his main camp near Saswad and himself took up his temporary residence in Poona. He posted one general Kutbuddin Khan at Lohgad with 7000 troops to guard the western passes.

Jay Sinh did not rely on armed preparations only. He employed private agents to induce Shivaji to submit of his own accord and avoid an unnecessary bloody war. He intimated to Shivaji that he himself was as solicitous of the Hindu religion as Shivaji, and that if the latter would willingly offer his submission to the Emperor, his own interests would be highly promoted. That he should not feel any derogation in such a course, Jay Sinh pointed to the honour he had gained by serving the Emperor, as the premier Hindu noble of the Mughal State.

Having safeguarded the western frontiers Jay Sinh moved from Poona to Saswad on 31st March and at once employed Dilir Khan in laying siege to the fort of Purandar. He despatched Daud Khan Qureshi to capture Rajgad, where Shivaji had his main treasure and offices. On 14 April a detached portion of Purandar known as Rudramal or Vajragad offered to submit. In the mean time Netaji Palkar, Shivaji's commandant, tried to capture Parenda but failed. Purandar, it seemed, would not long hold out, although its valiant defender Murar Bāji gave Dilir Khan a fore-taste of what the Mughals could expect from Shivaji's men.

Dilir Khan arrived before Purandar on 30 March and invested it with the numerous force he had brought. He opened a heavy fire against the fort with rapid effect. Murar Bāji tried his usual guerilla tactics of starving the besiegers out and setting fire to their ammunition. But these slow and imperfect methods had no effect on the well-equipped and richly supplied Mughal troops. Murar had with him only about two thousand select Mavla troops, all fired with the same zeal as himself. When the lower fort Rudramal fell into Dilir Khan's hands, he took up his residence at its foot known as Machi or the ridge. Thereupon the defenders took shelter in the upper fort and kept up an incessant fire with their small guns. They attacked the Mughals with such fury that once Murar himself pursued the Khan right up to his tent on the ridge where the two parties closed with each other in a deadly hand to hand combat. Many Marathas were cut down. Murar

Bāji lost one arm and his shield, but would not yield. He tied his maimed arm with his scarf and kept on hacking at the enemy. As he rushed against Dilir Khan himself, he was soon overpowered and had his head severed. His followers rescued the fallen trunk and sent it to Shivaji for the final rites. Still the Mughals obtained no access to the upper fort. The spot where Murar Baji fell is called Ranatemb meaning the hillock of the fight.

It was now the middle of April. Shivaji at Bhimgad east of Goa, had received on 14 March the first news of Jay Sinh and Dilir Khan's arrival at Poona and their formidable attacks in all directions. He hastened back and reached the vicinity of Purandar by the middle of April, halting probably at Shirwal, where he received the headless corpse of Murar Bāji, the sight of which awakened him to the dangerous situation that faced him. After some days of hesitation and deliberation he made up his mind to submit.

After messages had been exchanged between the two sides for some time Shivaji on 11 June 1665 accompanied by six Brahman counsellors rode in his Palki to Jay Sinh's tent in the middle of his camp near the plain of the Narayan temple of Pur about a couple of miles from Saswad. Jay Sinh wisely took the precaution of not conducting the negotiations behind Dilir Khan's back, as the latter acting like a spy might make an adverse report to the Emperor. On the day following Shivaji's arrival, that is on 12th June, Jay Sinh sent Shivaji with his own agent Rai Sinh to pay a visit to Dilir Khan in his camp. Shivaji went to Dilir Khan entirely unarmed. The Khan was mollified by this marked attention from Shivaji, presented him with two horses, a sword, a jewelled dagger and clothes, and personally conducted him back to Jay Sinh. When the Khan began to tie the sword on Shivaji, the latter said, "I should like to remain entirely unarmed; your good faith is my highest protection." Thereafter a free and frank conversation took place between the three chiefs and the terms were settled during the four days that Shivaji stayed in the Mughal Camp. He left it on 15 June and returned to hand over the forts which he had agreed to surrender.

We have to-day three main accounts of this important visit, first the full Persian reports made to the Emperor by Jay

Sinh himself, secondly the account recorded by Manucci, who was an eye-witness on the spot, and thirdly an interesting anonymous poetic account in Persian written by some intelligent person present in the camp and recently published under the caption Shivaji's letter to Jay Sinh. This last is an admirable piece of composition vividly depicting the atmosphere in the Mughal camp and supplying Shivaji's side of the affair, as the first of the three items gives the official Mughal version. On the basis of these three accounts we shall summarise the story of this grand event. Shivaji's Letter to Jay Sinh cannot be rejected as worthless simply because it was composed in the poetic vein. It deserves to be remembered that even official reports like Jay Sinh's are often intended to whitewash actual facts. Jay Sinh could not report to the Emperor Shivaji's actual grievances.

Jay Sinh writes, " After the arrival of the imperial army near Pabal, Shivaji's agents began to visit me and again up to my arrival at Poona they twice brought letters for me. But I gave no answer and sent them back in disappointment. He again sent me a long Hindi letter saying that he was a useful servant of the imperial threshold and would readily help in the conquest of Bijapur. I wrote to him in answer that " the imperial army was sent against you. If you desire your own life and safety, be a slave to the Imperial Court." When he was put to hard straits and our troops captured Rudramal, Shiva made a proposal, and begged to spare his life and property. I gave no answer and continued my war against him. On 20 May Shiva's Guru styled Raghunath Pandit arrived on a secret embassy and stated Shiva's terms of submission. I declined to negotiate with him. The Pandit went back and brought another message. I told him if Shiva consents to obey the Emperor's orders, he would be pardoned. On 9th June the Brahman went to Shiva and on the 11th he brought the news that Shiva had arrived. I sent my Bakhshi to conduct Shiva in."

Shivaji stayed with Jay Singh for three complete days, a period during which, apart from official business, the two chiefs must have talked about various matters of national and religious import and of the general state of Indian politics. Two such important personalities can hardly come together without arriving at some material results. At Jay Sinh's suggestion, Shivaji proceeded with his son Kirat-Sinh and met Dilir Khan on 13 June; and on the 15th Shivaji left the Mughal camp, after agreeing to a treaty by which twenty three of his important forts were to be at once delivered into the Mughal possession, he himself retaining only twelve minor ones. Kirat Singh accompanied Shivaji to take charge of the forts personally from him. Fort Kondhana or Sinhagad was at once given up to Kirat Sinh. Shivaji's mother and wife who were there left it, as also the whole garrison of seven thousand men. Kirat Sinh returned to his father on 18th June accompanied by Sambhāji who was to serve in the Mughal army. The keys of the vacated forts were forwarded by Jay Sinh to the Emperor.

Jay Sinh's letters to the Emperor appear after all to be formal official reports of the transactions and do not supply any clue as to how far he agreed or disagreed with Shivaji's views. This want is admirably made up by the Persian "Letter addressed to Jaysinh" in the name of Shivaji, appealing to his heart as a Hindu to appreciate and support the national and religious uplift undertaken by Shivaji in order to deliver his land from the oppressive Muslim yoke. Shivaji urged that as Hindus, they must both work together to win back their religious liberty and to prevent such persecution as was involved in the demolition and plunder of temples and forcible conversions; that Aurangzeb's power was mainly supported by the strength of the Rajput princes, and it was a shame as Shivaji pointed out, that a great ruler of the calibre of Jay Sinh should not raise even a finger against the Emperor's policy but meekly execute it by pulling the Hindu religion down. Frank private discussions could not have been avoided during the famous meeting. This is amply evidenced by Aurangzeb's own subsequent conduct. He suspected Jay Sinh of treachery and disgraced him publicly a year later when Shivaji escaped from Agra, with the connivance, if not with the active support, of Jay Sinh's son Ram Sinh.

This Persian metrical letter on the face of it reveals the surcharged atmosphere of the Mughal camp during the days of Shivaji's visit, which is admirably depicted even by Manucci. There was an unprecedented stir in the camp. Great vigilance prevailed there, lest some mischief should occur through the wily Shivaji. The small details mentioned in the letter could not have been reproduced unless the author had breathed that vivacious atmosphere. Shivaji brought to Jay Sinh's notice how he was being deluded into false hopes by the wily Emperor ; he removed all Jay Sinh's fears about treachery on his own part on account of the way he had behaved in the affair of Afzal Khan. But, urged Shivaji, people did not know that Afzal Khan had kept a reserve of 1200 Abyssinian troops in hiding near the place where they met ; and had therefore to act in the way he did to save his own life. The letter mentions the severe taunts that Shivaji personally conveyed to Jay Sinh. The latter, however, all along soberly maintained, "after all the Emperor was their master ; it is our duty to obey him and to be perfectly loyal to him." Thereupon Shivaji earnestly put him the plain question, "were you not equally bound to be loyal to Shah Jahan, when you were ordered to march under Dara Shukoh's command against the rebel Aurangzeb ? Were not Shah Jahan and Dara your masters ? Did they not put perfect faith in your honesty ? What happened to your loyalty then when you treacherously deserted them and joined Aurangzeb ? Don't you suppose you have been finally absolved from these heinous sins ? You will surely have to answer for them before the Final Arbiter, if not even in this world. Anyway, friend, beware of Aurangzeb. If you give me a helping hand, well and good ; if not, I am perfectly able to take care of myself. I have already cast my die, and am prepared to stand by it."

Manucci gives a few interesting details of Shivaji's visit to Jay Sinh, who tried to obtain success over Shivaji and avoid a result like that of Shaista Khan. When Shivaji's agents came to Jay Sinh, making various offers, Jay Sinh informed Shivaji through them, "If you put complete trust in me and follow my advice, I shall see that the Emperor promotes your interests highly." Shivaji accepted this advice, put perfect faith in Jay Sinh and went fearlessly to meet him, unarmed and unattended, into the very den of the lion. The whole camp was in an excited state upon Shivaji's arrival, lest some mischief should follow from his visit. But when it became known that he had come alone with no followers, the people in the camp felt easy. Jay Sinh provided for Shivaji's residence a tent adjoining his own. One evening as Manucci and Jay Sinh were playing at cards, Shivaji unexpectedly dropped in. All rose to receive him and when they were seated, Shivaji pointing to Manucci asked Jay Sinh who this young gentleman was, Manucci then about 25 years of age being some twelve years younger than Shivaji. Jay Sinh replied, "this young man was the leader of the Franks, (Firangies)." Thereafter the two, Manucci and Shivaji had a long conversation together on various topics, particularly the States of Europe, their strength on land and sea and their methods of warfare. Manucci spoke Urdu fluently and they had direct talks without an interpreter.

In due course Jay Sinh received the Emperor's reply confirming the treaty of Purandar ; and a similar letter addressed to Shivaji dated 5 September 1665 was also received, worded rather in stiff terms. When the Emperor's *farman* arrived, Jay Sinh invited Shivaji to come and receive it with due ceremony. Shivaji went six miles on foot with Kirat Sinh and welcomed the *farman* with fitting honours and obeisance. By the treaty of Purandar Shivaji agreed to join the Mughals in the conquest of Bijapur and executed his promise faithfully. As Shivaji was intimately acquainted with the local conditions, his co-operation in the coming war against Bijapur was found by Jay Sinh immensely valuable. Jay Sinh took charge of the ceded forts, but had not enough men to spare in order to garrison them all. Purandar, Sinhgad and Lohgad were the only ones which could be supplied with defensive forces and requirements. The walls and fortifications of a few others were demolished.

Thereafter Jay Sinh spent the wet season in completing his preparations for the war against Bijapur, in which Shivaji joined with a following of 9000 Mavlas under Netāji Pālkar. The combined armies started from Saswad on 25 November 1665 and reached Mangalvedhe on 18 December. Here Māloji Ghorpade of Mudhol and Ekoji from Bangalore came and joined the Bijapuri forces under Sharza Khan and Khawas Khan who had come from Bijapur to oppose the Mughals. A stiff battle took place in which Netāji Pālkar and Dilir Khan inflicted a severe defeat upon the Bijapuri forces. The two brothers Shivaji and Ekoji for the first time met personally in an open encounter. But after all the war did not turn out as successful for the Mughals as they had expected. Dilir Khan secretly reported to the Emperor the real or fancied wrongs he had received at the hands of Jay Sinh, and behaved like a spy on the movements and measures adopted by the latter. This was indeed an intentional contrivance used by the Emperor, who entertained grave suspicions that Jay Sinh sympathised with the Hindus of the Deccan. Any way this open conflict between the two top-men of the Mughal army affected the fortunes of the war very adversely. The Bijapur forces fought for life with unexampled valour and determination and were joined by the troops of Golkonda also. The moment for the extinction of these two States had not arrived.

Jay Sinh and Dilir Khan proceeded very near Bijapur, but the former on being affronted by the latter marched away towards Parenda. Shivaji offered to capture the fort of Panhālā and delivered an attack on it on 16 January 1666, but did not succeed in the attempt.

At this time a grievous breach occurred between Shivaji and Netāji Pālkar, which cannot be satisfactorily accounted for. It deserves to be carefully noticed and investigated as it has a close relation with Shivaji's history. Netāji was doubtless a valiant soldier, second only to Shivaji in tactics, and he had rendered long and valuable services to the Maratha State. A quarrel arose between them on some point of discipline; and while Jay Sinh's war with Bijapur was on, Netāji left Shivaji's service and joining the Bijapuri forces, created thereby a serious situation for Jay Sinh, who, by means of secret overtures took Netāji into the Mughal service and obtained for him a five thousand command from the Emperor (20 March 1666). We shall hear more of Netaji in due course.

CHRONOLOGY

VII

1665	June	15	Treaty of Purandar.
1666	Jan.	22	Death of Shah Jahan.
„	March	5	Shivaji starts for Agra.
„	May	12	Shivaji is presented to Aurangzeb at Court.
„	„	20	Jafar Khan presents Shivaji's petition to the Emperor.
„	„	29	Another petition from Shivaji presented.
„	June	8	Shivaji requests to be taken out of Ram Sinh's charge.
„	„	9	Shivaji sends away his retinue.
„	July	15	Shivaji obtains a loan from Ram Sinh.
„	„	„	Poet Parmānand first mentioned as at Agra.
„	Aug.	17	Shivaji escapes from Agra.
„	„	23	Poet Parmānand placed in detention.
„	Nov.	20	(or Sept. 12 ?) Shivaji reaches Rajgad.
„	Dec.	26	Parmānand brought back from Chandangaon.
„			Netāji Pālkar brought to the Emperor's court.
1667			Netāji made Muslim and sent to serve in Afghanistan.
1667	May		Jay Sinh recalled : is replaced by Muazzam and Jashvant Sinh.
„	„		Bahlol Khan besieged fort Rangna : Shivaji raises the siege.
„	Aug.	28	Death of Jay Sinh at Burhanpur.
„	Sept.		Adil Shah concludes treaty with Shivaji.
„	Dec.	11	The Portuguese make peace with Shivaji.
1668	March	9	Aurangzeb makes peace with Shivaji.
„	Aug.	5	Sambhāji joins the Mughal camp.
1668			Bijapur and Golkonda agree to grant Chauth to Shivaji.

CHAPTER VII

THE LION BEARDED IN HIS DEN.

[1666—1667]

1. Hesitation to visit Agra.
2. The Audience Hall.
3. The wonderful escape.
4. After effects, peace.

1. **Hesitation to visit Agra.**— Although Shivaji was shrewd enough to assume a submissive attitude towards Jay Sinh at Purandar, he cleverly made it a stepping stone to his future advancement. The treaty of Purandar was to him only a temporary set back, by no means a final extinction. After all Jay Sinh was a brother Hindu whom Shivaji meant to conciliate rather than to destroy. The treaty of Purandar was almost a stage-managed affair and should not be interpreted as a humiliation for Shivaji. He was not openly beaten. Jay Sinh was sanguine about effecting a permanent understanding between the Emperor and Shivaji. Could not this be satisfactorily secured if the two were to meet and arrange matters personally ? Shivaji had already agreed to serve the Emperor in the Deccan, and even in that connection he had carefully avoided offering his own person, but substituted in his place his own son of 8 years for the Emperor's service. There was a provision in the treaty for a personal visit of Shivaji to the Emperor. But as time passed, Jay Sinh considered it the best way to bring about a permanent reconciliation, more or less a first step to leading Aurangzeb back to the policy that had been adopted by the Great Akbar, of making friends with the Hindu princes. The experiment was worth trying. Jay Sinh repeatedly urged Shivaji to meet the Emperor personally and explain to him all the grievances that he had himself uttered in the Purandar camp. With equal force he urged upon the Emperor to receive a visit from Shivaji, test his hearty goodwill and convert him into a powerful support for the preservation of peace in the southern dominions. If only Shivaji could once meet the Emperor, thought Jay Sinh, and the latter shower on him all his kindly attentions and honours, he could

be won over to serve the Empire loyally. Thus Jay Sinh played the part of a mediator for reconciling the two opposite views into a beneficent union. History has pronounced this as Jay Sinh's blunder in not having judged his master's character correctly.

Jay Sinh offered Shivaji his personal guarantee that no harm would come to him from his visit to the Emperor. He assured Shivaji that the Emperor was anxious to meet him and to utilise his services for the conquest of Bijapur and Golkonda on which he had long set his heart. So while Aurangzeb probably suspected mischief from Shivaji in a personal visit, Shivaji had grave doubts about the sincerity of the Emperor, whose ways and methods were already well-known. He deceitfully betrayed his own brother Murad, cruelly encompassed the ruin of Dara Shukoh and Shuja, artfully confined his father and selfishly seized the throne for himself, not even sparing his own sons from his wrath. These were public acts which made Shivaji hopeless of receiving any signal favour by a personal visit. But there were other considerations which persuaded him to undertake the risk. A personal visit to the Emperor and his capital would give him a realistic idea of the inherent power of the Empire, so that he could judge for himself who could be his friends and who his foes at Court, and how far his dream of a Hindu Empire was practicable. In his own narrow sphere of the south, Shivaji was anxious to oust the Siddi from the vicinity of his capital on the west coast. Jay Sinh assured Shivaji that this object could be easily adjusted in a mutual discussion. Although, therefore, the prospect of a personal visit to the imperial capital was not very tempting to Shivaji, it held forth opportunities which made it worth a trial. He revolved the project in his own mind and with his mother and advisers for days together. Some matter-of-fact-men declared the step as dangerous and therefore highly inadvisable; but the priests, the astrologers and above all Shivaji's inner voice the Devi Bhavani, favoured the undertaking. Jay Sinh and his son Kirat-Sinh sent him solemn oaths and written promises that while at the capital both Jay Sinh and his eldest son Ram Sinh would guarantee his life and safety. The resolve was taken, the die was cast. Jay Sinh reported that Shivaji would soon arrive at the imperial Court.

These matters were under negotiation during the early months of 1666. Shivaji prepared for the worst and made as perfect arrangements as possible for his work being carried on in his absence. Jija Bai was to be the head of the administration with Moropant Peshwa, Nilopant Muzumdar and Pratāprao Gujar Senapati forming the executive Council. Shivaji made a tour of his districts, encouraging and inspiring local officials and guardians of forts. On Monday Falgun Shudha 9, 5 March 1666, he took his departure from Rajgad with his son Sambhāji and a select following of officials and servants and an escort of about 4000 men. Exact lists of those who accompanied him are not forthcoming, but Tānāji Mālusre, Yesāji Kank, Bāji Sharzerav Jedhe, Hiroji Farzand, Balāji Āvji, Nirāji Rāoji, Raghunath Ballāl Korde, Trimbak Sondev Dabir, and Madāri Mehtar are some of the prominent names mentioned in the available sources as his companions. The Emperor advanced him one lac of rupees for his travelling expenses and commanded that he should be accorded the honours of a Shahzada throughout the journey. The local official of every district through which Shivaji travelled was to accompany him in his jurisdiction.

On 5 April 1666 the Emperor wrote to Shivaji, "Your letter reporting that you have started, has been placed before me. Come here without delay with full confidence in my grace and perfect composure of mind. After you have obtained audience of me, you will be glorified with my royal favours and given permission to return home. I am sending you a resplendent Khilat."

When Shivaji reached Aurangabad crowds of citizens turned out to have a look at him. But the Governor Safshikan Khan did not come out to receive him, expecting that Shivaji would call on him. Shivaji noticed the affront and went straight to Jay Sinh's quarters. The latter at once reprimanded the Governor who came the next day, offering apologies for his remissness. About the middle of March Shivaji left Aurangabad and proceeded towards Agra by slow comfortable marches, patiently studying on the way men and matters of the Mughal Government and noting whatever was found pertinent to his purpose. No untoward incident is reported of this journey; a distance of about 500 miles was covered in nearly two months.

Shivaji was received by the Emperor in the Agra fort and not at Delhi as is commonly supposed. Agra was the favourite residence of Shah Jahan, where the celebrated Peacock Throne was located. When in 1658 Aurangzeb became Emperor, he proclaimed himself at Delhi and kept his father confined in the fort of Agra, which he never visited till after his father's death on 22 January 1666. When the time of mourning was over, Aurangzeb made his first public entry into the Agra fort and decided to celebrate his 50th lunar birthday, which fell on 12th May 1666, by holding his first grand Darbar with his seat on the Peacock Throne. As Shivaji was expected to reach Agra about the same time, it was arranged that his first audience with the Emperor should take place in that Darbar on 12th May. Aurangzeb was then at the height of his glory. He had just recovered from a serious ailment: all internal and external enemies had been humbled. He had not yet proclaimed his famous religious policy which later brought on him the Rajput war and other troubles. His generals had overcome the rebel Shivaji in a short easy campaign. Thus this birthday celebration of 1666 had a peculiar significance for Aurangzeb, which was to receive added importance from the presence of Shivaji. What proved to be the outcome of this proudest day for the Mughals, history has recorded.

2. **The Audience Hall.**—Contemporary letters have recently been discovered among the state archives of Jaipur which throw full and true light on the important events connected with Shivaji's visit to the Emperor and his miraculous escape. These events can now be accurately explained on the strength of this fresh evidence. Mirza Raja Jay Sinh was then the premier grandee of the Mughal Court and his success over Shivaji added lustre to his laurels. As he had constant dealings with the imperial Court, he had stationed his news-writers who despatched regular reports in Hindi and Persian to his capital Amber about every important transaction at the Court. These reports and letters which have now become available are of great historical importance, after remaining buried in oblivion for over two and a half centuries.

About twenty of these letters in Hindi pertain to Shivaji's visit and supply a graphic account of how he was received, how he took offence at the slight shown to him, and how he was dealt with during the three months of his confinement at Agra. One particular point about the presence of the poet Parmānand, author of the *Anupuran* or its Tamil name the *Shiva-Bharat*, among the followers of Shivaji at Agra has now been clearly established. These works recently recovered and published, have now a precious historical value, as the doubt about the contemporaneity of Shivaji and Parmānand is now set at rest.[1]

Parmānand's uncompleted epic brings the story of the Bhosles and the life of Shivaji down to the year 1661, and the portions subsequent to this date if at all written are missing. Parmānand was a Mahārāshtra Brahman who long lived at Benares and wrote his work at the request of curious local inquirers about the wonderful career of the Maratha hero. This Sanskrit poem was planned to consist of 100 cantos, of which only the first 31, with a portion of the 32nd, are now available.

We must now resume the story of Shivaji's visit to Agra. On that 12th of May the palace Hall Diwani-i-Am of Agra presented a unique spectacle. The whole square bristled with men and their varied equipment, and formed a grand exhibition of the highest Mughal splendour. The Emperor was weighed against various costly articles according to the Hindu fashion and then took his seat on the Peacock Throne. Let us quote from the eye witness' description of the part Shivaji played on this occasion :—

" A letter has been sent by Maharaj Kumār Rām Sinh to Shivaji asking him to arrive at Agra by the 11th of May to have the audience of the Emperor, who has ordered that the Kumar and Fidwi Khan should advance one day's march and welcome Shivaji on the way and conduct him to the capital. Tāj Sinh has been deputed by the Mirza Raja to accompany Shivaji all the way. On 11th May Shivaji reached Malik Chand's Sarai and halted there. Then Kumar Rām Sinh gave to Giridhar Lāl Munshi a special robe and a horse with

1. *House of Shivaji* by Sir Jadunath Sarkar.

silver trappings and said to him, "Do you go and convey my *Rām Rām* to Shivaji." So Giridhar Lāl went there with 40 horsemen, gave Shivaji his master's salutations and informed him of the arrangement made for their meeting. Shiva dismissed Giridhar Lāl after bestowing on him one robe and Rs. 200 cash.

"On 12th May Rām Sinh rode out to welcome Shivaji; and the two chiefs met each other at the Nurjung Garden. Tej Sinh told Shivaji, 'This is Kumār Rām Sinh' and next coming up to the Kumār's side pointed out Shivaji to him. The Kumār moved forward and embraced Shiva. Mukhlis Khan met Shiva next. The Kumār conducted Shivaji to a tent close to his own camp and welcomed him with music etc. Then Rām Sinh and Mukhlis Khan started leading Shivaji to the Court. In the mean time the Emperor had left the Diwāni--Am and taken his seat in the Diwan-i-Khās where Shivaji was conducted. The Emperor ordered Asad Khan Bakshi to bring Shivaji forward. Asad Khan led him upto the Emperor's presence. Shivaji presented one thousand Mohars and two thousand Rupees as his Nazar and Rs. 5000 as Nisar (propitiatory gifts being waved round). Sambhāji too was introduced to the Emperor and he offered 500 Mohars and 1000 Rs. as Nazar and Rs. 2000 as Nisar. Shivaji was made to stand in the place of Tahir Khan in front of Raja Rai Sinh. The Emperor neither talked with nor addressed any word to him.

"It was the Emperor's birthday and the betel leaf of the ceremony was distributed to the Princes and the nobles and Shivaji too got one. Next the *Khilats* for the occasion were presented to the Princes, to the Wazir Jafar Khan and to Raja Jashvant Sinh. At this Shiva became wrathful and fretted. He flew into a rage and his eyes became red. The Emperor noticed it and told the Kumar, "Ask Shiva what ails him." The Kumār came to Shiva's side, when Shivaji told him, "you have seen, your father has seen, your Padishah has seen what a man I am, and yet you have deliberately made me stand up so long. I cast off your *mansab*. If you wanted me to stand, you should have done so according to the right order of precedence." After saying this he turned his back to the throne and roughly walked away. The Kumār caught hold of his hand, but Shiva wrenched it away, came to one side and sat down. The Kumār followed him and tried to reason with him, but he would not listen and cried out, "my death-day has arrived. Either you will slay me or I shall kill myself. Cut off my head if you like, but I am not going to the Emperor's presence again."

"As Shiva could not be persuaded, the Kumar came back to the Emperor and reported the matter to him. The Emperor ordered Multafat Khan, Aquil Khan and Mukhlis Khan to go, console Shiva, invest him with the Khilat and bring him back to the presence. These three nobles came over and asked Shiva to wear the *Khilat*, but the latter refused, saying, "I don't accept the *Khilat*. The Emperor has deliberately made me stand below Jashvant Sinh. I am such a person and yet he has wilfully kept me standing. I decline the Emperor's *mansab*. I will not be his servant. Kill me, imprison me, if you like, but I will not wear the *Khilat*." So the nobles returned and reported this to the Emperor, who then told the Kumār to take Shiva away with himself to his own residence and persuade him to the proper course. Rām Sinh led Shiva away to his tents, seated him in his private chamber and reasoned with him. But Shiva would not listen. After keeping Shiva with him for an hour, the Kumār dismissed him to his own camp."

In the mean time how to deal further with Shivaji became a serious question with the Emperor. Many nobles advocated a severe punishment for such a gross breach of etiquette as he had committed. Rām Sinh on his part continued to send his agents and presents to Shivaji and tried to induce him to a reasonable course. Siddi Fulad the Police Prefect of the capital, visited Rām Sinh and conveyed a message from the Emperor intended to conciliate Shivaji. The next day, 13th May, Rām Sinh attended the Emperor's Darbar taking Shivaji's son along with himself. The Emperor gave the boy one full robe, a jewelled dagger and a pearl-necklace. In due course the Emperor decided either to kill Shiva or to confine him in a fortress. He ordered Siddi Fulad to remove Shiva to the house of Rad-Andaz Khan, a low-born fanatical young favourite of the Emperor, who was then Commandant of the Agra Fort. When Rām Sinh heard of it, he sent a message to the Emperor, saying, "Shivaji has come under a sacred guarantee of safety from me and my father. So kill me first and then deal with Shivaji as you like." Then the Emperor asked the Kumār to sign a bond of security for Shivaji that he might not escape or commit any harm. In the morning of 15 May Shivaji came to the Kumār's tent, gave him the solemn assurance of good conduct and Rām Singh signed the security bond.

One of the Jaipur letters thus describes Shivaji's appearance and retinue at Agra, "He has come alone with only a hundred retainers and his escort numbers 200 to 250 in all. Among the latter, 100 are mounted on their own horses and the rest are bargirs. When Shiva rides out in a Palki, many foot men wearing Turkish caps go before him. His flag is orange and vermillion-coloured with golden decorations stamped on it. In his train camels are few and meant for carrying luggage. He has a hundred *Banjaris.* All his high officers have Palkis to ride in ; so he carries many Palkis with him.

"At sight Shivaji's body looks lean and short. His appearance is wonderfully fair in complexion, and even without knowing who he is, one does feel instinctively that he is a ruler of men. His spirit and manliness are apparent. He is a very brave, high-souled man and wears a beard. His son is nine years old and is marvellously handsome in appearance and fair in complexion.

"Shivaji has come with a rather small contingent but with great splendour of equipment. A large elephant goes before him carrying his flag. An advance guard of troops precedes him. His force moves with grace and pomp. His Palki is completely covered with silver plates and its poles with gold plates. The public extol him for his manliness all the more, on account of his audacity and strong replies in the presence of the Emperor."

For more than three months from 12th May to 17th August Shivaji stayed at Agra, under confinement which became more rigorous as the days passed. How to remove the deadlock was the question which agitated both the Emperor's and Shivaji's minds during this interval. The former, however, made up his mind to put Shivaji to death, in what decent way was the only point he had to decide. Shivaji too understood what fate there was in store for him and set about making preparations to meet it. The Jaipur letters have the following entries on this point :—One day in a general talk in Rām Sinh's tent Shivaji said, "it is sheer destiny that has brought me here. Why did you not advise the Mahārajā (Mirzā Rājā) against sending me into the Emperor's hands?" Shivaji then paid some money to the Vazir Jafar Khan to win his support ; and on other courtiers too he spent more or less. He sent presents to many Umras to gain their favour. On 20th May Jafar Khan presented Shivaji's petition to the Emperor and got him to pardon Shivaji's offence and spare his life. Previous to this the Emperor had ordered Rām Sinh and Shivaji to go on duty to Kābul. But afterwards he rescinded that order. There were hopes that Shivaji would be taken to the Emperor and formally pardoned.

"On 29 May Shivaji wrote a petition to the Emperor saying, "If Your Majesty would restore all my forts to me, I will pay two crores of Rs. Give me leave to depart. My son will stay here in your service. I came here in full trust in your word. My loyalty is strong. Your Majesty is now at war with Bijapur. Let me go and fight there in your service." To this petition the Emperor replied, "Shivaji has gone off his head, because of my mildness towards him. How can he be given leave to depart for his home? Tell him firmly that he must not visit anybody, not even go to the Kumār's house." Thereafter strong patrols have been posted round Shivaji's residence."

8th June. Shivaji has petitioned the Emperor requesting, "issue orders for a residence for me, to which I can move, but do not keep me here in the custody of Rām Sinh." The Emperor replied, "Rām Sinh is a faithful servant, you must remain in his charge." So the Kumār's men are now keeping a watch over Shivaji in addition to the Kotwal's troops. Rām Sinh says that "if Shivaji escapes or kills himself, I shall have to answer for it to the Emperor." Therefore Tej Sinh and his retainers keep watch over the bed of Shivaji, while Arjunji, Sukh Sinh, and other Rajputs patrol around. Shiva, therefore, has sent word to Rām Sinh, take back the bond of security you have given to the Emperor and let the Emperor do what he likes with me." In the mean time the Emperor wrote to the Mirzā Rājā asking what course should be followed with regard to Shivaji and his replies are awaited."

On Friday 9th June Shivaji sent all his servants away,

saying "Go away, you all. Let none remain with me. Let me be killed if the Emperor desires it." Thereupon his men loaded their goods for departure. Shiva sent word to the Emperor directly through Fulad Khan, "I beg that my men be granted passports for the journey." These were obtained and Shivaji's retinue left Agra about 25th July.

16th June. Shivaji petitioned the Emperor asking permission to go to Benares and there pass his days as a religious recluse. The Emperor replied, "Let him become a *fakir* and live in the Allahabad fort. My Subahdar there will keep a good watch on him." Shivaji's residence is strictly patrolled by the Emperor's troops. The Kumār too enforces all strictness and caution. Rām Sinh takes Shiva's son to the Darbar.[2] No reply has been received by the Emperor from Jay Sinh. It is rumoured Shivaji is secretly soliciting some of the nobles for his release. He offered through them to the Emperor to be allowed to go personally to hand over the forts. The Emperor declined, saying, "Why need he go there himself? His men will yield the forts upon writing to them." Shivaji had run out of funds during his unexpectedly long stay at Agra. He had to spend heavily in bribes, presents and perquisites in order to secure his release. He had also to make large purchases. By the middle of July he appealed to Kumār Rām Sinh for a loan and obtained 66,000 rupees for which he gave a hundi on his officers in the Deccan to pay the Mirzā Rājā."

Days passed in this way. Jay Sinh wrote back strongly to the Emperor not to take severe steps against Shivaji but to conciliate him and utilise his services in the Deccan. He urged that the Emperor ought to respect the sacred oath and guarantee he had solemnly given to Shivaji that no harm would be done to him; that an Emperor's word is the most sacred thing in the world. An open violation of such guarantee would not only antagonise Jay Sinh, powerful as he doubtless was,

2. Sambhaji was then nine years old and used to visit the Emperor now and then. In giving an account of his past life in a sanskrit paper (dated 1680) he says he was, while at Agra, called upon to have a duel or a wrestling match by the Emperor (possibly with another boy of his age). He strongly refused to obey the Emperor.

प्रादुर्भूत बालभावेन्द्रप्रस्थाधिनाथानुज्ञात मल्लयुद्ध दत्ताज्ञाभंग [संभाजी दान-पत्र]

but would estrange all the other Rajput princes. This fear indeed deterred the Emperor from taking the extreme step of putting Shivaji to death.

Backdoor influences were at the same time urging the Emperor to take that extreme step. Shaista Khan's wife was bitter against Shivaji on account of the latter's raid upon the Khan's Camp at Poona. Aurangzeb's maternal aunt was married to the Vazir Jafarkhan, to whom Shivaji once paid a visit to explain matters. But Jafarkhan's wife prevailed upon her husband to dismiss Shivaji summarily, as she considered it dangerous to have in the house this dreadful devil, the perpetrator of that outrage against Shaista Khan as he was supposed to be able to take a sudden and long jump upon an adversary at a distance.

After these no details are available of Shivaji's residence at Agra upto 17th August, on which date he escaped in a wonderful manner. The plan was entirely of his own contrivance which revealed what a fertile brain he possessed. The event at once made Shivaji a conspicuous figure, as a divine agent specially appointed to uplift the Hindu religion. How he conceived the plan of escape and executed it with unfailing dexterity, is a perpetual riddle for the historian. We shall proceed to solve it, making the eye-witnesses speak.

3. The wonderful escape.—Thevenot the French traveller who was then at Agra and has recorded what he saw and heard on the spot, is the only intelligent eye-witness we have for this event. His account singularly corroborates the version of the Jaipur letters and explains the reason of Shivaji's visit. Thevenot writes, " Aurangzeb hearing the news of the sack of Surat and wishing to do away with Shivaji, expressed himself thus to the Rajas of his Court, amongst whom he knew Shivaji had many friends and told them that he highly esteemed Shivaji for his valour and wished he might come to Court, saying openly that he would take it as a pleasure to honour a hero like Shivaji at his Court. He commanded the Rajas to write to Shivaji and gave his royal word that he should receive no injury, he had now forgot what was past. Several Rajas wrote what the King had said and made themselves in a manner

sureties for the performance of his word, so that Shivaji made no difficulty in coming to Court and bringing his son with him.

"At first he met with all imaginable caresses, but some time after, Shivaji perceived a dryness in the King and boldly told him that he believed he had a mind to put him to death, though he had come on his Royal word to wait upon him without any constraint or necessity that obliged him to it ; but that His Majesty might have known what man he was, from Shaista Khan and the Governor of Surat ; that after all, if he perished, there were those who would revenge his death and that hoping they would do so, he was resolved to die with his own hands and drawing his dagger made an attempt to kill himself but was hindered and had guards set upon him.

"The King would have willingly put him to death, but he feared an insurrection of the Rajas. They already murmured at this usage notwithstanding the promise made to him, and all of them were so much the more concerned for him. This consideration obliged Aurangzeb to treat him well and to make much of his son. He told him that it was never in his thoughts to have him put to death, and flattered him with the hopes of a good government if he would go with him to Kandahar which he then designed to besiege. The King granted him passports for his troops coming from the Deccan. When he got these passports he resolved to make use of them for himself withdrawing from the Court. He gave the passports to his officers under pretence of calling his forces to provide him horses in certain places. When everything was ready Shivaji got himself and his son both carried privately in baskets (carried in pairs on bamboos) to the riverside. They crossed the river, mounted the horses that were ready and ran away telling the waterman (at the river) "go and acquaint the King that he had carried over Raja Shivaji." They rode day and night finding always fresh horses in the appointed places.

"Aurangzeb was extremely vexed at Shivaji's escape ; many believed that his escape was a false report deliberately given out and that he was in reality put to death. This raja is short and tawny with quick eyes that show a great wit."[1]

1. Foreign Biographies of Shivaji, p. 183.

The Jaipur letters and Thevenot's account tally in a great measure and may together be taken as the substantial truth. The perfidious conduct of Aurangzeb in inducing Shivaji to come to Agra and then trying to encompass his death through foul means was highly reprehensible. He was too timid to perpetrate the deed boldly. He was afraid of the public opinion which was none too favourable about his past conduct towards his father and brothers. Putting Shivaji to death in open violation of a sacred promise of the Emperor, would have quickly made Aurangzeb's name odious throughout India.

Aurangzeb was a man of a thoughtful introspective temperament, not prone to impulsive action. He had a masterly command over his feelings. After Shivaji's first outburst in the open court, there were three main alternatives before the Emperor : (1) to put him to death, (2) to convert him to Islam and utilize his services, (3) or to conciliate and send him back in fulfilment of his solemn word. There were advocates for each of these courses. The Emperor long wavered between the first two and latterly he made up his mind to do away with Shivaji, trying only to delude the public into believing that he had no hand in such a foul deed. He, therefore, tried to devise a course that would bring about the desired result, without implicating himself directly in it. For such a course Shivaji's vicinity to Rām Sinh's quarters was inconvenient, as Rām Sinh was the first person who was to be put off his guard as regards the Emperor's evil motives. Therefore a complaint was got up from the police that they could not keep a sufficient watch over Shivaji's movements in the open surroundings in which he lived as Rām Sinh's neighbour. The Emperor, therefore, ordered that on 18th August Shivaji should be removed to the house of Fidai Husain, which had been hurriedly completed and which was well suited for a prisoner's residence. When Shivaji was informed that he was to be removed to a new and more comfortable house, he understood what this change meant, and he escaped on the eve of the day appointed for the change of his residence. He had already asked Rām Sinh to cancel the bond of surety he had executed. He was anxious that Rām Sinh's position should not be compromised by his action.

To all appearances Shivaji talked of preparing for death.

The father hugged the son and bitterly mourned their lot, cursing the moment when they left their home. In desperation Shivaji often seemed to have given up all hope and made utterances calculated to accept anything that the Emperor would demand provided his life was spared. He begged each and every person of influence to intercede with the Emperor to have his life saved. Most of his men had already left him. He fell ill or pretended to be so. Only one or two servants Heroji Farzand and Madari Mehtar remained in attendance on him. In the evening of 17th August some one else slept in Shivaji's bed wrapped in coverings, and both Shivaji and Sambhāji escaped in separate baskets as narrated by Thevenot. Nirāji Rāoji, Dattāji Trimbak and Raghu Mitra are mentioned as having accompanied him. As soon as they reached their secret rendezvous, they mounted the horses that were kept ready for them by previous arrangement and rode away for the Deccan by way of Mathura.

The next morning Hiroji who had been sleeping in Shivaji's bed, also went out quietly telling the guards that Shivaji was fast asleep and that the sick man should not be disturbed. It seems Shivaji was not missed till about mid-day on the 18th. Fulad Khan himself came in and examined the spot to find that the bird had flown away. In extreme terror he went to the Emperor and reported that Shivaji had vanished by magic as no one was detected leaving his house by the guards who were closely watching the place. The Emperor was not so simple as to believe in witch-craft, and in extreme consternation sent round strict and expeditious orders to all governors and local officials to apprehend the runaways. Search parties were immediately despatched in all directions. Passes and fords were closed to traffic. Shivaji got the start of nearly one full day or at least 18 hours. The Emperor held Rām Sinh responsible for Shivaji's escape and commanded him to go personally and catch the fugitive. The Kumār went in search towards Dholpur. Fulad Khan in an outburst of violence declared that Shivaji had escaped through Rām Sinh's patrols. In a few days the Kumār was disgraced and forbidden the Court. It took some time to discover that he had slipped away by crouching down in the baskets of sweetmeats which used to be sent out. Those on duty were severely punished for their negligence. The inquiry went on for several days. The property left behind by Shivaji jewels, elephants, horses etc. was confiscated. Two days after Shivaji had left Agra, Trimbak Sondev and Raghunāthpant Korde were discovered and placed in confinement. They were subjected to severe torture by Fulad Khan and his underlings, but ultimately discharged on 3 April 1667, six months after Shivaji had reached home.

One of the Jaipur letters dated 15th July 1666 reported about Parmānand thus,—" Shivaji has a poet entitled Kavindra or Kavishwar to whom he has given a male and female elephant, one thousand rupees cash, a horse and full suit. Shivaji says as I am not able to go out, I will thus give away my horses and elephants and remain here as a Fakir."

A letter dated 23rd August from some local official says, " we have sent out orders to that effect to all the *paraganas*. To-day Manohardas Purohit and Nathurām report from Dausa that Parmānand Kavishwar had arrived there with two elephants, two camels, one horse, pack-bullocks, and forty runners. I have asked Manohardas to detain the poet and search the bullock packs thoroughly." The next letter of 28 December says, " Manohardas and Nathurām write to say Kavindra Kavishwar Parmānand of Shiva's service had been detained here. Later on an order came from the Mirzā Rājā to release and keep him under guard where he is. We made inquiries and learned that he had gone to Udai intending to proceed to Benares. So on hearing this news, I sent off four horsemen and fifteen footmen after him that very day. They overtook him in Chandangaon in the Hindaun Paragana and brought him back on Wednesday December 26. He now says, " I want to go to Delhi. Order me, therefore, what I should do with him. He carries much baggage." There is no further news in the Jaipur letters about the poet Parmānand.

The whole circumstantial evidence discloses one main fact that the world outside was extremely favourable to Shivaji, accusing the Emperor of treacherously violating his plighted word, an Emperor's word sacred for all time. If this were not the case, Shivaji could not have so easily escaped, or after having escaped would have been quickly seized. With wrong and unjust ways even mighty Emperors become powerless. After some time Rām Sinh was formally pardoned, but never again taken into that loving confidence which he had enjoyed before. It is also plain that Rām Sinh had no hand at all in Shivaji's escape. Shivaji's own genius and the way in which he had won the hearts of those about him, were mainly instrumental in his safe return. As little Sambhāji could not keep pace with his father in running away, he was placed at Mathura in charge of some faithful priests ; and the father himself travelled through the country of the Gonds on to Golkonda and Bijapur and suddenly appeared before his mother at Rajgad in the garb of a wandering mendicant on 12 September 1666 or on the 25th day after his leaving Agra.[1]

The news of this most thrilling dramatic achievement quickly resounded throughout the country. Every Indian home began to talk of the contrast,—a small slim figure all alone in that famous historic hall of Agra facing the mightiest and the most awe-inspiring monarch seated on the exalted Peacock Throne, surrounded by all his power and dignity. The incident sent an indescribable thrill throughout India and filled every Hindu breast with new hope and fresh courage on behalf of downtrodden humanity. Shivaji's reputation reached its zenith for having outwitted the wiliest and the mightiest Mughal Emperor. He at once became an all-India figure. His arrival in the homeland was hailed with peculiar joy, and grand celebrations were held throughout the Deccan. The forts pealed out salvoes of artillery announcing the event. As these *feu-de-joies* became unrestrained, Shivaji later on circulated standing orders prescribing the exact number of gunfire for specified important occasions. He rewarded all those individuals who had served him in his sore trial, Nirāji Rāoji, Bālāji Āvji, Hiroji Farzand, Raghunāthpant Korde, and Trimbak Sondev and others. Sugar was distributed in all forts in memory of the event. Shivaji was happy to find that his affairs had been satisfactorily conducted during his absence. The Mughal troops were harassing the land, but not a single act of treachery

1. This date is mentioned in the Jaipur *Akbarats*, see *House of Shivaji*, p. 151. But the Jedhe Chronology says he reached Rajgad on 2(November, that is 92 days after leaving Agra.

or desertion was noticed among Shivaji's officials, disclosing thereby to what perfection and order he had raised his State and his Government within a few years, and how the previous chaos and confusion had been removed.

But perhaps the highest gain which Shivaji derived from this adventure was that he came into direct contact with the men and politics, the currents and cross-currents of the imperial Court. He minutely noticed its strong and weak points and made full use of this experience in his future work. He concluded that the Mughal power was a hollow show, full of injustice, tyranny and corruption, and that it could be easily overthrown. Historians trace the decline of the Mughal Empire from this date of Aurangzeb's ascent to the zenith of power. Hereafter his slide down began, although slowly at first. Shivaji was ever on his brain and the Emperor continued mourning to the last day of his life the mistake he had committed in not putting Shivaji to death at once. He wrote in his will, "A moment's negligence in gathering correct news from the Kingdom leads to serious consequences and would have to be repented for life. I neglected to guard carefully that wicked Shiva, and have on that account to suffer these terrible hardships of war till my end."[1]

4. After effects, peace.—Shivaji's escape from the Emperor's custody at once nullified all the work of conquest that Jay Sinh had effected in the Deccan and increased the Emperor's anxieties. His visit to Agra benefited Shivaji more than if he had remained contented with the treaty of Purandar; he now felt himself no longer bound to observe that treaty. To guard against Shivaji, the Emperor thought of Netāji Pālkar whom Jay Sinh had recently admitted to the Mughal service, and who possessed valuable experience of war in the Deccan. Aurangzeb wrote to Jay Sinh to arrest Netāji and send him a prisoner to the Court, thinking perhaps that he would create further trouble in conjunction with Shivaji. So Netāji and his uncle Kondāji arrived at the capital, when the Emperor suggested to Netāji that if he would turn Muhammadan, he would be amply rewarded; if he declined, he would have to remain in life-long confinement. Netāji reluctantly agreed and was converted, re-

1. Sarkar's *Shivaji*, p. 157 and on.

ceiving the name of Muhammad Kuli Khan. He was then married to a Muslim lady and asked to accompany Mahabat Khan on war duty to Afghanistan. Here he remainded for 8 years, receiving high praise for the good work he did there. The future career of Netāji and his reconversion will be noticed in a later chapter.

Upon his return Shivaji for a time allowed himself rest and ease for recouping his shattered health and deliberating on the line of conduct he should now adopt towards the Mughals. Jay Sinh was still in the south with large armies, but Shivaji gave him no occasion to notice him. In fact Shivaji studiously avoided causing any irritation to the Mughals for some time. He directed his energies to consolidating his power in the Konkan and effecting a revenue settlement there. He had yielded formal submission to the Mughals by the treaty of Purandar, which he continued to observe in all outward appearance. He informed the Emperor that he had run away from Court for fear of his life, that he had no ill-will towards him personally, and that he was still as ready to serve the Emperor as he had stipulated. He wrote to Jay Sinh, "the Emperor has cast me off ; otherwise I intended to have begged him to allow me to recover Kandahar for him with my own unaided resources. If through your intercession I am pardoned, I shall send my son Sambhā to wait on the Prince and serve at the head of my followers wherever required."

"In May 1667," says the *Shakawali*, "Bahlol Khan and Ekoji Rāje besieged fort Rangnā. Shivaji Rāje attacked and raised the siege. A treaty of agreement was concluded in September between Shivaji and the Adil Shah." This proves that the Adil Shah at this time tried to regain his hold on south Konkon and that Shivaji wrested it back. Jay Sinh's position as the Mughal generalissimo in the south became untenable both on account of Shivaji's escape and his own failure before the armies of Bijapur. When Shivaji was in confinement at Agra, Jay Sinh urged his son Rām Sinh not to undertake the unpleasant task of guarding Shivaji, one Hindu prince watching over another. In this way both Jay Sinh and Rām Sinh fell in the estimation of the Emperor, who suspected them to be the agents responsible for Shivaji's escape. Some of Shivaji's Brahman followers who were arrested at Agra after Shivaji's flight, admitted, no doubt under torture, that Rām Sinh had played a mischievous game. Jay Sinh on the other hand kept on writing bitter letters to the Emperor expressing his severe anguish at the pass to which matters had come and reproaching his own ill-fate for the result. He was disgraced and recalled by the Emperor to the Court. Shahzada Muazzam was sent as Governor and arrived in May 1667 ; Jay Sinh delivered over the charge to the Prince at Aurangabad and set out on his northward journey, worn out by age and toil and by extreme disappointment at this public humiliation and the thought that his loyal life-long services had proved ineffectual in sustaining his honour and dignity. On the way he died at Burhanpur on 28 August 1667 (aged 62, born 1605).

At this moment Shivaji was not at all inclined to undertake any warfare against the Mughals ; and when he heard that Jay Sinh had been recalled, he probably breathed a sigh of relief as with all his persuasive powers he had found Jay Sinh either incorruptible or too much committed to the views of the Emperor, so that he could now welcome the return of the weak and indolent Muazzam and the open-hearted friendly Jashvant Sinh to the government of the Deccan. For the time being the implacable Dilir Khan was absent in a campaign against Devgad conquering the Gond country. Muazzam had all along resented the insubordinate spirit and spying nature of Dilir Khan, who wielded on that account an abnormal influence with the Emperor. Dilir Khan and Jashvant Sinh openly slighted each other, as the latter was the trusted counsellor of the Shahzada. Shivaji with his usual circumspection was fully posted in these internal details of the Mughal Government and did not fail to take full advantage of them.

Jashvant Sinh and the Shahzada welcomed with all their heart Shivaji's offer to serve the Emperor, knowing well that it was not possible to crush him. They recommended Shivaji's offer to the Emperor, who replied accepting the proposal and recognized Shivaji's title of "Raja." Sambhāji was sent to the Viceroy's Court at Aurangabad, had his first interview with him on 4th November and was then allowed to return home. In a letter dated 9 March 1668 Muazzam conveyed the Emperor's orders to Shivaji, conferring on him the title of "Raja" and agreeing to a peace, which lasted for two years.

On 5 August 1668 Sambhāji came back to serve in the Mughal Camp with his contingent headed by Pratāprāo Gujar and Niraji Rāoji. Sambhāji was created a commander of five thousand, and presented with a jewelled sword and an elephant. Jagirs for his expenses were assigned to him in Berar. This was Shivaji's peculiar method of securing substantial interests, practically losing nothing by his submission according to the treaty of Purandar. He soon got most of his forts also back as we shall see shortly. He was Aurangzeb's vassal in name. His relations with Bijapur also remained pacific. The European powers on the west coast sought his friendship. The Portuguese sent their agents to Shivaji and concluded a treaty of peace with him (11 December 1667). When the Mughal Emperor acknowledged him as a Raja, Bijapur and Golkonda began to deal with him as an independent king. Through Muazzam Shivaji secured the right of exacting *Chauthai* dues from those two States, thus treating them as his vassal territories. In order to avoid annual Maratha incursions for the exaction of these dues, they agreed to pay him a lump sum annually, Bijapur three and Golkonda five lacs. The year 1668 thus marks a rapid increase towards fullness of th last lunar phase of Shivaji's life.

CHRONOLOGY

VIII

1669 April 9	Emperor orders Hindu schools and temples to be demolished.
„ Sept. 4	Kashi-Vishweshwar temple pulled down and masjid built on its site.
1670 Jan.	Shivaji plunders Berar.
„ Feb. 4	Shivaji recaptures Sinhagad.
„ March 3	Kalyan and Bhivandi recovered.
„ April	Junnar, Ahmadnagar, Parenda plundered.
„ Oct. 3—6	Shivaji's second raid on Surat.
„ „ 16	Daud Khan routed at Vani Dindori.
„ Nov.	Shivaji raids Burhanpur and Karanja. Mahabat Khan appointed Mughal Governor.
1671 Jan. 5	Shivaji captures fort Salher.
„ monsoon	Dilir Khan sacks Poona.
„ Dec.	Mahabat Khan recalled : Bahadur Khan takes his place.
	Ikhlas Khan besieges Salher.
1672 Feb.	Mughals defeated before Salher.
	Fort Kanhergad bravely holds out for Shivaji.
	Shivaji's envoy, Qazi Haidar, meets Bahadur Khan and is confined at Parenda.
	Junnar and Ramnagar seized by Moropant.
	Bahadurgad built by Bahadur Khan.
„ Nov. 24	Death of Ali Adil Shah II.
1673 March 6	Fort Panhālā taken by Shivaji.
„ April 15	Battle of Umbrani : Bahlol Khan routed.
„	Pratāp Rao Gujar plunders Hubli.
1674 Feb. 24	Battle of Nesari, Pratāp Rāo killed.
„ March 23	Sampgaon plundered

CHAPTER VIII

STILL GREATER TRIUMPHS

[1668-1673]

1 Fresh wave of Mughal fanaticism.
2 Shivaji's reply, recovers lost forts.
3 Second sack of Surat and its sequel.
4 Bloody toll of Salher.
5 Panhala taken.
6 Pratap Rao Gujar sacrifices himself.

1. Fresh wave of Mughal fanaticism.—Soon after peace was concluded by Shivaji with the Emperor through the Shahzada, there occurred serious differences between that Prince and his overbearing lieutenant Dilir Khan of which Shivaji was not slow in taking advantage. The Emperor held the Khan in high esteem and credited his slanderous reports in preference to his son's statements. This produced a strong ill-feeling between them, the Shahzada being guided by Jashvant Sinh who was a great opponent of Dilir Khan. Their growing enmity came to a head just about the time that Shivaji was negotiating his peace and when the Emperor's attention was directed more to his preoccupations in north India involving as a consequence an utter neglect of the affairs in the Deccan. Sambhaji lived at Aurangabad under the guardianship of Pratāp Rāo Gujar and Nirāji Rāoji. They formed a close friendship with the Shahzada and Jashvant Sinh, all sharing the pleasures of hunting and the amusements of camp-life. This phase of Mughal-Maratha fraternity so disgusted Dilir Khan that he went to the length of reporting to the Emperor that the Shahzada was planning to depose him with the help of the Marathas. Thereupon the Emperor sent urgent and explicit orders to his son to place under immediate arrest the two Maratha officials Pratāp Rāo Gujar and Nirāji Rāoji. The Shahzada being friendly to the Marathas, contrived to communicate the news of this order privately to the two officials and thus enabled them to return home. This conduct further embittered the relations between Muazzam and

Dilir Khan and produced utter confusion in the Mughal administration of the Deccan. Just at this time Aurangzeb launched his cherished policy of persecuting his Hindu subjects by issuing on 9 April 1669 general orders "to demolish all the schools and temples of the infidels and put down their religious teaching and practices." A new large department was organized for a wholesale attack on the unbelievers throughout his dominions, and he called for periodical reports of what actual results were achieved as regards the demolition of schools and temples, the imposition of Jazia, the exclusion of the Hindus from public offices, the banning of Hindu fairs and festivities and similar measures.[1]

Aurangzeb was obsessed with the vain belief that Providence had given him his position and power only for exalting his own religion and putting down other faiths. In his view other religions could not stand in equality with his own. Soon after his father's death when he felt himself firm in his seat, he started on his life's mission with all the earnestness and vehemence he was possessed of. In this spirit of fanaticism he turned his arms first against the Bundellas, then against the Rajputs and lastly against the southern peoples to whom he was drawn by the rebellion of his son Akbar. Shivaji did not fail to remonstrate strongly and publicly against the mistaken policy of the Emperor which received its first formal demonstration in 1669 when the famous Kashivishveshvar temple was demolished. The Keshorai temples of Mathurā suffered a similar fate. So furious was Aurangzeb against the Krishna worship at Mathurā that he changed the name of the town to Islamabad. Ahmadabad and Ujjain were similarly treated. "Officers were appointed in a systematic plan, in all the cities and sub-divisions of the Empire, as Censors of Morals to enforce the regulations of Islam. The festivals of Divali and Holi were ruthlessly suppressed. A Director General was placed over the large number of officers employed in this grand task. The provinces of Bengal, Orissa, Assam and Rajputana suffered the same fate. The temples of Ambar, the capital of the loyal state of Jaipur were broken down later in 1680."

Neither age nor experience softened the rigour of Aurang-

1. Sarkar's Aurangzib, Vol. 3, p. 264-286.

zeb's religious policy. He confiscated all Hindu religious grants in Gujarat and remained deaf to all pleadings of pity and political expediency alike. When he was the Viceroy of Gujarat he had desecrated the temple of Chintamani at Ahmadabad in 1644 by slaughtering a cow in it and turning it into a mosque.

All these measures of the Emperor, who must, by his position, be the protector of all religions, and of all races, became well known throughout India and caused the deepest concern to all thinking men. Brilliant examples of tolerance and liberty of worship and conscience, were before the Indian public, like those of Akbar and Kabir. Shivaji certainly knew this and we may be sure that during his three months' sojourn at Agra he kept his eyes and ears open in order to devise measures to meet such attack on the Hindu religion, the most emergent question of the moment. Shivaji accepted the challenge and devoted his life to its solution.

The news of the demolition of the Vishveshwar temple at Benares on 4 September 1669 spread like wild fire and caused extreme consternation throughout the country. The masjid raised on the old shrine stands to-day as a living witness of the event. Shivaji at once set about measures to avenge the wrong and retaliate for the insult offered to his religion. At the beginning of 1670 he recommenced his aggression upon the Mughal territories in all directions, taking full advantage of the daily growing confusion in the Mughal administration of the Deccan. He began vigorously to recover the important forts he had surrendered to Jay Sinh. Early in January 1670 his troops plundered Berar and collected 25 lacs. Similar raids were carried out in the region of Ausa. At this moment the quarrel between the Shahzada and Dilir Khan had reached its height. Dilir Khan turned a rebel, and was about to be arrested and imprisoned under orders of the Emperor which had been previously obtained, but having got an inkling of the plan against him, he ran away into Malwa, leaving all his military equipage behind. The Shahzada and Jashvant Sinh pursued him and called upon Shivaji to take part in the chase. The Emperor's government became practically paralysed throughout the Deccan. Shivaji being supplied with correct news took advantage of the situation, and declared an open war by his famous capture of fort Sinhagad on February 4, 1670.

2. **Shivaji's heroic reply, Sinhagad recaptured.**—Of all the forts surrendered to Jay Sinh the most important was doubtless Sinhagad, for it was looked upon as the capital of the western regions and a key in the hands of those who had to govern them. Purandar ranked next to it. That is why Jay Sinh had insisted that Sinhagad should be the first to be handed over by Shivaji personally. He had after his visit to Jay Sinh in June 1665 personally delivered the fort to Kirat-Sinh. The fort was now most strongly held by a trusted and valiant Mughal commander named Uday Bhān Rāthod. No other fort was so well protected both by man and nature and now strongly guarded by the Mughals. He who possessed Sinhagad was the master of Poona.

There is evidence to show that Shivaji himself thought Sinhagad impregnable. He was, however, egged on to the venture by his mother Jija Bai in whose mind the public insult of the demolition of Kashivishveshwar was bitterly rankling. The ballad of Sinhagad says, when she found Shivaji hesitating on the question of retaking Sinhagad, which practically meant a sacrifice of some of his best soldiers and a challenge to the Emperor, she insisted on playing with him a game at dice and the wager was to be the capture of this fort. She demanded that if Shivaji lost the game he must pay the price. If he refused, she threatened him with a curse upon his newly erected *raj*,—a mother's curse! What was Shivaji to do?[2]

Shivaji certainly wanted the fort back, but believed that an attack on it would unnecessarily plunge him into a deadly war with the Emperor, which had been to some extent happily closed. He well knew that the fort could not be taken by any other means than by his brave soldiers scaling the walls

---

2. The reader may spend a little time in going over the ballad of Sinhagad so ably rendered by Acworth. Says Shivaji to his mother.—

"Oh lady, all my forts are thine,
But ask me not what is not mine."
"Beware a mother's curse," She cried
Its fire shall scorch thy kingdom wide.
Give me Sinhagad."

by means of rope-ladders stealthily walking in and opening the main gates, through which the storming party could rush in. Sinhagad is the only fort not vulnerable to artillery : there is no room where guns could be brought into position for a bombardment of it. All the sides are steep, upon one of which a narrow path now leads to the main gate for communication with the outside world. The difficulty was removed by Jija Bai who called in Tānāji Mālusre, Shivaji's dearest comrade and his brother Suryāji and prepared them for the venture with all the arts of motherly affection.

On the dark night of Magh 9 (4 February 1670) when the moon rose after midnight, Tānāji made the attempt, succeeded in capturing the fort but lost his life. With about 300 Mavlas he arrived at the fort after nightfall. A large number headed by Suryāji remained concealed near the main gate and Tānāji himself with his selected followers scaled the walls by means of an iguana and opened the gates by putting to the sword the few sentries that came out to oppose him. But all this could not be accomplished without making a noise. The guards were roused, an alarm was given and the commandant himself came out determined to defend the place to the last. A sanguinary action ensued in which both sides lost heavily including their leaders Tānāji and Uday Bhānu. The fort was captured and a huge bonfire announced the result to Shivaji at Rajgad. Next morning the dead body of Tānāji arrived in a palanquin to be received by Shivaji and Jija Bai, who grieved for the loss with poignant anguish. The fort had been recovered, but the lion Tānāji was no more.[3]

Tānāji's exploit is annually commemorated at the fort, which is practically still in tact in its original grandeur. Jija Bai at once sent for Tulsidās, a professional bard from Poona, and asked him to compose a ballad which sang in touching strains the valour and sacrifice of Tānāji Malusre. Shivaji amply rewarded the relatives of those who had fallen. Tulsidās'

3. Sinhagad is even to-day a rare sight not only for Mahārāshtrians but to travellers and visitors from all over India, who as a rule when they visit Poona, do not return without paying homage to Sinhagad at a distance of 18 miles thence, which motor buses now cover in half an hour for a few annas. From the foot the climb up is about 3 miles which one must do on foot.

ballad is still recited in stirring accents to thousands of listeners whose hearts are passionately moved to strong sentiments of pathos and patriotism. The quaint old language of the ballad as now before us may be taken as evidence of its historical accuracy. It has been rendered into English by Acworth.

When this principal fort fell, the others were not long in being taken, as none of them was so well defended. The defence of these forts could only be conducted by the devoted Mawlas, adept in a particular device perfected by the genius of Shivaji, who knew full well, in handing them over to the Mughals, that it would not be a difficult task to take them back. So they were peacefully handed over and now as peacefully got back. Purandar was attacked and taken on 8 March 1670, when its commandant Razi-uddin Khan was made a prisoner. At the same time Shivaji's men raided Chāndwad near Nasik and carried away the imperial treasure that was deposited there. An attempt was made on Mahuli, but its keeper Manohardas, Aurangzeb's trusted officer, successfully defended it and for the time Shivaji had to give up the attempt. Kalyan and Bhivandi were easily taken by putting to death the Mughal Governor Uzbeg Khan on 3 March 1670. Manohardas too failed to get timely reinforcements and himself delivered Mahuli to Shivaji on 16 June, thereafter joining another post under the Mughal government. Thus Shivaji got back the whole territory of north Konkan and quickly removed all traces of his former submission to the Emperor of June 1665. By the end of April 1670 Junnar, Ahmadnagar, Parenda and many other important Mughal possessions were raided and laid under heavy contribution by Shivaji's armies. There was one most valiant and efficient Mughal General, Daud Khan Qureshi, previously working under Dilir Khan at the siege of Purandar, who now did his best to resist this aggression of Shivaji manfully and for a time captured back fort Mahuli. We shall soon hear more of this Daud Khan.

3. **Second sack of Surat and sequel.**—Shivaji's active mind meditated fresh blows against the Emperor, and once more Surat attracted his attention. Having been informed that the Governor of Surat had recently died and that it had

no strong garrison, Shivaji at the head of a large force of fifteen thousand horsemen and some choice commanders, suddenly appeared before Surat on 3 October 1670. For three full days the town was mercilessly subjected to plunder and fire, nearly half the town being reduced to ashes. The European traders were cautious enough and had removed their valuable goods and treasure several miles away to the harbour of Swally, beyond Shivaji's reach. They did not oppose Shivaji, nor did he interfere with them. On the 3rd day when he learned that a large army was marching from Burhanpur for the relief of Surat, he retraced his steps after imposing an annual payment of 12 lacs upon the town by way of tribute and declaring his intention of renewing his attacks in case of failure to pay it. If the amount were regularly paid without demur, he proclaimed that he would do no injury to the peaceful merchants of that trading city. Two agents of the English factory at Surat waited upon Shivaji in his tent outside the town with presents of cloth, sword-blades, and knives. The Maratha King received them kindly and assured them that he would do no harm to the English, as they were his friends.

This time Shivaji collected from Surat a treasure worth 66 lacs and returned by way of Salher and Mulher. When he arrived in the vicinity of Chāndwad, he found his way barred by a large Mughal army led by the redoubtable Daud Khān Qureshi, who had obtained correct news of Shivaji's movements, and on the night of 16 October suddenly attacked him between Vani and Dindori with fury and determination. In this predicament how to save his men and treasure became a serious problem for Shivaji. He at once divided his force into four separate columns, each under a clever and resourceful leader, and decided to harass the Mughals in a guerilla fashion, avoiding open action as far as possible and giving out that he was going to make a sudden attack upon Aurangabad. A fifth and smaller body with the main booty of Surat managed to slip away through a secret pass, while the other divisions engaged the enemy. The ruse succeeded and the treasure was got safely away. But the action somewhere between Vani and Dindori proved most tenacious and costly on account of the determined onslaught made by the Mughals, under their various capable officers, Ikhlas Khan and Baqui

Khan, well directed by Daud Khan himself. This time Shivaji personally led the Marathas in an open and sanguinary action. On the whole three thousand Mughals and a few Marathas were killed. Four thousand horses were captured by the Marathas along with a number of officers and soldiers. They were subsequently released by Shivaji and allowed to go home. The famous Rai Bagan, the heroic wife of the Deshmukh of Mahur who had once before confronted Shivaji at the time of Kartalb Khan's discomfiture, now came forth to defend the Mughal cause, but she was overpowered and allowed to go home, completely subdued. As a result of this battle the Mughal power was neutralized for more than a month afterwards. Siddi Hilal the Mughal governor of Dindori transferred his services to Shivaji.

For several years after Shivaji's withdrawal from Surat the town used to shudder with panic every now and then, even at false alarms of the Marathas coming, so that the trade of this the richest port of India was practically destroyed. The alarm was revived throughout the following months of November and December and also fitfully throughout several succeeding years.[4]

Shivaji rapidly followed up his second sack of Surat by a sudden irruption into Berar, Baglan and Khandesh. Early in December he himself traversed Khandesh, capturing some forts of the Baglan district on the way. His Senapati Pratāp-Rāo Gujar plundered Bahadarpura, a suburb of Burhanpur, and quickly passing into Berar fell unexpectedly upon the rich and flourishing city of Karanja. Spoils to the value of a crore of rupees were carried away loaded on four thousand oxen and donkeys. The richest merchants of Karanja were carried away for the exaction of ransom. Shivaji from now on openly commenced his levy of Chauth on all the Mughal territories through which he passed. He meant to announce that all Maratha territories belonged of right to him and not to the Mughals.

4. The numerous and complicated details of this affair are interesting and may be studied minutely in the well arranged narrative given by Sir Jadunath Sarkar in his Shivaji and his Times, pp. 178-179.

4. **Bloody toll of Salher.**—While Shivaji was occupied in Berar and Khandesh, his Peshwa Moro Trimal Pingle made his way through north Konkan into Baglan, wresting from the Mughals Trimbak and some other forts, and passed *via* Mulher into West Khandesh levying contributions wherever he went, right, upto fort Salher, which is on the border of Khandesh and Gujarat. It was a post of the utmost strategic importance, for the possession of which a bitter conflict unprecedented in all Shivaji's life ensued, and several bloody battles were fought with heavy losses on both sides, proving thereby that Shivaji and his Marathas never shirked open fights when such were considered necessary. As Shivaji was returning from the plunder of Karanja, he was joined by a column under his Peshwa Moropant and the united division besieged the fort of Salher and captured it on 5 January 1671 after a short but desperate defence by Fathulla Khan its Mughal commander. The Mughal Government tried strenuously for a year to retake the place, when several memorable actions took place between the two contending parties.

The confusion in the Mughal government of the Deccan soon attracted Aurangzeb's attention. The second sack of Surat and the Maratha conquest of Baglan roused him to a sense of the grave situation. In November 1670 he sent to the supreme command of the Deccan the veteran Mahabat Khan. Another competent general Bahadur Khan was ordered from Gujarat as an additional support. Daud Khan and Dilir Khan were already there. The Emperor often talked of proceeding to the Deccan himself, but if his intention was really serious, it did not materialize, possibly owing to a want of nerve to face Shivaji personally. Many renowned Rajput officers were now posted to the Deccan. Mahabat Khan, Jashvant Sinh, Daud Khan and others all assembled at Aurangabad in January, paid their respects to Prince Muazzam, and fully deliberated upon measures for restraining Shivaji. But, as may be imagined, matters are not necessarily improved by many worthy men being brought together : the probability is that such wise heads differ radically and spoil the result, making the confusion worse confounded. They had mutual jealousies which prevented co-ordination and concerted action. It would be a tedious affair to detail the story of the present Mughal-

Maratha War and the recapture of Salher. During the monsoon months of 1671 the Mughals encamped at Parner, where the various commanders held daily entertainments such as music and dancing, where they all attended and made themselves merry when their soldiers were dying in numbers through pestilence in the camp. Four hundred dancing girls from the Punjab and Afghanistan lived in the Mughal camp and were patronized by the officers.[5]

The Emperor suspecting Mahabat Khan of a secret understanding with Shivaji, recalled him from the Deccan and appointed Bahadur Khan and Dilir Khan to that government. They rapidly came from Surat while Mahabat Khan was still in charge, and laid siege to Salher which was now in Maratha hands. In order to cripple Shivaji still further, Bahadur Khan and Daud Khan left the conduct of the siege to Ikhlas Khan and themselves made a detour upon Poona with a view to stopping Maratha succours proceeding to Salher. Bahadur Khan advanced towards Supa and Dilir Khan came upon Poona in December 1671. The latter massacred a large number of the innocent inhabitants of the place. But Shivaji was equal to the occasion. Pratāp Rāo Gujar, Anand Rāo Makāji, Moropant Pingle and other commanders of Shivaji played such havoc in Khandesh upon the small Mughal forces of Ikhlas Khan that Bahadur Khan and Dilir Khan had to retreat precipitately from the vicinity of Poona and hurry back to the north. Thereafter an obstinate and sanguinary battle took place before Salher in the first week of February 1672, in which the Mughals were completely routed. Ikhlas Khan and some thirty principal Mughal officers were wounded and captured and several thousand soldiers were slain. Moropant recaptured both Salher and Mulher, took prompt and ample measures for their future defence, and returned to report the success to his master. Says Sabhasad, "One Surya Rāo Kākde, Shivaji's companion in arms from childhood lost his life. More than ten thousand men were slain on the two sides with countless numbers of horses, elephants and camels. Rivers of blood flowed on the battle ground. The Marathas acquired by way of plunder six thousand horses, as many camels, one

5. Sarkar's Shivaji, P. 189.

hundred and twenty-five elephants, all the camp baggage of the Mughals with treasure and jewelry. This phenomenal victory was mainly due to the strategy and valour of Shivaji's Peshwa of whom a contemporary poet sang :—

"The valleys of Poona echo the name of Shivaji,
There roams his dauntless Peshwa,
He slaughtered the Mughals of Salher
Just as Arjun slaughtered the Kauravs of yore."[6]

The fight of Salher was an open action by Shivaji's men opposing the best equipped and most ably led Mughal armies, by no means partaking of the nature of guerilla warfare. The disaster to the Mughal arms led to the disgrace of Mahabat Khan at the hands of the Emperor, just in the same way as Jay Sinh five years before him had suffered. He was transferred to Afghanistan and died on the way thither, having served the Empire long and faithfully.

Sabhasad paints a glowing picture of the battle of Salher. Maratha captains and the Mavla troops overcame the most renowned Mughal commanders. The news rejoiced Shivaji's heart. He rewarded the messengers who brought the news with gold bracelets and wrist-lets. Sweets were widely distributed. Dilir Khan saved his life by flight. A large number of the Mughal wounded and captives fell into Shivaji's hands. They were properly nursed and were released with presents after their wounds had been treated. Some willingly accepted Shivaji's service. Thus Shivaji in a few years not only recovered his former position but became a match for the best generals and administrators of the Mughal Empire. His officers and men were so well trained that they could exhibit skill and initiative in every difficult situation. How one earnest leader can change the character of a whole nation and attain a swift rise to prosperity is well exemplified in this military organization of Shivaji.

---

[6] पुण्याच्या कप्या गर्जताती शिवाजी
तिथें नांदतो पेशव्या मर्द गाजी।
जशीं मर्दिलीं कौरवें पांडवानें
तशीं मारिलीं मोगलें पेशव्यानें ॥ **Sabhasad Bakhar P. 63.**

An illustration of this national change was now furnished by the fort of Kanhergad near Chāndwad, where Shivaji had appointed one Rāmāji Pangera as the keeper. The small fort was suddenly attacked by Dilir Khan with a very large force, when Rāmāji with a small but select band of 600 men faced terrible odds fighting with all their might, until nearly all the defenders were wounded and disabled but they succeeded in turning the enemy back with discomfiture. Such a spirit of service and sacrifice quickly permeated the whole Maratha nation at the magic lead of Shivaji. The terrible rout and the consequent debacle of the Mughal forces before Salher drove Aurangzeb to an extreme measure of reproach. He thus vented his wrath in bitterest terms in a letter to Dilir Khan and others.

"Why did you not die on the battle-field to avoid this disgrace to your master? Why do you live and report to me this dismal news? You very well know how the Adil Shah, the Kutb Shah, the Portuguese and the Siddis all court our favour and express an earnest desire to join our standard. If you had made such a common cause with all these and hunted Shivaji down from all sides, he could have been easily brought to his knees." But things are easier said than done.[6a]

In reply to these taunts Bahadur Khan and Dilir Khan rendered a piquant reply to the Emperor saying that:—

> "If the Emperor remembered that this same Shivaji had before so cleverly managed to effect his escape in a strange manner from the strictest imperial custody at Agra, our

6a. Compare similar description in

पर्णालपर्वतग्रहणाख्यान, २· ७—५२

मृतं किमिति नो तस्मिन् युद्धे सालेरि पर्वते ।
तेषां तत्क्रंदनं श्रुत्वा मया किंजीव्यतेऽधुना ॥
अफजलोपि हतो येन एकेनैव महामतिः ।
महाबलो महाबाहुरेदिलस्यातिसंमतः ॥
द्रष्टव्यं स्वामिभिस्तत्र कियद्यत्नेन रक्षितः ।
तथापि पक्षिवत्तूर्णं पुत्रेण सह निर्गतः ॥
ततस्तेनातिनिपुणं प्रविचार्य विवेकतः ।
काजी हैदर नामासौ प्रेषितो यवनोत्तमः ॥

own offence would not appear after all so very blameworthy."

Writes Sabhasad,

"The news (of the Mughal defeat before Salher) reached the Emperor and grieved him sorely. He did not make his public appearance for three days, saying "It seems God Almighty is pleased to deprive the Muslims of their Empire and bestow it upon an infidel. Why, I should rather die than live to see such results." The Emperor's foster-brother Bahadur Khan Koka, was then near the Emperor, when the latter uttered the above lamentation. He comforted the Emperor saying, "I am ready to go and retrieve the Mughal honour. I will attack Shivaji and humble him." The Emperor took comfort in this declaration and at once appointed Bahadur Khan to the government of the Deccan with Dilir Khan as his assistant. A local Marathi poet of the time thus described the Emperor's grief at the unbroken success of Shivaji :—

Just as one cannot weigh the waters of the ocean,
As one cannot gaze at the noonday sun,
As one cannot grasp a live coal in his fist,
So cannot I overcome this Shivaji.[7]

Soon after the battle of Salher Pratāp Rāo Gujar once more threatened Surat, but stayed his attack owing to other engagements. He, however, wrote a singular letter to the merchants and other people of Surat, which received an equally audacious reply from the Governor. These need not be repeated here : they show the pitch which the Mughal-Maratha antipathy had then reached.[8] Bahadur Khan and Dilir Khan informed the Emperor that Shivaji had sent them his own trusted ambassador Qazi Haidar for effecting an amicable settlement. But the Emperor would not think of making peace with Shivaji and ordered that the ambassador should be kept in confinement. He was then detained at Parenda, but soon effected his escape and returned to Shivaji's service. Obviously Shivaji intended to have his independent status formally re-

7 सरित्पतीचें जल मोजवेना । माध्यान्हिचा भास्कर पाहवेना ।
मुष्टींत वैश्वानर बांधवेना । तैसा शिवाजी मज जिंकवेना ॥

8. Sarkar's *House of Shivaji* Pp. 157-161.

cognized by the Emperor. As this effort failed he had to declare his independence to the world by a formal ceremony of coronation which soon after took place. By employing Qazi Haidar a Muslim Official for the delicate task of conducting peace negotiations, Shivaji showed that he entertained no class or religious prejudice, and that the Muslims loved him as much as the Hindus.

Soon after the capture of Salher and Mulher, the Peshwa Moropant descended into North Konkan and conquered the territories of Jawhar and Rāmnagar in June 1672, thus clearing Shivaji's direct way to Surat, which city on that account remained in constant alarm ever after. The Emperor was unable to prevent it. Although most of the forts in Baglan also surrendered to Shivaji, his birthplace the fort of Shivner remained in the Mughal possession right upto about 1755.

The Rajas of Rāmnagar had been receiving Chauth or one fourth of the land revenue from the Portuguese of Daman for a long time past to ensure their defence against koli raids. Shivaji, it is supposed, picked up this practice of exacting the levy of Chauth on the model of Rāmnagar. It soon developed into a formidable instrument for the expansion of the Maratha power, after Shivaji's death.[9]

Bahadur Khan and Dilir Khan took vigorous measures against Shivaji and exerted themselves most energetically in restoring the lost prestige of the Emperor. With a view to having a greater check upon Shivaji's central government at Poona, Bahadur Khan transferred the principal Mughal camp from Aurangabad to Pedgaon situated at a convenient bend of the river Bhima east of Poona. A large fort came to be constructed at Pedgaon during 1672 and onward and it was named Bahadurgad.

The three years 1669—1672 were a time of peculiar strain for Shivaji and his men. But it is this strain which called forth sacrifice, co-operation, and a sense of national unity and brotherhood, and stopped for a time the fissiparous tendencies of the Marathas. National unity and joint efforts thus came into being for the first time under the inspiring lead of Shivaji.

9. See शककर्ता शिवाजी P. 150.

Indeed this is the greatest service Shivaji did his nation as is testified to by Grant Duff.[10]

5. **Panhala taken.**—While engaged in dealing blows at the Mughal Empire, Shivaji continued nibbling at the possessions of Bijapur also. But on the whole there was peace between them since the expedition of Jay Sinh. This peace came to be disturbed on the death of Ali Adil Shah II on 24 November 1672, which caused a scramble for power among the officials and ministers of the Adil Shahi State. On this occasion Shivaji was engaged in consolidating his possessions from north to south along the Sahyadri range and was careful in holding strongly those forts and posts which had political and strategic significance. Like Sinhagad for the Poona region, the fort of Panhālā was coveted by him for the security of his southern section. His memorable fight at Panhālā with Siddi Jawhar Salabat Khan had before this proved fruitless and the fort had remained in Bijapuri possession since 22 September 1660 with a strong garrison to defend it against any sudden move on the part of Shivaji. When Sinhagad was secured by the death of the lion Tānāji Mālusre, Shivaji became ever more impatient to get back Panhālā, and concerted measures for its recovery. He assembled a band of valiant fighters at Rājāpur and asked Anāji Datto to lead them against Panhālā. Anāji obtained a clever co-worker Kondāji Ravlekar and arranged a sudden attack upon Panhālā on a dark night, nearly on the same plan that had been adopted by Tānāji Mālusre at Sinhagad two years before. Kondāji managed to obtain a secret entrance into the fort in disguise and seduced the garrison. On the night of 6 March 1673, the 13th dark moon of Phālgun, the Maratha Captain secretly scaled the walls with sixty select companions by means of rope ladders and suddenly created such a noise and confusion by means of trumpet calls and yells that the defenders did not realize what had happened and what was to be done. Kondāji's men opened the gates and Ānāji Pant's bands rushed in, sabring every one that came

10. "The highest legacy of Shivaji to his nation was not the territory and treasures he acquired but the example of service and sacrifice which he infused into the Maratha people."

to oppose them. They went straight to the Chief Keeper Babu Khan's residence and killed him outright. Nāgoji Pandit, Babu Khan's second in command, got such a fright that he ran away for his life. Thus with no one to lead the garrison, the fort fell easily into Maratha hands. A vast amount of buried wealth was recovered by threatening severe punishment. Shivaji received the news at Raigad and immediately repaired to Panhālā for making permanent arrangements for its defence. Satara and Parli were two other forts belonging to Bijapur in that sector and these were secured quickly. The Bijapur monarchy was hastening to its final extinction. Fort Parli was handed by Shivaji to Samarth Rāmdās for his shrine and named Sajjangad or the fort of the pious.

In heroic and lively strains this capture of Panhālā has been celebrated by the Sanskrit poet Jayrām Pindye and his account, absolutely contemporary, deserves a careful study.[11]

6. Pratap Rao Gujar's Sacrifice.—The Bijapurians could not take all this lying down. Khawas Khan, the minister in power, at once despatched Bahlol Khan with armies and provisions for wresting back Panhālā. The news of this fresh advance reached Shivaji, and deciding to encounter the Khan before he had proceeded far from Bijapur, Shivaji sent Pratāp Rāo Gujar and Ānand Rāo Makāji to oppose him. The two forces came into contact near Umbrani about 36 miles west of Bijapur. The Marathas hovered round the Bijapurians and starved them out. Unable to stand the privation any longer, the Muslim troops came out for an open action on 15 April 1673, when they were beaten with heavy loss. Bahlol Khan entreated Pratāp Rāo for quarters which he at once gave in a chivalrous spirit. The Khan was allowed to return, but he treacherously broke his word and started a quick offensive in another direction.

When Shivaji heard the full account of the battle of Umbrani he considered Pratāp Rāo's generosity entirely misplaced in allowing Bahlol Khan to go away unscathed when he was fully in the Maratha clutches. Shivaji imparted a strong reprimand to his commander about his conduct and ask-

11. *Parnala Parvata Grahanakhyan.*

ed him not to show his face to him again until he had brought Bahlol Khan to complete submission. Pratāp Rāo's pride was sorely touched by this unwonted censure from his master, and he immediately started in pursuit of the Khan, rightly guessing that the Khan would come out again at him if he would ravage the Kolhapur districts by levying a heavy blackmail. Pratāp Rāo left his headquarters first proceeding to the south and plundering the rich town of Hubli. Bahlol Khan, as expected, came against him with his full force, fired with a resolve to reconquer south Konkan from Shivaji. Bahlol Khan was soon joined by Sharza Khan and they together started their work with great fury and determination. Pratāp Rāo keenly watched for an opportunity to face Bahlol Khan in a personal combat, and having been informed by his spies of the Khan's exact position, fell upon him in the narrow pass of Nesari near Gad-Hinglaj about a mile to the north of the Ghataprabhā river. When Pratāp Rāo received the news, he was alone with only 6 or 7 of his own bodyguards, his main army far behind : but fired with anger and in reckless disregard of ordinary precautions, he set out and attacked the Khan's army. But how could eight men, however powerful and determined, hope to beat thousands ! These were all quickly cut down on 24 February 1674. Pratāp Rāo fell fighting like a brave warrior proving how dearly he loved his master's cause in preference to his own life. How much Shivaji mourned his Senapati's death and reproached himself for this sad result, can be better imagined than described.

Pratāp Rāo's help-mate Ānand Rāo Makāji was not far away when the former fell, and upon learning the news of his death hastened to avenge it. Bahlol Khan received timely help from Dilir Khan and extricated himself from the difficult situation in which he found himself. Ānand Rāo plundered Sampgaon the principal seat of Bahlol Khan's jagir, and carried away a plunder of 1½ lacs hons (23 March 1674). On his way back he was surprised by Bahlol Khan, but beat back the attacking force and returned home safely in high spirits. These events bring the story of Shivaji to the most glorious event of his life, his coronation.

CHRONOLOGY

CHAPTER IX

1674 June 6, Saturday	Shivaji crowned at Raigad.
„ Monsoon	Do. proposes peace to Bahadur Khan.
„ Sept. 24	Do. performs supplementary coronation.
„	Do. plunders Bahadur Khan's camp.
1674 Apr.-June 1676	Dilir Khan absent from the Deccan.
„	Ānnāji Datto besieges Ponda.
1675 March 22	Shivaji at Rājāpur, planning attack on Ponda.
„ May 5	Do captures Ponda, Karwar, & Sondha.
„ June 12	Rani of Bednore submits to Shivaji.
„ Novr. 11	Shivaji captures Satara; falls severely ill. Saint Rāmdās takes up residence at Parli.
„ „ 19	Bahlol Khan confines Khawas Khan and seizes power at Bijapur.
„	Sambhāji put under arrest at Shringārpur.
1676	Shivaji captures Khatāv.
1676 June 19	Netāji Pālkar reconverted to Hinduism.
„ Dec. 5	Pitāmbar Shenvi put under arrest.
1678 Sept.	Do dies.

CHAPTER IX

THE FULFILMENT[1]

[1674—1676]

1 The Coronation,—its true significance.
2 The Ceremony.
3 A year of unrest all round.

1. The Coronation,—its true significance.—Man is fond not only of work and achievement, but of exhibition and demonstration as well. By performing a splendid coronation ceremony in the old orthodox fashion, which had long been in abeyance for the Hindu nation, Shivaji revived the ancient custom and proclaimed the restoration of full Hindu sovereignty at least over one corner of India.

The ceremony consists of the erection of a throne and its formal occupation after a ritual bath and the sprinkling of holy waters accompanied by Vedic incantations. This was considered to be an excellent method for Shivaji's novel experiment of attracting public attention and confirming his ideal in the Indian imagination. Most of the Maratha nobles had the long established tradition of being addressed as "Rajas," but this did not mean actual kingship. Nor were there any Maratha kings of old who had celebrated the coronation ceremony since the days of the ancient Guptas. After long and deep deliberation with his counsellors, Shivaji conceived the plan of impressing not only on the Hindu but on the Muslim and Christian Powers of India as well, that the Marathas were now masters of their legitimate home, that the religious persecution of the past would no longer be tolerated, and that

[1] निर्जित्य सर्वानवनीमहेन्द्रान्
नृपः स सिंहासनमध्यरोहत् ।
योऽधत्त दिल्लीपतिचित्तशल्यं
अनन्यगच्छन्नृपतीतिशब्दम् ॥ शि. च. प्र. पृ. १२१

Victor over every other King on earth
This sovereign has mounted the throne ;
He has lanced the Delhi King's heart ;
Such alone we call "Lord of Men."

full religious liberty for all was the essence of the new State. The title of the Chhatrapati for the Maratha king was specially borrowed from Sanskrit works to convey this meaning.

At the same time Shivaji by this ceremony dealt a death-blow to the notion that he was a jagirdar of the Bijapur State and as such its bond servant, or that he was a mere robber. There were still some Maratha nobles who could not conceive an independent position and who hugged the idea that they were vassals of Bijapur. Such antiquated notions were to be for ever shattered : once an independent kingdom is formally proclaimed, the king could exercise the inherent right of levying taxes, of dealing with other Powers on terms of equality and prove that he was no longer to be looked upon as a mere upstart. There was also a prevalent notion even among his own clansmen that there no longer existed any Kshatriyas of ancient tradition and that there could now be no Kshatriya king after the great Parashuram had annihilated that caste. This palpably absurd social theory required to be knocked on its head by means of a bold stroke. With these various purposes in mind, Shivaji decided upon his own formal coronation and laboured to establish his lineal connection with the Sisodiā Kshatriya clan of the north.

By the beginning of 1673 the idea of a public coronation began to materialize, and when preparations were fully completed, the event took place at fort Raigad, on Friday 5 June 1674, the day of the sun's entering the constellation *Leo.*

The orthodox Brahman opinion was not favourable to Shivaji's claim to be recognised as a Kshatriya by blood, although he had proved this claim by action. More than a thousand years had passed since such a ceremony was last performed, and on that account men's memories had been entirely dimmed. All ancient learning of the Deccan had migrated to Benares after the invasion of Ala-ud-din Khilji and the Muslim conquest of the Deccan. Ancient families noted for hereditary learning like the Devs, the Dharmadhikaris, the Sheshas, the Bhattas, the Maunis, had left their hearths and homes at Paithan, with all their sacred books, and opened their new university of letters on the bank of the holy Ganges. The ignorant unthinking folks of Paithan had now no voice of authority left in them. Benares now began to dominate Hindu thought and learning. So Shivaji had to negotiate with Gaga Bhatt of Benares, a learned representative of that school of Hindu law-givers. He was invited to Raigad to arrange the details in such a way as to suit the needs of the present moment as much as to conform to the ancient usage.

During the reign of Akbar a learned Brahman of Benares named Krishna Narasinha Shesha wrote a work entitled *Shudrāchār Shiromani* (the head-jewel of the functions of the Shudra caste) wherein a theory was promulgated that there existed no Kshatriya caste in the present Kali age. The soul of Shivaji could not tolerate this humiliating position. The pronouncement of Krishna Shesha must be publicly refuted. So he sent a deputation of some learned Brahmans, Keshav Bhat Purohit, Bhalachandra Bhat, Somnathbhat Katre, to go to Udepur and other centres of Kshatriya tradition in North India and rally their opinion in favour of renovating the Kshatriya caste and declaring that caste being never extinct. The deputation was headed by Bālāji Āvji, the keeper of Shivaji's plans and a consummate diplomat. The avowed object of this regenerating movement was to purge society of stupid irrational notions, to put an end to the degradation that ignorance had inflicted in the spheres of the national language, the national religion and national patriotism.[2] The deputation sought out an equally versatile opponent to Krishna Shesha, in the person of Vishveshvar alias Gāgā Bhatta, whose ancestor Govind Bhatta, had left Paithan and taken up his residence at Benares early in the 16th century, and who was now ready to display his deep erudition and sharp dialectical powers and beat Krishna Shesha on his own ground. Govind Bhatta's descendants formed a large school of learning and opinion at Benares and produced numerous works of outstanding merit on religion, law and polity, which are even to-day taken as authoritative in Indian courts.[3]

2. स्वराष्ट्र-स्वधर्म-स्वभाषादिकांचा जगीं मान व्हावा असा हेतु साचा ॥

3. These are under the titles of मयूख, उद्योत, कमलाकर &c. व्यवहार मयूख by Nilakanth Bhatt, निर्णय कमलाकर or निर्णय सिंधु by Kamalakar Bhatt, दिनकरोद्योत by Dinkar Bhatt and a vast number of religious tracts and treatises are all well known to students of Hindu Law.

The Rajput princes respected the Bhatt family so highly that no ceremony could be completed in that part of India without some member of their learned family being present to officiate at the function. Vishveshwar alias Gāgā was himself an author of repute and has to his credit an important standard work, *Kāyastha-Dharma-Pradip,* in which the fanciful theories of the *Shudrāchār Shiromani* have been fully demolished and Kshatriya rites have been granted to the Kāyastha caste. At all social and religious conferences of Benares the Bhattas always received the honour of precedence. The deputation headed by Balaji returned after completing the preliminary arrangements.

Shivaji held consultations with his counsellors and his guru like Rāmdās, and having formed his decision sent his agent Govind Bhat Khedkar to escort Gāgā Bhatt to Raigad with all honours due to his position. The Bhatt arrived in due course and held consultations with prominent representatives of the various views on the subject of the Raja's coronation. He convinced his opponents about the necessity of looking upon Shivaji as a Heaven-sent warrior of undoubted Kshatriya characteristics and attributes as defined in the Smritis and the Bhagawadgitā. In Shivaji, he maintained, the merciful Almighty has once again incarnated himself in order to protect the people persecuted by Aurangzeb.[4] Gāgā Bhatt possessed great erudition and persuasive oratory and won over to his views most of the great intellects then living in Mahārāshtra. He was helped by the clever Bālāji Āvji under Shivaji's own direction.

Many distinguished guests were invited and brought to Raigad in special Palkis. An immense concourse of Pandits, diplomats, commanders, nobles, friends and relatives gathered at the capital. The coronation meant the performance of all the prescribed ceremonies of a twice born (*Dwija*) which in the case of Shivaji had been neglected and which required grand preparations, water brought in sacred jars from holy rivers, horses and elephants of healthy auspicious signs, skins of deer and tigers, fly-whisks and umbrellas of particular makes, gold jars of varied shapes, and last of all a gorgeous throne of such

4. See p. 34, Note 19.

shape and size as are enjoined in the scriptures. The construction of the various edifices and requirements, such as palaces, temples, tanks, gates, fortifications, guest-houses, offices, magazines and stores,[5] was carefully attended to.

Before the ceremonies began, Shivaji paid a visit of inspection to the Konkan regions, to Chiplun in particular, where he held a military review and issued some drastic orders quoted later, for the efficient performance of the various military duties. He returned to Raigad and appointed Hambir Rāo Mohite as *Senāpati* in the place of Pratāp Rāo Gujar recently killed. On the way from Chiplun Shivaji visited Pratāpgad, worshipped his family deity the Tuljā Bhavāni, presenting her a gold umbrella worth Rs. 56,000. On Jyestha Shuddha 4 Shak 1596 corresponding to 29 May 1674 Shivaji had his thread ceremony performed with due rites, and two days after, on Jyestha Suddha 6, his marriage with the chief queen was rehearsed with Vedic rites. *Punyahavachan*, sacrificial fire, penances and rites for averting evil (*Shantis*), were all duly executed in consonance with Vedic prescription and incantations of hymns.

2. **The Ceremony of his Coronation.**—After all these preliminary rituals came the principal function, which took place an hour before sunrise on Saturday Jyestha Shuddha 13 corresponding to June 6, 1674, when Shivaji ascended the throne and the royal umbrella was held over his head. He was dressed in costly clothes and ornaments. His family priest Balam Bhatt, son of Prabhakar, acted as the Chief ministrant, conducting the religious part of the ceremony. Shivaji was weighted against gold and other articles which were given away in charity. His weight is mentioned to have been 16000 hons, which comes to about 140 lbs (1 hon=7/24 tola). English letters give his weight as 150 lbs, which shews that he was not at all inclined to obesity. Henry Oxenden, a relative of the President George Oxenden of Surat, who was present at Raigad on deputation from the East India Company on that occasion by invitation, has left a realistic narrative of what he saw and heard personally about this grand ceremony.

5. An elaborate account of these has been recently published in *Shiva Charitra Sahitya*, Vol III, No. 123.

The throne was a raised seat rich and stately, nearly square in shape 13½ ft. by 12 ft. with four pillars at the four corners, to hold up the awning made of the cloth of gold. When Shivaji took his seat on it, the eight ministers stood around holding the various insignia of royalty in their hands. Beyond them stood the other officials, vassals, guests and distinguished visitors. Shivaji was sprinkled with holy waters and had sacred rice showered on him by the Brahmans and priests singing Vedic hymns to the accompaniment of offerings and the sweet strains of music. Gifts of money and clothes were distributed, Gāgā Bhatt the presiding priest getting one lac of cash in addition to costly clothes and ornaments. The subordinate priests received according to their ranks from 5 thousand to 25 Rs. each in cash. Other Brahmans received lesser amounts, no one getting less than 25 Rs. each. Ascetics, mendicants, recluses, hermits and all kinds of poor people that had assembled, received gifts, food and attention in various forms.

About 8 o'clock in the morning as soon as Shivaji became free from the religious performances, he gave an interview from the throne to Henry Oxenden. The latter was accompanied by his assistant and interpreter Nārāyan Senoy. The ambassador brought in presents, a ring, an English chain, a crest, a pair of wristlets set in jewels and a cluster of three large pearls all totalling to Rs. 3,000 in value. Return presents were given and the whole assembly was treated to *pan* and *attar*. Thereafter Shivaji went on an elephant in procession to the temple of Jagdishvar,[6] when flowers made of gold and silver were showered among the throng, shouting victory to Shivaji. How elephants could get up to the fort appears a marvel today.

The cost of the ceremony together with the construction of the throne and the edifices is estimated by Sabhāsad at Rs.

6. Note the verse carved there on stone :—

प्रासादो जगदीश्वरस्य जगतामानन्ददोऽनुज्ञया
श्रीमच्छत्रपतेः शिवस्य नृपतेः सिंहासने तिष्ठतः ।
श्रीमद्रायगिरौ गिरामविषये हीराजिना निर्मिता
यावच्चन्द्रदिवाकरौ विलसतस्तावत्समुज्जृंभते ॥

5 crores. This probably includes the fortifications and embellishment of the capital also. The ceremony alone is estimated by Sir Jadunāth to have cost about 50 lacs of rupees. Old Jija Bai was fortunate enough to have witnessed the coronation ceremony and along with it the fulfilment of her dream of an independent kingdom for her son. She died just 11 days after the grand function, at her residence at Pāchād at the foot of Raigad on 17 June, 1674, "rejoicing to see" as Sir Jadunāth writes, "before she closed her eyes that her son had reached the summit of human greatness, as the crowned king of the land of his birth, an irresistible conqueror, a strong defender of the religion, which was the solace of her life. A kind Providence seemed to have prolonged her life just long enough to witness the scene of his coronation." At Pāchād the dilapidated remains of her palatial residence with wells and ramparts still remind the curious visitor of that pious lady's devotion.

The coronation ceremony was modelled on the old Aryan traditions. A gold-laced flag accompanying the vermillion coloured national emblem, the grand royal umbrella, the gigantic drum, these were the usual appurtenances of pristine Hindu royalty and were revived on this national occasion. The orange coloured flag, it must be noted, was not newly introduced at the behest of Rāmdās. It was the Hindu national flag long before in use, habitually carried about by Maratha bands. The gold-laced costly emblem[7] was meant for parading on ceremonial occasions. The whole plan and varied construction of the capital, can even now be well conceived from the broken remains that exist to-day of the walls, the plinths, the grand market street, the gates and ramparts, the Gangā Sāgar tank, all in black hard stone.

Sir Jadunāth has added many interesting details of this ceremony, which a student will do well to study. A few extracts are given here. "The preparations took many months. The epics and political treatises were ransacked by a syndicate of Pandits and agents sent to learn the modern practice of Udepur and Jaipur. Invitations were sent to every part of India, Brahmans, nobles, local magistrates of the realm, agents of foreign states, distinguished visitors totalling eleven thou-

7. The भगवा झेंडा and जरी पटका.

sand people and with their wives and children making fifty thousand souls. All were fed with sumptuous meals for some months."

Apart from the ritual and the spectacular ceremony, the occasion was mainly used for giving a final shape to the constitution of the Maratha Kingdom, parts of which had been already introduced from time to time as necessity arose. Some of the eight ministers were already in existence, and possibly also the title of Chhatrapati itself. The Raja now assumed the formal titles, Maharaja Chhatrapati, Lord of the Throne, Head of the Kshatriya race.[8] Shivaji also started his own era of calculating time, which he called Raj-Shaka commencing from the date of his coronation, on account of which he is rightly called the 'Shakakarta,' "the maker of an Era" or a person who has changed the character of Time. Before him there were in vogue two calculations, the Vikram-Era and the Shaka-Era.[9] As for his official language Shivaji introduced Marathi in preference to Persian and Urdu, which Muslim rulers had imposed as a mark of their rule. Shivaji purposely borrowed Sanskrit phraseology for official purposes for which a special dictionary of court terms called the *Rajavyavahār Kosh* was prepared and adopted. This fine work was executed under the able direction of Raghunāthpant Hanumante by various learned Pandits among whom one Dhundirāj Lakshman Vyās is specially mentioned.[10] Similarly rules and regulations were framed for the conduct of administrative work, including forms of address, seals for the completion and authenticity of official documents. The most noteworthy features of Shivaji's constitution was the creation of the eight departments assigned

8. क्षत्रिय कुलावतंस, सिंहासनाधीश्वर, महाराज छत्रपति.

9. This Coronation Era introduced by Shivaji was in use to the end of the Marathi Raj in 1818. It is wrongly supposed to have been stopped by Nana Fadnis and Sakharam Bapu in 1777. They only prohibited the issue of formal letters in the name of Raja Shau II during the short period that elapsed between his adoption (15 Septr. 1777) and his formal Coronation on 20 Dec. 1777. This is how the note on p. 378 of the Dhadfale chronology (इ. वृ 1835) can be interpreted.

10. सोयं शिवछत्रपतेरनुज्ञां मूर्धाभिषिक्तस्य निधाय मूर्ध्नि ।
अमात्यवर्यो रघुनाथनामा करोति राजव्यवहारकोशम् ॥

to the eight different ministers styled the *Ashta Pradhans*, borrowed in the main (though not in its present developed form) from *Shukraniti* and other ancient works on Aryan polity. The names of the ministers and their official designations in Persian and Sanskrit are given below. The following four ministers had their seats on the right side of the throne :—

1. Peshwa—*Mukhya Pradhan* (the Prime Minister), Moro Trimal Pingle. The salary of the post was fifteen thousand hons a year.
2. Muzmudar, *Amātya* (Revenue Minister), Ramachandra Nilkanth, whose salary was twelve thousand hons a year.
3. Surnis, *Sachiv*, (Finance Minister), Ānāji Datto.
4. Waqenavis, *Mantri*, (Personal Adviser, Home Member or Chief Secretary), Dattaji Trimbak.

The following four had seats on the left side of the throne :—

5. Sarnaubat, *Senapati* (Commander-in-Chief), Hambir Rāo Mohite.
6. Dabir, *Sumant* (Foreign Minister), Rāmchandra Trimbak.
7. *Nyayadhish*, The Chief Judge, Rāoji Nirāji.
8. *Panditrāo* (Minister for Religion), Raghunāth Pandit. The salary of the last six was ten thousand hons. A hon was equivalent to about 3½ Rs.

It need not be mentioned how much this grand ceremony of Shivaji rejoiced the hearts of the Hindus in general and of the Marathas in particular and impressed the Hindu race with the appearance of a new defender to uphold their religion and liberty, which had suffered oppression under Muslim yoke for centuries past. In contrast the celebration must have as heavily depressed the Emperor. We have no evidence to show what the authorities at Bijapur and Golkonda felt at the news of Shivaji's coronation. They were fast hastening to their ignominious dissolution and they had hardly time to think of anything beyond their own survival from the declared greed of the Emperor.

Although this coronation ceremony established Shivaji as full fledged Kshatriya, there was certainly a small section which found fault with the ceremonial on the ground that the 6 June of 1674 was under unfavourable stars. One Nischalpuri Gosāvi, a learned monk versed in the Tantric lore of incantation, boldly came forth to denounce what Shivaji had performed and foreboded evil consequences if a rectification was not immediately effected, citing the deaths of Jija Bai and one of Shivaji's wife soon after the coronation as proof of the allegation. Shivaji was not the man to give cause for any unnecessary irritation in harmless matters like this. He silenced the clamour by acceding to Nischalpuri's demand of having a fresh coronation ceremony held on a smaller scale. For this he invited Nischalpuri to Raigad and performed a supplementary ceremony three months later on the *Lalita Panchami* day (24 September 1674) the details of which have been published.[11]

3. A year of unrest all round.—The last six years of Shivaji's short life from coronation to death bear an essentially different character from the previous period. His own health, usually so robust, began to deteriorate with domestic troubles, particularly the evil character which his son Sambhāji began to disclose in an increasing degree, and his anxieties to ensure the permanency of the State he had created by life-long effort. It is a common experience that it is easier to build a fortune than to preserve it. The coronation ceremony put a final seal on all the nation-building efforts Shivaji had put forth in the past. *But the Maratha State having thus come into being, had to be sustained and secured from internal conflicts as well as* external attacks. Like his ill-behaved son Sambhāji, his step-brother Ékoji too was by no means a friend to his cause. He inherited a certain prejudice against Shivaji and could not divest himself of a feeling of subordination to and dependence upon the Bijapur Sultan, which itself was then in its last

11. शिवराज्याभिषेक कल्पतरु, .B. I. Mandal Q. 10, 6.

throes of death. Both Bijapur and Golkonda were dragging on a precarious existence between Mughal aggression and Shivaji's ambition.

Bahadur Khan had assured the Emperor that he would do his best to bring the Maratha ruler down to his knees and neutralise the effect of his coronation ceremony. How could an Emperor tolerate an independent state in the midst of his possessions ? While the Raja was occupied with his coronation ceremonies at Raigad, reports reached him that Bahadur Khan was straining every nerve to undo all his work. Shivaji thereupon decided to strike the first blow. While the strong monsoon of 1674 was on, Shivaji sent his ambassador with proposals of peace to Bahadur Khan, to divert his attention. In the mean time Shivaji carried out a sudden raid upon the principal Mughal camp at Pedgaon on the Bhimā. He divided his forces into two parties, the smaller one of 2000 troops sought an open encounter with the Khan, who unwarily advanced about 50 miles to face the Marathas. When the Khan had thus been lured away from his base, the other and main division of the Marathas (more than 7000 strong) suddenly fell upon the Mughal Camp, set fire to all their tents and material and carried away more than a crore in plunder, including 200 select horses, which had been intended as a present for the Emperor. This happened in the month of July within a few weeks of the Coronation at Raigad. The attack was pressed during the next two months. Shivaji's men carried fire and sword through the Koli country of Jawhār and Rāmnagar. About the *Dussara* time (October) Shivaji himself led an expedition through Baglan, Khandesh and Berar, plundering the Mughal territory right from Aurangabad northward. Among other places Shivaji pillaged and burnt the English factory at Dharangaon near Erandole. The Mughal officer of the place Qutbuddin Khan Kheshgi bravely came forth to oppose Shivaji, but being routed with a loss of 300 men, he fled to Aurangabad for refuge, (November 1674).

Bahadur Khan found himself entirely thwarted on every side in dealing with Shivaji, and gladly entered into negotiations for the peace which Shivaji had been offering for some time. Shivaji agreed to restore 17 forts to the Emperor and allow his own son to be entertained as a six-thousand *mansab-*

dar in the Mughal army. The terms were reported to the Emperor, who sent his sanction. But by the time the negotiations came to be concluded, Shivaji assumed a different tone, and dismissed the Mughal ambassadors who had arrived for arranging the terms. The affair fell through with the result that Bahadur Khan was thoroughly lowered in the Emperor's estimation. "Bahadur Khan was like a petted child" said Shivaji. "He received a large bribe secretly from Shivaji, under the cloak of a tribute for his master and concluded a formal peace with the Marathas." (*Jedhe chronology.*)

For two years after Shivaji's coronation Bahadur Khan was left alone in charge of the Mughal interests in the Deccan, the indefatigable Dilir Khan having been recalled by the Emperor to the north, from April 1674 to June 1676. Aurangzeb soon perceived that Bahadur Khan was not equal to the task of subduing Shivaji and looked about for the best way of accomplishing that object. Why he himself did not come against Shivaji it is difficult to say. Possibly he did not like personally to take the lead. He consulted Dilir Khan on the subject and it was found that unless there was some one well acquainted with the geographical situation and the leading men of the Deccan, it would not be possible to subdue Shivaji. Such a man in their opinion was Netāji Pālkar who had long ago fallen out with Shivaji and being now a convert to the Muslim faith would, they conceived, support the imperial cause. Netāji alias Muhammad Kuli Khan, was sent for and he readily agreed to do his best in entrapping Shivaji if he was freely supplied with the necessary treasure and materials. The Emperor granted all that Netāji demanded and despatched him and Dilir Khan together for the destruction of Shivaji. They obtained news of Shivaji's movements and came upon him somewhere in the vicinity of Satara. One morning Netāji was suddenly missed from the Mughal Camp. He secretly rode away, came and met Shivaji privately and explained to him all that had happened. He had now been a Muslim convert for some eight years and had left his new family in the north. He solicited Shivaji for a reconversion and was at once admitted into the Hindu fold after performing the prescribed penance (*prayaschitta*) on 19 June 1676. Thus the Emperor's deep-laid plan of overcoming Shivaji was foiled.

Netāji continued thereafter in Shivaji's service and died an old man during Sambhāji's reign, but nothing is on record about this last phase of his life.

The State of Bijapur was now sinking deeper and deeper into ruin through a succession of ministerial revolutions. The boy Sultan Sikandar Adil Shah was on the throne with Khawas Khan as the principal minister wielding all authority. Aurangzeb urged his generals Bahadur Khan and Dilir Khan to subjugate the Adilshahi state now that it was in its weakest condition. Khawas Khan intrigued with Bahadur Khan, to whom he paid a personal visit on 19 October 1675 at a place on the banks of the Bhima. This visit was interpreted as a move on Khawas Khan's part to sell away the Adilshahi raj for some paltry selfish gain. Khawas Khan's rival Bahlol Khan got scent of this ruinous move, and at once put Khawas Khan under confinement at Bankapur and himself seized all power, (19 November 1675).

Shivaji was not slow to turn this opportunity to his advantage. The Portuguese of Goa too were equally alert in guarding their own realm, in case Shivaji succeeded in aggrandising his power at the expense of Bijapur, particularly on the coastal regions. Whenever there was any war on hand between some country Powers of India, it was the usual practice of these European maritime traders to make huge profits by supplying guns, arms and ammunition to the contending parties. This had attracted Shivaji's attention long since and he was anxious to develop his own naval resources and wrest both power and trade out of European hands. For this purpose he employed the consummate diplomat Pitāmbar Shenoi, who was well posted in the affairs and rivalries of these European traders and knew how to read and write their language. Through Pitāmbar's influence Shivaji borrowed the services of a few Portuguese naval and artillery experts from Goa and established his own ship-building yards and arsenals at Malwan. It was Pitāmbar Shenoi[12] who supplied Shivaji with valuable

12. A letter dated 6 December 1676 mentions that Pitāmbar was kept under arrest by Shivaji and all his papers and property confiscated. This shows Pitāmbar fell from Shivaji's favour for a time, but was upon inquiry absolved from blame and restored to office. Pitāmbar died about 1st September 1678.

details of the levy of the Chauth cess, which the Portuguese and some of the coastal powers were in the habit of paying and receiving. Shivaji adopted the system for his own purpose and developed it into a profitable instrument for the expansion of his *swarajya.*

From Kolaba to Malwan the west coast was already in Shivaji's possession with fortified bases at Kolaba, Suvarnadurg, Vijaydurg and Sindudurg. Chaul and Janjira were thorns for Shivaji lying in between. Immediately to the south was the important post of Goa, from which the Portuguese could check Shivaji's naval enterprises. South of Goa there were two more posts Ponda and Karwar, both strong and suitable, belonging to Bijapur, which Shivaji coveted in order to hold the Portuguese in restraint, and also to control the Siddi of Janjira. For executing his plan Shivaji soon after his coronation deputed Ānāji Datto to try and capture Ponda from the Bijapurians. Ānāji proceeded on his task in August 1674 and invested the place, which was valiantly defended by the Bijapuri keeper Muhammad Khan. As Ānāji found his efforts unavailing, Shivaji started for his support, reached Rājāpur on 22 March 1675 and thence despatched 40 vessels full of war material by sea to be used against Ponda. Shivaji himself proceeded against the place by land and besieged it on 8 April. Bahlol Khan ran to the rescue of Ponda, but was stopped on the way by Shivaji's men. Muhammad Khan soon found his position untenable and surrendered Ponda on 6 May 1675. Shivaji immediately strengthened the defences of the place and provided a strong and picked garrison for its future protection. He thus established his own counterpoise against Goa. His clever foresight could hardly be too much commended. He thereafter marched still southward and captured Karwar as well, with its marine fort called Sadāshivgad. He also annexed the neighbouring State of Sondha. This southern move extended Shivaji's responsibilities which required to be securely looked after. He created a fresh territorial division and appointed to its head an efficient officer Dharmāji Nāgnāth, just as Rāoji Somnāth was managing the district from Rajapur to Malvan. These two clever governors proved an effective check upon the Portuguese of Goa.

While in this region Shivaji's help was solicited by the

Rani of Bednur for bringing to submission her disloyal general Timannā who had defied her authority. Shivaji readily accepted the mission and extended his principle of Chauth to the Rani's jurisdiction. She agreed to pay the Chauth to Shivaji and purchased his protection. For this purpose he stationed Umāji Pandit at Bednur and completed the arrangements. He returned to Rājāpur on 12 June 1675, having at one stroke confirmed his hold on the western coast practically from Rāmnagar (near Daman) in the north to Basrur (port of Bednur) in the south. Soon after this he arrived at Raigad.

The fort of Satara also belonged to Bijapur and was captured by Shivaji on 11 November 1675. He liked the place very much, and at once took up his residence there, assigning the neighbouring fort of Parli to his *Guru* Ramdas, for whom he had recently conceived the highest reverence and from whom he received great comfort and solace in the midst of his numerous anxieties, which necessitated frequent mutual communication and exchange of visits. Thus during the year following his coronation Shivaji practically seized all the western territories of Bijapur, at the same time holding at bay Bahadur Khan the Mughal General in the manner already described.

Towards the end of 1675 when Shivaji was residing at Satara, he suddenly fell so seriously ill that reports spread abroad that he had died. A sudden and extreme depression took possession of his mind probably on account of his son Sambhāji's misbehaviour. "Sambhāji fell under disfavour and was kept confined with Umāji Pandit to give him lessons at Shringarpur.[13] Thereafter Sambhaji was for a time put under Rāmdās's care also. But there was no improvement in him. It seems Shivaji recovered his health in the early months of 1676 and stayed for a time at Panhālā. "He attacked Khatāv, pulled down its old fortifications, and created fresh defences," is an entry for 20 October 1676.[14]

13. See *Prabhat Shakavali*, Article 58 p. 29 of *Prabhat Bakhar*.
14. *Pashwa Deftar*, Vol. 45, p. 20.

CHRONOLOGY X

1672 April 21	Abdullah Qutb Shah dies.
„ Nov. 24	Ali Adil Shah II dies.
1675 March 17	Ekoji crowned at Tanjore.
1676	Shivaji decides upon his Karnatak expedition.
1677 Jan.	Shivaji's army moves against Koppal.
„ „	Shivaji leaves for Haidarabad.
„ March	The Miana brothers are humbled.
	Shivaji at Bhāgānagar.
„ April	Do Visits Shri Shaila.
„ May	Do captures Jinji.
„ „ 23	Do besieges Vellore.
„ July 5	Do humbles Sher Khan Lodi.
„ July 3rd week	Do encamps on the Coleroon, receives tribute from Choknath Nayak & a visit from his brother Ekoji.
„ „ 27	Do leaves Tanjore territories.
„ Nov. 16	Ekoji routed at Valigundapuram.
„ „	Shivaji reaches Gadag.
1678 Feb.	Sher Khan Lodi's son pays ransom and is released
1678 March 1	Shivaji's letter to Ekoji.
„	Treaty of peace between the two brothers.
„ July 22	Vellore captured by Shivaji's troops.
1679	Shivaji's letters to Dipa Bai and Raghunāth Pant.
1680 Jan.	Shivaji's last letter to his brother.

CHAPTER X.

THE CONQUEST OF THE SOUTH

[1677—1678.]

1 Expansion Southwards, necessity and opportunity.
2 Koppal seized.
3 Grand visit to Bhaganagar.
4 Bijapuri Karnatak seized.
5 The two brothers on their heritage.
6 Agreed division of patrimony.

1. Expansion southwards, necessity and opportunity.— Notwithstanding all the grandeur of his coronation and his assumption of the lofty titles of full sovereignty, Shivaji's actual dominions even now hardly extended beyond about 200 miles in length and far less in breadth, and did not cover even the whole of the Maratha country. The Siddi and the Portuguese were his nearest opponents on the west coast. The kingdoms of Bijapur and Golkonda remained a constant threat on his eastern flank, and although in themselves innocuous, they could serve as an easy instrument in the hands of the Mughals for attacking him. The Mughal pressure from the north was daily approaching his borders. His own brother too was now like him a crowned king and no less entitled to sovereignty. *Digvijay* or the conquest of the four quarters thus became a necessity of his situation, and was considered vital by the time-honoured tradition.

Although Shivaji was careful in husbanding his resources in all possible ways by benevolent administration, extension of cultivation and trade and by occasional plunder, his treasury had become empty. Enormous sums had been spent upon the coronation, on the forts, on the naval programme and on raising the huge armies required for his ambitious projects. So money became his immediate need.

As his path in the north was securely blocked by the Mughals Shivaji decided during 1676 to expand his power in the south and prepared for an expedition at a convenient moment by arranging the preliminaries. He was already secure in the possession of the west coast and only the east coast regions offered an outlet. Vellore, Jinji, Tanjore, were rich places and could, he considered, be easily assimilated in his Hindu Empire. He found a ready pretext for such a venture through the astute Golkonda minister Mādannā.

Madanpant or Mādannā was a respectable Hindu politician, who had recently organized the power and resources of the Kutbshahi kingdom in a satisfactory manner. The fertility of the east coast regions, the wealth of its famous diamond mines, the rich alluvial plains watered by several bountiful rivers, naturally attracted Shivaji towards the eastern belt of the Peninsula. The Muslims in the past had often devastated this soft Hindu land. Srirang Rai, the last prince of the old Vijaynagar dynasty, had long in vain exerted himself to save the old Hindu empire. But no substantial advance had been made in constructing a good orderly government in this part of the country. Shivaji decided to try his hand. The work belonged to the category of Hindu resurgence, which Shivaji had long ago undertaken and in which he now secured the ready help of Madan Pant of Golkanda and Raghunāth Nārāyan Hanumante of Tanjore.

Eknāth and his younger brother Madan were two Pandits of a Brahman family of Hanum-Konda in the Warangal district and are known to history as Ākannā and Mādannā. They first rose to eminence by dint of their innate capacity in the service of Mir-Jumla, the famous minister of the Kutbshah, who became at last too rich and powerful to obey his master. The Shah found Mādannā's services valuable in putting down the rebel, and thereafter employed him in reforming his administration. Mādannā served his master for many years with ability, loyalty and devotion. Well-versed in the languages and affairs of the south and likewise in Sanskrit and Persian, he could very ably manage the Kutbshahi State in the midst of the shifting politics of the day.

The year 1672 proved calamitous both to Bijapur and Golkonda. Abdulla the ruler of the latter state died on 21st April and Ali Adilshah of the former on 24th November following, thus facilitating intervention by the Mughals and the Marathas. The situation at both the places became so full of intrigue and confusion that the troubles of the two kingdoms cannot be well analysed without a full grasp of the fast changing details. Abdulla Kutb Shah had no son, but his eldest son-in-law Saiyad Ahmad tried to secure the throne for himself. Saiyad Muzaffar the Chief Commandant of the State forces, however, assisted Abul Hassan the younger son-in-law of the late Sultan, to gain the throne and himself exercised full powers of Government. But Abul Hassan soon asserted himself with the help of Madan Pant or Madan, overthrew the domineering Saiyad Muzuffar and raised Madan Pant to the position of his Chief Minister. The Shah conferred upon him the title of "Surva Prakāsh". This gave rise to two factions in the State, the Hindu and the Muslim, but Mādannā with great sagacity and tact managed to conduct the administration successfully and satisfactorily until the State came to be finally extinguished by Aurangzeb after murdering Madan Pant.

European travellers of the time have recorded their observations on the last days of Bijapur and Golkonda, in which Madan Pant has been represented as a versatile sweet-tempered person, while his elder brother Ākannā is described as whimsical and short-tempered. The latter was posted to the management of the Karnatak regions of the Kutb-Shahi State, but when Mādannā became the principal minister, he for a time appointed Ākannā as an ambassador to the Court of Bijapur and later made him the Chief Military Commandant. Both had a large family of cousins and nephews whom Mādannā employed in various offices in the State as he needed loyal subordinates for faithfully carrying out the reforms he introduced. The natural result of this policy was the preponderance of the Hindus in the Golkonda administration, which roused the jealousy of the Muslim section who obeyed no law and who started intrigue and foul play. This state of things gave Aurangzeb a useful handle to work its ruin.

While Golkonda was thus dragging on its wearisome existence, Shivaji stepped in to work out his policy of expansion. In this undertaking he had to deal with his own step-brother Ekoji who had just captured Tanjore and had himself crowned there on 17 March 1675 (the Hindu New Year's Day of Shak 1597 Rakshasa Samvatsar), probably in imitation of Shivaji's similar action in Mahārāshtra. This development requires a little more elucidation for which we must first study the relations existing between Ekoji and the Hanumante family who had long and loyally served Shahji in the Karnatak.

Like Dādāji Kondadev in Mahārāshtra Nāro Trimal Hanumante had been in Shahji's employ first under the Nizamshah and had later migrated with him to Bangalore. Soon after Nāropant died leaving two able sons Janārdan and Raghunāth, who in their turn continued to render faithful service to Shahji. Janārdan Pant's services were transferred to Shivaji while Raghunāth Pant continued to look after Shahji's interests in the Karnatak. After Shahji's death Raghunāth Pant served Ekoji with equal zeal and capacity. The principality of Tanjore was a vassal of Bijapur. Ekoji managed to take possession of it in 1675 under the advice and guidance of Raghunāth Pandit. Whether his coronation connoted a break from the vassalage of Bijapur is a moot point. It is sufficient for our purpose to note that Ekoji's administration under the wise guidance of Raghunāth Pant proved highly beneficial to the subjects. The Jesuit Missionary writes in 1676,—

"Vyankoji sought to make himself beloved by the people. The justice and wisdom of his government began to close the wounds of the preceding reign and to develop the natural resources of the country. By repairing the canals and tanks he gave fertility to the vast fields which had been left untilled for many years, and the last harvest (of 1676) has surpassed all that was seen before."[1]

But friction soon arose between Ekoji and his minister of which the cause is not clear. Ekoji must have felt jealous of Shivaji's achievements and did not like to merge his individuality in his brother's experiment, however advisable or alluring that might be to the outside public. Any way the friction between the two soon came to a head; Ekoji could no longer put up with the ways of the overbearing Pandit however wise he might have been. The Pandit threatened the master with resignation adding that he had capacity enough to carve out for himself a useful field of activity elsewhere. Ekoji at once gave him formal leave to depart. He left Tanjore with his whole family, giving out that he was proceeding to Benares to end his days there. On his journey north he

1. *Sarkār, House of Shivaji* p. 33.

thought out a grand ingenious plan of action having already been well-posted with the state of affairs at Golkonda, Bijapur and Raigad. He learned of Madan Pant's move to secure Shivaji's support on behalf of Golkonda : and as no one could then anticipate that the great regenerator of the Hindus was going to die prematurely, he rightly perceived that he could help that hero in his schemes of Maratha expansion in the south. Shivaji's early death and Aurangzeb's subsequent invasion of the south should not lead us to under-estimate the possibilities of the course of action adopted by Shivaji three years before his premature end. Having revolved a bold project in his mind, Raghunāth Pant first proceeded to Bijapur and having studied the situation of that state, visited Madan Pant at Bhāgānagar, whom he did not find it difficult to win over to his views. They meditated together long in private and matured plans of Hindu regeneration. They then took the Kutb-Shah into their confidence and persuaded him for his own safety to work in cooperation for a joint conquest of the south. The Shah agreed to receive a personal visit from Shivaji and pressed the Pandit to bring it about as quickly as possible. Hanumante, therefore, immediately repaired to Shivaji's residence and lucidly unfolded to him the grand plans of Hindu expansion in the south and discussed the pros and cons of the venture.

For a long time, however, Shivaji felt extreme hesitation and to strengthen his own inner voice, he thought it necessary to secure the blessing of some pious saints which in his difficulty he was wont to invoke. A Muslim Fakir named Bābā Yāqut lived at Kelsi near Dapoli, whose favour was sought by many a person in distress. Bābā Yāqut's tomb is even now held in veneration and receives from Government a grant for its up-keep and anniversary celebration, which has continued from Shivaji's time. There was another saint named Mauni Bovā at Patgaon, near fort Rangnā, now in the Kolhapur State jurisdiction. He used to be silent and never spoke a word. Shivaji visited both these saints and obtained their blessings for the hazard he was undertaking.[2]

2. Shivaji's sanad conferring Inam grants on this Mauni Bowa is dated 3rd May 1678, that is, soon after his return from the Karnatak expedition.

By the end of 1676 all preparations were complete and the plan was set in motion almost with clock-work regularity. It was given out that Shivaji was going to the south for demanding from his step-brother his legal share of their paternal property and accumulations which the latter had entirely usurped.

2. **Koppal seized.**—The Hindus of the south who had long been oppressed by the Muslims hailed Shivaji's expedition with all their heart, eager as they were to transfer their allegiance to Shivaji if he would extend them his protection. The fort of Koppal commanded the Bijapur possessions between the Krishna and the Tungabhadrā rivers and was securely held by two Afghan captains in Bijapuri service, Husain Khan Miana and his brother Abdul Rahim Khan. This "gate of the south" as Sabhāsad calls it, was of strategic importance for Shivaji's hold on the Karnatak. The Hindus of the Tungabhadrā regions had sent pathetic appeals to Shivaji to put down the atrocities perpetrated upon them by the Miana brothers. So when Shivaji decided to visit Golconda, he thought it necessary to subdue these two Afghan chiefs with a view to preventing them from threatening his rear from Koppal. When he arranged his march southward early in January 1677, he despatched a strong force in two divisions under Hambir Rāo Mohite and Dhanāji Jādhav to put down the Miana pathans and secure Koppal. Some stiff actions took place and the Marathas succeeded in inflicting severe defeats upon the Afghans. Abdul Rahim Khan was killed and his brother Husain Khan was taken alive. He surrendered the fort of Koppal to Hambir Rāo and was allowed to proceed wherever he liked. Hambir Rāo and Dhanāji both joined Shivaji at Bhāgānagar in March. The gate of the Eastern Karnatak was firmly secured and its possession opened the last memorable phase of Shivaji's life.

Shivaji left Raigad on an auspicious day in Magh (end of January 1677), leaving Moropant Pingle and Ānāji Datto in charge of the Government of the Deccan, to attend to the Mughals or other enemies, should they commit mischief in his absence. Raghunāthpant, Nirāji Rāoji, and his son Pralhād Nirāji proceeded to Bhāgānagar in advance to arrange the details of Shivaji's visit and to create a sense of perfect confidence and amity in the minds of the Golkonda authorities, who were naturally apprehensive at the prospect of the slayer of Afzal Khan appearing in their midst.[3]

3. **Grand Visit to Bhaganagar.**—From Raigad Shivaji proceeded to Vingorla probably to meet Mauni Bowā, and after receiving his benediction and accompanied by an army of 25 thousand well-equipped troops, made his way towards Bhāgānagar. Netāji Pālkar, Hambir Rāo Mohite, Ānand Rāo Makāji, Mānāji More, Suryāji Mālusre, Yesāji Kank, Dattāji Wāqenavis, the Pingle brothers, Nila Prabhu Parasnis, Bālāji Āvji, Shivaji Naik Punde, these and other trusted and competent associates are mentioned as having accompanied him. Strict instructions were issued to all the Maratha troops and rigidly enforced, that no injury or oppression was to be committed upon the Kutbshahi lands and their people. Shivaji exacted severe discipline in this respect and made some examples of drastic punishment. On arrival near Haidarabad, he was received by Madan Pant at the outskirts of the capital and was taken into the town in a grand procession. His troops and officials were gorgeously dressed. The town of Bhāgānagar was specially decorated. The citizens turned out in immense crowds to have a view of Shivaji and his men.

When Shivaji arrived at Qutb Shah's Dad Mahāl or Palace of Justice, he left his escort outside and entered the mansion with only five followers. The Shah came to the door of the hall, received Shivaji on terms of equality and led him to his seat by his side on the royal carpet. The minister Mādannā sat near them, the rest of the courtiers kept standing. The manly appearance of Shivaji and his men was most striking ; the guests were all honoured with presents of dresses and ornaments. This concluded the first or formal visit.

Thereafter the two potentates had many private interviews in which they freely talked of past occurrences and future plans. If the Shah had entertained any fear from Shivaji's presence, it was entirely dispelled after the free conversations they had with mutual benefit and understanding. In the meantime Mādan Pant entertained Shivaji at dinner at his own house

3. The Bakhar Shivadigvijaya is very eloquent on this Karnatak business. Bhāgānagar is the ancient name of Haidarabad.

where the minister's mother served Shivaji articles cooked with her own hand. The two brothers Mādannā and Ākannā sat during dinner by Shivaji's side and entertained him with talks and explanations covering various topics.

After long discussions and conferences a secret agreement was arrived at for the joint conquest of the southern regions of the east coast. The main clauses of the pact were that the Qutb Shah should pay 3,0000 hons daily to defray the expenses of the Maratha army ; that 5,000 Bhāgānagar troops should join the Marathas under Mirza Muhammad Amin ; the conquered territory should be equally divided between the two parties ; that they should jointly resist Mughal advance against either ; and for the proper execution of the stipulations, an accredited representative of Shivaji should be permanently posted at Bhāgānagar. In addition Shivaji agreed to pay 6 lakhs of hons by way of a yearly tribute to the Qutb Shah. It need not be mentioned that during the negotiations lasting for several days, mutual hospitality and entertainment went on smoothly all the time at the Kutbshahi capital. A grand expedition was immediately despatched for the southern operations, in which Shivaji nominated his two commandants Bāji Sarzerāo Jedhe and Yesāji Kank.

Happily we have a reliable account of Shivaji's work, his aims in the present undertaking, and his general attitude towards contemporary politics, preserved in his own letter addressed to Māloji Ghorpade of Mudhol from Bhāgānagar in March 1677. It runs thus[4]:—

"You are already aware how my late lamented father left the Nizamshahi State and accepted service under Bijapur during the regime of Ibrahim Adilshah and with what confidence that Shah treated him. My father's uppermost idea at the time was that whatever power he possessed should be utilized in raising the status of those Maratha Jagirdars who were wandering in search of livelihood, that they should attain distinction and confidence in managing the affairs of the State. With this object in view my father brought your father Bāji Ghorpade for an interview with the Adilshah and raised him to the status of an imperial commander. I know what great

4. Shivaji Souvenir Page 146.

deeds your father and you did since then during three regimes. It is a matter of sincere regret to me that your father forgetting all the good that my father had done to him, sided with Mustafa Khan in capturing him (my father). It was your father Bāji Ghorpade who undertook the hazardous enterprise and gave over my father as a captive in Mustafa's hands, a consummation which for years caused bitter enmity between your house and mine, resulting in open fighting and bloodshed on both sides. My people killed your father in a fight. Thus the enmity continued for a number of years; but now the time has arrived for rectifying the mistakes of the past: and with this view I now write this letter to explain the present political situation and advise you how to use it to mutual advantage.

"You are aware that there have been three Muslim states in the south, the Nizam Shahi, the Adil Shahi and the Qutb Shahi. Upon the first being destroyed by the Mughals, its great nobles came into the service of the Adil Shah after personal consultations and conferences. This Adil Shahi State, however, has now been seized by the Pathan Bahlol Khan. The Adil Shah is a minor, being a king only in name, but virtually under the Pathan's restraint; the throne, the umbrella and the fort of Bijapur are in the hands of the Pathan, a matter of evil portent to the interests of the Deccanis. If the Pathan is allowed to become powerful, he will surely ruin one and all the Deccani nobles. In order to obviate this, I have entered into a friendly understanding with the Qutb Shah, with whom I had purposely kept up amicable relations from the beginning, and who recently invited me for a personal visit in an autograph letter impressed with his own palm. I accepted his invitation and have met him. Upon learning that I had already declared myself an independent king, he excused me the usual Muslim ceremonials which he used to exact from one and all, viz., touching the ground with head before him. The Qutb Shah and I met on equal terms, both coming half way for the meeting. He received me most honourably and with sincere greetings. Holding me with his hand he seated me by his side and showed various marks of respect, cementing mutual friendship. After the customary ceremonials, we freely discussed political matters in which the Qutb-Shahi minister Madan Pant and I unitedly made certain proposals which the Shah cordially agreed to. He places such a high confidence in me that I now hold a very favourable position which I can well utilise in promoting the interests of the Marathas and in reducing the power of the Pathans of Bijapur.

" As soon as an agreement was reached on both sides, my most anxious plan was to take into confidence the great Maratha nobles, bring them for an interview with the Kutb Shah, to offer them fresh prospects in service and with their help extend the dominion both of the Shah and the Marathas. You know how keen I have been in consolidating the Maratha power by bringing together all the scattered elements for a united action. Inspired with these motives I have arranged with the Kutb Shah that he should employ you into his service. For this we must at once lay aside our hereditary enmity. You must discard all your suspicion about me. Take my honest word that I am anxious to promote your interests and enclose for your compliance the formal letter of invitation which the Kutb Shah has addressed to you through me. You are born of a high family. You must trust me and immediately on receipt of this letter, you must contrive to get away from the service of the Pathan and meet me at Bhāgānagar by rapid marches. Please do not lose this splendid opportunity : take time by the forelock, send me immediately in advance an envoy of your confidence to arrange details at least four days before you arrive for the actual interview. I am at this moment in such a strong position to promote your interests, that I am sure you will ever afterwards remember my good offices ; nay, your sons and grand-sons too will remember them with gratitude. Here is a rare opportunity by which you can profit at the hands of the Kutb Shah. Do not hesitate to come, or to give up your loyalty to the Adil Shah, nor should you allow any distrust about me to come in your way. In reality where is the Bijapur State now ? It came to an end when Khawas Khan was put to death, when the Pathan took possession of the city and the fort, and when the child king was imprisoned. The Adilshahi State no longer exists and you have no justification for serving it. You cannot call it your own. The Pathan will offer you inducements, which might prevent you from taking the step I advise. But you must remember that the Pathan will not care for you; and in the meantime the Kutb Shah, the various Maratha nobles and I, will soon swallow the Pathan up. You Marathas are my kith and kin. Your interest is dear to my heart. That is why I write so freely. The Kutb Shah and I can give you double of what the Pathan may promise you. Nay, whatever more is possible will surely be done to reward your services. I have renounced all suspicion about you from my mind and sacredly swear having done so, calling my Goddess Bhavāni to witness. I will not fail to keep my word. Fling away all suspicion about me, come to me at once and send your trusted envoy in advance with an oath in the name of your family God, that you on your part are as sincere as I am on mine. So let me have a sacred oath from you with your envoy. I shall never fail to advance your interests. What more shall I say?"

This important letter explains as nothing else does, the main object of Shivaji's life-endeavour. It was to have Maratha independence established on the principle of cordial co-operation of all the leading Maratha members. Shivaji was not opposed to the Muslim religion as he cordially agreed to support the Kutb Shah on condition of his protecting the interests of the Hindus. He entertained no rancour for his Ghorpade cousins, if they would come in and join in his national work. Evidently as the State of Bijapur was collapsing, he wished to prevent the Mughals from absorbing it. His plan was to share that prize with the Kutb Shah, himself taking the essentially Maratha lands and leaving the Telugu country to the Kutb Shah. This also supplies a clue to Shivaji's move against his brother of Tanjore.

4. Bijapuri Karnatak seized.—Intent on seizing the Bijapuri territories, Shivaji left Bhāgānagar about the end of March, and proceeded towards the south where his armies had already preceded him. He himself took this opportunity of visiting the famous shrines and places of pilgrimage on the way. He visited the confluence of the Krishnā and the Tungabhadrā known as the Nivritti or blissful Sangam, and performed acts of charity. His men in the meantime collected 5 lacs Hons by way of Chauth from Karnool and proceeded to Anantapur, while he himself went to Shri Shaila Mallikarjun, a famous shrine in a deep valley of the Krishnā, a rare secluded spot lavishly endowed by nature, which so enchanted his devotional instinct, that it was with difficulty that he could be snatched away from its charms, which engrossed his mind and kept him gripped for over ten days. In the first week of April he joined his main army at Anantapur.

Thereafter, travelling via Nandyal, Kadappa, Tirupati and Kalahasti, he reached the environs of Madras and despatched a body of 5,000 troops for the capture of Jinji, a fort belonging to Bijapur which was defended by the commandant Nasir Muhammad Khan. The Khan agreed to deliver the fort to Shivaji on receiving a jagir with an annual income of Rupees fifty thousand. Shivaji himself visited Jinji, pulled down its old fortifications and rebuilt the whole for permanent defence. He appointed Rāyāji Nalge to the command of the fort and Vithal Pildev Atre to look after the revenue affairs of the whole territory. He also introduced the Maratha system of revenue and accounts, which had proved successful in his Maval jagir. In fact Shivaji made Jinji the principal seat of his Karnatak government, having constructed official and residential buildings both for his civil and military administrators ; what we see there today is the survival of Shivaji's construction. All vestiges of Bijapur rule were removed.

This east coast region was very loosely held by Bijapur. It has already been noticed that Jinji was captured for Bijapur by the Vazir Khan Muhammad. That Vazir's son Nasir Muhammad now surrendered it to Shivaji. A Pathan noble of Bijapur named Sher Khan Lodi who resided at Valigandapuram near Trichinopoly, held sway over a considerable territory, practically independent of Bijapur. Another Bijapuri officer Abdulla Khan lived at Vellore. Sher Khan Lodi, ambitious but indolent, and desiring to oppose Shivaji's move, had secured the support of the French of Pondicherry. In the midst of this situation Shivaji took possession of Jinji and thence proceeded to Vellore on 23 May, and laid siege to that strong and famous post; but it could not be easily taken. There were two adjoining hills which Shivaji captured and from which he directed an artillery fire against the main rampart. As it seemed that the siege of Vellore would continue long, Shivaji entrusted the task to other hands and himself proceeded to the south against Sher-Khan Lodi. Vellore was captured a year later on 22 July 1678, after Shivaji had returned home from his southern conquest.

As Shivaji proceeded to the south Sher Khān opposed him with his forces in the vicinity of Tiruvadi. After repeated skirmishes Sher Khan found it impossible to resist Shivaji and offered to surrender. He came for a personal visit which took place on 5th July 1677, when he paid 20 thousand Hons as expenses, delivered his son as a hostage for the balance of his ransom, and effecting his own release ceded the whole country to Shivaji. The ransom was paid in February 1678 when the son was allowed to join his father. It will thus be seen how easily the whole coastal territory of the Karnatak from the Tungabhadrā to the Kāveri came into Shivaji's possession and how the Adilshahi Government was fast dissolving. Shivaji at once organized a regular system of defence and administration by importing twenty thousand hands from Mahārāshtra for revenue and military service.[5]

The large admixture of Maratha elements which is noticeable to this day in these far off Tamil and Kanarese lands, has its origin in the systematic efforts which Shivaji then made for the settlement of these fresh additions to his dominion. Traces of that Maratha system are even now visible.

5. **The two brothers on their heritage.**—After disposing of Sher Khan Lodi, Shivaji proceeded towards Tanjore to meet his step-brother Ekoji and adjust his relations with him. Shivaji encamped at Tirumalwadi on the Coleroon about ten miles north of Tanjore where Ekoji was expected to come on a visit. While at this place Chokkanath Nayak of Madura sent his agents with presents for Shivaji, who had demanded a heavy tribute. After a good deal of hesitation Chokkanath through the mediation of Raghunāth Pandit agreed to pay 6 lacs of Hons to Shivaji and the matter was settled.

In the meantime Ekoji arrived at Shivaji's camp to pay his respects. He was accompanied by his Peshwa Jagannāth Pant and a company of troops. The two brothers spent about a week together during the bright fortnight of Shravan (the third week of July). The first formal meeting took place in a

5. For Shivaji's southern activities see Martin's Account in Sen's Foreign Biographies. Martin's personal envoy met Shivaji and wrote his report, the best available contemporary narration of this Maratha invasion.

Shiva temple. During the interval they had many talks and dinners together both in public and private. But in the midst of the cordial and frank atmosphere outside, Ekoji evinced a peculiar reserve in his ways and did not disclose what attitude he intended to maintain towards his brother. Shivaji explained to him his own views and plans. Ekoji simply listened and did not signify whether and to what extent he agreed. He evidently felt overawed by Shivaji's great talents and masterful personality. Step-brothers are hardly ever affectionate to each other; their mothers were practically strangers and jealous through life. More than once Ekoji had appeared in open fight against Shivaji on behalf of Bijapur. Thus at this moment he felt altogether confounded in his brother's company. The Jedhe chronology mentions, " the two brothers met in the month of Shravan. Mutual suspicion led to a breach. Ekoji fled to Tanjore without taking his leave. Shivaji, therefore, captured his districts of Jagdevgad, Chidambaram, and Vridhachalam and laid siege to Kolar."

The real position of affairs between the two brothers is nowhere clearly recorded. What exactly Shivaji wanted from his brother has to be gathered from his letters, long but diplomatic, and from stray bits of references in the *Bakhars* and elsewhere. Shivaji said in effect :—

"We must both equally share our ancestral acquisitions. After our father's death you have alone enjoyed the whole without a single reference to me. I do not ask for a share of what you have earned by your effort. You may make whatever acquisitions you can, and God grant you strength for the same. But I must demand a share in what our father had left. For this you must produce recorded evidence upon which we should base our claims. I am ready to offer you help whenever you need it. You must speak out freely and without reservation what your position is." To this the only reply that Ekoji made was a vague one,—" I submit to your commands."

In this way they lived and talked for a week at the end of which Ekoji, feeling extreme irritation, probably at the pressure which Shivaji was slowly bringing to bear upon him, one night secretly escaped on a floating raft over the Coleroon back to Tanjore. Martin's envoy, an eye-witness writes :—" Sivaji demanded his share of his father's goods. He had written several times to Ekoji to come and meet him. The latter recoiled. At last he crossed the Coleroon and came to see Shivaji. The first conversation gave evidence of amity and tenderness, but when it came to negotiation, Ekoji discovered that his brother would not let him go unless he had satisfied him about his claims, and while he offered friendly words, he sought some means of withdrawing himself from such a bad strait. He succeeded therein one night. He had a raft kept ready on the banks of the river under pretext of necessity. He approached the banks of the river, threw himself into the raft and crossed to the other side. On receipt of this information Shivaji caused Ekoji's men who were in his camp to be arrested, among them one Jagannath Pandit, a Brahman, who commanded Ekoji's troops, a man of courage and ability. The brothers did not meet again."

Thereupon Shivaji despatched three clever agents to meet Ekoji in his palace and sent a personal letter to him with them, demanding a half share of his father's property on pain of reprisals. Shivaji gave his brother clearly to understand that no hesitation would be allowed, although in settling the actual amount, Ekoji's wishes would be respected, if he would come to terms. To this Ekoji replied,

" Whatever our father Shahji Raje acquired was by means of service to the Bijapur State against whom Shivaji Raje had all along rebelled and been disloyal, thereby causing harm to father. There is no ancestral property as such beyond what was acquired by service. I am even now the Bijapur Shah's loyal servant and as such would be guided by his orders."

Thus instead of conciliating Shivaji, Ekoji decided to put him down if the dispute resulted in a recourse to arms, and he called in the help of Madura and Mysore for that purpose. At the same time he reported the affair to Bijapur, but received no response from the authorities there. That Government was at the time not in a position to break with Shivaji. In this situation as Shivaji could not afford to stay longer in the south, he decided to return himself and left Bahir Rao Mohite, Hambir Rao and Raghunāth Pant with the major portion of his troops, to settle matters with Ekoji as they thought best. Shivaji began his return march from the bank of the Coleroon on 27 July. On the way back he seized all the territory of Ekoji on the north side of the Kaveri including the districts of Arni, Kolar, Hoskote, Bangalore, Bālapore and Shirā, and appointed his own officers to govern and defend them against any hostile attack. When Shivaji reached Gadag in November, he learned of an action having taken place; Ekoji had attacked Hambir-Rao Mohite, at Valigandapuram on 16th November and sustained a crushing defeat, his illegitimate brothers Pratāpji and Bhivji Raje, and his officer Shivaji Dabir were taken captives. Shivaji learned the details when he arrived in Mahārāshtra, and with a view to effecting a reconciliation he wrote a long letter of warning to Ekoji, which ranks as a document of rare value. It puts forth Shivaji's aims and policy clearly. This letter is full and authentic and is printed in the facsimile of Bālāji Āvaji's handwriting being dated 1 March 1678. In this letter, while demanding from his brother a full share of his father's acquisitions, he holds out a threat of severe reprisals, adding he was perfectly ready to adjust matters to his brother's satisfaction, but that he would not allow him to shirk the main demand. What Shivaji resented most was that Ekoji should ally himself with the Turks and Pathans of Bijapur who had been open enemies of the Hindus and whom it was Shivaji's life-mission to humble. Says he :—

"Gods and Goddesses have favoured me; through their favour I have been able to beat down the Turks. How could you hope to win against me with the help of these Turks? You should not have gone to the length of standing in open opposition to my armies. You cherished the wicked intention like Duryodhan's and caused unnecessary blood-shed. But what has come to pass cannot be remedied. You have only to take a lesson from what has occurred and give up your obstinacy. For thirteen long years you have usurped all father's property and now I have wrested away my share by force of arms. Please deliver to my officers Arni, Bangalore, Kolar, Hoskote, Shiralkot (Shira) and other minor districts including Tanjore: give up also a half share of the cash, ornaments, horses, elephants and other property and make your peace with me. I shall bestow on you a Jagir yielding three lacs annually of districts between the Tungabhadrā and Panhālā. Or if you do not wish to accept this as a gift from me, I shall request the Kutb Shah to confer on you a similar jagir in his dominion.

Thus I offer you two alternatives, choose whichever you like. Give up your obduracy and stop this domestic dissension. It is no use sulking. As an elderly person I have all along treated you affectionately and again repeat the same sentiments of your welfare. If you have the good sense to accept my advice, I am sure you will be happy and at ease. If not, you will only add to your distress, which it will not then be in my power to relieve."

It is evident from this that Shivaji, already ignoring the existence of the Bijapur State, required his brother to renounce it openly and disclaim all pretence of serving it. But this letter did not soothe Ekoji's heart. It grieved him all the more. His shrewd wife Dipā Bai came to his rescue and gave his disconsolate mind some sound advice and reconciled him to the inevitable. She managed to dismiss Ekoji's Muslim evil advisers and urged him to accept Raghunāth Pandit's counsel. Ekoji thereupon wrote a respectful letter to the Pandit and called him from Jinji for a personal visit. The Pant arrived in due course and had a cordial reception. Then the Pandit arranged the terms of an amicable settlement of the dispute between the two brothers. All necessary deeds and papers were prepared and despatched to Shivaji for approval and ratification.

Shivaji was highly gratified at this amicable settlement of a long-standing dispute and at once ratified the whole agreement. In soothing notes he replied to Ekoji and to his sister-in-law Dipā Bai, who had so cleverly managed to solve these delicate problems. He wrote to Raghunāth Pandit, "I cannot too highly commend the wisdom and foresight of my sister-in-law Dipā Bai, who with uncommon zeal and skill induced her husband to come to terms with me and thereby so satisfactorily solved a knotty question. I am supremely gratified at this happy result. In fact I was all along concerned to secure the best interest of my brother. In asking a half share I had his own lasting welfare at my heart. The paltry lucre was not my object. It was for the sake of higher aims, I had to make that stern demand. We must treat our servants and subordinates respectfully and effect lasting good of the State, which it behoves us both to serve with all our powers." These last lines clearly prove how anxious Shivaji was to raise the Maratha State to the height of glory and independence. Ekoji was solely guided by Muslim advisers who worked insidiously to undo Shivaji's life-work through Ekoji's instrumentality. These Muslim advisers were dismissed, and Raghunāth Pant was restored to his former position of a guardian, so that all cause for friction was finally removed in the course of a year after Shivaji's return from the Karnatak.

6. **Agreed division of patrimony.**—The agreement contained nineteen articles, the first ten of which unfold the plan for the moral and spiritual good of the Maratha State. The sixth article says, " No one who is wicked and an enemy of the Hindu religion should be harboured in the State. Such persons should be kept away from the power of doing harm." The whole dispute between the brothers and its conclusion unmistakably disclose that Shivaji's highest aim in the Karnatak expedition was to resuscitate and expand the Maratha State and create a lasting shelter for the Hindus in general, who had grown altogether helpless through centuries of ill-treatment.

The 12th article is politically significant and pertinent to the main point of dispute between the brothers. It says, " When a treaty of peace was effected between us (Shivaji and the Adil Shah) through our father's mediation (in 1662), the express stipulation laid down was that neither of us (Shivaji or Ekoji) should serve that State (Bijapur). We should help it whenever necessary not as servants but as well-wishers. We should hereafter strictly observe this understanding. Ekoji, therefore, should not hold himself a servant of that state. He may, when called up, help that State with a contingent of 5000 troops. He must exercise his supremacy over all the Poligars and potentates whom he has already subjugated."

This article makes it clear beyond the shadow of a doubt why Shivaji attacked Ekoji. While Shivaji proclaimed himself an independent monarch, he did not relish the spectacle of his own brother coming to oppose him on behalf of Bijapur on being guided exclusively by Muslim flatterers and holding himself a bond servant of a Muslim State, which he himself had all but conquered. In order to emphasize this aspect of his state policy, Shivaji laid down in the 15th article, " that the districts of Bangalore, Hoskote and Shiralkot (Shira) yielding a revenue of 2 lacks of Hons have already been conquered by us : when well managed they will soon be worth 5 lacs ; we assign these districts as a voluntary present to our sister-in-law Dipā Bai, wife of Ekoji. Ekoji may supervise their management but not lay claim to them. After Dipā Bai they will continue to her daughter or to any one else to whom she assigns them." Here Shivaji gives back practically all of Ekoji's possessions, redeeming them out of Muslim control. Nothing can be clearer than this final pronouncement of Shivaji's object in this last undertaking of his life.

Article 16 says, " We have conquered Tanjore and the adjoining districts of Ekoji worth about 7 lacs of Hons. These we hand over of our own free will to Ekoji as his own separate possession." Article 17 says, " We assign territory worth one lac to Raghunāth Pant in complete hereditary succession." Article 19 says, " Ekoji should look after the upkeep of the tomb of our father Shahji Raje." Evidently this filial duty was now assigned to Ekoji.[6]

These articles clearly demonstrate the nature of the dispute between the two brothers and Shivaji's object in this southern expedition. Ekoji was to be weaned away from his subordination to the Muslim power of Bijapur. In forwarding the treaty Shivaji wrote another affectionate letter to his brother. But Ekoji did not respond in the spirit in which Shivaji's scheme of a Swarajya was planned ; and although the dispute was apparently settled, Ekoji took to heart his loss of independence. He felt sorely grieved to find that Shivaji's officials took charge of all his possessions and administered them without reference to himself. He gave up all personal pleasures and enjoyment. When in due course this was reported to Shivaji, he wrote another loving letter full of sympathy and pathos about January 1680. Within three months thereafter Shivaji expired.

The death of Shivaji and the rapid changes that it brought about in the politics of the Deccan, involved the fate both of the Maratha and the Tanjore principalities, and although Ekoji survived Shivaji by nearly five years, we have no record to determine the Tanjore Rajah's aims and activities during that period. So far as Tanjore was concerned, Ekoji proved a wise and considerate ruler. He established his rule at Tanjore on

6. The whole treaty is quoted in the Shiva-digvijaya Bakhar.

a sound basis and provided means for its defence. His Rani Dipā Bai coming from the Ingle family, was a wise and influential lady, more or less after Jija Bai's pattern. She gave birth to three good sons Shahji, Sharfoji and Tukoji, who all ruled at Tanjore in succession and promoted arts and literature as well as the welfare of their subjects.[7]

Whatever results were achieved by Shahji and his son Ekoji in the spheres of politics and society, the credit for them must be equally shared by the Hanumante family also, particularly by Raghunāth Pant to whom Shivaji says, " I have endeavoured to rear up a number of my own co-workers and helpmates; but you belong to a different category. You have served our father and like him possess the power to correct and guide us when we cannot see our way. No other person can exercise such influence in our affairs. We look upon you fully in the place of our revered parent, and cannot too highly estimate your services." Raghunath Pant shared the noble aims of Shivaji and did his best to promote them. It is uncharitable and historically unjust to accuse him of selfish and mischievous motives in inducing Shivaji to undertake the Karnatak expedition for personal pique or love of lucre. Raghunath's brother Janārdanpant was also an able administrator working under Shivaji in the Deccan, as his brother did in the Karnatak under Ekoji.[8]

7. तीन पुरुषार्थ तिघे भूप । जियेचे पुत्र कुलदीप । दीपांबिका यथार्थरूप । नाम म्हणौनि शोभतसे ॥

Writes Raghunath Bhat Navahasta. (Gode's Research).

Her three sons are Kings,
The centre of men's desires,
The light of their royal house,
Truly has she been named *Dipambika*,
She shines like a lamp.

8. The introductory and the concluding portions of the *Rajvyavaharkosh* give a lucid account of the great work performed by the Hanumante family.

CHRONOLOGY

CHAPTER XI

1659 Sept. 5	Death of Sambhāji's mother, Sai Bai.
1676 Jan. 18	Khawas Khan put to death.
June	Bahadur Khan routed near Bijapur.
1677 August	Bahadur Khan resigns office : Dilir Khan in supreme command.
„ Sept.	Dilir Khan attacks Golkonda.
„ Dec.	Savitri Bai Desai humbled.
„ „ 23	Bahlol Khan dies, Siddi Mas'ud takes charge.
1678 April	Shivaji returns to Panhālā from the Karnatak ; Dilir Khan attacks Bijapur.
„ Sept. 18	Muazzam appointed to the Govt. of the Deccan.
„ Dec. 13	Sambhāji escapes from Panhālā.
1679 Feb. 25	Muazzam reaches Aurangabad.
„ April 2	Dilir Khan captures Bhupalgad.
„ April 3	Jazia re-imposed, Shivaji's letter of remonstrance to Aurangzeb.
„ August 18	Sambhāji and Dilir Khan besiege Bijapur.
„ Novr. 15	Dilir Khan raises the siege of Bijapur.
„ „	Shivaji's pact of friendship with Bijapur.
„ „ 20	Sambhāji leaves Dilir Khan's camp.
„ Dec. 4	Do reaches Panhālā : kept in confinement.
„ „ 31	Shivaji's visit to Rāmdās.
1680 Feb. 4.	Shivaji leaves Rāmdās and proceeds to Raigad.
„ March 7	Rājārām married to Pratāp Rao Gujar's daughter.
„ April 3	Shivaji dies.

CHAPTER XI

THE MOON SETS

[1678—1680]

1. Results of the Karnatak Campaign.
2. Public Remonstrance against Aurangzeb's intolerance.
3. Sambhaji's desertion.
4. Effort to reclaim Sambhaji fails.
5. The End.
6. Family and religious preceptors.

1. **Results of the Karnatak Campaign.**—Netāji Pālkar's desertion was a great blow to the aspirations of Dilir Khan and the expectations of the Emperor. The State of Bijapur was now managed by the Pathan minister Bahlol Khan with whom Dilir Khan effected a close friendship ; and the two formed fresh plans for the subjugation of both Shivaji and the Kutb Shah. Shivaji entertained a severe hatred for this Pathan who was ruining the old kingdom of Bijapur. Bahlol Khan put to death his Siddi competitor Khawas Khan on 18 January 1676, which acted as an open signal for a civil war in Bijapur. Bahadur Khan considered this a suitable opportunity for conquering Bijapur and with a large army came suddenly upon it. But he met with strong opposition, and was worsted in many sanguinary actions near Bijapur in June 1676. This sealed Bahadur Khan's fate in the eyes of the Emperor, to whom Dilir Khan had reported the utter incapacity of Bahadur Khan to cope with the situation in the Deccan. The Emperor thereupon recalled Bahadur Khan and entrusted the supreme command to Dilir Khan. Bahadur Khan gave up his office in August 1677 and in September Dilir Khan attacked Golkonda to punish Kutb Shah for joining Shivaji.

Shivaji's advance into the Karnatak was a great indirect blow to the Mughal Emperor's dreams of conquest. While Aurangzeb and Dilir Khan were planning finally to extinguish both Bijapur and Golkanda, Shivaji stepped in and practically seized the southernmost regions. His alliance with Golkonda proved a master-stroke, which upset Dilir Khan beyond calculation. Finding the allied troops of Kutb Shah and Shivaji absent in the south, Dilir Khan made a dash for Golkonda; but Mādannā being fully prepared to meet him, easily turned him back from the way. The news of this move and the Emperor's fresh measures for taking prompt action against Shivaji, compelled the latter to hasten back home leaving the completion of his Karnatak venture to other hands. On the way back Shivaji established a strong line of defensive posts right from Panhālā to Tanjore. While returning to his homeland towards the end of 1677, he met a slight opposition at Belvadi near Belgaum from the guardian Desai (i.e. Thanadar) of that post and his heroic wife Savitri Bai. Belvadi was captured after a month's attack by the heroic effort of Dādāji Raghunāth Prabhu Nadkar, and the distressed and humiliated lady was taken under protection by Shivaji.[1] He reached Panhālā in April 1678 after an absence of nearly fourteen months, having added to his dominions a territory yielding 20 lacs of Hons and containing a hundred forts.

In this latest exploit of Shivaji one must recognise the full play of his inherent genius. The Maratha kingdom was shaped into a real and compact unit; its scanty resources were strengthened; a band of young earnest men was trained in military and civil administration, so as to ensure the permanency of his achievement. Santāji Bhosle, Hambir Rao Mohite, Santāji Ghorpade, Janārdan Pant Hanumante, Keshav Trimal Pingle, Harji Mahādik, Dhanāji Jādhav and many other youthful energetic soldier-diplomats, who figured in later history so conspicuously, were initiated in state-craft in the fruitful field offered by this Karnatak expedition. Merit was critically tested and amply rewarded. Shivaji well understood the principle that the highest strength of the State lay in its efficient administration. Under his direction everyone felt inspired to do his duty and to sacrifice one's all for the good of the State. A healthy rivalry thus came into being to serve the State and earn the Raja's esteem. This benign policy won the hearts even of the rebellious Poligars and Deshmukhs of the Karnatak, who were indirectly influenced by his benevolent ways in severe contrast to the Muslim policy of the preced-

1. This memorable episode is well described in *Prabhu Ratnamala*, p. 82.

ing age and readily submitted to his rule. This healthy change was put to a real test during the difficult days of Sambhāji and Rājārām, when it was the cordial co-operation of the peoples of the south that enabled the Marathas to score phenomenal victories over the Emperor.

During Shivaji's absence in the Karnatak the Pathan Bahlol Khan of Bijapur died on 23 December 1677 and Siddi Mas'ud took up the control of that Government. Dilir Khan at once directed his attack upon Bijapur, when in his sore need Siddi Mas'ud applied to Shivaji for help in a pathetic letter, which ran thus : " We have been neighbours eating out of the same dish. You have doubtless as great a concern for the preservation of this State as I have. Let us join hands and in mutual co-operation destroy our common enemy the Mughals." Shivaji was touched by this appeal and at once prepared for an attack upon the Mughals. It can thus be realized how the two Muslim States were practically coming under Shivaji's heels and would have been easily absorbed by him, if his sudden death had not changed the course of events.

2. Public Remonstrance against Aurangzeb's Intolerance.—With Shivaji's return to his home-land unfortunately began the last chapter of his life. With a view to checking Dilir Khan he despatched some of his commanders to plunder the Mughal territory north of the Godavari up to Aurangabad and tried in vain to recapture Shivner, his birth place. Aurangzeb felt extremely uneasy at the rising tide of Shivaji's fortune and was utterly perplexed as to the means of overcoming him. He had already employed all his best generals and resources against him. Once again he appointed his son Muazzam to the Government of the Deccan on 18th September 1678, and this Shahzada reached Aurangabad on 25 February in the following year (1679). He was instructed to be guided entirely by Dilir Khan.

About this time there was a great stir in the country over the revival of the Jazia or poll-tax which had long been in abeyance and which the Emperor re-imposed by a fresh order dated 3rd April 1679. Shivaji at once wrote to the Emperor a well reasoned and spirited letter of protest against the measure, which was drafted by Nila Prabhu in eloquent Persian. This famous remonstrance clearly exposed the wrong-headed policy of Aurangzeb. "In strict justice," says Shivaji, "the Jazia is not at all lawful. If you imagine piety to consist in oppressing and terrorising the Hindus, you ought first to levy the tax upon Rajsinh who is the head of the Hindus. But to oppress ants and flies is neither valour nor spirit. If you believe in the Koran, God is the Lord of all men and not of the Muhammadans only. Islam and Hinduism are only different pigments used by the Divine Painter to picture the human species. To show bigotry for any man's creed and practices is to alter the words of the Holy Book. Your officers neglect to tell you of the true state of things and cover a blazing fire with straw." The appeal fell on deaf years. The Emperor was obdurate. He at this very juncture declared a war upon the Rajputs and thus flung himself into innumerable difficulties and disasters, which ultimately swallowed him up and ruined his Empire.

While the Raja was engaged in the south, Ānāji Datto and Moropant Pingle extended Maratha dominion along the west coast both southwards and northwards. They even went beyond Surat and plundered Broach. But these achievements were more than counterbalanced by the sudden desertion of Sambhāji to the Mughals, a contrivance of the astute Dilir Khan. This disaster dealt such a blow to Shivaji's heart that it may be said to have hastened his end.

3. **Sambhaji's desertion.**—Born in 1657, Sambhāji had lost his mother when he was only two years old. Of fine manly features Sambhāji's appearance was perhaps more commanding than his father's. At the age of 9 he accompanied his father to Agra, and upon his return was for a time stationed at Aurangabad as commandant of the Maratha contingent in Mughal service, when he came in direct contact with the loose life led by the Mughal grandees. It was at this time that he must have contracted the evil habits of addiction to sensual pleasures in severe contrast to the austere life of his father's surroundings. He freely shared the hunting pastimes of Muazzam. He had received the traditional education in reading and writing, accounts and sportsmanship, and in addition became well-versed in Sanskrit also in which Keshao Bhat Purohit and Kavikalash were his tutors. Soon after the coronation ceremony of 1674, complaints reached Shivaji's ears of

his son's evil habits. Shivaji kept him under surveillance at Shringārpore during 1676. He was also placed in the company of Rāmdās for some time. But his ways did not improve.

Upon his return from the Karnatak expedition in 1678, Shivaji noticed a distinct change for the worse in his son, and kept him in practical confinement at Panhālā. Sambhaji's high spirit revolted at this rigorous treatment, and in an evil moment he succumbed to the tempting offer made by Dilir Khan through secret spies. On the night of 13 December 1678 the Prince quietly escaped from Panhālā with his wife Yesu Bai and proceeded towards the Mughal camp at Bahadurgad to meet Dilir Khan, to whom he had already communicated his intention. The Khan felt immensely elated at the success of his game, and welcomed Sambhāji on the way at Karkam. The Khan immediately reported the affair to the Emperor and requested orders for entertaining Sambhāji with dignity. The Emperor certainly felt happy at the news, but conveyed to Dilir Khan his own grave suspicion that this might be a ruse on Shivaji's part for doing some mischief and warned him to be on his guard. Dilir Khan and Sambhāji then planned to proceed against Bijapur and on the way attacked Bhupalgad where, Sambhaji disclosed, a large amount of treasure and the families of several respectable Maratha nobles had been kept for safety under the trusted commandant Phirangoji Narsāla. Phirangoji could have fired his guns against the attackers, but refrained from fear of injuring his master's son and heir. After a severe hand to hand fight Dilir Khan captured the fort on 2nd April 1679, and put to death most of the inmates that fell into his hands. When Shivaji learned of the fall of Bhupalgad, he severely reprimanded Phirangoji for not firing on Sambhāji and putting such a sinner to death. After devastating Maratha territory, Dilir Khan and Sambhāji crossed the Bhimā at Dhulkhed on 18 August and marched to the vicinity of Bijapur where Siddi Mas'ud was in power, who in his distress implored Shivaji's help. Shivaji readily agreed and at once marched with two large contingents for the defence of Bijapur. In the mean time Dilir Khan laid siege to Bijapur, and for two months tried his utmost to capture the place. But Shivaji from outside severely handled the besiegers and dexterously supplied the defenders with necessaries and materials, so that

Dilir Khan was compelled to raise the siege and save his forces from destruction by a precipitate retreat on 14 November. Māloji Ghorpade of Mudhol at this time heroically defended Bijapur fully co-operating with Shivaji.

Thus sorely discomfited before Bijapur, Dilir Khan and Sambhāji turned to the west with a view to taking Panhālā. Siddi Mas'ud expressed his gratitude to Shivaji for having rendered timely help, and after honouring him with costly presents and dresses, gave him leave to depart. At this time an agreement was effected between the Bijapur Government and Shivaji, by which that Government renounced its right to the principality of Tanjore and confirmed to Shivaji all the territory he had seized between Kopbal and Jinji.

After all, Sambhāji's desertion did not benefit the Khan much. During their march towards Panhālā Dilir committed fearful atrocities upon the innocent populace of the various places on the way. At Tikota a large number of bankers and rich gentry had taken shelter with their hoarded wealth. Dilir Khan's cupidity was excited; he wantonly plundered the gentry and inflicted untold miseries upon innocent women and children, both Hindu and Muslim, many of whom killed themselves by jumping into wells to save their honour. Several thousand of these hapless people were taken prisoners and heavy ransoms demanded from them. This barbarous procedure chilled Sambhāji's ardour for Dilir Khan to such a degree that he strongly protested against it. From Tikota they proceeded to Athni, another wealthy mart, where the Khan expected to collect a rich booty. Here he laid violent hands only on the Hindus, who made piteous appeals to Sambhāji in the name of his father to intercede with the Khan for their safety and honour. And now Sambhāji's conscience was so keenly awakened that a complete estrangement took place between them. Dilir Khan taunted Sambhāji saying, "I am my own master: you have no business to teach me lessons in good conduct."

During all these months Shivaji had employed various means through secret agents to wean away Sambhāji from his sinister association. Their joint failure before Bijapur was reported to the Emperor who censured Dilir Khan and ordered him to put Sambhāji under arrest at once, and bring him a prisoner to Delhi; and he also replaced Dilir Khan by Bahadur

Khan in the Government of the Deccan. All this was going on secretly without Sambhāji's knowledge : but he did not fail to get scent of it and became afraid about his own safety. Mahādaji Nimbālkar to whom Sambhāji's sister was married, was then a noble in the service of the Emperor under Dilir Khan, and he roused Sambhāji to a sense of the dangerous situation in which he was placed. This remonstrance at once opened Sambhāji's eyes, and in the night of 20th November 1679 he with Yesu Bai in male disguise escaped secretly from Dilir Khan's camp at Athni with only ten followers and sought shelter with Mas'ud Khan of Bijapur. Dilir Khan on learning that Sambhāji had run away and was at Bijapur, sent his agents to Mas'ud Khan, and offered to pay him a heavy bribe for placing Sambhāji in his own custody. Mortally afraid of these sudden developments, Sambhāji left Bijapur secretly on the night of 30th November, joined a band of troopers whom Shivaji had specially stationed to watch his movements, and by long and strenuous marches rode into Panhālā on 4th December, after having been away for nearly one year. With his mother's death Shivaji's private life had become clouded with anxiety and unhappiness. His first wife Sai Bai, a gentle affectionate woman had been long dead and the gap was not properly filled up. Her son Sambhāji was growing up into a passionate reckless youth impatient of his father's control. The next queen-consort Soyra Bai possessed a character far from amiable. She planned, it is said, to supplant Sambhāji with her own son Rājārām, and gave Shivaji little rest by her ceaseless importunities and intrigues, particularly during the period when Sambhāji was away with Dilir Khan. Soyra Bai's obsession with this purpose disturbed the whole palace and embittered the relations between Shivaji and Sambhāji all the more. The lion-hearted king for once lacked the nerve to handle the delicate domestic situation.

4. Effort to reclaim Sambhaji fails.—While Shivaji was fighting in the environs of Bijapur against Dilir Khan, he devised an ingenious plan of creating a diversion in the Khan's rear. He divided his force, himself leading one division and sending Ānand Rāo Makāji to lead the other ; they suddenly struck against the Mughal possessions in the vicinity of Aurangabad. They plundered and devastated Jalnāpur and obtained enormous booty. Many rich residents of the city had taken shelter in the Darga of Saiyad Jan Muhammad, a Muslim saint. When Shivaji obtained news of this concealed wealth, he plundered the hermitage and carried away all the hoard deposited therein. Khafi Khan says that the saint cursed Shivaji for this act, in consequence of which the Raja soon after died.

The Mughals were quickly on Shivaji's track. When he was returning with the plunder of Jalnā, he was opposed by strong Mughal armies near Sangamner. Sidhoji Nimbālkar and Santāji Ghorpade faced the Mughals, obstructed their advance, and allowed Shivaji time to escape with the plunder to the fort of Patta. In the action that ensued near Sangamner Sidhoji was killed and Santāji after being routed took to flight. Portions of the plunder had to be given up and Shivaji returned to Raigad early in December.

As soon as Shivaji learned that Sambhāji had come back, prompt measures were taken for the defence of Panhālā lest Dilir Khan should come and attack it. But the Khan considered it an impossible task to attack Panhālā and turned his steps southward towards Kopbal, where he met with a severe reverse at the hands of Janārdan Pant Hanumante.

Shivaji lost no time in visiting Sambhāji at Panhālā, and spent something like a month in his son's company, trying to reclaim him to a sense of his duty and responsibility. But the prince showed no repentance or improvement in his ways.

As Sambhāji had received ample experience of life in Dilir Khan's camp, Shivaji did not purposely use any harsh measures towards him, but treated him with kindness and affectionate consideration. He employed a large staff of officials to prepare complete and detailed lists of the property of the Maratha State, the acquisitions of a life of strenuous labour and achievement. This was meant indirectly to impress Sambhāji with the idea of what one man could achieve and what responsibility rested on his shoulders in his prospective inheritance. These lists are minute and full and include every item trivial or costly, cash, ornaments, valuables, stores, provisions, arms, forts and property of every description.[2]

Father and son lived together for nearly a month at Panhālā, both deeply distressed at heart. But if human minds could be suddenly reclaimed by mere wordy advice or remonstrance, the world would be an entirely different place. "There was no repentance, no change in Sambhāji," says Sabhāsad. Shivaji was overtaken by a serious ailment. His future appeared altogether clouded to him, his health rapidly failed. That his own son should join his enemies was too much for the father to bear. He gave hurried orders for Sambhāji being kept in confinement at Panhālā and appointed Hiroji Farzand, Somāji Naik Banki, and Vithal Trimbak (grand-son of Murār Bāji and keeper of the fort) to watch him closely. He also asked Janārdan Pant to remove himself from Kopbal to Kolhāpur, exercise strict supervision upon Sambhāji and prevent him from committing further mischief. Shivaji in a despairing mood started to seek solace at Sajjangad in the company of the saint Rāmdās.

5. **The End.**—One can only imagine the serious agonies of Shivaji's mind at this time. It was all very well to wage a relentless war against the Emperor and administer him a severe threat in an open letter of remonstrance. But who was to undertake this grand task in his absence? He who could so wonderfully devise his means of escape from Agra was now powerless before his own son. He vividly felt his end approaching and the concern about the future of the Maratha State weighed heavily on his bosom. Shivaji's second son Rājārām was just ten years old: his mother Soyrā Bai, the principal queen, was by no means an accommodating lady. Shivaji's ministerial cabinet was in no sense a homogeneous or united body. The two powerful ministers Moropant Pingle and Ānāji Datto were so openly at logger-heads with each other, that Shivaji himself entertained grave fears that without a competent master to control them, the ministers alone would not be able to carry on the affairs of the State smoothly for a moment. When parting from Sambhāji at Panhālā Shivaji told him, "We now proceed to Raigad, where Rājārām's marriage

2. See the Legacy of Shivaji—Sarkar's House of Shivaji, pages 165-172, as also Sabhāsad and other Bakhars, where the full lists are printed.

awaits our presence; thereafter we shall soon return here and talk about future plans. You are our eldest son; and we have naturally every reliance on you." The Waquenasi note on Rāmdās records "The Maharaja came to visit (Rāmdās) on Paush Shukla 9 (December 31) and stayed till Magh Shukla 15 (4 Feb). Every day passed in ceremonial and attention. The Samarth discussed fully matters of State and philosophy of life. For three full days the Maharaja was unconscious in deep contemplation. The Samarth inferred that the Maharaja's end was near." Shivaji left for Raigad on 4 February, where Rājārām's thread ceremony was performed on 7th March 1680, and a week later on 15 March Rājāram was married to Pratāp Rāo Gujar's daughter Janki Bai. A week later on 23 March Shivaji had an attack of fever, which soon proved fatal. Some officials were called to his bed-side. When all hope of life seemed to be lost, messengers were sent to Sambhāji Rājā at Panhālā, with a proposal for dividing the raj between the two sons. This Sambhāji refused to accept. All inmates of Raigad were overcome with extreme grief. The holy water of the Ganges was administered to the dying Raja. Thus Shivaji expired at midday, on Saturday, Chaitra Sh. 15, Shake 1602 (3 April 1680), Raudra year, in the presence of Rāmchandra Nilakanth, Pralhād Nirāji and Bālāji Āvji. Neither the Peshwa Moropant nor the Sachiv Ānāji Datto was near.

6. **Family and religious preceptors.**—As Shivaji's *gurus* the following are mentioned among many others whose blessings he never failed to seek :—

(1) Tukārām Bāwā.
(2) Samarth Rāmdās.
(3) Bābā Yākut of Kelsi.
(4) Mauni Bāwā of Patgaon.
(5) Nischalapuri Gosāvi.
(6) Parmānand Bāwā of Polādpur.
(7) Jayarām Swāmi of Wadgaon.
(8) Nārāyan Dev of Chinchwad.
(9) Rangnāth Swāmi of Nigdi,
(10) and his brother Vithal Swāmi.
(11) Bhānudas Bāwā, descendant of Eknāth.

(12) Anand Murti of Brahmanāl.
(13) Bodhle Bāwā of Dhāmangaon.
(14) Trimbak Nārāyan of Bārāmati.

Wives and Children.

1. Sai Bai Nimbālkar—married 17 April 1640, died 5 September 1659 ; one son and three daughters:- Sambhāji born 14 May 1657 ; Sakwār alias Sakhu Bai married to Mahādaji Nimbālkar ; Ranu Bai married into the Jādhav family ; Ambikā Bai married to Harji Raje Mahādik of Tarle.
2. Sagunā Bai Shirke, married 1641. Had one daughter, Nani Bai alias Rajkuwar married to Jānoji Shirke Malekar.
3. Soyara Bai Shirke married about 1660 ; died 1681 ; had one son Rājārām born 14 February 1670 and one daughter Bālābai alias Dipā Bai married to Visaji Rao.
4. Putlā Bai Mohite, married 1653, became Sati.
5. Lakshmi Bai Vichare married before 1656.
6. Sakwār Bai Gaikwad, married January 1657 ; had one daughter Kamaljā Bai married to Jānoji Pālkar.
7. Kashi Bai Jādhav married 8 April 1657.
8. Gunavantā Bai Ingle married 15 April 1657.

Shivaji thus had eight wives and eight children, 2 sons and 6 daughters. Besides two illegitimate wives are mentioned. Only three out of these wives were alive at the time of his death. Putlā Bai became Sati, Soyrā Bai was put to death by Sambhāji, and Sakwār Bai was long kept a prisoner in Aurangzeb's camp in the Deccan with Yesu Bai and Shahu.

CHRONOLOGY

CHAPTER XII

1659	Siddi Khairyat of Janjirā overcome.
1672 April	Shivaji's first visit to consult Rāmdās.
1672	English envoy Ustick visits Shivaji.
1673	English envoy Niccolls visits Shivaji.
1674	Visit of the English envoy, Oxenden.
1675	Visit of the English envoy, Austen.

CHAPTER XII

SHIVAJI'S CHARACTER AND WORK.*

1. The Amatya's tribute.
2. Shivaji and Ramdas.
3. Shivaji and a Hindu Samrajya.
4. The Eight Ministers, and administration.
5. Forts on land and sea.
6. Army organisation.
7. The navy and the Siddi of Janjira.
8. Shivaji's Relations with the English.
9. Was Shivaji a mere plunderer ?
10. Estimate of Shivaji by thinkers and writers, 1—8.
11. Conclusion.

1. The Amatya's tribute.—We cannot see the full height of a gigantic tree when we stand beneath it. So, too, a hero's true greatness is perceived only when he is viewed from a distance in time. It is, therefore, a wonder how Shivaji's character, policy and achievements were so correctly judged by one of his own ministers, Rāmchandra Nilakanth. This officer had filled the post of Amātya (or Accountant General) under him for ten years, and afterwards showed signal capacity by successfully organising the national defence and ensuring concerted action between scattered elements during Mahārāshtra's life-and-death struggle with all the forces of the Mughal Empire, after Sambhāji's tragic death and the flight of Rājārām from the homeland. He wrote a sort of political testament for the guidance of the succeeding kings, which is known as the Ajnāpatra.[1]

I shall begin by giving here some extracts from this wonderfully penetrative analysis of Shivaji's character and aims :

* संत बोलतात,

राजे भ्रष्ट यवन जाले, ठायीं ठायीं दोष घडले,

मग यांहीं अवतार घेतले, कलिपाप हरावया ॥

The Saints have said :

The corrupt Muslims have become our Kings,
Everywhere misdeeds have cropped up,
Then He incarnated Himself
To remove the sins of this dark age.

1. This has recently been translated from the Marathi original into English by Professor S. V. Puntambekar of the Benares Hindu University.

"The epoch-maker Chhatrapati was at first a Muslim's dependent but he managed from the age of fifteen to free his small jagir of Poona and based his future greatness on that small beginning, entirely relying on his own effort and initiative.

"He judged the capacities of men and created his own helpmates and servants by enabling them to do great things, so that he could succeed in what appeared impossible at the beginning. He welded the scattered elements of his people into a united body and with their help accomplished his main object. He was surrounded at first by three powerful states the Adilshahi, the Kutbshahi and the Nizamshahi, besides the *Subhas* of the Mughal Emperor, each maintaining a lac of troops. There were besides these the Siddis, the French, the English, the Dutch, with smaller chiefships like Rāmnagar, Sondha, Bidnur, Mysore, Trichinopoly and the various local Palegars with clansmen like the Morays, the Shirkes, the Sāvants, the Nimbālkars, the Ghātges, etc.

"All these he encompassed with the extraordinary power of his own ingenuity. He overcame every enemy, some he openly attacked, some he compelled to accept a fight, some he surprised by means of ingenious contrivance, others he weakened by involving them in mutual dissensions, sometimes secretly fomenting quarrels ; others he confounded by sudden raids upon their camps and habitations. Some he boldly met in open combat, some he won over through tempting offers, some he boldly went to visit personally, some were scattered through curious stratagem.

"He audaciously built his own forts and shelters in alien jurisdictions; in the case of some who were already strongly entrenched in naval bases, he raised his own rival sea-forts. His navy forcibly entered some inaccessible ports. In this way dealing differently with different opponents he established an independent kingdom of his own stretching from Salher and Ahiwant in West Khandesh to Tanjore on the Kaveri, with unchallenged supremacy, erecting for its defence hundreds of forts and several sea-bases with extensive market places. He created his own regiments of 40 thousand paid troops, in addition to about 70 thousand *shilledars* or hired troopers, and an infantry of some two lacs, a treasure which could be counted by crores, choice jewelry and material provision of every indispensable article. Thus he elevated his Maratha nation consisting of 96 clans to an unheard of dignity, crowning the whole achievement by occupying an exalted throne and assuming the title of Chhatrapati. All this he did for the defence of his religion, for putting Gods and Brahmans in a position enabling them to have their proper functions performed without molestation. Under Shivaji's rule robberies and injustice became unknown, and his commands came to be strictly obeyed by all. He plunged the most powerful Mughal Emperor Aurangzeb into an ocean of grief. Indeed this miracle is a special creation of God Almighty through Shivaji's instrumentality."

So much for the best contemporary estimate of him. We can say that Shivaji's principal service lies in his having quickly transformed the inherent lawlessness of the Maratha people into a national solidarity by his unequalled leadership, enabling them to attain to the foremost place among the various races of India. We know well what a factious, turbulent and riotous life the Maratha clans of the western hills used to lead for centuries before the rise of Shivaji. They had been wasting their energy in internecine disputes, obeying no law, no authority and making life and property hopelessly insecure in the land. Shivaji correctly gauged the situation ; he at first heartily joined the mass, and by quickly gaining their confidence established such a complete hold upon their contentious but valiant spirits, that they soon learned to render implicit obedience to him; and under his leadership they put forth a united national effort in defence of their country's liberty. The roving undisciplined bands soon came to realize the value of willing comradeship, and followed their leader in weal and woe. Shivaji succeeded not only in establishing his own independence, but also in bringing about the necessary solidarity among the scattered warring elements of his homeland, so that the Marathas were transformed into a nation and a power of the first rank in Indian politics. He placed before the nation the higher ideal of *Swarajya*, of political emancipation from the chains of grinding slavery that held down his country for centuries together. The semi-wild hill tribes of the Sahyadri range, the common peasantry of the Desh country, and the military feudal lords who held the country of foreign *Sultans*, he welded into a powerful nation state, that successfully challenged the might of the Mughal Empire. Shivaji was manifestly a highly gifted personality, ready to meet any danger, always possessing supreme self-confidence, at once stern and kind-hearted, an ideal king of the type which Kālidās has immortalized in his famous description of Dilip.[2]

2. **Shivaji and Ramdas.**—The rank materialism of the present day has so blinded us that without a special effort and a particular study of the essential ingredients of the atmosphere which Shivaji breathed, we can form no accurate estimate of what he thought, believed and achieved. His aim in life was primarily spiritual rather than political. He severely resented Muslim interference with the religious practices of the Hindus, and tried to make his land safe for sincere believers of every creed. As this could not be done without political power, he had of necessity to achieve that power.

A large number of papers of his period has lately been printed, which particularly disclose this phase of Shivaji's endeavour. Gods, Brahmans, Saints, and Shrines are words ever present in his mind, as these papers reveal. It is a historical fact that wherever Shivaji went, be it Agra, Karwar, Tanjore or elsewhere, his first concern was to find out the celebrated shrines of the vicinity and the men of saintly character and learning that congregated at such places. He goes by sea to Basrur and pays a devout visit to Gokarn Mahableshwar at Karwar. Later when he went to Bhāgānagar and thence proceeded to the south, he spent a long time at Shrishaila Mallikārjuna, getting into a trance from which he could be roused with difficulty. Saints and sacred places were in those days the repositories of knowledge, learning, piety, and information in the various branches of life. Often he used to lose sight of his objective and suddenly get into a mystic pensive mood, after having met with some souls of extraordinary spiritual power. He never undertook a serious task without first consulting his *gurus*. Shivaji made no distinction in this respect between a Hindu and a Muslim saint. He honoured all with equal respect. At his capital Raigad he erected a special mosque for

2. अधृष्यश्चाभिगम्यश्च, *Raghuvansha*, I. 16 and others.

Muslim devotees in front of his palace in the same way, that he built there the temple of Jagadishvar for his own daily worship.

The famous saint Rāmdās was the *guru* from whom Shivaji received formal initiation and to whose shrine he made grants of land which are found recorded in a sanad in which the royal donor eloquently describes his feelings of reverence and devotion. There are two opposite views on the question of Shivaji's relations with Rāmdās, one school of writers maintaining that this saint was the sole inspirer of Shivaji's work in the political field as well as in his spiritual life. The other view is that Rāmdās had hardly any share in Shivaji's constructive work as a king. Rāmdās certainly appeared in the region round about Satara, just about the time that Dādāji Kondadev and Shivaji took possession of Sinhagad (1644). From this date onward the two persons made Mahārāshtra their main field of activity for over thirty years; and they must certainly have heard of each other's work and felt respect for it. Rāmdās' description of the best man (*Uttama Purusha*) occurring in his *Dāsabodha*, seems to me to convey a deep inner meaning, pointing to his having just before heard of Shivaji's suppression of Afzalkhan. So one may justifiably maintain that instead of Rāmdās inspiring Shivaji in his political ideals, it was Rāmdās who was led to effect a change in his outlook and teaching, after observing a clear demonstration of the hero as King in the person of Shivaji. Thereafter Rāmdās began to feel that no religion could stand and thrive without a strong leader of men coming forth to defend it; in other words, that political power was necessary for maintaining religious liberty. The truth appears to be this. Rāmdās at first confined his teaching only to the spiritual regeneration of society coupled with practical hints for making life a success. He established a chain of monasteries throughout the land where physical education was imparted with special attention to the formation of bodily strength and character. The presiding deity in these *mathas* was the athletic demi-god Hanuman. But to look upon these monasteries as secret training centres of Shivaji's political activity or as institutions for political spying to help him, is mere guess work of twentieth century Indian politics.

When did Shivaji and Rāmdās first come together? Both had their field of activity in Māharāshtra and must have heard and learnt of each other for a good long time before they had a personal meeting. Such a meeting presupposes that the two may have an intimate contact together, long quiet talks and mutual discussions so as to influence each other's future plans. There is no evidence nor any likelihood that such a purposeful and consultative meeting between Shivaji and Rāmdās took place before the known one of April 1672 (Chaitra of Shaka 1594), which is mentioned by Diwākar Gosāvi in his letter. It was after this admittedly first meeting, that their contact began to grow closer and that Shivaji received his formal initiation (*Upadesh*) from the *guru*. From 1672 onwards they met frequently and consulted each other; and their mutual respect grew in an increasing degree till the end. Thenceforward Shivaji indeed found great solace in the *guru's* company.

During the unhappy closing days of Shivaji's life, his vision came to be dismally clouded for various reasons, and he purposely went to seek advice from his *guru* and spent a month in his company at Sajjangad. The question was, as Shivaji was visibly dying, who should conduct the affairs of the Maratha State, seeing that Sambhāji had proved himself hopelessly unfit. Taking a dispassionate view of the situation as we know it now, Rāmdās, if he had had the inclination to handle political matters, should have called together when Shivaji was there on a visit to him, the principal officials and publicly declared some definite scheme of succession for their execution. Such a course would have averted the perilous situation which developed from the absence of a formal declaration of Shivaji's heir. Instead of this Rāmdās at that visit of Shivaji merely gave expression to the conventional blissful sentiments of satisfaction at Shivaji's achievements, which we find embodied in that exquisite poem *Anand-Vana-Bhuvan*, summarizing the hero's life-work.

Shivaji's other *gurus* have been mentioned elsewhere.

3. **Shivaji and a Hindu Samrajya.**—It is necessary to inquire whether Shivaji ever entertained a desire to found a Hindu empire for the whole of India. There is no knowing

what would have happened if he had been vouchsafed the long life which his opponent Aurangzeb enjoyed, or at least if he had lived ten years longer than he did. His base was certainly broad enough to sustain any expansion of his small Maratha kingdom in the Deccan. He had practically subjected the territories south of the river Godavari. His main object was to win religious freedom and not territory. He certainly would have been foremost to defend the Hindu religion all over India. "*Hindavi-Swarajya*" was the title he has used for his national scheme in one of his letters (to Dādāji Naras Prabhu in 1645), meaning thereby that he wanted to strive for a Hindu religious autonomy for the whole country. Saṃbhāji in his Danapatra calls him *Haindava-dharma-Uddharaka*.[3] Shivaji's famous letter to Aurangzeb breathes such a spirit. Although he died prematurely, his ideals did indeed continue to inspire his successors for more than a hundred years after him, particularly the Peshwas right upto the time of Mahadji Sindia, who tried to free the Hindu holy places of north India from Muslim control, and who indeed obtained from the Emperor Shah Alam a *firman* prohibiting the slaughter of cows throughout the country. Peshwa Bālāji Rāo in one of his letters boasts of being a true disciple of Shivaji, meaning that he followed the latter's ideals. Shivaji's levy of *Chauthai* and *Sardeshmukhi* was conceived in the spirit of an all-India instrument of expansion. A poet of Mirza Raja Jaysinh's court credits his patron with the feat of having "subjected kings like Shivaji who aspired to the imperial seat of Delhi."[4]

Shivaji voluntarily undertook a journey to the court of Aurangzeb, a hazardous venture, which discloses a desire on his part to see for himself how far northern India was prepared for the restoration of a Hindu empire after several hundred years of continuous Muslim rule. The line quoted above discloses a general public desire to depose Aurangzeb as he was

3. हैन्दवधर्मोद्धारक the regenerator of the Hindu religion.

4. येन श्रीजयसिंहेन दिल्लींद्रपदलिप्सवः
शिवप्रभृतिभूपाला वशं नीता स्वतेजसा ॥
जयसिंहप्रशस्ति, राजवाडे सं॰ ले॰

the enemy of the Hindu religion. The moment Shivaji escaped from the Emperor's custody, Hindu India hailed him as a heaven-sent deliverer, and thereafter northern scholars, poets, priests and chiefs began to flock to Shivaji's court. Poet Bhushan[5] and Chhatrasāl Bundelā are instances of this nation-wide impulse. Even Gāgābhatt was induced to preside at the coronation ceremony, mainly on account of the prevailing sentiment all over north India in favour of Shivaji's uncommon personality.

Similarly one cannot sufficiently admire the method he adopted for the defence of his kingdom by means of land and sea-forts, the four rocky naval bases forming the spinal cord of Maharashtrian independence, which even the great Mughal Emperors had never thought of. At all these naval bases he established docks for the construction and repair of armed and trading vessels with fresh gun-foundries which excite our admiration even now. This was a provision both for the expansion of trade and security against hostile attacks, of which the famous Maratha Captain Kanhoji Angria and his house took full advantage for more than half a century after Shivaji had passed away. The Abbé Carre reports that Shivaji had studied geography in minute details with the help of specially prepared charts. Shivaji's ships opened a fresh trade to Arabia and outside, a source of income hardly understood in those days of narrow vision. He removed the time-honoured ban on sea voyage by Hindus, and in opposition to the orthodox practice admitted Muslim converts back into Hindu fold, as the cases of Bajaji Nimbalkar and Netaji Palkar amply prove, as an innovation not then allowed by contemporary Hindu society. Shivaji's new State required a new court language in preference to Persian, which meant a sure sign of slavery ; so he adopted Marathi for this purpose and constructed a Sanskrit dictionary of specially coined court terms, known as the Raj-vyavahar-kosh.*

5. Bhushan is now supposed to have visited Shahu and not Shivaji. But he certainly voiced the sentiments current about Shivaji.

* See foot-note 10, p. 214.

The comprehensive and many-sided arrangements of Shivaji's coronation ceremony were a revival to strike the popular imagination and remind it of ancient imperial tradition, which had fallen into oblivion ever since the days of the ancient Guptas and Harshavardhan, more than ten centuries before.

But one thing is quite clear that in defending the Hindu religion, Shivaji was in no way actuated by any hatred towards the Muslims as a sect or towards their religion. Full religious liberty for all was his ideal and the practice in his State. He revered Muslim saints like Bāwā Yāqut of Kelsi to whose shrine he made a grant which is still being enjoyed. He had many devoted Muslim servants and followers who whole-heartedly co-operated with him. His chief naval commanders were Muslims, Daulat Khan and Siddi Misri. Madāri Mehtar a *farrash* (chamberlain) was a servant near his person, who helped him in his flight from Agra. Shivaji's confidential foreign secretary (*Munshi*) was one Mulla Haidar, who wrote his Persian correspondence and who was once deputed to Bahadur Khan the Mughal viceroy in the Deccan to negotiate a peace.[6] A considerable portion of the population under Shivaji's rule was Muslim, but it all lived as contented and free as his Hindu subjects.

4. **The Eight Ministers.**—The Aryan theory of the state had laid down elaborate schemes from which Shivaji accepted his division of departmental work among eight ministers, a measure admirably suited to the needs of his time, which is still in evidence all over the world. Shivaji clearly laid down definitions of these ministers' duties and responsibilities. Among the institutions brought into being by Shivaji this departmental division of work among ministers is the most noteworthy. This system was borrowed by Shivaji from the ancient Hindu tradition embodied in Sanskrit works on polity. Under Muhammadan rule there used to be only two main officers, one *Diwan* or the revenue minister, and the other the *Bakshi* or the head of the military establishment. The provincial head or Subahdar was vested with full civil and military powers. It must, however, be borne in mind that Shivaji's ministry of eight depart-

ments can in no sense be likened to the present ministerial cabinets under responsible government or democratic rule. Shivaji assigned no separate independent powers to his ministers. His was merely a convenient system for dividing administrative work; and six out of his eight ministers were bound, in consonance with the needs of the time, to conduct military operations when required, along with their respective duties. It is, therefore, misleading to compare this division of work instituted by Shivaji with the governments of our present times controlled by cabinets responsible to parliaments. Modern cabinets have independent powers and they often overrule the monarch. But Shivaji was a thorough autocrat, and although he freely sought advice from his ministers, he as often overruled their advice and dictated his own measures as he thought best. Of the eight ministers, the Peshwa or Prime minister, was to exercise supervision over the rest and to conduct the government in the absence of his master. The salary of the Prime Minister was 15000 Hons a year, which works out at Rs. 4375 a month at the rate of about 3½ Rs. the exchange value of the Hon, quite a substantial reward for the service rendered, and the more so when we bear in mind the purchasing power of money in those days. The other ministers were (2) the Amātya (in charge of the revenue), (3) the Sachiv (in charge of finance), (4) the Senāpati (commander-in-chief), (5) the Mantri (personal adviser) and the (6) Sumant (foreign minister). The Amātya received a salary of 12,000 Hons yearly or Rs. 3,500 a month. The two remaining ministers (7) the Nyāyādhish (minister of justice) and the Panditrav (minister of charities and religion) were not expected to go out on expeditions, but were to have stationary offices at the seat of government. The salaries of these last six were 10 thousand Hons a year or nearly Rs. 3000 a month.

Shivaji as an intensely practical administrator, clearly saw the danger of distributing land in lieu of service. To his ministers and the other servants he always made cash payments. Rāmachandra Pant Amātya has lucidly described the

6. This Mulla Haidar served Shivaji till his death, and thereafter having disagreed with Sambhāji he joined the Emperor's service and in 1700 was the Chief Kazi at Delhi. See p. 215, footnote.

dangers and pitfalls of conferring gifts of land for military and other services under a government. The jagir system Shivaji considered harmful to the interests of the State. He mercilessly confiscated the landed *watans* of previous regimes and allowed no middlemen as landholders between the cultivators and the Government. Writes the Amātya, "The king is the supreme owner of all lands. To him the Zamindars do not render proper loyalty. Nor do they remain contented with what they possess. They are unjust to the cultivators of the soil. They erect independent fortifications, defy the master, grasp what does not belong to them, commit robberies outside. Once their position is fairly strengthened, they use it as a base for further expansion, (Did not Shivaji do the same ?). If a foreign enemy invades a country, these land-holders often openly join him, secretly convey to him important information. Thus they become a fruitful source of weakness to the State. A jagirdar is rarely honest."

The creation of ministerial departments was a matter of gradual growth, developing as Shivaji's work began to grow. They were not all created at the time of his coronation, although formal confirmation and promulgation of their definite duties were effected at the time of that ceremony.

Administration.—The whole dominion of Shivaji was fluctuating and fluid in its area, as he was all along engaged in building up and extending his kingdom. He divided it into three main provinces, the northern division from Poona to Salher, being under his Peshwa Moropant Pingle and including north Konkan also. Southern Konkan upto north Kanara was in the viceroyalty of Anāji Datto, while the southern Desh districts roughly from Satara to Dharwar and Kopbal were under Dattājipant Waqnis. The newly conquered districts south of the Tungabhadrā, namely, Arni, Vellore, Jinji, &c. were administered by Harji Mahādik, Shivaji's son-in-law. There were many scattered outlying districts, where specially trusted and competent agents were appointed from time to time. The Mughal territory was to be subjected to the levy of the Chauth contribution. All this territory old and new contained, as contemporary records tell us, 240 forts, of which 111 were newly built by him. His annual revenue has been calculated at seven crores of Rupees, but possibly it was much less in actual realisation. He collected a large amount of treasure and other valuable articles which it is impossible to calculate even with tolerable accuracy in terms of modern currency. Besides the land revenue there were cesses according to local conditions.[7]

When one comes to examine Shivaji's administration, one can easily detect a few broad principles which he shrewdly brought into force as he proceeded building up his *swarajya*. They are :—

1. The country was to be defended against enemies by means of well garrisoned forts ;

2. All services were to be paid in cash and not by grants of land ;

3. Servants were employed on the principle of merit and not heredity ;

4. Revenue was not to be collected through Zamindars or middlemen but through a well-supervised government agency ;

5. The system of farming lands was abolished; in other words, land revenue was never auctioned ;

6. All government work was divided among well defined separate departments[7] ;

7. Equal opportunity was offered in the public service to all castes ;

8. Expenditure was so budgeted as to lay by some surplus every year.

It will be noticed that all well regulated governments of modern times have adopted these principles in their administration. The first basis of this system was laid down by Dādāji Kondadev, who in his turn had copied it from Malik Ambar. Shivaji selected the best points of all previous systems. Justice was mostly entrusted to the village panchāyats, so that the task of policing the country became automatically simplified.

7. *Vide* का० सं० प० या० ले० २; भा० व० २ मराठ्यांचें दप्तर; इ० सं० पे० द० मा०; ऐ० वि० वि० १ पृ० २१.

Shivaji always gave as much importance to preservation as to acquisition. Some of the ministers on military duty outside were drawing certain advantages which the ministers doing civil duty at headquarters were denied. Once when such a complaint reached Shivaji, he made an important pronouncement and declared that preservation of the raj was a task in no way inferior to fresh acquisition, and that the ministers and servants doing duty at home should be as well rewarded as those who were out on active service.[8]

I may here quote one recorded instance of how strict and impartial Shivaji was about alienating government lands. His son-in-law Pilāji Shirke, husband of his daughter Rajkuwar, had rendered meritorious service in arranging a friendly understanding between Shivaji and Lakham Sāvant of Kudal. In return for his good work Pilāji Shirke demanded from Shivaji the grant of the Deshmukhi Vatan of Dābhol. In a typical but firm and sweet reply Shivaji wrote to Shirke, "Our Maratha government does not allow grants of land to any body. But recognising your good work for the State and in addition the family relationship we bear with your house, we will think of bestowing the Dābhol Deshmukhi on the son of our affectionate daughter Rajkuwar, when she gets one."[9]

It was only new personal grants which Shivaji disallowed. But he generously continued old religious grants and even made fresh endowments to both Hindu and Muslim shrines.

While Shivaji erected forts of his own, he did not allow any private individuals under his rule to build their own fortifications. He purposely dismantled several old private fortresses which were likely to endanger his position. Writes Amātya in this connection, "Zamindars when threatened by the enemy are apt to join him and cause harm to our State. Such deserters should be traced, captured and punished. In case their capture becomes impracticable, their sons and relations should be apprehended ; the womenfolk should be made slaves. Examples should be made of such treasonous practices even by resort to the method of poisoning such offenders."

---

8. Raj. 8. 10. योगक्षेम, acquisition and preservation.
9. Letter, *Shiva-Charitra Sahitya* 3.438.

5. **Forts on land and sea.**—Of all measures of defence the most prominent that was devised and persistently developed by Shivaji was his system of forts. These became a necessary adjunct of the guerilla method which he developed from his father's example. There are three distinct lines of such forts which can be recognised even at the present day, although all these forts were either purposely dismantled during the British regime or fell into decay through neglect, as the method of warfare has now been completely revolutionized. The main forts are on the tops of the Sahyadri range ; there are two more lines of them, one on the eastern and the other on the western spurs of the mountain range. In addition, there are some built by him on difficult rocks on the sea-coast. Some towns in the plains had also been strongly fortified long before Shivaji, such as Ahmadnagar and Sholapur. Sindhudurg of Malvan, Vijaydurg, Suvarnadurg and Kolaba were the main naval fortifications which even today inspire awe and admiration for Shivaji's ingenuity. Of all his forts Raigad, his capital, reveals the great importance which Shivaji attached to these forts and the lavishness with which he poured money on their construction. Almost the first fort constructed by him was Pratāpgad which was at first intended to be only a seat of the goddess Bhavāni whom he installed therein. For grasping the significance of Shivaji's conception of defending his country by means of these forts, an actual visit to some of them today is indeed necessary. Visitors to Poona from all over India and abroad, hardly fail to visit Purandar and Sinhagad in the vicinity of that town.

The construction of these forts is worth noting. Only one difficult passage is kept in the bosom of the fortifications, not to be easily detected. When the principal entrance is securely closed and guarded, no enemy can reach the inside. Guns, ammunition, grain and other requisites used to be stored inside, so that the defenders could hold out for almost any length of time. Raigad is so extensive inside, that large numbers of cattle and men could have their life's requisites for years on end. A plentiful supply of water inside the forts was the first necessity in their construction. There were natural springs upon most of the hills, while elsewhere special tanks were built. Shivaji prepared and circulated minute regulations for the conduct of the garrison and the defence in case of attack or siege. The classical and sonorous names given to most of these forts, excite one's interest and admiration for the ingenuity of Shivaji's Pandits in coining them.

Most of these forts possess a history of their own, and wonderful reminiscences, which have gathered about them in local tradition, bring to a visitor's mind a picture of those old days. What minute care and observation Shivaji personally bestowed upon the construction of his forts can be understood from the following extract out of an old description of the fort of Malvan which Shivaji named Sindhudurg : "Sindudurg is a star in the firmament, an ornament of pride to the Maharaja's raj, just as every Hindu house has for its front decoration the *tulsi*-basin. The gods obtained only fourteen gems, but Shivaji added this fifteenth to the number. When he came to Rājāpur for the first time he minutely examined the various rocks locked in water and dotting the western coast, and was struck with the position of the rock islet opposite Malvan. He at once called together the fishermen of the place and gathered from them all details of that frowning sea-monster. It was difficult of direct approach except with a zigzag serpentine sea-passage, through which only a small fishing boat could make its way. Large ships could have no access to it. Shivaji rewarded the Kolis liberally and at once employed them as enterprising sailors. He consulted the astrologers and selected an auspicious day to begin the foundation. He ordered five hundred stone-dressers and two hundred iron-smiths, purchased two hundred tons of iron-metal and started the work of construction. A grand inauguration ceremony was held, sugar was distributed, feasts and dinners were lavishly given amidst music and rejoicing. One hundred Hons were distributed in charity to appease the sea-goddess along with cocoanuts, dresses, and other offerings. Three thousand skilled artizans, some of whom were specially obtained from the Portuguese government of Goa, were at once engaged for the various jobs. A guard of five thousand Mavlas was set up ; a budget of one crore of Hons was sanctioned. All possible measures against damage by the waves or the danger of an enemy were taken. Shivaji appointed Govind Vishvanāth Prabhu as the Chief supervisor of the works and himself returned to Raigad. Within three years a mighty bleak black spot arose on the fortress and then the Maharaja made his formal ceremonial entry into it with a salvo of guns. He named it Sindhudurg." [10]

6. **Army Organisation.**—Little need be said on Shivaji's army. The forts formed an adjunct to his main fighting forces, which had only two branches, troopers and foot-soldiers, the latter mostly garrisoning the forts. Shivaji mixed freely with all kinds of men and possessed an intuitive capacity for judging their character and ability. Most of his soldiers were either directly selected by him or guaranteed by those about him who shared his confidence. Small muskets, swords and shields, or small daggers and spears were the weapons then mostly in use. There were two main classes of troopers, *Silledars* and *Bargirs*. Siledars were the higher type who brought in their own horses and weapons, and received a larger pay, while the bargirs were direct employees, receiving their accoutrement from government. Large camps of troops were formed at convenient places with thousands of horses and magazines of weapons and stores of provisions. Shivaji was fond of horses and procured select animals of the Arab, the Kathiawadi and other breeds. Bodies of spies were attached to each regiment, whose officers arranged the troop-movements in consonance with the information supplied by the spies. These spies formed the most efficient branch of Shivaji's army. How minutely Shivaji regulated the affairs of the army can be judged from the following letter which was circulated by him as standing orders to all the revenue and military officers.

"To Jumledars, Havaldars, and Karkuns, in charge of the army stationed at Chiplun, 16 April, 1673.

10. *Chitra Gupta bakhar*—pp 132-34. A few names of Shivaji's forts will interest the reader,—प्रचंडगड, प्रकाशगड, प्रच्चितग०, प्रबळग०, प्रवालग०, प्रसन्नग०, प्रसिद्धगड ; भूधरगड, भूपालगड, भूमंडनगड, भूषणग० ; महिपतगड, महिमंडनग०, वल्लभगड, वर्धनगड, वसंतगड, वंदनगड, विशालगड, विश्रामगड Chapter VII of the Amātya's Rājniti is devoted to the subject of forts; the Shivaji Souvenir gives a description of all Shivaji's forts.

I have made arrangements for a cavalry regiment being cantoned at Chiplun, as it cannot possibly return to the up country at this advanced season. Owing to the stay of this regiment at Chiplun, all the grain and other necessaries that were stored for the rainy season in the Subha of Dabhol, have been almost exhausted, entailing hardship and no end of distress upon the people of the district by the grain, forage and every other article having been appropriated for the use of the army. There are yet twenty days of the hot Vaishakh month to pass.[11] The severity of the season now prevents any change in encampment. As provisions are urgently required, I have ordered the officers to collect whatever grain could be had from the various forts and thus provide for men and horses. Now you will ask for any amount of rations of grain and grass, feed recklessly while the supplies are available, and when these are exhausted during the height of the rainy season, you will get nothing. Hence the present supplies must be made to last till the end of the rainy season. You must, therefore, without complaint accept whatever rations the Karkuns will daily give you and nothing more should be asked ; so that all will get tolerably enough to keep men and horses from starving. You must not, therefore, grumble and quarrel with the officers or trouble them for every trifling requirement. No one should enter the store-rooms and make free use of the provisions kept therein. Men and horses must continue to accept whatever is given them and make things going. Some will make fires for cooking purposes in places where there are stacks of hay. Some will take live-coal for smoking pipes and carelessly set fire to the stacks lying about. When one shed takes fire, it will soon extend to the whole encampment and cause incalculable damage. Should a mishap of the kind occur, no amount of punishment of officers and cultivators will replace the loss ; not a piece of timber would then be available to construct the sheds and no shed could be constructed at a moment's notice. You must all take note of this situation, keep a watch in the camp and see that nothing untoward happens, while men are cooking food or burning grass. If you keep lights burning at night, mice might carry away the lighted

11. So the letter is written about Vaishakh Shudh 10 = 16 April 1673.

wick and cause mischief. All such accidents must be scrupulously guarded against. You must be particularly careful about fires breaking out. Every precaution should be taken to save the grass and the sheds. Then only can the horses live through the long rainy season. If you fail, there is an end to all horses and stables and food. Then you will begin to rob the people ; some will take away the grain of the poor cultivators, some will take away their bread, others grass and wood, some carry away their vegetables and other provisions. When you behave that way, the poor peasants will find life impossible and run away. Some will starve. Then they will think you are worse than the Mughals, who overrun the countryside. Thus all the curses of the peasants and the horses will descend on you. Know this well, whether you are *sipahi* or a foot-soldier and behave yourselves. Some of you may be staying in different villages in government stables or otherwise. You have no business to trouble the rayats in any way, no business to stray outside your place. The Sarkar has given you your share from the treasury. Whatever one wants, whether grain, grass for cattle or fuel or vegetables, you should duly buy it, if it comes round for sale ; or you should go to the open bazaar and buy it. You must not force anybody or quarrel with anybody. The supplies that have been assigned to the government stables must last for the whole rainy season. The Karkuns are instructed to give rations with an eye to economy. You must take what you are given, so that you will never be reduced to starvation. You will have some food everyday and the horses will gain strength. You must not lose temper with the Karkuns or enter the store-rooms violently and seize the articles. The men attached to the stables will make fires, some will make their hearths and cook at wrong places, some will light their smoking pipes without noticing that the hay is lying about. Thus there will suddenly occur an accident. When one room catches fire, the whole place will be burnt down. Therefore, let due warning be given to all. Officers should always be going about to see that everything is safe. Therefore it is, that I write to you in such detail. All the Jumledars, Havaldars and Karkuns should hear this letter being read to them and act up to it. We shall keep ourselves informed frequently, nay every day, and punish those who disobey. Whosoever behaves in contravention of this order will be severely punished and dishonoured."[12]

Insistence on order, implicit obedience and the strictest discipline were the rules which distinguished Shivāji as a ruler far in advance of his age, as is illustrated by the manner in which he regulated the behaviour of his troops during their campaigns of conquest or plunder. "A grand Darbar was held on the Dassara day when all the men, their horses and equipment were minutely examined and the regulations clearly explained. No molestation of women, children, Brahmans, husbandmen and cows was allowed during war. All plundered articles were to be delivered upon return to headquarters, when special rewards in money, dresses and titles were bestowed for good work, and severe punishment inflicted upon delinquents, who had kept back or misappropriated articles of plunder. After returning from a plundering expedition, he saw to it that every article seized by his men was properly delivered to his officers. Every member of his army was supplied with a memo of his private belongings when he started on the march, and on return was required to give up whatever he possessed over and above his original list. Honest dealings were handsomely rewarded and the least dereliction punished with severity." Every soldier, before being enlisted in the service had to produce two sureties for good conduct. The relatives of those who had fallen on service or duty were compensated. When Shivaji attacked a town, he was an adept in discovering secret hoards, so that people came to credit him with supernatural powers. His simple style of life has been highly commended by the French envoy Germain, who visited him at Tiruvadi in July 1677. He wrote, "The camp of Shivaji was without pomp, without women ; there were no baggages, only two tents but of simple cloth, coarse and very scanty, one for him and the other for his prime-minister."[13]

7. **The navy and the Siddi of Janjira.**—Shivaji early in his career saw the necessity of having a strong and inde-

12. Source-book of Mar. History—P. 117,
Shivaji Souvenir. P. 150.
13. *Foreign Biogr.* P. 306.

pendent navy of his own, as much for the protection as for the expansion of his resources by means of foreign trade. More than a hundred years before Shivaji, the Nizam Shah of Ahmadnagar had established his own navy at Janjira and placed in command of it Siddi Yaqut Khan a daring Abyssinian immigrant well-versed in naval art (1490). He was charged with the two-fold function of the supervision of the coastal trade and the safe conveyance of Muslim pilgrims to Mecca. Thus was created the small State of Janjirā which has survived centuries of political change.[14]

When Shivaji attacked Kalyan and seized the Bijapuri portion of north Konkan, he was severely opposed by this Siddi chief with his numerous following of daring sailors. Thus it became necessary for Shivaji to create his own navy in order to check the activities of the Siddi and strengthen his own power on the west coast. In this way there arose a perennial source of rivalry and war between these two powers throughout the Maratha period.

Shivaji's war with the Siddi commenced in 1657 and continued upto his death, having been marked in the interval by some very stiff engagements. In 1659 he sent his Peshwa Moropant Pingle and Vyankoji Datto (brother of Ānāji) with a strong naval force to put down the Siddis. Siddi Khairyat was overcome and compelled to accept terms, by which all the territory of the Siddis was to be handed over to Shivaji except the island fort of Janjirā itself. Whilst these operations on the west coast were going on, Shivaji was attacked by Afzal Khan with the result that his hold upon the Siddi was released. By the time Mirza Raja Jaysinh appeared on the scene, the Siddi transferred his allegiance to the Mughal Emperor, and under the latter's support increased his power to a considerable extent with an additional base at Surat. Shivaji also had in the meantime increased his navy, and prepared for a renewal of his contest with the Siddi by building the four strong fortresses of Sindhudurg, Vijaydurg, Suvarnadurg and lastly Kolaba, with adequate naval equipment for each. Ibra-

14. Janjirā is a corruption of the Arabic word *Jazira* meaning an island. It is situated at the mouth of the Rajpuri creek, Yaqut Khan became the hereditary title of the Siddi Chief of Janjirā.

him Khan and Mainak Bhandāri were his trusted naval commanders. They succeeded for a time in establishing a strong check upon the various powers of the west coast from Kalyan to Karwar, including the Portuguese of Goa. The last named considered it a wise policy to conciliate Shivaji by agreeing to supply him with guns and ammunition of western make, whenever required.

Under the backing and encouragement of the Mughals, the Siddis' strength steadily grew and a continuous war between them and Shivaji was the result, a full narration of which cannot be attempted here.[15]

8. **Shivaji's relations with the English.**—This subject has been already treated in so far as the factors of Rājāpur were concerned. There was really no conflict of interest between Shivaji and these merchants of the East India Company. The Dutch and the English, unlike the Portuguese, had then no intention of making land acquisitions in India and confined their activities to trade, which profited them as much as it did the Indian princes. The island of Bombay had just been acquired by the English from their Portuguese neighbours, and as Surat was constantly under the threat of an attack from Shivaji, the English were planning to shift their headquarters from Surat to Bombay. The incident of Rājāpur rankled in their hearts, but no actual collision occurred. After his escape from Agra Shivaji's power rapidly increased, and the English became anxious to secure his good will in order that their trading operations might not suffer. With this object in view the President of Surat sent envoys to Shivaji from time to time, Ustick in 1672, Nicolls in 1673, Henry Oxenden in 1674, and Austen in 1675. Of these the visit of Oxenden to Raigad at the time of Shivaji's coronation is historically noteworthy, as that Englishman has left a full and accurate account of what he saw and heard of that important event in Shivaji's life. Oxenden brought Shivaji presents from the Company along with their congratulations. A treaty of mutual trade and friend-

15. Students will do well to refer to his letter dated 19th January 1675 addressed to his officer at Prabhāvali on naval equipment—Raj. 8.31.

ship was then arranged between them and their relations remained cordial during Shivaji's life-time.

9. **Was Shivaji a mere plunderer ?**—Shivaji has been often called a plunderer and a rebel. One must examine his life minutely to determine what this charge exactly meant. Every patriot has felt bound to rebel against the existing alien government, and it would be no wonder if Muslim writers set Shivaji down as such. Even the Marathi writers exult in calling him a pund (rebel) for having liberated his land from foreign yoke. As soon as he attained the required power, he organized a regular government and advanced the interests of the subjects over whom he ruled. But he cannot be charged with being a wicked wanton plunderer. He plundered the towns and territory of the enemy as a legitimate act of war. There is no instance of his having plundered innocent people or princes who were not at war with him. Even the Muslim historian Khafi Khan absolves him from this charge. He never molested religious places such as musjids. He respected the holy Koran when obtained in plunder and returned it with due reverence. It was a strict rule in his army never to molest women, children or holy men in the course of a raid. Prisoners of war were very kindly treated and released after their wounds had been dressed.

His usual practice when he arrived before a town, was to call upon the wealthy and leading merchants to make a reasonable contribution towards the expenses of his war, and if it was willingly paid, he never used force. But when such willing compliance was refused, he exacted forcibly what he could collect. In most cases Shivaji's plunder was a war levy, more or less of the type of that extorted by the present day governments of the world, who legally impose and exact money during times of stress in the form of tax or contribution. Shivaji was careful not to harm poor innocent husbandmen by depriving them of their means of livelihood. He imposed large fines upon well-to-do merchants and seized their secret hoards ; or he carried away enemy treasures while they were on the way. When an enemy was defeated, he plundered his camp and took away the tents, animals, stores and whatever else could be obtained. These wise and considerate methods of Shivaji were mostly adhered to throughout the best days of Maratha government. Shivaji took great pains to acquire correct information about his objectives through his efficient spies and acted upon it with the least molestation possible.

10. Estimate of Shivaji by thinkers and writers.— The opinion of a Maratha on his national hero may be suspected of being tainted by blind adoration or national vanity. I shall therefore give here only estimates of Shivaji's character formed by foreigners, most of them belonging to the race that had fought four sanguinary wars to wrest the overlordship of India from the hands of Shivaji's successors in office.

(1) Elphinstone in his *History* aptly summarizes Shivaji's character thus :—

"The son of a powerful chief Shivaji had begun life as a daring and artful captain of banditti, had ripened into a skilful general and an able statesman and left a character which has never since been equalled or approached by any of his countrymen....It required a genius like his to avail himself as he did of the mistakes of Aurangazeb by kindling a zeal for religion and through that, a national spirit among the Marathas. It was by these feelings that his government was upheld after it passed into feeble hands and was kept together, in spite of numerous internal disorders until it had established its supremacy over the greater part of India."

(2) Sir Richard Temple writes in his *Oriental Experience*,

"Raigad according to the sagacious suggestion of Shivaji's father was occupied as the last and the greatest of the Maratha strongholds. There it was that Shivaji established himself finally as sovereign of western India. It was here that Shivaji reigned and here too he died after having rebelled, plundered, fought and ruled for about thirty years. In this fort he collected the wealth and riches of half India, treasures in Spanish dollars, sequins, and the coins from all southern Europe and all Asia.

"Shivaji was not only a bold man but he had the peculiar power of arousing enthusiasm in others and he was the man who raised an abject race from nothingness up to empire. Besides, Shivaji was a great administrator. He founded many institutions which survived for more than one century."

(3) *Says Acworth,*

"But Shivaji's mere acquisitions constitute an altogether imperfect measure of the power he exercised and evoked. No man perhaps then living had a keener and juster appreciation of his own strength and the weak points of his opponents. He alone among his countrymen thoroughly gauged the sources and direction of both. He saw that the time had come when the Maratha nation might be made anew and he made it. He saw that with all its swelling pretentiousness, its enormous wealth, the vast numbers of its subjects, nothing but the shell of its old energy and power was left to the Muhammadan Dominion, that the vices and the jealousies of autocratic rule had eaten away the heart of it. Shivaji from the first day kept his eye steadily fixed on the vast project of Hindu reconquest, and both as a captain and as a statesman in each of which capacities he was pre-eminently great, his conduct shows an unswerving adherence to certain leading principles of action and administration, which he had prescribed to himself as the adequate and necessary means to an end.

"Shivaji's claim to greatness is of course not to be criticised by the ethics of the nineteenth century. Though he was ruthless in attaining his object, he was completely free from the detestable passion for gratuitous cruelty as well as from any disposition to indulge in it as a gratification of temper.

"The whole career of Shivaji was one of struggle and stress. It was essential to him to push his projects as secretly, as unostentatiously and in such a way as to attract as little notice as possible. The character of Shivaji far transcends that of his mighty foe Aurangzeb. Religion was a dominant feature in both, but in Aurangzeb it was degraded into pettiest, narrowest and most malignant bigotry. The gaoler of his father, the assassin of his brothers, the suspicious and dreadful tyrant of his sons, too conscious of faithlessness in himself to have faith in others or to inspire it, his statesmanship mere cunning, his energy the peddling industry of a clerk, opposed to such a national and religious upheaval as is without a parallel in the history of India and which was guided by an intellect as far reaching and profound as his own was limited and shallow, he was born to be the architect of ruin ; and if Shivaji was an incarnation of divinity, specially created for Hindu conquest and dominion, Aurangzeb seems equally to have been sent into the world for the express purpose of disintegrating the Muhammadan empire.

"While Shivaji's genius as a captain is universally recognised, scant justice is done to his constructive and administrative abilities and to the permanence of his idea, both of conquest and government."[16]

(4) *Writes S. M. Edwardes,*—

"The success of Marathi poets and saints from Jnaneshwar to Shridhar (1300-1700) in overcoming the prejudices of caste was only partial and temporary. Far more efficacious was the rise of Shivaji to power and his constant association with himself in his task of political and military administration, of men who in many instances were not Brahmans. With Prabhus acting as his civil and military officials, with Marathas and Bhandaris forming the bulk of his land and naval forces, with Kolis or Ramoshis acting as his comrades in hazardous enterprises, and with Mahars and Mangs holding his hill forts, the general mass of the people certainly obtained a clearer and more practical idea of a common nationality and the limitations of an exclusive caste system, than they could ever have obtained, wholly illiterate as they were, from the public repetition of quotations of Tukārām or Nāmdev, of Eknāth or Rāmdās."

(5) *Says Bernier* (in 1666),—

"This man, Sevagi, is exercising all the powers of an independent sovereign ; laughs at the threats both of the Mogal and the King of Vizapur, makes frequent incursions and ravages the country on every side from Surat to the gates of Goa. He distracts the attention of Aurangzeb by his bold and never-ceasing enterprizes and affords so much employment to the Indian armies that the Mogal cannot find the opportunity of conquering Vizapur. How to put down Shivaji is become his object of chief importance."

16. Introduction to the *Ballads of the Marathas* XX.

(6) *The contemporary English merchants of Surat wrote,—*

"Shivaji is the fairest friend, noblest enemy, and the most politique Prince."

"He will continue victorious even to a miracle."

"Shivaji Raja, ambitious to be famed mighty conqueror, marched into Karnatak and with a success as happy as Caesar's in Spain, he came, he saw, and he conquered. He has taken two very strong Ghurs or rocks, being no less dexterous thereat than Alexander the Great and become master of Bijapur. He has vowed to his God never to sheath his sword till he has reached Delhi and shut up Aurangzeb in it. It is too well known that Shivaji is a second Sartorius and comes not short of Hanniball for stratagems. He loved his country but was not partial to any one. He had many Muslims in his service and the head of his navy was a Muslim. But he could not tolerate the conversion of his Hindu brethren to either Islam or to Christianity. The underlying reason for his vengeance upon Aurangzeb was the religious policy of that monarch."

(7) *Khwafi Khan says,—*

"Shivaji had always striven to maintain the honour of the people in his territories. He persevered in a course of rebellion, in plundering caravans, and troubling mankind ; but he entirely abstained from other disgraceful acts and was careful to maintain the honour of women and children of Muhammadans when they fell into his hands. His injunctions upon this point were very strict, and any one who disobeyed them received punishment.

(8) *Spoke Sir Jadunath Sarkar at the Shivaji birthday celebration in Madras in* 1928,—

"Shivaji's political ideals were such that we might accept them even today without any change. He aimed at giving his subjects peace, universal toleration, equal opportunities for all castes and creeds, a beneficent, active and pure system of administration, a navy for promoting trade and a trained militia for guarding the homeland. Above all he sought for national development through action and not by lonely meditation. Every worthy man, not only the natives of Mahārāshtra but also recruits from other provinces of India who came to Shivaji, were sure of being given some task, which would call forth his inner capacity and pave the way to his own rise to distinction, while serving the interests of the State. The activities of Shivaji's government spread in many directions and this enabled his people to attain to a full and varied development such as all modern civilized states aim at.

"All this national expansion proceeded from the initial energy of one man. Shivaji was the central power-house of the new Mahārāshtra. He had the supreme royal gift of quickly judging every man's character and capacity and choosing the best instrument for every task that he wanted to be done. But he was a self-taught man, he never visited any great capital, court or camp. His administrative and military systems perfectly suited to his country and age, were his own creation. Everything proceeded from his own heart and brain. Therefore the historian of Shivaji at the end of a careful study of all the records about him in eight different languages, is bound to admit, that he was not only the maker of the Maratha nation, but also the greatest constructive genius of medieval India. States fall, empires break up, dynasties become extinct, but the memory of a true 'hero as King' like Shivaji, remains an imperishable historical legacy for the entire human race,

The pillar of a people's hope,
The centre of a world's desire,

to animate the heart, to kindle the imagination and to inspire the brain of succeeding ages to the highest endeavours, as saint Rāmdās truly said.[17]

17. शिवचरित आठवावें । कीर्तिरूपें ॥
शिवराजाचें आठवावें रूप । शिवराजाचा आठवावा प्रताप ।
शिवराजाचा आठवावा साक्षेप । भूमंडळीं.

In a similar strain speaks Raghunathpant Hanumante also, when he says :

क्रमेण जित्वा स दिशश्चतस्रो
राजा शिवच्छत्रपतिः प्रतापात् ।
निःशेषयन्म्लेच्छगणं समस्तं
पाति स्म पृथ्वीं परिपूर्णकामः । [Contd. next page.

11. **Conclusion.**—Shivaji was a genius far in advance of his times. He conceived and carried out most of the reforms and measures usually associated in our days with a civilized state. While his political activities with reference to an independent Maratha sovereignty have been commonly understood, his reforms in the social, religious and economic spheres of a full national life, have received scant justice. He certainly was a champion of Hinduism, but was no bigot. He treated all religions with equal respect. His modernizing spirit is well exemplified in the significant titles he deliberately adopted at his coronation. He styled himself the pinnacle of the glorious Kshatriya caste, thereby giving a direct lie to the current orthodox view that during the Kali age there survived only the two castes, the highest and the lowest, the Brahman and the Shudra. § Another title he assumed gave him the right to deal on equal terms with the existing monarchs of Delhi and Bijapur as well as the Rajput princes of ancient origin. The chief of every Maratha clan used them to be addressed as a raja : but Shivaji to assert his overlordship assumed the title of Maharaja Chhatrapati to suit the ancient vedic conception.

Judged even by the strictest standard Shivaji stands out unmistakably as a unique personality, not only in his own time but in the modern age as a whole. In the midst of the surrounding darkness he shines forth as a brilliant luminary far ahead of his day. The India of Shivaji's days could not stand comparison with the fast rising west in scientific knowledge and political advancement. Europe had just then emerged out of the dark ages and was rapidly progressing in practical sciences. The discovery of gunpowder, the use of the mariner's compass, the invention of the art of printing were giving Europe leadership in temporal power and prosperity, and an ascendency over the backward races of the

"There rules the Chhatrapati Shivaji after having valiantly and gradually conquered territories in the four quarters, up-rooted the Muslim powers, and with his objective fully accomplished." Such a person is termed a Punyashloka (of unspotted fame) according to the Aryan ideal. भोसलवंशावलि by Gagabhatt, Hanumante's प्रशस्ति of the राजव्यवहारकोश, संभाजीदानपत्र and similar Sanskrit pieces deserve a close study.

§ कलौ आद्यन्तयोः स्थितिः । See pages 208, 209 and 214.

world outside. Constantinople had fallen, America had been discovered, Bacon had changed the traditional scholastic learning into new channels of discovery and experiment. Nothing was held sacred or sacrosanct from the inquiring mind. Europe had turned its back on the dead past and was marching on in a hopeful and buoyant mood, while the lights dimmed and ceased to burn in this land of the east, and it sank more and more into the morass of superstitious ignorance and hopeless despair.

It is this gloom which Shivaji's sudden appearance dispelled pointing to a new path of national uplift. All the greater credit is due to Shivaji for it, because he did all this on his own initiative. No Bacon had appeared in India to point out a new way to human advancement. Even his guru Rāmdās did not dream of a new path. Shivaji gathered together and trained a large number of followers, exceptionally capable though not comparable to himself, who carried on his work after him with a determination which has become a romance in Maratha history. It is no exaggeration to say that he is the creator of the Maratha nation, or as Sir Jadunath has aptly put it, "the last great constructive genius and nation-builder that the Hindu race has produced. He called the Maratha race to a new life. He raised the Marathas into an independent self-reliant people, conscious of their oneness and high destiny, and his most precious legacy was the spirit that he breathed into his race. He has proved by his example that the Hindu race can build a nation, found a state, defeat enemies ; they can conduct their own defence, protect and promote literature and art, commerce, industry ; they can maintain navies and ocean-trading fleets of their own and conduct naval battles on equal terms with foreigners. He taught the modern Hindus to rise to the full stature of their growth. Shivaji has shown that the tree of Hinduism is not really dead, that it can rise from beneath the seemingly crushing load of centuries of political bondage ; that it can put forth new leaves and branches. It can again lift up its head to the skies."

CHRONOLOGY

CHAPTER XIII

1670 Feb. 24	Birth of Rājārām.
1680 April	Rājārām enthroned as Chhatrapati.
„ June 18	Sambhāji gets possession of Raigad.
„ July 20	Sambhāji confines Rājārām & becomes Chhatrapati.
„ August 23	Sambhāji issues his Dānapatra.
„ Octr.	Death of Moropant Pingle : his son made Peshwa.
„ Novr.	Sambhāji opens campaign against the Mughals.
1681 Jan. 16	Sambhāji crowned.
„ „	Prince Akbar proclaims himself Emperor.
„ April	Prince Akbar is defeated near Ajmere & flees.
„ May 9	Prince Akbar crosses the Narmadā for the south.
„ „ 20	Prince Akbar informs Sambhāji of his plans.
„ June 1	Prince Akbar arrives at Pali (Padshahpur).
„ „	Azam Shah in pursuit of Akbar.
„ August	Attempt to poison Sambhāji.
„ Septr. 8	Aurangzeb leaves Ajmir for the Deccan.
„ Octr.	Annāji Datto put to death by Sambhāji : also Bālāji Āvji, Soyra Bai, & others.
„ Novr. 13	Aurangzeb arrives at Burhanpur.
„ „ „	Sambhāji visits Akbar at Pāli.
„ Dec.	The Siddi of Janjirā attacks Maratha territory.
1682 early months	Fierce fighting at Janjira between the Siddi and Dādji Raghunath.
„ March 22	Aurangzeb reaches Aurangabad.
„ April	Akbar despatches Shiab-uddin Khan to Nasik against Sambhāji.

1682 May 22	Sambhāji writes letters to Rāmsinh planning the deposition of Aurangzeb.
Dec.	British envoys meet Sambhāji at Raigad.
1683	Sambhāji attacks the Portuguese at Chaul & Goa.
„ Feb.	Akbar collects troops.
„ Autumn	Aurangzeb disheartened : holds conferences with his commanders.
„ Octr.	Sambhāji victorious against the Portuguese.
„ Novr.	Sambhāji retires from Goa.
1684 Feb.	Akbar & Kavi Kalash concert measures against Aurangzeb.
1684 July 27	Azam Shah's envoy meets Kavi Kalash.
„ August 20	Akbar rejects his brother's offer of peace.
„ Dec.	Akbar and Kavi Kalash meet for consultation.
1685 Jan.	Sambhāji devastates Berar, Khandesh and Broach.
„ March 27	Aurangzeb invests Bijapur.
1686 Sept. 12	Aurangzeb reduces Bijapur.
1687 Jan. 28	Aurangzeb invests Golkonda.
.. Feb.	Akbar left for Persia and Durgādās for Rājputana.
„ Oct.	Battle of Wāi : Hambir Rao Mohite killed.
„ „ 1	Aurangzeb captures Golkonda.
1688 Jan.	Akbar reaches Ispahan in Iran.
„ Ending months	Kavi Kalash fights the Shirkes and escapes to Vishālgad.
1689 Jan.	Sambhāji and Kalash leave Vishalgad & halt at Sangameshwar.
„ Feb. 1	Sambhāji and Kalash captured.
1689 March 11	Sambhāji and Kalash put to death.
1696	Durgādās with Akbar's daughter meets Aurangzeb at Brahmapuri.
1704	Death of Akbar in Iran.

CHAPTER XIII

SAMBHAJI THE VIOLENT

[1680—1689]

1. Accession.—The great Shivaji had passed away without naming his successor. He left two sons behind : the elder Sambhāji, then twenty-two years old, though brave and intrepid, had misbehaved himself and was, therefore, not trusted by his father, but was kept confined in the fort of Panhālā. The younger Rājārām, then just ten years old, having been born on 24 February 1670, was at the end of the mourning period for his father, placed on the throne at Raigad, by his mother Soyarā Bai, a woman of vain ambition but wanting in statecraft. She was supported in her course by Shivaji's confidential secretary Bālāji Āvji, who wrote letters in his own hand to the Killedar of Panhālā, explaining the step that was taken, and calling upon him to keep a strict watch on Sambhāji. But the news of Shivaji's death could not be long concealed from Sambhāji, who killed the Killedar, took possession of Panhālā and prepared for a march on Raigad. Senapati Hambir Rao Mohite, who was near Karhād not far from Panhālā, and who had received no intimation of Soyara Bai's plans, went over to Sambhāji. In the mean time two of Shivaji's prominent ministers, Moropant Pingle and Ānnāji Datto, who had supported Soyarā Bai's plans, became confused by the alarming news of Sambhāji's proceedings, as they were moving towards Panhālā under orders to keep him from doing mischief. Sambhāji managed to capture and confine them both at Panhālā under a rigorous watch. Determined to put down Soyarā Bai and her supporters, Sambhāji marched on Raigad with a force of twenty thousand men and meeting with

no resistance, got possession of the capital on 18 June and formally ascended the throne on 20 July, after putting Rājārām and Soyarā Bai in close confinement. In gratitude for this easy success, he immediately made a formal grant to his family goddess Bhavāni of ten thousand gold Hons a year.[1] Matters thus appeared to move smoothly. Moropant Pingle died in October, and Sambhāji appointed his son Nilopant to the Peshwāship. The formal ceremony of coronation was performed on 10 January 1681, Magh Shudh 7. The disturbed atmosphere of Mahārāshtra soon assumed its normal peaceful tenor.

2. **Akbar's flight to Sambhaji.**—The wanton war which the Emperor Aurangzeb started against the princes of Rājputānā in 1679, and which Shivaji had denounced in a vigorous open letter of remonstrance, now brought serious consequences to Sambhāji in a curious manner. Aurangzeb's son Akbar, who had been conducting the operations under his father's supervision, vainly struggled against the powerful Rajput combination. Of the several sons of Aurangzeb this Shahzada Akbar was the most dearly loved one; because by reason of his having lost his mother in infancy, he was personally brought up by the father with tender care and affection. He grew to be the most clever and competent of his brothers and was frequently employed by his father in state affairs requiring firm and delicate handling. When Aurangzeb wanted to suppress the Rāthod rising, he entrusted the command of his armies to Akbar and gave him personal instructions how to conduct the operations. The war proved disastrous, spread like a contagion, and united the states of Rājputānā in a common desperate opposition. Akbar spent a year vainly struggling against heavy odds, and suffering terrible losses in the wild and rugged country in which the operations had to be conducted. He, therefore, entered into peace talks with the Rajputs, and proposed to his father that the war should be closed on honourable terms which the Rajputs were ready to accept. He held private consultations with the valiant Rāthod leader Durgā-

1. This is an unpublished Sanskrit document bearing the clear date of 23 August 1680 and signed by Sambhāji and his ministers. It gives many useful details of his own and his ancestors' lives.

dās, who made pathetic appeals to Akbar's generosity in the following terms.

"Why is the Emperor so unkind to us? We are his loyal servants and shall continue so if we are left in peace and in subordinate alliance to the Emperor, following the policy of the great Akbar. But if relentless war is inflicted upon us, we shall never yield so long as the last drop of Rajput blood remains in our veins." Akbar saw the position clearly and advised his father to conclude the war. But Aurangzeb was not going to be guided by such sober policy. He scolded Akbar in severe terms. Akbar took the rebuke to heart, and impelled by Durgādās and his valiant bands, he openly revolted against his father and proclaimed himself emperor, just about the time that Sambhāji was celebrating his own coronation at Raigad, early in January 1681. Aurangzeb thus came to face a dangerous situation. He was at Ajmere watching the course of events. As the Rajputs headed by Akbar marched upon him, so delicate became Aurangzeb's position, that he was at his wits' end how to extricate himself from the fate which he had once imposed on his own father. Space does not allow a full recitation of the ruse which the ingenious Emperor employed to save himself from falling a prisoner into his son's hands. He succeeded in inflicting a defeat upon his enemies with the result, that both Akbar and Durgādās had to flee for their lives to the south, and take shelter with king Sambhāji, finding their escape blocked in other directions. They eluded the pursuing armies and crossed the Narmada on 9th May, whence Akbar wrote the following letters to Sambhāji two days after.

"Since his coming to the throne, my father the Emperor Aurangzeb has formed the deliberate resolution of putting down the Hindus. This is the sole cause of his war against the Rajputs. While in the eyes of God all men are His equal children and deserve impartial protection from their ruler, I became convinced that by such extreme measures, my father would lose his hold on the country and decided to oppose him in this disastrous move. I am, therefore, coming to you as a friend, as your kingdom is out of the Emperor's reach. The valiant Durgādās Rāthod accompanies me. Please do not entertain any false suspicions about my intentions. If by the grace of God I succeed in my endeavour to depose my father I shall remain only the nominal master and shall let you exercise all the power. We shall fully cooperate in putting down the Emperor. More when we meet in person."

Again on 20 May Akbar wrote, "most probably my letter has not reached you, otherwise you would have sent me a reply. It is proper you should not fail in sending letters to me. What more except the desire of meeting you?" Later on similar letters were addressed to Sambhāji by Akbar's Diwan.[2]

Akbar himself quickly followed this letter and journeying through Khandesh and Baglan *via* Nasik and Trimbak into north Konkan, arrived on 1st June at Pāli near Nāgothnā, 25 miles north of Raigad. Here Sambhāji's men met and accommodated him. This village Pāli on account of the Shahzada's residence, came thenceforward to be named Pādshāhpur. Immediately on his arrival at this place, the western monsoon made its usual appearance, adding in no small degree to the discomforts of a small hut thatched with hay, with mud walls plastered in cowdung and covered with white cloth. Here the Mughal Prince had now to live, a youth who had been brought up in the splendid palaces of Delhi, where even the carpeted marble floor was never too soft for his feet. Sambhāji at once sent Hiroji Farzand and Netaji Pālkar to wait upon the Prince with a present of a pearl necklace, an aigrette and 1000 *mohurs*. They provided him accommodation and rations only of the barest kind. Netāji Pālkar, the only elderly person who had knowledge of the imperial life and manners of the north, was posted to remain with Akbar, charged with the duty of looking after his comforts. Hiroji returned to Raigad to report to the king upon the event.

The contact of these two strange figures, Sambhāji and Akbar, could not under the circumstances be expected to be helpful to either, although at heart they both ardently wished to support each other in their common endeavour to put down the Emperor. But how was Sambhāji to put implicit faith in the professions of a dearly loved son of his father's bitterest enemy? Might he not be a spy specially employed to put the valiant Maratha prince off his guard, and thereby encompass

2. House of Shivaji, by Sir J. Sarkar, p. 180.

the ruin of the newly established Maratha raj, now that the great Shivaji was no more? Sambhāji's own domestic situation, already difficult and depressing enough, was not calculated to inspire trust in others, much less in a princely guest of Akbar's type. Sambhāji had no friend or confidant to advise and guide him in matters of state. He well knew he was disliked by everybody ever since his father's days, and could exact obedience only at the point of the sword. On the other hand, Akbar's advent into Mahārāshtra particularly at an inhospitable season, without previous notice or expectation, was too much for poor Sambhāji to afford either comfort or convenience to his worthy guest. Possibly they did not know even each other's language wherein they could freely express their sentiments. Sambhāji's minister Kavi Kalash was the only common medium. The four rainy months were utterly wasted in preliminary talks. When they ended, Sambhāji and Akbar had their first formal meeting on 13th November 1681.

Whatever the real cause of the final breach between these two young princes might have been, they both tried their utmost to support each other sincerely through six long years, from June 1681 to February 1687. It is unfortunate that their efforts were not crowned with success.

3. **Aurangzeb descends into the Deccan.**—Aurangzeb had long dreamt of completing the task of subjugating the whole Indian continent which his worthy ancestors had vainly tried to accomplish; and now that Shivaji was dead, the conquest of the south appeared to him comparatively easy; and when at Ajmere he learnt in June 1681 that Akbar had fled to Sambhāji for shelter, he realised the gravity of his situation and immediately despatched his second son Azam Shah in pursuit, himself following him in September after completing measures of security for his northern Empire. He was accompanied by most of his tried commanders, his sons and grandsons with all the best provision he could make in equipment and finances. Aurangzeb reached Burhanpur on 13 November 1681, and advancing further south took up his residence at Aurangabad on 22 March 1682.

Hiroji Farzand and other thoughtful persons who visited Akbar and Durgādās at Pali, now realized, here was a splendid opportunity for Sambhāji to complete his father's task of releasing his homeland from the Mughal grasp and organize a spirited resistance to Aurangzeb's aggression. But these officers were sadly disappointed in Sambhāji that he possessed neither the character, nor the capacity required for a task of such immense magnitude and for leading the nation to victory in its hour of trial. Shivaji was an adept in grasping every opportunity that came in his way, but not so Sambhāji, whose impatient and suspicious temperament smelt treason and disloyalty in all his captains and helpmates. The Emperor learnt every detail about the activities of both Sambhāji and Akbar through a net-work of spies and took full advantage of it. He offered inducements to Sambhāji's followers and sowed sedition among them. Sambhāji at the same time came to be involved in dissensions in his own family and government at Raigad, thus weakening his position in an immense measure.

4. **Bloody beginning of Sambhaji's reign.**—In order to understand Sambhāji's present situation the reports sent by the English and the French merchants prove extremely valuable; and a few points are here extracted from this source. Sambhāji made a good start after having got possession of Raigad without much effort. A report of 20 August 1680 says. "Sambhāji Rajah intends to give Bahadur Khan, the Mughal Subhedar, battle in the open field and has sent him word as such." 10 November 1680. "We are alarmed of Maratha forces being abroad. A party of horse and foot is reported to be marching towards Surat, another against Burhanpur and a third to keep Bahadur Khan in play." [3]

November 1680. "Although the officers of the Karnatak had recognized Sambhāji Rajah as their sovereign, they nevertheless were in fear on receiving the news that the new king had caused to be arrested and put in fetters many Brahmins among the principal officers of the late Shivaji, among others Janārdan Pandit. No good is predicted of the government of Sambhāji from his having arrested officers of such importance and experience. The Killedar of Jinji and other chief officers have

3. *House of Shivaji*, by Sir Jadunath, pp. 179-214, gives fresh material on Sambhāji.

received orders from Sambhāji Raja to arrest Raghunāth Pandit. But the affair has not yet been pushed forward."

21 June 1681. "Sultan Akbar is at Pāli. He is a white man of middle stature of about 25 years of age. He is lodged in a large house covered with straw. It is lined with white Calico and spread with ordinary carpets. He sits open, with but one man of note Durgādās, a Rajput in great esteem with his master. He has about five hundred horse and but fifty camels. Sambhāji Raja's men keep guard. Four or five days ago came to him from Sambhāji Rajah a person of great esteem, Hiroji Farzand with a letter and presents."

16 July 1681. "Akbar's force increases daily. He hath now 1500 horse and five or six thousand more at Trimbak. Sambhāji is daily expected to wait on him and conduct him to Burhanpur. From thence they intend to march for Delhi."

30 August 1681. "Sambhāji hath been in great danger of his life. He had like to have been dispatched by poison put into a dish of fish. But a boy privy to it prevented his eating it. It was given to one of his servants and a dog. Both died in a few hours. Those that conspired against him were Ānāji Pandit, Kesho Pandit, Pralhād Pandit etc.; all are laden with iron."

8 September 1681. "The conspirators against Sambhāji, Ānāji Pandit, Rāmrāja's mother and Hiraji Farzand would have brought Sultan Akbar in, but he would not. He immediately gave Sambhāji notice of it by a messenger."

12 October 1681. "Sambhāji is not at Rairi. For plotting against his life he has put to death Ānāji Pandit, Hiraji Farzand, Bālāji Prabhu, Somāji Datto and five more, bound and put under elephant's feet. Twenty more are to suffer death. The Raja will march to Burhanpur with Akbar in a few days."

27 October 1681. "Rāmrāja's mother is dead, by report, poisoned by Sambhāji's contrivance."

This explains Sambhāji's situation. Having discovered a plot against his own life, he at once arrested and put to death all those whom he suspected to be involved in the affair, including his step-mother Soyarā Bai. She belonged to the Shirke family, and so Sambhāji's wrath fell upon the Shirkes, as supporters of the lady ; several of them were mercilessly slaughtered. These atrocities occurred during the three months from August to October 1681. As Sambhāji was occupied in the investigation of the plot, he could not meet the Shahzada immediately on his arrival. The harsh punishments which he inflicted upon the offenders, alienated most of his servants. The atmosphere about him became charged with suspicion and hatred for him, and practically continued so till his end. His fury against all those who were rightly or wrongly supposed to be implicated in the plot against him, continued to inflame him throughout his reign. Mānāji More, Gangādhar Pant, Vāsudev Pant, Rāoji Somnāth, Pralhād Nirāji and some others were subjected to hardships and confinement at different times.

As Sambhāji grew extremely distrustful of his father's faithful servants, he had none about him to whom he could entrust his affairs. He, therefore, selected an utter foreigner to be his adviser, the famous Kavi Kalash, a Brahman of Kanauj, who had long been a family priest of the Bhosles at Prayag and whose acquaintance Sambhāji had probably made as early as 1666 on his return journey from Agra after escaping from his confinement. Kavi Kalash is a title meaning the prince of poets. He was certainly a versatile scholar and a poet of a high order, who wrote works in Sanskrit and Hindi and received the popular appellation of Kaviji or Kabji. He must have arrived in the Deccan on the occasion of Shivaji's coronation if not earlier, and had been employed to teach Sanskrit and the Puranas to Sambhāji. Some of the pieces composed by him are extant. His name Kavi-Kalash came to be corrupted into Kalusha, now a household word in Mahārāshtra meaning an instigator of strife. An old chronicle says that one Keshav Bhat Kabji, a north India Brahman versed in magic and incantation, possessed Sambhāji's mind. This Keshav Bhat must be the same as this Kalusha. He had a sweet persuasive tongue. His mastery of Hindusthāni and foreign breeding probably formed the chief recommendation in the eyes of Sambhāji to secure his confidence in a moment of exasperation and distrust. Recent research proves that Sambhāji was fond of the tantric rites, *i.e.* effecting results through certain magical processes, so common in that age.

Lacking the towering self-confidence and resourcefulness of his father, Sambhāji searched in vain for overcoming his tremendous difficulties, both domestic and foreign, and clutched at such vain remedies, to which usually a weak and distracted mind is so prone and which certainly proved his ultimate ruin. We have no means of ascertaining how far Kalusha was responsible for introducing Sambhāji into the vices and drug habits, with which report credits him. An excitable temperament like Sambhāji's hardly needs extraneous causes to foster such evil propensities in him. Kalusha's official title was *Chhandogamatya,* i.e. the minister of Vedic learning.

The motto on Sambhāji's own seal and that adopted by Kalusha are characteristic of their mental attitude and views on life. The ostentatious vein of those seals is obvious.*

Popular tradition in Mahārāshtra charges Kalusha with having been the Emperor's spy, slyly trying to bring about Sambhāji's ruin. There is absolutely no proof to support such as allegation. Sambhāji nominally continued his father's council of eight ministers, but practically entrusted all matters of administration to his favourite Kalusha, for whom he created an additional post of *Chhandogamatya.*

5. **Grand projects.**—Sanskrit poems have been discovered whose authorship doubtless goes to Sambhāji, showing that he was well tutored in old Sanskrit learning under the direc-

---

* श्रीशंभोः शिवजातस्य मुद्रा द्यौरिव राजते।
यदंकसेविनो लेखा वर्तते कस्य नोपरि ॥

"This seal of Sambhāji, born of Shivāji, shines like the sky. What cannot his favourites overcome?"* The seal of Kalusha runs thus :—

विभ्रिरार्थिमनीषाणामवश्योर्नयवर्त्मनां
शेवधिः सत्रे सिद्धीनां मुद्रा कलुशहस्तगा ।

"This seal, stamped by the hand of Kalusha, satisfies the desires of the needy, offers opportunities for the righteous and forms the source of all successful projects. Quite a number of papers with this seal have been discovered, which in addition contain pompous phrases applied to Kalusha, conveying both a religious import and an adeptness in political state-craft such as

"आज्ञापत्र धर्माभिमान, कर्मकांडपरायण, दैवतैकनिष्ठाप्राहिताभिमान, सत्यसंध, समस्त-राजकार्यधुरंधर, विश्वासनिधि, कविकलश, छंदोगामात्य."

tion of his father. The Sanskrit *dana-patra* alluded to before, bears his own Sanskrit endorsement. He writes in it that he had it prepared on his own initiative. And now Sanskrit letters have been discovered in the archieves of Jaipur, written to Rajah Ram Sinh of Amber, both by Sambhāji and Kavi Kalash, enfolding a grand project of dethroning the Emperor Aurangzeb in co-operation with Akbar and Durgādās. These letters were sent by Sambhāji with his special agent Pratāp-Sinh, who was authorised to arrange the details personally. Sambhāji offered to lead a large and well equipped army through Gujarat into north India and called upon Rām Sinh to join them with an equal quota of his own Rajput troops for a combined dash upon Delhi and its capture for Akbar, thus taking advantage of the Emperor's absence in the south. "We cannot", says Sambhāji, "endure any longer the persecution that this wicked Emperor is inflicting upon the Hindu race and religion, and are prepared to sacrifice everything, our treasure, our land, our forts and even our lives, in an attempt to put him down. With this resolve we have for these two years entertained at our court our honoured guests Akbar and Durgādās, and have waged a ceaseless strife upon Aurangzeb. We have put to death many a brave captain of his, captured several, released some, either after exacting heavy ransoms or out of compassion. Many effected their escape by offering bribes. The moment has now arrived when the Emperor himself can be captured and made prisoner, so that we can carry out our religious functions without molestation. If you muster courage and co-operate with us, what is there to prevent success crowning our endeavours? You well remember how your own son the young Krishna Sinh was treacherously put to death by the Emperor. You are only to follow in the footsteps of your father, the revered Mirza Raja Jai Sinh, who helped Aurangzeb in acquiring for him the throne of Delhi as against his elder brother Dara Shukoh."

The date wanting in this Sanskrit letter of Sambhāji can fortunately be supplied from a similar letter addressed to the same Rām Sinh of Jaipur on 22 May 1682 by Akbar. It says, "Aurangzeb's treatment of the Hindus has become manifest and is known to you. As for instance, in the affair of Kumar Kishan Sinh, though it happened owing to his youthfulness, yet it too was a sign of bigotry on the part of Alamgir which he displays to that community in every way. Therefore, out of my regard for the hereditary servants of our house, who have generation after generation been treated with kindness by our august dynasty, I exalt and cherish you by conferring on you the title of Mirza Raja and the *mansab* and cash reward of your father and on your son Bishun Sinh that *mansab* which you held when you were a Kumar.

"Hope for the daily increasing favours of my Imperial Majesty and be ready with your ears alert for the news of my coming. When I march with my victorious army towards Hindustān, you should join my followers and exert yourself greatly in my Imperial service, which will be the cause of your being favoured at court and honoured. The usual jewels and robes of honour are not being sent to you on account of the insecurity of the roads." [4]

These two Sanskrit and Persian letters singularly and independently corroborate each other. The grand project of the two young enthusiasts, one styling himself the Emperor and the other a Chhatrapati, had nothing inherently weak in it. Only it required a genius like that of Shivaji to execute it. Durgādās and Akbar were capable men and with the dashing valour of Sambhāji added, there was in it every promise of success. Writes Sir Jadunath : "For more than a year after his arrival in the Deccan, the Emperor accomplished nothing notable in spite of his immense resources. In truth he was at this time passing through a domestic and mental crisis which has been entirely concealed by the Persian Court-historians. The unexpected rebellion of Akbar, whom he loved most among all his sons, as he in one of his letters calls upon God to witness, had totally shaken his faith in his family, and he did not know whom to trust or where he would be safe. Hence his policy for some time after his arrival in the Deccan, was hesitating, suspicious, watchful and seemingly capricious or self-contradictory." [5]

Aurangzeb knowing that Sambhāji and his own rebel son

4. *House of Shivaji*—p. 184, by Sir Jadunath. For the Sanskrit letter see P. V. Kane Commemoration Volume.

5. *Hist. of Aurangzib*, IV, p. 304.

would specially work their way to the north through northern Konkan and Gujarat, despatched Shihab-ud-din Khan with Dalpat Bundella to take possession of some of the Maratha key forts near Nasik, and thus block the path of the rebels in that direction. In April 1682 Shihab-ud-din laid siege to the fort of Ramsej seven miles north of Nasik. The Maratha killedar so gallantly defended the fort, that the Mughals failed to make any effect upon it, and learning that Rupāji Bhosle and Mānāji Moré were fast coming upon them with a relieving force, the Khan retired from Ramsej after suffering heavy losses. Dalpat Bundella was wounded with a stone. At this dismal failure Aurangzeb felt so heavily grieved that he threw off his *pagri* and swore never to put it on again till he had driven the enemy out of his country.

6. **Aurangzeb's discomfiture.**—The season of 1682 and 83 indeed offered a good chance for a sudden attack either upon the Emperor's head-quarters, as Akbar was persistently suggesting, or for a dash through Gujarat into Rajputana. Why such a move was not made we have no means of knowing. But during that first year of Aurangzeb's invasion, his position was certainly very precarious, and he got so frightened that during the autumn of 1683 he called to his presence all his army leaders for a personal consultation to determine upon the right plan for a speedy victory. The Emperor was very uneasy even suspecting the loyalty of his eldest surviving son Shah Alam, who was reported to be in collusion with Akbar. He felt imminent danger to his own life in this land of that 'satan' Shivaji and his 'devilish' comrades. Every Mughal soldier always stood in fear of a sudden premeditated Marāthā attack upon their main camp, resulting in terrible havoc to life and property. At the above mentioned conference with his generals, the Emperor gathered that they were all afraid to face the Marāthās. He then called upon his eldest son to lead an expedition against Sambhāji. The son replied, "I can do so only if you recall Amir Khan from Afghanistan and appoint him my deputy." But the removal of that man from the north-western frontier meant the loss of that part of his Empire. A realistic picture of the Emperor's sore predicament is well revealed in the contemporary writ-

ings of the European merchants. A Surat letter reports on 19th June, 1783 " the Mughal is grown very crazy and his mind continually alters. In all likelihood he will not live much longer. Sultan Akbar hath the good will of most ". " The king is extraordinarily peevish and uneasy because of Sultan Akbar. Sultan Azam, Begam Jahanzeb Banu and Dilir Khan are degraded for suspicion of being kind to Akbar." The Emperor felt a suspicion against Prince Azam. He summoned the Prince and Dilir Khan to his presence. They delayed coming. Dilir fell under the Emperor's punishment."[6] He took poison to avoid the Emperor's wrath. Dilir Khan had been the most trusted of Aurangzeb's generals and had served him faithfully in the Deccan for over twenty years. That such a faithful servant should have to commit suicide, shows how perverse the Emperor had then grown.

After a full inquiry into the condition of affairs in the different theatres of the war and receiving correct reports from the various commanders and officers, Aurangzeb arranged a fresh plan of campaign against Sambhāji's dominions and assigned definite duties to each general. The task of simultaneously attacking Sambhāji and the Portuguese, as the latter were reported to be harbouring Akbar, was assigned to Shah Alam, Aurangzeb's eldest son, and was carried out by him, at first with some success. But Shah Alam suffered such dreadful privations in that expedition that the Emperor for the present gave up his attempt against Akbar and Sambhaji, and directed his attention to the subjugation of Bijapur and Golkonda, the two Muslim States from whom Sambhāji received occasional support and who, being both Shias in their faith, had long been objects of particular execration to the fanatic Emperor. He moved his armies to the south early in 1685, invested Bijapur on 27 March and captured it after a heroic resistance on 12 September 1686. Similarly Golkonda was invested on 28 January 1687 and it surrendered to him on 1st October of that year. So during these three years his main attention had been withdrawn from the Maratha country. Abul Hasan Tanashah the king of Golkonda was kept in confinement at Daulatabad.

6. Vide Sarkar's Aurangzeb, Vol. IV, pp. 305-307.

7. **The Portuguese cowed by Sambhaji.**—Here we must go back a little and trace Sambhāji's occupations on the west coast. After the first outburst of his vindictive fury, things settled down at Raigad and he moved out to attend to the Siddi of Janjirā and the Portuguese of Chaul, these neighbours of Sambhāji having been called upon by the Emperor to join in his war against the Marāthā king. The Siddi was the Emperor's admiral and now being egged on to attack Sambhāji, he furiously raided Maratha territory right up to the foot of Raigad towards the end of 1681. Sambhāji at once accepted the challenge and launched his whole naval force of 150 fighting ships and some five thousand select sailors against Janjira and invested the place both by land asd sea. Dādji Raghunāth Prabhu Mahadkar, Sambhāji's intrepid general[7] created terrible havoc against the Siddi in the early months of 1682, when Siddi Kasam defended his position with great heroism. But just at this moment the Emperor arrived in the Deccan and Sambhāji was compelled to raise the siege of Janjira in order to meet the fearful attacks that were directed against him by the Mughal forces in several other directions.

The Portuguese were called upon by the Emperor to wage war against Sambhāji. They dared not remain friends with the Marāthās in the presence of the Mughal might, now directed particularly against Sambhāji's dominions in the Konkan, as it was here that both Sambhāji and Akbar made their inimical moves against the Emperor. Aurangzeb employed his sons and grand-sons and his best generals to secure the forts and passes in north Konkan and capture both his rebel son and the Marāthā king by all possible means. The British trading establishments at Surat and Bombay, the Dutch factory at Vengurla, the Portuguese strong-holds on the west coast were all cowed into abject submission, thus making Sambhāji's situation all the more precarious. Although thus hemmed in by enemies all round, Sambhāji continued to resist boldly and conduct a heroic war, so that he for a time kept at bay the bravest

7. Dādji Raghunāth Prabhu Mahadkar is the same person who subjugated Savitri Bai Thanedarin of Belvadi, in Dec. 1677. He also distinguished himself in a war with the Siddi of Janjira in 1682. Nilakanth Trimbak Prabhu Mahadkar, the Peshwa of Sambhāji Raja of Kolhapur in 1727, belonged to the same family.

generals of Aurangzeb and even threatened his very bases at Ahmednagar and Aurangabad.

The British at Bombay were called upon both by the Emperor and Rajah Sambhāji to join in, but cleverly managed not to come into scrape with either by sending their envoys to both in order to preserve their neutrality.

During 1683 Sambhāji personally attacked the Portuguese at Chaul and Goa. The Portuguese Governor Tavora felt consternation at being placed between the Mughal 'monster' and the Marāthā 'devil', and was reduced to such straits that he found his situation hopeless. This situation is eloquently explained by the Italian Manucci then present at Goa. The heroic fight before Phonda between Sambhāji and the Portuguese during the months of October and November of 1683 and the former's capture of that stronghold, practically annihilated the Governor's hopes of defending Goa. He in his extremity opened the grave of their great protector, St. Xavier, held a congregation in that holy presence of priests and populace and offered prayers in an all night vigil for the rescue of his nation's fortunes. The Saint did indeed work a miracle. As Goa was on the point of surrendering, Sambhāji suddenly retired having received news of a Mughal army threatening his rear, led by Shah Alam the Emperor's eldest son, who came upon Sambhāji's track under pressure from his father. The Maratha king had to beat a hurried retreat in order to save his life and forces from capture. This happened towards the end of November 1683. Goa was thus miraculously saved and the incident marked the decline of the Maratha king's fortunes. The Sāwant of Wadi in the immediate neighbourhood of Goa. was also incited by the Emperor to oppose Sambhāji and was severely threatened to be put out of existence if he declined.

These momentous events indeed form an exciting chapter of Maratha history. Sufficient details are available in the Portuguese and Persian languages as regards the constant friction that continued between Sambhāji and Shahzada Akbar and which ultimately disconcerted their plans of a combined stand against the Emperor. The resources of Aurangzeb proved too much for the poor efforts of these two fiery youths. How could the small poor territory of Konkan stand against the might of the magnificent Mughal Empire controlling the vast

Indian continent? That they did hold out even for some years and strike terror into Aurangzeb's heart, is in itself an achievement worthy of great credit. Again and again did Akbar urge upon Sambhāji's attention the advisability of making a sudden sweep upon the Emperor's central camp and effecting a complete rout of his powerful armies. But such a daring project required a genius like that of Shivaji to execute it. Sambhāji, brave as a lion personally, lacked the patient calculating forethought and vigilance essential for the success of such an extensive and large scale undertaking.

8. **Sad end of Akbar.**—Absence of recorded evidence prevents one from knowing, how Sambhāji and his ally Akbar were occupied during the three years that the Emperor was engaged in the conquest of Bijapur and Golkonda, and why they did not utilize the opportunity to their own advantage. It seems the two had severe disagreement on several points connected with the conduct of their operations. Akbar probably felt after his close experience during the few years that he was in Maharāshtra, that Sambhāji, far from possessing any of his father's great qualities, was decidedly incompetent to handle the grave situation that had arisen for them, or make a proper use of the opportunities that came in their way. Akbar indeed felt the net being tightened closely round him by his father and was terribly frightened for his life, as there was every likelihood of his being discovered and captured by the numerous agents roaming about the land. His sister Zinat-un-Nisa Begam who looked after her father's household, was trying her best to bring about a reconciliation between them. But Akbar well knew what his fate would be if he went back to his father. He became convinced that if he had to save his life, it was no use wasting his time with Sambhāji. The princes of Rajputana repeatedly urged him to come over to their shelter, so that they could together rise against the Emperor and take possession of Delhi. But Akbar's resources were very poor; he had no money, nor men; Sambhāji himself being hard up, could render no help to him. Besides, his way to Rājputānā was securely blocked both through Gujarat and Khandesh.

Sambhāji's vicious and intemperate habits must also have disgusted the Shahzada, so that a severe estrangement came about between them. Akbar was fed up with the miserable life of a wandering fugitive in an inhospitable land, with no brighter prospect. For three years in succession rumours of Sambhāji and Akbar going to start on a raid on Surat, struck terror into the hearts of the people of Gujarat. Kalusha and Akbar kept constantly moving between Kolhāpur, Rājapur, Vengurla and Sangameshwar, as these places repeatedly occur in the letters of those days. Some disaffected servants and commanders of Aurangzeb continued to help Akbar secretly. A few glimpses of Akbar's life are available in Sir Jadunath's *House of Shivaji*. On 17 February 1683, the following news reached the Emperor through his spies. " The 'rebel' (Akbar) had newly enlisted 2000 horse and two thousand foot. Their salary is paid by the 'wretch' (Sambhāji). The 'rebel' made a Hindu dancing girl Muslim and kept her in his harem and gave her the pearl necklace and other things presented to him (by the Maratha king). When the news of it reached to (the) 'wretch,' he sent to the 'rebel' to say, " I had offered the necklace and other things for your royal use." The 'rebel' replied, " I am an Emperor's son and shall do as I like." Thereupon the 'wretch' sent him a message to send back the troops he had under him. Thus the 'rebel' finding himself helpless, set fire to his house, assumed the guise of a *faqir* and started for Goa. Then the 'wretch' wrote to the Portuguese not to let the 'rebel' enter their territory. For this reason they kept him out. So the 'rebel' has turned back and taken his abode at the place where he formerly used to remain."

Akbar to Kavi Kalash, 20 Feb. 1684. " Immediately on receipt of this, set out to see me. God forbid, that through delay the affair should take a different turn. Know the matter to be urgent." Again on 27 July 1684. " Received your letter. As for the envoy of Muhammad Azam, who has arrived there, I do not know why he has come and what agreement you have made with him. You can make peace if you consider it expedient for yourself. I am not myself much inclined towards peace. Do not remain careless relying on peace. You know best what is for your future benefit." Akbar writes to Kavi Kalash on 20 August 1684. " The question of peace is entirely at the discretion of the Raja and yourself. As for the peace with the 'Feringis' in which you have dragged me as an intermediary, I do not know how the affair has been concluded. Inform me what agreement has been made with the envoy of Muhammad Azam. What is the state of the Bijapur business ?"

November 1684. "Received your two letters. You have fixed 30 November as the date of your interview with us. But these are the days of Ashura (ten holy days of Muharram). Inform me after fixing the 11th or 12th of the month for your interview. On that day my standards will march out of Sakharpen and arrive at Malkāpur. You ought to come there on that date and see me. Thereafter you may go to Kolhapur." In December 1684, Akbar writes, "it is very good you have come. I too have come to Malkāpur. It is proper that the interview and the business should be quickly concluded. What more except longing to see you ?"

On 18 January 1685 Akbar writes to Sambhāji. "Cream of grand Rajahs, chief of august princes, devoted follower, Chhatrapati Rajah Sambhāji. Know that the facts about the defeat of the Mughals and the firm stand made by Kavi Kalash have reached me. Kavi Kalash is a very good and faithful servant of yours. God forbid that he be ruined through jealousy. You ought to do everything to protect him. It is certain that the Mughals have gone away and that you have marched towards Khelnā. If you so wish, I will also go and join you in the campaign."

This correspondence shows that Sambhāji and Akbar were deliberating upon some grand plan. At the beginning of 1685 Sambhāji did actually invade Broach and carried away a good deal of plunder from Gujarat, cutting up the Emperor's troops that came to oppose him on his return journey near Nasik. But this solitary transaction did not materially affect Akbar's prospects. Ultimately in sheer desperation he managed to engage a British cargo vessel on which he embarked at Rājāpur in February 1687 and sailing *via* Vengurla to Muskat, reached Ispahan in Iran in January 1688 after nearly a year's journey. Here he remained for the rest of his life, a wanderer from home and a constant threat to his father's northern possessions. Fortunately for Aurangzeb Akbar's prolonged stay in Persia proved as ineffective to his ambition as his six years' residence in Mahārāshtra. Manucci quotes a long and instructive letter[8] addressed by Akbar to his father a little while before his death in 1704. He died in November of that year, a broken-hearted but spirited soul experiencing the cursed lot of a Mughal prince. Letters often passed between the father and the son and even communication through personal agents was long kept up between them, with eloquent promises of pardon and earnest request for return from the Emperor. But up to the very last Akbar turned a deaf ear to all such entreaties conveyed by his father, sister or friends.

9. **The Chivalrous Durgadas.**—It is necessary here to complete the story of Durgādās also, as it materially affects Aurangzeb's plans and measures. After saying good-bye to Akbar at Rajāpur in February 1687, Durgādās returned to Jodhpur and continued throughout his long life steadfastly to organize the Rajput clans in order to wrest Marwar back from the Emperor's control. Akbar's son Buland Akhtar and his daughter Safiat-un-Nisa were in his charge and were brought up by him in Marwar with great care and solicitude for their comfort and breeding. Durgādās employed a Muslim theologian to instruct them in their own faith. When Aurangzeb learned of Akbar's flight to Iran, he sent his own trusted agent Ishwardas Nagar[9] to Durgādās and effected a reconciliation with him. Durgādās with Akbar's daughter, then over 16 years of age, came to visit the Emperor at Brahmapuri in 1696. The following memorable dialogue between the grand-father and the grand-daughter is preserved in history :—

Aurangzeb : As you have passed all your life among non-Muslims, you must be altogether ignorant of our faith. So you must at once start the study of the *Koran*.

Safiat : You are wrong, grand-papa. The revered Durgādās not only provided for all my physical comforts, but also employed a Muslim lady to teach me religion. I know all the *Koran* by heart.

Aurangzeb : Oh, how good of Durgādās. How do you think I should reward him for all his services ?

8. *Storia-do-mogor*, Volume IV, pp. 171-177.

9. This Ishwardas has written a full history of Aurangzeb's life in Maharashtra which forms a valuable source of information for that period.

Safiat : Ask Ishwardas about it and he will tell you."

The Emperor then conferred a small jagir upon Durgādās and the latter returned to Jodhpur. Akbar's son Buland Akhtar was still in Rājputānā, whom Durgādās kept like a pawn in his hand to serve as a threat in case the Emperor did any wrong to the interests of the Jodhpur raj. Ajit Sinh, the posthumous son of Jashvant Sinh had now come of age and claimed his father's patrimony, but was not yet recognized by the Emperor. Durgādās informed the Emperor that he would deliver Buland Akhtar, provided Ajit Sinh was restored to his father's dominions. This was agreed to and the Emperor was able to recover his grandson only after he had carried out the promises made to Durgādās. In 1689 Ajit Sinh was given a *mansab* in the imperial army with several Parganas as his jagir. Durgādās on getting letters-patent and being put in actual possession of the lands assigned to him, came to Aurangzeb with Buland Akhtar *via* Ahmadabad and Surat. Ajit Sinh later grew up to be one of the strong Rajput potentates wielding power and influence in the post-Aurangzeb regime of Mughal decadence. But it was the genius of Durgādās which organized the Rajput opposition that Aurangzeb had to face, no less in intensity than his Maratha enemies. Durgādās died long after Aurangzeb's death and received signal honours from his successors. Durgādās is called the "flower of Rajput chivalry." Rajput mothers pray to God for sons as brave as Durgādās.[10]

10. Sambhaji captured.—The Emperor employed Shihab-Uddin Firoz-Jang and his son, Chinkilich Khan, the future Nizam-ul-mulk Asaf Jah I, to harass Sambhāji's possessions in north Konkan and Baglan. They succeeded in winning over several prominent followers of Sambhāji. He retaliated with equal vigour. In the beginning of 1685 Sambhāji's troops devastated Mughal lands from Aurangabad to Burhanpur and carried away enormous booty which was sold in special marts and openly advertised in advance. At least seventeen large cities are mentioned as having been completely sacked in

10. **ए माता पूत एसा जिन जेसा दुर्गादास.** A long and interesting account is given by Sarkar, *Aurangzeb*, Vol.III and Volume V, pp. 284-292 to which the curious reader is referred.

these inroads of Sambhāji. While the Emperor was engaged in his war against Bijapur and Golkonda, Sambhāji took up his residence at Panhāla in order to be able to keep an eye upon the former's movements.

The conquest of the two remaining Muslim kingdoms of the Deccan at once increased the Emperor's prestige and resources. He obtained enormous hoards of money, bodies of trained troops and stocks of arms and provisions that had been long accumulated is those two capitals. Aurangzeb could employ all these against the declining fortunes of Sambhāji, who had exhausted all his father's treasure and added little new income during his seven years of mis-government and war. When he was deserted by Akbar, he had no comrade left to share his misfortunes. Aurangzeb retired from Bijapur and encamped at Akluj[11] on the Bhima near Pandharpur, in order to concentrate all his power and energy against the hapless Sambhāji. One of the Bijapur generals named Sharza Khan, a clever and watchful man conversant with the terrain of the Maratha country, invaded the Satara district. Sambhāji's Senapati Hambir Rao Mohite came to oppose him. An action was fought between them near Wai towards the end of 1687, in which Hambir Rao lost his life on the battle-field. He was the last of Sambhāji's supporters and his loss sealed the Raja's fate. A kind of encircling movement was started against him in all directions. Sambhāji was deserted by most of his followers and came to be surrounded by swarms of Mughal parties, occupying the difficult passes and stopping communication between Panhālā and Raigad, where Sambhāji was known to be moving.

The hilly regions below the Sahyadri range between Kolhāpur and Satara were long held by the Shirkes, who had become Sambhāji's mortal enemies and had out of revenge deserted to the Emperor. They now played their game, watched Sambhāji's movements and communicated them to the Mughal officers. For about a year after Hambir Rao's death, Sambhāji and Kavi Kalash struggled on as best they could. In November 1688 Kavi Kalash had a severe brush against the Shirkes and being hotly pursued, saved his life by taking shelter on the fort

11. About 50 miles above Brahmapuri.

of Vishālgad. When Sambhāji heard this news at Raigad, he at once attacked and put down the Shirkes near Sangameshwar and joined Kalash at Vishālgad. But their situation soon became critical, on account of most of their followers being seduced. The Shirkes reported the secret movements of Sambhāji and Kavi Kalash to the Emperor's agents. One Shaikh Nizam, a former officer of Golkonda who was posted at Kolhāpur with instructions to pounce upon Sambhāji at a moment's notice, obtained news of Sambhāji's movements. During January 1689 Sambhāji and Kalusha organized their party and started from Vishālgad to proceed to Raigad by the Ambā Ghat. Shaikh Nizam receiving information that Sambhāji and Kavi Kalash were halting at Sangameshwar, suddenly fell upon them on 1st February 1689, and apprehended them with a few of their followers after a light skirmish in which some of Sambhāji's men lost their lives and a few escaped to Raigad. Why Sambhāji and Kalusha tarried at Sangameshwar it is difficult to say. They had nimble horses, perhaps better than those of their pursuers and could have easily escaped to Raigad even after the arrival of their captors. Māloji Ghorpade whose father Shivaji had killed but who faithfully served Sambhāji to the last, sacrificed his own life trying to save that of his master. Shaikh Nizam seated Sambhāji on his own elephant and the other captives were accommodated on horses and camels. All immediately afterwards moved back from Sangmeshwar towards the Emperor's camp by the Ambā Ghāt.

11. **Tragic death.**—The Emperor received the news of Sambhāji's capture at Akluj, where it caused a wild outburst of rejoicing. A great terror had been lifted from the hearts of the imperialists. The Emperor felt that this success had put the crown on his recent victories over Bijapur and Golkonda, and now afforded him the cherished satisfaction of returning to Delhi in the triumph of a completed task. He at once left Akluj and proceeded to Bahadurgad, where the captives were brought under the guard of Hamid-uddin Khan. By the Emperor's orders the captive Maratha King was made a mark of public ridicule. Four miles outside the encampment Sambhāji and Kavi Kalash were dressed as buffoons in long fools' caps with bells fixed on them, mounted on camels and brought

to Bahadurgad with drums beating and trumpets pealing. Hundreds of thousands of spectators lined the roads gazing at these unhappy captives, as if they were a kind of wild beasts or demons. Thus degraded they were slowly paraded through the entire camp, extending over miles in length and finally brought to the Emperor, who then sat in full Darbar for the occasion. At the sight of the prisoners Aurangzeb descended from the throne and kneeling down on the carpet bowed his head to the ground in double thankfulness to the Giver of this crowning victory. After he had a quiet look at the prisoners, they were removed to their cell.

Next day, the Emperor sent his trusted personal officer Ruhulla Khan to talk to Sambhāji and make him an offer of his life on condition, that (1) he surrendered all his forts, (2) disclosed all his hidden treasures, and (3) declared the names of those Mughal officers who were in league with him. Fretting with bitterness of soul at having been publicly insulted and driven to desperation, Sambhāji spurned the offer of life with all the vehemence he could gather, loosened his tongue in abuse of the Emperor and his Prophet, giving free vent to his long pent up sentiments against the Muslim faith, and scurrilously asked for one of Aurangzeb's daughters as the price of his friendship. The envoy dared not report to the Emperor the foul language he had heard, but conveyed only a hint of its purport. For once Sambhāji hehaved with a stoic firmness worthy of the great Shivaji, and fully atoned by the manner of death for all the sins he had committed in life.

Aurangzeb lacked the magnanimity of the Greek monarch Alexander. He had not the heart to tolerate the open insult he had received from his worst enemy, who in his eyes had sinned beyond hope of pardon. That very night Sambhāji's eyes were blinded and the next day the tongue of Kavi Kalash was cut out. Sambhāji stoically bore the tortures heaped upon him in order to extract his secrets. After a fortnight's torture and insult, the captives were removed with the imperial camp from Bahadurgad to Koregaon on the river Bhima and there put to a cruel and painful death on 11th March 1689, the Amavasya day of the month of Falgun, their limbs being hacked off one by one and their flesh thrown to the dogs. Their severed heads were stuffed with straw and exhibited in the chief cities of the Deccan to the accompaniment of drum and trumpet. These heads were later discovered in a thorny bush at the village of Vadu and secretly cremated by some kindly souls at Tulapur on a spot where the two rivers the Bhima and the Indrayani meet.

Writes Ranade, "Aurangzeb's dream, which he cherished throughout his life, had thus been accomplished before he had been six years in the Deccan. The whole country from the Narmadā to the Tungabhadrā lay at his feet. It seemed as if Shivaji and the men whom he led to victory had lived and died in vain. The great deluge against which Shahji and Shivaji had struggled to protect the country for over sixty years, now swept over the land, carrying everything before it and there seemed no signs of any possible resistance."

Thus perished the second Maratha Chhatrapati, accomplishing by his death, as the sequel will show, the task of destroying Aurangzeb's hopes and conquest, which his own short life in vain tried to bring about. The fearless manner in which he met his end, united and steeled the hearts of the Maratha nation as nothing else would have done, and nerved them to avenge the death of their sovereign.

CHRONOLOGY

CHAPTER XIV.

1689 Feb. 9	Rājārām proclaimed King.
,, March 25	Zulfiqar Khan besieges Raigad.
,, April 5	Rājārām escapes from Raigad.
,,	Matabar Khan overruns North Konkan.
,, August	Santāji raids the Emperor's camp at Koregaon.
,, Septr.	Rājārām leaves Panhālā for Jinji.
,, Novr. 3	Raigad falls into Mughal hands along with Shahu and Yesu Bai.
,, ,, 15	Rājārām reaches Jinji and forms his court.
,, ,, 30	Zulfiqar Khan moves towards Jinji.
,, Dec. 18	Aurangzeb leaves Koregaon for Bijapur.
1690	The Emperor's camp moves to Galgale.
,, March 2	Rājārām's inspiring appeal to Bāji Sarzarao and others.
,, June	Zulfiqar Khan arrives before Jinji and besieges it.
1691	Zulfiqar in great straits before Jinji.
,, Octr. 4	Aurangzeb despatches Asad Khan and Kambaksh to succour Zulfiqar Khan.
,, Dec. 16	Asad Khan and Kambaksh arrive before Jinji.
1692 Dec. 13	Ali Mardan Khan defeated and captured near Kanchi by Santāji Ghorpade.
	Kambaksh kept under arrest by Asad Khan.
1693 Jan. 1	Ismail Khan Maka defeated by Dhanāji Jadhav.
,, ,, 5	Santāji raids Zulfiqar Khan's camp at Desur.
,, ,, 23	Mughal forces retire from Jinji to Wandiwash.

1694	Rājārām's queens join him at Jinji.
	Death of Pralhād Nirāji at Jinji.
1695 May	Aurangzeb removes his camp to Brahmapuri.
„ Octr.	Rāmchandra Pant holds a conference at Vishalgad and plans an offensive.
„ Novr.	Aurangzeb despatches Khanazad Khan to put down the Marathas in the Karnatak.
„ „ 20	Kasim Khan meets his death at Duderi : Khanazad Khan obtains release by ransom.
1696 Jan. 20	Himmat Khan and son killed in battle by Santāji Ghorpade.
„ Feb. 26	Santāji defeats Hamid-ud-din Khan.
„ April	Santāji demands reward for his services.
„ June 9	Birth of son Shivaji to Tārābai.
„ „	Santāji deprived of his office of Senapati.
1696 June	Santāji defeats Dhanāji at Aiwargudi and puts to death Amrit Rao Nimbālkar.
1697 March	Santāji routed near Bijapur and again near Dahigaon.
„ June	Santāji murdered by Nāgoji Mane.
„ Dec.	Rājārām escapes from Jinji.
1698 Feb. 7.	Zulfiqar Khan captures Jinji.
„ „ 22	Rājārām reaches Vishālgad.
„ May 23	Birth of Sambhāji (second son of Rājārām).
„ Oct.	Rājārām establishes capital at Satara.
1699	Battle of Talner : Hussain Ali Khan captured by the Marathas.
„ Oct. 31	Rājārām starts ravaging Mughal territory.
„ Dec. 22	Marathas raid the Emperor's camp at Brahmapuri.
1700 March 2	Death of Rājārām at Sinhagad.

CHAPTER XIV

RAJARAM THE QUIESCENT

[1689—1700]

1. Two stars of dazzling brilliancy.
2. Fall of Raigad, and Ramchandra Pant's leadership.
3. Maratha Trek to Jinji.
4. The Emperor's movements.
5. Jinji besieged.
6. The Maratha aims.
7. Besiegers besieged.
8. Heroic deeds of Santaji.
9. Santaji's tragic end.
10. Guerilla warfare described.
11. Rajaram escapes, Jinji falls.
12. Rajaram's death and character.

1. Two stars of dazzling brilliancy.—Rājārām, the younger son of Shivaji, was at the time of Sambhāji's death, nineteen years old, having been born on 24 February 1670. The news of Sambhāji's capture did not take long to reach Raigad. Rājārām was then in nominal confinement in the fort, whose commander, under the advice of the veteran Yesāji Kank, brought him out and proclaimed him king on 9th February, i.e. a week after Sambhāji had been seized. This procedure did not fail to disillusion the Emperor and prove that the Maratha monarchy was not at an end. Pralhād Nirāji, Mānāji More and others who had been unjustly confined by Sambhāji, were set at liberty and restored to their offices. In order to nip this revival of the Maratha royal power in the bud, the Emperor at once despatched his able commander Itikad Khan (afterwards surnamed Zulfiqar Khan, Nusrat Jung, son of Aurangzeb's long standing minister Asad Khan), with orders to invest Raigad and to capture both that fort and the new Maratha king. The Khan arrived before the fort on 25 March 1689 and at once laid siege to it. The inmates were terribly dismayed by this fresh onslaught and held frequent consultations under the direction of Yesu Bai, the widowed queen of Sambhāji, a wise and patient woman intensely devoted to her nation's cause. She heartened the drooping spirits of the Maratha garrison by her brave words and offered the following sound advice: "Raigad is doubtless a strong fort and can hold out long ; but it is hazardous that we should all remain confined in this one small spot. In order to distract the Emperor's attention, I should advise you that Rājārām with his wives and followers should clear out before the siege becomes too stringent. I can stay here with my little son Shāhu and defend the capital, fearlessly awaiting the result. Our principal commanders should carry on their usual harassing operations in all directions against the Mughal forces, and convince them that the death of their King has made no difference in our resistance."

This disinterested and far-sighted counsel touched every Maratha soul and was at once acted upon. The leaders took solemn oaths of remaining faithful to Shahu as their Chhatrapati and carrying on the warfare in his name till the country was liberated from the enemy's possession. Accordingly Rājārām slipped out of Raigad on 5 April, proceeded to Pratāpgad and despatched his wives and party for safety into the difficult fortresses of Vishālgad and Rāngnā. Some of the other leaders, Rāmchandra Pant Amātya, Pralhād Nirāji and Shankaraji Malhār Sachiv, also left Raigad and in mutual consultation from different places commenced an unprecedented campaign of fire, plunder and brigandage into the Mughal territory, using a net work of spies to obtain information of the enemy's movements.

While Zulfiqar Khan was busily engaged in operations before Raigad, the Emperor captured several other important Maratha forts such as Salher, Trimbak, Rajgad, Rohida, Torna and Mahuli, which had formed the scenes of the early exploits of Shivaji. Matabar Khan, a shrewd and circumspect general with great organizing capacity, was appointed by the Emperor to hold and administer the important region of north Konkan, now known as the district of Thana, which contained several forts of strategic importance. For nearly fifteen years Matabar Khan held this post with valour and skill and supplied valuable resources to the Mughal captains from his base at Kalyan, where many buildings still preserve his memory.

But some of Rājārām's young helpmates, particularly Santāji Ghorpade and Dhanāji Jādhav, made wonderful progress in the plan that was adopted. They fell upon Mughal detachments and sometimes routed them so thoroughly that succours could not reach Zulfiqar Khan in time for his operations against Raigad. While Rājārām was cantoning at Pratāpgad, Santāji Ghorpade and Vithoji Chavān accomplished an extraordinary feat of valour and dexterity, which struck terror into the Emperor's heart. With a few selected followers they made their way on a dark night through torrents of rain to the Emperor's camp at Koregaum. They fell upon his own royal tent, cut down the supporting ropes and the huge cloth edifice came down in a crash, killing the inmates, including, as was at first supposed, the Emperor himself. They carried away the sets of large gold top-balls of the tent and other valuables and presented them to Rājārām at Pratāpgad. Afterwards it was discovered that Aurangzeb by chance was passing that night in his daughter's tent and thus escaped death. The incident clearly illustrates the nature of Maratha tactics and gave the Emperor a sure foretaste of what he was to expect in future. "In the long history of his struggle with the Marathas after the sun of Maratha royalty had set in the red cloud of Sambhāji's blood and the people's war had begun, Santāji Ghorpade and Dhanāji Jadhav were the two stars of dazzling brilliancy which filled the Deccan firmament for nearly a decade, and paralyzed the alien invader," writes Sir Jadunath.

Soon a Mughal force came to Pratāpgad and Rājārām had to leave it and take up his residence at Panhālā. Shaikh Nizam, the captor of Sambhāji, came against Panhālā, but was completely routed and put to flight from the foot of that fort, thereby saving Rājārām from a fate similar to that of his brother. In the meanwhile Santāji fell upon Zulfiqar Khan's besieging army, and brought away five elephants and an amount of valuable plunder. The three Ghorpade brothers, Santāji, Bahirji and Māloji were rewarded by Rājārām with the respective titles of *Mamulkat-madar*, *Hindurao* and *Amir-ulumrao*, by which their descendants are still distinguished in the Deccan.

2. Fall of Raigad and Ramchandra Pant's leadership.—Of all Maratha forts nature has made Raigad so inaccessible to an enemy that it could hold out for years on end. Constructed on a large plateau it can maintain cattle and grow enough food and other necessaries of life required by a large garrison. After a thorough search Shivaji and his father selected this site and added to its natural defence such fortifications as human ingenuity could devise. But Shivaji's foresight was helpless against human treachery. This very weakness of Maratha character helped Zulfiqar Khan to capture Raigad on 3rd November 1689 after a siege of 8 months. Suryāji Pisāl of Wāi, one of the important officers in charge of the defence, opened the gates to the Khan on a promise of getting the Deshmukhi Vatan of Wāi which he had long coveted. With the fall of Raigad Yesu Bai, her young son Shāhu and a large number of loyal followers were captured and carried by Zulfiqar Khan in triumph to the Emperor. But his joy at this success was only short-lived. With one voice the Maratha leaders, great and small, pledged themselves to a heroic effort to avenge the national insult of their Chhatrapati having been brutally murdered and his son and wife carried away in captivity. Writes Ranade, " Just when its country's fortune was at the lowest ebb and everything seemed to be lost beyond hope, these very misfortunes served to rouse a band of patriots who had been trained in Shivaji's school, to resolve, resourceless and penniless as they were, to secure their national independence and drive Aurangzeb's armies back into Hindustan." At the head of this band was Rājārām who was hailed by the nation, as the very spirit of his father, although he possessed none of the latter's capacity or skill in the management of affairs. But he had an amiable docile temperament and a mild liberal disposition, cheerfully accepting what his worthy counsellors suggested in their wisdom.[1] His chief adviser at first was Pralhād Nirāji, the son of Shivaji's Minister of Justice Nirāji Rāoji, and reputed to be the wisest man of his time among the Marathas.

But the credit of organizing the scattered Maratha nation against the Emperor's power goes principally to Rāmchandra Nilkanth, ancestor of the present Amātya family of Bawda, who had been trained under Shivaji but had fallen in insignificance during the fitful rule of Sambhāji. The Pant possessed a peculiar genius for recognizing merit in men and harnessing

1. The bakhar-writer styles him (स्थिरबुद्धि) of a steady, quiescent nature.

it to promote the national interests. Rājārām thus describes Rāmchandra Pant's services. "This Maratha kingdom is a gift from Heaven. Rāmchandra Pant saved it in its dreadful crisis by carefully picking up the merits and capacities of men, inspired them with a spirit of service and devotion and employed them in appropriate spheres. With uncommon foresight he employed national resources to the best advantage. He successfully thwarted the heroic efforts of Aurangzeb who with his mighty resources came down upon the Maratha land determined to conquer it. Providence crowned Rāmchandra Pant's endeavours with success and frustrated all the cherished desires of the Emperor." Rāmchandra Pant was no soldier, and hardly moved from his base on any military expedition. He possessed the rare virtue of keeping his subordinates ever contented and willing to execute his commands. From his base at Vishālgad he kept a vigilant eye upon the doings of the numerous Maratha leaders, employed over an extensive field of war stretching from Burhanpur in the north to Jinji in the south.

Out of a number of young spirited chiefs who wholeheartedly executed the projects and commands of Rāmchandra Pant, we have space to mention only four, two Brahmans and two Marathas. Parashurām Trimbak Pratinidhi, ancestor of the present chief of Aundh, and Shankarāji Nārāyan Sachiv (the founder of the present Sachiv family of Bhor), were mainly occupied in defending, holding and recapturing the important forts of Shivaji's homeland. Santāji Ghorpade and Dhanāji Jadhav were employed in destroying the enemy's field armies and crippling the material resources of the Mughal generals roving over the vast region of Mahārāshtra and the Karnatak.

3. **Maratha Trek to Jinji.**—When Rājārām's position at Panhālā was found untenable, it was decided that he with a few followers should save himself by flying to Jinji, a stronghold about 60 miles south-east of Madras and about 40 miles inside from the coast of Pondicherry. "As if he had prescience of coming events, Shivaji by his conquests and alliances formed a new line of defence in southern India in the Kaveri valley to which he could retire in case of necessity." Indeed a continuous line of Maratha possessions from Supa, Sampgaon, Kopbal and Bangalore, to Vellore, Jinji and Tanjore

had since been kept up. Such a necessity now arose and Rājārām secretly escaped from Panhālā to Jinji after undergoing many perils and hair-breadth escapes from the Mughal pursuers on the way. Leaving Panhālā at the end of September 1689, Rājārām reached Vellore in a month, deluding the pursuers with various stratagems, and arrived at Jinji on 15 November. Here he now established his residence having been joined in due course by most of his ministers and commandants, Santāji and Dhanāji supplying the necessary convoy guarding the front and the rear. Indeed, Rājārām owed his life to these two watchful generals and the men serving under them. Keshav Purohit, a priest of Rājārām, long in his employ for explaining the Puranas, accompanied the party from Panhālā to Jinji and has vividly described the Maratha king's journey and its perils in a stirring Sanskrit poem called *Rājārām-Charita*.

Jinji soon became the centre of Maratha activity, where the whole Court was assembled and formed, reviving the Council of eight ministers with an addition of the ninth called the Pratinidhi now specially created for providing a position for Pralhād Nirāji, who had rendered extraordinary services. Tanjore in that vicinity was already a Maratha capital, being at this time ruled by Shahji the eldest son of Ekoji and cousin of Rājārām. Writes Keshav Purohit, " the Chiefs of the Karnatak lands hailed Rājārām as an uncommon hero and made his cause their own. They brought him presents of money, provisions and materials, and having been actuated with a spirit of vengeance against Muslims, offered every kind of service to the Maratha king."[1] A few Muslim Chiefs also made common cause with the Marathas under the belief that they were being persecuted without reason. This indeed helped the extension of Maratha influence over the Karnatak regions.

कर्नाटविषयैर्भूपैरेकीभूय महीपतेः। उपायनानि दत्तानि धनानि विविधानि च। सेना बहुविधाः स्वीया दानमानप्रतोषिताः। प्रेषितास्तस्य सैवायै म्लेंच्छसंमर्दनक्षमाः॥ २ . ३—४.

4. **The Emperor's movements.**—The Maratha tactics quickly upset the Emperor's plans, of which the student must take note. The removal of the Maratha Court to the distant Jinji created fresh problems for him. To watch the affairs of Jinji and concert measures for putting down the growing

Maratha power became his immediate concern. He left his camp of Koregaon on 18 December 1689 and removed to Bijapur and after a few months stay at that place, moved still further south and pitched his camp on the Krishna at Galgale, 34 miles south-west of Bijapur. Here he spent nearly three years visiting Bijapur at intervals. By that time the Maratha pressure had increased in Mahārāshtra ; and the Emperor in 1695 moved his camp back to Brahmapuri on the south bank of the Bhimā not far from Pandharpur. This place he renamed Islampuri, and here he stayed for over four years from May 1695 to October 1699. By the end of this time Rājārām had returned to Mahārāshtra, the fort of Jinji having fallen to the Mughals ; but as the Marathas sheltered in their strong western forts proved practically invincible, the Emperor took the fatal resolve of personally marching against them and demolishing these inaccessible haunts of his enemy.

His officers and soldiers had by then become utterly wearied of camp life, away from their homes now for 17 years, and urged the Emperor to return to Delhi after concluding some kind of peace and understanding with the Marathas. The Emperor felt sorely disappointed at this turn of events, and as he could no longer trust his officers, he himself undertook the arduous campaigns for the reduction of the hill forts of Satara and others. After capturing Satara in 1700, he encamped during the rains at Khawaspur on the river Mān. Here he encountered a severe disaster, his whole camp was washed away by unexpected floods. The uproar woke him from sleep and while running out in the dark he slipped and became lame for the rest of his life. During the next three years he fixed his monsoon camp at Poona and other adjacent places. In 1703 he captured Sinhagad and then encamped at Poona, which he named Muhiyabad. But the captured forts could not be long held in subjection : they were all recovered by the Marathas by the year 1705.

During all this time the miseries and hardships which the Emperor and his troops had to suffer went on increasing. They had to trudge through knee-deep mud and raging streams, dragging heavy guns, baggage and ammunition to hills and ramparts, thousands of feet high, not for one or two years but conducting such warfare in a foreign land continuously for a quarter of a century. This would have proved a feat of uncommon heroism if it had had an element of sentient reason in it. History finds in it only a comic picture of obstinacy with tragic results both to Aurangzeb's Empire and the humanity of India. Towards the end, the Emperor's fighting machine broke down ; risings became common, which required his attention and once more he moved to the south, into the Raichur Doab against the Bedar Chief of Wakinkheda and Surapur. After two years of vain struggle in that quarter he realized that his whole life had been entirely wasted and returned north in utter weariness and despair (... Ahmadnagar, in the midst of severe molestation and mortification caused by Maratha arrogance. Here he finally gave up his ghost on 20 February 1707. It is against the background of these moves of the Emperor, that the Maratha struggle can be properly understood.

5. **Jinji besieged.**—We must now go back to the year 1689, a year so full of rapid developments in the annals of this Mughal-Maratha struggle, the capture and death of Sambhāji, the fall of Raigad and the flight of Rājārām to Jinji, all occurring within a few months' time. Immediately on Zulfiqar Khan's arrival at Koregaon with Shāhu and his mother as captives, the Khan was ordered to pursue Rājārām into the eastern Karnatak. He left the Emperor's camp on 30th November, arrived before Jinji in the following June and at once laid siege to that fort. The siege lasted for nearly 8 years and has for various reasons become memorable in history : and although the place was captured at the end of that long struggle, the Maratha king had already escaped back to Mahārāshtra, thus adding to the disappointments and misfortunes of the Emperor.

The credit of retrieving the Maratha fortunes goes mainly to two men of uncommon ability, Rāmchandra Pant Amātya the consummate planner and Santāji Ghorpade Senapati the adroit executor. Santāji is called the perfect master of guerilla warfare. Santāji as a boy had served Shivaji and possibly Sambhāji also : but there is no evidence on record how he was occupied during the rule of the latter unfortunate monarch. Santāji suddenly emerged from oblivion in the sore need created by the fall of Raigad, when he was called upon to defend his

Chhatrapati and the Maratha raj. Writes Sarkar,[2] "Santāji had an inborn genius for handling large bodies of troops spread over a wide area, changing his tactics so as to take prompt advantage of every change in the enemy's plans and condition and organizing combined movements. The success of his tactics depended on the rapid movement of his troops and on his subordinates carrying out his orders punctually to the minute. He, therefore, insisted on implicit obedience from his officers and enforced the strictest discipline in his army by drastic punishments. As Khafi Khan writes, "Santa used to inflict severe punishments on his followers. For the slightest fault he would cause the offender to be trampled to death by an elephant." "His greatest monument is the abject fear he inspired in the ranks of the Mogul army, which faithfully reflected in the curses and abuses invariably used as the epithet to his name by Persian histories. As will be seen later Santāji's boastful and defiant demeanour made him odious to his master and his harsh ways made him equally disliked by his subordinates. This proved the cause of his ruin."

Dhanāji Jādhav was of a different type. Coming from the same family to which Shivaji's mother Jija Bai belonged, he supported and co-operated with Santāji wherever he was called upon to do so. Equally brave and fearless, Dhanāji possessed a milder temperament and certainly a sweeter tongue. The Mughal troops looked upon Dhanāji with such awe that Khafi Khan narrates how Mughal troops used to ask their horses, when they refused to drink, whether they had seen Dhanāji reflected in the water. Early in their career Dhanāji and Santāji inflicted a severe defeat upon Sharza Khan, alias Rustam Khan, as he was coming to capture the fort of Satara in May 1690.

6. **The Maratha aims.**—The aims of the Maratha government in prosecuting the arduous struggle against the Mughals are repeatedly stated in clear terms in the orders and charters issued by their rulers during this period of war. Hanumant Rav Ghorpade and his relation Krishnāji are definitely told on 4 June 1691 that,[3] "Having clearly grasped your

2. *Aurangzeb*, Vol. V, p. 128.
3. Sh. Ch. Sa. 5.767 in B. I. M. Quarterly 16.1.

readiness to quit the Mughal service and return to the king's for defending the Mahārāshtra Dharma, i.e., the cherished desire of the Maratha nation, we are assigning to you for your own personal expenses and those of your troops, an annuity of six lacs Hons (Rs. Twenty-five lacs) the first half of which, viz. three lacs is to be paid as soon as you establish possession over (1) the Raigad district, (2) the district of Bijapur, (3) the district of Bhāgānagar (Haiderabad) and (4) the district of Aurangabad, at the rate of ¾ of a lac for each of these items. The other half of the annuity, viz., three lacs more, will be paid as soon as you capture Delhi. You must loyally execute our commands, and our government will then continue their favour towards you." This is a typical instance out of many, which sets down the Maratha aims as a crusade of a religious character and of an abnormal magnitude. It was a severe and direct attack upon the Mahārāshtra religion, that their Chhatrapati was put to a cruel death and not allowed even the usual funeral rites. It should be noted that these aims included even the conquest of Delhi, so as to make the whole sub-continent of India safe for the Hindu religion, and no more destruction of temples and idols was to be tolerated. Aurangzeb's armies were mostly composed of Hindus, that is, the northern Rajputs and the southern Marathas: it was certainly his duty to respect the sentiments of those who served him. Rājārām's Government deliberately weaned away many Maratha Chiefs who had accepted Mughal service. Aurangzeb profusely offered lands, titles and rewards as inducements to Maratha leaders to renounce their king and accept his service. By way of counteraction the Maratha Government adopted the same methods. This religious motive of the present war appears to have been continued as a national demand throughout the later Maratha expansion directed by the Peshwas.

This statement of the Maratha aims is not confined to a few rare documents, but runs through most of the writings detailing the political transactions of the Maratha Government of that period. On 22 March 1690 Rājārām from Jinji assures Bāji Sarzarav Jedhe Deshmukh of Kari of his support, and inspires him how they should exert themselves in their national cause. "We have enlisted on arrival in the Karnatak forty thousand cavalry and a lac and a quarter of infantry. The local Palegars and fighting elements are fast rallying to the Maratha standard. Our raj now has a peculiar message for the people, and you as one of them already suffer the agonies of the wrongs inflicted upon it by the Mughals. You must now put forth the sacrifice required on behalf of our religion. We have despatched Keso Trimal Pingle to Mahārāshtra with a treasure of a lac of Hons, guarded by an escort of forty thousand armed men with Santāji and Dhanāji at their head. As soon as this party arrives in your part of the country, you must join it with your following with the utmost expedition, in order to overcome the common enemy. In fact the enemy is nothing of himself : it is people like you who have raised him into that importance. If our Marathas had not joined him, he would have been nowhere. You alone possess the nerve to overcome this Aurangzeb. He has wronged you by threatening to convert you to his religion. He has already converted Netaji and Sābāji Ghatge and Jānoji Rāje, in addition to several Brahmans also. He also entertains further deep-rooted motives of a sinister nature against our nation, of which you must beware. The Nimbālkars and the Mānes have already deserted him and his ranks are being rapidly thinned. God is helping us. We are sure to succeed." This letter only one among many is in the handwriting of Khando Ballāl, Rājārām's Chitnis and shows the depths to which the heart of the Maratha nation was stirred in this heroic crusade.

Without a careful study of such documents no correct judgment can be formed of this phase of Aurangzeb's activities in the south. This opposition was a supreme effort to save the Maratha hearth and home. The Hindu-pad sovereignty of the future days was to the Marathas from the beginning a sacred and dear question of preserving their religion, which was found impossible in the absence of political power. Animated by a desire to avenge their wrongs, the Maratha bands spread over the vast territories from Khandesh to the south coast, over Gujarat, Baglan, Gondvan, and the Karnatak, devastating Mughal stations, destroying their armies, exacting tribute, plundering Mughal treasures, animals and stocks of camp equipage. The Emperor soon found himself unable to cope with these methods. He could fight any large army in the open field, but the guerilla tactics, of stealthy secret attacks from inaccessible places and at awkward unsuspected hours, proved too much even for his vast and splendid resources. The Marathas were inured to all kinds of hardship. They could feed upon the most simple food, stand inclement weather, and so proved veritable ghosts to the average Mughal fighter.

Rāmchandra Pant took effective measures against the Maratha deserters to the Emperor. If a chief or man was discovered to side with the Mughals, their families and relations, their wives and children were arrested and sternly dealt with, so that life became intolerable in Mahārāshtra for such deserters, traitors and renegades. The Pisāl Deshmukhs of Wai who had surrendered Raigad to the Mughal force, had to undergo unbearable persecution for years and were reduced to the utmost misery, although they were amply rewarded by the Emperor for having accepted the Muslim faith. The respectable Beg family of Junnar had to suffer similar persecution.[4]

Yesu Bai from her confinement in the Mughal camp did not fail to keep constant contact with the Maratha leaders, and secretly supported them by sending out useful news, and frequent hints through private messengers, who went to and fro between the two camps on various pretexts. On Yesu Bai's advice Rājārām conveyed to Jinji his wives and their retinue. They sailed in a ship from Vengurla on the west coast escorted by the two brothers Lingo Shankar and Visāji Shankar, trusted relatives of Khando Ballāl Chitnis. They owned cargo ships plying in the western sea, which conveyed these ladies safely to the south in 1694.[5] The party consisted of Rājārām's three wives, Tārā Bai, Rājas Bai and Ambikā Bai and their retinue. They disembarked at Honāvar and travelling by the land route through the Bednur territory, reached Jinji safely in due course, unmolested by the pursuing enemy. While at Jinji Tārā Bai gave birth to a son (9 June 1696) and Rājas Bai did the same also two years later (23 May 1698). These two sons, named Shivaji and Sambhāji respectively, figured in the later developments of the Maratha State and originated the Kolhapur branch of the Chhatrapati's house.

4. Vide Pisal Papers, Rajwade, III, Nos. 56—64.

5. Vioaji Shankar's services are seen rewarded in a document dated 19 October 1694. P. D. 31.60.

7. **Besiegers besieged.**—The main object of the Maratha administrators and generals at this time was to release their Chhatrapati from Jinji, save him from a fate similar to his brother's, and liberate the Maratha territories from the Mughal control. The Emperor was by no means blind or ignorant on these points. Through obstinacy he pursued rigorous measures of war in preference to some kind of understanding or accommodation for putting an end to the hostilities. If he had taken a reasonable line of action and employed means to end the war on honourable terms, the Maratha rulers would certainly have welcomed that course and even accepted Aurangzeb's suzerainty, remaining content with a small subordinate principality in the Deccan. Several well-wishers of the Emperor did not hesitate to persuade him to this line of conduct. But he stoutly resisted it and suffered the consequences. The Marathas in retaliation managed to raise armies and develop a system of harassment, conquest and expansion, by which they regained not only their *Swarajya* of Shivaji's days, but also the right to levy *Chauthai* and *Sardeshmukhi* over the lands of Mahārāshtra and the Karnatak. Many of the original leaders died in the attempt, but their half-finished work was continued by the next generation with redoubled devotion and success.

For the first few years of the present phase of the war, Jinji formed the main objective of the Emperor's efforts for putting down the Marathas. Zulfiqar Khan exerted himself to the utmost, but was severely hampered by the hostile surroundings in which he was placed. He realized the hopelessness of subduing the Marathas under the prevailing conditions and tried for a time the policy of conciliating them. Very often the troops of Dhanāji and Santāji pressed him so hard from without, that instead of his besieging Jinji, he often found himself and his host surrounded and starved, so that in his extremity he had to raise the siege and seek replenishment of his forces in the outlying districts, during the summer of 1691.

At the end of 1692 Ali Mardan Khan a daring Mughal officer in charge of Kanchi, boldly came out and encountered Santāji Ghorpade with a view to preventing him from falling upon Zulfiqar Khan. A stiff action was fought on 13 Dec. 1692 in which Ali Mardan Khan was defeated and taken prisoner to Jinji, where he had to pay a large ransom to effect his release. Ismail Khan Maka, another Mughal general, was similarly dealt with by Dhanāji, (9 Jan. 1693). Thus Zulfiqar Khan found himself in sore straits. His two valiant helpmates Daud Khan Panni and Sarfaraz Khan also turned against him, making his situation precarious. His only recourse was to send frequent piteous appeals to the Emperor for reinforcements.

On receipt of such pressing appeal for help and funds, the Emperor sent him fresh contingent under his own son Kam Baksh and his minister Asad Khan, father of Zulfiqar Khan. But the arrival of these two important personages on the scene of Jinji towards the end of 1691, only created fresh complications and did anything but remove Zulfiqar Khan's difficulties. Kam Baksh followed the example set earlier by his brother Akbar. Asad Khan and Zulfiqar Khan charged the Prince with collusion with the Marathas and openly placed him under arrest in Dec. 1692. The confusion became worse confounded, when a false report went round that the Emperor had died. The two Khans abandoned their operations before Jinji and being severely pressed by the Marathas retired to Wandiwash under the most distressing circumstances, which are vividly described in Martin's Memoirs.

Zulfiqar and Asad Khan in utter despair of opposing the Marathas or even of saving themselves and the Emperor's son Prince Kam Baksh under their care in the siege camp before Jinji, paid a large sum to Rājārām and his minister and were thus permitted to withdraw to Wandiwash without serious opposition. This lame conclusion of their wonderful victories caused a rupture between the Maratha generals and Rājārām. Martin writes "The commanders who had come to Jinji from Mahārāshtra in December 1692, were extremely irritated that Rāmrājā without their participation, by the advice of his minister alone, had made a treaty with the Mughals. They bore a particular grudge against Rājārām's minister whom they accused of having received a large sum for allowing the Mughals to escape safely, when the Marathas could have held them all at their discretion, i.e., Kam Baksh, the Wazir Asad Khan and Zulfiqar Khan along with a large number of persons of rank who were in the army. The Maratha commanders represented that they could have extracted large sums as their ransom, besides being able to secure an advantageous treaty with the Emperor himself by restoring to him men of such importance. Santāji Ghorpade was so incensed by this conduct of Rājārām that he withdrew his troops to some leagues from Jinji. It was believed that Rājārām had acted in gratitude. He well knew that Zulfiqar could have easily taken Jinji. This mutual accommodation between Rājārām and Zulfiqar Khan was the result of a secret understanding, which they had formed in view of the expected death of the Emperor and the inevitable war of succession among his sons, so that Asad Khan and Zulfiqar planned to establish themselves as independent sovereigns in the southern peninsula with the kingdom of Golkonda as their share and the kingdom of Bijapur as the share of Rājārām." "Rājārām managed to appease Santāji by paying him a visit and also presents. Such squabbles throw a lurid light on the confused and mismanaged operations of the Mughal-Maratha war extending over the vast regions of Mahārāshtra and the Karnatak. For a time Santāji became the master of the situation and reaped the utmost advantage.

It is easy to understand why the siege of Jinji dragged on so languidly and how much on that account the Emperor became exasperated, when he was apprized of the true state of things at Jinji. To remedy the situation he despatched another competent and trusted general Kasim Khan, posting him midway on the road to Jinji so that he could crush the bands of Santāji and Dhanāji and enable Zulfiqar Khan to prosecute the siege without outside molestation. He instructed Zulfiqar Khan to capture both Jinji and Rājāram at a stroke. Kasim Khan, although an opium-addict as Khafi-Khan records, was indeed a tried and resourceful general, and was enthusiastic in carrying out the heavy task that was entrusted to him. But how he too was over-matched by the superior genius of Santāji has become a dazzling episode in the history of Indian warfare, to which it is now necessary to advert before taking up the story of Jinji.

8. Heroic deeds of Santāji.—On the occasion of the Dasarā celebration of October 1695, Rāmchandra Pant called

6. Sarkar's *House of Shivaji*, XIII, p. 219.

together at Vishālgad most of the responsible Maratha leaders for a conference and a personal consultation, with a view to taking stock of the situation as developed by the various scattered units wanting in cohesion and acting independently of each other, and for concerting effective measures to conduct a further offensive, as much to meet the danger signified by the Emperor's appointment of Kasim Khan, as to secure a rapid victory. They planned fresh grand operations: two main parties were formed, one to devastate the northern portions of the Mughal territories, and the other to operate in the region of the Tungabhadrā, so as to overcome Kasim Khan and relieve the pressure against the Chhatrapati at Jinji. Santāji agreed to execute the latter portion of the scheme, and Dhanāji was asked to remain in the region of Bijapur keeping an eye on the Emperor's moves as well as being ready to support Santāji if any danger threatened him. The Emperor was then camping at Brahmapuri, where he was soon apprized of the plans formed by Ramchandra Pant. He immediately despatched another tried general Himmat Khan to prevent Santāji from committing mischief. The two Mughal generals undertook what may be called a pincer movement to hem in Santāji both from front and behind. Dhanāji got scent of this move and made rapid marches towards the Karnatak to save the situation if it became serious. The Emperor became extremely ill at ease about the fate of his armies before the combined manoeuvres of Santāji and Dhanāji. Kasim Khan also reported to the Emperor how the situation was developing against him and pressed him for more troops and war material. In this crisis Aurangzeb selected another trustworthy young enthusiast, a rising star of his Court, Khanazad Khan, son of the revered Ruhulla Khan and despatched him with all haste to the south with a party of his own select body-guard, and several more tried officers, such as Safshikan Khan and Muhammad Murad Khan.

With such grand arrangements speedily set in motion, the Emperor felt confident that all would go well. These generals marched through the Karnatak regions and joined Kasim Khan at the beginning of November 1695. How Santāji overcame this critical situation is a marvel in the art of war. He was well served by his numerous spies, knew the terrain, as the sequel shows, changed his movements to suit the shifting situation and managed to win signal success out of what had appeared to be a terrific ordeal.

When Kasim Khan received the report that a noble of the high rank of Khanazad Khan was coming to his help, he thought it necessary to accord him a fitting reception. He ordered from Adoni costly tents, furniture and dining sets of high value, and arranged a gorgeous camp for his honoured guest, not suspecting danger in these open preparations. The Naik of Chitradurg who had been wronged by Kasim Khan, secretly communicated to Santāji all the vulnerable points of the Mughal arrangements and the shrewd Santāji was not slow to take full advantage of it. He arranged his troops in three parties assigning definite tasks to each, so as to fall upon the various Mughal chiefs separately, before they could join. Just before Kasim Khan's arrival at the decorated camp for the reception of Khanazad Khan, Santāji suddenly swooped down upon it in the small hours of the morning and set the whole place on fire. No sooner was the occurrence reported to Kasim Khan than he hurriedly attacked Santāji and was himself shortly after joined by Khanazad Khan. Santāji was quite prepared for such an eventuality and had kept a concealed reserve force near, which suddenly fell upon these attackers and caught them between two opposing bodies. Unable to withstand the withering fire of the Marathas, the two Khans escaped in consternation to a small neighbouring citadel called Duderi, about 22 miles east of Chitaldurg. "The imperialists, giving up all plan of fighting took the road to Duderi in confusion, reached the place in extreme difficulty and were invested."[7] Santāji quickly followed and at once closely surrounded the place, which had in it no food or water and which was not prepared to stand a long siege. The Mughals found themselves in extreme peril during three days of want and starvation and exposure to the deadly effect of the Maratha guns. Kasim Khan was addicted to a regular use of opium which he could not now procure and died on 20th November 1695 in agonies consequent on such privation. It was reported that he swallowed poison and put an end to his life for fear of being disgraced by the Emperor. Poor Khanazad Khan appealed to Santāji's

7. Sarkar's *Aurangzeb*, V. 113.

mercy and surrendered. Santāji was not wanting in magnanimity to a fallen foe. He accepted Rs. 20 lacs by way of ransom in addition to all the belongings of the camp, worth about 30 lacs more, gave his own escort to accompany the noble Khan back to the Emperor's presence, with a personal message to him to take back this human treasure, as his own worst enemy. Kasim Khan had already paid for his sins.

9. **Santaji's tragic end.**—As these developments were being reported to the Emperor, he had already despatched another brave general Hamid-ud-din Khan with a full fighting train to the relief of the first two forces. Another Mughal officer Himmat Khan Bahadur who was not far off, also came in hurriedly to pounce upon the Marathas. Santāji encountered Himmat Khan and his son in a sanguinary action near Basawa-Pattan in which both the father and the son were routed and killed (20 January 1696). Then came Hamid-ud-din Khan who was able with his fresh troops to inflict a defeat upon Santāji and put him to flight (26 February), as his men were already fully exhausted and wearied after months of severe fighting. The story of these wonderful achievements of Santāji reverberated throughout the land causing high admiration in Maratha hearts and extreme depression in those of the Mughals. But Santāji was now to experience a sudden fall. Providence had not provided him with a suave tongue or an agreeable temper. There was only one person whom Santāji respected and obeyed, and that was Rāmchandra Pant who was far away in Mahārāshtra.

A large number of the letters that passed between them during all these years has been published and these clearly show how difficult Rāmchandra Pant found the task of handling Santāji. The general is here repeatedly admonished to be sweet and accommodating towards his co-workers and superiors and particularly towards the Chhatrapati. Santāji's biting tongue and boastful demeanour had more than once disgusted Rājārām. After these unequalled successes over the various Mughal generals, Santāji went straight to Jinji (April 1695), and demanded an adequate reward for his services. But Rājārām and Santāji had become gradually so estranged that a severe altercation took place between them, which soon rose to bitter invective. Both were touched to the quick. Santāji openly charged Rājārām with pusillanimity and disburdened his mind to some such effect. "Your position is all due to me. I can make and unmake the Chhatrapati." This was too much even for the mild temper of the King. Santāji was at once dismissed from his office of Senapati and Dhanāji appointed in his place.[8]

How could it be expected that a hero of Santāji's calibre, a winner of a hundred battles would meekly submit to such insult, or hand over his office to a successor without striking a blow? The Emperor had already advertised a prize on Santāji's head. It is not necessary to suppose that the Mughals had any hand in bringing about a mortal ill-feeling between Dhanāji and Santāji. From words they came to blows over the question as to which of them should hold the Senapati's office. In June 1696 they fought an action near Aiwargudi on the river Manimukta near Kanchi, in which Dhanāji was worsted and his valiant young partizan Amrit Rao Nimbalkar was taken prisoner, whom Santāji cruelly trampled to death under the feet of an elephant. This Amrit Rao's sister Rādhā Bai was married to Nāgoji Māne of Mhaswad near Satara. Nāgoji was playing a game of selfish ambition and intriguing with the Emperor for the destruction of Santāji. In this he was encouraged by his wife Rādhā Bai out of a desire to avenge the death of her brother. The monsoon months of 1696 passed critically for Santāji on the one hand and for Rājārām and Dhanāji on the other. As Santāji was not to be easily overcome, his followers were seduced and won over by secret methods. In this destructive game Nāgoji Māne had a principal share. Santāji's ranks came to be slowly thinned and his strength fearfully weakened. Indeed many instances are found recorded of Maratha Sardars constantly plying between the two opposing camps during this long drawn war in which time-serving selfishness and divided loyalties played no small part.

Rājārām ordered Dhanāji to capture Santāji and bring him a prisoner before him. Santāji then fled away, being hotly pursued by Dhanāji from the Karnatak into Mahārāshtra. During the flight they fought an action near Bijapur in which

8. Vide P. D. 31.68 dated 27 Oct. 1696; Sanads and Letters by Mawji and Parasnis, p. 177.

Santāji sustained a severe defeat in March 1697, and to save his life he made his way into the hills of Mahadev east of Satara. He had only a few personal servants left with him in his solitary wanderings. Nāgoji Māne hung on his track. One hot noon in June 1697 as Santāji came to a spring and was having his bath, some armed men suddenly fell upon him, cut off his head and brought it to Nāgoji Māne, who immediately rode with it to the Emperor's camp at Brahmapuri and presented the head to him. In return Nagoji obtained the promised reward and a handsome jagir from the Emperor, who was highly pleased with this end of his mortal enemy.[8] Santāji is now remembered as the past master of guerilla warfare, the highest and best instrument which enabled the Marathas to attain a rapid rise before the development of artillery warfare in India. The death of this unmatched hero was a severe blow to the Maratha fortunes.

10. **Guerilla warfare described.**—This peculiar form of war-fare called by the Marathas Ganimi-Kava requires a word of explanation. The Marathas took pride in being called *ganims* or "plunderers," and developed their peculiar method of fighting which the chronicler Chitnis thus describes. "The Mughal forces are huge in numbers, standing firm only in open ground. The Marathas on the other hand suddenly erupt at one place to-day and tomorrow elsewhere some fifty miles away. Then they come round again and execute unexpected raids, making only a show of a fight, plunder and fly away. They fall upon foraging parties, attack weakly held Mughal posts, capture strategic points and thus inspire confidence among their followers. They devastate Mughal territory from the river Godavari to Bhaganagar, carrying away pack animals, horses and elephants, create confusion among the enemy, and remain concealed in unfrequented thickets widely apart and make a sudden dash upon the Mughal armies proceeding to-

8. There are various versions of the circumstances under which Santāji met his tragic death. The exact truth is nowhere recorded. Passions were then running high and gave colour to a variety of tales. Sir Jadhunath has tried his best to evolve a most likely story after consulting the Persian, French and other sources. See his *House of Shivaji*, pp. 215-238 ; also his *Aurangzib*, Vol. V.

wards Jinji, occasionally engaging in an open encounter and any how preventing them from reaching their destination. The Emperor found himself non-plussed how to overcome these pests. They seemed to be ubiquitous and illusive like the wind. When the attacking Mughal forces had gone back, the scattered Marathas, like water parted by the oar, closed again and resumed their attack as before." "If a Mughal officer resisted the Marathas and was defeated and captured by them, he had to provide his own ransom, and the Emperor would often dismiss such unfortunate sufferers on the suspicion of cowardice. Hence it was safer for a Mughal commander to bribe the Marathas than to fight them. Certainly it was cheaper. Worse than these, many imperialists made a concert with the enemy and enriched themselves by robbing the Emperor's own subjects and innocent traders.[9]

"Thus the Marathas held their life as trash and defended their raj. They were rewarded with lands and titles. On the one side stands the Emperor with his whole might, countless forces, immeasurable treasure carried in thousands and thousands of train-carts; on the other side these scanty numbers of the poor Marathas carefully husbanding life and resources but relentlessly acting like packs of wolves against Mughal hordes and creating dearth of comfort in the midst of their own plenty.[10]

Santāji left behind him an inspiring name and a large family of brothers and nephews, who fortunately did not imbibe his spirit of insubordination and irascible temper: nor did they entertain any traces of hatred towards Dhanāji Jādhav, who had been already exalted to the position of the *Senapati.* They all joined him in continuing the war with full cordial co-operation, and when after the fall of Jinji, Rājārām and his Court returned to Mahārāshtra, it was the combined effort of all the Ghorpades that conquered and saved the distant Karnatak lands for the Maratha dominion, leaving a precious legacy to one of their distinguished descendants, Murār Rao of Gutti, whose career extending over more than half a century of troublesome times, forms an important part in Maratha his-

9. *Rajaram's life* by Chitnis, pp. 41-43; Sarkar: Vol. V. p. 12.
10. Grant Duff, Vol. I, p. 338, describes this guerilla warfare.

tory. Gajendragad, Sandur, Kapsi, and other small principalities in the south are still extant as reminders of the departed glory of the Ghorpades.

11. **Rajaram escapes, Jinji falls.**—The death of Santāji at once transferred the scene of hostile activities from the Karnatak to Mahārāshtra. The Emperor was vehemently urging Zulfiqar Khan to make a rapid conclusion of the siege of Jinji and sent him severe reprimands against his dilatory methods. In December 1697 Rājārām managed to escape from the besieging forces, reached Vellore and returned to Mahārāshtra, the news of which made the Emperor furious against Zulfiqar Khan, who would certainly have been degraded and punished if the Emperor had been on the spot. The Khan at last reported that Jinji had been captured on 7 February 1698, after allowing the ladies of Rājārām unmolested exit to their home. They returned to Vishālgad in due course. Pralhād Nirāji's son Nāro Pralhād was taken captive and put to death, in order to satisfy the Emperor that some persons were captured as prisoners and put to death. Zulfiqar Khan was rewarded with the title of Nusrat Jung. Historians compare this long siege of Jinji to the siege of Troy of Grecian antiquity. The possession of Jinji did not avail the Mughals much. They transferred their seat of government from Jinji to Arcot.

Rājārām after escaping from Jinji, proceeded to Vishālgad, (22 Feb. 1698), eluding the Emperor's strong parties on the route. He at this time made some overtures for peace directly to the Emperor, but the latter declined the offer and continued the war relentlessly. As soon as the Chhatrapati arrived in the Maratha land, it became necessary to have a capital from which the Maratha Government could act. Both Raigad and Jinji had been lost. Vishālgad was too inaccessible for purposes of easy communication so necessary in administrative work. The fort of Satara, therefore, was selected as a suitable centre well protected by nature, and here Rājārām established his seat about the Dassara time of 1698. Satara was, however, soon afterwards captured by Aurangzeb, but retaken by the Marathas in 1704. It again became the seat of Maratha Government after the return of Shāhu from the Mughal camp in 1708 and acquired the name of Shahunagar.

Rājārām during 1698 and the next year made an extensive tour of his country, established contact with local officers and the guardians of forts, and cheered up by his personal presence the drooping spirits of his wearied soldiers. During this tour of inspection, he discovered clear evidence of the decline of the Mughal power. The Emperor was already too old to control the extensive and conflicting elements of his government. Every soldier was tired of the war in which the Emperor obstinately persisted and in which no Mughal had any heart. The Emperor's sons and officers looked more to their personal prospects than to the details of war and thought only of the eventual changes that were sure to follow the Emperor's death. Buland Bakht, the Raja of Devgad, who like the Maratha kings, was manfully resisting Mughal aggression in his territory, sent his agents to Rājārām proposing a combined attack upon the northern possessions of the Emperor. Rājārām thereupon deputed Nemāji Sinde with some other chiefs to ravage Khandesh and Berar and exact *Chauth* from those districts. Early in 1699 Nemāji encountered the Mughal governor of Talner, Husain Ali Khan, captured him in a sanguinary action and released him after exacting a fine of two lacs from him. This news distressed the Emperor beyond measure.

At the Dasara season of 1699 Rājārām himself set out from Satara accompanied by several young leaders of future fame such as Khanderao Dābhāde, Parsoji Bhosle, Haibatrao Nimbālkar, with Dhanāji Jādhav at their head. They gave out that they were going to march upon Surat and plunder that rich town. The Emperor in order to ward off this danger, despatched a strong body of his troops against them. Several skirmishes occurred between the Maratha raiders and these Mughal detachments. During November Rājārām himself was stopped from proceeding to the north by Zulfiqar Khan and was compelled to turn back. He came straight to Brahmapuri for raiding the Mughal camp and if possible taking possession of Shahu. Indeed how high the Maratha spirits had risen at this moment is evidenced by Rājārām's letter addressed to Vithoji Babar on 22 December 1699 in which he writes, "We have arrived at Sinhagad and have launched the full force of our armies against the Emperor. The Senapati Dhanāji, Nemāji Sinde, Persôji Bhosle and other leaders have led a furious attack upon the imperial camp of Brahmapuri and captured the Emperor's own daughter along with several prominent families. Thereafter they fell upon a convoy of ten thousand pack animals carrying supplies to the imperial forces which were marching upon Satara. The enemy has lost all courage, and can make no effect against fort Satara. We now take no account of this powerful Emperor whom, God willing, we shall soon put to rout. You must do your best in this joint effort. We are rewarding your services in an ample measure."[11]

12. **Rajaram's death and character.**—At this moment of triumph and rising hope, however, the Maratha nation was ordained to suffer a serious loss. Rājārām found the strain of camp life unbearable and his health suddenly gave way. He became ill on the way during his march and had to be carried in a palanquin at a time when Satara was being besieged by the Emperor : so Rājārām made for Sinhagad where he expired immediately after arrival on 2 March 1700, having just completed 30 years of his life. This untimely death of their Chhatrapati following Santāji's tragic end, was another serious blow to the rising fortunes of his nation. One of his wives Ambikā Bai burnt herself on hearing of her husband's death, but the two other wives Tārā Bai and Rājas Bai, long survived him and played their part in future politics.

Rājārām's character and capacity have been already described in the preceding pages. He possessed no dash or initiative, nor did he ever evince any personal valour. He was only ten years of age when his father died and had received no education during his detention on the fort of Raigad at the hands of his elder brother. Rājārām has left no writing behind like the Sanskrit and Hindi compositions of Sambhāji. His mother was put to death and Rājārām had no congenial company in his boyhood. At the death of Sambhāji, sheer chance brought Rājārām to his father's throne. He fortunately obtained wise and able counsellors in Rāmchandra Pant and Pralhād Nirāji, and equally brave warriors in Santāji and Dhanāji. There is not a single occasion recorded in his life on which Rājārām showed personal daring or capacity for government.

11. *History of the Pratinidhis*, Vol. 3, p. 451.

When his mentor Pralhād Nirāji died in 1694, Rājārām's affairs went rapidly on the decline. That he could not handle Santāji properly or at least prevent his murder, is a sad commentary on his power of control. His mind and body were both weak, due possibly to dissipation and the use of opium to which he is said to have been addicted. His virtue was of a negative kind, non-interference. What Rājārām lacked was amply made up by his spirited queen Tārā Bai as the sequel will show.[12]

Just before Rājārām's death the Emperor tried to seduce Rāmchandra Pant and Parashurām Pant from allegiance to their master by means of a singular trick. He wrote letters to the two offering inducements, and contrived that the one addressed to Rāmchandra Pant should fall into the hands of Parashurāmpant and vice versa. The two grew suspicious of each other for a time, but soon learned the real motive of their common enemy.

During the regime of this Chhatrapati Rājārām, one serious departure from Shivaji's policy came about through the force of circumstances, *viz.* the system of conferring lands on military commanders for their services. Shivaji had strictly prohibited the grant of land on any account for services rendered to the State, which he always paid in cash. But during the confused situation created by the war and the presence in the Deccan of the Emperor, his whole Court and his huge armies, Shivaji's healthy precept had to be given up. The Emperor himself offered gifts of land to the Maratha gentry by way of inducements, and unless similar inducements were offered by the Maratha government, it could not raise the required armies for the conduct of the war. The Maratha leaders and soldiers were openly asked to ravage Mughal territories and conquer lands on promise that these would form their own hereditary possession, when the Maratha *raj* would come to be fully established. These leaders of Maratha bands had to borrow funds

12. Rājārām's seal contains a motto which can thus be rendered in English : "Like the King Rāma of old this seal of King Rāma shines forth, impelled by the motive of inspiring all people alike with a sense of their national duty."

धर्मप्रद्योतिताशेषवर्णा दाशरथेरिव । राजारामस्य मुद्रेयं विश्ववंद्या विराजते.

from bankers on the mortgage of their prospective conquests, and created personal interests in the lands they laid their hands on. Started indeed as a measure under the stress of war in order to put down the Emperor's sinister designs, this system of jagirs came to be the virtual foundation of the future Maratha rule. In the long run it proved to be a ready instrument both for the rapid expansion and the equally rapid ruin of the Maratha Empire. Masses of published papers confirm this view and supply ample evidence of it.[13]

---

13. See Rājwāde, Vol. 8.52.

CHRONOLOGY

CHAPTER XV

1696	Balaji Vishwanath Sar-Subahdar of Poona.
1700 March 2	Death of Rajaram ; Shivaji II crowned by Tarabai.
„ Apr. 21	Aurangzeb captures Satara and Parli forts.
„ Aug. 17	Shahu reported as ailing.
1701 May 28	Aurangzeb captures Panhala.
1702 June 4	Aurangzeb captures Vishalgad.
„ ending months	Balaji Vishwanath defends Sinhagad.
1703 April 8	Aurangzeb captures Sinhagad.
„	Aurangzeb encamps at Poona ; orders Shahu's conversion.
„ Novr.	Shahu married and entrusted to Kam Bakhsh for negotiating his release.
„	Ray-Bhanji Bhosle accepts Emperor's service.
1704	Fort Satara recaptured by the Marathas.
1705 April 17	Yesubai's letter of distress in captivity.
„	The Marathas ravage Mughal territory beyond the Narmada.
1706 Feb. 6	Shahu temporarily released.
1707 Feb. 20	Death of Aurangzeb.

CHAPTER XV

RETRIBUTION

[1700—1707]

1. Tarabai opposes the Emperor.
2. Shahu in captivity.
3. Contact with Balaji Vishwanath.
4. Raybhanji Kaka.
5. Piteous appeal of Yesubai.
6. Tragedy of Aurangzeb's life.
7. Aurangzeb's death.
8. Tarabai triumphant.

1. Tarabai opposes the Emperor.—Rājārām died at Sinhagad on 2 March 1700, a little over a month before his newly established capital Satara followed the fate of Raigad ten years before. Since the return of Rājārām from Jinji the aged Emperor, sorely disappointed in his hope of overcoming the Marathas and feeling that his commandants did not exert themselves earnestly enough in the tasks assigned to them, had taken upon himself the work of personally leading his forces in the difficult region of the western Ghats. His officers and soldiers became wearied of this continuous camp life and its interminable hardships. Yet the Emperor would not flinch. With the greatest effort in 6 years (1699-1704), he was able to capture only four major forts with a few minor ones of no importance to his strategy. These were Satara (21 April 1700), Panhala (28 May 1701), Vishalgad (4 June 1702) and Sinhagad (8 Apr. 1703). Even these were only nominally secured mainly by payment of money and were quickly recaptured by the Marathas after a year or so, as soon as the Emperor had turned his back upon Maharashtra and proceeded to the Berad country in the south. It is noteworthy that during the siege of Vishalgad Sawai Jaisinh, the young ruler of Jaipur, played a conspicuous part both in the arduous task of fighting and in the subsequent negotiations for its surrender, whereby he established relations of amity with some of the Maratha leaders and the young Shahu, who was then living as a captive in the imperial camp. This early contact proved a prominent factor in the Mughal-Maratha relations as they afterwards developed in the hands of the first two Peshwas.[1]

The conquered forts were all given new names in the Muhammadan style by the Emperor, but those names have not survived in popular use. Satara was renamed Azam-tara, Parali Navrastara, Panhala Nabishahdurg and so on. But the conquest of Sinhagad in 1703 gave such supreme satisfaction to the Emperor's heart that he gave it the significant name *Bakshinda Baksh*, "a reward given by the Almighty."

As soon as Rāmchandra Pant Amātya learnt of Rājārām's death, he repaired to Sinhagad and immediately issued letters conveying the news to the various captains encouraging and begging them all to continue to perform their duties as before, and to exert themselves even more vigorously, remembering that the destinies of their nation were in their keeping. He also invited some prominent persons to attend the funeral rites of the late king, and held deliberations with them on the future plans. In deference to Tarabai's wishes her little son Shivaji, less than four years old at the time, was a few months later crowned Chhatrapati at Vishalgad,[2] although the rightful succession of Shahu was not excluded. Indeed, so far as the war was concerned, Tarabai for a time inspired greater vigour and enthusiasm among the whole Maratha nation than her husband had done. Unfortunately, her hopes and position came soon to be seriously weakened by the discovery that her little son was deficient in mental powers and not competent to manage the concerns of the State. For the present, however, Tarabai exhibited wonderful powers of organization and inspired one and all with a sense of devotion to the national service. Panhala and Vishalgad, both inaccessible strongholds, were selected as the Chhatrapati's residence, and on this account the Emperor doubtless directed his next effort to their capture during the years 1701 and 1702.

2. Shahu in captivity.—In order to follow clearly the Mughal-Maratha struggle in its essentials, it is necessary here

1. For details of Aurangzeb's last effort and struggles, the reader is referred to Sir Jadunath's full account.

2. They mostly resided at Panhala also, but the throne was never removed to Panhala.

to take particular note of the manner Shāhu led his life in the Emperor's camp, as he was destined to be the future Chhatrapati of the Marathas. When Raigad was captured by Zulfiqar Khan on 3rd November 1689 Sambhāji's Rani Yesubai, then about 30 years of age and her young son Shāhu of seven years, two illegitimate sons of Sambhāji named Madan Sinh and Madhav Sinh, Rani Sakwarbai, the sole surviving widow of the great Shivāji, with a following of about 200 men and women were captured and taken to the Emperor's camp. Here they had to spend seventeen years in captivity which dimmed all their hopes in this world; and although ultimately Shāhu came out of the bitter trial safe, there was during the interval constantly hanging over his head the sword of an unknown fate, well acquainted as he was with the Emperor's methods of dealing with an opponent, blinding an enemy, converting him to his faith or imprisoning him for life. Those who accuse Shāhu of pusillanimity, engendered by the luxuries of a soft palace life, forget that he never had been to Delhi and seen the palace life of that capital. He had constantly to undergo the same privations and hardships as the fighting members of the Emperor's camp, in addition to being a closely watched prisoner, a pawn in the Emperor's game to be utilized as occasion would require.

During the eight months that had elapsed between the death of Sambhāji and the capture of Raigad, the Emperor had a sufficient foretaste of the audacity and toughness of the Maratha nation, which made him wiser in dealing with these fresh captives. He naturally became more cautious and politic than vengeful as in the case of Sambhāji. He abandoned all thought of making short work with these innocent and hapless captives, and ordered that Shāhu and his mother should be accommodated in enclosed quarters near his daughter's, and adjoining his own residential tent ; and that their servants and followers should have another detached spot assigned to them, certainly within the main enclosure, but at a long distance from each other, in order to prevent easy or frequent communication between the two parties. These servants' quarters came to be known as the "Rani's Bazaar". Sufficient subsistence allowance within the limits of bare existence, was here assigned to each member of the party according to his rank to appease

Maratha sentiment. Towards Shāhu himself Aurangzeb deliberately adopted an attitude quite the reverse of that towards his father. He styled Shāhu as the legitimate Maratha king and gave him the title of "Raja", with the nominal dignity of a seven-thousand commander.

Throughout the Emperor's residence in the Deccan, his domestic affairs were looked after by his daughter Zinat-un-Nisa Begam, an intelligent, pains-taking and kind-hearted lady, unmarried, now 47 years old (born on 5 October 1643), to whose care the Emperor entrusted the prisoners Shāhu and Yesubai.[3] The Begam was born of the same mother as the Emperor's rebel son Akbar, and like him entertained a tender feeling for the Marathas, being by nature of a pious philosophical outlook upon life. She, therefore, felt a deep interest and compassion for Yesubai and her son, who on this account developed a sense of filial reverence for her, which endured long after Aurangzeb's death. This Zinat-un-Nisa built a mosque at Delhi out of her own private money and died in 1721. When, therefore, Balaji Vishwanath led an expedition to Delhi in 1718, Zinat-un-Nisa must have, one may presume, helped Yesubai's release and return. She was certainly instrumental in letting Shāhu go back to the Deccan from the river Narmada in 1707.

Any way this lady's kind offices doubtless softened the rigours of Shāhu's imprisonment and in a great measure ameliorated the prisoners' lot. For whatever the wishes or command of the Emperor might be, their immediate execution was in the hands of the Begam. A woman alone could sympathise with the lot of Sambhāji's widow. Jyotyaji Kesarkar, Bhaktaji Huzra and Banki Gaikwad are mentioned out of the many followers of Shāhu, as having kept up close touch between these Maratha inmates in the camp and the warring Marathas outside it.

In her dealings with the Emperor, Yesubai feigned from the beginning an attitude of hostility towards Rājārām and his

3. This is presumably the same lady who is known in popular anecdotes to have pleaded for Shivaji's life being saved during his visit to Agra in 1666 and whose hand Sambhaji is said to have asked for, just before he was put to death.

Government. She declared that Rājārām saved his own life by escaping, and purposely allowed her to be captured at the fall of Raigad ; and that now they all looked to the Emperor's mercy for their safety and comfort. This attitude was long and successfully kept up in order to lull the Emperor's suspicion about her treachery. Shahu's real name was Shivāji, and on arrival at the camp, Aurangzeb called him Shivāji the *Sav* (honest) in contrast with his wily grand-father. This word *Sav* is said to have been corrupted into Shāhu (Sādhu, Sahu) by which name he thereafter continued to be known. Although to all appearance Aurangzeb treated him kindly, his object was to make use of him as circumstances would require in his project of subduing the Maratha country. Once or twice Rājārām tried to effect Shāhu's release by means of a sudden and secret attack upon the camp : but these attempts failed. Once, it is recorded, when Shāhu came to make his obedience to the Emperor, the latter asked him, " I am ready to send you back to your uncle, are willing to go ? " " No ", replied Shāhu, " My uncle is my enemy, as he was my father's too. If I go to him, he will keep me in rigorous confinement. I will go back only when Your Majesty puts me firmly on the throne as a legitimate sovereign of the Marathas." What to do with Shāhu was thus a source of perennial anxiety to the Emperor. He often thought of converting him to the Muslim faith and making him a vassal-prince ruling the Maratha land. He omitted no occasion for creating disunion in the Maratha nation by asserting Shāhu's claim against Tarabai's son. But these attempts did not prove successful in his life-time.

Shāhu thus acquired no education to fit him for life. He practised some riding, hunting and swordsmanship within the limits of the camp. He learnt to write Modi characters, and letters are extant in which he has fully and freely expressed his sentiments in that script. He did not know Sanskrit, nor did he have occasion to learn his own religion or the traditional Hindu mythology. On the contrary, placed as he was, he developed respect for the Muslim faith through intimate contact with the orthodox life of the Mughal court pattern. It may truly be said that he knew more of the Muslim religion than of his own. But his mind grew alert, quick and watchful, and tossed as he was in the midst of the turmoils of a raging war, he had plenty of thrilling experiences and acquired a sturdy common sense, a discerning faculty to assess correctly the merits and weaknesses of human character, a mortal fear to do wrong and a genial philanthropic temperament. The life of the Mughal camp was sufficiently varied and not altogether monotonous, and Shāhu freely participated in it.

With his advance to manhood Shāhu's troubles increased beyond measure, particularly after 1699, when the Emperor himself set out on the work of capturing the difficult Maratha forts. While the news of Rājārām's premature death gladdened the Emperor's heart, it distressed Shāhu's so acutely that he became ill and was for a time confined to bed. The malady affected his mind and body to some extent. It is recorded that on 26 August 1700, Shāhu who was ailing, paid a visit to the Emperor and made his bow when the latter said, "Raje, you look very weak and pale." Hafiz Ambar who was standing by, explained the reason by saying, "The Raja does not touch *dal* and rice. He feeds only on sweets : his religion enjoins that in a state of imprisonment, a Hindu should not eat a full dinner but must live on light refreshments." Thereupon the Emperor ordered, "Take him to Hamid-ud-din Khan. He will cure the ailment." This dyspepsia leading to fever and jaundice seems to have troubled Shāhu long. It is mentioned that he took the bath of recovery on the 4th June preceding.

Rājārām's death and the accession of Tarabai to power in the Maratha State considerably changed the state of affairs in the Deccan. Before this, the Emperor had succeeded in setting up an administration for the conquered territories, particularly the country between Satara and Aurangabad. Most of the leading families and the common populace of this region, chiefs and sardars, bankers and accountants had accepted the Emperor's service. The papers of various families in this tract of the country, such as the Purandares, the Bokils, the Atres, the Joshis, the Gijres, the Devs of Chinchwad, the Brahmes of Chakan and so on have been printed. The members of these families were regularly employed by the Emperor in the various branches of the administration, but at the same time the Maratha Chhatrapati also claimed their services and allegiance, so that a kind of double government continued for some years, the Mughals ruling by right of conquest and the Marathas by right of possession. Friction and rivalry of a serious nature thus went on, dividing the loyalties of the common residents and of the average officials during the time of the war, and even later after hostilities had been formally closed by the Emperor's death. It was during this period of double government that Shāhu came to cultivate a more or less intimate contact with some of these local families and their prominent members, particularly money-lenders, who often satisfied his immediate needs of money and did other services to relieve his difficulties. This is quite plain from the various records of his reign, in which he acknowledges these obligations with gratefulness and rewards them by gifts of land and money. He always considered it his pious duty to remember and repay every act of kindness shown to him during this hard period of captivity extending over seventeen years.[4]

3. **Contact with Balaji Vishvanath.**—One outstanding figure hitherto entirely unknown to the world outside, now appears on the stage of Maratha politics and works in favour of Shāhu, viz., Bālāji Vishvanāth Bhat, whom later on Shāhu appointed his Peshwa and who was instrumental in changing the entire character of the Maratha Government. When and how Shāhu came to know him and why he decided to raise him to the first position in the State, are questions which have not been convincingly solved. He was a hereditary Deshmukh of Shriwardhan on the west coast under the jurisdiction of the Siddis of Janjira, and appears to have migrated to the region of Poona possibly during the last days of Shivaji's reign. Definite evidence is available that he was the Sarsubahdar of the Poona division since 1696 and of the Daulatabad division from 1704 onwards, under orders of the Maratha Government. We possess letters issued by Ramchandra Nilkanth Amātya and other ministers to Balaji Vishvanath, calling upon him to ex-

4. A modi *bakhar* containing 143 pages, the first 16 and the last few missing, exists at the Osmania University, Haiderabad (Dec.), which records some interesting details of Shāhu's life in captivity. A few stray leaves of this same book were discovered at Poona and printed in 1915 by the Bh. I. S. Mandal, *Tritiya-Sammelan Vritta*, pages 85-90.

plain certain matters, to execute certain measures and occasionally reprimanding him for dereliction of duty. In 1702 when the Emperor invested Sinhagad, Balaji Vishvanath, writing on behalf of the Senapati Dhanāji Jadhav, sent an insistent request to his co-worker Ambāji Trimbak Purandare for a supply of gun-powder which was urgently needed for the defence of that fort against Tarbiat Khan the Artillery officer of Aurangzeb. To rise to the position of a Sarsubahdar in 1696 Balaji must have served in the lower grades of the Rajah's service for a long time before. But his antecedents are altogether unknown. We know that after capturing the fort of Sinhagad in April 1703, the Emperor cantoned at Poona during the monsoon months of that year, when it is presumed, the question of Shāhu's conversion and release seriously agitated Aurangzeb's mind. He issued orders that on a certain day Shāhu should be converted to the Muslim faith, a measure which dreadfully distressed Shāhu and his mother. They gave up eating food, began to starve themselves and begged the Begam Saheb to intervene in their favour and plead with the Emperor to cancel his order for his conversion.

But the Emperor was obdurate, and only relented so far as to concede that Shāhu would be spared on condition that two prominent Maratha youths offered themselves for conversion in his place ; his order once issued must have its course. Shāhu then begged Khandoji and Jagjivan, two sons of Shivaji's Senapati Prataprao Gujar, who were his companions in captivity in the Emperor's camp, to offer themselves for the sacrifice. They were accordingly converted and renamed Abdur-Rahim and Abdur-Rahman. Shāhu later gave these two men in Inam the village of Salgaum which is near Parli and is still enjoyed by their descendants,—both the Hindu and the Muslim branches living in amity and neighbourhood close to each other.

In the month of November 1703 two suitable brides were selected for Shāhu, one from the Sinde family of Kanerkhed and the other a daughter of Manaji Rustumrao Jadhav of Sindkhed, and Shāhu was married to them with fitting ceremony under the Emperor's direction. A third intelligent lady named Virubai was selected to supervise Shāhu's harem and remained ever after with him as an illegitimate wife.

We may presume that Balaji Vishvanath as the representative of the Maratha Government at Poona, must have had a private hand in these affairs of Shāhu and might even have been consulted. His services must have been laid under requisition by the Mughal officials for supplies of provisions and materials of war. Balaji certainly carried out his duties securely in Poona in the midst of Mughal hosts occupying the country, and formed intimate contacts with several local families and persons of influence. His diplomatic skill and circumspect conduct, on the one hand in guarding the interests of his own nation in the midst of war, and, on the other, in forming friendships with several Mughal officials of high rank, became quite obvious under the delicate circumstances of the double government then prevailing, and must have been closely noticed and appreciated by Shāhu who was on the spot. It is also said that Balaji had secret means of approach to Begam Zinat-un-Nisa's counsels and through her, guarded Shāhu's interests at great risk to his life. The words applied to him by Shāhu viz. "a servant of incomparable ability,"* convey indeed a testimony involving personal experience.

4. **Raybhanji Kaka.**—Shivaji's father Shahji had several illegitimate sons, one of whom by name Raybhanji managed to get into the Mughal employment about 1703 and helped Shāhu to the best of his power. He was then popularly known as Bhanji Kaka. The Emperor created him a commander of six thousand and often employed him as a medium of communication with the Maratha Government. After 1703 the Emperor began to entertain serious ideas of closing the war on honourable terms and returning to Delhi. It was in this connection that he found Raybhanji serviceable, as his close personal association with men and affairs of the Deccan during the last several years gave him a unique position. Raybhanji lived to see Shāhu properly crowned at Satara at a later date.

To all appearances the Emperor showed deep interest and great concern in the well-being of Shāhu, and thought it the best means of closing the war to release him and send him to claim from his aunt his paternal right to the Maratha throne.

* अतुल पराक्रमी सेवक.

The Emperor's anxiety at this time was two-fold, to ensure the peaceful succession to his throne after his own death, and to conciliate the Marathas by offering them such terms as they could accept but as would not damage his prestige. On these points he took serious counsel with his best advisers and entrusted the affairs of the Deccan to his beloved son Kam Baksh with Zulfiqar Khan as his guide, leaving northern India to be shared by the other two sons. Such a division of his Empire between his three sons was long contemplated by him. On 27 November 1703 the Emperor called up Shāhu and entrusted his person to Kam Baksh with instructions to open negotiations with Dhanāji Jadhav about the release of Shāhu. Thereupon Dhanāji was consulted and he offered to close the war on condition that the Maratha King should have the right to levy *Chauth* and *Sardeshmukhi* dues upon the six subhas of the Deccan, in lieu of which the Marathas would protect the country. Dhanāji also agreed to take charge of Shāhu and swear allegiance to the Emperor, provided the prominent leaders of Maratha bands were received by him in open Darbar and honoured with dresses, so that all might feel that the Maratha kingdom of Shivaji's days had been restored to Shāhu as a recognised feudatory of the supreme Mughal authority. These terms were agreed to and invitations were sent round to the chiefs of the Maratha army. Soon these leaders assembled in Dhanaji's camp close to the Emperor's, each with his full quota of troops. When the Emperor saw this huge Maratha assemblage, his suspicious nature became alarmed ; he feared that this was a Maratha trick, an intentional ruse to capture his own person. He forthwith broke up the intended negotiations, to the great joy of the Marathas who were unwilling to accept Mughal suzerainty after all the sacrifices of years of war. It appears evident that Dhanāji and Shāhu had open conferences at this time, in the presence of Kam Baksh and Zulfiqar Khan, and possibly Balaji Vishvanath was then a confidential adviser of Dhanaji. This accounts for Dhanaji's respect for Shahu just before the battle of Khed in 1707 and his quick desertion of Tarabai's cause.

After 1703 a year or two passed in such wrangling without any definite move by the Emperor about Shāhu's future, when one more unsuccessful effort was made by the Emperor on his return journey from Surapur to Ahmadnagar in 1706. He made Shāhu write personal letters to some of the Maratha leaders inviting them to join him, gave Shāhu a *khilat* of farewell leave, actually released him from his own camp, and ordered him to go and rule his kingdom in obedience to Kam Baksh. Shahu's residential tents were removed and pitched in Zulfiqar Khan's quarters on February 6, 1706. But no Maratha Chief came to join Shāhu. It was evident to the Maratha leaders that this would prove a clear device for dividing Maratha ranks and starting a civil war among them. Though Shāhu was at large, he would not care to escape and incur the risk of either creating strife in the Maratha nation or being captured again by the Emperor, as Zulfiqar Khan was secretly instructed to watch his movements.

5. **Piteous appeal of Yesubai.**—The last years of Aurangzeb's life, as the student knows, were fearfully clouded with darkness about the future of the Deccan or of the vast Empire outside. Extreme misery and want prevailed in the Mughal camp, where not a single bright face could be seen. For years the Mughal soldiery had received no pay; and utter hopelessness overcame them all. We can thus imagine to what sorry straits Shāhu and his mother with their followers had been reduced in these last two years of the Emperor's life. A Marathi letter addressed by Yesubai to the head of the shrine of Moraya Dev of Chinchwad, begging for a loan, eloquently explains the situation and deserves reproduction here. It is dated 19 April 1705 from Ahmadnagar, and runs thus: After compliments, "My son Daji has accompanied the Emperor and we were sent here along with the Zanana some five months ago. We are here experiencing a dreadful predicament caused by want of provisions and cash. Our assigned allowances have not long been paid to us, all cash was either plundered by the Marathas or appropriated by the Muslim officials. For a long time past we have had to live on loans, but now no banker hazards a loan to us. My debt already amounts to seven thousand and we are heavily pressed for its repayment. It is indeed providential unkindness that such extreme misery should befall the great Shivaji's daughter-in-law. Every passing moment adds to our trouble. In this extremity we approach your

Holiness as our last resort, and beseech you to relieve our sufferings. If you can kindly send me a loan of seven thousand rupees with the bearer Rayaji Jadhav, we can pay back our debt to the bankers here and obtain further sums from them. The bearer will fully explain our situation. I will pay back this loan to your Holiness as soon as better days return. I am a poor, ignorant, illiterate woman of the Chhatrapati's house and am reduced to such misery. Your Holiness must not reject my prayer out of memory of what my worthy father-in-law might have done for your Holiness' shrine. Trusting you will not disappoint me &c."

6. **Tragedy of Aurangzeb's life.**—The Emperor's last three years in the Deccan were the darkest in his long reign. The Marathas constantly hovered round the Mughal camp and carried away everything they could lay their hands on. Even when they surrendered their forts to the Emperor, they hardly left anything valuable in them, so that these captured forts proved mere dry rocks and stones difficult to be protected and replenished. They could be held only by those who were used to the hard and rugged life of Maharashtra and not by the heavily-armoured Mughal soldiers. The keenly observant Manucci's pen has given graphic accounts of these last years of Aurangzeb's life. As Sir Jadunath Sarkar writes, " The wastage of the Deccan war, which raged intensely for over twenty years, was a hundred thousand lives of soldiers and followers and three times that number of animals, elephants, horses, camels and oxen, for each of those years. In the imperial camp pestilence was always present and the daily mortality was heavy from the immense number of men crowded together, the accumulation of filth and flies and the unbearable stench. His soldiers and camp followers suffered unspeakable hardships in marching over flooded rivers, muddy roads, and broken hilly tracks. Posters disappeared, transport beasts died of hunger and overwork, scarcity of grain was ever present in the camp. His officers were awfully wearied. Aurangzeb burst into wrath at any suggestion of return to north India and taunted the unlucky counsellor with cowardice and love of ease. One by one the old, able and independent officers of his earlier years passed away, and he was now surrounded only by timid cycophants

and upstart nobles of his own creation, who would never venture to contradict him in his errors, nor give him honest counsel. The mutual jealousies of his generals ruined his affairs, so that the Emperor had to conduct every operation in person and nothing would be done. The Marathas find their raids of late immensely beneficial. As soon as they arrive into a district, the Mughal officer in charge of it sends his agents to the Maratha leaders and negotiates the amounts to be paid. If they don't get the stipulated sum, plunder and fire are the result. The Maratha king is now all powerful. He has a hundred thousand well trained fighting men in his charge : so he is not afraid of giving an open fight to the Emperor. It is now the Maratha Raja's turn to inspire the same terror among the Mughals which Aurangzeb in his earlier days used to do among the Marathas."[4]

The last words of the above description doubtless refer to Tarabai and her son. The Emperor's return from Devapur to Ahmadnagar appeared like a mourning procession. The Marathas hovered round his army like vultures and created a havoc. During these last years the Marathas started distant expeditions into Malwa and Gujarat. They ravaged Burhanpur, Surat, Broach and other wealthy towns. Hindurao Ghorpade and his sons and relatives extended their sway southward over the Karnatak.

Things were equally bad in north India, where the people were up in arms. The Bundelas under Chhatrasal asserted their independence. The Rajputs were all combined in revolt. The Jats and the Sikhs rose in rebellion. The disruption of the Empire had already begun. These were the results of Aurangzeb's war in the Deccan. The Marathas had their revival in these chaotic conditions and practically swept all India during the next century.

7. **Aurangzeb's death.**—The last few months of Aurangzeb's life witnessed the final break-down. He had no money : no funds reached him from outside. The Marathas became aggressive. The Emperor's own wives and daughters

4. Sarkar, *Aurangzeb*, V. p. 14 &c.

came to the point of starving. With a united voice they all pitieously pleaded for a return to Agra. They said, "It is now thirty years since we have been wandering in foreign land, suffering the hardships of camp life all the while. We were then young and full of youth. Now we have grown old and decrepit. Let us go back to Agra and die peacefully in our homes, without the fear of these vultures tearing us. Let us have peace at least in death." The Emperor replied, "Don't fear, I have made every provision for your future." His sole companions were now, his daughter Zinat-un-Nisa, already an old maid and his last wife Udepuri Begam, a low animal type of a partner, whose son Kam Baksh broke his father's heart by freaks of insane folly and passion. These last years of the Emperor's life were darkened by domestic bereavements. His best loved daughter-in-law Jahanzeb-Begam died in Gujarat in March 1705. His rebel son Akbar had died in Iran in 1704 but the authentic news of his death reached the Emperor in 1705. His gifted daughter Zeb-un-Nisa ended her days in prison at Delhi. His eldest surviving and capable son was a closely watched prisoner for over ten years and now his youngest sister Gauhar-Ara Begam died in 1706. In May of the same year his daughter Mihar-un-Nisa and her husband both died together in Delhi and the next month died Buland Akhtar, the son of Akbar. Azam Shah, the Emperor's second son tried to murder Kam Baksh. So Aurangzeb sent both these sons away from his death-bed. Four days after sending away Azam Shah from his side, the aged and worn out figure now left in utter loneliness was seized with a severe fever: for three days he insisted on coming to the court-room and saying the five daily prayers in full congregation. On Thursday 19th February Hamid-un-din by the advice of astrologers, submitted a petition for giving away an elephant worth Rs, 4000 in charity for averting evil stars. The dying man wrote across the petition, "the giving away of an elephant in charity is a custom of the Hindus and star-worshippers. Give instead Rs. 4000 to the Chief Kazi for distribution among the poor. Convey quickly to the first station and consign to dust this heap of dust (his own body)." During these last days he dictated two pathetic letters to his sons Azam Shah and Kam Baksh entreating them to be friendly and loving. He also prepared a will and placed it under his pillow, proposing a peaceful partition of his Empire among his three surviving sons. On the morning of Friday 20 February Aurangzeb came out of his bed-room, went through his morning prayer. Gradually unconsciousness crept on, his fingers continuing to move over the beads of his rosary and his lips to gasp out the Kalimah till about 8 o'clock, when all was over. Thus perished one of the mightiest and most remarkable figures in the world's history. His son Azam Shah arrived two days after and performed the burial of his father's body at Khuldabad, now called Roza, in a low simple tomb without any marble platform.[5]

8. **Tarabai triumphant.**—After the death of Rajaram Tara Bai's voice became supreme in Maharashtra, as she managed affairs in the name of her son. Unfortunately she had serious differences of policy with the veteran Rāmchandra Pant, who with Dhanāji Jadhav kept up his contact with Shāhu and tried to bring him back as their next Chhatrapati. As this move was violently opposed by Tara Bai, Rāmchandra Pant remained a mere apathetic onlooker and ceased to take the same active part in her government that he had done during Rājārām's life. The published papers make hardly any mention of Rāmchandra Pant hereafter. Tara Bai, mainly with the support of Parashuram Trimbak, Dhanāji and Shankaraji Narayan, prosecuted the war with singular zeal and success, inflicting terrible hardships upon the Mughals as described above. She deserves all the credit for the Maratha nation's emerging successfully out of the dreadful war with power to control the destinies of India during the eighteenth century. The great ability of Tara Bai is attested to even by Muslim writers. She constantly moved from fort to fort directing operations and inspiring her followers. Girjoji Yadav, the guardian of the fort of Panhala, was her personal and confidential agent through whom her commands were communicated outside. This Girjoji belonged to the large Yadav family of Karhad. Although Satara was recaptured by the Marathas, in 1704, Tara Bai made Panhala her central station from which she issued her commands in the name of her young son.

---

5. Sarkar's *Aurangzib*, Volume V.

A contemporary Maratha poet thus sings the achievements of Tara Bai :—

"Our goddess Tulja is blessing us,
The Emperor's power has come into our hands;
Victory is garlanding young Shivaji's neck.
Delhi is humbled;
The Lord of Delhi has lost his lustre,
Tara Bai the Rani of Rama is terribly angered.
Remember, you folks, God Shankar commands all this.
He has delivered into the hands of the great Destroyer
All the armies of the Lord of Delhi.
Indra's court is now laughing
At the misery of Delhi's Lord.
The Queen of Rama ranges in frown on the battle-field;
Take care oh Mughals,
The final end is near,
The jewelled crest of the Bhoslas,
The giver of good fortune, Raja Shiva,
Now shines on the throne.[6]

The rise of Shāhu synchronizes with that of the Peshwās and involves the eclipse of Rāmchandra Pant Amātya, the great regenerator of the Maratha nation. That this connecting link between the old order and the new, became extinct was indeed a national loss. This chapter can be fittingly concluded by quoting the eloquent passage in which Ranade has stressed the importance of this Maratha war of independence.[7]

"If all these dangers were averted and a new force communicated to the people, the credit of it must be ascribed to Aurangzeb's ambition. The twenty years war was brought to a happy termination. Aurangzeb stirred the people of Maharashtra to their inmost depths and it was the hard discipline of this war which cemented the national and patriotic instincts of their leaders, and during the next three generations carried them as conquerors to the farthest part of India. Without

6. Rise of the Maratha Power, pp. 192-196.

revenues, without armies and without resources of any kind, they managed to raise armies, retake forts and develop a system of conquest by which they regained not only the Swaraj but also the right to levy Chauthai and Sardeshmukhi all over the Deccan and the Karnatak. Mere free-booters and plunderers never could have obtained success in such a war. It was a higher moral force which brought out all the virtues of the best men of the nation, daring heroism, noble endurance, administrative skill, hope which rose higher with every disappointment, an unshakable faith, devotion to high ideals, a sense of brotherhood, a spirit of self-sacrifice, and a trust in the final success of their cause. It is as a school for such discipline that this War of Independence will always remain the most glorious period of Maratha history."

INDEX